CRIMINAL JUSTICE AND LAW

ENFORCEMENT BOOKS

OF

CORAL GABLES PUBLISHING COMPANY, INC.

South Miami, Florida   33143

CONSTITUTIONAL LAW

KLEIN'S   **CONSTITUTIONAL LAW FOR CRIMINAL JUSTICE PROFESSIONALS, 3rd Edition**

IRVING J. KLEIN, B.S., J.D., PROFESSOR EMERITUS OF LAW AND POLICE SCIENCE, JOHN JAY COLLEGE OF CRIMINAL JUSTICE, CITY UNIVERSITY OF NEW YORK

The book is designed as a classroom text and covers the following subjects by chapters: The Constitutional Process, History of the Adoption of the Constitution, States Rights to Arrest, Detain and Punish, Absorption of Bill of Rights, First Amendment, Fourth Amendment - Search and Seizure, Fifth Amendment, Sixth Amendment Trial Guarantees, Eighth Amendment, Reserved Powers of the Tenth Amendment, Civil Rights of the Constitution, Plea Bargaining, Entrapment, Civil Rights Cases and Legislation, Constitution of the United States of America -1787, Glossary of Legal Terms, 55 Relevant Edited Cases of the United States Supreme Court, Table of Cases, Index, and annual supplements containing relevant United States Supreme Court Cases.

Hard cover - smythe sewn
865 pages
ISBN 0-938993-12-7

1992 (with updated annual supplements)
L.C. 91-076152

KLEIN'S   **PRINCIPLES OF THE LAW OF ARREST, SEARCH, SEIZURE, and LIABILITY ISSUES**

IRVING J. KLEIN, B.S., J.D., PROFESSOR EMERITUS OF LAW AND POLICE SCIENCE, JOHN JAY COLLEGE OF CRIMINAL JUSTICE, CITY UNIVERSITY OF NEW YORK

This book is a horn-book that may be used as a classroom text for those teachers who do not wish to have their students brief United States Supreme Court cases, and still know and understand the Anglo-

Saxon origin of the law of arrest, search and seizure, and the present liability issues of law enforcement personnel. It is kept up to date so that it may be used as a reference source by practitioners and students. It contains the following subjects by chapter: Constitutional Basis for Arrest, Law of Search and Seizure, Liability of Law Enforcement Officers, United States Constitution, Glossary of Legal Terms, Table of Cases, and Index.

Paperback
302 pages   1994
ISBN   0938993-16-X   L.C. 94-070088

KLEIN'S   **THE LAW OF ARREST, SEARCH, SEIZURE and LIABILITY ISSUES - PRINCIPLES, CASES AND COMMENTS**

IRVING J. KLEIN, B.S., J.D., PROFESSOR EMERITUS OF LAW AND POLICE SCIENCE, JOHN JAY COLLEGE OF CRIMINAL JUSTICE, CITY UNIVERSITY OF NEW YORK

This book is designed as a classroom text or collateral reading source for those teachers who like to combine horn-book law with edited cases that students may brief and recite their briefs in class. It is kept up to date by pocket part annual supplements. It is an extension of Professor Klein's horn-book on the same subject. This too may be used as a reference source by practitioners and students. It contains the following subjects by chapter: The Constitutional Basis for Arrest, Search and Seizure, Liability of Law Enforcement Officers, 34 edited relevant cases of the United States Supreme Court, United States Constitution, Glossary of Legal Terms, Table of Cases, and Index.

Hard cover - smythe sewn
744 pages   1994
ISBN   0-938993-17-8   L.C. 93-074910

CORRECTIONS

SECHREST AND COLLINS'   JAIL MANAGEMENT AND LIABILITY ISSUES

DALE K. SECHREST, D. CRIM. ASSISTANT PROFESSOR CRIMINAL JUSTICE DEPARTMENT, FLORIDA INTERNATIONAL UNIVERSITY, PRESENTLY ASSOCIATE PROFESSOR OF CRIMINAL JUSTICE AT CALIFORNIA STATE UNIVERSITY, SAN BERNADINO, CALIFORNIA, AND WILLIAM C. COLLINS, J.D., OLYMPIA WASHINGTON

This book is designed as a classroom text and as a guide to

Administrators of Jails and Prisons. It covers the following subjects by chapters: Administration, Censuring Facility Safety and Security, Staffing the Faculty, Managing the Inmate Population, Rights to Minimal Care, Contracting for Services, Planning the New Facility, Reaching for Professionalism, References, Name Index, and Subject Index.

Hard cover - smythe sewn
225 pages   1989
ISBN   0-938993-05-4   L.C. 88-064044

POLICE ADMINISTRATION

HOGGES' A QUALITY CIRCLE APPROACH TO POLICE COMMUNITY RELATIONS

RALPH HOGGES, ASSOCIATE DEAN OF FACULTY AND CHAIRPERSON, DIVISION OF GENERAL STUDIES, FLORIDA MEMORIAL COLLEGE

This book is designed as a collateral classroom text and covers the following subjects by chapter: A Brief Definition of Police Community Relations, Why Police Community Relations Fail, Why Utilize the Quality Control Circle, Planning Developing, Implementing and Evaluating your Police Community Relations Program, Overview of Police - Community Relations, Police Culture, Police Personality, Police Officer Cycle, Police Stress, Police Moral, Interpersonal Communications, Cultures, Prejudice and Discrimination, Police Quality Control Interaction, Blacks and Police Officers, Hispanics and Police Officers, Asians and Police Officers, Whites and Police Officers, Follow up by Management, Feed back to Participants, and Conclusion.

Paperback
78 pages   1988
ISBN   0-938933-03-8   L.C. 88-80358

Irving J. Klein, B.S., J.D.

Professor Emeritus of Law and Police Science
John Jay College of Criminal Justice
City University of New York

THE LAW OF ARREST, SEARCH, SEIZURE,

AND LIABILITY ISSUES -

PRINCIPLES, CASES AND COMMENTS

CORAL GABLES PUBLISHING CO., INC.
South Miami, Florida 33143

Library of Congress Catalog Card Number: 93-74910

Klein, Irving J.
      The Law of Arrest, Search, Seizure and Liability Issues - Principles, Cases and Comments

      Includes indexes.
      1.   United States - Constitutional Law. 2. Criminal Justice, Administration of - United States. 3. Criminal Justice, Personnel - United States. 4. Arrest - United States. 5. Search and Seizure - United States I. Title.
      KF9630.K55 1994   345.'73'05   93-74910
      ISBN 0-938993-16-X

Editing
  and
Design: Marta Arias-Klein, Ed.D.
           Linda Diamond
           Ovidio Hidalgo-Gato, J.D.
           Michael R. Klein, J.D.
           Lissette Marin

Printed in the United States of America
1 2 3 4 5 6 7 -

Dedicated to my dear wife, Dr. Marta A. Klein, whose encouragement and help were largely responsible for the completion of this work.

PREFACE

This book is being printed in two forms. One form is a hard cover book, bound in smyth sewn fashion to withstand many years of use, and updated annually by supplements reflecting the latest decisions made by the United States Supreme Court. This hard cover book will contain edited cases that may be used as a source for students' briefs. The other form will be a paperback book, known as a horn-book, that contains a review of the law of arrest, search and seizure, in summary narrative form. It will not contain edited cases. Both forms will contain decisions of the United States Supreme Court relating to arrest, search and seizure as well as the development of the Fourth and Fourteenth Amendments of the United States Constitution.

Both forms of this book, however, can whet the appetite of the reader to delve further in the study of law. Those who will read the hard cover volume will have the advantage of reading interesting experiences of other people. In a way, when one reads a decision of the Court it is almost like reading a mystery novel. The facts of a case are usually written in the beginning of the Justices' decision and then the Justice writes about the reasons that he/she and colleagues, who join in the decision, have used to decide the case. Naturally this is based, in most instances, on the concept of stare decisis (to stand by decided cases).

As I read these decisions, I think of it as a challenge as to what I believe the final decision will be, much as when one reads a mystery novel, and guesses who the culprit is.

I intend to continue my practice of updating the hard cover volume annually, wherein the Coral Gables Publishing Co., Inc. publishes a supplement that is designed to fit in the inside of the pocket part in the back of the book. I further intend to write new updated volumes of the soft cover book as the need arises.

I have epitomized and analyzed decisions of the Court that I believe are most relevant to the law of arrest and search and seizure, to assist those persons charged with the responsibility of enforcing our criminal laws, methods to apprehend, supervise, adjudicate and convict accused persons within the framework of constitutional procedures. I have drawn on my experiences as a police officer, social worker, county prosecutor, defense counsel and college professor in an effort to make this text interesting and readable. You will notice that my style of writing is similar to my talking to you in a lecture. I write more about this in my first chapter's introduction. I hope my efforts have been realized.

The names of the cases are in bold face type for easier reading. Parallel citations have been included where they were found to exist at the time of this writing. Some cases are so recent that such citations have not yet been made available.

As you know it takes some time before the finalized decisions of the Court are made available in the hard cover copies of the United States Reports published by the United States government. Thus, full citations for the United States Reports are not included for the cases decided in more recent cases.

You will note that in my analysis of a case I refer to the Court, using an upper case C for the word Court. This means that I am referring to the United States Supreme Court. This practice is used for the sake of brevity.

As you are aware, several new associate justices have been placed on the bench of the Court in recent years. When the decisions are read, there are many surprises in the viewpoints of various justices. It is obvious to me that the Court is in transition to a new phase after what was thought to be a firmly consolidated conservative majority.

There appears to be a group of moderately conservative justices. They are David Souter, Sandra O'Connor and Anthony Kennedy. They seem to be very cautious in deciding cases and have a hesitancy to overturn precedents. They don't always vote together but the general tone is present. They appear to want to restrict federal judges in the reevaluation of sentences of state courts, particularly in Fourth Amendment cases on search and seizure.

It appears to me that Justice Souter is the most unpredictable in his decisions. He has independence that made him a frequent dissenter. He confronts some of the Court's contradictions and tries to make some continuity of precedents and to avoid those that do not.

Justice Thomas seems to have an alliance with

Justice Scalia. He appears to vote together with Justice Scalia in most instances of the non-unanimous cases. There is no doubt that Justice Thurgood Marshall who was replaced by Justice Thomas, would have voted on the other side of issues.

Justice Ginsburg who has joined the Court for the 1993-94 Term is the first Justice nominated by a Democratic President in 26 years. While one never completely knows how a new justice will act on issues, it appears that she will be more liberal than Justice White, whom she replaces.

While I usually only write about the majority decision in a case because it is my intent to advise the student what the law is, it is interesting to read the dissents that I have included in some of the edited cases. These are sometimes written with sarcastic venom by the dissenters. Even the majority opinions sometimes sharply criticize the reasons of the dissenters. In short, I believe that there are many heated arguments going on between the justices on many issues. I believe that this is a good sign that no one justice is in a position to dictate his or her opinion to the others and in the end, reason probably prevails.

One reading this book is exposed to the evolutionary process of constitutional guarantees afforded to those who are accused of crime. Some United States Court decisions, included in the text are no longer considered as binding by law. Later cases, which have modified or changed the principle of law of the older cases, are included to bring the content up to date as of January 1994. This pedagogical approach was used to enable the student to observe the evolutionary changes in our law.

There are two basic methods to study law. The first is the "case method" and the second is the "horn-book method." Some students and professors have indicated that they prefer to use both methods simultaneously.

The "case method" is designed to help the student remember the principle of law of the case relating to a factual pattern which occurred in the case. Thus the student learns to understand the law by inductive reasoning, and then is able to apply this principle of law to other cases having similar facts.

The procedure under the "case method" requires a student to read the decision, summarize it in writing pursuant to the directions received from the teacher, and recite in class the results of the summary, emphasizing the primary principle of law. This is a student brief.

Cases, as the term is used in this book, mean the published reports of controversies that have come before a court wherein the court renders a decision, including the reasons for the final conclusion, which is the judgment.

The cases found in this book are appellate court decisions. Most court trials are recorded in a court stenographer's minutes and are not ordinarily transcribed unless an appeal is made. If an appeal is made, the appealing party has the record transcribed and printed. It is then sent to the proper appellate court, and some courts permit photocopies in lieu of printing. The appellate court consists of more than one jurist, one of whom is assigned to write an opinion. This procedure is described fully as it relates to the United States Supreme Court in section, 1.41 infra.

The student's brief should not be confused with a lawyer's brief. The latter is a memorandum of law submitted to the judges to assist the court to arrive at a decision. The "case method" causes the student to read the case more carefully, perhaps several times, to extract the essentials expressed, so that concepts are more firmly implanted in the mind. It also establishes a permanent notebook for reference. Its final attribute is that it develops the ability of the student to reason logically.

Each professor has a favorite method to brief a case. The procedure that I have used successfully is as follows:

- Name of Case (title of action)
- Citation (address where the case can be found)
- History (legal history of what happened to this case in the lower courts)
- Principle of Law (summary of the decision as it relates to the point in the book that is being studied)
- Facts (the facts of the original apprehension of petitioner and/or appellant)
- Decision (the reasoning of the Court in arriving at its judgment)
- Judgment (final determination of the Court as it relates to the instant case).

The "horn-book method" is the study of a horn-book,

which is a treatise on a field of law written by someone who has spent years studying cases and statutes in that discipline. The author presents a systematic and logical body of legal principles that the courts and other judicial or quasi-judicial tribunals apply in deciding controversies. The horn-book consists of general rules and conclusions based on court decisions and is therefore the product of inductive reasoning.

Legal citations have been referred to as the address where the case can be found. This means that if a student were to go to a legal library the case may be found in the volume and page number indicated in the citation. For example, the case STONE v POWELL, 428 U.S. 465, 96 S.Ct. 3037, 49 L.Ed.2d 1067 (1976), has been cited. This means that the decision of Stone v Powell may be found in three parallel places, viz.. Volume 428 of the United States Reports at page 465, Volume 96 of the Supreme Court Reporter at page 3037, and Volume 49 of the Lawyers Edition of the United States Supreme Court Reports, second series at page 1067. This case was reported by the Court during the 1976 Term and hence (1976) at the end of the citation denotes that fact. Reports of the United States Supreme Court are first published as "slip decisions." The official edition is published by the United States Government Printing Office. Three unofficial editions are published. They are United States Law Week, Commerce Clearing House Supreme Court Bulletin, and the Criminal Law Reporter. Slip decisions are published shortly after the decision is handed down and hence they are subject to revision. The citation of the "slip decision" is indicated by docket number, court, and date of decision (not Term of Court), e.g. HOLLOWAY et al v ARKANSAS, No. 76-5856, U.S. Sup. Ct., April 3, 1978 (46 L.W. 4289), or C.C.H., Sup.Ct.Bull. or Cr.L. citations may be used.

Limited repetition will be observed as one reads through the pages of this book. This design was intentionally adopted to conform with the pedagogical method that first tells the student what is going to be discussed, next tells it, and finally, tells what has been told.

Chief Justice Rehnquist said that the Court's doctrine of adhering to its own precedents is at its strongest in cases involving property and contract rights "because, people make commercial arrangements in reliance on those cases." "By contrast," he said, "the call of precedent is at its weakest in cases about rules of procedure or evidence. It is particularly weak in cases originally decided over vigorous dissents by 5-4 votes." I cannot agree that stare decisis is more important to contract law than it is to individual rights that are so precious to our fundamental liberty.

There is another shift taking place in the discipline of constitutional law. That shift manifests itself in the actions of state courts. Constitutional scholars now believe that United States Supreme Court interpretations are becoming no more than persuasive authority for the construction of similar state provisions. The Supremacy Clause of the United States Constitution does not require conforming interpretations of state and federal constitutions as long as a defendant's state right is not enforced to the prejudice of a broader federal right. To put it another way, a state court may give a defendant greater constitutional rights than those afforded to the defendant by the United States Supreme Court.

This does not mean that the state courts are going off in an entirely new direction. State rulings on constitutional laws are adaptations of United States Supreme Court doctrines. This would seem to indicate to the serious teacher, student or practitioner that if he or she is looking for guidance in an area covered in this text, the annual supplement, if any, should be consulted first, the main volume next, to be followed by researching the most recent cases in the involved state or regional digest to ascertain the law. Naturally, the use of Sheppards to update the material is helpful as well as Westlaw or Lexis. Few of us have the time, facilities or funds to complete all of this research but we can try with the tools available to us to do a comprehensive job, if the case merits it.

Again, I wish to thank many people who helped in the preparation of this work. Foremost is the help and encouragement given to me by my wife, Dr. Marta Arias-Klein, now a retired Professor of Criminal Justice of Nassau Community College, Garden City, New York. I am also thankful for the editing and suggestions provided to me by my son, Professor Michael R. Klein, also of Nassau Community College.

Invaluable assistance has been given to me by so many academicians almost too numerous to mention. However, it would be ungrateful if I omitted mention of

President Jay Sexter, of Mercy College, Dobbs Ferry, New York; Professors T. Kenneth Moran, Henry Morse, Christopher Morse, Richard Koehler, and President Gerald W. Lynch, all of John Jay College of Criminal Justice; Doctor Thomas A. Reppeto, President of the Citizen's Crime Commission of New York City, formerly Dean at John Jay College of Criminal Justice; Professor Thomas Kissane of Iona College, New Rochelle, New York, and so many professors throughout the United States. I would like to mention each and everyone of them, who have given me encouragement by their comments on the need for such a book as this. However, I hope that those academicians omitted understand that it would be impracticable to mention all of them. My secretary, Lissette Marin, deserves particular mention. She has put up with my foibles and has repeated typing materials several times until we both were satisfied with the results.

Finally, everyone knows, but seldom thinks about the fact, that only the title and author's name appears on the cover of a book and in some cases, the name of the publisher. However, the people who create the printed page, the editors, the typists, the typesetters, the printers, the shipping clerks, the office staff, the truckers, and the creators of the binding, the paper, etc. are each very important in the final result. Most times these individuals are anonymous even to the author. Linda Diamond and Ovidio Hidalgo-Gato, J.D., our word processing geniuses, worked closely with me in producing the final product.

I have retired from day to day teaching at John Jay College of Criminal Justice, but President Gerald W. Lynch has graciously named me as Professor Emeritus of Law and Police Science and an office has been made available to me at the college. Accordingly, I would appreciate it if my readers find any errors or wish to make any suggestions for the improvement of the book, that they write to me at John Jay College of Criminal Justice C.U.N.Y., Law, Police Science, and Criminal Justice Administration Department, 899 Tenth Avenue, New York, NY 10019.

Thank you.

Irving J. Klein

January, 1994

TABLE OF CONTENTS

CHAPTER 1 CONSTITUTIONAL BASIS FOR ARREST

CHAPTER 2 SEARCH AND SEIZURE

CHAPTER 3   LIABILITIES OF LAW ENFORCEMENT OFFICERS

DECISIONS FIRST REFERRED TO IN CHAPTER ONE

DECISIONS FIRST REFERRED TO IN CHAPTER TWO

CHAPTER 1   CONSTITUTIONAL BASIS FOR ARREST

Contents

1.1 Introduction

This book is designed to acquaint practitioners and students of criminal justice with the laws of arrest and search and seizure as they exist at the time of the initial publication, and kept up to date by annual pocket part supplements.

I would like readers to imagine that I am lecturing to them throughout the text portion of the book. The only shortcomings to this method of instruction that I can think of are that the reader is not able to ask questions of me, nor participate in class discussions, that I believe are a desirable component in the learning process. Notwithstanding these impediments, I believe that if this book is used as a text book for course study, the professor, or instructor, will be able to fill in for me, to make the use of the book a stimulating learning experience.

I believe that for one to understand and fully appreciate the principles of law discussed in the following pages it is necessary that the reader have an understanding of some of the foundations upon which the laws of arrest and search and seizure are based.

For some readers, they may believe that I am insulting their intelligence by including the introductory material. For others, it may be the first time that they come in contact with it and will enlarge their mental horizon.

As I write this, I am reminded of something I have told students in my classrooms from my personal experience. I am referring to the many professional conferences that I have participated in as panelist and as a listener. As a listener, I found that much that I was listening to, coming from eminent and knowledgeable panelists, I already knew. However, invariably, I came away from the experience learning many new concepts that I did not know.

With this in mind, I suggest that all readers, spend a little time reading this chapter, with my hope that the reader, who has a background in this area, will learn something new that I have included herein.

The practitioners know the law of arrest, search and seizure, and practice it according to the law. They and their employers, whether it be the United States of America, a state, a county, a city or a governmental authority of any kind, will be protected from a civil or

3

criminal judgment.

Of equal importance is the fact that a law enforcement officer who is honestly attempting to do a conscientious job, can work effectively within the framework of the United States Constitution, if properly trained and motivated. It is very discouraging for a law enforcer to arrest someone for a crime that the arrestee committed, without any question, yet the defendant is permitted to exit the courtroom as a free person because the arrest was made outside the bounds of the constitutional limitations. If our society is to prevail, special motivation must find its way into the law enforcement community in the United States of America. This book is being published in two forms. One will consist only of a horn-book, the other will contain, in addition to the horn-book portion, an addition wherein I have included edited relevant cases from which a student may prepare a student's brief for classroom discussion.

§ 1.2   Constitutional Law

In order for the reader to understand the arrest and search and seizure laws, it is necessary that he/she understands the basics of constitutional law. For this reason, I have incorporated herein some of the material that I have included in another book that I have written, entitled Constitutional Law for Criminal Justice Professionals, now in its third edition. It is published by Coral Gables Publishing Company, Inc., under ISBN # 0-938993-12-7.

§ 1.3   Constitutional Law Defined

Constitutional law is defined very loosely because it escapes a precise definition. In its broadest sense, the term *constitutional law* designates that branch of jurisprudence which deals with the formation, construction, and interpretation of the Constitution by

4

the President, Congress, court decisions, rulings of public officials, as well as governmental practices and customs.

§ 1.4   Common Law Defined

In order to understand the concept of constitutional law, the student must have an understanding of the phrase *common law*. This has been defined by case law as follows:

As distinguished from law created by the enactment of legislatures, the common law comprises the body of those principles and rules of action, relating to the government and security of persons and property which derive their authority solely from usages and customs of immemorial antiquity, or from the judgments and decrees of the courts recognizing, affirming, and enforcing such usages and customs; and, in this sense, particularly the ancient unwritten law of England. 1 Kent, Comm. 492; **WESTERN UNION TEL. CO. v. CALL PUB.CO.**, 181 U.S. 92, 21 S.Ct. 561, 45 L.Ed. 765; **STATE v. BUCHANAN**, 5 Har. & J. (Md) 365, 9 Am.Dec. 534; **LUX v. HAGGIN**, 69 Cal. 255, 10 P. 674; **BARRY v. PORT JERVIS**, 64 App. Div. 268, 72 N.Y.S. 104; **U.S. v. MILLER** 236 F. 798, 800 (D.C.).
    As concerns its force and authority in the United States, the phrase designates that portion of the common law of England (including such acts of parliament as were applicable) which had been adopted and was in force here at the time of the Revolution. This, so far as it has not since been expressly abrogated, is recognized as an organic part of the jurisprudence of most of the United States. **BROWNING v. BROWNING**, 3 N.M. 371, 9 P. 677; **GUARDIANS OF POOR v. GREENE**, 5 Bin (Pa.) 557; **U.S. v. NEW BEDFORD BRIDGE**, 27 Fed.Cas. 107; **HAGEMAN v. VANDERDOES**, 15 Ariz. 312, 138 P. 1053, 1056, L.R.A. 1915A, 491, Ann.Cas. 1915D, 1197; **INDUSTRIAL ACCEPTANCE CORPORATION v. WEBB** Mo.App. 287 S.W. 657, 660.
    It has also been said that the common law is that the body of law and juristic theory which was originated, developed and formulated and is administered in England, and has obtained among most of the states and peoples of Anglo-Saxon stock. **LUX v. HAGGIN**, 69 Cal. 255, 10 P. 674.

§ 1.5   Changes in Law

Law may be changed in three basic ways. One is by legislative enactment. This occurs when the legislature, be it Congress, a state legislature, or a local legislative body, presents a bill that is passed and enacted into law without a veto by the executive branch of government. Another method is by constitutional amendment, the procedure for which is included in the document itself. The third method is by interpretations given to the Constitution or statutes by courts, legislative bodies, executive departments of government and administrative agencies of government. The third method of changing the law is the one which we will be largely concerned with in the pages which follow in this text.

§ 1.6   Citations Explained

Throughout the text are references to and quotations from cases. For example, you might see **LUX v. HAGGIN**, 69 Cal. 255, 10 P. 674. In law, the numbers and letters following the name of a case are known as *citations*. They refer to a designated book in which can be found the full text of the named case. **LUX v. HAGGIN** can be found in volume 69 of the California Reports, page 255. It is also available in volume 10 of the Pacific Reporter, page 674. **THE CITY OF TOPEKA v. ROBERT MOODBERRY**, 191 Kan. 304, 380 P.2d 371, can be found in volume 191 of the Kansas Reports, page 304 and in volume 380 of the Pacific Reporter, second series, page 371.

§ 1.7   Federal Cases

Most of the cases considered in this text are cases that have been decided in federal courts. These sometimes are referred to as *federal cases*. Some have their origin in state courts, having gone through the state court system and then finding their way to the

United States Supreme Court. For example, **BETTS v. BRADY** is cited 316 U.S. 455, 62 S.Ct. 1252, 86 L.Ed. 1595 (1942). The case may be found in volume 316 of the United States Reports, page 455; in volume 62 of the Supreme Court Reports, page 1252; and in volume 86 of the Lawyers' Edition, Supreme Court Reports, page 1595, for the year 1942.

§ 1.8   United States Supreme Court Cases

Cases appear in the United States Supreme Court in four basic ways. The first and most common method is by a writ of certiorari. This is a common law writ in which a petitioner asks for a writ from a higher court, and it is issued. The writ directs the lower court to send the whole record of the case up to the higher court for review. The petition for the writ is made in the first instance to a higher court.

Another method to get the United States Supreme Court to review a case is by means of an appeal from a lower court decision. Appeals may be made as a right only in designated cases.

The third and least used method is a certification of a question of law. This type of review occurs when a lower appellate court believes that they should not decide a question of law and they certify the question of law, send it on to the United States Supreme Court, and ask that court for guidance to decide a case pending before the lower court.

The fourth method is indicated in Article III of the Constitution. "In all cases affecting ambassadors, other public ministers and consuls, and those in which a state shall be a party, the Supreme Court shall have original jurisdiction."

§ 1.9   Article III, the Judicial Article

There are provisions in Article III of the United States Constitution providing for original jurisdiction

of the United States Supreme Court, but these are not
pertinent to the law enforcer's role and hence will be
omitted in this discussion.

It is interesting to note that at present, the
United States Supreme Court does not have to consider
every case that comes before it except those where
appellant has a right of appeal. A minimum of four
justices of the Court must conclude that a substantial
federal question of law exists before the Court is
required to review a decision of a lower court when the
case comes before the Court on a writ of certiorari.

Article III of the Constitution concerns itself with
the judicial power of the United States. This is the
article of the Constitution from which the United States
Supreme Court derives its power and authority.

§ 1.10   Checks and Balances

We are all familiar with the system of checks and
balances that was built into the structure of the
Constitution.   The framers were largely young and
practical men. They knew well the principle that power
begets power, and they were determined to do all they
could to prevent one branch of the government from being
more powerful than the other two branches. Accordingly
they established the executive power (Article II),
wherein the executive branch of the government was
charged with the responsibility of implementing the laws
as promulgated by the legislative power (Article I) and
as interpreted by the judicial power (Article III).   In
this way each power acts as a check and balance on the
others.   We need look no further than the Watergate
scandal to see how efficiently the concept of checks and
balances operates.   When the executive branch took too
much power unto itself, it was impeded and checked by the
legislative and judicial branches.

I could think of no greater example of the greatness
of the American Constitution and how it has worked than
when I compared it with an incident which occurred to me
when I engaged in a conversation with a Portuguese youth
in the Lisbon, Portugal, airport in 1972. My wife and I

were in a lounge free of all other persons except this youth. After exchanging pleasantries in his obvious attempt to be friendly and practice the English language, he furtively looked about the terminal and said in a scarcely audible voice, "Is it true that you have free speech in the United States?" I replied that we have free speech and that I was a professor of constitutional law and we often studied cases in class where the courts have granted persons the right to freely express their opinions. I advised him, however, that the right of free speech did not include the right to incite a riot or falsely alarm persons in a crowded theater that there was a fire in progress when in fact that was not the case.

The youth appeared to be overwhelmed because he looked around again in the same furtive manner and exclaimed, "We have the right of free speech in our constitution, but if people say anything against the government, they are put in jail."

This short conversation with this young man increased my understanding of the constitutional process of our government more than all that I had previously learned through reading United States history.

We can verbalize about individual rights in the United States, but the Constitution might be a worthless document similar to that of the 1972 Portugal Constitution if it were not for the important division of governmental power and authority—the system of checks and balances—coupled with the desire of our military officers for an ordered society based upon the rule of law as opposed to the rule of man.

We, in the United States of America, are most fortunate to have a governmental structure that is subject to the will of the majority of the people, which over the years has represented a middle-of-the-road doctrine.

The Prime Minister of England, William E. Gladstone (1809-1888), once said, when speaking about the American Constitution, that it is "the most wonderful work ever struck off at a given time by the brain and purpose of man."

§ 1.11   The Constitution, A Living Document

The Constitution has been able to survive and is a living thing because it contains so many vague words and phrases which need to be interpreted by human beings of future generations. Examples of these terms are "full faith and credit," "necessary and proper," "general welfare," and "unreasonable search and seizure."

For example, the reasonableness of a search in 1960 might be different from that in 1975 or the year 2000. Certainly in 1950 it would have been considered unreasonable for commercial airline passengers to be searched and their luggage searched and x-rayed prior to boarding. Who among us who use the commercial airlines is not comforted when a thorough search of all passengers is conducted before they are permitted to board the flight?

§ 1.12   Vague Words in the Constitution

We can consider the vague word concept a little further if we examine the word "commerce" as it is used in Section 8, Article I, where the Constitution in delineating the powers of Congress reads: ".... To regulate Commerce with foreign Nations and among the several States, and with Indian Tribes." While much credit may be accorded to the foresight of the framers of the document, no person at that time in their wildest imagination could foresee that we would be using the airways for travel or for sending messages or transmitting photographs. However it has been possible, under the interstate commerce clause, to bring order into these industries when without it we might have had complete chaos. The Constitution is a living instrument—ever changing to meet new problems confronting the American people, their way of life, and their well-being.

§ 1.13   Power Granted and Limited by the Constitution

The Constitution contains a preamble followed by seven articles and twenty-six amendments. It has three major objectives:

1. It establishes the framework or structure of government.
2. It delegates or assigns the powers of government.
3. It restrains the exercise of these powers by governmental officials in order that certain individual rights may be preserved.

In summary, one might say that the Constitution establishes the framework of government by granting and limiting its powers.

§ 1.14   Historical Background of the Constitution

While it is not the intention of this text to deal extensively with the historical events leading to the establishment of Anglo-Saxon law and the conflict between the colonies of America with England, it is however felt that it is necessary to understand certain historical fundamentals from which grew the establishment of our system of government under the Constitution of the United States of America.

The reader is no doubt aware that colonies were established along the eastern seaboard as a result of several different reasons. Some settlers came for what they called "Religious Freedom." Others came because they were deported because of criminal activity in England. Others came to seek their fortunes in the New World. Others were pirates who established home ports from which they could attack and plunder ships on the high seas.

§ 1.15   Procedural Rights for the Accused

The development of procedural safeguards for persons

accused of crime is a fascinating chronicle in the annals of Anglo-American law. The safeguards are based upon two underlying assumptions of democracy:

1. The sanctity of the individual against the government;
2. Government by law rather than by man.

These rights were obtained at a very high price, through the blood, sweat, and tears of many generations of men and women. Fair trial as we know it today took centuries to evolve. It was an outgrowth of the Magna Carta (1215), the Petition of Rights (1628), and the Bill of Rights (1689).

§ 1.16   Bill of Rights

The first ten amendments to the United States Constitution are called the Bill of Rights. The rights enumerated therein were not new to the colonies. Eight state constitutions gathered these rights into separate provisions called a Declaration of Rights, or a Bill of Rights. Connecticut and Rhode Island, for example, had these rights in their original charter from England. The most influential of the states' Bill of Rights was the Virginia Bill of Rights of 1776. It greatly influenced the final document that was ratified by the thirteen new states.

§ 1.17   Offenders' Rights Under Early Common Law

There were no procedural safeguards in early English history for those accused of crimes. There was a procedure known as the hue and cry. In some respects it was similar to programs being used in some cities and rural areas today. In essence, victims of crimes would raise a hue and cry. Then all the inhabitants of the community would arm themselves to seek the felon. We would call this a vigilante system today. At this juncture, the present-day vigilante system and the ancient hue and cry procedure take separate paths. In the hue and cry, the felon had a precarious existence. If captured, there would be a hastily convened court. If capture was resisted, a member of the community could legally kill the fugitive. Usually, there was little chance of exoneration or even for an impartial jury. Accused persons could say nothing before the court in their defense. They were usually executed by being hanged, beheaded, or thrown from a cliff by the aggrieved or a relative of the aggrieved. If they were caught, they were almost certain to endure severe sanctions. If the accused escaped, he/she would be declared an outlaw and therefore not entitled to the protection of the law. There was no right to appeal and the suspect could be executed without first being indicted. Outlaws who were captured with stolen goods on them could be executed summarily by a member of the community. Under the above conditions it was understandable that many state conventions balked at entering a government without fundamental safeguards of a bill of rights.

§ 1.18   Administration of Criminal Justice

The courts in interpreting the Tenth Amendment to the Constitution have held consistently that the administration of criminal justice is principally the function of the states, unless in so doing they offend some fundamental principle of justice, thereby violating a constitutional right.

§ 1.19   Rule of Law

The rule of law was most eloquently expressed by Prof. Albert V. Dicey when he wrote:

"No man is punishable or can be lawfully made to suffer in body or goods except for a distinct breach of law established in the

13

ordinary legal manner before the ordinary courts of the land. In this sense the rule of law is contrasted with every system of government based on the exercise by persons in authority of wide arbitrary or discretionary powers of constraint.

.... We mean in the second place, when we speak of the "rule of law" as a characteristic of our country not only that with us no man is above the law but ... that here every man, whatever be his rank or condition, is subject to the ordinary law of the realm and amenable to the jurisdiction of the ordinary tribunal.

.... There remains yet a third and a different sense in which the "rule of law" or the predominance of the legal spirit may be described as a special attribute of English institutions. We may say that the constitution is pervaded by the rule of law on the ground that the general principles of the constitution (as for example the right to personal liberty, or the right of public meetings) are with us the result of judicial decisions determining the rights of private persons in particular cases brought before the courts. **CAMPBELL v. HALL** (1774) Leefe 655; K.&L. 487. It should be noted, however, that the origin of parliament may not be traced to judicial decision and the independence of judges has rested on statute since the Act of Settlement (1701)."

The English constitution, from which the Constitution of the United States of America evolved, was an unwritten constitution and body of laws that developed from treaties, agreements, statutes, and court decisions.

It is difficult for an American to comprehend that as the English were developing a constitution raising the status and individual liberty of its inhabitants, the converse was true in much of the civilized world. It is said that when Voltaire came to England, his feeling was that he had passed out of the realm of despotism to a land where the laws might be harsh but where men were ruled by law and not by caprice.

To point up his despair, Voltaire was sent to the Bastille for a poem which he had not written, nor did he know who had written it, nor did he agree with its message. Voltaire had other experiences in his struggle against arbitrary power. He finally saved his life and property by accepting exile from France.

Prof. Dicey's third rule of law is not applicable to the study of the American Constitution. Even though the Constitution of the United States of America specifically declares certain rights to its inhabitants, it has remained for the courts to guarantee these rights through judicial interpretation.

In summary, the rule of law as we know it in the United States dictates an absolute supremacy of regular law in contrast to arbitrary power. It even excludes wide discretionary authority on the part of government. People may be punished for a breach of law, but they shall not be punished for anything else. It further means that there shall be equality before the law regardless of the influence that the litigants may possess through wealth or politics.

§ 1.20   Right to Personal Freedom

The English theory was and is that the freedom of a person is not a special privilege but is the result of the ordinary law of the land, which is enforced by the courts.

The Star Chamber Abolition Act of 1641 guaranteed to the English subject that a writ of habeas corpus was available against the King and the Council. In England and in the United States the right of personal liberty means essentially that a person shall not be subjected to arrest, imprisonment, or other physical or mental coercion unless there is a legal reason for such action. The law provides a remedy for those whose liberty has been taken away sans legal justification. As indicated above, the Star Chamber Abolition Act of 1641 provided for a writ of habeas corpus, which made the King and the Council accountable to the court.

15

§ 1.21   Writ of Habeas Corpus

One of the fundamental guarantees afforded the inhabitants of the United States is the writ of habeas corpus. The United States Constitution reinforces this guarantee by providing in Article I, Section 9, subdivision (2), "The privilege of the Writ of Habeas Corpus shall not be suspended, unless when in Cases of Rebellion or Invasion the public Safety may require it." A writ of habeas corpus may be defined as an order from a court to a named person or official to produce the body of a confined person before the court. The court then hears evidence to determine the legality of the detention of the incarcerated person. This right is so basic to our system of government that various states have provided statutory sanctions against jurists who fail to comply with a petition for a writ of habeas corpus. New York State provides by statute that if a judge refuses to issue a writ of habeas corpus, with respect to an incarcerated person who has not had the legality of his detention previously determined by habeas corpus proceedings, the judge forfeits to the person detained $1000 to be recovered by an action in his name or in the name of the petitioner to his use. (N.Y.) C.P.L.R. 7003. New York further provides by statute that any officer who shall deliver to a demanding state in an extradition case the person in custody, in disobedience of a writ of habeas corpus, commits a felony. (N.Y.)C.P.L. 570.26. Florida provides in Section 79.01, Florida Statutes, as interpreted by **CHASE v. STATE** 93 Fla. 963, 113 So. 103, 54 A.L.R. 271, where the court held that this is a writ of a person's right not subject to the court's discretion. It is also found in Section 13, Article I, of the Florida Constitution as follows:

> The writ of habeas corpus shall be grantable of right, freely and without cost. It shall be returnable without delay, and shall never be suspended unless, in case of rebellion or invasion, or suspension is essential to public safety.

Section 79.5, Florida Statutes, provides for a civil

liability of $300 against a person who fails to bring a prisoner before the court within three days of his being served with a writ of habeas corpus. The writ of habeas corpus has general recognition in all states.

While the right to a writ of habeas corpus is a fundamental right, in order to be eligible in Federal District Court to obtain such a writ from a state court prosecution, it is necessary to exhaust all state remedies as to federal claims. **ROSE v. LUNDY**, 455 U.S. 509, 102 S.Ct. 1198, 71 L.Ed.2d 379 (1982) codified in 28 U.S.C. 2254.

However in **CASTILLE ET.AL. v. PEOPLES**, 489 U.S. 346 109 S.Ct. 1056, 103 L.Ed.2d. 380, 44 Cr.L. 3145 (1989), the Court held that where a claim has been presented to the state courts for the first and only time in a procedural context, merits will not be considered unless "there are special and important reasons therefore." This is not fair presentation for purposes of an exception to the exhaustion requirement. The case was remanded to the Court of Appeals to determine whether the requisite exhaustion now exists because respondents claims are now procedurally barred in state court by a statute of limitations.

The writ of habeas corpus guarantee has some limitations established by the Court. In **STONE v. POWELL** 428 U.S. 465, 98 S.Ct. 3037, 49 L.Ed.2d 1067 (1976) the Court indicated that federal habeas corpus review would no longer be available to state defendants on the issue of unreasonable search and seizure where the state has provided a full and fair litigation of a Fourth Amendment claim.

Subsequently, the Court extended the concept of denial of federal habeas corpus relief in **MCCLESKEY v. ZANT**, Superintendent, Georgia Diagnostic and Classification Center,—U.S.—, 111 S.Ct. 1454, 113 L.Ed.2d. 517, 49 Cr.L. 2031 (1991) where the petitioner had been convicted of murder and a related crime and was sentenced to death. An occupant of an adjacent jail, a government informer, obtained a confession of the murder from the petitioner and testified in the trial with respect to this murder from the petitioner and boasted about it. He appealed the conviction, and after the State Supreme Court affirmed, he filed an unsuccessful

petition for state habeas corpus relief alleging, inter
alia, that his statements to the informer were arrived at
by a situation created by the state to induce him to make
incriminating statements without the assistance of
counsel in violation of **MASSIAH v. UNITED STATES** 377 U.S.
201. He then filed a first federal habeas corpus
petition which did not raise a Massiah claim and a second
state petition, both unsuccessful. He then filed his
second federal habeas corpus petition basing a Massiah
challenge on a statement made by the informer to police
two weeks before trial.

The Court in a 6-3 decision held that his failure to
raise a Massiah claim in his first federal habeas
petition constituted an abuse of the writ and affirmed
the Court of Appeals in its characterization that this
was an abuse of the writ situation.

In **STRINGER v. LEE ROY BLACK, COMMISSIONER,
MISSISSIPPI DEPARTMENT OF CORRECTIONS**, 503 U.S.
_____, 112 S.CT. 1130, 117 L.ED.2d 367, 50 Cr L 2094
(1992), the Court, in a 6-3 decision, held that federal
habeas corpus relief may be available to a petitioner
whose death sentence became final before a decision of
this Court that was more favorable to him was decided.
But, he may not rely on the more favorable decision if
the later decision involved a new rule of law. The
appellate court must first decide, however, whether the
later decision in question announced a new rule, i.e.,
was not dictated by precedent existing when his judgment
became final. If the answer is yes and neither of two
exceptions apply, not applicable in the instant case, the
decision is not available to the petitioner. Second, if
the decision did not announce a new rule, it is
necessary to inquire whether granting the relief sought
would create a new rule because the prior decision is
applied in a novel setting thereby extending the
precedent. The Court did not precisely say it, but your
author believes, that the finality requirement will
preclude review in such a case.

It may be also said that the federal habeas corpus
relief is appropriate when no new rule was enunciated by
the Court and relied on by the petitioner after the
petitioner was sentenced. This reasoning by the Court
promotes the interest in finality, predictability and

comity underlying the new rule jurisprudence.

§ 1.22   HABEAS CORPUS - NON RELEVANCE TO NEW LAW

The issue of reference in a trial to defendant's silence after he was given a 'Miranda Warning' arose in **BRECHT v. ABRAHAMSON**, _____ U.S._____, 113 S.Ct. 1710,123 L.Ed.2d 353, 53 Cr L 2023(1993). In that case the defendant shot and killed his brother-in-law. He never indicated that it was an accidental shooting until he testified at the trial. He was convicted and brought a habeas corpus petition. Basically, on the grounds that the prosecutor permitted the jury to know that he had previously said nothing about an accident.

The Court held that different standards apply in a habeas corpus petition, that is known as collateral review, as opposed to coming up on certiorari, where it is considered a direct review. For example, new constitutional rulings always apply retroactively in direct review but seldom apply in collateral review. The main interest is in finality of conviction that came to the end of the direct review process.

The Court held that the mention of petitioner's failure to state at any time prior to his trial testimony that the shooting was an accident did not "substantially influence" the jury's verdict.

A 1993 case captioned **LEONEL TORRES HERRERA, PETITIONER v. JAMES A. COLLINS, DIRECTOR TEXAS DEPARTMENT OF CRIMINAL JUSTICE, INSTITUTIONAL DIVISION,** _____ **U.S.** _____, _____ **S.Ct.** _____, _____ **L.Ed.2d.** _____ 52 Cr L 2090 (1993), refined the right to Federal habeas corpus relief still further. In that case the petitioner was found guilty after trial of the capital murder of one police officer. Approximately 6 months after sentencing, he pled guilty to a related capital murder of another police officer. He had been sentenced to death on the trial of the death of the first police officer. His cases went through many proceedings in the Texas courts and a Federal habeas corpus proceeding all of which were unsuccessful. Approximately ten years had passed when he sought a second habeas corpus in Federal court. His latest petition claimed by affidavits of other persons that he was innocent of both police officers' deaths and his deceased brother was the perpetrator. He contended that this was newly discovered evidence.

This reached the Court and in several opinions, that concurred in part on a 6-3 basis, the majority held that his claim of innocence did not entitle him to Federal habeas corpus relief in that his claim had to be evaluated in light of the previous ten years of proceedings in this case. After a fair trial in which he was found guilty, his presumption of innocence disappears. The Court further said that Federal habeas corpus does not set to correct errors of fact, but to insure that individuals are not imprisoned in violation of the Constitution. The Court said that Executive Clemency could be the petitioner's relief but not Federal habeas corpus.

In reading this case, I couldn't help but guess that the petitioner might have been persuaded to confess to the second police officers death to shield someone else because he was already sentenced to death. After his brother died, he probably decided to get affidavits from others exonerating himself from both killings.

§ 1.23   Bills of Attainder and Impeachment

A bill of attainder pertains to a right of personal freedom. Such a bill is crucial to the preservation of the English and American concept of due process of law. Article I, Section 9, subdivision (3), of the United States Constitution notes, "No Bill of Attainder or ex post facto Law shall be passed." It also appears in Article I, Section 10, as a limitation on state power.

The English experience with bills of attainder was disastrous. *Bills of Attainder* can be defined as legislative acts, no matter what their form, that apply to named individuals or to easily ascertainable members of a group in such a way as to inflict punishment on them without a judicial trial. **UNITED STATES v. BROWN**, 381 U.S. 437, 448 (1965).

A bill of attainder was a Tudor weapon whereby

20

Parliament could vote a person to death without a regular trial. It was not uncommon to still the voice of a political enemy by passing a bill of attainder. This type of action was supplanted with the device known as impeachment, which was far less ghastly. Apparently impeachment was first used in the Good Parliament of 1376. This was done by Parliament, presuming the idea that it was the highest court in the land and still retaining the concept that the King can do no wrong. The House of Commons acted as a sort of grand jury in presenting offending ministers to the Upper House for trials of high offenses. Even though the King could do no wrong, it was still an offense to give the King bad advice or even obey bad orders given by him. In this way, Parliament had complete control over finances, reasonable control over legislation, and a little control over policies.

The framers of the United States Constitution, armed with the knowledge of what had occurred in England, provided for the remedy of impeachment as a method of keeping control over the executive. U.S. Const., Art. II, Sec. 4. Executions were no longer necessary.

§ 1.24   Ex Post Facto Law

Article I, Section 9, subdivision (3), and Section 10, of the United States Constitution, previously indicated, prohibits the enactment of an ex post facto law. An *ex post facto law* has been defined as "every law that makes an action done before the passing of the law which was innocent when done, to be criminal and punishable as a crime; every law that aggravates a crime or makes it greater than when it was committed; every law that alters the legal rules of evidence and requires less or different testimony than the law required at the time of the commission of the offense in order to convict the offender." **HILL v. STATE OF TEXAS** 171 S.W.2d 880 (1943). The courts have construed ex post facto laws to be applicable only to criminal statutes that work to the disadvantage of the defendant. **CALDER ET WIFE v. BULL ET WIFE**, 3 U.S. 386, 1 L.Ed. 648 (1798).

A refinement of the application of ex post facto laws appeared in **COLLINS, DIRECTOR OF TEXAS DEPARTMENT OF CRIMINAL JUSTICE v. YOUNGBLOOD** 497 U.S.—, 110 S.Ct. 2715, 111 L.Ed. 30, 47 Cr.L. 2180 (1990). This case involved a conviction for aggravated assault wherein Youngblood was convicted and was sentenced to life imprisonment and a $10,000 fine. His conviction and sentence were affirmed on direct appeal and he sought a writ of habeas corpus in state court, arguing that Texas law did not authorize both a fine and prison term for the offense and asked for a new trial. The court recommended that the writ be granted but before the Court of Criminal Appeals considered the writ, a new statute was passed allowing an appellate court to reform an improper verdict assessing a punishment not authorized by law. The Court of Criminal Appeals reformed the verdict by eliminating the fine and denied the request for a new trial.

The respondent argued that the new law violated the Ex Post Facto Clause Article I Sec. 10 and filed a writ of habeas corpus in Federal District Court which was denied. The Court of Appeals reversed. The Court, through Rehnquist, CJ. joined by 5 other justices held that the Texas statute allowing reformation of improper verdicts does not punish a crime an act previously committed, which was innocent when done, nor make more burdensome the punishment for a crime, after its commission, nor deprive one charged with a crime of any defenses available according to law at the time it was committed. Its application to respondent therefore is not prohibited by the Ex Post Facto Clause Article I Sec. 10. The Court of Appeals was reversed.

§ 1.25   Writ of Assistance

A writ of assistance was an ancient writ issuing from the court of exchequer to the sheriff commanding him to aid the king's tenants by knights' service or to the king's collectors, debtors, or accountants to enforce payment of their own dues so that they in turn could pay their dues to the kings. In effect, it put the creditor in possession of lands owned by the debtor when the

22

sheriff could not execute against any other property. For a detailed discussion of this writ see **MARBELHEAD LAND CO. v. LOS ANGELES COUNTY**, (D.C. 276 F. 305).

§ 1.26   Early Function of the United States Government

The government conceived by the framers of the Constitution was to maintain law and order and to protect life, liberty, and property from both internal and external threats. The state government was to protect the health, morals, and welfare of its inhabitants. Individuals were to be left free to follow their own interests in competition with other individuals without interference from government.

At the time of the ratification of the Constitution, approximately 75% of the American people were farmers, while the rest were small craftsmen, tradesmen, merchants, professional men, or seamen.

Around 1900 this composition of the people came to an end as a result of the Industrial Revolution, the growth in population, and the rise of giant industrial corporations. The immigrants from Europe came in droves as they flocked to the cities and industrialized centers looking for work and living accommodations. The economic life of the country changed as rural populations moved to the cities and the attitude toward government changed. The industrialized society caused the individual to be less and less self-sufficient and the people looked to the government for help.

§ 1.27   Supreme Court Supervisory Powers

The United States Supreme Court has supervisory powers over federal criminal justice by virtue of Article III of the United States Constitution. While Article III established and defined the judicial power of the United States in one Supreme Court, it delegated to Congress the power to create lower federal courts. The supervisory powers are inherent in interpretation of the Constitution, a role the Supreme Court has assumed since

Chief Justice Marshall's decision in **MARBURY v. MADISON**, 1 Cranch 137, 5 U.S. 368, 2 L.Ed. 60 (1803), where Chief Justice Marshall elevated a court of law into an important organ of government. Although judicial review was not expressly granted by the Constitution, it was first asserted in **MARBURY v. MADISON** (supra). In that case, Marshall, who was an ardent Federalist, favored a strong national government and distrusted the people's capacity for self-government.

The Federalists were defeated in the election of 1800, but they tried to maintain their influence by finding positions for loyal followers between the time of the election of 1800 and the inauguration on March 4, 1801. In January 1801, President Adams, a Federalist, named his Secretary of State John Marshall, as Chief Justice of the United States. The lame-duck Congress passed the Judiciary Act of 1801, which created many new judgeships in lower courts and also provided that the next vacancy of the Supreme Court should not be filled. This act reduced the number of justices of the Court from six to five, making the appointment of a justice by the new Democratic-Republican President, Thomas Jefferson, all but impossible. A number of commissions for justices of the peace for the District of Columbia were not signed by midnight on March 3, 1801, by the outgoing Secretary of State, John Marshall, and were in the Secretary of State's office waiting delivery when Jefferson became President. Jefferson ordered his new Secretary of State, James Madison, not to deliver some of the commissions to the "midnight appointees."

William Marbury was one of the "midnight appointees" whose commission as justice of the peace for the District of Columbia had not been delivered. He and three other appointees petitioned the Supreme Court for a writ of mandamus to compel Secretary of State Madison to deliver the commissions. This had been a common law writ that had English origin.

It was thought that Marshall, being a Federalist, would order Madison to deliver the commissions and thereby initiate a struggle between the Court and the executive branch of government. To most people's surprise, he did not order this. Although he found fault with Madison for failing to deliver the commissions,

Judiciary Act of 1789 was passed by Congress

Marshall held that the Court could not compel Madison to act because the statute cited by Marbury and the other petitioner was unconstitutional. They had relied on Section 13 of the Judiciary Act of 1789, which stated that the Supreme Court could issue writs of mandamus in "cases warranted by the principles and usages of law, to any courts appointed, or persons holding office under authority of the United States." Marshall stated that this act enlarged the original jurisdiction of the Supreme Court beyond that stated in Article III of the Constitution. In that Article, original jurisdiction was conferred on the Supreme Court in only two types of cases; those "affecting ambassadors, other public ministers and consuls, and those in which a state shall be a party." Since Marbury's suit did not fall into either of these categories, Marshall ruled that the suit should not have been brought initially to the Supreme Court. Further, since there was a contradiction between the law of Congress and that of the Constitution, the Supreme Court had a clear duty to maintain the higher law of the Constitution and to declare the legislative act unconstitutional.

Thus, we see the principle of the supervisory power of the Supreme Court developed. To use the words of Howard L. McBain as he expressed them in the Bacon Lectures on the Constitution of the United States, "Some Aspects of Judicial Review," published by Boston University, Heffernan Press, 1939:

> " The concept of judicial review rests upon an extraordinarily simple foundation. Stripped to its essence, it is almost too plain for stating. The Constitution is the supreme law. It was ordained by the people, for ultimate source of all political authority. It confers limited powers on the national government. These limitations derive partly from the mere fact that these powers are enumerated—the government cannot exercise powers not granted to it—and partly from certain express prohibitions upon its powers or upon the manner of their exercise. If the government consciously or unconsciously oversteps these

25

limitations there must be some authority competent to hold it in control, to thwart its unconstitutional attempt, and thus to vindicate and preserve inviolate the will of the people as expressed in the Constitution. This power the courts exercise. This is the beginning and the end of the theory of judicial review".[2]

§ 1.28   State Constitutions

The custom of establishing a written constitution was an outgrowth of trading-company royal or proprietary charters. It was a means of establishing fundamental written law. Vattel, who wrote a pamphlet on the *Laws of Nations* which had some popularity in America, insisted that the fundamental law ought to be a fixed and written document. It is interesting to note that none of the state conventions during 1776 and 1777 submitted their results to the people for approval. Each merely proclaimed a new constitution to be in operation. The early state constitutions were not democratic in nature according to present-day standards. Most constitutions required a property qualification in order to have voting privileges. In order to be a governor or legislator the aspirant had to have considerable wealth.

§ 1.29   Concept of Judicial Review

Judicial review was an outgrowth of the revolutionary philosophy. Its basis was that the legislature should have limited power with an independent judiciary combined with a separation of powers. James Otis had argued in the Writs of Assistance case that an act against the supreme Constitution was void and that it was the duty of the *courts* to "pass the law into disuse."

---

[2]McBain, <u>Some Aspects of Judicial Review</u>, BACON LECTURES ON THE CONSTITUTION (1939).

26

§ 1.30   Bill of Rights

There was much infighting within the state conventions and olive branches were offered in the form of a Bill of Rights which would be attached to the document at the first opportunity.

James Madison had at first proposed that the content of the original document be altered to include the provisions of the Bill of Rights. After much debate in both houses, a compromise resulted in the passage by Congress of the Bill of Rights which was followed by the adoption of the first ten amendments to the Constitution.

It should be noted that James Madison did not initially agree with the Tenth Amendment in that he believed that "powers must necessarily be admitted by implication." The ten amendments were finally adopted by Congress in 1789 and by the states within two years of the establishment of the government.

With this historical insight into the development of the Constitution of the United States of America, the student is brought to the realization that it was not created overnight; that it was the result of trial and error worked on by the best minds of the time; that it was fraught with economic implications; and that it was accomplished by the blood, sweat, tears, and dedication of many persons with opposing viewpoints. It is said that a compromise exists where no one is completely satisfied and no one is completely dissatisfied. This is the nature of the Constitution of the United States. Its general terms have left to future generations the job of interpreting its clauses in the light of contemporary thinking.

§ 1.31 Distribution of Powers and Reservation of Powers

Hence we now have a legacy of a document which derives its power from the people to the government. Where the government is one of enumerated powers with a legislature to make the laws, an executive to implement the laws, and a judiciary to interpret the laws. Occasionally we find a hybrid situation develops and is

given constitutionality by the Court. Such a situation
arose in **TOUBY v. UNITED STATES**,—U.S.—, 111 S.Ct. 1752,
114 L.Ed.2d 219, 49 Cr.L. 2169 (1991). In that case the
Controlled Substance Act Section 201 (h) of 98 Stat 2071,
21 U.S.C. Sect. 811 (h) gave the Attorney General the
authority, upon compliance with specified procedures, to
add new drugs to five "schedules" of controlled
substances. The Attorney General added a drug known as
"EUPHORIA" to the list temporarily. This was done to
combat the drug trade in their ability to quickly concoct
what became known as "designer drugs." It took between
6-12 months to comply with the procedure while drug
traffickers were flooding the market. The Attorney
General meanwhile subdelegated enforcement authority of
these drugs to the Drug Enforcement Administration. The
question arose in this case as to whether this was an
unconstitutional act on the part of the Attorney General.
The Court rejected the separation of powers argument
saying that the principle does not speak to the manner in
which authority is parcelled out within a single branch.
     Another argument presented by the petitioners is
that the method bars judicial review. The court rejected
this argument also because another section of the Act
authorizes judicial review of a permanent scheduling
order. Concomitant with this, we have in the Tenth
Amendment provision that if the enumerated power of
government is not expressly given to the United States
government, it is therefore reserved to the states to
exercise this power. One of the basic powers not
specifically given to the government of the United States
was the power over the health, welfare, and morals of the
state inhabitants. This is commonly referred to as the
police power. However, through the concept of implied
power as construed by the United States Court, there has
been a gradual incursion into the police power of the
states.
     It is the judicial and police power which we will be
concerned with in the following chapters of this book.

§ 1.32   Constitutional Judicial Review

Article VI of the Constitution reads:

> *This Constitution, and the Laws of the United*
> *States which shall be made in Pursuance*
> *thereof; and all Treaties made, or which shall*
> *be made, under the Authority of the United*
> *States, shall be the supreme Law of the Land;*
> *and the Judges in every State shall be bound*
> *thereby; any Thing in the Constitution or Laws*
> *of any State to the Contrary notwithstanding.*
> . . .

This Article was the source of much controversy initially. State judges went along their own merry way in deciding cases contrary to the intent of the Constitution. The first Chief Justice of the United States Supreme Court was John Jay. He thought so little of the office that he sought and won the "higher" office of Governor of the State of New York.

It was not until John Marshall, the fourth Chief Justice, took the position that the office came to be one of the most influential forces in government. A case decided by his court within two years after he began his service in the Court caused the Constitution to assume significant new directions. This was accomplished through his leadership, referred to supra in § 1.27, supra.

The case was **MARBURY v. MADISON**, 5 U.S. 368, 2 L.Ed. 60, decided in 1803, and it provided for judicial review to examine the language of the Constitution, to invalidate any lower form of law found by the courts to be in violation of the Constitution which is the "supreme Law of the Land." John Marshall implemented what he and his associate judges believed the framers of the Constitution had in mind. They were perhaps buttressed in this opinion by the writings of James Otis.

It is ordinarily necessary that a litigant must raise a constitutional issue on the trial of the action in order for a higher court to reconsider the issue on appeal. However in **AMEDEO v. ZANT**, 486 U.S. 214, 108

S.Ct. 1771, 100 L.Ed.2d. 249, 43 Cr.L. 3043 (1988), the
Court held that where a petitioner for Habeas Corpus
relief had made a procedural default in which no record
had been made in the trial of a constitutional objection
to the method of selection of petitioner's jury, the
conviction may be considered on appeal and reversed. In
this case there was an objection to the method of
selection wherein the prosecutor sent a memorandum to the
Putnam County Jury Commissioners that was intentionally
designed to result in under representation of black
people and women in the master jury lists from which all
grand and petit juries were drawn. The memorandum was
uncovered by one of plaintiff's attorneys while preparing
an appeal. The Court held that by the officials'
concealment of the evidentiary basis for the challenge,
the failure to raise this issue at the trial was
adequately explained for the purpose of the "cause" prong
of the test for excusing such defaults.

A showing that the factual or legal basis for a
claim was not reasonably available to counsel, or that
some interference by officials made compliance
impracticable constituted cause.

§ 1.33   Limitations on Judicial Power

There is a proclivity for a person who has ascended
the bench to think that God has died and the judge
assumes the role of God. The Constitution has guarded
against this phenomenon by the system of checks and
balances previously described. Notwithstanding this
system, we often find cases wherein the judicial power is
abused. The Constitution as interpreted by the Marshall
decisions ultimately protects the litigant from this
human frailty.

A famous example of overbearing judicial temperament
occurred in **SHEPPARD v. MAXWELL**, 384 U.S. 333, 86 S.Ct.
1507 (1966), where the presiding judge was more
interested in his image with the media than he was with
the concept of fundamental fairness of trial.
Unfortunately, not every litigant has the resources to
take cases to the United States Supreme Court, and

admittedly there are still judges who abuse the powers of their office.

It is, however, interesting to note that one by one each of the states is enacting legislation to review the judicial temperament of judges, their competence, and their right to remain in office or to be reappointed.

Your attention is directed to the following sentences in the **MARBURY v. MADISON** case (supra):

> "From these, and many other selections which might be made, it is apparent, that the framers of the constitution contemplated that instrument as a rule for the government of courts, as well as legislature. Why otherwise does it direct the judges to take an oath to support it? .... Why does a judge swear to discharge his duties agreeably to the constitution of the United States if that constitution forms no rule for his government? .... and that courts as well as other departments, are bound by that instrument."

In **MARTIN v. HUNTER'S LESSEE**, 14 U.S. 562, 4 L.Ed. 97 (1816), and **COHENS v. VIRGINIA**, 19 U.S. 82, 5 L.Ed. 257 (1821), the United States Supreme Court applied the theory of judicial review to decisions of state courts.

§ 1.34   Means by Which Cases Reach the United States Supreme Court

Any lawyer who has been in general private practice can tell you of experiences which he/she has had where an irate client comes to the office and says substantially, "I don't care what it costs, I want to take this case to the United States Supreme Court." Little does the client know that the probability of the United States Supreme Court's deciding his case is very small because appeal, as a right, exists only in a small number of designated cases. Even if a constitutional issue is involved, the workload of the Court is so large that, of necessity, the Court must screen its case load to consist of those matters where a substantial federal question is involved. The word "substantial," being nebulous, creates problems, but the Justices of the Court have the final word in this area. The largest number of cases reaching the Court are by way of writ of certiorari.

§ 1.35   Federal Court Structure

Section 1, Article III, provides that "the judicial power of the United States shall be vested in one Supreme Court, and in such inferior courts as the Congress from time to time, ordain and establish."

To implement this provision, Congress passed the First Judiciary Act in 1789. By the terms of the Act, a federal court system was established which was substantially unchanged for almost a century. It set up the power of the Supreme Court to supervise state courts dealing with federal constitutional issues and set up a system of federal courts operating throughout the nation instead of only in the nation's capital.

§ 1.36   United States District Courts

The court of original jurisdiction in federal matters is called a United States District Court. It might be called the United States District Court for the Eastern District of New York or the United States District Court for the Southern District of Florida.

The district courts are scattered throughout the fifty states and their number is set by Congress. The number of courts varies from time to time depending on legislation, log rolling in Congress, and need. There is at least one district court in each of the states. United States District Courts, as their name implies, have jurisdiction over all federal matters, both criminal and civil, except a few disputes which start in the specialized legislative courts or the Supreme Court.

§ 1.37   Court of Appeal

The United States Courts of Appeal are the next higher court in the federal system. At one time were referred to as the Circuit Court of Appeals. The older cases refer to them as such. The name was changed by Congress in 1948.

These courts hear appeals from District Courts and from important independent regulatory commissions. These courts usually represent the end of the appellate procedure because the case seldom goes to the United States Supreme Court for reasons which will be explained later.

There are eleven circuits for these courts plus one for the District of Columbia. Each has a designated number except the court in the District of Columbia which is designated as United States Court of Appeals for the Federal Circuit. It is therefore obvious that territory of a United States Court of Appeals includes more than one state's boundaries. A panel of three judges usually reviews cases in that court.

§ 1.38   United States Supreme Court

This is the highest court of the federal system. It presently consists of a Chief Justice and eight Associate Justices. I emphasize the word "presently" in the preceding sentence because Congress has the power to change that number through legislation and, in fact, it has on several occasions.

However, it has not been changed by Congress since 1869. There was a great possibility of a change during the Franklin Roosevelt administration with his "packing the court" idea but the reason for the legislation disappeared and with it went the legislation. The legislation proposed that the number of justices be increased. In this way, Roosevelt hoped to appoint persons to the Court who would find social legislation passed by Congress to be constitutional.

The United States Supreme Court has original as well as appellate jurisdiction. Article III, Section 2, reads as follows:

> "In all Cases affecting Ambassadors, other
> public Ministers, and Consuls, and those in
> which a State shall be a Party, the supreme
> Court shall have original Jurisdiction.   In
> all other Cases before mentioned, the supreme
> Court shall have appellate Jurisdiction, both
> as to Law and Fact, with such Exceptions, and
> under such Regulations, as the Congress shall
> make".

For all practical purposes, however, the Supreme
Court is an appellate court.

The Supreme Court hears the following appeals where
federal questions are involved:

1.   From the highest state court;
2.   Directly from United States Districts Courts in
     some cases (explained more fully later in this
     chapter);
3.   From United States Courts of Appeals;
4.   From legislative courts (e.g., Court of Military
     Appeals).

The Supreme Court and lower courts in the federal
system are called constitutional courts if they are
legislated into being by virtue of Article III of the
Constitution. On the other hand, if Congress legislates
a court into being under the implied powers given to it
in other than Article III of the Constitution, the court
is then known as a legislative court.   The basic
difference is the requirement of appointment to Article
III judges in that they be appointed for life or good
behavior and can only be removed by impeachment, whereas
the legislative judicial appointments need not carry
these qualifications.

Congress has legislated the procedure by which a
case may be entertained by the United States Supreme
Court. There are three basic methods. One is by a writ
of certiorari, another is by certification, and the third
is by appeal. Some of the older cases appeared by the
common law writ of error but that was discontinued in

1928 and the substitute is generally an appeal.

§ 1.39   Writ of Certiorari

A writ of certiorari in Supreme Court practice is obtained by an unsuccessful litigant in a lower court by presenting a petition to the Supreme Court to review a lower court's decision. The opposing litigant may file answering briefs showing reasons why the writ should not be granted. Should the court decide that a substantial federal question is involved, it issues a writ to the lower court to send the entire record of the case in the court below to the United States Supreme Court for review. A very small percentage of the petitions for the writ are granted. That is why you will often see in a citation cert. den. (meaning certiorari is denied).

§ 1.40   Certification

The better nomenclature for this type of review might be certification of a question of law. This review is not controlled by the litigants. It occurs when a United States Court of Appeals or the Court of Claims is looking for guidance in deciding a case that is presently before that tribunal. The court will send certified questions of law to the United States Supreme Court with the hope that the Supreme Court will render a decision so that the lower court will, in effect, render a decision in the case before it, which it will believe will not be reversed by the United States Supreme Court if it should reach that body. This method of review, however, is seldom used.

§ 1.41   Appeal

This is the method most laymen have heard about but know very little about. The term "appeal" as used in

United States Supreme Court procedure refers to a method of review, which is a matter of right of a party to an action. Therefore the Supreme Court is obligated to review emanating from state courts in two situations as follows:

1. Where the validity of a treaty or statute of the United States is questioned and the state court has held it to be invalid;
2. Where the validity of a state law has been questioned on the ground that it contravenes the Constitution, treaties, or law of the United States and the state court sustains its validity.

In addition to the above mandatory reconsideration, the Supreme Court may review by appeal a decision of a United States Court of Appeals when a federal statute is held to be unconstitutional in a suit where the United States is a party or where a state statute is held by this court to be unconstitutional or repugnant to the laws of the United States or treaties of the United States. Some cases of the United States District Courts are reviewed directly by the United States Supreme Court on appeal if they are deemed by the court to be of sufficient importance and that they must be settled by the Supreme Court as quickly as possible.

Direct appeals from the United States District Court to the Supreme Court are allowed as follows:

1. Where the district court has held an act of Congress unconstitutional;
2. Where either a one-judge or three-judge district court has rendered a judgment in a suit brought by the United States to enforce:
    (a) the Interstate Commerce Act;
    (b) the Antitrust Laws;
    (c) the Federal Communications Act;
3. Suits brought by private parties in district court to restrain the enforcement of state or federal statutes because of unconstitutionality;
4. Suits brought in district courts before a three-judge bench where the court grants or denies an injunction setting aside orders of the Interstate

Commerce Commission.

It should be noted with great emphasis, however, that even though an appeal may be a matter of right to a litigant, a minimum of four justices have to decide that a substantial federal question exists before the entire Court will review a case on appeal. Accordingly, while every litigant who has a right to appeal does get judicial review of a sort in the United States Supreme Court, the full Court may never render a decision as to the merits of the case.

§ 1.42   Decision-Making Method of the United States Supreme Court

Few people are privy to the inner workings of how a case is decided in the United States Supreme Court.

The machinations at the Supreme Court are similar to a secret society. Little is known by the general public or bar as to how a case is decided by that Court. The justices do not speak about a case other than the written decisions. Of all the other branches of government, the Supreme Court is the least accountable. This is so because of the cardinal principle of our government that we shall have an independent judiciary.

Behind the robed figures that one sees on the bench of the court, however, are people, each with his/her own foibles, prejudices, and experiences of life. Given such a group, it is natural to assume that these jurists have differences of opinion which cause personal irritations between them.

There is a weekly conference usually scheduled for Wednesday afternoon and all day Friday. At these conferences cases are discussed. The Justices arrive punctually at 9:30 AM. In the center of the oak-paneled room is a massive mahogany table which is surrounded by nine high-backed chairs and many carts. These carts are wheeled in to the room before the conference, and they contain information on cases that each Justice thinks he may need to intelligently discuss a pending case. They pour themselves coffee from a silver urn and shake hands.

This apparently has been the custom since 1888. Following this, they sit down to argue their points.

As has been pointed out earlier in this text, not every case that finds its way to the hallowed chambers of the United States Supreme Court is decided by that Court. Some of the conferences are for the purpose of deciding what cases are worthy of their full consideration.

Copies of each case go to every Justice. Some of the Justices delegate the function of reading the petitions for review to their clerks and then rely on the clerks' summarizing memos. Mr. Justice Brennan had the reputation of personally reading virtually all of the petitions which ask for review.

Each Justice then makes his/her own decision as to whether the case presents a substantial federal question requiring a decision by the United States Supreme Court. If one Justice believes that such a substantial federal question exists, he asks that it be placed on the conference list for discussion. Most of the petitions for review, however, do not arouse a Justice's interest and are placed on "the dead list." If a case is placed on "the dead list," that case is not decided by the Court.

When a case is placed on the conference list, it requires the vote of at least four Justices to grant it review. The result of this voting are usually kept secret. On occasion, if a Justice believes very strongly that a case should be considered by the Court for review and the vote, after it has been placed on the conference list, is negative, the Justice who felt so strongly about it writes a dissenting opinion with respect to the Court's refusal to hear and decide the case. There have been times when such a dissenting opinion resulted in a reconsideration at a subsequent conference list and because of the persuasiveness of the dissenting Justice's opinion, other Justices have changed their votes to place the matter on the Court's calendar.

After the Court agrees to hear the case, it is scheduled for oral argument some months later. Meanwhile, lawyers for opposing sides file written briefs usually consisting of sixty to eighty pages. Often friends of the Court also supply the Court with their briefs. When the appointed day arrives, each side has one-half hour for oral argument. The Justices often ask questions of the attorneys who are arguing their cases.

At the following Friday conference, these cases are again considered by the Justices. Beginning with the Chief Justice and then the Associate Justices in the order of their seniority, each expresses his/her view. At length a vote is taken but this time the junior Justice votes first. Presumably, this method is used so that the junior Justice's vote will not be influenced by the vote of the senior Justices.

No one, except the Justices, is permitted in the conference room. All notes are taken by the Justices themselves. If the Chief Justice is on the majority side, he will assign an Associate Justice to write the decision or may elect to write it himself. The dissenters decide among themselves who is going to write the decision.

There is a rule that up until the moment that an opinion is announced in public, each Justice may change his/her mind. It appears that this frequently happens. The shifts in their votes are a result of changes in the Justices' minds based upon their efforts to apply their knowledge and experience to their understanding of the facts of the case.

Each Justice has three law clerks to assist him/her. Naturally, each Justice has his own method in writing opinions. Some write initial opinions after extended research. They then give these opinions to their clerks to add, delete, or check out the veracity of the reasoning and citations. Then a conference is held which might extend to the early hours of the morning, whereby each comma, period, or phrase is checked out between the clerks and the Justice. Finally, a completed document is submitted to the other Justices. Following this, "joint memos" are sent, hopefully, to the Justice who wrote the opinion. Sometimes other Justices recommend additional or different language to the authoring Justice, and he/she must decide whether or not to change the original opinion to meet the requirements of the other Justices. When minor differences occur, the point may be omitted entirely. When this occurs, scholars may have difficulty understanding what the Court had in mind because of a step being missed in the Court's reasoning process.

Each time a new draft of an opinion is circulated, any change is indicated in the margin by means of a black line. Many decisions require many draft corrections before they are finally agreed upon and announced.

United States Supreme Court Justices are reported to be working six or seven days a week. If one computes the overtime, they may be said to work eight or ten days a week.

From the above, it becomes quite apparent that the law of the land as interpreted by the United States Supreme Court is not created without serious deliberation and compromise.

§ 1.43   Genesis of Anglo-Saxon Law Enforcement

We have discussed the Anglo-Saxon and American concept of freedom of the individual. Now we shall treat the other side of the coin. As has been shown, the framers of the Constitution, recognizing the will of the people for protection from enemies from within, provided that the states have an obligation to provide for the arrest of malefactors.

There was no organized police force in Anglo-Saxon history until 1829 when Sir Robert Peel persuaded the English Parliament to pass an act creating a police force for the city of London. He, therefore, is sometimes referred to as the father of the concept of an organized police force to keep the peace; hence, the affectionate name of "Bobbies" which the London police still bear.

Prior to 1829, the Crown appointed sheriffs and constables. They were the only peace officers and they had the authority to call upon the citizens to form a posse comitatus which would assist in making an arrest of a suspect. From this idea we have evolved the concept of a citizen's arrest. It had been the duty of the citizen to make an arrest and this has continued to this day with a modification of the word "duty" to that of a "right" of a private citizen to make an arrest. He is no longer under any duty unless he is called upon to assist a peace officer. In that case, many states today provide by statute that a refusal to assist a peace officer in making an arrest when requested to do so by the peace officer results in the commission of a criminal offense by the refusing citizen.

At common law, most arrests were made after the issuance of a warrant. There was a distinction between less grievous and more grievous crimes and they were given the nomenclatures of misdemeanors and felonies respectively.

In misdemeanor cases, both the peace officer and the private citizen could not lawfully effect an arrest without a warrant unless the crime was a breach of the peace committed in their presence. Felonies, however, being far more serious, and the possibility of flight by the perpetrator being greater because of the severity of the punishment, called for more drastic action. Accordingly, in the case of a felony, a peace officer or a private person, acting without a warrant, could make an arrest for a felony actually committed, if it were committed in his presence or if he had reasonable grounds to believe that the person to be arrested had committed the felony. Thus we see developed through common law, an obligation by the executive branch of government to maintain the peace and to arrest, detain, and punish violators.

Most states have by statute adopted the original common law concept of arrest but have enlarged it to give greater authority of arrest to peace officers. Some states have further divided the duties of a peace officer to add that of a police officer with added power and responsibilities. (N.Y.) Criminal Procedure Law. 140.10; 140.25.

(Tenn.) Tennessee Code, Section 40.803,reads as follows:

"Grounds for arrest by officer without warrant-An officer may, without a warrant, arrest a person:

(1) For a public offense committed or a breach of the peace threatened in his presence.

(2) When the person has committed a felony, though not in his presence.

(3) When a felony has in fact been committed, and he has reasonable cause for believing the

person arrested to have committed it.
(4)   On a charge made, upon reasonable cause, of
      the commission of a felony by the person
      arrested."

However, Section 40.816 of the Tennessee Code is as follows:

"Grounds for arrest by private persons-No fee
allowed-A private person may arrest another:
(1)   For a public offense committed in his
      presence.
(2)   When the person arrested has committed a
      felony, although not in his presence.
(3)   When a felony has been committed, and he has
      reasonable cause to believe that the person
      arrested committed it.
      Provided, that a private person who
      makes an arrest of another pursuant
      to the provisions of Sections
      40.816-40.823, shall receive no
      arrest fee or compensation
      therefor."

A close reading of the powers of arrest of a private
person as compared to those of an officer in Tennessee
reveals that the private person has almost as much power
to arrest as that of an officer, but there are civil
restraints available in the nature of an action for false
imprisonment, seeking money damages where a private
person unlawfully arrests another.

§ 1.44   Constitutional Basis of Arrest

The Constitution of the United States has provisions
regarding arrest, search, and seizure. As had been
indicated previously, the framers of the Constitution
were fearful of creating another monarchy with omnipotent
powers. Accordingly, the Fourth Amendment, along with the
remaining Bill of Rights, was proposed during the first
Congress by James Madison.

The Fourth Amendment adopted in 1791 reads as follows:

> *"The right of the people to be secure in their persons, houses, papers, and effects, against unreasonable searches and seizures, shall not be violated, and no Warrants shall issue, but upon probable cause, supported by Oath or affirmation, and particularly describing the place to be searched, and the person or things to be seized."*

History has demonstrated that there was extensive litigation relating to the construction the United States Supreme Court would give to this amendment. Between 1914 and 1962, federal law enforcement officers were strictly bound by its direction while state law enforcement officers in some states were not bound by it. **WEEKS v. UNITED STATES**, 232 U.S. 383, 34 S.Ct. 341, 58 L.Ed. 652 (1914). Colorado was one state which had previously had its own interpretation of reasonable search which was different from the federal rule. The United States Supreme Court sustained Colorado's right to arrest and convict persons whose Fourth Amendment rights had been violated. In **WOLF v. COLORADO**, 338 U.S. 25, 698 S.Ct. 1359, 93 L.Ed. 1782 (1949), MR. JUSTICE FRANKFURTER, speaking for a majority of the court, said in a 5-4 decision,

> ".... the security of one's privacy against arbitrary intrusion by the police-which is the core of the Fourth Amendment-is basic to a free society. It is therefore implicit in "the concept of ordered liberty" and as such enforceable against the states.... Accordingly, we have no hesitation in saying that were a State affirmatively to sanction such police incursion into privacy, it would run counter to the guarantee of the Fourteenth Amendment. But the ways of enforcing such a basic right raise questions of a different order."

The court continued by discussing the exclusionary rule which forbade the introduction of such unreasonably seized evidence and the use of the exclusionary rule in federal prosecutions as well as some state jurisdictions. The court then went on to say:

> "We cannot, therefore, regard it as a departure from basic standards to remand such persons, together with those who emerge scatheless from a search, to the remedies of private action and such protection as the internal discipline of its police, under the eyes of an alert public opinion may afford. Granting that in practice the exclusion of evidence may be an effective way of deterring unreasonable searches, it is not for this Court to condemn as falling below the minimal standards assured by the Due Process Clause a State's reliance upon other methods which, if consistently enforced would be equally effective.... The public opinion of a community can far more effectively be exerted against oppressive conduct on the part of the police directly responsible to the community itself than can local opinion, sporadically aroused, be brought to bear upon remote authority pervasively exerted throughout the country."

In essence, the court said that if a state violated a person's Fourth Amendment rights, the person could not take advantage of an exclusionary rule but could sue the officer and bring public opinion to bear to have the officer disciplined. However, the evidence was admissible and the conviction will not be disturbed.

In 1963, **KER v. CALIFORNIA**, 374 U.S. 23, 24 Ohio Op.2d 201, 10 L.Ed.2d 726, 83 S. Ct. 1623, the court held that legality of arrests by state and local police officers are to be judged by the same constitutional standards as those of the federal government.

For some time there was a question as to whether the Fourth Amendment applied to mere arrests of persons. This was laid to rest in **HENRY v. UNITED STATES**, 361 U.S.

44

98, 80 S.Ct. 168, 4 L.Ed.2d 134 (1959), where the court said the statute states the constitutional standard, for it is the command of the Fourth Amendment that no warrants for either searches or arrests shall issue except upon probable cause, supported by oath or affirmation, and particularly describing the place to be searched, and the persons or things to be seized. Note that the court included the words "searches and arrests" in its determination.

The Court explained the constitutional necessity for a "promptly after arrest" determination of probable cause in a warrantless arrest situation in **GERSTEIN v. PUGH**, 420 U.S 103, 113, 95 S.CT. 854 (1975), 43 L.ED.2d 54, where the Court stated ". . . the Court has never invalidated an arrest supported by probable cause solely because the officers failed to secure a warrant." In **RIVERSIDE COUNTY, CALIF. v. McLAUGHLIN**, 500 U.S. _____, 111 S.Ct. 1661, 114 L.Ed.2d 49, 49 Cr L 2103 (1991), the Court further defined the meaning of "promptly after arrest" to include a period of up to 48 hours. The Court said "Where an arrested individual does not receive a probable cause determination within 48 hours, the burden shifts to the government to demonstrate the existence of a bona fide emergency or other extraordinary circumstance which cannot include intervening weekends or the fact that in a particular case it may take longer to consolidate pretrial proceedings."

§ 1.45   Arrest Defined

The reader is no doubt conversant with the layman's concept of the meaning of arrest. Many times the courts are called upon to distinguish between an arrest and the taking of a person into custody for the purpose of investigation. It is frequently said that the officer invited the suspect to come to the police station to answer some questions and the suspect complied with the invitation. Defense attorneys frequently ask the officers what the officer would have done had the suspect refused. This question is based upon probabilities and should not be permitted as a legally admissible question.

A legal definition of arrest which has been given much authority contains the following elements:

1. The purpose or intention to effect the arrest under real or pretended authority;
2. Actual or constructive seizure or detention of the person to be arrested by the person having present power to control him;
3. Communication by the arresting officer of intention or purpose then and there to make the arrest;
4. Understanding by the person to be arrested that such is the intention of the arrester. **U.S. v. RAIDL**, 250 F.Supp. 278, 280.

A careful reading of the elements indicated above reveals that an arrest may be effected under pretended authority. If the authority is lacking the officer and/or governmental agency in which he/she is employed may be liable for money damages as a result of a civil action in unlawful arrest. The officer may also be liable for criminal and civil sanctions for arresting a person in violation of his constitutional rights. (Title 42 U.S.C. 1983, 18 U.S.C. 241, 18 U.S.C. 242.) These will be treated in much greater detail in a later portion of this text. In **MIAMI v. ARONOWITZ**, 141 S.2d 784 (Fla. 1959), the court held that a traffic officer's stopping the movement of vehicular traffic was not an arrest.

No governmental entity is permitted to enact a statute that is vague. If it would be otherwise, "men" would read into a statute what they wished and a possible violator would not have fair warning. An example of this occurred in a California statute that required a person who wanders on the streets to provide "credible" and "reliable" identification when stopped by police. This statute was declared unconstitutional because it contained no standards on what would satisfy the identification requirement and it was deemed vague on its face. **KOLENDER v. LAWSON**, 33 Cr.L.3063 (1983).

NEW YORK v. P.J. VIDEO INC., 475 U.S. 868, 106 S.Ct. 1610, 89 L.Ed.2d. 871, 39 Cr L 303 (1986), concerned a warrant that was issued to search and seize obscene video cassettes that were available for rent and sale in a video store. A confidential criminal investigator of the

District Attorney's Office of Erie County had executed an affidavit attached to a search warrant application wherein he summarized the theme of and conduct depicted in each movie. The New York courts suppressed the evidence on the grounds that the warrant in such a case required a higher probable-cause standard for issuing warrants to seize such things as books or movies than for warrants to seize weapons or drugs. The state court held further that there was insufficient information in the affidavits in this case under the higher standard requirement, to believe that the movies were obscene under New York law. In a 6-3 decision the Supreme Court held that no "higher probable-cause standard was required by the First Amendment for issuances of the warrant in question and the evidence should not have been suppressed."

§ 1.46   Valid Arrest and Search Warrant Requirements

You will remember that I previously indicated the terms of the Fourth Amendment. You will also remember that a comment was made that this amendment has been the subject of much litigation. We have also discussed how the United States Supreme Court has construed this amendment to be applicable to arrest situations.

We will now direct our attention to some requirements that the courts have construed as being necessary in every warrant of arrest. Foremost among these is the requirement that the warrant be supported by probable cause. Probable cause was defined in **CARROLL v. UNITED STATES**, 267 U.S. 132, 162, 45 S.Ct. 280, 288, 69 L.Ed. 543, 555 (1925), as "the facts and circumstances within (the officers') knowledge and of which they had reasonable trustworthy information were sufficient in themselves to warrant a man of reasonable caution to believe that a particular offense had been or was being committed." (See §2.22 for further discussion on this topic.) The probable cause must be found in the first instance by the officer who applies for the arrest warrant. However, his basis for probable cause must be reviewed by a detached magistrate or other judicial

officer. If probable cause is found by the detached
magistrate or other judicial officer, the order for the
arrest is issued.

In practice, the general format for applying for
either a search warrant or an arrest warrant is that the
officer will prepare and execute an affidavit detailing
all facts which either he/she or a police informant had
observed. If an informant is used, the officer must
indicate the past reliability of the informant. The
officer must buttress the information of the informant by
his/her own personal observations or the observations of
a fellow officer who, in the line of duty, imparted the
information to the officer who is executing the
affidavit. The detached magistrate or judicial officer
then makes an individual appraisal based upon the
information in the affidavit. If he/she feels that
probable cause exists based upon an evaluation of the
facts and the credibility of the fact observer, he/she
will issue a warrant to the officer to arrest the named
person or search the premises particularly described in
the warrant for the particular evidence sought.

Jurisdictions may vary with respect to the times of
the day that the warrant may be executed and how long the
warrant is effective.

After the warrant is issued, the officer then
executes the warrant by either arresting the named person
or making the seizure of the particularly described
evidence and place to be searched. The next court
appearance is sometimes called a "Return." In effect, the
officer returns to the court and makes a report to the
court as to what he/she has found as a result of
executing the warrant.

The foregoing procedure is only a general analysis
of how a warrant is obtained, executed, and returned.
Local practices may vary but generally the above
procedure is used and has met with favor in the courts.
See **COOLIDGE v. NEW HAMPSHIRE**, 403 U.S. 443, 91 S.Ct.
2022, 29 L.Ed.2d 564 (1971). In this case the United
States Supreme Court treats the requirement for an
independent magistrate or judicial officer. In **SHADWICK
v. CITY OF TAMPA**, 407 U.S. 345, 92 S.Ct. 2119, 32 L.Ed.2d
783 (1972), the court held that a court clerk who was not
a lawyer could fulfill the requirement of a judicial

officer establishing probable cause to issue a warrant
for a violation of a city ordinance.

§ 1.47   Search Warrant - Independent Source Required

The 1988 Court appeared to be stretching to validate
seizures of contraband. The Court, in a rather unusual
procedure vacated a judgment of conviction and remanded
two cases to the First Circuit Court of Appeals with
instructions that it remand to the District Court for
determination whether a warrant-authorized search of a
warehouse was an independent source of challenged
evidence. **MURRAY v. UNITED STATES** and **CARTER v. UNITED
STATES**, 487 U.S. 588, 108 S.Ct. 2529, 101 L.Ed.2d. 472,
43 Cr L 3168 (1988).

The essential problem in these cases was that the
Federal law enforcement officers forced entry of a
warehouse in South Boston, Massachusetts, without the
benefit of a warrant. They made observations of the
presence of large burlap bags that were later found to
contain marijuana. They left the premises without
disturbing the bales. They kept the building under
surveillance and did not re-enter it until they obtained
a search warrant. All during this time the building was
unoccupied. In applying for the warrant, the agents did
not mention the prior entry, and did not rely on any
observations made during that entry. The warrant was
issued about eight hours after the initial entry.
Thereupon, the agents immediately entered the warehouse
and seized 270 bales of marijuana and notebooks listing
customers for whom the bales were destined. The Court
noted that if the search warrant was based on an
independent source, the evidence should not be
suppressed.

The unusual procedure that I indicated above was
because the majority decision consisted in a plurality of
four justices. JUSTICE BRENNAN and JUSTICE KENNEDY took
no part in the consideration or decision of this case.
Three justices joined in dissenting opinion and one
justice filed an independent dissenting opinion. JUSTICE
KENNEDY had recently been appointed to the Court and

hence there were ten Justices accounted for in the report of this decision.

§ 1.48   Uniform Arrest Act

As indicated previously, the police officer who invites a suspect to come to the police station is not deemed to be arresting that person. There has been much confusion in this area for many years. Accordingly, a Uniform Arrest Act was adopted by the Interstate Commission on Crime. It contains the following provisions concerning detention:

"1.   A peace officer may stop any person abroad whom he has reasonable ground to suspect is committing, has committed or is about to commit a crime, and may demand of him his name, address, business abroad and whither he is going.

2.   Any person so questioned who fails to identify himself or explain his actions to the satisfaction of the officer stopping him, may be detained and further questioned and investigated.

3.   The total period of detention provided for by this section shall not exceed two hours. Such detention is not an arrest and shall not be recorded as an arrest in any official record. At the end of the detention period the person so detained shall be released unless arrested and charged with a crime."

The statute has been adopted by several states and has been upheld as constitutional. The United States Supreme Court has not yet decided the constitutionality of this statute. However, suppose the subject of the detention stands mute when he is accosted by the police officer. Does this give the officer sufficient grounds to detain him for up to two hours? On the other hand, suppose the subject makes incriminating statements at the time of his first contact with the officer. The officer asks him a question without giving the subject Miranda warnings, and the subject makes incriminating statements. Can these statements be used at the later trial? Was the subject compelled to identify himself and explain his actions to the satisfaction of the officer or face a detention of up to two hours? Were his Fifth Amendment self-incrimination rights violated? These and other interesting constitutional questions have not been answered and will probably be discussed further by the United States Supreme Court in the future.

§ 1.49   Stop and Frisk

The right of an officer to stop and frisk a suspect for weapons has been firmly established through a landmark decision in the case of **TERRY v. OHIO**, 392 U.S. 1, 440 Ohio Op.2d 383, 88 S.Ct. 1868, 20 L.Ed.2d 889 (1968). This case is edited and included in part II of the hard covered form of this book.

New York State, Florida, Ohio, and other states have codified what had been apparent through common law decisions. New York Section 140.50 of the Criminal Procedure Law reads as follows:

"Temporary questioning of persons in public places; search for weapons-
1.   In addition to the authority provided by this article for making an arrest without a warrant, a police officer may stop a person in a public place located within the geographical area of such officer's employment when he reasonably suspects that such person is committing, has committed or is about to commit either (a) a felony or (b) a Class A misdemeanor defined in the penal law and may demand of him his name, address and an explanation of his conduct."

Florida's similar statute is:
"901.151 Stop and frisk law
(1)   This section may be known and cited as the

"Florida stop and frisk law."

(2)   Whenever any law enforcement officer of this
        state   encounters   any   person   under
        circumstances which reasonably indicate that
        such person has committed, is committing, or
        is about to commit a violation of the criminal
        laws of this state or the criminal ordinances
        of   any   municipality   or   county,   he   may
        temporarily detain such person for the purpose
        of ascertaining the identity of the person
        temporarily detained and the circumstances
        surrounding his presence abroad which led the
        officer to believe that he had committed, was
        committing, or was about to commit a criminal
        offense.

(3)   No person shall be temporarily detained under
        the provisions of subsection (2) of this
        section longer than is reasonably necessary to
        effect the purposes of that subsection. Such
        temporary detention shall not extend beyond
        the place where it was first effected or the
        immediate vicinity thereof.

(4)   If at any time after the onset of the
        temporary detention authorized by subsection
        (2) of this section, probable cause for arrest
        of person shall appear, the person shall be
        arrested. If, after an inquiry into the
        circumstances which prompted the temporary
        detention, no probable cause for the arrest of
        the person shall appear, he shall be released.

(5)   Whenever any law enforcement officer
        authorized to detain temporarily any person
        under the provisions of subsection (2) of this
        section has probable cause to believe that any
        person so temporarily detained, or is about to
        detain temporarily, is armed with a dangerous
        weapon and therefore offers a threat to the
        safety of the officer or any other person, he
        may search such person so temporarily detained
        only to the extent necessary to disclose, and
        for the purpose of disclosing, the presence of
        such weapon. If such a search discloses such a
        weapon or any evidence of a criminal offense

it may be seized.
(6)   No evidence seized by a law enforcement
      officer in any search under this section shall
      be admissible against any person in any court
      of this state or political subdivision thereof
      unless the search which disclosed its
      existence was authorized by and conducted in
      compliance with the provisions of subsections
      (2)-(5)."

A case decided with the Terry case was the **SIBRON v.
NEW YORK** case, 392 U.S. 40, 88 S.Ct. 1889, 20 L.Ed.2d
917. The officer had plenty of time in this case to
secure a warrant and the stop and frisk was for the
purpose of finding narcotics, not weapons. Therefore the
Court invalidated the search.

§ 1.50   The Moving Motor Vehicle Problem

The right of a police officer to stop a driver of a
moving motor vehicle because of suspicious actions by the
driver of the automobile has been a particularly
troublesome area of constitutional law. The problem
arises because of the possible abuse of this privilege by
law enforcement personnel. Frequently if a driver is
driving a new shiny car and the driver is young, or if
the driver is apparently of a different ethnic group or
color of skin from the dominant population in a
particular community, or if the driver is driving slowly
accompanied by others in the vehicle and they are in a
ghetto area, or if the driver violates a traffic law, the
suspicions of the police officer are aroused. Many
excellent arrests have been made under these conditions.
On the other hand, many persons have been stopped and
questioned under the same conditions who were doing
nothing illegal. They resent the intrusion into their
privacy by the police and get the impression that they
are living in a police state. Obviously, there must be
some balance between these opposing views.
The United States Supreme Court has met this problem
on a case-by-case basis. In **CARPENTER v. SIGLER**, 419 F.2d

169, the United States Court of Appeals for the Eighth Circuit held that suspicious actions by a driver of an automobile occurring at about 3:30 A.M. warranted the officer to stop the car and ask one of the occupants to step out. As the occupant got out of the car, a noise of metal hitting metal was heard by the officer and this noise was apparently caused by the exiting offender as he labored to get out of the car. The officer beamed his light on the floor of the car and found two crowbars there. The court held that the prior activity of the driver raised sufficient justification for the officers to stop the car. However, in **HARRIS v. U.S.**, 390 U.S. 234, 88 S.Ct. 992, 19 L.Ed. 2d 1067 (1968), the court held that **FBI** agents who had received information regarding interstate shipment of stolen property and seeing two persons drive to a residence on two occasions and load cartons into a car and drive away, did not have probable cause for a warrantless search. The issues presented in arrest and search of the occupants of an automobile and a search of the parties and the automobile are more extensively discussed in § 2.28 infra.

The question was fully answered in **MICHIGAN DEPARTMENT OF STATE POLICE v. SETZ**, 496 U.S.444, 110 S.Ct. 2481, 110 L.Ed.2d. 412, 41 Cr L 2155 (1990). In that case Michigan State Police established a program to set up highway checkpoints to stop and briefly detain all motorists passing through such checkpoints to detect and deter drunk drivers. As a result of an approximate one hour and fifteen minute test on a single night between midnight and approximately 1:15 am police officers stopped 126 vehicles; each stop lasted approximately 25 seconds. Two were detained for investigation and were eventually arrested for drunk driving. A legal contest was begun the day before this incident occurred with the claim that this procedure was a violation of the Fourth Amendment. The Michigan courts agreed that it was, basing their decision on **BROWN v. TEXAS**, 443 U.S. 47 (1979) that held that in a balancing test the checkpoints were not effective enough to justify the intrusion of a highway stop.

The Court in a majority decision written by Rehnquist, C.J. held that this type of stop was similar to a border stop in **UNITED STATES v. MARTINEZ-FUERTE**, 428

U.S. 543, upholding a balancing test in checkpoints for detecting illegal aliens, and he balanced the need to save lives and save injuries of persons who have been killed or injured by intoxicated drivers in favor of the sobriety checkpoints. It was not a violation of the Fourth Amendment.

§ 1.51   Statutory Authority to Stop Vehicles

All states have statutes which authorize law enforcement officers to stop vehicles to inspect these vehicles. When one gets a license to drive a vehicle, it is a license and nothing more. It is revocable for cause and one does not have a constitutional right to drive an automobile. He does, however, have a constitutional right to equal protection under the law and equal privileges and immunities. If he complies with the statutes as others do, he must be treated as others are treated. Reasoning thus, if driving is a privilege and not a right, and if a condition for the privilege of driving a vehicle is that the driver is subjecting himself and his vehicle to inspections by designated law enforcers, then the statute authorizing law enforcement personnel in the line of their duty to inspect drivers and their vehicles is constitutional. The question remains, however, does this statute give authority to law enforcement officers to stop and question passengers in the automobile?

§ 1.52   Detention for Fingerprints

The right to take fingerprints from a person who has been lawfully arrested has been held to be elementary by the courts. In **SMITH v. U.S.**, 324 F.2d 879 (D.C.Circ 1963), the court said, "We find no error in the admission of the palm print of Smith, taken the day before trial for purposes of comparison with the palm print of the victim's credit card. Unlike the situation in **BYNUM v. UNITED STATES**, appellant here was in lawful custody at the time the prints were recorded... and it is elementary that a person in lawful custody may be required to submit to photographing and fingerprinting as part of routine identification processes."

However, the problem arises when the police take the fingerprints of suspects who are not in lawful custody and whose prints are taken for the purpose of connecting the suspect to the commission of a crime. This type of case arose in **DAVIS v. MISSISSIPPI**, 394 U.S. 721, 89 S.Ct. 1394, 22 L.Ed.2d 676 (1969).

In the Davis case, the defendant and several other black youths were taken to police headquarters where they were questioned in connection with an alleged rape of an eighty-six-year-old white woman. They were questioned briefly and fingerprinted. Several days later the defendant was jailed and fingerprinted again. His fingerprints were found to match those on the window of the victim's home. The United States Supreme Court in an opinion by Brennan, J., expressed the view of six members of the Court in holding that since the defendant's detention by the police was unlawful, his fingerprints were obtained in violation of the Fourth and Fourteenth Amendments, so as to be inadmissible at his trial.

§ 1.53   Doctrine of Close Pursuit

The nations of the world, as well as the states of the union, have had to protect themselves from the lawbreaker who would commit a crime in one jurisdiction and then flee to freedom in another jurisdiction. We are all acquainted with the western films of yore where the bad man (usually wearing the mustache or beard and with black horse and clothing) would race for the border to gain his freedom. To counteract this situation, many nations have entered into treaties to extradite persons accused of crimes. The states have also entered into agreements called compacts.

Interstate compacts are authorized by Article I, Section 10, of the United States Constitution. As the text of this section reads, it is necessary for Congress to consent to an agreement or compact between states. It has been found that this device has been very useful for

the solution of regional problems which require
continuing administration and regulation. One of these
problems particularly of interest to law enforcement has
been the case of the fleeing offender.

For this reason, a uniform close pursuit act has
been promulgated and has been adopted by many states. The
Massachusetts statute reads as follows:

> "*10A.Authority of officer of another state to
>   arrest felon*
> Any member of a duly organized state,
> county or municipal peace unit of another
> state of the United States the laws of which
> contain provisions substantially equivalent to
> the provisions of this and the following
> sections, who enters this commonwealth in
> fresh pursuit, and continues herein in such
> fresh pursuit, of a person in order to arrest
> him on the ground that he has committed a
> felony in such other state shall have the same
> authority to arrest and hold in custody such
> person as members of a duly organized state,
> county or municipal peace unit of this
> commonwealth have to arrest and hold in
> custody a person on the ground that he has
> committed a felony in this commonwealth. This
> section shall not be construed so as to make
> unlawful any arrest in this commonwealth which
> would otherwise be lawful.
>
> *10B. Proceedings after arrest*
> If an arrest is made in this commonwealth
> by an officer of another state in accordance
> with the provisions of the preceding section
> he shall without unnecessary delay take the
> person arrested before a justice, associate
> justice or special justice of a court of
> record in the county in which the arrest was
> made, who shall conduct a hearing for the
> purpose of determining the lawfulness of the
> arrest. If such justice, associate justice or
> special justice determines that the arrest was
> lawful he shall commit the person arrested to

await for a reasonable time the issuance of a rendition warrant by the governor of the state from which he fled. If such justice, associate justice or special justice determines that the arrest was unlawful he shall discharge the person arrested.

10C. Partial invalidity
     If any part of sections ten A and ten B is for any reason declared void, it is declared to be the intent of said sections that such invalidity shall not affect the validity of the remaining portions of said sections."

10D. Citation of law; uniform construction
     Sections ten A to ten C, inclusive, may be cited as the uniform extraterritorial arrest or fresh pursuit law, and shall be so interpreted and construed as to effectuate their general purpose to make uniform the law of the states which enact similar laws.

§ 1.54   Extradition

The reader know that a matter of extradition was treated as one of comity between the states according to the Articles of Confederation, the predecessor of the United States Constitution. Although the Constitution in Article IV, Section 2 provided ".... A Person charged in any State with Treason, Felony or other Crime, who shall flee from Justice and be found in another State, shall on Demand of the Executive Authority of the State from which he fled, be delivered up, to be removed to the State having Jurisdiction of the Crime," the matter remained one of comity between the states. This was reinforced by **KENTUCKY v. DENNISON**, 24 HOW.66. (1861). After 126 years that case was reversed by **PUERTO RICO v. BRANSTAD**, 483 U.S. 219, 107 S.Ct. 2802, 97 L.Ed.2d. 187, 41 Cr L 3359 (1987), which held that if all requirements of the Constitution and the Extradition Act (18 U.S.C. 3182) are complied with by the Governor of the demanding state, the

Governor of the asylum state is subject to a Federal Court order in the nature of mandamus, to cause the delivery of the fugitive to agents of the demanding state or commonwealth.

The concept of extradition of criminal defendants from one jurisdiction to another was greatly expanded in **UNITED STATES v. HUMBERTO ALVAREZ - MACHAIN,** _____ U.S. _____, 112 S.Ct. 2188, 119 L.Ed.2d 441, 51 Cr L 2154 (1992). This case involved the abduction of a medical doctor from his office in Guadalajara, Mexico by private persons acting on behalf of DEA officials. He had been indicted in the United States for participating in the kidnap and murder of a United States Drug Enforcement special agent, Enrique Camarena-Salazar and a Mexican pilot working with him, Alfredo Zavala-Avevar. The DEA believed that the respondent participated in the murder by prolonging agent Camarena's life so that others could further torture and interrogate him.

Mexico and the United States had an Extradition Treaty whereby each nation could request the other nation for the return of a criminal fugitive. There was nothing indicated in this treaty specifically prohibiting either nation from causing the abduction of a person within its jurisdiction to the other jurisdiction. Based on the absence of language to that effect, the Court held in a 6-3 decision that the abduction of the respondent in this case did not require his repatriation to Mexico and he could stand trial in the United States.

§ 1.55   Absorption Defined

Absorption is a term that has been commonly applied to a rule of constitutional law that when the United States Supreme Court declares that a right given to United States citizens as provided for in the Bill of Rights of the Constitution is applicable to the action of state and local government, the right is thus absorbed and the inhabitant may not be lawfully denied that right by the actions of any governmental authority within the jurisdiction of the federal or state governments.

§ 1.56   Fourteenth Amendment

The Fourteenth Amendment to the United States Constitution came about as a response to the turmoil following the War between the states. The black people of the southern states were, to a large extent, homeless and unemployed. Many of the communities in which they and their white masters had lived were devastated. Southern legislatures enacted laws compelling the former slaves to return to the service of their former masters as employees. They were not permitted to own or rent their own land nor to engage in their own business. Vigilante groups of white people terrorized the blacks.

Congress, meeting at the close of the Civil War, set up military governments in the former Confederate States and three new constitutional amendments were added, as well as many statutes applying to civil rights in an effort to protect the black persons.

The Thirteenth, Fourteenth, and Fifteenth Amendments which read as follows, were the nation's effort to find a solution to the problems of reconstruction:

"*Amendment 13 Section 1—Neither slavery nor involuntary servitude, except as a punishment for crime whereof the party shall have been duly convicted, shall exist within the United States, or any place subject to their jurisdiction.*

Section 2—Congress shall have power to enforce this article by appropriate legislation.

Amendment 14 Section 1—All persons born or naturalized in the United States, and subject to the jurisdiction thereof, are citizens of the United States and of the State wherein they reside. No State shall make or enforce any law which shall abridge the privileges or immunities of citizens of the United States; nor

> shall any State deprive any person
> of life, liberty, or property,
> without due process of law; nor deny
> to any person within its
> jurisdiction the equal protection of
> the laws. . . .
>
> Section 5—The Congress shall have power
> to enforce, by appropriate legislation,
> the provisions of this article.

Amendment 15   Section 1—The right of citizens of
the United States to vote shall not
be denied or abridged by the United
States or by any State on account of
race, color, or previous condition
of servitude.

> Section 2—The Congress shall have power
> to enforce this article by appropriate
> legislation."

In order for a person to fully understand the search
and seizure law, as it presently exists, I believe it to
be important that the reader understands the development
of the Fourteenth Amendment as it now applies to State
action. Some of the following material does not
specifically relate to search and seizure but the
development of the amendment as it applied to other
rights is connected in theory to search and seizure
practices today and in the future.

During the 1865-66 session of Congress, a Joint
Congressional Committee on Reconstruction was set up to
conduct an investigation into reports of racial violence
in the South (United States Commission on Civil
Rights—Law Enforcement: A Report on Equal Protection in
the South, 6-10,1865). The results of this investigation
culminated in the adoption of the first of many federal
civil rights laws in 1866.

The statutes were designed to punish by fines and
imprisonment, or both, those persons who under color of
any law, statute, ordinance, regulation, or custom
subjected any inhabitants of any State, Territory, or

District to a deprivation of any rights, privileges, or
immunities secured or protected by the laws of the United
States or to different punishment, pains, or penalties
because the person was an alien or by reason of his color
or race.

A statute enacted during this period which passed
into oblivion but has been resurrected in recent years is
now embodied in 42 U.S.C. 1983. It has become known to
law enforcement officers as Section 1983. It was
originally known as the Klu Klux Klan Act of 1871. It
creates a civil cause of action, enforceable in the
federal courts against any person, acting under color of
state law, who deprives another of rights, privileges, or
immunities secured by the Constitution or laws of the
United States. There have been recent actions resulting
in judgments against law enforcement personnel where the
allegations were that these persons conspired against the
plaintiff to deny the plaintiff the enumerated rights.

The Fourteenth Amendment created questions
concerning the extent to which the provisions of the Bill
of Rights would be made applicable to state action. The
first cases dealing with the problem which were decided
by the United States Supreme Court were the
Slaughterhouse cases, 83 U.S. 36, 16 Wall 36, 21 L.Ed.
394 (1873). In these cases butchers challenged a state
law which granted a monopoly to slaughter all animals in
the New Orleans vicinity for a period of twenty-five
years. The challenges to the statute relied upon the due
process and equal protection clause and privilege and
immunities clause of the Fourteenth Amendment. The
court rejected the petitioner's claims but in so doing
did not rule on anything other than the privileges and
immunities clauses. The Court said that the right to
follow a trade or profession without state interference
in the form of a monopoly was not a "privilege or
immunity" of citizens of the United States. The Court
contended that the equal privilege and immunity clauses
would give equal rights to seek the protection of
government, to assert claims against the government, the
right to hold office, etc., but not the unfettered right
to engage in a trade or profession.

You will remember that the Bill of Rights was
included in the Constitution at the behest of several

states who would not ratify the document unless it was amended in short order to include these rights. Some made it a condition of their ratification. The fear, at that time, was that a strong national government might take away the individual's right to personal liberty. There was no comparable fear that the states might accomplish the same ends. It was thought that the Bill of Rights, as contained in the first ten amendments of the United States Constitution, was applicable only to the federal government. That view, held by many, was reinforced when in 1833, Justice Marshall speaking for the Court in **BARRON v. BALTIMORE**, 32 U.S. 243, 8 L.Ed. 672, held that the Fifth Amendment's requirement that private property not be taken for public use, without just compensation did not apply as a protection against a local government which had diverted a stream in such a manner so as to damage the plaintiff's property. Marshall contended that the limitations in the Constitution's First Amendment, "Congress shall make no law ...." indicated a limitation on the national government and by implication a limitation on the amendments which followed the First Amendment. In effect, the court was adhering to the principle of dual citizenship, i.e., citizen of the United States and citizen of the state of his domicile.

In the **Slaughterhouse cases** (supra), the Court, speaking through Mr. Justice Samuel F. Miller, said that " ... there is a citizenship of the United States and a citizenship of a State which are distinct from each other .... We think this distinction and its explicit recognition in this amendment (Fourteenth Amendment) gives great weight to this argument, because the next paragraph of this same section which is the one mainly relied on by the plaintiffs in error [old method of describing appellant], speaks only of privileges and immunities of citizens of the United States and does not speak of those citizens of the several states .... The language is, 'No State shall make or enforce any law which shall abridge the privileges or immunities of citizens of the United States.'" In practical effect, we find the majority of the Court held, if a citizen of a state is denied equal privileges and immunities by state action, his recourse is only to the state courts and to the state legislature. The Court contended that the Fourteenth Amendment was adopted for the protection of discrimination against blacks as a class or on account of their race or a denial of equal justice in state courts. There were, however, three strong dissents in this case by Mr. Justice Stephen J. Field and concurred in by Mr. Justice Noah H. Swayne and Mr. Justice Joseph P. Bradley.

The student should take note that often when a strong dissent is written, as the personnel of the court changes over the years, the dissenting minority is joined by others of like mind and the previous dissent may become the holding of the Court. This is the slow deliberate changing of our laws which makes revolution unnecessary, for if the argument for change has merit, there is a great likelihood that a change will take place. This is precisely what happened in the development of the court construction of the Fourteenth Amendment.

The Fourteenth Amendment has been a much litigated one but the later Supreme Court decisions have dealt very sparingly with the privileges and immunities aspect and have broadened the scope of the amendment by enlarging on the meaning of the due process and equal protection clauses. **LOCHNER v. NEW YORK**, 198 U.S. 45, 25 S.Ct. 539, 49 L.Ed. 937 (1905), was such a case. In this case the court struck down a state statute which limited the number of hours an employee in a bakery or confectionery establishment could work. It limited the amount to a maximum of sixty hours in one week on an average of ten hours a day. The statute was included in the Labor Law of New York State, and it made it unlawful for an employer to require an employee to work in excess of the prescribed hours. Ostensibly, the legislature enacted this statute in the belief that it was properly exercising its rights under the police power to protect the health, welfare, and morals of its people.

Lochner was convicted and lost all New York State appeals. He then brought the case to the United States Supreme Court. Mr. Justice Rufus W. Peckham delivered the opinion of the Court. He stated that "such a statute interferes with the right of contract between an employer and an employee .... The general right to make a contract

64

in relation to his business is part of the liberty of the
individual protected by the Fourteenth Amendment of the
Federal Constitution .... Under the provision no State
can deprive any person of life, liberty or property
without due process of law. The right to sell labor is
part of the liberty protected by this amendment unless
there are circumstances which exclude the right." The
Justice went on to explain that the State does retain
police powers which relate to the safety, health, morals,
and general welfare of the public and if a statute is a
legitimate exercise of its police powers, it has the
right to enact such a statute. However there is a limit
to the police power. He said "the question necessarily
arises: Is this a fair, reasonable and appropriate
exercise of the police power of the State, or is it
unreasonable, unnecessary and arbitrary interference with
the right of the individual to his personal liberty or to
enter into those contracts in relation to labor which may
seem to him appropriate or necessary for the support of
himself and his family? .... It seems to us that the real
object and purpose were simply to regulate the hours of
labor between master and his employees (all being men,
sui juris) in a private business not dangerous in any
degree to morals or in any real and substantial degree to
health of the employees. Under such circumstances the
freedom of master and employee to contract with each
other in relation to their employment, and in defining
the same, cannot be prohibited or interfered with without
violating the Federal Constitution. . . ."
    Here, too, there was a strong dissent by Mr. Justice
Harlan with whom Mr. Justice White and Mr. Justice Day
concurred. Mr. Justice Holmes wrote a strong dissent on
his own.
    We therefore find a slim majority of one writing the
law for that day. This, as every student knows, has
changed so that today there are many state statutes
limiting the hours of work. The reason that they are now
not a violation of the Fourteenth Amendment is that after
the Lochner case, the Supreme Court continued the same
construction of the due process and equal protection
clauses in **ADKINS v. CHILDREN'S HOSPITAL**, 261 U.S. 525,
43 S.Ct. 394, 67 L.Ed. 785 (1923), but in **WEST COAST
HOTEL CO. v. PARRISH**, 300 U.S. 379, 57 S.Ct. 578, 81

L.Ed. 703 (1937), the Court specifically overruled the Adkins case. In the West Coast Hotel Co. case the court sustained a state statute which set up minimum wages and conditions of labor for women and minors. The court in substance said that the community may direct its lawmaking power to correct an abuse which springs from employers' selfish disregard of the public interest.

The Fourteenth Amendment has been construed in the criminal branch of the law also. The due process and equal protection clauses were discussed in **PALKO v. CONN.**, 302 U.S. 319, 58 S.Ct. 149, 82 L.Ed. 288 (1937). Palko was indicted and tried for murder in the first degree. A jury found him guilty of second degree murder. A Connecticut statute permitted the state to appeal rulings and decisions "upon all questions of law arising on the trial of criminal cases." The state appealed and was successful. A new trial was ordered and after trial, Palko was found guilty of First Degree Murder and was sentenced to death. He appealed to the Supreme Court on the grounds of his being placed in double jeopardy in violation of the Fifth and Fourteenth Amendments.

The Court in an opinion by Mr. Justice Benjamin N. Cardoza discussed the relationship of the Fifth Amendment provision that no person shall be held to answer for a capital or otherwise infamous crime unless on presentment or indictment of a grand jury and that no person shall be compelled in any criminal case to be a witness against himself, and spoke of **DEJONGE v. OREGON**, 299 U.S. 353, 57 S.Ct. 255, 81 L.Ed. 279 (1937), and **HERNDON v. LOWRY**, 301 U.S. 242, 57 S.Ct. 732, 81 L.Ed. 1066 (1937), and other cases which had made the Fourteenth Amendment applicable to the States with respect to freedom of speech, freedom of the press, the free exercise of religion, the right to peaceable assembly, or the right of counsel to one accused of crime. Mr. Justice Cardoza said, "In these and other situations immunities that are valid as against the federal government by force of the specific pledges of particular amendments have been found to be implicit in the concept of ordered liberty, and thus through the Fourteenth Amendment become valid as against the states .... The right to a trial by jury and immunity from prosecution except as the result of an indictment may have value and importance. Even so, they are not of the

66

very essence of a scheme of ordered liberty. To abolish them is not to violate a 'principle of justice' so rooted in the traditions and conscience of our people as to be ranked as fundamental .... Few would be so narrow or provincial as to maintain that fair and enlightened system of justice would be impossible without them. What is true of Jury trials and indictments is true also, as the cases show, of the immunity from self incrimination .... This too might be lost and justice still be done .... If the Fourteenth Amendment has absorbed them (privileges and immunities) the process of absorption has had its source in the belief that neither liberty nor justice would exist if they were sacrificed .... On which side of the line the case made out by the appellant has appropriate location must be the next inquiry and final one. Is that kind of double jeopardy to which the statute has subjected him a hardship so acute and shocking that our policy will not endure it? Does it violate those 'fundamental principles of liberty and justice which lie at the base of all our civil and political institutions?'.... The answer surely must be 'no.'"

In this case the state successfully based its argument on the premise that the first trial was not free from substantial error and it should be permitted a trial without a substantial error. The court held that the appellant was not deprived of any privileges or immunities that were granted him as a citizen of the United States.

This case stands for the proposition, however, that if a state denies a state citizen of a fundamental principle of liberty and justice which lies at the base of all of our civil and political institutions, the citizen will be protected against state action by invoking the Fourteenth Amendment due process clause and for such a transgression by a state, the Fourteenth Amendment had absorbed the Bill of Rights given to federal citizens against federal action.

The Palko case was followed by others among which we find **SNYDER v. MASSACHUSETTS**, 291 U.S. 97, 54 S.Ct. 330, 78 L.Ed. 674 (1941), which held that the Fourteenth Amendment was applicable against state action when it violated principles of justice so rooted in the traditions and conscience of our people as to be ranked as fundamental and **LISENBA v. CALIFORNIA**, 314 U.S. 291, 62 S.Ct. 280, 86 L.Ed. 166 (1941), where the court held a state liable for the administration of fundamental fairness essential to the very concept of justice.

For example, the student will find that the due process clause of the Fourteenth Amendment and the equal protection clause of the amendment brought about the absorption of many of the rights of the Bill of Rights into state action. **CHICAGO, B & Q CO. v. CITY OF CHICAGO**, 166 U.S.226, 17 S.Ct. 581, 41 L.Ed. 979 (1897); **LOCHNER v. NEW YORK**, 198 U.S. 45, 25 S.Ct. 539, 49 L.Ed. 937 (1905). Other cases relating to search and seizure will be explained and cited to show the development of the Fourteenth Amendment in chapter 2.

§ 1.57   Fourth Amendment

> *"The right of people to be secure in their persons, houses, papers, and effects, against unreasonable searches and seizures, shall not be violated, and no Warrants shall issue, but upon probable cause, supported by Oath or affirmation, and particularly describing the place to be searched, and the persons or things to be seized."*

The Fourth Amendment to the United States Constitution was construed by the United States Supreme Court for many years as a protection against unreasonable searches by federal law enforcement officers. The lawyers of our nation, however, pounded at the door of the courts until the door finally gave way. A fuller explanation of the evolution of the theory of the Fourth Amendment application to state action as well as federal action appears in chapter II of this book.

An overview would not be complete, however, without referring to the case of **MAPP v. OHIO**, 367 U.S. 643, 81 S.Ct. 1680, 6 L.Ed.2d 108 (1961). This was the case that opened the door to a new body of state law dealing with unreasonable search and seizure by state law enforcement officers. Prior to this decision, there were basically two sets of rules governing unreasonable search and seizure by governmental authority. They were the Federal Rule and the State Rule. The Federal Rule was much more restrictive on government agents than the State Rule. Much will be said about the development of these rules in Chapter 2, infra.

§ 1.58   Police Power

The term "police power" as it relates to governmental authority has been interpreted as the power "to prescribe regulations to promote the health, peace, morals, education and good order of the people, and to legislate so as to increase the industries of the state, develop its resources, and add to its wealth and prosperity." **BARBIER v. CONNOLLY**, 113 U.S. 27, 5 S.Ct. 357, 28 L.Ed. 923 (1885).

It will be noted that the federal government is one of delegated powers which were so delegated by the colonies. Those powers not delegated to the federal government were expressly retained by the states through the Tenth Amendment, which reads:

> *"The powers not delegated to the United States by the Constitution, nor prohibited by it to the States, are reserved to the States respectively, or to the people."*

This has come to be known as the Reserved Powers Amendment.

There was no delegation of the police power to the United States and hence the police power is one of those powers retained by the states. Therefore, we have a proliferation of state law enforcement agencies, each originally having autonomous control and direction.

It is said by some that there are over forty thousand independent governmental police departments in the United States. It is quite evident that such a structure for law enforcement is not a practical solution to the criminal justice problems confronting the United States today. Many small departments with their own power structure and their duplication of services with state or county law enforcement make for an almost impossible and wasteful system of law enforcement in this country. The advent of the airplane, the fast automobile equipped with citizens band radio, the cellular mobile telephone, the fast-moving boat, the increase in white-collar and computer-related crime, and the web of organized crime into legitimate businesses have all made the small police department incapable of properly performing its duty to prevent crime and arrest violators of law.

The Law Enforcement Assistance Administration was Congress's answer to the problem. This agency of the central government was empowered to do research in the criminal justice discipline and to turn over money to local police authorities. In return, on a quid pro quo basis, the police departments receiving this money gave up some of their autonomy to the Law Enforcement Assistance Administration. Since most local communities were hard pressed financially, the communities accepted this money.

It is obvious that power begets power and the police power requires control. A Houston, Texas, ordinance made it unlawful to "in any manner...interrupt any policeman in the execution of his duty." In **HOUSTON, TEXAS v. HILL** 482 U.S. 451, 107 S.Ct. 2502, 96 L.Ed.2d. 398, 41 Cr L 3273 (1987), the Court held this to be an unconstitutionally broad statute. It found that arrests were made by the police for, inter alia, "arguing, talking, interfering, failing to remain quiet, refusing to remain silent, verbal abuse, cursing, verbally yelling, talking loudly, and walking through a scene."

The Court also held a District of Columbia statute that made it unlawful to display within 500 feet of a foreign embassy any sign that tends to bring a foreign government into "public odium" or "public disrepute" to be a content-based restriction on political speech in a public forum that is not sufficiently narrowly tailored to serve the compelling governmental interest in preserving the dignity of foreign officials and, therefore, violates the First Amendment. **BOOS ET AL, PETITIONER v. BARRY, JR., MAYOR OF DISTRICT OF COLUMBIA, 11ET AL.**, 485 U.S. 312, 108 S.Ct 1157, 99 L.Ed. 333, 42

Cr L 3093 (1988).

§ 1.59   Custodial Interrogation

When a person suspected of criminal activity is taken into custody by law enforcement officers, he/she is usually in a state of shock when that person is a neophyte of this experience. It once was said by a person of middle age, who had no prior police record, that when he was arrested for intoxicated driving and placed in a police detention cell, he saw his whole life go down in shambles when the iron gate of the cell slammed shut. For the average American law abiding person who has had no criminal contact with the police, it is a harrowing experience to have his/her liberty curtailed in this way. The Court has decided that when a person is in the custody of the police for interrogation purposes, if the police deny that person the aid of counsel after a request for counsel's assistance, the police are denying that person a fundamental right to the assistance of counsel as provided for in the Sixth Amendment as it was made applicable to the states by the due process clause of the Fourteenth Amendment. **ESCOBEDO v. ILLINOIS**, 378 U.S. 478, 84 S.Ct. 1758, 12 L.Ed.2d 977 (1964). Any evidence obtained as a result of this interrogation was to be excluded from the trial. The Court held that when the process shifts from investigatory to accusatory—when its focus is on the accused and its purpose is to elicit a confession—our adversary system begins to operate, and, under the circumstances here, the accused must be permitted to consult with his/her lawyer.

The Escobedo case was followed by **MIRANDA v. ARIZONA**, 384 U.S. 436, 86 S.Ct. 1602, 16 L.Ed.2d 694 (1966). The Court extended the Escobedo rule and defined that custodial interrogation beyond the circumstances when the accused asks for counsel to be present. The Court said that it is the duty of the police to inform the suspect of his right to counsel even if he does not specifically ask for it. The language of the Court follows:

Our holding will be spelled out with some specificity in the pages which follow but briefly stated it is this: the prosecution may not use statements, whether exculpatory or inculpatory stemming from custodial interrogation of the defendant unless it demonstrates the use of procedural safeguards effective to secure the privilege against self-incrimination. By custodial interrogation, we mean questioning initiated by law enforcement officers after a person has been taken into custody or otherwise deprived of his freedom of action in any significant way. As for the procedural safeguards to be employed, unless other fully effective means are devised to inform accused persons of their right of silence and to assure a continuous opportunity to exercise it, the following measures are required. Prior to any questioning, the person must be warned that he has a right to remain silent, that any statement he does make may be used as evidence against him, and that he has a right to the presence of an attorney, either retained or appointed. The defendant may waive effectuation of these rights, provided the waiver is made voluntarily, knowingly, and intelligently. If however, he indicates in any manner and at any stage of the process that he wishes to consult with an attorney before speaking there can be no questioning. Likewise, if the individual is alone and indicates in any manner that he does not wish to be interrogated, the police may not question him. The mere fact that he may have answered some questions or volunteered some statements on his own does not deprive him of the right to refrain from answering any further inquiries until he has consulted with an attorney and thereafter consents to be questioned.

The Miranda case was decided simultaneously with **VIGNERA v. NEW YORK**, **WESTOVER v. UNITED STATES**, and **CALIFORNIA v. STEWART**. These cases raised a furor within the police agencies of the United States. However, acting true to form, the police of the nation learned to live with the decision. They prepared printed cards which were distributed to members of the force, the contents of which were to be read to prisoners at the first available and reasonable opportunity. Signs were posted in station houses in conspicuous places to give the prisoner adequate warnings. Where English and another language were frequently used, the signs might be in two or several languages. They became known in the police profession as the "Miranda Warnings."

Miranda was not the final word of the court with respect to custodial interrogation and right of counsel. In **MICHIGAN v. MOSELY**, 423 U.S. 96, 96 S.Ct. 321, 46 L.Ed.2d 313 (1975), a defendant asserted his Miranda rights and the interrogation ceased. About two hours later another interrogation was commenced for another crime (homicide). The Court said that the fact that one in custody initially asserts Miranda rights does not rule out absolutely the possibility of a subsequent valid waiver. Counsel need not be present before a later waiver is possible. The Court, in effect, said that the right to cut off questioning was in fact honored in this case. The first detective immediately ceased his interrogation. The second detective fully advised the defendant of his Miranda rights. The second questioning was a "reasonable interpretation" of the defendant's earlier refusal to answer questions about the first crime (robbery). However, in a Ninth Circuit Court of Appeals case, it was held that officers cannot ignore a clear indication of desire to remain silent. **UNITED STATES v. KINSMAN**, 540 F.2d 1017 (1976). Other cases have held that officers must allow defendant to contact an attorney even though retained counsel is unavailable.

The waiver must be an intelligent waiver. See effect of influence of drugs. **UNITED STATES v. COX**, 487 F.2d 634 (5th Cir. 1973); intoxication, **KENNEDY v. STATE**, 499 S.W. 842 (Ark. 1973), **HART v. STATE**, 224 S.E. 2d 755 (Ga. App. 1976). Even an attorney is fully entitled to Miranda warnings. **STATE v. STEIN**, 360 A. 2d 347 (N.J. 1976).

In **BECKWITH v. UNITED STATES**, 425 U.S. 341, 96 S.Ct. 1612, 48 L.Ed.2d 1 (1976), the Court rejected the "focus" test of Escobedo and Miranda. In that case agents of the Intelligence Division of the Internal Revenue Service did not arrest petitioner but met with him in his home. The Court said, "An interview with government agents such as (this one) simply does not present the elements which the

Miranda court found so inherently coercive as to require
its holding." The Court did not find Beckwith in a
custodial situation.

In **BREWER v. WILLIAMS**, 430 U.S. 387, 97 S.Ct. 1232,
51 L.Ed. 424, 45 L.W. 4287 (1977), the Court reversed a
conviction of a defendant who was found guilty of murder
when he gave information as to the location of the victim
while he was in custody of the police on a long
automobile ride to a place of detention. The defendant
had been represented by counsel and the police had
promised that they would not interrogate the prisoner
while enroute. Notwithstanding this, the police, knowing
that the prisoner was a deeply religious Christian,
worked on his emotions by intimating that it was a shame
that the victim was not able to get a Christian burial
because no one knew where she was. The prisoner then led
the police to the location where she was buried in a
shallow grave. It appears that the Court wanted to
punish the police for not keeping their word and this
case acts as a warning to any law enforcement officer
than an agreement made is not to be broken or the
defendant's case will be dismissed.

In **GEDERS v. UNITED STATES**, 425 U.S. 80, 96 S.Ct.
1330, 47 L.Ed.2d 592 (1976), it was held that a trial
court's order directing the defendant not to consult with
his attorney during a regular overnight recess was held
to be a violation of defendant's right to counsel.

The claim that the Miranda warnings were not
understood by the prisoner reached the Court in **WAINRIGHT
v. SYPES**, 432 U.S. 72, 97 S.Ct. 2497, 53 L.Ed.2d 594, 21
Cr.L. 3177 (1977). In that case the petitioner claimed
that he did not understand the Miranda warnings and made
a statement to the police which inculpated himself in a
murder. Prior to and during the trial, there was no
motion to suppress these statements and he was convicted.
The issue was first raised on appeal and the Court was of
the opinion that the fact that it was first raised on
appeal precluded habeas corpus relief absent a showing of
actual prejudice and cause for his failure to make a
timely objection.

In **MASSACHUSETTS v. WHITE**, #77-1388 (1978), the
Court affirmed by a 4-4 decision that a defendant legally
intoxicated could not waive his right to remain silent

and consult a lawyer.

Once an accused has invoked his right to counsel under **MIRANDA v. ARIZONA**, 384 U.S. 466 (1966), he may not be subjected to further interrogation until counsel has been made available to him, unless the accused initiates further communications, exchanges, or conversations with the police. In **EDWARDS v. ARIZONA** 451 U.S. 477, 101 S.Ct. 1880, 68 L.Ed.2d. 378, reh den (US) 101 S.Ct. 3128, 69 L.Ed.2d. 984, 29 Cr.L. 3037 (1981) the petitioner was in custody and was given Miranda warnings. He asked for counsel and questioning ceased. The following day the police returned, gave him Miranda warnings again, and for an unknown reason, the petitioner implicated himself in the crime of robbery, burglary, and 1st degree murder. Counsel had not been supplied to him after his first request the previous day. The Court held that his conviction was reversed. There was no direction for a remand for a new trial in this case.

MICHIGAN v. JACKSON, 475 U.S. 625, 106 S.Ct. 1404, 89 L.Ed.2d. 631, 39 Cr L 3001 (1986), extended this right from the Fifth Amendment, Miranda doctrine to the Sixth Amendment right of counsel concept if police initiate interrogation after a defendant's assertion, at an arraignment or similar proceeding of his right to counsel, any waiver of the defendant's right to counsel for that police initiated interrogation is invalid.

When a suspect is interrogated by police in a custodial setting and when the suspect invokes his right to counsel, the suspect may not be interrogated further by the original interrogators or others, while he remains in custody, even if the subject of the offense is wholly unrelated to the crime as to which he has already requested counsel, unless counsel has been provided to the suspect as the suspect initiates further communication with officials **ARIZONA v. ROBERSON**, 486 U.S. 675, 108 S.Ct. 2093, 100 L.Ed.2d. 704, Cr L 3085 (1988).

In **RHODE ISLAND v. INNES**, 446 U.S. 291, 100 S.Ct. 1682, 64 L.Ed.2d. 297 (1980), an off-hand remark was made to defendant by police officer, that a handicapped child at a nearby school might find the gun. This lead defendant to tell where the gun was. The Court held that this did not constitute interrogation. It held further that in cases like this, interrogation might occur when the suspect could reasonably be expected to be particularly vulnerable, i.e., an express question is asked by the police.

In **NEW YORK v. QUARLES**, 467 U.S. 649, 104 S.Ct. 2626, 81 L.Ed.2d. 550 (1984), the majority held in a 5-1-3 decision that a police officer need not recite Miranda warnings before asking a custodial suspect immediately at the time of arrest, "where is the gun," when the officer had knowledge that the suspect was reported to have recently possessed a gun and the gun was not in the possession of the suspect at the time of the arrest. The question could reasonably be said to have been prompted by the officer's concern for public safety. In that case the apprehension was made in a supermarket and other persons were present. The Court thus enunciated a "PUBLIC SAFETY" exception to the Miranda warnings.

In **BERKEMER v. MCCARTY**, 468 U.S. 420, 104 S.Ct. 3138, 82 L.Ed.2d 317 (1984) it was held that an officer need not give Miranda warnings to a driver of a motor vehicle in a routine traffic stop before the officer asks the driver questions. However, once the motorist has been detained pursuant to a traffic stop, and thereafter is subjected to treatment that renders him "in custody" for practical purposes, he is entitled to the full panoply of protections prescribed by Miranda.

The Court modified **BREWER v. WILLIAMS**, supra, in **NIX v. WILLIAMS**, 467 U.S. 431, 104 S.Ct. 2501, 81 L.Ed.2d. 377, 35 Cr.L. 3119 (1984) where volunteers were searching for the body of a 10 year old girl. The respondent had been arrested and was being transported to a place of incarceration. The police informed his counsel that during the drive they would not question the respondent. However, one of the officers began a conversation with the respondent that resulted in him making incriminating statements and directed the officers to the child's body. A systematic search of the area by 200 volunteers was then terminated. The Court held that these were different facts from Brewer (supra) because in the instant case, the volunteers would have discovered the body without the aid of the respondent. The Court held further that the evidence pertaining to the discovery and the condition of the body was properly admitted in the

76

second trial (no evidence was introduced as to how police found the body in the second trial) on the ground that the body ultimately or inevitably would have been discovered even if no violation of any constitutional provision had taken place... .If the prosecution can establish by a preponderance of the evidence that the information ultimately or inevitably would have been discovered by lawful means, then the deterrence rational has little basis, and the evidence should be received.

Another decision of importance to police and prosecutorial personnel is found in **OREGON v. ELSTAD**, 468 U.S. 298, 105 S.Ct. 1285, 84 L.Ed.2d. 22, 36 Cr.L. 3167 (1985). There the respondent was picked up at his home as a burglary suspect. At his home he made an incriminating statement without having been given Miranda warnings. Later at the station house, he was given Miranda warnings and he then decided to give a written confession without the assistance of counsel. The Court held that the Fifth Amendment guarantee against self incrimination does not require suppression of a confession, made after proper Miranda warnings and a valid waiver of rights, solely because the police had obtained an earlier voluntary statement without the prior Miranda warnings having been given.

In **ARIZONA v. MAURO**, 481 U.S. 520, 107 S.Ct. 1931, 95 L.Ed.2d. 458, 41 Cr L 3081 (1987), the Court whittled away at the Miranda rule, as it seems to be doing on a steady basis in a 5-4 decision. In that case the defendant was in custody for killing his son. He had indicated that he did not wish to answer any questions until a lawyer was present. The police ceased questioning and placed the prisoner in the office of the police captain. The prisoner's wife insisted that she be allowed to speak with her husband. The police were reluctant to permit this but finally acceded to her request when she agreed to have an officer present with her during the conversation. The officer assigned brought a tape recorder into the room which was placed in plain sight. The prisoner said, inter alia, that she should not answer questions until a lawyer was present. At the subsequent trial, the tape recording was introduced into evidence to rebut his insanity defense. The Court held that this was not the result of a police interrogation or its functional equivalent and the tape recording was inadmissible as evidence.

The Court has held that the failure of the police to inform the suspect of all the possible subjects of interrogation does not constitute official "trickery" sufficient to invalidate the suspects waiver of the Fifth Amendment privilege. **COLORADO v. SPRING**, 479 U.S. 564, 107 S.Ct. 551, 93 L.Ed.2d. 954, 40 Cr L 3194 (1987). In the above case, the suspect was not forewarned that he would be questioned about a homicide which he initially denied having committed but at a subsequent interrogation he confessed to the crime. He had signed written Miranda waivers prior to questioning on both interrogations.

It is sometimes amazing as to what a lawyer will conceive as an argument to represent a client's interest. Sometimes the lawyer is successful and I call them the "unsung heroes of history." However they are not always successful in their quest for a new rule of law. Such a situation arose in **PATTERSON v. ILLINOIS**, 487 U.S. 1210, 108 S.Ct. 2389, 101 L.Ed.2d. 261, 43 Cr L 3146 (1988). In that case, a murder occurred as a result of a gang fight between two rival gangs in Cook County, Illinois (Chicago). An investigation by the local police determined that Tyrone Patterson, the petitioner herein, had been one of the perpetrators and he was indicted for the murder. He had been apprehended one day prior to the indictment and held in police custody while the police were completing the investigation.

When he was apprehended, he was told of his Miranda rights and volunteered to answer questions put to him by police. On the next day, he was informed that he was indicted for murder. He asked the police officer who informed him of the indictment about particulars of who was also indicted. Upon learning that one particular member of the gang had been omitted from the indictment, he asked "[W]hy wasn't he indicted, he did everything." He also began to explain that there was a witness that would support his account of the crime. Thereupon, the police officer interrupted petitioner and handed him a Miranda waiver form containing five specific warnings as suggested by the Court in **MIRANDA v. ARIZONA**. The officer read it aloud, as petitioner read along with him. Petitioner initialed each of the five warnings and signed

78

the waiver form. Then the petitioner gave a lengthy statement to the police officers concerning the murder, describing the role of each of his fellow gang members in the crime. Later that day, he confessed involvement, the second time, to an Assistant State's Attorney after he had acknowledged to the Assistant State's Attorney that he had signed the waiver and understood his rights. At this time the petitioner was seventeen years of age.

In a 6-3 decision, the Court held that this was an intentional relinquishment or abandonment of a known right or privilege and that he was sufficiently aware of his right to have counsel present during the questioning and that his statements should not be suppressed.

In **DUCKWORTH v. EGAN**, 492 U.S. 195, 109 S.Ct. 2875, 106 L.Ed.2d. 166, 45 Cr L 3172 (1989) the police questioned a suspect after they had read a full Miranda Warning to him that also included the statement that if he could not afford a lawyer, one would be appointed for him "if and when you go to court." He read and signed a waiver form providing this information. Twenty-nine hours later, he signed a different waiver form and confessed to the stabbing. He sought suppression of this confession and this was denied. Following conviction he sought habeas corpus review in Federal District Court and the writ was denied. The Court of Appeals reversed saying that the words "if and when you go to court" was constitutionally defective because it denied the indigent accused a clear and unequivocal waiving of the right to appointed counsel before interrogation and linked that right to a future event.

The Supreme Court held that informing a suspect that an attorney would be appointed for him "if and when you go to court" does not render Miranda Warnings inadequate.

In **BUTLER v. MCKELLAR, WARDEN**, et al, 494 U.S.__, 110 S.Ct. 1212, 108 L.Ed.2d. 347, 46 Cr L 2165 (1990), the petitioner whose conviction for a capital offense had become final on direct appeal, filed for habeas corpus relief in the Federal District Court. His argument for relief was based upon the fact that on the same day that the Federal Court of Appeals denied a rehearing of an appeal, the Court handed down its decision in **ARIZONA v. ROBERSON** 486 U.S. 675 (1988), wherein the Court held, inter alia, that when a suspect invokes his rights to counsel in any pending case, the suspect may not be interrogated further by his original interrogators, or others while he remains in custody on any case unless counsel has been provided to the suspect.

In the BUTLER case, he had been arrested and charged with a separate assault charge for which he had retained counsel. While he was in custody, he was informed that he was a suspect in a murder case. He was informed of his Miranda rights but signed waiver of rights form and made incriminating statements. These statements were admitted, over objection, in the murder trial and he was convicted. He argued that he should be entitled to the protection enunciated in **ARIZONA v. ROBERSON**, supra, but the Court agreed with the Court of Appeals that ROBERSON did not apply retroactively on collateral review. His interrogation was conducted according to the guidelines established at that time.

The Court with Justice Scalia as the writer of the opinion in **McNEIL v. WISCONSIN** __U.S. __, 111 S.Ct. 2204, 115 L.Ed 2d 158, 49 CrL 2247 (1991), made another dent in the armor set by **MIRANDA v. ARIZONA** 384 U.S. 436 (1966). In the McNeil case the Court held that a suspect's invocation of the Sixth Amendment to counsel by his appearance at a judicial proceeding concerning a formally charged offense does not serve as an invocation of the Fifth Amendment based on right to have counsel present during custodial interrogation of the suspect without the presence of counsel. In this case the suspect was charged with armed robbery and was represented by a public defender at a bail hearing. While in jail on that charge, he was questioned by police about a murder in another city. He was advised of his Miranda rights, signed forms waiving them and made incriminating statements relating to the crimes in the other city. He was then formally charged. His pretrial statements were admitted after a denial at a suppression hearing, and he was convicted. The Court held that his invocation of the right to counsel during a judicial proceeding pursuant to the Sixth Amendment did not constitute an invocation of his right to counsel derived from **MIRANDA v. ARIZONA** from the Fifth Amendment's guarantee against compelled self incrimination. The statements were not to be suppressed.

The question of the necessity of Miranda warnings

came up again in a sobriety test conducted on videotape in a police booking facility in **PENNSYLVANIA v. MUNIZ** __ U.S. __, 110 S.Ct. 2638, 110 L.Ed. 2d 528, 47 CrL 2165 (1990). In that case a driver of an automobile was apprehended for drunk driving and had all of the usual manifestations of an intoxicated person. He was brought to a police booking facility and subjected to a sobriety test in which the officer's questions and the subject's responses were recorded on videotape and audio. He was not given Miranda warnings. He claimed that this was custodial interrogation requiring the administration of Miranda warnings and thus should be suppressed.

The responses and questions relating to the date of sixth birthday were not allowed by the Court, but all other responses were allowed on the theory that this was not custodial interrogation. The Court majority said this was similar to **SCHMERBER v. CALIFORNIA** 384 U.S. 757 (1966) where blood extraction was permitted as not being the fruit of custodial interrogation.

See Section 2.50 **ILLINOIS v. PERKINS** for additional relevant information.

To this date, it appears that we have not heard the last word from the Court on Miranda warning requirements. The trend seems to be towards an erosion of defendant's rights in this area of the law.

CHAPTER 2   SEARCH AND SEIZURE

Contents

The Fourth Amendment to the United States Constitution provides:

The right of the people to be secure in their persons, houses, papers, and effects, against unreasonable searches and seizures, shall not be violated and no Warrants shall issue but upon probable cause, supported by Oath or affirmation, and particularly describing the place to be searched, and the persons or things to be seized.

§ 2.1   History of the Exclusionary Rule

The reader probably knows that the United States Constitution provides for the theory of checks and balances where each major branch of the government, i.e., the Executive, Legislative, and Judicial, acts as a check and balances the power of the other branches of government. In this way, no one branch is able to have complete authority to administer the governmental processes. Each branch of the government is a complete unit in itself and theoretically is not to be dominated by others. It sometimes happens, however, that a strong President, acting with a majority of his own political party in the legislative branch, can get legislation passed, but in the final analysis, the Supreme Court, consisting of persons enjoying the highest prestige and having lifetime positions, acts as a leveling influence against unconstitutional legislation.

You will recall that the executive power is exercised by the President of the United States or the Governors of the respective States. You will also remember that the implementation or enforcement of laws is the responsibility of the executive branch of government. Hence the State, City, or County police departments and agencies are arms of the executive branch of government.

The United States Constitution, we say, gives basic fundamental rights to citizens and persons within our geographical borders. If these rights are denied to these people by the legislative or executive branches of government, it then becomes the responsibility of the judicial branch of government to see that this condition is corrected.

The Fourth Amendment to the United States

Constitution dealing with unreasonable search and seizure had at first been intended to limit only the central federal government from the infringement of this right of United States citizens. With the passage of the Fourteenth Amendment to the United States Constitution, lawyers were finding new meaning in that document that one wonders whether the framers and proposers of the original Fourth Amendment and the Fourteenth Amendment had any idea of at the time of adoption.

The United States Supreme Court does not have the power to send an army into the field to enforce a judgment of the court but it must rely upon the integrity of the executive branch to enforce its decisions. Because of the nature of people, if one has some power, inherently he/she grabs more power unless restrained in some manner. The police of the nation, given certain powers, were frequently obsessed with the idea that they could do anything they wanted to do with suspected persons, in the interest of effective law enforcement. The United States Supreme Court devised what has come to be known as the exclusionary rule. In essence the rule provides that if the court finds that the conduct of the police deprived the defendant/petitioner of a substantial constitutional right, all evidence secured as a result of such conduct would not be admissible on the trial of the defendant. Without this evidence in the trial record, no impartial trier of the facts, be it the judge, trying the case without a jury, or the jury, could find that the defendant was guilty. The defendant, however, is required to object to the introduction of this tainted evidence by the procedural device known as a motion to suppress. This is merely an application to the trial court, preceding the actual trial, to conduct a hearing as to whether the defendant has been denied any constitutional right and whether any evidence was obtained as a result of this denial. If the trial judge finds that there was a denial of a constitutional right, the judge will grant the motion to suppress and the prosecutor must find other evidence or move the court for dismissal of the case against the defendant for the reason that he/she has insufficient admissible evidence to convict the defendant.

The concept of the exclusionary rule developed

slowly in our legal system. It had been employed to prevent abuses of the privileges of self-incrimination of the Fifth Amendment in **BOYD v. U.S.**, 116 U.S. 616, 6 S.Ct. 524, 29 L.Ed 746 (1886). In this case compelled statements were elicited from the defendant by the police. The court, however, had a greater problem in the cases involving Fourth Amendment unreasonable searches. In **WEEKS v. U.S.**, 232 U.S. 383, 34 S.Ct. 341, 58 L.Ed. 652 (1914), the court held that any evidence obtained by federal officers in violation of the Fourth Amendment would be barred from a federal prosecution. However, they did permit state officers to secure the evidence in accordance with the state rules of evidence and then hand this evidence over to the federal officers for federal prosecution. This came to be known as the **"Silver Platter Doctrine"** on the theory that the state officers could engage in practices forbidden to federal officers and then hand over the evidence on a theoretical "Silver Platter" to the federal officers.

At that time many states were operating under the theory enunciated by Mr. Justice Benjamin Cardozo when he was Chief Judge of the Court of Appeals of the State of New York, where in **PEOPLE v. DEFORE**, 242 N.Y. 13, 150 N.E. 585 (1926), he said at 242 N.Y. 13, 21, "The criminal is to go free because the constable has blundered"; and at page 23, "The pettiest police officer would have it in his power through overzeal or indiscretion to confer immunity upon an offender for crimes the most flagitious. A room is searched against the law, and the body of a murdered man is found. . . . The privacy of the home has been infringed and the murderer goes free"; and at 242 N.Y. 13, 24, "The question is whether the protection for the individual would not be gained at a disproportionate loss of protection for society. On the one side is the social need that crime shall be repressed. On the other, the social need that law shall not be flouted by the insolence of office."

The Supreme Court decided a similar case in **WOLF v. COLORADO**, 338 U.S. 25, 69 S.Ct. 1359, 93 L.Ed. 1782 (1949), where it held that a state officer, enforcing a state law, was not controllable by the Fourth Amendment in that this amendment was directed towards governmental abuse and the state officer was in the guise of a private person. The concept being that with respect to state officers' actions, he was acting in conformity with a rule of evidence in the state and the state had a reserved right to enact and implement its own rules of evidence. It is apparent that the Supreme Court was stretching to validate state action in **WOLF v. COLORADO** (supra) because the Court also indicated that an unreasonable search and seizure by a state officer violates the federal constitution by violating the due process clause of the Fourteenth Amendment, but it did not require the exclusion of the evidence in state courts.

The "Silver Platter Doctrine" was discontinued as a result of the court's decision in **ELKINS v. UNITED STATES**, 364 U.S. 206, 80 S.Ct. 1437, 4 L.Ed.2d 1669 (1960), where it held that the evidence seized by state officers by an unreasonable search and seizure could not be admitted into evidence in a federal prosecution.

The court, however, still did not interfere with the admissibility of evidence by state law enforcement officers in state courts except where the evidence was obtained by a search and seizure accomplished by coercion, violence, or brutality to the person such as "shocks the conscience." **ROCHIN v. CALIFORNIA**, 342 U.S. 165, 72 S.Ct. 205, 96 L.Ed. 183 (1952). This was a case where a stomach pump was employed to regurgitate narcotics swallowed by the defendant/petitioner.

The court continued to deal with the problem in **IRVINE v. CALIFORNIA**, 347 U.S. 128, 75 S.Ct. 381, 98 L.Ed. 561 (1954), wherein they limited Rochin to situations involving coercion, violence, or brutality to the person. In **BREITHAUPT v. ABRAM**, 352 U.S. 432, 77 S.Ct. 408, 1 L.Ed.2d 448 (1957), a blood sample was taken under the watchful eye of a physician. The sample was taken from the defendant while he was unconscious and it was determined that he had a high alcoholic content in his blood and this was used against him in connection with a vehicular homicide case. In that case the court upheld the conviction because the court found no coercion, violence, or brutality employed by the police.

The court overruled **WOLF v. COLORADO** (supra) when it decided **MAPP v. OHIO**, 367 U.S. 643, 81 S.Ct. 1684, 6

L.Ed.2d 1081 (1961), wherein the court stated that:
".... The efforts of the courts and their officials
to bring the guilty to punishment, praiseworthy as
they are, are not to be aided by the sacrifice of
those great principles established by years of
endeavor and suffering which have resulted in their
embodiment in the fundamental law of the land ....
Because there can be no fixed formula, we are
admittedly met with recurring questions of the
reasonableness of searches, but less is not to be
expected when dealing with a Constitution, and, at
any rate reasonableness is in the first instance
for the [trial judge] to determine .... We hold
that all evidence obtained by searches and seizures
in violation of the Constitution is, by the same
authority, inadmissible in a state court."

The "Burger Court" was more law-and-order-oriented
than the "Warren Court" and recent decisions appear to
give greater authority to law enforcement officers to
make searches without a warrant. In **UNITED STATES v.
SANTANA,** 427 U.S. 38, 96 S.Ct. 2406, 49 L.Ed.2d 300
(1976), the court held that when the police observed
petitioner possessing contraband while she was standing
in the doorway of her house, her retreat to the interior
vestibule of the house, taking the contraband with her,
did not give her protection of the unreasonable search
provisions of the Fourth and Fourteenth Amendments.

In **UNITED STATES v. WATSON,** 423 U.S. 411, 96 S.Ct.
820, 46 L.Ed.2d 598 (1976), the court again decided in
favor of a warrantless search. This case was based upon
18 U.S.C. 3061(a)(3) which expressly authorized postal
inspectors to make arrests without a warrant for a felony
when they had probable cause to believe that the person
to be arrested had committed or was committing such a
felony. The court wrote, ".... The duty of law
enforcement officers to seek a warrant 'where practicable
to do so' is merely a rule of 'judicial preference' and
not one of constitutional dimensions. . . ."

From a reading of these 1976 cases relating to
alleged violations of Fourth and Fourteenth Amendments
and from other later cases, it appears that the court is
lowering its threshold for exclusion of evidence based

upon alleged violations of the Bill of Rights. There are, however, many states whose highest court has required a higher threshold where more rights are granted to an arrestee than those which are required by the federal government. They decide their cases based upon the Bill of Rights as enunciated in their state constitutions. In a text such as this, it would be impractical to indicate the threshold in each state and, hence, if there is any doubt on the part of the reader, he/she is referred to the latest decisions in his/her jurisdiction.

Thus we have the present trend of the law with respect to the exclusionary rule as it applies to unreasonable search and seizure. Its applicability to other fundamental rights of the Bill of Rights of the United States Constitution are not relevant to the subjects in this book, and therefore have been not been included.

§ 2.2   Search Warrants

A search warrant is an order in writing in the name of the People signed by a neutral and detached magistrate, directed to a peace officer, commanding him/her to search for personal property and bring it before the court.

A search warrant is obtained by a law enforcement officer by applying to a detached neutral magistrate that he/she issue such a warrant. In order to do this constitutionally and to preserve the record, the officer is required to indicate by way of an affidavit what probable cause exists for the issuance of such a court order. After reading the affidavit setting forth facts which in the officer's opinion give the officer probable cause to make the search to obtain evidence to arrest the defendant for violation of some law, the detached, neutral magistrate makes his/her own conclusion as to whether probable cause exists. If the necessary probable cause exists, the judicial officer will sign an order, which is usually prepared beforehand by the prosecutor. This order will direct the law enforcement officer to make a search and if the evidence sought is found, to bring the evidence and the person described in the warrant before the court. The returning of the evidence and/or the named person before the court has come to be known as the "return."

§ 2.3   **Probable Cause Regarding Search Warrants**

Probable cause and reasonable grounds are almost synonymous. The reason that the Court has insisted that a neutral detached magistrate view the circumstances of probable cause is that the Court has manifested a preference for arrest under search warrants on the grounds that interposing an orderly procedure whereby a neutral and detached magistrate makes the decision is better than allowing those engaged in the competitive enterprise of ferreting out crime to make hurried decisions which would be reviewable by a magistrate only after the fact and by hindsight judgment. "In a doubtful or marginal case a search warrant may be sustainable where without one it would fall." **UNITED STATES v. VENTRESCA**, 380 U.S. 102, 85 S.Ct. 741, 13 L.Ed.2d 684 (1965). The court treated the problem of judicial determination of probable cause in **AGUILAR v. TEXAS**, 378 U.S. 108, 84 S.Ct. 1509, 12 L.Ed.2d 723 (1964), where it struck down a state search warrant issued on the basis of an affidavit which recited only that the police "have received reliable information from a credible person" and "do believe" that defendant possesses narcotics at described premises because the affidavit contained "mere conclusions," not enabling the magistrate to "judge for himself the persuasiveness of the facts relied on ... to show probable cause." The affidavit should have indicated specific facts which led them to their conclusion and did not give proof that the informant was credible or reliable. A magistrate may require the testimony of the informer before he signs the warrant. The problem of the requirement of a neutral and detached magistrate issuing the warrant was met squarely by the court in **COOLIDGE v. NEW HAMPSHIRE**, 403 U.S. 443, 91 S.Ct. 2022, 20 L.Ed.2d 564 (1971), where the Attorney

General of the State of New Hampshire, acting as a Justice of the Peace, under New Hampshire Law in force at that time, issued a search warrant. The court held that this action did not satisfy the requirements of the Fourth and Fourteenth Amendments in that the Attorney General was not detached but was interested in the prosecution of the case.

§ 2.4   Identity of Informants Regarding Search Warrants

The government is sometimes confronted with a serious problem in decision making when at a motion to suppress and controvert a warrant hearing, the defendant's counsel asks the affiant of the application for the warrant for the identity of the informant. Anyone who has any familiarity with informers knows that they do not want to be identified. In some cases their very life depends upon their anonymity. At the very least, their future use to law enforcement is extinguished.

Those students who are familiar with the law of evidence will know that in a trial of an action, hearsay evidence is not admissible unless it falls within certain long used and reliable exceptions. However, in a motion to suppress, in most jurisdictions, hearsay evidence is admissible. In this way it is possible for the officer to testify that an informer told him something even though the informer is not available for cross-examination.

The conversation between a law enforcement officer and an informant is privileged, much like that of husband and wife, attorney and client, penitent and clergyman, and other privileged communications. However, where disclosure of an informer's identity or of the contents of his communication is relevant and helpful to the defense of the accused or it is essential to a fair determination of the cause, the privilege must give way. **ROVIARO v. UNITED STATES**, 353 U.S. 53, 77 S.Ct. 623, 1 L.Ed. 639 (1957); **RUGENDORF V. UNITED STATES**, 376 U.S. 528, 84 S.Ct. 825, 11 L.Ed.2d 887 (1964). In Roviaro, the defendant was charged in two counts with (1) an illegal sale of heroin to "John Doe" and (2) illegal transportation of heroin. The court reasoned that "John Doe" was a participant in the transportation charge and that "John Doe" was an informer. In this factual pattern, the court said the government should be required to supply the identity of the informant or suffer dismissal.

MCCRAY v. ILLINOIS, 386 U.S. 300, 87 S.Ct. 1056, 18 L.Ed.2d 782 (1967), was another case treating the question of whether an informer need be identified at the insistence of the defendant. In that case petitioner was arrested for possession of narcotics and heroin was found on his person. A preliminary hearing on a motion to suppress was held and the arresting officers testified that an informant who had supplied reliable information on about twenty previous cases told them that he had observed McCray selling narcotics at a certain corner and then accompanied the police to that corner and pointed out McCray. Both officers were asked for the name and address of the informant, but objections to these questions were sustained and petitioner's motion was denied. He was subsequently convicted. The court reasoned that the arresting officers testified in open court fully and in precise detail as to what the informer told them and as to why they had reason to believe his information was trustworthy. Each officer was under oath. Each was subject to a searching cross-examination. The judge was obviously satisfied that each was telling the truth and for that reason he exercised discretion conferred upon him by the established law of Illinois to respect the informer privilege. "Nothing in the Due Process Clause of the Fourteenth Amendment requires a state court judge in every such hearing to assume the arresting officers are committing perjury...."

The court denied the petitioner's right to cross-examine the arresting officers on the identity of the informer reasoning that the claim of the petitioner of violation of his Sixth Amendment right of cross-examination can not be sustained because it would follow from this argument that no witness on cross-examination could ever constitutionally assert a testimonial privilege including the privilege compelling self-incrimination guaranteed by the Constitution itself.

The author believes that to assume that every
policeman who testifies is telling the truth is an
absurdity. However, the court probably took the right
course of action in this case in deciding as it did
because if it had decided to the contrary, the law
enforcement officer's most valuable asset, the informer,
would be destroyed and many serious crimes would not
otherwise be solved.

In **PEOPLE v. VERRECHIO**, 23 N.Y.2d 489, 245 N.E.2d
222 (1969), a New York Court of Appeals case where the
officer testified that an informant of past reliability
had told him that the defendant "usually had heroin," the
court, per Burke, J., held:

> Obviously the information imparted was extremely
> vague and lacking in specifics and the source of
> the informer's information is nowhere detailed so
> that it could as readily be rumor or outright
> fiction as personal knowledge of fact.... On these
> facts we are presented with a "rare" case in which
> identity should be disclosed unless the officer's
> observations provide objective verification of the
> details of the information supplied by the
> informer.

This was not a reversal of McCray (supra) but
followed Roviaro (supra), and New York chose to place a
higher threshold on the right of confrontation and cross-
examination in cases where the information relayed to the
officer by the informant was extremely vague. Each state
may do this with respect to its own constitution and
their courts' interpretation of it. On the other hand,
as each right of the Bill of Rights of the Federal
Constitution is absorbed by virtue of the Fourteenth
Amendment, each state is required to give the basic
threshold of rights to its inhabitants as is declared by
the United Supreme Court.

Another case where the state refused to identify the
informant referred to in an affidavit supporting the
issuance of a search warrant occurred in **COLORADO v.
NUNEZ**, 465 U.S. 324, 104 S.Ct. 1257, 79 L.Ed.2d 338,
(1984), where the state court suppressed evidence seized
because the state refused to identify the informant who

94

gave the police officer the initial information leading to the issuance of the search warrant. The Court dismissed the writ as improvidently granted saying that it appeared that the judgment of the court below rested on independent and adequate state grounds. This appears to be an extension of **MICHIGAN v. LONG**, infra, in § 2.28. In the Nunez case, three concurring justices joined in a dissenting decision wherein they said that this decision confers on trial courts in Colorado discretion to do far more than the Federal Constitution minimally requires. The Federal cases require disclosure of the identity of the informant when there is a showing of a reasonable basis in fact to question the accuracy of the informant's recitals.

§ 2.5   Particularity in Search Warrants of Place and Person to Be Searched and Seized

The Fourth Amendment proscription respecting the particularity of the description of the place to be searched and the person or things to be seized was inserted to prevent a recurrence of a General Warrant or a Writ of Assistance which had previously existed in England. Accordingly, the courts have required law enforcement officers to be precise in their requests for search warrants. Typographical errors in the descriptive part of the warrant may not prove fatally defective but care should be taken to avoid them. If the address indicated is 2300 S. State Street when it should have been 2310 S. State Street, the warrant can withstand attack if the apartment number is correct. **PEOPLE. v. WATSON**, 26 Ill.2d 203, 186 N.E.2d 326 (1962). Often an address has a deep lot and there is a building adjacent to the street and another building in the rear of the one adjacent to the street. This must be specifically described. So too must a particular apartment number or floor number in a building be particularly described so as to comply with the particularity requirement of the Amendment. In Watson (supra) the Illinois Supreme Court held that a warrant is sufficiently descriptive if it enables the officer, with reasonable effort, to identify the place. If the property is sufficiently recognizable from the description to enable the officer to locate the premises with definiteness and certainty it is adequate. The constitutional safeguard is designed to require a description which particularly points to a definite ascertainable place so as to exclude all others.

Because of freedom afforded to the press under the First Amendment, in obscenity cases, great particularity of the things to be seized is required. A Quantity of Copies of **BOOKS v. KANSAS**, 378 U.S. 205, 84 S.Ct. 1723, 12 L.Ed.2d 809 (1964).

States vary as to the particularity requirement but it is safe to say that if an officer exercises the greatest care in his description of the place to be searched, what he is seeking, and the person to be seized, the warrant will withstand a motion to controvert.

§ 2.6   No Delay in Execution of Search Warrants

A search warrant is a procedural device which is prescribed by both state and federal statute.   The statute may vary from state to state in its particular requirements but if there is no time limit for its execution indicated in the statute, the common law rule of reasonable time attaches.   Some states require an authorization to that effect if the warrant is to be executed at night.   N.Y.——Criminal Procedure Law 690.45(5).

§ 2.7   Search Warrants and Seizure of Nondescribed Contraband

If an officer, pursuant to a search warrant, enters a premises and in searching for the items described on the search warrant in the particularly described location observes a revolver unlawfully possessed or a machine gun or other contraband, it is his/her duty to seize this contraband along with the items described in the warrant and the seizure is valid. **HARRIS v. UNITED STATES**, 331 U.S. 145, 67 S.Ct. 1098, 91 L.Ed. 1399 (1947). Such items are admissible in evidence under the theory that they have been seized as incidental to a lawful arrest. **CHIMEL v. CALIFORNIA**, 395 U.S. 752, 89 S.Ct. 2034, 23 L.Ed.2d 685 (1969). The difficult problem arises, however, when the items mentioned in the search warrant are not found but other contraband is found. In that case the officer is to seize the contraband anyway but when the defendant moves for a motion to suppress, he may be successful in suppressing the evidence so obtained. Notwithstanding this, the contraband is not returned to the defendant but is confiscated.

§ 2.8   Search Warrants and Seizure of Authorized Objects

A search warrant may not be validly issued to seize objects which are not unlawfully held. It cannot be used in civil actions as a substitute for an action in replevin or a warrant of attachment. The statutes of the various states indicate with specificity the type of items which may be seized. Generally, they are issued upon property which was stolen or embezzled, or when the property was used as a means of committing a felony, or when the property is either in the possession of a person who intends to use it as a means of committing a crime, or if the property is in possession of another to whom such person delivered it for the purpose of concealing it or preventing it form being discovered. It is recommended that the reader consult the criminal procedure statute of his/her state to ascertain local requirements for the authorized objects of a search warrant.

§ 2.9   Good Faith Exception

In the year 1980, the courts appeared to begin a trend which appears to represent the thinking of many law enforcement persons with respect to the situation where an arresting officer makes an arrest under conditions which, if it were strictly construed, would result in the dismissal of criminal charges against a defendant who is obviously guilty of the crime charged, when the officer made an effort to comply with constitutional safeguards, but made a good-faith error. Such a situation arose in **U.S. v. WILLIAMS**, 622 F.2d. 830, 27 Cr.L. 3293 (1980) where in the United States Court of Appeals for the Fifth Circuit, the court in an en-banc decision held that evidence obtained by police conduct that is alleged to be unlawful shall not be suppressed if the government establishes that the conduct, if mistaken or unauthorized, was taken in the reasonable good-faith belief that it was proper. The United States Supreme Court denied certiorari in 449 U.S. 961 which leaves this decision to be followed in other circuits. Other circuits and some state courts did just that. As of that time, as known to the author, the 2nd and 4th Circuit as well as California, Florida, Georgia, Montana, New Hampshire, Colorado and Virginia had followed it.

The denial of certiorari by the Supreme Court in the Williams case has been followed by other denials of other cases such as **U.S. v. SINDONA** 636 F.2d. 792, Cert. den. 451 U.S. 912, 101 S.Ct. 1984, 68 L.Ed.2d 302 (1980) and **U.S. v. ASLOUNY**, 629 F.2d. 830 Cert. den. 449 U.S. 1111, 101 S.Ct. 920, 66 L.Ed.2d. 840 (1980).

As of this writing, it has not been adopted as a federal statute but movement is being made in that direction. It therefore appears that the good-faith exception is with us for some time to come.

The Supreme Court delivered a decision in **GATES v. ILLINOIS**, 462 U.S. 213, 103 S.Ct. 2317, 76 L.Ed.2d 527, 51 LW 4709 (1983) that appears to skirt the problem of the good-faith exception. In that case, a search warrant was obtained for the auto and residence of a husband and wife drug dealing team. The Illinois courts suppressed the evidence on the ground that the police application for the warrant failed to satisfy a two pronged test announced in **AGUILAR v. TEXAS**, 387 U.S. 108 and **SPINELLI v. UNITED STATES**, 393 U.S. 410, i.e. (1) revealing the informant's "basis of knowledge" and (2) providing sufficient facts to establish either the informant's "veracity" or the "reliability" of the informant's

report. The Supreme Court wrote that it would not pass
on the question of whether or not to exclude evidence
obtained in the reasonable belief that the search and
seizure was consistent with the Fourth Amendment since it
was not presented or decided by the Illinois courts.
However they announced a new concept which they called
the "totality of the circumstances" approach and
abandoned the two pronged test. They explained that the
task of the issuing magistrate is simply to make a
practical, common sense decision whether, given all the
circumstances set forth in the affidavit before him,
there is a fair probability that contraband or evidence
of a crime will be found in a particular place. And the
duty of the reviewing court is simply to ensure that the
magistrate had a substantial basis for concluding that
probable cause existed. In the instant case, the Court
held that the issuing magistrate had a substantial basis
for concluding that probable cause to search respondent's
home and car existed. The Illinois courts were reversed.
This case greatly expands the power of law enforcement
agencies to get convictions.

An extension of the "totality of the circumstances"
approach was made by the Court in **U.S. v. LEON**, 468 U.S.
897, 104 S. Ct. 3105, 82 L.Ed.2d. 677 (1984). In the
Leon case, the police initiated a drug-trafficking
investigation by surveillance of the respondent's
activities. Based on an affidavit summarizing the police
officer's observations, a facially valid search warrant
for three residences and automobiles was obtained and
executed.

The searches produced large quantities of drugs and
other evidence. Respondents were indicted for federal
drug offenses, and motions to suppress were filed and
granted in part. The District Court concluded that the
affidavit was insufficient to establish probable cause,
although recognizing that the officer had acted in good
faith.

The Supreme Court held that the Fourth Amendment
exclusionary rule should not be applied so as to bar the
use of the prosecution's case-in-chief of evidence
obtained by officers acting in reasonable reliance on a
search warrant issued by a detached and neutral
magistrate but ultimately found to be invalid.

   Hence the good faith exception to the exclusionary
rule, long in incubation, finally saw the light of day.
A fortiori, **MASSACHUSETTS v. SHEPPARD**: 468 U.S. 981, 104
S.Ct. 3424, 82 L.Ed.2d 737, 35, Cr.L. 3296 (1984).
   In **MARYLAND v. GARRISON**, 480 U.S. 79, 107 S.Ct.
1013, 94 L.Ed.2d. 72, 40 Cr L 3288 (1987), Baltimore
police officers had a warrant to search the person of
Lawrence McWeble and "the premises known as 2036 Park
Avenue third floor apartment." They met McWeble in front
of the building and used his key to enter the first floor
hallway and to the locked door at the top of the stairs
to the third floor. They had previously made an exterior
examination of the premises and an inquiry of the utility
company. Nothing was revealed in the investigation to
indicate that there were two separate apartments on the
third floor. When they entered the third floor, unknown
to the police, there were two apartments. Both apartments
had their entrance doors open. The officers searched
Garrison's apartment and found contraband. When it was
explained to them that there were two separate
apartments, they discontinued any further search, but
seized the contraband and arrested Garrison. The
validity of the search was questioned and the Maryland
Court of Appeals held the search invalid. The Court
reversed in a 6-3 decision holding that the Maryland
Court of Appeals did not decide the case on a "plain
statement" that the decision rested upon adequate and
independent state grounds, see **MICHIGAN v. LONG**, 463 U.S.
1032, 1042, (1983), and that it decided it on a Maryland
constitutional provision in pari materia with the Fourth
Amendment and therefore the Court said it has
jurisdiction. It went on to hold that the warrant was
valid on the known facts when it was issued; and that the
purposes justifying a police search strictly limit the
permissible extent of the search. The Court has also
recognized the need to allow some latitude for honest
mistakes that are made by officers in the dangerous and
difficult process of making arrests and executing search
warrants. Although the Court had previously indicated in
STONE v. POWELL, 428 U.S. 465 and **MICHIGAN v. LONG**,
supra, that it was not going to relitigate alleged Fourth
Amendment constitutional violations of state cases where
full and fair hearings had been held where the grounds

100

for the determination were based on a "plain statement" that the decision rests upon adequate and independent state grounds, it appears to this author that the Court is straining to decide state cases where the good faith exception is not being adhered to on the grounds that the state may give greater protection to its inhabitants against unreasonable search and seizure than the protections found in the Fourth Amendment.

The good faith exception to the exclusionary rule applied only to good faith mistakes made by police officers who were in possession of search warrants. The Court extended this exception to a police officer who acted on the authority of a state statute authorizing an administrative search where the statute was declared unconstitutional by a United States District Court on the day following the search. In **ILLINOIS v. KRULL** et al, 480 U.S. 905, 107 S.Ct. 1160, 94 L.Ed. 626, 40 Cr.L 3327 (1987), the Court held that a police officer who entered an automobile wrecking yard pursuant to a state statute authorizing him to do so may seize stolen autos found therein and the contraband is not to be suppressed in a trial for the possession of stolen property, notwithstanding that the authorizing statute was held to be unconstitutional on the day following the search.

As certain as day follows night, the question of civil liability of good faith searches by law enforcement officers, acting without a proper search warrant found its way to the Court in **ANDERSON v. CREIGHTON**, et al, 483 U.S. 635, 107 S.Ct. 3034, 97 L.Ed.2d. 523, 41 Cr L 3396 (1987). That case involved an F.B.I. agent but it is believed that its holding could also be applied to non federal law enforcement officers. The Court essentially held that a federal law enforcement officer is entitled to summary judgment of dismissal of a complaint for damages under the Fourth Amendment if he can establish, as a matter of law, that a reasonable officer could have believed that the search that was conducted comported with the Fourth Amendment even though it actually did not.

§ 2.10   Force Necessary for Execution of Search Warrants

During the 1960's few police departments were free from the cry of police brutality. In recent years this complaint has markedly diminished as more police departments become professionalized.   Unfortunately, there are still some departments against whom many complaints of police brutality are still made.   It is noteworthy at this point, however, that with the Burger Court's decision in **RIZZO v. GOODE**, 423 U.S. 362, 96 S.Ct. 598, 46 L.Ed.2d 561 (1976), the Court held that twenty complaints of incidents in a city of three million residents and seventy-five hundred policemen "established neither a conspiratorial design nor departmental policy actively promulgated by the named petitioners to deprive them of their constitutional rights."   In that case petitioners were seeking injunctive relief against the Mayor and City Government to prevent further police brutality. Statutes usually give the police the right to use reasonable force in effecting an arrest.   This inferentially includes reasonable force to obtain evidence from one who is attempting to conceal it or destroy it.

To be defensive against complaints of police brutality and a Title 42 U.S.C. 1983 action, a member of the force executing a search warrant should use only such force as is necessary to accomplish the intended purpose and no more.

The statutes usually provide that when an officer executes a warrant he has the authority to break both outer and inner doors if, after giving notice of his authority and purpose and demanding entrance, he is refused admittance.   18 U.S.C. 3109.   This sounds wonderful in theory but any experienced officer knows that an experienced potential defendant will have the evidence down the toilet, or in a fire at a fireplace, or swallowed, or thrown out of a window by the time the officer makes his/her entrance.   The statute does not indicate the time between the notice, the refusal of entry, and the right to break the door down and begin the race to the toilet or other places of activities mentioned above.   From personal experience, this time interval is little short of a simultaneous action or the evidence is irretrievably gone.

The question of whether law enforcement officers, possessing a valid search warrant, can detain forcefully the occupants of a premises being searched until they had completed the search came on to be heard in **MICHIGAN v. SUMMERS**, 452 U.S. 692, 101 S.Ct. 2587, 69 L.Ed.2d. 340, 29 Cr.L. 3097 (1981).

In that case, police officers executing a search warrant of a house for narcotics, came upon the respondent, George Summers, as he was descending the front steps. They requested assistance to gain entry and detained him while they searched the premises. After finding narcotics and ascertaining that Summers was the owner of the house, they searched him and found heroin in his possession. He alleged that his personal search was a violation of the Fourth Amendment. The State Courts upheld his theory, but the United States Supreme Court held, inter alia, that for Fourth Amendment purposes, a warrant to search for contraband founded on probable cause implicitly carries with it the limited authority to detain occupants of the premises while a proper search is conducted.

§ 2.11   Reasonable Searches

The Fourth Amendment prohibits unreasonable searches and seizures by the government. It does not prevent reasonable searches. Naturally, the term "reasonable" has a nebulous meaning but it is subject to court interpretation, much like other terms used in the document. What may be reasonable today may not have been reasonable yesterday.

Whether a search is reasonable or unreasonable within the meaning of the Fourth Amendment is a judicial question and Congress could enact no law declaring reasonable a search which the courts hold to be unreasonable, though it could pass an act prohibiting searches that were unreasonable. **U.S. v. BATEMAN**, D.C. Cal., 278 F. 231. In **AGNELLO v. U.S.**, C.C.A.N.Y. 290 F. 671, affirmed in part and reversed in part on other grounds in 269 U.S. 20, 46 S.Ct. 4, 70 L.Ed. 145 (1925), the court held that it was within the judicial function to determine whether a search is reasonable within the meaning of the Fourth Amendment to the federal Constitution.

The courts have construed searches to be reasonable under the following circumstances:

1. Consent Search
2. Probable Cause Search
3. Open Fields Doctrine
4. Search Incidental to a Lawful Arrest
5. Plain-view Search
6. Inventory Search
7. Automobile Search Under Restricted Conditions
8. Administrative Search
9. Close Pursuit
10. Custom and Immigration Officers Search
11. Reasonable Suspicion Search
12. Aerial Search
13. Garbage Search
14. Warrantless Search of Probationer
15. Drug Testing of Certain Employees
16. Stop and Frisk Search
17. Valid Search Warrant Search
18. Open Fields Doctrine Search
19. Hot Pursuit Search
20. Reasonable Suspicion Search
21. Public Bus Search
22. Search Within Scope of Lawful Statutes
23. Detention Search
24. Reasonable Searches by School Authorities

§ 2.12   The Consent Search

The consent search is one which is permissible as a reasonable search in theory. The courts, however, tend to disbelieve the officers' testimony in many of these cases because they reason that a defendant knowing his rights with respect to searches of his person or property would ordinarily not consent to such a search. Notwithstanding this, there have been many cases where evidence has been admitted into the trial based upon a consent search. In this situation the subject of the search is waiving a constitutional right.

§ 2.13   Public Bus Search

In **FLORIDA v. BOSTICK**, ___ U.S. ___, 111 S.Ct. 2382, 115 L.Ed.2d 389, 49 Cr L 2269 (1991), the Court held that it was not necessarily a seizure when Broward County officers boarded a Miami to Atlanta bus stopped in Ft. Lauderdale, Florida, and without particularized suspicion, engaged the defendant in conversation where he sat. After telling him that he could refuse, they requested his consent to search his bags. He gave permission and they found cocaine in one bag. The Court in an opinion by Justice O'Connor with Rhenquist C.J. and White, Scalia, Kennedy and Souter, JJ. held that the case was remanded to the Florida Supreme Court to evaluate the seizure question under the correct legal standard, i.e., that this Court has held that the Fourth Amendment permits police officers to approach individuals at random in airport lobbies and other public places to ask them questions and to request their consent to search their luggage, so long as a reasonable person would understand that he or she could refuse to cooperate. This case requires the Court to determine whether the same rule applies to police encounters that take place in a bus.

§ 2.14   Voluntary Nature of Consent

If a constitutional right is waived, the courts must conduct an inquiry as to the voluntary nature of the waiver and carefully evaluate the evidence with a presumption against waiver which must be rebutted and overcome by the prosecution. This does not mean that a person giving a consent to a search must be advised that he has a right to refuse because any defendant who was the subject of a search authorized solely by his/her consent could effectively frustrate the introduction into evidence of the fruits of that search by simply failing to testify that he/she in fact knew that s/he could refuse to consent. In **SCHNECKLOTH v. BUSTAMONTE**, 412 U.S. 218, 93 S.Ct. 2041, 36 L.Ed.2d 854 (1973), it was held that "…. when the subject of a search is not in custody and the State attempts to justify a search on the basis of his consent, the Fourth and Fourteenth Amendments require that it demonstrate that the consent was in fact voluntarily given, and not the result of duress or coercion, express or implied. Voluntariness is a question of fact to be determined from all the circumstances, and while the subject's knowledge of a right to refuse is a factor to be taken into account, the prosecution is not required to demonstrate such knowledge as a prerequisite to establishing a voluntary consent.

In **U.S. v. MENDENHALL**, 446 U.S. 544, 100 S.Ct. 1870, 64 L.Ed.2d. 497, reh, den, (U.S.) 100 S.Ct. 3051, 65 L.Ed.2d. 1138, 22 Cr.L. 3127 (1980), a young black woman who met a profile of the Drug Enforcement Administration with respect to possibly being a person unlawfully carrying narcotics was stopped in the Detroit Metropolitan Airport upon her arrival on a flight from Los Angeles. Her driver's license and her airline ticket had two different names. After returning both items to her, one Drug Enforcement Agent asked her if she would accompany him to the airport DEA office for further questioning and she agreed. At the office, the agent asked her if she would allow a search of her person and handbag and told her that she had a right to refuse. She agreed and handed her purse to the agent. A female police officer was summoned to conduct the search of her person, and she too asked the respondent whether she consented to the search. Respondent began to disrobe and took two packages from her undergarments and handed them to the policewoman. One of the packages appeared to contain heroin. She was then arrested for possessing heroin. A motion to suppress was denied in the District Court but reversed in the Court of Appeals. The United States Supreme Court reversed the Court of Appeals saying, inter alia, the fact that the respondent was 22 years old and had not been graduated from high school and was a Negro accosted by white officers while not irrelevant were not decisive .... A person has been "seized" within the meaning of the Fourth Amendment only if, in view of all of the circumstances surrounding the incident, a reasonable person would have believed that he was not free to leave, and as long as the person to whom questions are put remains free to leave, and as long as the person to whom questions are put remains free to disregard the questions and walk away, there has been no intrusion on that person's liberty or privacy as would require some particularized and objective justification.

Another case involving a drug courier occurred in **FLORIDA v. ROYER**, 460 U.S. 491, 103 S.Ct. 1319, 75 L.Ed.2d. 229, 32 Cr.L. 3095 (1983). In that case the suspect had purchased an airline ticket in Miami under an assumed name. Two detectives decided that the subject fit the "drug courier profile", and upon request, but without consent he produced his driver's license with his correct name. He explained that a friend had made the reservation for the airline ticket for him. Without returning the airline ticket or his driver's license, the detectives identified themselves and asked him to accompany them to a small room adjacent to the concourse. Also without his consent, one detective retrieved his checked luggage and brought it to the room. He procured a key to one bag and opened it. The detectives found that it contained marihuana. The second piece of luggage had a combination lock on it and the suspect said that he did not know the combination, but he did not object to its being pried open by the officers. This too contained marihuana. He was then told that he was under arrest. Motion to suppress was denied in the trial court, reversed in the District Court of Appeal. This case came to the Court on a writ of certiorari to the District Court of Appeal of Florida.

A strong and sarcastic dissent was written by Justice Rehnquist joined by Chief Justice Burger and Justice O'Connor. However the majority held that the defendant was illegally detained in the small room and thus the search of the luggage without his consent was tainted by his illegal detention.

§ 2.15   Capacity of Consenting Person

The person giving the consent must also have the capacity to consent. Consider, if you will, the situation of a uniformed police officer knocking on the door of an apartment to gain entrance because of a noise complaint. Consider also that a young child of approximately ten years of age responds to the officer's knock and seeing the huge man in uniform at the entrance to the apartment, becomes frightened and invites the officer into the apartment. While in the apartment under these circumstances, the officer is told to leave the apartment by the father of the child. Let us assume further that there is no noise or other apparent violation of law observed by the officer. The query in this situation is whether the officer should gracefully leave or engage in a verbal contest with the father? The answer should be that he should leave gracefully because there is a question as to the competency of the child to consent to a search of the apartment or his/her competency to admit the officer under those conditions. The competency of the person authorizing the search also arises when a landlord, spouse, innkeeper, partner, agent, employee, or servant gives the consent.

It has been held that the consent of a joint owner or user of property or premises may be effective against another. **FRAZIER v. CUPP**, 394 U.S. 731, 89 S. Ct. 1420, 22 L.Ed.2d 684 (1969). A consent to search a rented hotel room violated the constitutional rights of a person who rented the room. **STONER v. CALIFORNIA**, 376 U.S. 483, 84 S.Ct. 889, 11 L.Ed.2d 856 (1964). A landlord's consent to search a house is not effective against a tenant, otherwise tenants' homes would be "secure only in the discretion of the landlord.": **CHAPMAN v. U.S.**, 365 U.S. 610, 81 S.Ct. 776, 5 L.Ed.2d 828 (1961).

§ 2.16   Consent by Spouse

It appears that a spouse may validly consent to a search of property and/or premises which is jointly used by them but not to property or premises which is not jointly occupied and therefore a wife cannot consent to the search of a husband's garage which is used solely by him. **CABEY v. MAZURKIEWICZ**, 3 C.C.A. 7/29/70. This is not a uniformly accepted rule and the reader is encouraged to research cases in the subject jurisdiction to ascertain the latest rulings of the court.

§ 2.17   Consent by School Authorities

There is some uncertainty as to whether a teacher or principal can authorize the search of a student's locker. The argument is advanced that the faculty member stands in the position of in loco parentis of the student while the student is at school and thus has the capacity to consent to the search. One such case where the consent search was upheld is in N.Y., **PEOPLE. v. OVERTON**, 249 N.E.2d 366 (1969).

In another case, **NEW JERSEY v. T.L.O.**, 469 U.S. 325, 105 S.Ct. 733, 83 L.Ed.2d. 720, 36 Cr.L. 3091, (1985), the Court held that the Fourth Amendment requires that unreasonable searches and seizures applies to searches conducted by public school officials and is not limited to searches carried out by law enforcement personnel. In carrying out searches mandated by state statutes, they act as representatives of the State, not as surrogates of the parents of the students. However, school officials need not obtain a warrant before searching a student who is under their authority. The legality of a search of a student should depend on reasonableness, under all of the circumstances, of the search. Under ordinary circumstances, where there are reasonable grounds to believe that the search will turn up evidence that the student has violated either the law or the rules of the school, the search is valid.

§ 2.18   Consent by Parent

As an extension of **PEOPLE. v. OVERTON** (supra), we can assume that a parent may consent to a search on behalf of a minor child. However in **BUMPER v. NORTH CAROLINA**, 391 U.S. 543, 88 S.Ct. 1788, 20 L.Ed.2d 797

(1968), the grandmother of a defendant who thought that the police had a search warrant acquiesced to the search of the family's house, but when the warrant was a mere piece of paper purporting to be a warrant, it was held that the search was invalid.

§ 2.19   Consent - Apparent Authority

In **ILLINOIS v. RODRIGUEZ** 497 U.S. 177, 110 S.Ct. 2793, 111 L.Ed.2d 148, 47 CrL 2186 (1990) there was, in my opinion, an extension of the good faith exception, but in this case there was no warrant. The police contend that they reasonably believed that the person who opened the door to a premise occupied by her former male friend was her own apartment shared with her former friend. She lead them to the apartment after they responded to an assault complaint at the apartment of her mother. They found her with signs of severe bleeding and she told them that the respondent had assaulted her severely that day in an apartment at another location. She accompanied the police to the apartment as "our" apartment and said that she had clothes there. The respondent was sleeping when they entered the apartment. The police observed in plain view, drug paraphernalia and containers filled with white powder that they correctly believed was cocaine (confirmed by later analysis). They went to the bedroom where Rodriguez was sleeping and found additional containers of white powder in two open attache cases. The officers arrested Rodriguez and seized the drugs and related paraphernalia.

A Fourth Amendment violation was claimed. The Court, by Justice Scalia, in a 6-3 decision held that when the officers had reasonable cause to believe that the victim lived there, even though unknown to them, she had vacated the apartment weeks earlier, they did not violate the Fourth Amendment. That amendment does not prohibit reasonable searches but only unreasonable searches. The reasonableness of a police determination of consent to enter must be judged not by whether the police were correct in their assessment, but by the objective standard of whether the facts available at the moment would warrant a person of reasonable caution in the belief that the consenting party had authority over the premises. The case was remanded to the appellate court to determine whether the police reasonably believed that the female victim had authority to the entry of respondent's apartment.

§ 2.20   Revocation of Consent

There is uncertainty as to whether a consent search can be withdrawn after the consent was given. **STRONG v. UNITED STATES**, 1st C.C.A., held that a defendant may revoke his consent while the search is in process.

§ 2.21   Summation of Consent

The courts require the government to rebut a presumption that the defendant did not give his/her consent. It should therefore be evident that great proof by the government is required to sustain this burden. This can be accomplished by written consents signed by the defendant prior to the search, spelling out the terms of the consent, or by the presence of a disinterested witness who will testify as to the oral communication of the defendant's consent. When there is the slightest doubt that the defendant does not comprehend the English language, the law enforcement officer should make certain that the defendant is made fully aware of the request to search in his native tongue or in sign language, if he/she is unable to speak and/or hear.

§ 2.22   Probable Cause Search

The probable cause search is one which is decided almost on the ad hoc basis with certain general rules. As stated previously, the court has the power to determine the reasonableness of a search. **AGNELLO v. U.S.** (supra). A judicial definition of probable cause appears in **CARROLL v. UNITED STATES**, 267 U.S. 132, 162, 45 S.Ct. 280, 288, 69 L.Ed. 543, 555 (1925), where Chief Justice Taft wrote that probable cause was said to exist where "the facts and circumstances within (the officers') knowledge and of which they had reasonably trustworthy information were sufficient in themselves, to warrant a person of reasonable caution" to believe that a particular offense had been or was being committed. Probable cause is not to be confused with mere suspicion on the part of an officer. He/she must set forth in testimony at a suppression hearing and/or trial, evidence which would be sufficient in itself to cause a reasonably prudent person to believe that a particular offense was being committed.

In **TERRY v. OHIO**, 392 U.S. 1, 88 S.Ct. 1868, 20 L.Ed.2d 889 (1968), an experienced officer observed the defendants "casing" a jewelry store and when he stopped them and patted them down he found two revolvers. The Supreme Court said: "It would have been poor police work indeed for an officer of 30 years' experience in the detection of thievery from stores in this same neighborhood to have failed to investigate this behavior further."

Where there is sufficient time to get a warrant, absence of the warrant will cause an exclusion of the evidence. One such case occurred when Federal Narcotics Agents, who had information about persons on an Amtrack train, had dogs sniff for marijuana when the train arrived in Boston, Massachusetts. They found a footlocker containing the contraband and waited until the respondents had claimed the luggage and were loading it into a trunk of a car, whereupon three persons were arrested. The footlocker and the prisoners were taken to the Federal Building in Boston. About one and a half hours after arrival at the Federal Building, the footlocker was opened without respondents' consent and the contraband was discovered. The Court affirmed the suppression of these items, indicating that the agents should have gotten a warrant under these circumstances. **U.S. v. CHADWICK**, 433 U.S. 1, 97 S.Ct. 2476, 53 L.Ed.2d 538, 21 Cr.L. 3169 (1977).

A law enforcement officer whose observations cause him to reasonably believe that a traveler is carrying luggage containing narcotics may briefly detain the luggage pursuant to **TERRY v. OHIO**, 392 U.S. 1 (1968) but a warrantless detention for one and a half hours of this luggage when the agents had several hours notice of when and where the defendant would arrive was unreasonable. **U.S. v. PLACE**, 462 U.S. 696, 103 S.Ct. 2637, 77 L.Ed.2d. 110, 33 Cr.L. 3186 (1983).

§ 2.23   Open Fields Doctrine

The Fourth Amendment gave special protection to "persons, houses, papers and effects and does not extend to the open fields," **HESTER v. UNITED STATES**, 265 U.S. 57 (1924). This rule was litigated and extended in **OLIVER v. UNITED STATES**, 466 U.S. 170, 104 S.Ct. 1735 80 L.Ed.2d. 214 (1984) where Kentucky State Police had received information that marihuana was being grown on petitioner's farm. They investigated and found a locked vehicle entrance gate with a "No Trespassing" sign. They walked around a foot path that was on one side of the gate, and continued to walk along the road for several hundred yards. The officers found a field of marihuana over a mile from petitioner's home. A motion to suppress was granted by the District Court, holding, inter alia, that the fields were highly secluded; they are bounded on all sides by woods, fences and embankments and cannot be seen from any point of public access. The court concluded that this was not an "open field." The Court of Appeals for the Sixth Circuit sitting en banc reversed and it came to the United States Supreme Court on certiorari. The Court held that an individual may not legitimately demand privacy for activity conducted out of doors, in fields, except in the area immediately surrounding the home.

The Court expanded the open fields doctrine in **UNITED STATES v. DUNN**, 480 U.S. 294, 107 S.Ct. 1134, 94 L.Ed.2d. 326, 40 Cr L 3313 (1987) where it included a barn that was located 60 yards from a home and outside a fence surrounding the home, and where the police could

believe on the basis of objective facts known to them,
that the barn was not being used for the intimate
activities of the home.

§ 2.24   Search Incidental to a Lawful Arrest

Once an arrest takes place, the usual police
practice is to "book" the prisoner. This means that
he/she is taken to a police building or other location
and his/her pedigree is recorded. Prior to detention,
certain property should be removed from the prisoner.
This will include items which might facilitate escape,
might be used to injure him/herself or another, might be
used to deface property, or might be valuable property to
be held by the police for safekeeping or for the purpose
of preventing destruction of evidence. In order to
implement these requirements the officer will search the
prisoner in the presence of the recording or booking
officer. Frequently contraband is uncovered in the
prisoner's clothing in this way. This contraband is
lawfully seized and may be introduced into evidence at a
trial if the original arrest was valid.

The history of the right of police officers to
conduct searches incident to a lawful arrest has been
somewhat inconsistent. In **WEEKS v. UNITED STATES**, 232
U.S. 383, 34 S.Ct. 341, 58 L.Ed.2d 652 (1914), the
Supreme Court held that if the original arrest was
lawful, the officers were at liberty to look throughout
the premises where the arrest occurred. **AGNELLO v.
UNITED STATES**, 269 U.S. 20, 46 S.Ct. 4, 70 L.Ed. 145
(1925), declined to sustain a search of a house several
blocks from the scene of the arrest. This concept was
further restricted in **CHIMEL v. CALIFORNIA**, 395 U.S. 752,
89 S.Ct. 2034, 23 L.Ed.2d 685 (1969), where the court
restricted the search incidental to a lawful arrest to
the person of the arrestee and the area from within which
he might have obtained a weapon or something that could
have been used as evidence against him. In **U.S. v.
EDWARDS**, 415 U.S. 800, 98 S.Ct. 1234, 39 L.Ed.2d 771
(1974), it was held that a search of a prisoner's
clothing while he is in custody may be made without a

warrant as a search incidental to a lawful arrest.   In
U.S. v. ROBINSON, 414 U.S. 218, 94 S.Ct. 467, 38 L.Ed.2d
427 (1973), the defendant was arrested for driving after
revocation   of   his   driver's   license.   The   officer
searched the defendant and found fourteen capsules of
heroin.   The Court held that this was admissible evidence
as incidental to a lawful arrest.   In **GUSTAFSON v.
FLORIDA**, 414 U.S. 260, 94 S.Ct. 488, 38 L.Ed.2d 456
(1973), the Court similarly held that where a search of
a person arrested for driving without a valid driver's
license occurred and where marijuana was found on the
person arrested, the marijuana was admissible in evidence
as incidental to a lawful arrest.

An   extension   of   **CHIMEL v. CALIFORNIA**,   supra,
occurred in **MARYLAND v. BUIE**, 494 U.S. 325, 110 S.Ct.
1093, 108 L.Ed. 2d 276, 46 Cr L 2132 (1990), where Prince
George County police officers acting under authority of
an arrest warrant visited a suspect's home to make an
arrest for an armed robbery of two suspects.   Six or
seven officers proceeded to the suspects house after
reasonably ascertaining that he was home by means of a
telephone call.   The house had also been kept under
police surveillance before their entry.   Once inside,
they fanned out through the first and second floors.
Corporal James Rozar announced that he would "freeze" the
basement so that no one could come up and surprise the
officers.   With his service revolver drawn, he twice
shouted into the basement, ordering anyone down there to
come out.   When a voice asked who was calling, Rozar
announced three times: "This is the police, show me your
hands."   Eventually, a pair of hands appeared at the
bottom of the stairwell and Buie emerged from the
basement.   He was then arrested, searched and handcuffed
by Rozar.   Detective Joseph Frolich entered the basement
"in case there was someone else" down there.   He noticed
a red running suit lying in plain view on a stack of
clothing and seized it.   Such a running suit was
allegedly worn by one of the armed robbers in this case.

After the case had gone through the state courts
where the admissibility of the running suit was hotly
contested in split decisions, the Court accepted the case
and found that the Fourth Amendment permits a properly
limited protective sweep in conjunction with an in-home

115

arrest when the searching officer possesses a reasonable belief based on specific and articulable facts that the area to be swept harbors an individual posing a danger to those on the arrest scene. The case was remanded to the Maryland Court of Appeals to determine whether there was reasonable suspicion by the officer to fear for his safety or the safety of others in the premises. If they so find, the open view status of the red running suit would make it admissible in the trial. Chimel was distinguished in that in Chimel, there was a "top to bottom" search and that in Buie, the search may be conducted only when justified by a reasonable, articulable suspicion that the house is harboring a person posing a danger to those on the arrest scene.

§ 2.25   Arrest Warrant—No Authority to Search Third Person

An arrest warrant in the possession of a law enforcement officer gives that officer the authority to enter the suspects' own premises to effect his arrest. **PAYTON v. NEW YORK**, 445 U.S. 602, 603. Further, no warrant is required to apprehend a suspected felon in a public place, **U.S. v. WATSON**, 423 U.S. 411 (1976), but when law enforcement officers have an arrest warrant for a suspect, the officer has no authority to enter the residence of a third person in search of the suspect and thus any entry made under these circumstances absent a search warrant for the particular premises is an unconstitutional search. Hence any contraband thus seized, even if it was in full view, is subject to suppression. **STEAGOLD v. UNITED STATES**, 451 U.S. 204, 101 S.Ct. 1642, 68 L.Ed.2d. 38, 29 Cr.L. 3007 (1981).

§ 2.26   Plain-View Search

The plain-view search is another exception to the requirement that a search warrant is necessary to conduct a legally sufficient search and seizure. This concept was best explained by Mr. JUSTICE POTTER STEWART in **COOLIDGE v. NEW HAMPSHIRE**, 403 U.S. 443, 91 S.Ct. 2022, 29 L.Ed.2d 564 (1971), when he wrote: "It is well established that under certain circumstances the police may seize evidence in plain view without a warrant. But it is important to keep in mind that, in the vast majority of cases, (any) evidence seized by the police will be in plain view, at least at the moment of seizure. . . . An example of the applicability of the plain view doctrine is the situation in which the police have a warrant to search a given area for specified objects, and in the course of the search come across some other article of incriminating character. Where the initial intrusion that brings the police within plain view of such an article is supported, not by a warrant, but one of the recognized exceptions to the warrant requirement, the seizure is also legitimate. . . ."

In the **UNITED STATES v. SANTANA**, 427 U.S. 38, 96 S.Ct. 2406, 49 L.Ed.2d 1300 (1976), the court held for the principle that what is knowingly exposed to the public is not protected.

Under the plain-view doctrine, the following conditions must be present in order to have the evidence admissible:

1.   The officer is lawfully present;
2.   The discovery is inadvertent;
3.   The object is incriminating.
     Coolidge v. New Hampshire (supra).

In **TEXAS v. BROWN**, 460 U.S. 730, 75, L.Ed.2d. 502, 103 S.Ct. 1535 (1983) 33 Cr.L. 3001 (1983) the Court upheld a seizure of a tied-off, opaque balloon when an officer had lawfully stopped an automobile in a routine driver's license checkpoint, and based on his knowledge and experience he believed that the balloon contained heroin which in fact it did.

When an officer lawfully arrests a person and then escorts him to his home for the purpose of securing credentials to establish the arrestees identity, any contraband, observed by the officer in plain view in the premises may be lawfully seized by the officer and used as evidence against the arrestee. **WASHINGTON v. CHRISMAN**, 455 U.S. 1, 102 S.Ct. 812, 70 L.Ed.2d, 778, 30 Cr.L. 3041 (1982).

Another example of this concept was to be found in **MARYLAND v. MACON**, 472 U.S. 463, 105 S.Ct. 2778, 86 L.Ed.2d. 370, 37 Cr.L. 3111 (1985) where an officer entered an adult book store where he made a purchase of an obscene magazine. After conviction and a denial of a motion to suppress, the case was decided by the United States Supreme Court. The Court held that this premises was open for the public and the transaction was a sale in the ordinary course of business. The money used to make the purchase was retrieved but never introduced in the trial. This money was the only "fruit of the arrest" and was not introduced in evidence.

In **ARIZONA v. HICKS**, 480 U.S. 321, 107 S.Ct. 1149, 94 L.Ed.2d. 347, 40 Cr L 3320 (1987), a divided Court held that where a police officer was lawfully in a premise and had a suspicion that two sets of expensive stereo components that he observed there were stolen, his actions to read and record the serial numbers and moving some of the components including a turntable, took it out of the plain view exception, and the items were lawfully suppressed in the trial of the defendant for a robbery and possession of the stolen stereo components.

The plain view doctrine for a constitutional search was expanded in **HORTON v. CALIFORNIA**, 496 U.S. 128, 110 S. Ct.2301, 110 L.Ed.2d 112 (1990). In that case a police officer who was investigating an armed robbery obtained a search warrant of the accused's home based on probable cause. The warrant authorized a search of the home but only for the stolen property. The officer made the search but did not find the stolen property. However, he found the robbery weapons in plain view. The officer testified that while he was searching for the stolen property, he was also interested in finding other evidence connecting the accused with the crime. The trial court refused to suppress these items and it was affirmed by the California Supreme Court. The United States Supreme Court upheld his conviction saying that the inadvertent provision of **COOLIDGE v. NEW HAMPSHIRE** did not command a majority of that Court and the plain view doctrine does not require an inadvertent finding of the items.

§ 2.27   Inventory Search

When an officer makes an arrest, the arrestee is "booked" as previously indicated. If the arrestee is in possession of a vehicle, many times the vehicle must be safeguarded by the police. In order to do this, police agencies have devised recording methods to fix responsibility should anything of value be later found to be missing. Therefore an inventory of the vehicle and its contents are noted and recorded. It sometimes occurs that items indicating the commission of a crime are present in such vehicles and the problem arises as to whether such items are admissible in evidence against the arrestee. The courts have decided that this is a normal method of inventory which is necessary for the police to perform their sworn responsibility and all items secured thereby are admissible as an inventory search. There is a close distinction between this concept and that of "incidental to arrest" situations. Usually the term incidental to an arrest applies to the arrestee's person and the area to which he may reach to secure a weapon. **CHIMEL v. CALIFORNIA** (supra). In **SOUTH DAKOTA v. OPPERMAN**, 428 U.S. 364, 96 S.Ct. 3092, 49 L.Ed.2d 1000 (1976), it was held that where the police impounded a vehicle for a traffic violation and an inventory search of the unlocked area of the vehicle followed, the contraband seized as a result of this search was admissible in evidence as being according to standard police procedures and the search was reasonable.

A police officer who had lawfully arrested a person was held to be acting properly when he inventoried the contents of a shoulder bag arrestee had been carrying and the amphetamine pills contained therein were admissible as evidence against the arrestee. **ILLINOIS v. LAFAYETTE**, 462 U.S. 640, 103 S.Ct. 2605, 77 L.Ed.2d. 65, 33 Cr.L. 3183 (1983).

In **COLORADO v. BERTINE**, 479 U.S. 367, 107 S.Ct. 738, 93 L.Ed.2d. 739, 40 Cr L 3175 (1987), the police were

119

given authority to open a closed backpack in which were found various containers having controlled substances, cocaine paraphernalia and a large amount of cash. This was done while inventorying an auto van that had been impounded after the driver was arrested for driving while under the influence of alcohol.

However, where the Florida Highway Patrol had no policy regarding the opening of closed containers in an inventory search, a search of a closed container in the trunk of an impounded vehicle was a violation of the Fourth Amendment pursuant to **FLORIDA v. WELLS** 495 U.S. 1, 110 S.Ct. 1632, 109 L.Ed.2d 1, 47 CrL 2021 (1990).

§ 2.28   Automobile Search

As indicated in the preceding section, an automobile may be legally searched for inventory purposes and contraband found therein can be admissible in evidence. There are other situations where probable cause may exist for a police officer to search an automobile. An automobile is capable of being moved quickly from one location to another. In some cases it would be futile to first apply for a search warrant because by the time the warrant is obtained and executed, the evidence would have disappeared.

In **CARDWELL v. LEWIS**, 417 U.S. 583, 94 S.Ct. 2464, 41 L.Ed.2d 325 (1974), the court sustained the admissibility of paint scrapings taken from the exterior of a car and an observation of the tread of a tire on an operative wheel. An automobile similar in color and model to defendant's car had been seen leaving the scene of a crime. This similarity was corroborated by comparison of the paint scraping taken from the victim's car with the color and paint of defendant's automobile. The defendant had repair work done on his car immediately after the death of the victim. He also had a nexus with the victim on the day of death. All of this provided reason to believe that the car was used in the commission of the crime for which Lewis was arrested.

The automobile search may also be conducted under

the incidental-to-lawful-arrest doctrine if the officer can show that he/she believed he/she was in danger and therefore searched the vehicle to protect him/herself. However, **CHIMEL v. CALIFORNIA** (supra) limited the area to be searched under this doctrine.

Frequently an automobile is stopped by a police officer for a traffic violation. Upon stopping the automobile, the officer may see contraband in plain view. This contraband is admissible in evidence.

Another situation involving a lawful search of a moving vehicle occurred in **CARROLL v. U.S.**, 267 U.S. 132, 45 S.Ct. 280, 69 L.Ed. 543 (1925), where the court permitted evidence to be admitted which had been secured by federal officers after they justified their actions by indicating to the court that they had probable cause to stop the moving vehicle. Another case upholding the right of officers to make this kind of search was **CHAMBERS v. MARONEY**, 399 U.S. 42, 90 S.Ct. 1975, 26 L.Ed.2d 419 (1970).

MR. JUSTICE REHNQUIST writing for the majority in **RAKUS v. ILLINOIS**, 436 U.S. 954, 99 S.Ct. 421, 58 L.Ed.2d 387 (1978), held that passengers in an automobile that they did not own or lease had no standing to object to the lawfulness of a police search of the automobile because the Fourth Amendment rights are personal rights.

A 1979 case involving an automobile search occurred in **PROUSE v. DELAWARE**, 440 U.S. 648, 99 S.Ct. 1391, 59 L.Ed.2d 660, 24 Cr.L. 4168. In that case the police conducted random stops of motor vehicles without any apparent violation of law taking place. The Court held this to be a Fourth and Fourteenth Amendment violation. This decision does not prevent a roadblock of all vehicles where the officer might ask for identification, as long as all persons and vehicles are treated similarly.

Another 1979 case where the Court reversed a random automobile stop and search was **KRETCHMAR v. NEBRASKA**, 440 U.S. 978, 60 L.Ed.2d 237, 99 S.Ct. 1793 (   ), 25Cr.L. 4001.

An interesting automobile search by Border Patrol Officers lead to a clarification and expansion of the law enforcement officers' right to search a moving vehicle. In **U.S. v. CORTEZ**, 449 U.S. 411, 101 S.Ct. 690, 66

L.Ed.2d. 621, 28 Cr.L. 3051 (1981), Border Patrol
Officers had discovered distinctive human footprints in
the desert. They deduced that on several occasions,
groups of between 8 and 20 persons had been guided
through the desert from Mexico by the same individual
into Arizona and that they were entering the United
States illegally. The prints indicated that they stopped
at an isolated point on a road and were picked up on
clear nights between 2:00 a.m. and 6:00 a.m.

Based on this information, they stationed themselves
at a point on the road where they believed the pickup
vehicle would pass. Indeed it did pass, once in either
direction, within the estimated time that it would take
to go to the point of pickup and return with its human
cargo. When it returned the officers stopped the vehicle
which was being driven by the respondent. Cortez and
another respondent, Hernandez-Lorea were found in the
vehicle wearing shoes which matched with the suspect
desert footprints. There were illegal aliens in the
vehicle. The Supreme Court held that the objective facts
and circumstantial evidence in this case justified the
investigative stop of respondent's vehicle. The Court
went further in saying that the totality of the
circumstances must be taken into account ... the evidence
must be weighed as understood by those versed in the
field of law enforcement. Notice that the Court did not
say that the officers were aware of a repeated practice
and that they might have secured a search warrant for
another occasion. It is the author's view that some
earlier courts would have required a search warrant in
this case. We can therefore see that the Berger Court of
1981 is leaning towards enlargement of the search powers
of law enforcement officers.

On July 1, 1981, the United States Supreme Court
handed down two closely related decisions involving
automobile searches. In the first case reported **ROBBINS
v. CALIFORNIA**, 453 U.S. 420, 101 S.Ct. 2841, 69 L.Ed.2d
744, 29 Cr.L. 3115 (1981), California Highway Patrol
officers stopped petitioner's car because it was
proceeding erratically. They smelled marihuana smoke as
he opened the car door. They then searched the vehicle
and found in the luggage compartment two packages wrapped
in green opaque plastic. Upon unwrapping the plastic

packages, they found that they contained bricks of marihuana. He was charged with various drug offenses, including the possession of the marihuana bricks. His suppression motions were denied and he was convicted. The conviction was affirmed twice by the California Court of Appeal because the United States Supreme Court had remanded it to that court for further consideration in light of **ARKANSAS v. SAUNDERS**, 442 U.S. 753, 443 U.S. 903.

After granting a writ of certiorari, the United States Supreme Court held that unless a closed container found in an automobile is such that its contents may be said to be in plain view, those contents are fully protected by the Fourth Amendment .... To fall within such exception, a container must so clearly announce its contents whether by its distinctive configuration, transparency, or otherwise, that its contents are obvious to the observer. The Court held that this was not the situation in the instant case and the opening of the package without a search warrant violated the Fourth Amendment and Fourteenth Amendments.

The second case had a contrary result. In **NEW YORK v. BELTON**, 453 U.S. 454, 101 S. Ct. 2860, L.Ed.2d 768, 29 Cr.L. 3124 (1981) the respondent was in a vehicle stopped by a New York State policeman because of an excessive speed violation. Other occupants were in the vehicle but none of the occupants owned the car or were related to the owner. The officer smelled burnt marihuana and had seen on the floor of the car an envelope marked "SUPER GOLD" that he associated with marihuana. He frisked all four occupants of the vehicle after announcing that they were all under arrest and split them up into four separate areas of the Thruway at this time so that they would not be in "physical touching area of each other." He then picked up the envelope marked "SUPER GOLD" and found it contained marihuana. After giving Miranda warnings, he searched each of them. Following this, he searched the passenger compartment of the car. On the back seat he found a black leather jacket belonging to Belton. He unzippered one of the pockets and discovered cocaine. Placing the jacket in his automobile, he drove the four arrestees to a nearby police station. The Court held that the search of the jacket was not a violation of

the Fourth Amendment and Fourteenth Amendment under the
theory of **CHIMEL v. CALIFORNIA** 395 U.S. 752, wherein it
was held that a lawful custodial arrest creates a
situation justifying the contemporaneous warrantless
search of the arrestee and of the immediately surrounding
area. Not only may the police search the passenger
compartment of the car in such circumstances, they may
also examine the contents of any containers found in the
passenger compartment. The author believes that the
Court was stretching to validate this search because it
could be argued that when the search of the passenger
compartment occurred, the trooper was not in danger that
Belton could have, at that time, reached into his jacket
to get a weapon or to destroy evidence as was the theory
in **CHIMEL v. CALIFORNIA**, supra. Nevertheless, this case
expands the authority of the police officer to search the
passenger compartment of an auto after a lawful arrest
has taken place so long as it is reasonably
contemporaneous with the arrest.

The holding of **ROBBINS v. CALIFORNIA** (supra) was
short lived when in June of 1982 the Court handed down
U.S. v. ROSS, 456 U.S. 798, 102 S. Ct. 2157, 72 L.Ed.2d.
572, 31 Cr.L 3051 (1982). In that case the Court
rejected the holding in **ROBBINS v. CALIFORNIA** (supra) and
held that police who have probable cause for a vehicle
search under the "automobile exception" to the Fourth
Amendment's warrant requirement may search without a
warrant, every part of that vehicle and its contents,
including closed containers, that may conceal the object
of the search. The Court also rejected that part of
ARKANSAS v. SAUNDERS, 442 U.S. 753 (1979) that suggested
that a warrantless search of a container found in an
automobile could never be sustained as part of a
warrantless automobile search. This decision caused much
confusion in the final outcome of cases with respect to
trials in progress between the Robbins decision, July 1,
1981 and the time of Ross, June 1, 1982.

In **MICHIGAN v. LONG**, 463 U.S. 1032, 103 S.Ct. 3469,
77 L.Ed.2d. 1201 (1983), two police officers patrolling
a rural area at night saw a car traveling erratically and
at excessive speed. When the car swerved into a ditch,
the officers investigated and were met by respondent, the
sole occupant of the car, the driver appeared to be under

the influence of something. When he opened the door of his vehicle, the officers observed a hunting knife on the floorboard on the driver's side. They patted him down and found no weapons. A flashlight beamed into the car revealed an open pouch containing marihuana under the armrest on the front seat. The trunk of the car was then searched and the officers found some more marihuana. The Michigan State Supreme Court suppressed the marihuana taken from the passenger compartment holding it was an illegal search. The United States Supreme Court remanded the issue of the legality of the trunk search. The Court held further that it would no longer give advisory opinions in state court matters when the state court references to state law constituted adequate and independent state grounds. It will no longer look beyond the opinion under revision. This case came to the United States Supreme Court by a writ of certiorari. In the author's opinion, it was an extension of **STONE v. POWELL**, 428 U.S. 465, 98 S.Ct. 3037, 49 L.Ed.2d. 1067 (1976) where the court indicated that federal habeas corpus review would no longer be available to state defendants on the issue of unreasonable search and seizure where the state had provided a full and fair litigation of a Fourth Amendment claim.

While it appeared for a time that the federal court doors were closed to unreasonable search and seizure claims where the state had provided full and fair litigation, in **KIMMELMAN v. MORRISON**, 477 U.S. 365, 106 S.Ct. 2574, 91 L.Ed.2d. 305, 39 Cr L 3187 (1986), the Court held that the preclusion of habeas corpus review in the Federal District Court did not apply where Sixth Amendment ineffective assistance of counsel claims are founded primarily on incompetent representation with respect to Fourth Amendment issues. In that case, the defense attorney completely failed to seek pretrial discovery which led to his failure to file a timely motion to suppress evidence seized from the petitioner's home.

FLORIDA v. LUZ PIEDAD JIMENO, __U.S. __, 111 S.Ct. 1801, 114 L.Ed.2d 297, 49 CrL 2175 (1991), decided May 23, 1991, validated a police search of a closed container found in a car that Jimeno had been operating and had given consent to the officer to search the car. The

Court held that this consent included the contents of anything found in the car. In the instant case, the police found a closed container and found cocaine in it. Justice Marshall and Justice Stevens dissented saying substantially that an individuals consent to search the interior of his car should not be understood to authorize a search of closed containers inside the car. This was one of Justice Marshall's last decisions before he retired.

However in the LONG case (supra), the Court held that the state court decided the case on Federal grounds and the Court would take jurisdiction. It further ruled that the officers' action was reasonable and it reversed the Michigan Supreme Court decision.

Another case involved an investigatory stop of a passenger automobile and a trunk with a camper traveling in tandem on a highway that was under surveillance for suspected drug traffic. Both vehicles appeared to be traveling together. A Drug Enforcement Administration agent, patrolling the highway noticed these vehicles. The pickup truck was apparently overloaded. After following them for about 20 miles, he decided to make an investigative stop and radioed the South Carolina State Highway Patrol for assistance. When the state officer responded, they attempted to stop the two vehicles. The passenger automobile pulled over to the side of the road but the truck continued on pursued by the state officer. The D.E.A. agent identified himself and attempted unsuccessfully to contact the state officer. He then radioed the local police for help. In the meantime, the state officer had stopped the truck and told the driver that he would be held until the D.E.A. agent arrived. The D.E.A. agent, left the passenger automobile driver with the local police and arrived at the location of the detained truck about 15 minutes after the truck had been stopped. Upon smelling marijuana coming from the truck, he opened the rear camper without the driver's permission and found burlap bags containing marihuana therein. He arrested the driver and returned to the passenger vehicle and then arrested the driver of that vehicle. The case came before the United States Supreme Court because motions to suppress had been granted below.

The Court held that the evidence should not be

126

suppressed because in evaluating the reasonableness of an investigative stop, the Court examines "whether the officer's action was justified at its inception and whether it was reasonably related in scope to the circumstances which justified the interference in the first place," citing **TERRY v. OHIO** (supra). They held further that although brevity is an important factor in determining whether the detention is unreasonable, courts must also consider the purposes to be served by the stop as well as the time reasonably needed to effectuate those purposes. Here the D.E.A. agent diligently pursued his investigation and clearly no delay unnecessary to the investigation was involved. **U.S. v. SHARPE**, 470 U.S. 675, 105 S.Ct. 1568, 84 L.Ed.2d 605 (1985).

The automobile exception was extended to include a mobile motor home located in a public parking lot. **CALIFORNIA v. CARNEY**, 471 U.S. 386, 105 S.Ct. 2006, 85 L.Ed.2d 406 (1985).

In **CALIFORNIA v. ACEVEDO**, 500 U.S. _____, 111 S.Ct. 1982, 114 L.Ed.2d 619, 49 Cr L 2207 (1991) the Court enlarged law enforcement powers in automobile search cases. In that case the Santa Ana California Police Department had received information from a federal DEA in Hawaii that a package of marijuana was seized by them that was destined to be picked up at a Federal Express office in Santa Ana, California. Instead the DEA sent it to Officer Coleman of the Santa Ana Police Department with instructions to take it to the Santa Ana Federal Express office and arrest the person who picked it up. The addressee picked up the package and was followed by Officer Coleman to an apartment in the city and he was observed to carry the package into the apartment. About 1 1/2 hours later the addressee was observed leaving the apartment and dropped the box and paper that had contained the marijuana into a trash bin. Officer Coleman left the scene to get a search warrant, leaving other officers at the location. About 35 minutes later the remaining officers saw Richard St. George leave the apartment carrying a blue backpack, which appeared to be half full. The officers stopped him as he was driving off, searched the backpack and found 1 1/2 pounds of marijuana.

About 25 minutes later, Charles Steven Acevedo

entered the apartment, and about 10 minutes later, he
came out carrying a brown paper bag, the size of one of
the wrapped marijuana packages sent from Hawaii. Acevedo
walked to an auto in the parking lot, placed the bag in
the trunk and started to drive away. Whereupon the
officers, fearing the loss of the evidence, stopped him,
opened the trunk and found the marijuana.

The defendant moved for the suppression of the
marijuana but the motion was denied. On appeal the
California Court of Appeal, Fourth District reversed,
saying that the marijuana should have been suppressed.
The U.S. Supreme Court held in a 6-3 decision that police
may search a container within an automobile where they
have probable cause to believe that it holds contraband
or evidence.

§ 2.29   Administrative Search

Tax assessors, health inspectors, fire inspectors,
and building inspectors all belong to that category of
persons who, in order to properly do their mandated jobs,
must have access to the interior of buildings. When they
are denied entrance, a controversy arises. Some persons
object to these visits on constitutional grounds. The
United States Supreme Court has upheld the right of these
inspections as administrative searches where there is an
objection but only after a warrant has been secured and
properly executed. **CAMARA v. MUNICIPAL COURT**, 387 U.S.
523, 87 S.Ct. 1727, 18 L.Ed.2d 930 (1967).

In the case of welfare investigators, however, the
court had held otherwise. In **WYMAN v. JAMES**, 400 U.S.
309, 91 S.Ct. 381, 27 L.Ed.2d 408 (1971), the court
sustained the right of a welfare investigator to visit
the home of a client where aid to a dependent child was
being received, on the grounds that it was not
unreasonable for Fourth Amendment limitations where the
requirement served the paramount needs of the child;
there was reasonable advance notice given concerning the
date of the visit; neither forcible nor surreptitious
entry of the home would take place; and visits occurred
at reasonable times of the day. The court further held

that such a visitation was not a search in the traditional criminal law context of the Fourth Amendment and the consequence of refusal to allow a home visit is not a criminal prosecution but the termination of benefits, thereby allowing a choice to the client.

In **MICHIGAN v. CLIFFORD**, 464 U.S. 287, 104 S.Ct. 641, 78 L.Ed.2d. 1477 (1984), arson investigators entered a premises five hours after firefighters had left the premises. They had no administrative warrant, but conducted a search and found objects which in their opinion caused the fire and were deliberately placed there for that purpose. The Court held that the evidence seized in that search was obtained in violation of respondent's right under the Fourth and Fourteenth Amendments because it was not authorized by consent or exigent circumstances.

The problem of "chop shops" where stolen vehicles are taken to have their parts dismantled and sold to unsuspecting persons looking to purchase used auto parts is widespread. New York State and many other governments have enacted statutes authorizing law enforcement persons to conduct an inspection of junkyards who are licensed to carry on this business. Such a statute usually includes the following directions: The establishment is required to maintain a record of all motor vehicles, trailers and major component parts thereof, coming into his possession together with a record of disposition of any such motor vehicle, trailer or part thereof, and shall maintain proof of ownership for any motor vehicles, trailer or major component part thereof while in his possession. The Court held in **NEW YORK v. BURGER**, 482 U.S. 691, 107 S.Ct. 2636, 96 L.Ed.2d. 601, 41 Cr L 3299 (1987), that there are three criteria that must be met for a warrantless search of a commercial establishment. They are (1) A "substantial" government interest... (2) necessary to further [the] regulatory scheme (3) the statute's inspection program... [must] provid[e] a constitutionally adequate substitute for a warrant. In the instant case, officers visiting a junk yard, were told that the proprietor had no "police book" and were permitted into the yard; checked V.I.N. of vehicles; checked them on the police computer; found many of them to be stolen; and made the arrest of the proprietor. A divided Court said that the New York regulatory scheme satisfies the three criteria necessary to make reasonable warrantless searches.

The reader's attention is directed to **ILLINOIS v. KRULL**, et al, Section 6.9, for a discussion of an alleged unconstitutional administrative search.

§ 2.30   Prisoners—Privacy of

A prison inmate has no reasonable expectation of privacy in his prison cell entitling him to protection of the Fourth Amendment against unreasonable searches. **HUDSON v. PALMER**, 468 U.S. 517, 104 S.Ct. 3194, 82 L.Ed.2d.393 (1984). In that case a prisoner sustained a shakedown search of his cell and locker by correction officer Hudson, and a fellow officer. The officers discovered a ripped pillow case in a trash can near respondent's cell bunk. Charges against Palmer were instituted for destroying state property and he was found guilty after a hearing. Palmer later brought a pro se action under 42 U.S.C. 1983 claiming that the shakedown search was instituted solely to harass him and they had brought false charges against him in violation of his Fourteenth Amendment right not to be deprived of property without due process of law and that Hudson intentionally destroyed certain of his non contraband personal items during this search.

The Court further held that there was no Fourteenth Amendment Due Process Clause violation because respondent had adequate post-deprivation remedies under Virginia law for any loss suffered.

§ 2.31   Hot-Pursuit Searches

Let us assume that a police officer arrives at the scene of a robbery shortly after the perpetrator has left the premises. Let us further assume that the officer gets a good description of the perpetrator and is told that the malefactor was seen entering a premises. Does the police officer have to wait to get a warrant to enter the premises in hot pursuit of the accused? The answer is no. In **WARDEN v. HAYDEN**, 387 U.S. 294, 87 S.Ct. 1642, 18 L.Ed.2d 782 (1967). It was held that this type of search was a reasonable search for items having some evidentiary bearing on the case under investigation.

In another case where officers searched for a defendant where the offense was a non jailable one, the Court held otherwise. In **WELSH v. WISCONSIN**, 470 U.S. 753, 104 S.Ct. 2091, 80 L.Ed.2d. 732 (1984) the defendant had driven his automobile erratically and swerved off the road into an open field and stopped. No property damage or personal injury occurred. The defendant was observed by a witness who suggested that he wait for assistance. Ignoring the witness' suggestion, he exited from the vehicle and walked away. The police arrived, checked the registered owner and went to the defendant's house. They were permitted to enter by the defendant's stepdaughter and they found the defendant nude in his bed. He was then arrested for driving a motor vehicle while under the influence of an intoxicant in violation of a Wisconsin statute which provided that a first offense was a noncriminal violation subject to a civil forfeiture proceeding for a maximum fine of $200.00.

The United States Supreme Court held that the warrantless, night-time entry of petitioner's home to arrest him for a civil, non jailable traffic offense was prohibited by the Fourth Amendment.

However, in **U.S. v. HENSLEY**, 469 U.S. 469 U.S. 1, 105 S.Ct. 675, 84 L.Ed.2d. 604 (1985) the Court held that where the police had stopped a vehicle because they had received information from another police department that the described vehicle and its occupants were wanted in connection with a robbery, the police did not violate any Fourth Amendment right in that they may briefly stop a person suspected of involvement in a past crime, ask questions, or check identification in the absence of probable cause, because it promotes the strong government interest in solving crimes and bringing offenders to justice.

A case that determined that what police contended was a hot-pursuit case (close pursuit) was decided by the Court not to be such a case. The case was **MINNESOTA v.**

OLSON, 491 U.S. 91, 110 S.Ct. 1684, 109 L.Ed.2d 85, 47 CrL 2031 (1990). In that case, the defendant was suspected of being the driver of the getaway car used in a robbery-murder. After recovering the murder weapon and arresting a suspected murderer, the police surrounded the home of two women with whom they believed Olson had been staying. When police telephoned the home and told one of the women that Olson should come out, a male voice was heard saying "tell them I left."

Without getting a warrant, and with weapons drawn, they entered the home, found Olson hiding in a closet and arrested him. Shortly thereafter he made an inculpatory statement. The trial court rejected a suppression motion with regard to the statement and he was convicted of murder, armed robbery and assault. The Minnesota Supreme Court reversed, ruling that Olson had sufficient grounds to challenge the legality of the warrantless entry, and that his statement was tainted and should have been suppressed. The Court affirmed the State Supreme Court. The moral is - when law enforcement has a choice - get the warrant.

§ 2.32   Custom and Immigration Searches

The Fourth Amendment commands that searches and seizures be reasonable. What is reasonable depends upon all of the circumstances surrounding the search or seizure itself, **NEW JERSEY v. T.L.O.**, 469 U.S. 325, 105 S.Ct. 733, 741-744, 83 L.Ed.2d 720 (1985). The permissibility of a particular practice is judged by "balancing its intrusion on the individual's Fourth Amendment interests against its promotion of legitimate governmental interests." **UNITED STATES v. VILLAMONTE-MARQUEZ**, 462 U.S. 579, 103 S.Ct. 2573, 2579, 77 L.Ed.2D 22 (1983); **DELAWARE v. PROUSE**, 440 U.S. 648, 654, 99 S.Ct. 1391, 1396, 59 L.Ed.2d 660 (1979); **CAMARA v. MUNICIPAL COURT**, 387 U.S. 523, 87 S.Ct. 1727, 18 L.Ed.2d. 930 (1967).

Customs officers and immigration officers are given greater latitude in searching without a warrant, pursuant to Congressional authorization to the Executive

Plenary Authority to search at the border with probable
cause or without probable cause or with a warrant. The
Court long recognized Congress' power to police entrants
at the border. **BOYD v. UNITED STATES**, 116 U.S. 616, 623
S.Ct. 524, 528, 29 L.Ed.2d 746 (1886). The Court stated
in **UNITED STATES v. 12 - 100 FT REELS OF FILM**, 413 U.S.
123, 125, 93 S.Ct. 2665, 2667, 37 L.Ed.2d 500 (1973) . .
. The Constitution gives Congress broad comprehensive
powers "[t]o regulate commerce with foreign nations,
"Art, § 8, cl. 3. Historically such broad powers have
been necessary to prevent smuggling and to prevent
prohibited articles from entry.". . . "Routine searches
of the persons and effects of entrants are not subject to
any requirement of reasonable suspicion, probable cause,
or warrant, on less than probable cause. Automotive
travelers may be stopped at fixed check points near the
border without individualized suspicion, even if the stop
is based largely on ethnicicity, **UNITED STATES v.
MARTINEZ-FUERTE**, 428 U.S. 543, 562-563, 96 S.Ct. 3074,
3085, 49 L.Ed.2d. 1116 (1976).

These cases reflect longstanding concern for the
protection of the integrity of the border, particularly
because of the national crisis in law enforcement of
illicit narcotics. **UNITED STATES v. MENDENHALL**, 446 U.S.
544, 100 S.Ct. 1870, 64 L.Ed.2d 497 (1980).

Title 19 U.S.C. § 1582 provides that "all persons
coming into the United States from foreign countries
shall be liable for detention and search authorized . .
. . [by customs regulations]." Customs agents may "stop,
search, and examine" any "vehicles, beast or person" upon
which an officer suspects there is contraband or
"merchandise which is subject to duty." § 482; see also
§§ 1467, 1481; 19 CFR §§ 162.6, 162.7 (1984).

Expectation of non privacy is not only at the border
but also in the country's interior. **CARROL v. UNITED
STATES**, 267 U.S. 132, 154, 45 S.Ct. 280, 285, 69 L.Ed.2d
543 (1925); CF. **FLORIDA v. ROYER**, 460 U.S. 491, 515 103
S.Ct. 1319, 1333, 75 L.Ed.2d 229 (1983). In **UNITED
STATES v. MONTOYA de HERNANDEZ**, infra at 5534, the search
for 88 balloons containing cocaine hydrochloride in the
petitioner's alimentary canal took place at the
international borders. In a case involving customs
officers, it was held that when a custom officer opened

133

a container as it arrived from Calcutta and observed marihuana in the container, it was not an unreasonable search when the container was closed and shipped to addressee. When the addressee exited from his premises with the container, while an application was being made for a search warrant, the Court held that a D.E.A. was acting lawfully when he arrested the addressee and opened the container while he possessed no search warrant. **ILLINOIS v. ANDREAS**, 463 U.S. 765, 103 S.Ct. 3319, 77 L.Ed.2d 1003 (1984).

U.S. Customs agents have been held to have authority to make "suspicionless" boarding of sailboats in a channel leading to the open sea for purpose of examining vessel's documentation pursuant to 19 U.S.C. 158(a). **U.S. v. VILLAMONTE-MARQUEZ**, 51 L.W. 4812.

Drug Enforcement Agents of the federal government appear to have similar authorization to detain and search air passengers at airports that the United States Custom Officers have pursuant to **U.S. v. SOKOLOW** 490 U.S. 1, 109 S.Ct. 1581, 104 L.Ed.2d. 1, 45 Cr L 3001 (1989). In that case the petitioner made a round trip flight from Honolulu International Airport to Miami, Florida, in July, remaining in Miami for only 48 hours. The D.E.A. knew at the time that he was stopped that he paid $2,100.00 for two round-trip plane tickets from a roll of $20.00 bills; he travelled under a name that did not match the name of his telephone listed; his original destination was Miami, a source city for illicit drugs; he appeared nervous during his trip, and he checked none of his baggage.

The Court held that the D.E.A. agents had a reasonable basis to suspect that respondent was transporting illegal drugs on these facts and reversed the Court of Appeals decision that held that the District Court should have suppressed the evidence. The case was remanded to the Court of Appeals for further proceedings consistent with the Courts decision (reinstate the conviction).

§ 2.33   Identity Stop

In **IMMIGRATION AND NATURALIZATION SERVICE v. DELGADO**, 468 U.S. 210, 104 S.Ct. 1758, 80 L.Ed.2d. 247 (1984) agents of the service conducted three surveys of a garment factory seeking illegal aliens. During the surveys, each of them lasting two to three hours, I.N.S. agents positioned themselves near the factory exits, while other agents moved systematically through the factory, approaching employees, and, after identifying themselves, they asked the employees a maximum of three questions relating to their citizenship. If they were satisfied with the reply or credentials of each employee, they would move on to the next. Agents were placed at the exit doors and the employees were permitted to do their work and were free to walk around the factory. The union, citizen employees and those with permanent resident cards brought actions, later consolidated, in Federal District Court seeking declaratory and injunctive relief. The District Court granted summary judgment for the I.N.S., but the Court of Appeals reversed holding that the surveys constituted a search in violation of the Fourth Amendment. It was reviewed by the United States Supreme Court. That Court held that the surveys were not a seizure and the Court further held that interrogation relating to one's identity or a request for identification by the police does not, by itself, constitute a Fourth Amendment seizure. Unless the circumstances of the encounter are so intimidating as to demonstrate that a reasonable person would have believed he was not free to leave if he had not responded, such questioning does not result in a detention under the Fourth Amendment. If one of the respondent employees had in fact been seized or detained there would have been a seizure. However, their disposition indicated that none of them were seized or detained. They therefore had no standing to litigate the issue. The Court of Appeals was thus reversed.

U.S. v. ROSS (supra) was extended in **U.S. v. JOHNS**, et al, 469 U.S. 478, 105 S.Ct. 881, 83 L.Ed.2d. 890 (1985) when United States Custom officers had probable cause to search lawfully stopped trucks and smelled marijuana. They took packages from the trunks to a

D.E.A. warehouse and three days later government agents opened some of the packages and took samples that later proved to be marijuana. No search warrant had ever been obtained. The Court held that the warrantless search of the trucks was not unreasonable because it occurred three days after the packages were unloaded from the trucks. Ross did not establish that the warrantless search of a vehicle need to occur contemporaneously with its lawful seizure. Nor does Ross or other "vehicle search" decisions of this Court suggest that warrantless searches of containers must invariably be conducted "immediately" as part of the vehicle inspection of "soon thereafter."

§ 2.34   Reasonable Suspicion Search

An alimentary canal search is one in which the suspect swallows the contraband, much as what happened in **ROCHIN v. CALIFORNIA** 342 U.S. 165, 72 S.Ct. 205, 96 L.Ed.2d. 183 (1952) where a stomach pump was used to extract the contraband. You will recall that in that case the Court held that this kind of action shocked the conscience and declared it unconstitutional. However, in **U.S. v. ELVIRA MONTOYA DE HERNANDEZ,** 437 U.S. 531, 105 S.Ct. 3304, 87 L.Ed.2d 381 (1985), 37 Cr.L. 3175 (1985) a border search case, the Court upheld the search of a woman who had swallowed 88 balloons containing cocaine hydrochloride. The search was initiated after much delay by a customs officer's suspicion that respondent was an alimentary canal smuggler. After giving respondent other options, which could not be implemented, a court order was obtained for an x-ray and a rectal search. A physician conducted the rectal search and retrieved one of the aforementioned balloons. She subsequently defecated the remaining balloons over a 4 day period. The Court held that the detention of a traveler at the border, beyond the scope of a routine customs search and suspicion, is justified at its inception if custom agents, considering all the facts surrounding the traveler, is smuggling contraband in her alimentary canal.

An extension of the Reasonable Suspicion Search concept to a search of a home occurred in **MARYLAND v.**

BUIE, supra, in § 2.24. A detailed explanation of this case appears in that section.

Another example of the reasonable suspicion concept is found in **ALABAMA v. WHITE**, 496 U.S. 325, 110 S.Ct. 2412, 110 L.Ed. 301, 47 CrL 2148 (1990), where a police stop of a vehicle, followed by a consent search was approved by the court. Here the stop was initiated by an anonymous tip to police describing certain actions that the respondent was about to take in proceeding to a well described automobile at or about a designated time, and her proceeding along the shortest route to a named motel, and the fact that she would be in possession of cocaine in a brown attache case, all were considered by the Court to have been borne out by the officer's observational testimony. This was held to be sufficient reasonable suspicion in the "Totality of the Circumstances" to permit police officers to stop the vehicle.

The following consent search where the suspect consented to the search and gave the officers a key to open the attache case where cocaine was found was held to be sufficient grounds to conduct an investigatory stop; this was a 6-3 decision.

§ 2.35   Aerial Search

The aerial search, an old weapon of law enforcement, has been given the approval of the United States Supreme Court in **CALIFORNIA v. CIRAOLO** 476 U.S. 207, 106 S.Ct. 1809, 90 L.Ed.2d. 210, 39 Cr.L. 3106 (1986) where police officers, receiving a tip that marijuana was growing in respondent's back yard which was enclosed by two fences and could not be observed at ground level, secured a private plane and flew over respondent's land at an altitude of 1,000 feet. The officers, who were trained in marijuana identification, identified plants growing in a 15 by 25 foot plot. They photographed the area with a standard 35 mm camera and then obtained a search warrant and executed it. The Court, in a 5-4 decision, held that it was unreasonable for respondent to expect that his marijuana plants were constitutionally protected from being observed with the naked eye from an altitude of 1,000 feet. No search warrant by the police was required.

A further refinement of this principle was decided by the Court in **FLORIDA v. RILEY**, 488 U.S. 445, 109 S.Ct. 693, 102 L.Ed.2d. 835, 44 CrL 3079 (1989). In the Riley case a Florida county sheriff, acting upon an anonymous tip that marijuana was being grown in a greenhouse located on Riley's property made an initial ground level observation of the property outside the perimeter of it, but could not make any observations of the contents of the greenhouse. Thereupon he made observations from a helicopter flying at about 400 feet and found what he believed to be marijuana plants growing in the partially covered greenhouse. The main issue that was presented in this case was that the helicopter was flying at less than 500 feet which is the lowest altitude permitted by the FAA for fixed winged aircraft.

The Court held that the FAA permits helicopters to fly below the 500 feet limit and thus the helicopter in this case was not violating any law; did not interfere with the respondent's normal use of his greenhouse or other parts of the curtilage; that intimate details connected with the use of the home or curtilage were not observed; and that there was no undue noise, wind or dust, or threat of injury. Accordingly, a search warrant issued as a result of that observation should not be suppressed.

§ 2.36   Garbage Search

In **CALIFORNIA v. GREENWOOD** and **VAN HOUTON**, 486 U.S. 356, 108 S.Ct. 1625, 100 L.Ed.2d. 30, 43 Cr L 3029 (1988), the Court held that the police do not require a warrant to search garbage that had been left at the curb and removed by a defendant's regular trash collector who gave the trash to the police. Accordingly, any criminal evidence secured in this fashion is not to be suppressed.

§ 2.37   Warrantless Search of Probationer

Probationers are persons who have been found guilty

of a crime and who are placed under the supervision of a probation officer in lieu of being incarcerated. As such, they are not entitled to the constitutional protection to be free from warrantless searches of their persons or homes by probation officers pursuant to governmental rule or regulation so long as there are reasonable grounds to believe the presence of contraband and the supervisor gives approval. **GRIFFEN v. WISCONSIN**, 483 U.S. 868, 107 S.Ct. 3164, 97 L.Ed.2d. 709, 41 Cr L 3424 (1987).

§ 2.38   Automobile Roadblock

In **BROWER v. INYO COUNTY** 489 U.S. 593, 109 S.Ct. 1378, 103 L.Ed.2d. 628, 44 CrL 3175 (1989), the Court defined a roadblock as a seizure but left the issue as to whether or not it was an unreasonable search to be decided on remand to the Court of Appeals to determine whether the District Court erred in concluding that the roadblock was not unreasonable. In that case a civil rights action was brought against police who had set up a roadblock to stop the plaintiff's decedent while he was speeding and driving a stolen automobile. They placed a tractor-trailer truck across the road beyond a bend in the road and allegedly beamed the headlights of a police vehicle opposite to the decedent's movement on the road that allegedly blinded him, causing him to strike the trailer and was killed thereby.

§ 2.39   Drug Testing Employee

There has been much controversy as to whether employees, both public and private, have a constitutional right to be free from random tests for alcohol and/or controlled substances that might be in their bodies and affect their job performance. In **SKINNER v. RAILWAY LABOR EXECUTIVES ASSOCIATION**, 489 U.S. 602, 109 S.Ct. 1402, 103 L.Ed.2d. 639, 44 CrL 3178 (1989), the Court held that the Federal Railroad Administration regulations that require private railroads to administer blood and

urine tests to railroad employees involved in certain
train accidents and fatal incidents, and that further
authorize railroads to administer breath and urine tests
following accidents, incidents and rule violations,
constitute a "search" within the meaning of the Fourth
Amendment, but the compelling governmental interest in
railroad safety outweighs the tests' limited intrusion
upon the privacy interests of employees in the
pervasively regulated railroad industry, and therefore,
testing in the absence of a warrant or individualized
suspicion is reasonable under the Fourth Amendment.

The Court was more restrictive in the 5-4 decision
of **NATIONAL TREASURY EMPLOYEES UNION v. VON RAAB**, 489
U.S. 656, 109 S.Ct. 1384, 103 L.Ed.2d. 685, 44 CrL 3192
(1989). In that case, the United States Custom Service
invoked a suspicionless drug testing program for
employees seeking promotion or transfers to positions
involving the interdiction of illegal drugs or requiring
the carrying of firearms or to handle "classified"
material. The Court again held that this was a search
within the meaning of the Fourth Amendment and was
reasonable insofar as the program applied to employees
seeking promotion to positions involving the interdiction
of drugs or requires them to carry firearms. The Court
remanded the case to the Court of Appeals to determine
whether the category of employees is narrowly drawn to
include only those who are likely to gain access to
sensitive material.

§ 2.40   Electronic Surveillance and Wiretapping

The issue of whether the use of electronic
surveillance and/or wiretapping was a violation of
unreasonable search and seizure has gone full circle in
the courts. Naturally, the country's founders had no
idea that one day telephones, wireless, radio and
electronic devices would be available to infringe on the
privacy of the individual in his home, on the street, or
in his place of business.

The problem was given attention in **OLMSTEAD v.**

UNITED STATES, 277 U.S. 438, 48 S.Ct. 564, 72 L.Ed. 944 (1928). That case involved the tapping of telephone wires which led to information leading to the petitioner for the crimes of conspiracy to import, possess, and sell liquor unlawfully. There was no trespass into any real property of the defendant. The wiretaps were made in the basement of an office building and on the streets near the petitioner's house. The court held that pursuant to common law, the admissibility of evidence was not affected by the illegality of the means by which it was obtained. It held further that the tapping of telephone lines, as was done in this case, was not a search and seizure as was contemplated by the fourth Amendment. The court said that if Congress wanted to protect the secrecy of telephone messages, it could, by direct legislation, make it inadmissible in federal criminal trials.

Mr. JUSTICE BRANDEIS wrote a strong dissent to this opinion, calling attention to the fact that by the laws of Washington, wiretapping was a crime. Pierce's Code, 1921 Section 8976 (18). He went on to say, "Decency, security and liberty alike demand that government officials shall be subjected to the same rules of conduct that are commanded to the citizen .... If the government becomes a lawbreaker, it breeds contempt for law; it invites every man to become a law unto himself; it invites anarchy." This terminology was later to be heard in many cases that followed where the exclusionary rule was invoked by the court to keep law enforcement practices within the confines of the constitutional limitations.

Congress yielded to the court's direction six years later, when it enacted Section 605 of the Federal Communications Act which provided:

".... (N)o person not being authorized by the sender shall intercept any communication and divulge or publish the existence, contents, substance, purport, effect or meaning of such intercepted communication to any person."

With the tremendous advances in technology, law enforcement agents are now able to monitor the location of articles and the conversations of persons in buildings, vehicles and practically any private area by means of electronic beepers. A question of a beeper intrusion was considered by the United States Supreme Court in **U.S. v. KNOTTS**, 400 U.S. 276, 103 S.Ct. 1081, 73 L.Ed.2d 55, 32 Cr.L. 3069 (1983). In that case the Court held that a warrantless monitoring of an electronic tracking device ("beeper") inside a container of chemicals did not violate the Fourth Amendment when it revealed no information that could have been obtained by visual surveillance. Following the Knotts case, in 1984, the case of **U.S. v. KARO**, 468 U.S. 705, 104 S.Ct. 3296, 82 L.Ed.2d. 530, came before the Court. Here, an informant permitted a (D.E.A.) agent to place a beeper in a can along with other cans filled with ether. A Court order was obtained allowing the placement. The ether was to be used to extract cocaine from clothing. The ether and the beeper were taken to successive locations. Finally, the agents determined by the use of the beeper, and observations that it was in one of the defendant's houses and they secured a search warrant for the house. Upon executing the warrant, they found cocaine illegally possessed therein and made the arrests. After having reached the United States Supreme Court, the Court held that no Fourth Amendment interest of any respondent was infringed because it was neither a search nor a seizure since it contained no information that Karo wished to keep private. However, the monitoring of a beeper in a private residence, a location not open to surveillance violates the Fourth Amendment rights of those who have a justifiable interest in the privacy of the residence. In this case however, the government had sufficient probable cause for the issuance of the warrant without the use of the beeper, and hence the seizure of the cocaine pursuant to a search with a warrant was not a violation of the Fourth Amendment.

You will note that in Section 25.18, (8) (a) that appears in Section 2.49 of this book under the headnote OMNIBUS CRIME CONTROL AND SAFE STREET ACT, it is required that "Immediately upon the expiration of the period of the order, or extension thereof, such recordings shall be made available to the judge issuing such order and sealed under his directions."

In **UNITED STATES v. FILIBERTO OJEDA-RIOS** et al. 495

U.S.257, 110 S.Ct. 1845, 109 L.Ed.2d. 224, 47 CrL 2060 (1990), the Supervising United States Attorney neglected to comply with this sealing requirement as to some of the wiretap tapes that were recorded and the defendants sought suppression of these tapes. The Court held that the case should be remanded to determine whether a reasonable explanation was contained in the suppression hearing. If it was first advanced in the appeal process, it would have no merit. The statute should be strictly construed.

This case should act as a caveat to all whose responsibility it is to make certain that at the proper time, the wiretap recordings are properly sealed pursuant to the instructions of the judge who signed the wiretap order.

§ 2.41   Fruit of the Poisonous Tree

Section 501 of the Federal Communications Act provided a fine not exceeding $10,000 or imprisonment for a term not exceeding one year, or both, for willful violations of Section 605. The section made no mention of the exclusion of evidence seized in violation of the act but the courts have so interpreted it on the grounds that it was obtained in violation of Section 605 on the grounds that such evidence was tainted as fruit of the poisonous tree. To remove all incentive by law enforcement authorities to violate the act, the United States Supreme Court in **NARDONE v. UNITED STATES**, 302 U.S. 379, 58 S.Ct. 275, 82 L.Ed. 314 (1937), adopted the exclusionary rule to exclude in federal trials all evidence, leads, and other derivative evidence which becomes available as a result of illegal interceptions. This idea was reiterated in **WONG SUN v. U.S.**, 371 U.S. 471, 83 S.Ct. 407, 9 L.Ed.2d 441 (1963). In this case federal narcotic agents made an unlawful entry and an unauthorized arrest. As a result of this action, heroin was found at another location and another defendant was arrested. The Court reversed and remanded, saying that ".... verbal evidence which derives so immediately from an unlawful entry and an unauthorized arrest ... is no

less the 'fruit' of official illegality than the more
common tangible fruits of the unwarranted intrusion."
     Sometimes it is not an easy matter to detect what is
and what is not a poisonous tree case.   In **TAYLOR v.
ALABAMA**, 457 U.S. 687, 102 S.Ct. 2664, 73 L.Ed.2d 314, 31
Cr.L. 3118 (1982) the defendant was arrested on the basis
of an uncorroborated tip, without a warrant and without
probable cause.   The crime charged was a robbery of a
grocery store.   His fingerprints were taken and Miranda
warnings were given.   After being advised that his
fingerprints matched those on some grocery items and
after a visit from his girlfriend, he made a confession.
HELD: A   confession   obtained   through   custodial
interrogation after an illegal arrest should be excluded
unless intervening events break the original connection
between the arrest and the confession.
     TAYLOR v. ALABAMA, supra, was stretched in **NEW YORK
v. HARRIS**, 495 U.S. 14, 110 S.Ct. 1640, 109 L.Ed.2d. 13,
47 CrL 2025 (1990). In that case the police had probable
cause to arrest Harris for murder. They entered his home
without a warrant, and read him his Miranda rights. They
reportedly secured an admission of guilt in the home.
They arrested him, took him to the police station and
again gave him his Miranda rights. Whereupon he signed
a written inculpatory statement. The New York trial
court suppressed the first statement but admitted the
second inculpatory statement signed in the police
station. The Appellate Division affirmed, but the Court
of Appeals reversed. The Court reversed the Court of
Appeals saying, inter alia, that Harris' statement taken
at the police station was not the product of being in
unlawful custody. Neither was it the fruit of being
arrested in the home rather than somewhere else. Here,
the police had a justification to question Harris prior
to his arrest; and therefore, his subsequent statement
was not an exploitation of the illegal entry into Harris'
home. While the opinion of the justices varied with the
opinion of Rehnquist, CJ. joined by 4 other justices,
however all justices concurred in the result.

§ 2.42   Standing to Object

A defendant in a federal criminal trial could only object to the use of evidence secured by violation of Section 605 if s/he was an actual party to the intercepted conversation. **GOLDSTEIN v. UNITED STATES**, 316 U.S. 114, 86 L.Ed. 1312, 62 S.Ct. 1000 (1942).

In **UNITED STATES v. SALUCCI**, et.al., 448 U.S. 83, 100 S.Ct. 2547, 65 L.Ed.2d. 619, 27 Cr.L. 3241 (1980), the Court held that defendants charged with possession may only claim the benefits of the exclusionary rule, if their own Fourth Amendment rights have been violated. In this case the police had a search warrant of one of the respondent mother's apartment where stolen mail was found. The court held the seizure constitutionally valid in that the respondent had sustained no violation of their own Fourth Amendment rights even though the trial court held that the affidavit used to support the warrant did not show probable cause. The Court further held that the respondents in this case did not have "automatic standing" to challenge the legality of the search. A fortiori, in **RAWLINGS v. KENTUCKY**, 448 U.S. 98, 100 S.Ct. 2556, 65 L.Ed.2d. 633, 27 Cr.L. 3245 (1980) the court did not allow "automatic standing" to challenge Fourth Amendment violation where a defendant had placed drugs in the purse of an acquaintance where she admitted ownership of the drugs to the police at the scene of the arrest in a spontaneous reaction to the discovery of the drugs in the purse.

§ 2.43   Section 605 Violations in State Courts

In 1913, in **WEEKS v. UNITED STATES**, 232 U.S. 383, 34 S.Ct. 341, 58 L.Ed. 652 (1914), the Court first adopted the exclusionary rule for evidence seized in violation of the Fourteenth Amendment. In 1952 the issue of Section 605 came before the United States Supreme Court as to whether the exclusionary rule applied to state court trials when state officers violated the provisions of Section 605. **WOLF v. COLORADO**, 338 U.S. 25, 69 S.Ct. 1359, 93 L.Ed. 1782 (1949), decided that issue when the Court said that it would not be applicable to state trials in that each state was free to adopt its own rules of evidence.

§ 2.44   Silver-Platter Doctrine Revisited

In view of the fact that the states could have their own rules of evidence, a system of cooperation developed whereby state law enforcement officers would cooperate with federal law enforcement officers in effecting arrests. The procedure was for the state officers to violate Section 605 or any other Fourth Amendment direction, seize the evidence and/or arrest the perpetrator, book and arraign the arrestee before a magistrate who would turn over the evidence and the defendant to federal authorities for prosecution. This came to be known as the "silver platter doctrine."

This doctrine continued until 1937 when in **ELKINS v. UNITED STATES**, 364 U.S. 206, 80 S.Ct. 1437, 4 L.Ed.2d 1669 (1960), the court held that evidence seized by state agents in violation of standards of the Fourth Amendment could not be used by federal agents in federal prosecutions.

§ 2.45   Electronic Device Intrusion

SILVERMAN v. UNITED STATES, 365 U.S. 505, 81 S.Ct. 679, 5 L.Ed.2d 734, was to be decided by the court in 1961. In that case an electronic spike mike which penetrated the heating duct system of the suspect's house was a sufficient invasion of a private premises to be an unreasonable search and seizure. **BERGER v. NEW YORK**, 388 U.S. 41, 87 S.Ct. 1873, 18 L.Ed.2d 1040 (1967), finally laid the Olmstead decision to rest in a historical grave. The Berger case invalidated a New York statute which permitted application to court, by law enforcement officers, for an ex parte order permitting eavesdropping under prescribed conditions. The court held that the Fourth Amendment right of privacy was enforceable against the states and that the statute was too broad and was a trespassory intrusion.

KATZ v. UNITED STATES, 389 U.S. 347, 88 S.Ct. 507, 19 L.Ed.2d 576 (1967), followed this. Katz was subjected to an electronic listening and recording device which had been attached to the outside of a public telephone booth where he was transmitting wagering calls from Los Angeles to Miami and Boston in violation of a federal statute. No warrant had been issued for this intrusion. The court held that "One who occupies it (telephone booth) shuts the door behind him and pays the toll that permits him to place a call is surely entitled to assume that the words he utters into the mouthpiece will not be broadcast to the world...." The court refused to retroactively validate the conduct of the FBI because they probably could have obtained a warrant for the actions that the agents engaged in.

In the **UNITED STATES v. DONOVAN**, 429 U.S. 413, 97 S.Ct. 658, 50 L.Ed.2d 652 (1977), the Court held that the government has a responsibility to inform the judge who issues the wiretap order of the identities of those persons whose conversation is to be overheard, but it is not a constitutional requirement that all those likely to be overheard engaged in incriminating conversations be named.

The Court in another case held that a pen register that records telephone numbers dialed from a monitored telephone does not intercept wire or oral communications within the meaning of the federal electronics eavesdropping statute. It sustained a district court's order to a telephone company to provide reasonable technical assistance for the installation of a pen register and to be compensated for its service was held not to be an abuse of discretion. **U.S. v. N.Y. TELEPHONE CO.**, 434 U.S. 159, 98 S.Ct. 364, 54 L.Ed.2d 376, 22 Cr.L. 3001 (1977).

§ 2.46   Federal and State Fourth Amendment Rights Joined

MAPP v. OHIO, 367 U.S. 643, 160 Ohio Op.(2d) 384, 81 S.Ct. 1680, 6 L.Ed.2d 1081 (1961), in a 5 to 3 decision, finally merged the federal and state exclusionary rules with respect to Fourth Amendment violations. The state was no longer permitted to admit evidence in state trials which violated the dictates of the Fourth Amendment. This was accomplished by the court by reading the Due Process Clause of the Fourteenth Amendment along with the Fourth Amendment so as to make Fourth Amendment rights which were applicable to United States citizens with respect to the federal government applicable to all inhabitants against both federal and state governments.

§ 2.47   Bullet—Removal from Suspect's Body

Sometimes the law may appear to work an injustice to society. This conclusion is reached by many layman when a bullet is lodged in a suspect's body who probably committed a crime; the bullet is necessary to connect this person to the alleged crime; and the Court prohibits the surgery necessary to extract the bullet. The situation occurred in **WINSTON v. LEE**, 470 U.S. 753, 105 S.Ct. 1611, 84 L.Ed.2d 662 (1985). The Court held that the proposed surgery in this case would violate respondents right to be secure in his person and the search would be "unreasonable" under the Fourth Amendment. However the Court said further that the reasonableness of surgical intrusions beneath the skin depends on a case-by-case approach in which the individuals' interest in privacy and security are weighed against society's interests in conducting the procedure to obtain evidence for fairly determining guilt or innocence. In this case the bullet was lodged substantially deep in suspect's body.

§ 2.48   Deadly Force

The apprehension of a criminal suspect by the use of deadly force has been limited by the Court's decision in **TENNESSEE v. GARDNER**, 471 U.S. 1, 105 S.Ct. 1694, 85 L.Ed.2d. 1 (1985). That case held a Tennessee statute unconstitutional that permitted police to use deadly force to prevent the escape of suspected felons. The Court said that it violated the Fourth Amendment prohibition against unreasonable seizures because it permits the use of deadly force against an apparently unarmed, nondangerous fleeing suspect; such force may not be used unless necessary to prevent the escape, and the officer has probable cause to believe that the suspect poses a significant threat of death or serious physical injury to the officer or others.

§ 2.49   Omnibus Crime Control and Safe Streets Act

On July 23, 1965, recognizing the urgency of the nation's crime problem and the depth of ignorance about it, President Johnson established the Commission on Law Enforcement and Administration of Justice. This commission conducted extensive studies into the problem and this culminated in a comprehensive report published in 1967 entitled "The Challenge of Crime in a Free Society."

The nation was disturbed at the state of criminal justice and at this writing, it is still disturbed. Much money and man/woman hours have been spent on this problem and the solution has not surfaced to date. In response to the problem, Congress enacted the Criminal Justice Act of 1964, the Narcotic Addict Rehabilitation Act of 1966, the Juvenile Delinquency Prevention and Control Act of 1968, the Gun Control Act of 1968, Title III of the Omnibus Crime Control and Safe Streets Act of 1968 (relating to wiretapping and electronic surveillance), and Title XI of the Organized Crime Control Act of 1970 (relating to regulation of explosives).

The statutes indicated above were designated to be included in the Attorney General's First Annual Report dated September 1, 1972, available from the Superintendent of Documents, United States Printing Office, Washington, D.C. 20402, stock number 2700-0160.

Title III of the Omnibus Crime Control and Safe Streets Act of 1968 (relating to wiretapping and electronic surveillance) is particularly relevant to this text. The student should read it and analyze its

149

provisions keeping in mind the following guidelines:

1. What crimes are involved?
2. Who may authorize surveillance?
3. What specifically is required?
4. What is the time limitation on the authorization?
5. When is no prior judicial authorization permitted?

TITLE 18 U.S.C   CHAPTER 119
     WIRE AND ELECTRONIC COMMUNICATIONS INTERCEPTION
     AND INTERCEPTION OF ORAL COMMUNICATIONS

§ 2510.   Definitions
        As used in this chapter—

(1) "wire communication" means any aural transfer made
in whole or in part through the use of facilities for the
transmission of communications by the aid of wire, cable,
or other like connection between the point of origin and
the point of reception (including the use of such
connection in a switching station) furnished or operated
by any person engaged in providing or operating such
facilities for the transmission of interstate or foreign
communications for communications affecting interstate of
foreign commerce and such term includes any electronic
storage of such communication, but such term does not
include the radio portion of a cordless telephone
communication that is transmitted between the cordless
telephone handset and the base unit;

(2) "oral communication" means any oral communication
uttered by a person exhibiting an expectation that such
communication is not subject to interception under
circumstances justifying such expectation, but such term
does not include any electronic communication;

(3) "State" means any State of the United States, the
District of Columbia, the Commonwealth of Puerto Rico,
and any territory or possession of the United States;

(4) "intercept" means the aural or other acquisition of

the contents of any wire, electronic, or oral communication through the use of any electronic, mechanical, or other device;

(5) "electronic, mechanical, or other device" means any device or apparatus which can be used to intercept a wire, oral, or electronic communication other than—

(a) any telephone or telegraph instrument, equipment or facility, or any component thereof, (i) furnished to the subscriber or user by a provider of wire or electronic communication service in the ordinary course of its business and being used by the subscriber or user in the ordinary course of its business or furnished by such subscriber or user for connection to the facilities of such service and used in the ordinary course of its business; or (ii) being used by a provider of wire or electronic communication service in the ordinary course of its business, or by an investigative or law enforcement officer in the ordinary course of his duties;

(b) a hearing aid or similar device being used to correct subnormal hearing to not better than normal;

(6) "person" means any employee, or agent of the United States or any State or political subdivision thereof,and any individual, partnership, association, joint stock company, trust, or corporation;

(7) "Investigative or law enforcement officer" means any officer of the United States or of a State or political subdivision thereof, who is empowered by law to conduct investigations of or to make arrests for offenses enumerated in this chapter, and any attorney authorized by law to prosecute or participate in the prosecution of such offenses;

(8) "contents", when used with respect to any wire, oral, or electronic communication, includes any information concerning the substance, purport, or meaning of that communication;

(9) "Judge of competent jurisdiction" means—

(a) a judge of a United States district court or a United States court of appeals; and

(b) a judge of any court of general criminal jurisdiction of a State who is authorized by a statute of that State to enter orders authorizing interceptions or wire, oral, or electronic communications;

(10) "communication common carrier" shall have the same meaning which is given the term "common carrier" by section 153(h) of title 47 of the United States Code;

(11) "aggrieved person" means a person who was a party to any intercepted wire, oral, or electrical communication or a person against whom the interception was directed;

(12) "electronic communication" means any transfer of signs, signals, writing, images, sounds, data, or intelligence of any nature transmitted in while or in part by a wire, radio, electromagnetic, photoelectronic or photooptial system that affects interstate or foreign commerce, but does not include--

(A) the radio portion of a cordless telephone communication that is transmitted between the cordless telephone handset and the base unit;

(B) any wire or oral communication

(C) any communication made through a tone-only paging device; or

(D) any communication from a tracking device(as defined in section 3117);

(13) "user" means any person or entity who-

(A) uses an electronic communication service;

and

(B) is duly authorized by the provider of such service to engage in such use;

(14) "electronic communications system" means any wire, radio, electromagnetic, photooptical or photoelectronic facilities for the transmission of electronic communications, and any computer facilities or related electronic equipment of the electronic storage of such communications;

(15) "electronic communication service" means any service which provides to users thereof the ability to send or receive wire or electronic communications;

(16) "readily accessible to the general public" means, with respect to a radio communication, that such communication is not--

(A) scrambled or encrypted;

(B) transmitted using modulation techniques whose essential parameters have been withheld from the public with the intention of preserving the privacy of such communication;

(C) carried on a subcarrier or other signal subsidiary to radio transmission;

(D) transmitted over a communication system provided by a common carrier, unless the communication is a tone only paging system communication; or

(E) transmitted on frequencies allocated under part 25 , subpart D,E, or F of part 74, or part 94 of the Rules of the Federal Communications commission, unless, in the case of a communication transmitted on a frequency allocated under part 74 that is not exclusively allocated to broadcast auxiliary services, the communication is a two -way voice communication by radio;

153

(17) "electronic storage" means--

(A) any temporary, intermediate storage of a
wire or electronic communication incidental to the
electronic transmission thereof; and

(B) any storage of such communication by an
electronic communication service for purposes of
backup protection of such communication; and

(18) "aural transfer" means a transfer containing the
human voice at any point between and including the point
of origin and the point of reception.

§ 2511.   Interception and disclosure of wire or oral communications prohibited

(1) Except as otherwise specifically provided in this
chapter any person who—

(a) intentionally intercepts, endeavors to
intercept, or procures any other person to intercept
or endeavor to intercept, any wire, oral, or
electronic communication;

(b) intentionally uses, endeavors to use, or
procures any other person to use or endeavor to use
any electronic, mechanical, or other device to
intercept any oral communication when—

(i) such device is affixed to, or
otherwise transmits a signal through, a wire,
cable, or other like connection used in wire
communication; or

(ii) such device transmits communications by
radio, or interferes with the transmission of
such communication; or

(iii) such person knows, or has reason to
know, that such device or any component thereof

has been sent through the mail or transported in interstate or foreign commerce; or

(iv) such use or endeavor to use (A) takes place on the premises of any business or other commercial establishment the operations of which affect interstate or foreign commerce; or (B) obtains or is for the purpose of obtaining information relating to the operations of any business or other commercial establishment the operations of which affect interstate or foreign commerce; or

(v) such person acts in the District of Columbia, the Commonwealth of Puerto Rico, or any territory or possession of the United States;

(c) intentionally discloses, or endeavors to disclose, to any other person the contents of any wire, oral or electronic communication, knowing or having reason to know that the information was obtained through the interception of a wire, oral, or electronic Communication in violation of this subsection; or

(d) intentionally uses, or endeavors to use, the contents of any wire, oral, or electronic communication,knowing or having reason to know that the information was obtained through the interception of a wire, oral, or electronic communication in violation of this subsection;

shall be punished as provided in subsection (4) or shall be subject to suit as provided in subsection (5)

(2)(a)(i) It shall be unlawful under this chapter for an operator of a switchboard, or an officer, employee, or agent of a provider of wire or electronic communication service, whose facilities are used in the transmission of a wire communication, to intercept, disclose, or use that communication in the normal course of his employment while engaged in any activity which is a necessary

incident to the rendition of his service or to the
protection of the rights or property of the provider of
that service, except that a provider of wire
communication service to the public shall not utilize
service observing or random monitoring except for
mechanical or service quality control checks.

(ii) Notwithstanding any other law, providers of wire
or electronic communication service, their officers,
employees, agents, landlords, custodians, or other
persons, are authorized to provide
information,facilities, or technical assistance to
persons authorized by law to intercept wire, oral or
electronic communications or to conduct electronic
surveillance, as defined in section 101 of the Foreign
Intelligence Surveillance Act of 1978, if such provider,
its officers, employees, or agents, landlord, custodian,
or other specified person, has been provided with--

(A) a court order directing such assistance
signed by the authorizing judge, or

(B) a certification in writing by a person
specified in section 2518(7) of this title or the
Attorney General of the United States that no
warrant or court order is required by law, that all
statutory requirement have been met, and that the
specified assistance is required,

setting forth the period of time during which the
provision of the information, facilities, or technical
assistance is authorized and specifying the information,
facilities, or technical assistance required.   No
provider of wire or electronic communication service,
officer, employee, or agent thereof, or landlord,
custodian, or other specified person shall disclose the
existence of any interception or surveillance or the
device used to accomplish the interception or
surveillance with respect to which the person has been
furnished a court order or certification under this
chapter, except as may otherwise be required by legal
process and then only after prior notification to the

Attorney General or to the principal prosecuting attorney of a State or any political subdivision of a State, as may be appropriate. Any such disclosure, shall render such person liable for the civil damages provided for in section 2520. No cause of action shall lie in any court against any provider of wire or electronic communication service, its officers, employees, or agents, landlord, custodian, or other specified person for providing information, facilities, or assistance in accordance with the terms of a court order or certification under this chapter.

(b) It shall not be unlawful under this chapter for an officer, employee, or agent of the Federal Communications Commission, in the normal course of his employment and in discharge of the monitoring responsibilities exercised by the Commission in the enforcement of chapter 5 of title 47 of the United States Code, to intercept a wire or electronic communication, or oral communication transmitted by radio, or to disclose or use the information thereby obtained.

(c) It shall not be unlawful under this chapter for a person not acting under color of law to intercept a wire, oral, or electronic communication, where such person is a party to the communication or one of the parties to the communication has given prior consent to such interception.

(d) It shall not be unlawful under this chapter for a person not acting under color of law to intercept a wire, oral, or electronic communication where such person is party to the communication or where one of the parties to the communication has given prior consent to such interception unless such communication is intercepted for the purpose of committing any criminal or tortious act in violation of the Constitution or laws of the United States or of any State,

(e) Notwithstanding any other provision of this title or section 705 or 706 of the Communications Act of 1934, it shall not be unlawful for an officer, employee, or agent of the United states in the normal course of his official duties to conduct electronic surveillance, as defined in section 101 of the Foreign Intelligence Surveillance Act of 1978, as authorized by that Act.

(f) Nothing contained in this chapter or chapter 121,or section 705 of the Communications Act of 1934, shall be deemed to affect the acquisition by the United States Government of foreign intelligence information from international or foreign communications, or foreign intelligence activities conducted in accordance with otherwise applicable Federal law involving a foreign electronic communications system, utilizing a means other than electronic surveillance as defined in section 101 of the Foreign Intelligence Surveillance Act of 1978 and procedures in this chapter and the Foreign Intelligence Surveillance Act of 1978 shall be the exclusive means by which electronic surveillance, as defined in section 101 of such Act, and the interception of domestic wire and oral communications may be conducted.

(g) It shall not be unlawful under this chapter or chapter 121 of this title for any person--

   (i) to intercept or access an electronic communication made through an electronic communication system that is configured so that such electronic communication is readily accessible to the general public;

   (ii) to intercept any radio communication which is transmitted-

      (I) by any station for the use of the general public, or that relates to ships, aircraft, vehicles, or persons in distress;

      (II) by any governmental, law enforcement, civil defense, private land mobile, or public safety communications system, including police and fire, readily accessible to the general public;

(III) by a station operating on an authorized frequency within the bands allocated to the amateur, citizens band, or general mobile radio services; or

(IV) by any marine or aeronautical communications system;

(iii) to engage in any conduct which--

(I) is prohibited by section 633 of the Communications Act of 1934; or

(II) is excepted from the application of section 705(a) of the Communication Act of 1934 by section 705(b) if that Act;

(iv) to intercept any wire or electronic communication the transmission of which is causing harmful interference to any lawfully operating station or consumer electronic equipment, to the extent necessary to identify the source of such interference; or

(v) for other users of the same frequency to intercept any radio communication made through a system that utilizes frequencies monitored by individuals engaged in the provision of the use of such system, if such communication is not scrambled or encrypted.

(h) It shall not be unlawful under this chapter--

(i) to use a pen register or a trap and trace device(as those terms are defined for the purposes of chapter 206 (relating to pen registers and trap and trace devices) of this title); or

(ii) for a provider of electronic communication service to record the fact that a wire or electronic communication was initiated or completed in order to protect such provider, another provider furnishing service toward the completion of the wire or electronic communication, or a user of that service, from fraudulent, unlawful or abusive use of such service.

(3)(a) Except as provided in paragraph (b) of this subsection, a person or entity providing an electronic communication service to the public shall not intentionally divulge the contents of any communication (other that one to such person or entity, or an agent thereof) while in transmission on that service to any person or entity other than an addressee or intended recipient of such communication or an agent of such addressee or intended recipient.

(b) A person or entity providing electronic communication service to the public may divulge the contents of any such communication--

(i) as otherwise authorized in section 2511 (2)(a) or 2517 of this title;

(ii) with the lawful consent of the originator or any addressee or intended recipient of such communication;

(iii) to a person employed or authorized, or whose facilities are used, to forward such communication to its destination; or

(iv) which were inadvertently obtained by the service provider and which appear to pertain to the commission of a crime, if such divulgence is made to a law enforcement agency.

(4)(a) Except as provided in paragraph (b) of this subsection or in subsection (5), whoever violates subsection (1) of this section shall be fined under this title or imprisoned not more than five years, or both.

(b) If the offense is a first offense under paragraph (a) of this subsection and is not for a tortious or illegal purpose or for purposes of direct or indirect commercial advantage or private commercial gain, and the wire or electronic communication with respect to which the offense under paragraph (a) is a radio communication that is not scrambled or encrypted, then--

(i) if the communication is not the radio portion of a cellular telephone communication, a public land mobile radio service communication or a paging service communication, and the conduct is not described in subsection (5), the offender shall be fined under this title or imprisoned not more than one year, or both; and

(ii) if the communication is the radio portion of a cellular telephone communication, a public land mobile radio service communication or a paging service communication, the offender shall be fined not more than $500.

(c) Conduct otherwise an offense under this subsection that consists of or relates to the interception of a satellite transmission that is not encrypted or scrambled and that is transmitted--

(i) to a broadcasting station for purposes of retransmission to the general public; or

(ii) as an audio subcarrier intended for redistribution to facilities open to the public, but not including data transmission or telephone calls,

is not an offense under this subsection unless the conduct is for the purposes of direct or indirect commercial advantage or private financial gain.

(5)(a)(i) If the communication is--

(A) a private satellite video communication that is not scrambled or encrypted and the conduct in violation of this chapter is the private viewing of that communication and is not for a tortious or illegal purpose or for purposes of direct or

indirect commercial advantage or private commercial
gain; or

(B) a radio communication that is transmitted on
frequencies allocated under subpart D of part 74 of
the rules of the Federal Communications Commission
that is not scrambled or encrypted and the conduct
in violation of this chapter is not for a tortious
or illegal purpose or for purposes of direct or
indirect commercial advantage or private commercial
gain,

then the person who engages in such conduct shall be
subject to suit by the Federal Government in a court of
competent jurisdiction.

(ii) In an action under this subsection--

(A) if the violation of this chapter is a first
offense for the person under paragraph (a) of
subsection (4) and such person has not been found
liable in a civil action under section 2520 of this
title,the Federal Government shall be entitled to
appropriate injunctive relief; and

(B) if the violation of this chapter is a second
or subsequent offense under paragraph (a) of
subsection (4) or such person has been found liable
in any prior civil action under section 2520, the
person shall be subject to a mandatory $500 civil
fine.
(b) The court may use any means within its
authority to enforce an injunction issued under
paragraph (ii)(A), and shall impose a civil fine of
not less than $500 for each violation of such
an injunction.

(3) Nothing contained in this chapter or in section 605
of the Communications Act of 1934 (48 Stat. 1143; 47
U.S.C. 605) shall limit the constitutional power of the
President to take such measures as he deems necessary to
protect the Nation against actual or potential attack or

other hostile acts of a foreign power, to obtain foreign intelligence information deemed essential to the security of the United States, or to protect national security information against foreign intelligence activities. Nor shall anything contained in this chapter be deemed to limit the constitutional power of the President to take such measures as he deems necessary to protect the United States against the overthrow of the Government by force or other unlawful means, or against any other clear and present danger to the structure or existence of the Government. The contents of any wire or oral communication intercepted by authority of the President in the exercise of the foregoing powers may be received in evidence in any trial hearing, or other proceeding only where such interception was reasonable, and shall not be otherwise used or disclosed except as is necessary to implement that power....

§ 2512. Manufacture, distribution, possession, and advertising of wire, oral, or electronic communication intercepting devices prohibited

(1) Except as otherwise specifically provided in this chapter, any person who intentionally--

(a) sends through the mail, or sends or carries in interstate or foreign commerce, any electronic, mechanical, or other device, knowing or having reason to know that the design of such device renders it primarily useful for the purpose of the surreptitious interception of wire, oral, or electronic communications;

(b) manufactures, assembles, possesses, or sells any electronic, mechanical, or other device, knowing or having reason to know that the design of such device renders it primarily useful for the purpose of the surreptitious interception of wire, oral, or electronic communications, and that such device or any component thereof has been or will be sent through the mail or transported in interstate or foreign commerce; or

(c) places in any newspaper, magazine, handbill, or other publication any advertisement of-

> (i) any electronic mechanical, or other device knowing or having reason to know that the design of such device renders it primarily useful for the purpose of the surreptitious interception of wire, oral, or electronic communications; or

> (ii) any other electronic, mechanical, or other device, where such advertisement promotes the use of such device for the purpose of the surreptitious interception of wire, oral, or electronic communications,

knowing or having reason to know that such advertisement will be sent through the mail or transported in interstate or foreign commerce,

shall be fined not more than $10,000 or imprisoned not more than five years, or both.

(2) It shall not be unlawful under this section for-

(a) a provider of wire or electronic communication service or an office, agent, or employee of, or a person under contract with, such a provider, in the normal course of the business of providing that wire or electronic communications service, or

(b) an officer, agent, or employee of, or a person under contract with, the United States, a State, or a political subdivision thereof, in the normal course of the activities of the United States, a State, or a political subdivision thereof, to send through the mail, send or carry in interstate or foreign commerce, or manufacture, assemble, possess, or sell any electronic, mechanical, or other device knowing or having reason to know that the design of such device renders it primarily useful for the purpose of the surreptitious interception of wire, oral, or electronic communications.

§ 2513. Confiscation of wire, oral, or electronic communication intercepting devices

Any electronic, mechanical, or other device used, sent, carried, manufactured, assembled, possessed, sold, or advertised in violation of section 2511 or section 2512 of this chapter may be seized and forfeited to the United States. All provisions of law relating to (1) the seizure, summary and judicial forfeiture, and condemnation of vessels, vehicles, merchandise, and baggage for violations of the customs laws contained in title 19 of the United States Code, (2) the disposition of such vessels, vehicles, merchandise, and baggage or the proceeds from the sale thereof, (3) the remission or mitigation of such forfeiture, (4) the compromise of claims, and (5) the award of compensation to informers in respect of such forfeitures, shall apply to seizures and forfeitures incurred, or alleged to have been incurred, under the provisions of this section, insofar as applicable and not inconsistent with the provisions of this section; except that such duties as are imposed upon the collector of customs or any other person with respect to the seizure and forfeiture of vessels, vehicles, merchandise, and baggage under the provisions of the customs laws contained in title 19 of the United States Code shall be performed with respect to seizure and forfeiture of electronic, mechanical, or other interception devices under this section by such officers, agents, or other persons as may be authorized or designated for that purpose by the Attorney General.

§ 2515. Prohibition of use as evidence of intercepted wire or oral communications

Whenever any wire or oral communication has been intercepted, no part of the contents of such communication and no evidence derived therefrom may be received in evidence in any trial, hearing, or other proceeding in or before any court, grand jury, department, officer, agency, regulatory body, legislative committee, or other authority of the United States, a State, or political subdivision thereof if the disclosure of that information would be in violation of this chapter.

§ 2516.   Authorization for interception of wire, oral, or electronic communications

(1) The Attorney General,Deputy Attorney General, Associate Attorney General, or any Assistant Attorney General, any acting Assistant Attorney General, or any Deputy Assistant Attorney General in the Criminal Division specially designated by the Attorney General, may authorize an application to a Federal judge of competent jurisdiction for, and such judge may grant in conformity with section 2518 of this chapter an order authorizing or approving the interception of wire or oral communications by the Federal Bureau of Investigation, or a Federal agency having responsibility for the investigation of the offense as to which the application is made, when such interception may provide or has provided evidence of-

(a) any offense punishable by death or by imprisonment for more than one year under sections 2274 through 2277 of title 42 of the United States Code (relating to the enforcement of the Atomic Energy Act of 1954),section 2284 of title 42 of the United States Code(relating to sabotage of nuclear facilities or fuel), or under the following chapters of this title: chapter 37 (relating to espionage), chapter 105 (relating to sabotage), chapter 115 (relating to treason), or chapter 102 (relating to riots), chapter 65 (relating to malicious mischief), chapter 111 (relating to destruction vessels), or chapter 81 (relating to piracy);

(b) a violation of section 186 of section 501(c) of title 29, United States Code (dealing with restrictions on payments and loans to labor organizations), or any offense which involves murder, kidnapping, robbery, or extortion, and which is punishable under this title;

(c) any offense which is punishable under the following sections of this title: section 201 (bribery of public officials and witnesses),section 215 (relating to bribery of bank officials), section 224 (bribery in sporting contests), subsection (d), (e), (f), (g), (h), or (i) of section 844 (unlawful use of explosives),section 1032 (relating to concealment of assets), section 1084 (transmission of wagering information), section 751 (relating to escape), section 1014 (relating to loans and credit applications generally; renewals and discounts), sections 1503, 1512, and 1513 (influencing or injuring an officer, juror, or witness generally), section 1510 (obstruction of criminal investigations), section 1511 (obstruction of State or local law enforcement), section 1751 (Presidential and Presidential staff assassination, kidnapping and assault), section 1951 (interference with commerce by threats or violence), section 1952 (interstate and foreign travel or transportation in aid of racketeering enterprises), section 1958 (relating to use of interstate commerce facilities in the commission of murder for hire), section 1959 to violent crimes in aid of racketeering activity), section 1954 (offer, acceptance, or solicitation to influence operations of employee benefit plan), section 1955 (prohibition of business enterprises of gambling), section 1956 (laundering of monetary instruments), section 1957 (relating to engaging in monetary transactions in property derived from specified unlawful activity), section 659 (theft from interstate shipment), section 664 (embezzlement from pension and welfare funds), section 1343 (fraud by wire, radio, or television), section 1344 (relating to bank fraud), sections 2251 and 2252 (sexual exploitation of children), sections 2312, 2313, 2314 and 2315 (interstate transportation of stolen property), section 2321 (relating to trafficking in certain motor vehicles or motor vehicle parts),section 1203 (relating to hostage taking), section 1029 (relating to fraud and related activity in connection with access devices), section 3146 (relating to penalty for failure to appear), section 3521(b)(3) (relating to witness relocation and assistance), section 32 (relating to destruction of aircraft or aircraft facilities), section 1963 (violations with respect to racketeer influenced and corrupt organizations), section 115 (relating to threatening or retaliating against a Federal official), and section 1341 (relating to mail fraud), section 351 (violations) with respect to congressional, Cabinet, or Supreme Court assassinations, kidnapping, and assault), section 831 (relating to prohibited transactions involving nuclear materials), section 33 (relating to destruction of motor vehicles or motor vehicle facilities), section 175 (relating to biological weapons), or section 1992 (relating to wrecking trains);

(d) any offense involving counterfeiting punishable under section 471, 472 or 473 of this title;

(e) any offense involving fraud connected with a case under title 11 or the manufacture, importation, receiving, concealment, buying, selling, or otherwise dealing in narcotic drugs, marihuana, or other dangerous drugs, punishable under any law of the United States;

(f) any offense including extortionate credit transactions under sections 892, 893, or 894 of this title, or

(g) a violation of section 5322 of title 31, United States Code (dealing with the reporting of currency transactions);

(h) any felony violation of sections 2511 and 2512 (relating to interception and disclosure of certain communications and to certain intercepting devices) of this title;

(i) any felony violation of chapter 71 (relating to obscenity) of this title;

(j) any violation of section 1679a(c)(2) (relating to destruction of a natural gas pipeline) or subsection (i) or (n) of section 1472 (relating to aircraft piracy) of title 49,(sic) of the United States Code;

(k) any criminal violation of section 2778 of title 22 (relating to the Arms Export Control Act);

(l) the location of any fugitive from justice from an offense described in this section; or (sic)

(m)(sic) any felony violation of sections 922 and 924 of title 18, United States Code (relating to firearms); and

(m)(sic) any conspicracy to commit any of the foregoing offenses.

(n) any violation of section 5861 of the Internal Revenue Code of 1986 (relating to firearms); and

(o) any conspiracy to commit any offense described in any subparagraph of this paragraph.

(2) The principal prosecuting attorney of any State, or the principal prosecuting attorney of any political subdivision thereof, if such attorney is authorized by a statute of that State to make application to a State court judge of competent jurisdiction for an order authorizing or approving the interception of wire or oral

communications, may apply to such judge for, and such judge may grant in conformity with section 2518 of this chapter and with the applicable State statute an order authorizing or approving the interception of wire or oral communications by investigative or law enforcement officers having responsibility for the investigation of the offense as to which the application is made, when such interception may provide or has provided evidence of the commission of the offense of murder, kidnapping, gambling, robbery, bribery, extortion, or dealing in narcotic drugs, marihuana or other dangerous drugs, or other crime dangerous to life, limb, or property, and punishable by imprisonment for more than one year, designated in any applicable State statute authorizing such interception, or any conspiracy to commit any of the foregoing offenses.

(3) Any attorney for the Government (as such term is defined for the purpose of the Federal Rules of Criminal Procedure) may authorize an application to a Federal judge of competent jurisdiction for, and such judge may grant, in conformity with section 2518 of this title, or order authorizing or approving the interception of electronic communications by an investigative or law enforcement officer having responsibility for the investigation of the offense as to which the application is made, when such interception may provide or has provided evidence of any Federal felony.

§ 2517.   **Authorization for disclosure and use of intercepted wire, oral, or electronic communications**

(1) Any investigative or law enforcement officer who, by any means authorized by this chapter, has obtained knowledge of the contents of any wire, oral, or electronic communication, or evidence derived therefrom, may disclose such contents to another investigative or law enforcement officer to the extent that such disclosure is appropriate to the proper performance of

the official duties of the officer making or receiving the disclosure.

(2) Any investigative or law enforcement officer who, by any means authorized by this chapter, has obtained knowledge of the contents of any wire, oral, or electronic communication or evidence derived therefrom may use such contents to the extent such use is appropriate to the proper performance of his official duties.

(3) Any person who has received, by any means authorized by this chapter, any information concerning a wire, oral, or electronic communication, or evidence derived therefrom intercepted in accordance with the provisions of this chapter may disclose the contents of that communication or such derivative evidence while giving testimony under oath or affirmation in any criminal proceeding in any court of the United States or of any State on in any Federal or State grand jury proceeding.

(4) No otherwise privileged wire, oral, or electronic communication intercepted in accordance with, or in violation of, the provisions of this chapter shall lose its privileged character.

(5) When an investigative or law enforcement officer, while engaged in intercepting wire, oral, or electronic communications in the manner authorized herein, intercepts wire, oral, or electronic communications relating to offenses other than those specified in the order of authorization or approval, the contents thereof, and evidence derived therefrom, may be disclosed or used as provided in subsections (1) and (2) of this section. Such contents and any evidence derived therefrom may be used under subsection (3) of this section when authorized or approved by a judge of competent jurisdiction where such judge finds on subsequent application that the contents were otherwise intercepted in accordance with the provisions of this chapter. Such application shall be made as soon as practicable.

§ 2518.   Procedure for interception of wire, oral, or electronic communications

(1) Each application for an order authorizing or approving the interception of a wire, oral, or electronic communication shall be made in writing upon oath or affirmation to a judge of competent jurisdiction and shall state the applicant's authority to make such application.   Each application shall include the following information:

(a) the identity of the investigative or law enforcement officer making the application, and the officer authorizing the application;

(b) a full and complete statement of the facts and circumstances relied upon by the applicant, to justify his belief that an order should be issued, including (i) details as to the particular offense that has been, is being, or is about to be committed, (ii) except as provided in subsection (11), a particular description of the nature and location of the facilities from which or the place where the communication is to be intercepted, (iii) a particular description of the type of communications sought to be intercepted, (iv) the identity of the person, if known, committing the offense and whose communications are to be intercepted;

(c) a full and complete statement as to whether or not other investigative procedures have been tried and failed or why they reasonably appear to be unlikely to succeed if tried or to be too dangerous;

(d) a statement of the period of time for which the interception is required to be maintained.   If the nature of the investigation is such that the authorization for interception should not automatically terminate when the described type of communications has been first obtained, a particular description of facts establishing probable cause to believe that additional communications of the same type will occur thereafter;

(e) a full and complete statement of the facts concerning all previous applications known to the individual authorizing and making the application, made to any judge for authorization to intercept, or for approval of interceptions of, wire, oral, or electronic communications involving any of the same persons, facilities or places specified in the application, and the action taken by the judge on each such application; and

(f) where the application is for the extension of an order, a statement setting forth the results thus far obtained from the interception, or a reasonable explanation of the failure to obtain such results.

(2) The judge may require the applicant to furnish additional testimony or documentary evidence in support of the application.

(3) Upon such application the judge may enter an ex parte order, as requested or as modified, authorizing or approving interception of wire, oral, or electronic communications within the territorial jurisdiction of the court in which the judge is sitting, if the judge determines on the basis of the facts submitted by the applicant that—

(a) there is probable cause for belief that an individual is committing, has committed, or is about to commit a particular offense enumerated in section 2516 of this chapter;

(b) there is probable cause for belief that particular communications concerning that offense will be obtained through such interception;

(c) normal investigative procedures have been tried and have failed or reasonably appear to be unlikely to succeed if tried or to be too dangerous.

(d) except as provided in subsection (11),there
is probable cause for belief that the facilities
from which, or the place where, the wire, oral, or
electronic communications are to be intercepted are
being used, or are about to be used, in connection
with the commission of such offense, or are leased
to, listed in the name of, or commonly used by such
person.

(4) Each order authorizing or approving the
interception of any wire, oral, or electronic
communication shall specify—

(a) the identity of the person, if known, whose
communications are to be intercepted;

(b) the nature and location of the communications
facilities as to which, or the place where,
authority to intercept is granted;

(c) a particular description of the type of
communication sought to be intercepted, and a
statement of the particular offense to which it
relates;

(d) the identity of the agency authorized to
intercept the communications, and of the person
authorizing the application; and

(e) the period of time during which such
interception is authorized, including a statement as
to whether or not the interception shall
automatically terminate when the described
communication has been first obtained.

An order authorizing the interception of a wire, oral, or
electronic communication under this chapter shall, upon
request of the applicant, direct that a provider of wire
or electronic communication service, landlord, custodian
or other person shall furnish the applicant forthwith all
information, facilities, and technical assistance
necessary to accomplish the interception unobtrusively

and with a minimum of interference with the services that such service provider, landlord, custodian, or person is according the person whose communications are to be intercepted. Any provider of wire or electronic communication service, landlord, custodian or other person furnishing facilities or technical assistance shall be compensated therefor by the applicant for reasonable expenses incurred in providing such facilities or assistance.

(5) No order entered under this section may authorize or approve the interception of any wire, oral, or electronic communication for any period longer than is necessary to achieve the objective of the authorization, nor in any event longer than thirty days. such thirty-day period begins on the earlier of the day on which the investigative or law enforcement officer begins to conduct an interception under the order or ten days after the order is entered. Extension of an order may be granted, but only upon application for an extension made in accordance with subsection (1) of this section and the court making the findings required by subsection (3) of this section. The period of extension shall be no longer than the authorizing judge deems necessary to achieve the purposes for which it was granted and in no event for longer than thirty days. Every order and extension thereof shall contain a provision that the authorization to intercept shall be executed as soon as practicable, shall be conducted in such a way as to minimize the interception of communications not otherwise subject to interception under this chapter, and must terminate upon attainment of the authorized objective, or in any event in thirty days. In the event the intercepted communication is in a code or foreign language, and an expert in that foreign language or code is not reasonably available during the interception period, minimization may be accomplished as soon as practicable after such interception, An interception under this chapter may be conducted in whole or in part by Government personnel, or by an individual operating under a contract with the Government, acting under the supervision of an investigative or law enforcement officer authorized to conduct the interception.

(6) Whenever an order authorizing interception is entered pursuant to this chapter, the order may require reports to be made to the judge who issued the order showing what progress has been made toward achievement of the authorized objective and the need for continued interception. Such reports shall be made at such intervals as the judge may require.

(7) Notwithstanding any other provision of this chapter, any investigative or law enforcement officer, specially designated by the Attorney General or by the principal prosecuting attorney of any State or subdivision thereof acting pursuant to a statute of that State, who reasonably determines that—

(a) an emergency situation exists that involves--

(i) immediate danger of death or serious physical injury to any person,

(ii) conspiratorial activities threatening the national security interest or

(iii) conspiratorial activities characteristic of organized crime

that requires a wire, oral, or electronic communication to be intercepted before an order authorizing such interception can with due diligence be obtained, and

(b) there are grounds upon which an order could be entered under this chapter to authorize such interception,

may intercept such wire, oral, or electronic communication if the application for an order approving the interception is made in accordance with this section within forty-eight hours after the interception has occurred, or begins to occur. In the absence of an order, such interception shall immediately terminate when the communication sought is obtained or when the application for the order is denied, whichever is earlier. In the event such application for approval is denied, or in any other case where the interception is terminated without an order having been issued, the contents of any wire, oral, or electronic communication intercepted shall be treated as having been obtained in violation of this chapter, and an inventory shall be served as provided for in subsection (d) of this section on the person named in the application.

(8)(a) The contents of any wire, oral, or electronic communication intercepted by any means authorized by this chapter shall, if possible, be recorded on tape or wire or other comparable device. The recording of the contents of any wire, oral, or electronic communication under this subsection shall be done in such way as will protect the recording from editing or other alterations. Immediately upon the expiration of the period of the order, or extensions thereof, such recordings shall be made available to the judge issuing such order and sealed under his directions. Custody of the recordings shall be wherever the judge orders. They shall not be destroyed except upon an order of the issuing or denying judge and in any event shall be kept for ten years. Duplicate recordings may be made of use or disclosure pursuant to the provisions of subsections (1) and (2) of section 2517 of this chapter for investigations. The presence of the seal provided for by this subsection, or a satisfactory explanation for the absence thereof, shall be a prerequisite for the use or disclosure of the contents of any wire, oral, or electronic communication or evidence derived therefrom under subsection (3) of section 2517.

(b) Applications made and orders granted under this chapter shall be sealed by the judge. Custody of the applications and orders shall be wherever the judge directs. Such applications and orders shall be disclosed only upon a showing of good cause before a judge of competent jurisdiction and shall not be destroyed except on order of the issuing or denying judge, and in any event shall be kept for ten years.

(c) Any violation of the provisions of this subsection

may be punished as contempt of the issuing or denying judge.

(d) Within a reasonable time but not later than ninety days after the filing of an application for an order of approval under section 2518 (7)(b) which is denied or the termination of the period of an order or extensions thereof, the issuing or denying judge shall cause to be served, on the persons named in the order or the application, and such other parties to intercepted communications as the judge may determine in his discretion that is in the interest of justice, an inventory which shall include notice of—

(1) the fact of the entry of the order or the application;

(2) the date of the entry and the period of authorized, approved or disapproved interception, or the denial of the application; and

(3) the fact that during the period wire, oral, or electronic communications were or were not intercepted.

The judge, upon the filing of a motion, may in his discretion make available to such person or his counsel for inspection such portions of the intercepted communications, applications and orders as the judge determines to be in the interest of justice. On an ex parte showing of good cause to a judge of competent jurisdiction the serving of the inventory required by this subsection may be postponed.

(9) The contents of any intercepted wire, oral, or electronic communication or evidence derived therefrom shall not be received in evidence or otherwise disclosed in any trial, hearing, or other proceeding in a Federal or State court unless each party, not less than ten days before the trial, hearing, or proceeding, has been furnished with a copy of the court order, and accompanying application, under which the interception

was authorized or approved. This ten-day period may be waived by the judge if he finds that it was not possible to furnish the party with the above information ten days before the trial, hearing, or proceeding and that the party will not be prejudiced by the delay in receiving such information.

(10)(a) Any aggrieved person in any trial, hearing, or proceeding in or before any court, department, officer, agency, regulatory body, or other authority of the United States, a State, or a political subdivision thereof, may move to suppress the contents of any intercepted wire or oral communication, or evidence derived therefrom, on the grounds that—

(i) the communication was unlawfully intercepted;

(ii) the order of authorization or approval under which it was intercepted is insufficient on its face; or

(iii) the interception was not made in conformity with the order of authorization or approval.

Such motion shall be made before the trial, hearing, or proceeding unless there was no opportunity to make such motion or the person was not aware of the grounds of the motion. If the motion is granted, the contents of the intercepted wire or oral communication, or evidence derived therefrom, shall be treated as having been obtained in violation of this chapter. The judge, upon the filing of such motion by the aggrieved person, may in his discretion make available to the aggrieved person or his counsel for inspection such portions of the intercepted communication or evidence derived therefrom as the judge determines to be in the interests of justice.

(b) In addition to any other right to appeal, the United States shall have the right to appeal from an order granting a motion to suppress made under paragraph (a) of this subsection, or the denial of an application for an order of approval, if the United States attorney shall certify to the judge or other official granting such motion or denying such application that the appeal is not taken for purposes of delay. Such appeal shall be taken within thirty days after the date the order was entered and shall be diligently prosecuted.

(c) The remedies and sanctions described in this chapter with respect to the interception of electronic communications are the only judicial remedies and sanctions for nonconstitutional violations of this chapter involving such communications.

(11) The requirements of subsections (1)(b)(ii) and (3)(d) of this section relating to the specification of the facilities from which, or the place where, the communication is to be intercepted do not apply if--

(a) in the case of an application with respect to the interception of an oral communication--

(i) the application is by a Federal investigative or law enforcement officer and is approved by the Attorney General, the Deputy Attorney General, the Associate Attorney General, an Assistant Attorney General, or an acting Assistant Attorney General;

(ii) the application contains a full and complete statement as to why such specification is not practical and identifies the person committing the offense and whose communications are to be intercepted; and

(iii) the judge finds that such specification is not practical; and

(b) in the case of an application with respect to a wire or electronic communication--

(i) the application is by a Federal investigative or law enforcement officer and is approved by the Attorney General,the Deputy Attorney General, the Associate Attorney General, an Assistant Attorney General, or an acting Assistant Attorney General;

(ii) the application identifies the person believed to be committing the offense and whose communications are to be intercepted and the applicant makes a showing of a purpose, on the part of that person, to thwart interception by changing facilities; and

(iii) the judge finds that such purpose has been adequately shown.

(12) An interception of a communication under an order with respect to which the requirements of subsections(1)(b)(ii) and (3)(d) of this section do not apply by reason of subsection(11) shall not begin until the facilities from which, or the place where, the communication is to be intercepted is ascertained by the person implementing the interception order. A provider of wire or electronic communications service that has received an order as provided for in subsection (11)(b) may move the court to modify or quash the order on the ground that its assistance with respect to the interception cannot be performed in a timely or reasonable fashion. The court, upon notice to the government, shall decide such a motion expeditiously.

§ 2519.   **Reports concerning intercepted wire, oral, or electronic communications**

(1) Within thirty days after the expiration of an order (or each extension thereof) entered under section 2518, or the denial of an order approving the interception, the issuing or denying judge shall report to the Administrative Office of the United States Courts—

(a) the fact that an order or extension was applied for;

(b) the kind of order or extension applied for (including whether or not the order was an order with respect to which the requirements of sections 2518(1)(b)(ii) and 2518(3)(d) of this title did not apply by reason of section 2518(11) of this title);

(c) the fact that the order or extension was granted as applied for, was modified, or was denied;

(d) the period of interceptions authorized by the order, and the number and duration of any extensions of the order;

(e) the offense specified in the order or application, or extension of an order;

(f) the identity of the applying investigative or law enforcement officer and agency making the application and the person authorizing the application; and

(g) the nature of the facilities from which or the place where communications were to be intercepted.

(2) In January of each year the Attorney General, an Assistant Attorney General specially designated by the Attorney General, or the principal prosecuting attorney of a State, or the principal prosecuting attorney for any political subdivision of a State, shall report to the Administrative Office of the United States Courts—

(a) the information required by paragraphs (a) through (g) of subsection (1) of this section with respect to each application for an order or extension made during the preceding calendar year;

(b) a general description of the interceptions made under such order or extension, including (i) the approximate nature and frequency of incriminating communications intercepted, (ii) the approximate nature and frequency of other communications intercepted, (iii) the approximate number of persons whose communications were intercepted, and (iv) the approximate nature, amount, and cost of the manpower and other resources used in the interceptions;

(c) the number of arrests resulting from interceptions made under such order or extension, and the offenses for which arrests were made;

(d) the number of trials resulting from such interceptions;

(e) the number of motions to suppress made with respect to such interceptions, and the number granted or denied;

(f) the number of convictions resulting from such interceptions and the offenses for which the convictions were obtained and a general assessment of the importance of the interceptions; and

(g) the information required by paragraphs (b) through (f) of this subsection with respect to orders or extensions obtained in preceding calendar year.

(3) In April of each year the Director of the Administrative Office of the United States Courts shall transmit to the Congress a full and complete report concerning the number of applications for orders authorizing or approving the interception of wire, oral, or electronic communications pursuant to this chapter and the number of orders and extensions granted or denied pursuant to this chapter during the preceding calendar year. Such report shall include a summary and analysis of the data required to be filed with the Administrative Office by subsections (1) and (2) of this section. The Director of the Administrative Office of the United States Courts is authorized to issue binding regulations dealing with the content and form of the reports required to be filed by subsections (1) and (2) of this section.

§ 2520.   Recovery of civil damages authorized

(a) **In general.** -- Except as provided in section 2511(2)(a)(ii) any person whose wire, oral, or electronic communication is intercepted, disclosed, or intentionally used in violation of this chapter may in a civil action recover from the person or entity which engaged in that violation such relief as may be appropriate.

(b) **Relief.**-- In an action under this section, appropriate relief includes--

(1) such preliminary and other equitable or declaratory relief as may be appropriate;

(2) damages under subsection (c) and punitive damages in appropriate cases; and

(3) a reasonable attorney's fee and other litigation costs reasonably incurred.

(c) **Computation of damages.**--(1) In an action under this section, if the conduct in violation of this chapter is the private viewing of a private satellite video communication that is not scrambled or encrypted or if the communication is a radio communication that is transmitted on frequencies allocated under subpart D of part 74 of the rules of the Federal Communications Commission that is not scrambled or encrypted and the conduct is not for a tortious or illegal purpose or for purposes of direct or indirect commercial advantage or private commercial gain, then the court shall assess damages as follows:

(A) If the person who engaged in that conduct has not previously been enjoined under section 2511(5) and has not been found liable in a prior civil action under this section, the court shall assess the greater of the sum of actual damages suffered by the plaintiff, or statutory damages of not less than $50 and not more than $500.

(B) If, on one prior occasion, the person who engaged in that conduct has been enjoined under section 2511(5) or has been found liable in a civil action under this section, the court shall assess the greater of the sum of actual damages suffered by the plaintiff, or statutory damages of not less than $100 and not more than $1,000.

(2) In any other action under this section, the court may assess as damages whichever is the greater of--

(A) the sum of the actual damages suffered by the plaintiff and any profits made by the violator as a result of the violation; or

(B) statutory damages of whichever is the greater of $100 a day for each day of violation or $10,000.

(d) **Defense.**-- A good faith reliance on--

(1) a court warrant or order, a grand jury subpoena, a legislative authorization, or a statutory authorization;

(2) a request of an investigative or law enforcement officer under section 2518(7) of this title; or

(3) a good faith determination that section 2511(3) of this title permitted the conduct complained of;

is a complete defense against any civil or criminal action brought under this chapter or any other law.

(e) **Limitation.**--A civil action under this section may not be commenced later than two years after the date upon which the claimant first has a reasonable opportunity to discover the violation.

§ 2521.   Injunction against illegal interception

Whenever it shall appear that any person is engaged or is about to engage in any act which constitutes or will constitute a felony violation of this chapter, the Attorney General may initiate a civil action in a district court of the United States to enjoin such violation.   The court shall proceed as soon as practicable to the hearing and determination of such an action, and may, at any time before final determination, enter such a restraining order or prohibition, or take such other action, as is warranted to prevent a continuing and substantial injury to the United States or to any person or class of persons for whose protection the action is brought.   A proceeding under this section is governed by the Federal Rules of Civil Procedure, except that, if an indictment has been returned against the respondent, discovery is governed by the Federal Rules of Criminal Procedure.

§ 2.50   Use of False Friends

No police agency can be effective unless it utilizes the services of undercover agents.   There is an old cliche that a detective is as good as his informant and no more.   The courts have recognized this need; however, they have placed certain restrictions on its use where other fundamental rights are infringed upon by undercover agents.   If, for example, an undercover agent represents himself to be a physician who is treating the defendant and exacts privileged information as a result of this role, the courts have said that this is a violation of fundamental right.   **N.Y.—PEOPLE. v. LEYRA**, 302 N.Y. 353, 98 N.E.2d 553.

There are six leading cases in this area of law that were decided by the United States Supreme Court.   They are **ON LEE v. UNITED STATES**, 343 U.S. 747, 72 S.Ct. 967, 96 L.Ed.1270 (1952); **LOPEZ v. UNITED STATES**, 373 U.S. 427, 83 S.Ct. 1381, 10 L.Ed.2d 462 (1963); **HOFFA v. UNITED STATES**, 385 U.S. 293, 87 S.Ct. 408, 17 L.Ed.2d 374 (1966); **OSBORN v. UNITED STATES**, 385 U.S. 323, 87 S.Ct.

429, 17 L.Ed.2d 394 (1966); **UNITED STATES v. RUSSEL**, 411 U.S. 423, 93 S.Ct. 1637, 36 L.Ed.2d 366 (1973); and **WEATHERFORD v. BURSEY**, 429 U.S. 545, 97 S.Ct. 837, 53 L.Ed.2d 30, 20 Cr.L. 3059 (1977).

In each of these cases the defendant petitioner relied on and confided in friends who later turned out to be government informers. The Supreme Court in divided decisions upheld the right of law enforcement authorities to use undercover false friends of the accused to get a conviction.

A slight deviation from this false friend doctrine took place in **MAINE v. MOULTON**, 474 U.S. 159, 106 S.Ct. 477, 88 L.Ed.2d. 481, 38 Cr.L. 3037 (1985). A codefendant who agreed to cooperate with the police was equipped with a body transmitter and then went to meet the other defendant to plan for their upcoming trial. The non-cooperating defendant made incriminating statements during this conference, some of which were used at trial. The United States Supreme Court held that the non-cooperating defendant was denied his right to counsel and affirmed the decision of the Supreme Judicial Court of Maine that held that the statements made by the non-cooperating defendant should be suppressed and remanded for a new trial.

A later case involving a similar issue occurred in **KUHLMANN v. WILSON**, 477 U.S. 436, 106 S.Ct. 2616, 91 L.Ed.2d. 364, 39 CrL 3207 (1986), where the respondent was confined in a cell with another prisoner who had agreed to act as a police informant. Respondent made incriminating statements to the informer who reported them to the police. Respondent moved to suppress the statements on the ground that they were obtained in violation of his First Amendment right to counsel. The case is a classic example of "never give up" motto of many attorneys. He went through the state courts and was unsuccessful. He applied to the Federal District Court on habeas corpus and was unsuccessful. He applied to the Federal District Court on habeas corpus and was unsuccessful in 1973. In 1980, he made several attempts in the state courts based upon a later United States Supreme Court decision and he was unsuccessful. Then he brought another habeas corpus petition in Federal District Court in 1982. The District Court denied relief but the Court of Appeals reversed. The United States Supreme Court held that if the defendant demonstrates that the police and their informant took some action, beyond merely listening, that was designed deliberately to elicit incriminating remarks, the defendant is entitled to an order of suppression. They found that in this case, the police did not go beyond listening to the defendant and hence reversed the Court of Appeals.

The Court decided differently when the informant in the same cell block was an undercover agent. In **ILLINOIS v. PERKINS** 496 U.S. 292, 100 S.Ct. 2394, 110 L.Ed.2d. 243, 47 CrL 2131 (1990), the Court concerned itself on whether Miranda warnings are necessary in this type of situation. The respondent was incarcerated on another charge and an undercover agent was placed in the same jail cellblock with the respondent and was able to get precise information on a murder that the respondent had committed. The Court in a 7-1-1 decision held that no Miranda warnings were necessary before asking questions that may elicit an incriminating response. The statements at issue in this case were voluntary and there is no federal obstacle to their admissibility.

§ 2.51   Privileged Communications

There are certain conversations between persons which, pursuant to common law, are privileged and are not admissible in evidence against an accused. Some states and the federal government have given these privileges further imprimatur by statutory enactment.

The privileges which now exist in many jurisdictions are conversations between spouses in the furtherance of the marriage relation, between attorney and client, physician and patient, clergyman and penitent, and newspaper reporter and his source information.

It is not the purpose of this text to treat these privileges in great detail because it is thought that such treatment belongs to a course in the law of evidence, and may be found in a text that I have written, entitled Law of Evidence for Criminal Justice Professionals, now in its third edition, published by West Publishing Co., St. Paul, MN 55164. However, it should be noted here that if a common law privilege or statutory privilege is invaded by undercover government agents, the courts will suppress the evidence as a violation of due process under the Fourteenth and Fourth Amendments to the United States Constitution. **PEOPLE v. LEYRA** (supra).

§ 2.52   Police Observation - Not a Search

It is a natural response for most people to feel intimidated if police officers in a police cruiser appear to be singling attention on that person. This situation arose in **MICHIGAN v. CHESTERNUT**, 486 U.S. 567, 108 S.Ct. 1975, 100 L.Ed.2d. 565, 43 CrL 3077 (1988), where a marked police cruiser containing four police officers engaged in routine patrol duties in metropolitan Detroit followed Michael Mose Chesternut when he began to run from a corner where he had been standing. He did this after he saw the patrol car nearing the corner where he was located. The police followed Chesternut around the corner to (as was testified to by one police officer) see where he was going. They quickly caught up with him and drove alongside him for a short distance. As they drove alongside him, the officers observed Chesternut discard a number of packets he pulled from his right-hand pocket. One of the officers retrieved and examined the packets and Chesternut stopped running. Based on the officer's experience as a paramedic, the officer believed that the packets contained codeine. He then arrested Chesternut for the possession of narcotics.

At the station house the police discovered in Chesternut's hatband, another packet of pills, a packet containing heroin and a hypodermic needle. The evidence was suppressed in the Michigan Courts on the grounds that the defendant having run at the sight of the police, did not justify the search and was violative of his Fourth Amendment rights. The Court, however, reversed the lower court's decision by holding that the test for determining whether law enforcement officers investigative pursuit of an individual constitutes a Fourth Amendment "seizure" is whether under all the circumstances surrounding the incident, a reasonable person would have believed that he was not free to leave. Police officers who followed a man for a short distance when he ran upon seeing this patrol car, but who in no way, signified an attempt to capture him or intrude on his freedom of movement, did not "seize" him for constitutional purposes and therefore were not required to have an objective basis for suspecting him of criminal activity. The Court accordingly reversed the lower court's and reversed the dismissal of the action.

In a later decision, **CALIFORNIA v. HODARI**, __U.S.__, 111 S.Ct. 1547, 113 L.Ed.2d. 690, 49 CrL 2049 (1991), a policeman in Oakland, California, was on patrol with another officer in an unmarked police vehicle in a high crime area. With the intuition of an experienced police officer, he saw something he didn't like. Four or five youths were huddled around a small red car parked at the curb. The officers were dressed in street clothes except that they wore jackets with "Police" embossed on both front and back. When the youths saw the officer's car approaching, they took flight. They all went in different directions.

The officers gave chase. One officer remained with the police vehicle and gave chase after the red car. Hodari ran with a companion through an alley. The other officer left the police vehicle and ran around the block in the street. Hodari, while running through the alley and later in the street, intermittently looked behind him to see if the officers were following him. Suddenly he and the officer who had run around the block came face to face in the street. Thereupon Hodari tossed away what appeared to be a small rock. The officer tackled Hodari, handcuffed him, and radioed for assistance. Hodari was found to have $130.00 in cash and a pager on his person and the rock tossed away was crack cocaine.

The question of the crack cocaine seizure was considered by the Court. The Court held that Hodari was not seized until he was tackled. The cocaine was not the fruit of a seizure and thus was not to be suppressed. This was a 7-2 decision by Justice Stevens joined by Justice Marshall.

§ 2.53   Conversations Not Protected by Fourth Amendment

There are many types of situations where the Fourth Amendment does not protect the contents of conversations. The Fourth Amendment is only designed to protect secrecy. Therefore if the conversation is not concealed in any way, it would be admissible at trial. If it can be shown that there is a threat to national security and the President proves that it was reasonable and it shall not be otherwise used or disclosed, except as is necessary to implement his/her power to obtain foreign intelligence information deemed essential to the security of the United States or to protect national security, he may eavesdrop without a warrant and the evidence is admissible at trial.   Omnibus Crime Control and Safe Streets Act of 1968—Title III, § 2511(3).

In every case where a government undercover agent is used, the speaker bears the risk that his friend is a government agent. If participants to a conversation make no effort to be secret, their conversation thus becomes public. For example, let us assume that two persons are engaged in a conversation in an airplane or train and they are conversing in a loud tone of voice, apparently not concerned that their conversation is being overheard by others. The use of this conversation against them at a trial would not be subject to the suppression order because they are not being deprived of their privacy in any way.

§ 2.54   Access to Federal Courts

The defendant in a state court who had an unlawful search and seizure problem from the time of **MAPP v. OHIO** had relatively easy access to the Federal Court after he/she had exhausted all state remedies. This was done by a petition for a writ of habeas corpus to a United States District Court within the Circuit of the State Court handling the matter. If the District Court denied the Habeas Corpus petition, the petitioners would appeal the denial to the Court of Appeals within the same Circuit as the United States District Court. If the

Court of Appeals affirmed the District Court's denial, the petitioner asked the United States Supreme Court for a writ of certiorari directed to the highest Court of the State from which the case arose, for the purpose of review. The procedure has been severely limited since the Court decided **STONE v. POWELL**, 428 U.S. 465, 96 S.Ct. 3037, 49 L.Ed.2d 1067 (1976). In that case the Court said that if a defendant in a state court had a full and fair consideration of their reliance on the exclusionary rule with respect to allegedly unlawfully seized evidence by the state courts at a trial and on direct review, the prisoner may not be granted federal habeas corpus relief on the ground that evidence obtained in an unconstitutional search or seizure was introduced at his trial.

Where a state prisoner brings a petition for a writ of habeas corpus to the Federal District Court, based on an alleged violation of a constitutional right, the petition should be denied, if it is shown that the petitioner was barred by a procedural default, from raising a constitutional claim on direct appeal without showing cause for and actual prejudice from the default. **ENGLE v. ISAAC**, 456 U.S 1001, 102 S.Ct. 1558, L.Ed.2d 783, 31 Cr.L. 3001 (1982). In that case the petitioner had not raised constitutional claims pursuant to an Ohio Rule of Criminal Procedure 30 and the Ohio Supreme Court dismissed his appeal.

If trial errors of a constitutional nature occur and the defendant fails to make a contemporaneous objection, the defendant is not able to get a collateral review by the United States Supreme Court unless it falls within the "cause and actual prejudice" standard under which a convicted defendant must show both "cause" excusing his double procedure default and "actual prejudice" resulting from the errors of which he complains. **U.S. v. FRADY**, 456 U.S. 152, 102 S.Ct. 2287, 71 L.Ed.2d. 816, 31 Cr.L. 3013 (1982).

§ 2.55   Suppressed Evidence - Impeachment Tool

In **U.S. v. HAVENS**, 446 U.S. 620, 100 S.Ct. 1912, 64 L.Ed.2d 559, 27 Cr.L. 3136 (1980) the Court allowed previously suppressed evidence to be used for impeachment purposes where a defendant's statement made in response to proper cross examination reasonably suggested by the defendant's direct examination, are subject to otherwise proper impeachment by the government albeit by evidence that had been illegally obtained and is inadmissible as substantive evidence of guilt, citing **HARRIS v. NEW YORK**, 401 U.S. 222 and **OREGON v. HASS**, 420 U.S. 714. In the instant case, the respondent arrived at Miami International Airport with another male person from Peru. As a result of a customs search, the other persons T shirt revealed pockets sewn into it containing cocaine. The respondent's luggage was searched and T shirts were found therein that had matching pieces of cloth cut out to that of the sewn pockets. These T shirts were suppressed by the District Court but when respondent took the stand in his trial, he denied knowledge as to the presence of T shirts in his luggage with pieces of the cloth missing. The evidence of the T shirts was admitted, over objection, and the jury was instructed to consider this evidence only with respect to the defendant's credibility. The Court of Appeals reversed but the United States Supreme Court held that it was proper to use this suppressed evidence for impeachment purposes.

In **JENKINS v. ANDERSON, WARDEN**, petitioner claimed that he acted in self defense in a homicide charge. However, he failed to notify the governmental authorities until two weeks after the killing. On his trial, he testified that he had acted in self defense and the prosecutor questioned him, over objection, about his two week silence. The Court held that this was no violation of his constitutional rights saying, inter alia, that while the Fifth Amendment prevents the prosecution from commenting on the silence of a defendant who asserts the right to remain silent during his criminal trial, it is not violated when a defendant who testified in his own defense is impeached by his prior silence. **JENKINS v. ANDERSON, WARDEN**, 447 U.S. 231, 100 S.Ct. 2124, 65

L.Ed.2d. 86, (1983).

§ 2.56   Seizure of Possessory Interest In Property
             Protected by Fourth Amendment - Mobil Homes

In **KATZ v. UNITED STATES**, 389 U.S. 347, 88 S.Ct. 507, 19
L.Ed.2d 576 (1967) the Court held that a violation of the
privacy of a telephone conversation constituted a search
and seizure. In **SODAL, et al. v. COOK COUNTY, ILLINOIS,
et al.**, ___U.S.___,113 S.Ct 538, 121 L.Ed.2d 450, 52 Cr
L 2031 (1992) the court extended the seizure doctrine
controlled by the Fourth Amendment to the non court
ordered assistance rendered in Deputy Sheriffs of Cook
County, Illinois, in the removal of a mobile home,
located in a trailer park, by the park owner.
      In the above case, the owner of a trailer park had
not obtained an eviction order and this fact was known to
three Deputy Sheriffs and a Deputy Lieutenant Sheriff who
were all present while employees of the trailer park,
disconnected connections of the subject trailer and moved
the trailer out of the park, over the objections of the
trailer's owner. One Deputy Sheriff told the owner that
"he was there to see that (Sodal) didn't interfere with
(Willoway's) work." Willoway was the name of the trailer
park's owner.
      In a unanimous decision by J. White, the Court held,
inter alia, citing **UNITED STATES v. JACOBSEN**, 466 U.S.
109, 113 where the Court explained that the first clause
of the Fourth Amendment:

      "protects two types of expectations, one involving
      'searches'the   other   involving 'seizures'. A
      'search' occurs when an expectation of privacy that
      society is prepared to consider reasonable is
      infringed. A 'seizure' of property occurs where
      there is some meaningful interference with the
      individual's possessory interests in that
      property."

The Court went on to say that "What matters is the
intrusion on the people's security from governmental

194

interference on the people's security from governmental
interference."... "The facts alleged suffice to
constitute a "seizure" within the meaning of the Fourth
Amendment, for they plainly implicate the interests
protected by that provision."
        The reader may wonder how the violation by
government officers violated the Fourth Amendment when
there was no criminal activity involved in this case.
The answer to that is that Sodal had brought a Title 42
Section 1983 damage action against the Sheriffs and Cook
County for civil damages and the case had been dismissed
in the United States District Court, and the U.S. Court
of Appeals for the Seventh Circuit, sitting en banc,
affirmed the trial court wherein it held, inter alia,
that the Fourth Amendment would be triviolized if it was
called into play in suits involving property interests
when liberty or privacy were not at stake. The United
States Supreme Court could not concur with the lower
courts in this interpretation.

§ 2.57   Racketeer Influenced and Corrupt Organizations
           Act (RICO)

        A new weapon of law enforcement has been introduced
in various prosecutions wherein the proceeds of criminal
activity are confiscated by the government. It is known
as a combination of two statutes. They are the Racketeer
Influenced and Corrupt Organizations Act (RICO) and the
Civil Remedies for Racketeering Activity Act (CRRA).
These were initially federal acts but many states have
adopted similar statutes.
        If you are interested in reading the text of the
federal RICO statute and its criminal and civil
penalties, they may be found in 18 U.S.C.A. 1961, 1962,
1963, 1964 of chapter 96.
        Indiana has such a law and it was applied against
Fort Wayne Books Inc. and also against Ronald W.
Sappenfield in connection with their operation of adult
bookstores. The police seized the assets and the
bookstores as a result of arrests for misdemeanor
obscenity violations and the cases found their way into
the United States Supreme Court. In essence the Court

said that the Indiana statutes were constitutional. The
Court further held that the United States Supreme Court
had jurisdiction to hear the cases but the bookstores and
their contents could not be seized until there was a
judicial determination of the obscenity.

To seize the bookstores and their contents prior to
a judicial determination of obscenity is a First
Amendment and Fourth Amendment violation. **FORT WAYNE
BOOKS INC. v. INDIANA, ET. AL. AND SAPPENFIELD, ET. AL.
v. INDIANA,** 489 U.S. 109 S.Ct. 916, 103 L.Ed.2d. 34, 44
Cr. L. 3039 (1989)

CHAPTER 3   **LIABILITIES OF LAW ENFORCEMENT OFFICERS**

Contents

§ 3.1 Caveats to the Reader

In summation, I do not believe a treatise such as this is complete, unless I bring to the attention of the reader certain caveats, the knowledge thereof, will prevent a miscarriage of justice and many sleepless nights. They are contained in the following sections.

§ 3.2 Civil Weapons Available for Violations of Civil Rights

As the Due Process Clause of the Fourteenth Amendment continues to be interpreted by the Court in a way that almost every violation of the Bill of Rights has been incorporated into state law, it becomes increasingly necessary for state personnel and especially state law enforcement persons to be aware of the laws to prevent a devastating damage action against them. One of the weapons which is being used by aggrieved persons is a civil action instituted in the federal court under authority of 42 U.S.C. 1983.
This statute reads as follows:

"Every person who, under color of any statute, ordinance, regulation, custom, or usage, of any State or Territory, subjects, or causes to be subjected, any citizen of the United States or any other person within the jurisdiction thereof to the deprivation of any rights, privileges, or immunities secured by the Constitution and laws, shall be liable to the party injured in any action at law, suit in equity, or other proper proceeding for redress."

The phrase "under color of any statute, ordinance, regulation, custom or usage" has been applied to police officers who misuse their authority. A state could not be expected to violate the statute in the present-day setting. However, a police officer acting on his/her own could do so while acting under the guise of a police officer.
The statute, along with 18 U.S.C. 241 and 18 U.S.C. 242, was adopted in 1871. It was initially known as the

Ku Klux Klan Act and was designed to afford a federal remedy to aggrieved persons who suffered constitutional deprivations at the hands of the Ku Klux Klan. The Klan claimed as its members the leading citizens of the community as well as the lowest and, hence, state law enforcement was not interested in protecting persons who were the subject of Klan action. Nevertheless, the law was rarely invoked successfully until 1941 when the Court decided the **UNITED STATES v. CLASSIC**, 313 U.S. 299, 61 S.Ct. 1031, 85 L.Ed. 1368, wherein the Court said, "Misuse of power, possessed by virtue of a state law and made possible only because the wrongdoer is clothed with authority of state law, is action taken 'under color of state law.'" Accordingly, the stage was set for a meaningful redress of an aggrieved person's claim. A line of cases then developed to hold the officer accountable in attempts of circumvention of the law. For example, an officer cannot escape liability by being dressed in plain clothes and while riding in an unmarked car. **CATLETTE v. UNITED STATES**, 132 F.2d 902 (4th Circ. 1943). Of utmost importance to the officer should be the knowledge that the Court has held that neither the city (employer) nor the police department of which he is a member is liable in damages for the officer's behavior. The officer is the one who must pay the judgment if it is found that there is liability.

　　　　Federal law enforcement agents are not subject to this statute.

　　　　It was not until the 1960s, however, that this law was rediscovered and it became popular to sue state law enforcement persons. In **MONROE v. PAPE**, 365 U.S. 167, 81 S.Ct. 473, 5 L.Ed.2d 492 (1963), the plaintiffs, husband and wife along with their children, had gone to bed for the night when thirteen Chicago policemen broke into their apartment during the early morning hours. The plaintiffs were caused to get out of bed and to stand naked while the officers ransacked every room, ripping mattress covers and emptying drawers. The husband was then taken to the police station and held on open charges for ten hours during which time he was questioned about a murder which had taken place two days prior to the arrest. He was not taken before a magistrate even though one was available and he was denied contact with his family or an attorney. The policemen had no search

warrant for the initial intrusion and no written charges
were lodged against him. He was released after the long
interrogation. His action against the thirteen officers
was successful.

If, however, an officer acts in good faith and a law
under which he acted is later declared to be
unconstitutional, the officer cannot be held liable for
damages. **PIERSON v. RAY**, 386 U.S. 547, 87 S.Ct. 1213, 18
L.Ed.2d 288 (1967).

In a case brought under 42 U.S.C. 1983, the
petitioners sought pecuniary as well as injunctive
relief. The Court held that the responsible authorities
were not found to have affirmatively sanctioned any
constitutional deprivations, and thus no equitable relief
would be granted. **RIZZO v. GOODE**, 423 U.S. 362, 96 S.Ct.
598, 46 L.Ed.2d 56 (1976).

It should be noted that pursuant to **IMBLER v.
PACHTMAN**, 424 U.S. 409, 94 S.Ct. 984, 47 L.Ed.2d 128
(1975), the court held that prosecutors and judges are
not subject to suits under this statute but they are
liable under 18 U.S.C. 241 and 18 U.S.C. 242.

Later, **MONELL v. DEPARTMENT OF SOCIAL SERVICES**, 436
U.S. 658, 98 S.Ct. 2018, 56 L.Ed.2d 611 (1978), overruled
MONROE v. PAPE, 365 U.S. 167, 81 S.Ct. 473, 5 L.Ed.2d 492
(1961). In the Monell case, the Court permitted
plaintiffs to sue local government for monetary,
declaratory, or injunctive relief where the action was
grounded on allegations of an unconstitutional policy,
statement, ordinance, regulation, or decision officially
adopted by the body's officers or where constitutional
deprivation was visited on the plaintiffs pursuant to
governmental "custom" even though such custom had not
received formal approval through the body's decision-
making channel. It further held that local governmental
officials were "persons" under Section 1983 in those
cases where local government would be able to be sued in
its own name. A municipality could not be held liable
under Section 1983 solely on a respondeat superior theory
and stare decisis did not bar overruling of **MONROE v.
PAPE**.

In **SMITH v. WADE**, 461 U.S. 30, 103 S.Ct. 1625, 75

L.Ed.2d. 632, 33 Cr.L. 3013 91983), a prison guard was found liable for punitive damages where he was found to be guilty of gross negligence, or gregarious failure to protect a youthful inmate from harassment, beating and sexual assault.

An interesting case involving a police officer's liability arose in **HARING v. PROSISE**, 462 U.S. 306, 103 S.Ct. 2368, 76 L.Ed.2d. 595, (1983). In that case a defendant pleaded guilty to a charge of manufacturing a controlled substance. At the hearing, one of the arresting officers testified regarding the search of the defendant's apartment that led to the discovery of the contraband material prior to their obtaining a search warrant. No objection was made at the time of trial to the search but while defendant was confined, he filed a pro se action for damages under 42 USC 1983. The Court held that even though the defendant made no objection to the search at the time of trial or sentencing, he was not barred from prosecuting the action later if it was not previously litigated, even though Virginia had a collateral estoppel policy which would bar his subsequent civil challenge to police conduct. The author recommends that in cases where a plea is negotiated, if there is any possible civil liability on the part of law enforcement personnel, that an agreed statement be recorded in open court that the state, city, county and village, its officers employees and/or agents are to be relieved of any civil or criminal liability in connection with the search, arrest and/or confinement of the defendant, as a condition for the acceptance of the plea by the presiding judge.

BRANDON v. HOLT, 469 U.S. 464, 105 S.Ct. 873, 83 L.Ed.2d. 878 (1985) appears to have modified MONELL (supra). In the **BRANDON v. HOLT** case, the Director of Police of the Memphis Police Department was named as a defendant in a civil rights action under 42 U.S.C. 1983. The lower courts rejected plaintiff's contention that the suit against the Director of Police was being brought against him in his representative capacity. However, the United States Supreme Court held. The City was not named as a defendant because the complaint was filed before **MONROE v. PAPE** (supra). There is a distinction between suing a government official in his individual capacity and suing him in a representative capacity. In this case

he was being sued in a representative capacity and thus
a judgment against a public servant "in his official
capacity" imposes liability on the entity that he
represents.

In **OKLAHOMA CITY v. TUTTLE**, 471 U.S. 808 105 S.Ct.
2427, 85 L.Ed.2d. 791, 37 Cr.L. 3067 (1985) the Court
held that a city could not be held liable for a 42 U.S.C.
1983 violation by a single incident of unusual excessive
use of force by a police officer.

Municipalities sued for damages under 42 U.S.C. 1983
for constitutional violations are not entitled to
qualified immunity on the good faith of their officials.
OWENS v. CITY OF INDEPENDENCE, 445 U.S. 622, 100 S.Ct.
1398, 63 L.Ed.2d. 673, reh den, 446 U.S. 993, 100 S.Ct.
2979, 64 L.Ed.2d. 850, 27 Cr.L. 3047 (1980). This was a
case where the petitioner, a Chief of Police of
Independence, Missouri was dismissed by the City Manager
without notice of reasons, charged, that his dismissal
was without a hearing in violation of his constitutional
rights to procedural and substantive due process in
violation of his constitutional rights. The petitioner
brought an action under 42 USC 1983 against city
officials in the City. The District Court entered
judgement for respondents. The Court of Appeals affirmed
saying although the petitioner's Fourteenth Amendment
rights were violated all respondents were entitled to
qualified immunity from liability based on the good faith
of the officials involved. The Supreme Court reversed.

In **CARLSON v. GREEN**, 454 U.S. 944, 102 S.Ct. 484, 70
L.Ed.2d. 254, reh den 454 U.S. 1093, 102 S.Ct. 661, 70
L.Ed.2d. 633. (1980) Same case below, 649 F.2d. 285 the
Court held that a **BIVENS v. SIX UNKNOWN FEDERAL NARCOTICS
AGENTS**, 403 U.S. 388, remedy was available to a mother
whose son had died in a federal prison in Indiana after
he had suffered personal injuries while in prison and
petitioner claimed that her son's Eighth Amendment rights
were violated by prison officials by failing to give him
proper medical attention. She asserted jurisdiction
under 28 USC Section 1331(a). In this case, there were
additional jurisdiction problems in that the damages were
limited to that provided by Indiana's survivorship and

wrongful death laws which the trial court said was insufficient to meet Section 1331 (a)'s $10,000 jurisdictional amount requirement. The Court of Appeals reversed, saying that the federal common law (Bivens) allows survival of the action. The Supreme Court affirmed.

The case of **STONE v. POWELL**, 428 U.S. 465, 96 S.Ct. 3037, 49 L.Ed.2d. 1067, 19 Cr.L. 3333 (1976) prevented a state prisoner from bringing a federal habeas corpus challenge to an adverse state court ruling on a motion to suppress unconstitutionally seized evidence when the state courts had a full and fair hearing.

In **ALLEN v. CURRY**, 452 U.S. 965, 101 S.Ct. 3118, 69 L.Ed.2d. 977, 28 Cr.L. 3009 (1980) the defendant had made a motion in a Missouri court to suppress evidence. The motion was denied and he was later convicted. No assertion was made that he was denied a full and fair hearing in state court and he was thus barred from federal habeas corpus relief. He brought an action for damages under Title 42 Section 1983 and the defense claimed that the matter of constitutionality was res judicata in the state court and that the Federal District Court should dismiss the case based on the theory of collateral estoppel. The two lower courts disagreed on this issue. The Supreme Court granted certiorari and agreed with the prosecution.

Punitive damages are usually incorporated into a statute to cause the potential wrongdoer to think at least a second time when the perpetrator is about to commit an offense. It is used as an additional deterrent to prevent violations of law. Title 42 Section 1983 of the United States Code provides for punitive damages against an offender with the deterrent effect in mind. The question then arose as to whether this was to apply to a Municipality as well as an individual who had been found liable under this statute.

In the case of **CITY OF NEWPORT ET AL v. FACT CONCERTS, INC. and MARVIN LERMAN**, 453 U.S. 247, 101 S.Ct. 2748, 69 L.Ed.2d. 616, 29 Cr.L. 3105 (1981) after disposing of procedural questions, which are not relevant to our studies, the Court held that considerations of public policy do not support exposing municipalities to punitive damages for malicious or reckless conduct of its officials.

203

There was a serious question as to the civil liability of assigned counsel who represent indigent defendants as to whether they were liable under Title 42 Section 1983 of the United States Code. Many members of the private bar, not wishing to expose themselves to potential civil liability under this statute, were refusing to represent these clients. The matter was finally determined when on December 14, 1981 Supreme Court handed down its decision in **POLK COUNTY ET AL PETITIONERS v. RUSSEL RICHARD DODSON**, 454 U.S. 312, 102 S.Ct.445, 70 L.Ed.2d. 509, 30 Cr.L. 3033 (1981) where the court held that a public defender does not act "under color of state law" when performing a lawyer's traditional functions as counsel to an indigent defendant in a state criminal proceeding.

In that case, Martha Shepard, an attorney in the Polk County, Iowa, Offender Advocate's Office, moved for permission to withdraw as counsel on the ground that respondent's claims were legally frivolous. The respondent brought suit under Title 42 Section 1983 for damages on the grounds that the attorney had failed to represent him adequately in an appeal to the Iowa Supreme Court. The United States Supreme Court dismissed the action on the theory indicated above. The attorney is however still liable under a common law malpractice claim but there are certain limitations on that claim, not relevant to a study of constitutional law.

Mentally retarded persons who are involuntarily committed in a state institution, have a Title 42 Section 1983 cause of action for failure of those in charge of the institution to provide safe conditions of confinement, freedom from unreasonable bodily restraints, and such minimally adequate training as reasonably required of such interests but the proper standard for determining whether the state has adequately protected such interests and rights is whether professional judgment was exercised. This can be established by proof of a qualified professional's judgement that is entitled to a presumption of correctness. **MILLS v. ROGERS**, 457 U.S. 291, 102 S.Ct. 2442, 73 L.Ed.2d. 2616, 31 Cr.L. 3071 (1982).

Ordinarily it is incumbent upon a litigant seeking redress against a state for violations of a federal constitutional right to exhaust state remedies before the Federal Court is authorized to entertain jurisdiction. However in **PATSY v. FLORIDA BOARD OF REGENTS**, 457 U.S. 496, 102 S.Ct. 2557, 73 L.Ed.2d. 172, 31 Cr.L. 3089 (1982) the United States Supreme Court held that in a Title 42 Section 1983 case, there is no exhaustion requirement except in the case of adult prisoners bringing actions pursuant to that law.

Police officers have thought themselves to be highly vulnerable to an 1983 civil rights action. Judges have been held immune to this cause of action in **PIERSON v. RAY**, 386 U.S. 547; prosecutors in **IMBLER v. PACHTMAN**, 424 U.S. 409; legal aid attorneys in **POLK COUNTY, ET AL, v. DODSON** 454 U.S. 312, 102 S.Ct. 445, 70 L.Ed.2d. 509, 30 Cr.L. 3033 (1981); and in 1983 in the case of **BRISCOE v. LAHUE**, 460 U.S. 325, 103 S.Ct. 1108, 75 L.Ed.2d. 96, 32 Cr.L. 3073 (1982) the Court held that a police officer is immune from suit for damages under 42 USC 1983 brought by a former criminal defendant on the basis, as alleged, that the officer perjured his testimony at the defendant's criminal trial.

We usually think of a Title 42 Section 1983 action as applicable to an officer of government who deprives someone of civil rights in violation of the United States Constitution. In **WEST v. ATKINS** this concept was expanded to include a private physician's actions when, while under contract to North Carolina to provide orthopedic services at a state-prison hospital on a part-time basis, treated a prisoner in an allegedly inadequate manner. The Court held that since a State law prohibited the prisoner from employing or electing to see a physician of his own choosing the physician who is under contract with the State to provide medical services to inmates at a state prison on a part-time basis and "under color of State law, is within the meaning of 1983 when he treats an inmate. **WEST v. ATKINS**, 487 U.S. 42, 108 S.Ct. 2250, 101 L.Ed.2d. 40, 43 Cr L 3091 (1988).

The Court held in **WILL v. MICHIGAN DEPARTMENT OF STATE POLICE**, 491 U.S. 58, 109 S.Ct. 2304, 105 L.Ed.2d. 45, 45 Cr L 3087 (1989), that neither a state nor its officials acting in their official capacities are "person(s)" under 42 U.S.C. 1983 who may be sued for

205

depriving a citizen of constitutional or statutory rights
while acting under color of law. This is not contrary to
MONELL v. NEW YORK CITY DEPARTMENT OF SOCIAL SERVICES,
436 U.S. 658 (1978), which held that a municipality is a
person under section 1983, since States are protected by
the Eleventh Amendment while municipalities are not. The
Court held that a suit against state officials in their
official capacities is not a suit against the officials,
but rather is a suit against the officials office and
thus is no different from a suit against the state
itself. This was a 5-4 decision in which there were
strong dissents by Justices Brennan, Marshall, Blackman,
and Stevens.

In **GRAHAM v. CONNOR**, 490 U.S. 386, 109 S.Ct. 1405,
104 L.Ed.2d. 443, 45 Cr L 3033 (1989), the Court was
confronted with a case involving a claim of police
officers using constitutionally excessive force in
subjecting a free citizen to an arrest, investigative
stops or other seizure of his person. In that case the
plaintiff, Dethorne Graham, brought a Title 42, Section
1983 action for damages because of what he claimed was an
excessive use of force against him.

It appears that Mr. Graham was a diabetic and he
felt the symptoms of a diabetic insulin reaction coming
on. In such a case it is imperative that the diabetic
ingest sugar to counter this reaction. He requested a
friend to drive him to a convenience store to purchase
orange juice. He entered the store and became impatient
when he found a number of people waiting to be served.
He quickly exited the store and asked his friend to drive
him to another friend's house. Connor, a police officer,
became suspicious, and followed the car in which Graham
was a passenger. He made an investigatory stop, ordering
the pair to wait until he found out what happened in the
store. Connor's back-up officers arrived at the scene,
handcuffed Graham, in spite of the fact that Graham's
driver and friend informed Connor that Graham was
suffering from a "sugar reaction." One of the back-up
officers rolled Graham over on the sidewalk, and cuffed
his hands tightly behind his back ignoring his friend's
pleas to get him sugar. Another officer said "I've seen

206

a lot of people with sugar diabetes that never acted like this. Ain't nothing wrong with the M.F. but drunk. Lock the S.B. up." Several officers then lifted Graham up from behind, carried him over to his friend's car, and placed him face down on its hood. He had been unconscious at this time. While on the hood of his friend's care, he regained consciousness and asked the officers to check his wallet for a diabetic decal that he carried. One of the officers told him to shut up and shoved his face against the hood of the car. A friend of Graham's brought orange juice but the officers refused to let him have it. Finally, officer Connor received a report that Graham had done nothing wrong at the convenience store and released him. Graham sustained a broken foot, cuts on his wrists, a bruised forehead, and an injured shoulder. He also claims to have developed a loud ringing in his ear that continued to the day of the appeal in the United States Supreme Court. This is a bizarre course of events that might have been at least partially avoided if the officers had been made knowledgeable of the symptoms of insulin reaction. The author believes that if it was found that their employer had not taught its officers of the possibility of confusing this reaction with the symptoms of alcoholic intoxication or drug intoxication, the employer should have been named as a party defendant in this action. While it is difficult for an officer to arrive at a proper diagnosis in the case of indulgence in a controlled substance case, all the officers had to do in this case where they said that he was drunk, would have been to smell his breath. If he had an alcoholic breath, he might be intoxicated with alcohol, but if he had no alcoholic breath, this would rule out the characterization of one of the police officers saying, "Ain't nothing wrong with the M.F. but drunk."

Returning to the legal issues involved in this case, the District Court granted respondent's motion for a directed verdict that included whether the force was applied in a good faith effort to maintain and restore discipline or maliciously and sadistically for the very purpose of causing harm. The Court of Appeals affirmed, rejected Graham's argument that it was error to require him to prove that the allegedly excessive force was applied maliciously and sadistically to cause harm and

SECTION 3.2   Civil Weapons Available for Violation of
                     Civil Rights

holding that a reasonable jury could not find that the
force applied was constitutionally excessive.
     The Supreme Court reversed the Court of Appeals in
holding that the reasonableness standard of the Fourth
Amendment should control this situation.   The Court
continued by writing, "Determining whether the force used
to effect a particular seizure is "reasonable" under the
Fourth Amendment, requires careful balancing of the
nature and quality of the intrusion on the individual's
Fourth Amendment interests at stake." **UNITED STATES v.
PLACE**, U.s. 696 (703) (1983).
     BURNS   v.   REED, —U.S.—,   111   S.Ct.1934,   114
L.Ed.2d.547, (1991) decided May 30, 1991, held that State
prosecutors had absolute immunity from actions for
damages under 42 U.S.C. 1983 for participation in
probable cause hearing, but enjoy only qualified immunity
for their actions in giving advice to police officers.
     The issue here was he had advised police officers
that they could interrogate an Indian woman while she was
under hypnosis.   While the subject woman was under
hypnosis she referred to herself and the assailant as
"Katie."   Interpreting this as support for their
multiple-personality theory, the officers detained the
woman (Burns) and sought the advice of Reed (a State
prosecutor).   He told them that they "probably had
probable cause to arrest her."
     During a probable cause hearing, one of the officers
in response to Reed's questioning testified that Burns
had confessed to the shootings of her sons while they
slept. Neither Reed nor the officer informed the judge
at this hearing that the "confession" was obtained under
hypnosis or that Burns had consistently denied her guilt.
     The Court reaffirmed absolute immunity from damages
under 42 U.S.C. 1983 pursuant to **IMBLER v. PACHTMAN** 424
U.S. 409 (1976) where a prosecutor was acting in a quasi-
judicial role as the advocate of the state but when his
actions were taken pursuant to his investigative or
administrative duties, he would receive only qualified
immunity accorded to police officers. Here the Court
held that he was acting in an investigative, or
administrative duty in advising the police officers how

                           208

to get the confession out of her. The fact that neither the police or Reed advised the judge at the probable cause hearing that the confession was obtained while she was hallucinated and that she had otherwise consistently denied her guilt all caused the immunity defense to fall.

§ 3.3   Criminal Weapon Available for Violations of Civil Rights

Under the common law, if one is aggrieved, the injured party may elect his remedy either at civil law or criminal law. Both remedies were not simultaneously available. However, most states have enacted legislation making both remedies available for one injury. These statutes are said to be in derogation of the common law. So, too, has Congress made simultaneous criminal statutes available to an aggrieved who under color of state law has been deprived of a federal constitutional or statutory right. The remedy is to be found in 18 U.S.C. 241 and 18 U.S.C. 242.

It is to be noted that a criminal action requires proof beyond a reasonable doubt whereas a civil action merely requires a preponderance of the credible evidence, i.e., mere tipping of the scale of justice, for the action to be successful. Accordingly, a conviction under the criminal remedy of Sections 241 and 242 infra is more difficult to accomplish than a recovery under Section 1983 supra. If the officer violates a local law as well as the federal law, he/she may be prosecuted in both jurisdictions.

18 U.S.C. 241 provides as follows:

"If two or more persons conspire to injure, oppress, threaten or intimidate any citizen in the free exercise or enjoyment of any right or privilege secured to him by the Constitution or laws of the United States, or because of his having so exercised the same; or

If two or more persons go in disguise on the highway, or on the premises of another, with intent to prevent or hinder his free exercise or enjoyment of any right or privilege so secured-

209

They shall be fined not more than $5,000.00 or
imprisonment not more than ten years or both."

   Prior to 1966, this statute was thought to apply to
private persons not connected with the government.
However, the Court decided otherwise in that year in the
case of **UNITED STATES v. PRICE**, 383 U.S. 787, 86 S.Ct.
1152, 16 L.Ed.2d 267. This case grew out of the murder
of three civil rights workers, Andrew Goodman, Michael
Schwerner and James Chaney, in Mississippi. They were
intercepted by a deputy sheriff, taken to a lonely, dark
road and the deputy was there joined by two other law
enforcement officers and fifteen private persons who
collectively arranged to kill the young workers. The
Federal Justice Department instituted the procedure for
indictments under Section 241 for conspiring to "injure,
oppress, threaten and intimidate" the three victims "in
the free exercise and enjoyment of the right... not to be
deprived of life or liberty without due process of
law...." The United States District Court dismissed the
indictments reasoning that § 241 did not embrace
conspiracies to deprive an individual of due process of
law. However, the United States Supreme Court held that
to act under color of law does not require that the
accused be an officer of the state. "It is enough that
he is a willing participant in joint activity with the
State or its agents. Those who took advantage of
participation by state officers in accomplishment of the
foul purpose alleged must suffer the consequences of that
participation." The Court further held that the rights
covered in the statute included those rights of the
Fourteenth Amendment.
   18 U.S.C. 242 reads as follows:

"Whoever, under color of any law, statute,
ordinance, regulation or custom, wilfully
subjects any inhabitant of any State,
Territory or District to the deprivation of
any rights, privileges, or immunities, secured
or protected by the Constitution or Laws of
the United States.... shall be fined not more

than $1,000 or imprisoned not more than one
year, or both."

The Court interpreted the word "wilful" as requiring
a specific intent to deprive a person of a right which
had been made clear and definite either by express terms
of the Constitution or by laws of the United States, or
by decisions interpreting them. **SCREWS v. UNITED STATES**,
325 U.S. 91, 65 S.Ct. 1031, 89 L.Ed. 1495 (1945).

§ 3.4   Prisoners Rights Violation by Deliberate Indifference of Custodian

In **WILSON v. SEITER**, ___ U.S.___, 111 S.Ct.2321,
115 L.Ed.2d. 271, 49 Cr L 2263 (1991), the Court held
that in order for a prisoner to be successful in a Title
42 Section 1983 action, the complaint must prove that the
officials acted with the requisite mental state, i.e.,
deliberate indifference to their plight. In that case
the allegations in the complaining affidavit indicated
overcrowding, mixing of healthy inmates with others
having mental and physical ailments, excessive noise,
inadequate heating and cooling and lack of sanitation;
but not the state of mind of the respondents.

The majority however made clear that claims
involving particular conditions such as overcrowding and
inadequate cooling can be dismissed before the lower
court reaches the mental element, on the ground that they
do not attain the level of seriousness, required by the
objective proving of the Eighth Amendment. The court
cited **RHODES v. CHAPMAN**, 452 U.S. 337 (1981) holding that
some conditions can interact to produce a constitutional
violation does not mean that all prison conditions are a
"seamless web" for Eighth Amendment purposes.

Glossary of Legal Terms

The following glossary of legal terms is not intended to be exhaustive. It may be used by the student as an easily available aid to a better understanding of the text portion and the edited decisions contained in the preceding pages.

Ab Initio: From the first; from the beginning

Abstention: In constitutional law this term is sometimes used by a federal court when it declines to exercise its jurisdiction over a matter, pending a final determination of it in the courts of a state.

Abuse of Discretion: Legal name given to a court review of the actions of a trial court or administrative officer where petitioner claims that discretion exercised was arbitrary, discriminatory, and/or unreasonable.

Abuse of Process: The use of legal papers for a purpose other than intended by law, resulting in unlawful harassment to the recipient.

Accessory: One who aids in the commission or attempted commission of an offense or in assisting a perpetrator of an offense to avoid apprehension.

Accomplice: A person who voluntarily acts with another to commit or attempt to commit an offense, both persons having a shared criminal purpose.

Accusation: A charge of wrongdoing made against a person. It may include a prosecutor's information, a grand jury indictment, or a complainant's formal affidavit of complaint.

Acquittal: A finding that a defendant is not guilty of the offense for which he/she was charged.

Actus Reus: The guilty act as opposed to the mens rea which is the guilty mind.

Ad Hoc: For this particular purpose.

Adjudication: The judicial determination of a controversy between parties wherein judgment is pronounced. May also apply to administrative tribunals.

Admissible Evidence: All means by which any alleged matter of fact is proved or disproved which is permitted into a trial record pursuant to the law of the court's jurisdiction.

Admission: In criminal law, the voluntary statement made or an act done which is contrary to a person's position on trial. It falls short of a confession which is a direct acknowledgment of guilt.

Adversary: An opponent in a legal controversy.

Affiant: The person who subscribes his/her signature to an affidavit.

Affidavit: A statement in writing subscribed by a signature of a person which was affixed under oath before a notary public, a magistrate, or a commissioner of deeds.

Affirm: To attest to the truth of a statement or the act of an appellate court indicating that the ruling or decision of the lower court was correct.

A Fortiori: All the more; a term which is used which draws a conclusion by giving a reason; to the same effect.

Aid and Abet: To intentionally assist another to attempt to or to commit a criminal offense.

Alibi: A provable account of a person's whereabouts at a particular time which negates that person's involvement in a criminal offense.

Amicus Curiae: Friend of the court. Used frequently where nonlitigants submit memoranda of law to assist the court to render a decision in a pending matter.

Arraignment: A proceeding wherein the accused is informed of the nature of the charges against him/her. This is done before a judge or a magistrate. The accused

213

is asked how he/she pleads to the charges and bail conditions are sometimes set pending a trial at a later date.

Arrest: The initial taking into custody of a person by law enforcement authorities to answer for a criminal offense or violation of a code or ordinance.

Assault: Any unlawful attempt to inflict bodily injury upon another, accompanied by the apparent present ability to do the act.

Assignment of Error: An allegation made by appellant against trial judge charging error which is the ground for reversal.

Attainder: In common law, a mark of infamy given to a convicted felon resulting in loss of all civil rights. See bill of attainder.

Attempt: An overt act, beyond mere preparation, to commit an offense.

Bail: A pecuniary or other security accepted by a court or duly authorized officer to insure the appearance of a defendant at every stage of the proceedings up to final incarceration, dismissal, payment of fine, and/or sentence of probation.

Bailiff: A court attendant or court officer.

Bar: (Attorneys): Duly licensed attorneys are designated as being admitted to the bar of courts.

Bar (Procedure): A barrier to relitigating the same issue (position in court room). Defendant standing before the judge is called "prisoner at bar" (partition in court room separating judge, court personnel and attorneys litigating the instant case from others in court room).

Barrister: English practitioner of law who functions as a trial counsel.

Battery: The touching of another person done willfully and in anger.

Bench: The place where the judge or judges sit while in a courtroom.

Bench Warrant: A court order directing a law enforcement officer to seize a named person and bring that person before the court.

Bill of Attainder: A legislative act designed to inflict punishment upon a named person or persons without the benefit of a judicial trial. A legislature however has power to quell disorder in the chamber and may punish and/or incarcerate for contempt as long as accused has opportunity to appear and respond to charges.

Brief (Court use): A written argument presented to a judge, panel of judges, or an administrative law judge to persuade that person to decide an issue presently before the tribunal in favor of one of the litigants.

Brief (Student use): An epitome of a written decision which the student writes as an aid to remembering the legal history, questions of law, facts of the case, opinion and judgment of the court.

Burden of Proof: The requirement of a litigant to persuade the trier of the facts that the allegations made against the other party to an action are true. In criminal law, the government is required to prove its case beyond any reasonable doubt. In civil cases, the party bringing the action is required to prove the allegations by a preponderance of evidence. In administrative hearings, the allegations must be proven by substantial evidence or by clear and convincing evidence.

Caveat: A warning.

Certiorari: A common law writ issued from a higher court to an inferior court, commanding the inferior court to certify and send the record of a particular case, previously decided by the inferior court, to the higher court for review of the inferior court's actions in the case.

Circumstantial Evidence: Secondary facts from which a rational inference may be logically arrived at to prove a principal fact.

Citation: A written or printed command to a person to appear before a court on the day and time indicated. Also used as a location in a publication where a legal case may be found.

Civil Liberties: Courses of action that a person is entitled to which are immune from governmental interference. They may be limitations of governmental action, e.g., liberty of free speech guaranteed in the First Amendment of the United States Constitution.

Civil Rights: A course of action which a person is entitled to which is defined by positive laws enacted by government, e.g., right to bring a civil action against the government pursuant to statutory authority.

Clear and Convincing: A standard of proof beyond a mere preponderance but not as much as beyond a reasonable doubt. Usually that quantum of proof required of a party to prevail in an administrative tribunal. Similar to substantial evidence.

Clear and Present Danger: A limitation on the unfettered exercise of free speech such as shouting "fire" in a crowded theater when in fact there is no fire or no danger present.

Collateral Attack: A challenge to a judgment brought about indirectly and not by direct appeal, e.g., habeas corpus petition instead of appeal of a prior rendered judgment.

Collateral Estoppel: The determination of litigated facts is binding on those parties in all future proceedings against each other. The constitutional prohibition against double jeopardy enables a defendant to plead collateral estoppel if a primary issue was previously litigated and defendant's contention prevailed at former trial.

Comity: A judicial courtesy wherein one court yields to another court of concomitant jurisdiction based on the concept that a court which first asserts its jurisdiction will not be interfered with by another court, e.g., judgments of courts of competent jurisdiction of foreign nations are not interfered with by other state or federal courts based on comity.

Common Law: A system of jurisprudence which is derived from Anglo-Saxon law from principles, rather than rules, based on justice, reason, and common sense, judicially originated. The principles change with the needs of the community.

Competent (Court): One having proper jurisdiction.

Competent (Person): Capacity to understand and act reasonably.

Competent (Witness): Capacity to understand.

Confession: A direct acknowledgment of guilt.

Conjugal Visitation (Prison): Permission to engage in sexual intercourse between the inmate and his/her spouse.

Contempt of Court: An act or an omission tending to obstruct or interfere with the orderly administration of a court or to affect the dignity of a court.

Corporal Punishment: Pain inflicted upon a person as a means of correction or to prevent recidivism, e.g., whipping of a prisoner.

Crime: Any act which the government has declared to be contrary to the public good, which is declared by statute to be a crime and which is prosecuted in a criminal proceeding. In some jurisdictions crimes only include felonies and/or misdemeanors.

Crime against Nature: Deviant social behavior relevant to sexual acts, e.g., sodomy; sexual intercourse with a dead body.

Cruel and Unusual Punishment: Amorphous term which cannot be defined with specificity. Punishment which is shocking to reasonable persons. United States Supreme Court interprets this phrase on an ad hoc basis.

Custodial Interrogation: The confinement of a person by law enforcement agents/officers. The person is not free to leave and is questioned about a crime.

De Minimus: Insignificant; of no importance; not important enough to take the time and attention of the court.

Demurrer: An answer to a complaint which declares that even if all of the facts stated in the complaint are true, it does not state a cause of action. The court ruling on a demurrer may grant summary judgment for the prevailing party, thus terminating the case.

De Novo: To start for another time from the beginning.

Deposition: A statement of a person reduced to writing which is subscribed under oath or affirmation.

Dictum (Obiter dictum): A statement made by the court which is included in a judicial opinion and is not necessarily pertinent to the facts of the instant case. A dictum is not considered to be binding on future cases.

Discovery Process: Pretrial procedure whereby litigants supply information to their adversary before trial, which is necessary to the other party's position at trial.

Dismiss (Appeal): To place parties in same position as if no appeal were taken.

Dismiss (Legal): To terminate a court case without a trial.

Diversity of Citizenship: Where citizens of different states are litigants in an action. It may be cause for federal court jurisdiction if other requirements are met.

Domicile: A place of permanent residence where a person intends to return when absent. A person may have only one domicile but may have many residences.

Double Jeopardy: A person who is tried again for a crime which has been litigated to an acquittal or conviction is said to be twice placed in jeopardy if tried again for the same offense. A mistrial or appeal does not prevent a second trial unless the mistrial was the result of brash behavior by the prosecution in a obvious attempt to try the defendant at another time.

Due Process: A phrase without a fixed meaning. It has been interpreted by the U.S. Supreme Court as requiring a government to exercise fundamental fairness in the administration of criminal justice.

En Banc: By the full court.

Enjoin: A command by a court to do or refrain from doing a specific act.

Et Seq.: And the following.

Evidence: All matter of proof offered in a trial to prove or disprove an issue of fact.

Exclusionary Rule: A judicially contrived procedure which prevents evidence unconstitutionally obtained by law enforcement officers from being introduced into evidence at a criminal trial and is not to be considered by the triers of the facts of the case in arriving at a verdict.

Exculpatory: Statements or evidence which tends to prove that a person was not the perpetrator of a criminal offense.

Execute: The killing of a prisoner by authority of the government; the signing of a legal instrument.

Ex Post Facto Law: A law which declares designated behavior to be a crime which, when committed, was noncriminal; or increases the punishment after it was committed; or diminishes the requisite proof for conviction.

Fair Hearing: An extra judicial hearing usually authorized by statute to determine a controversy in an administrative tribunal. It must be conducted in a manner which includes an opportunity for all sides to

219

present evidence, e.g., 42 U.S.C.A. Sect. 602(a)(4) requiring fair hearing prior to termination of welfare benefits.

Felony: A crime for which a person may be imprisoned for at least a year and a day.

First Impression: The first time that a question of law has been decided by a court.

Frisk: The patting down of the outer clothing of a person who is suspected of carrying a concealed weapon.

Fruit of the Poisonous Tree Doctrine: If a law enforcement officer obtains information from a defendant in an unconstitutional manner, although that evidence is not used at the defendant's trial, other evidence ascertained as a result of the illegally obtained evidence is also excludable from the trial, based on the doctrine of the fruit of the poisonous tree. Such other evidence has been held to be admissible, however, for impeachment when defendant testifies.

Full Faith and Credit: Phrase applied to the United States Constitution which requires the "public Acts, Records and Judicial Proceedings of one state to be respected by each of the sister states, Art. 4, Sec. 1.

Grand Jury: A body of people (usually 23) who serve as part of the criminal justice system. The grand jury's function is to investigate and indict persons for crimes or render information or presentments for crimes committed in its territorial jurisdiction. It may also find that a complaint of criminal activity is not worthy of an indictment or information.

Guilty (Criminal): The finding beyond a reasonable doubt, by a jury or judge presiding without a jury, after a trial, or after a judicial confession of guilt, that a defendant committed the crime charged.

Habeas Corpus Writ: A court order requiring a person who has custody of another person to be present in court with the detainee so that the court can inquire as to the

220

legality of the detention. Writs of Habeas Corpus may be directed to a Commissioner of Prisons and may also be used in child custody and elderly guardianship litigation.

Harmless Error: Error conducted during a trial which an appellate court has concluded does not affect a defendant's substantial right to cause a reviewing court to reverse the judgment of the trial court.

Head Note: Summary of facts, questions of law, decision and judgment of a case.

Hearing: A proceeding where evidence is taken to determine issues of fact. It may be an administrative hearing, e.g., police agency disciplinary hearing; suppression hearing (to determine whether evidence was unconstitutionally seized); prima facie hearing (to determine if allegations constitute a crime). Some hearings do not require formal rules of evidence.

Hearsay Rule: In the law of evidence hearsay is not generally admitted into evidence unless the material offered is one or more of the recognized exceptions. (See Klein's *Law of Evidence for Police*, 2nd Edition. West Publishing Co., 1978). It is evidence which is restating what another person either orally said or wrote, when it is offered for the truth of the assertion.

Hung Jury: A trial jury which cannot agree on a verdict according to the number set forth by law in its jurisdiction. Most criminal courts require a unanimous vote for conviction. Some require a substantial majority, e.g., 10-2. A retrial does not subject the defendant to double jeopardy.

Ibid: In the same book or on the same page. It avoids repetition of source data.

Immunity: Usually a right of absolution from prosecution for a criminal act given to a witness to a crime in exchange for information given to a Grand Jury or prosecutor. A Grand Jury or a prosecutor has power to grant immunity.

Impeachment: Term applied to questions directed toward a witness who is testifying under cross-examination in an attempt to obtain contradictory statements to affect the credibility of the witness.

In Camera: In chambers of the judge. Chambers can mean the judge's office or it could mean the robing room adjacent to the court room.

Incriminate: To involve either one's self or another as responsible for criminal conduct.

Inculpatory: Tending to involve one's self or another as responsible for criminal conduct; incriminate.

Independent Source: Information acquired by a law enforcement agency which is not tainted by any violation of a constitutional right.

Indictment: A formal written accusation drawn up by a prosecutor and presented to a Grand Jury which then investigates the charge. If a prima facie crime is found, the foreman of the Grand Jury endorses the indictment as a "True Bill." If the charges are not substantiated, "No True Bill" is found and the indictment is so endorsed. It usually applies to felony offenses only.

Informant: A person who supplies information to a law enforcement officer referring to the commission of a crime or to some set of facts requiring the attention of the law enforcement agency.

In Loco Parentis: In the place of a parent.

Interrogation: Questioning of a person to ascertain facts.

Issue (In courtroom setting or controversy): A certain point of law or fact which is in dispute.

Judge (Trial Judge): The presiding officer in a trial whose duty it is to see that a fair, impartial, and orderly trial is conducted, adhering to the Constitution of the United States, the Constitution of the State (if

222

state jurisdiction), the laws of the court's jurisdiction and the rules of the court. The judge is an impartial arbiter who rules on the admissibility of evidence and motions of various types and instructs the fact triers as to the law of the case. Some jurisdictions give judges the title of "Justice."

Judgment: The final determination of the rights of parties to a lawsuit, whether civil or criminal, which determination is made by a judge or panel of judges, and which is entered in the clerk's records of the case.

Jury Charge (Judge's charge to jury): At the end of the testimony of a jury trial, each side indicates that it "rests." Thereupon it is the duty of the trial judge to explain the law of the case to the jury before it goes to the deliberation room. This is called "the Judge's Charge."

Lesser Included Offense: A crime or violation of law which is part of a more serious crime. A crime having less aggravating elements than a more serious crime which carries greater sanctions (punishment), e.g., larceny is a lesser included offense of robbery.

Lineup: A procedure where law enforcement officers select a number of persons to stand or sit next to each other to be viewed by witnesses or victims of crime to ascertain whether any or all of the selected persons committed a criminal offense. This is usually done before a one-way mirror with a suspect's attorney present and the proceedings are recorded.

Litigation: A controversy between parties which is brought to a court for determination of the issues.

Magistrate: A judicial officer authorized to conduct preliminary hearings, set bail conditions, administer oaths, and issue warrants. Most jurisdictions do not authorize magistrates to conduct trials of criminal offenses. A judge may also be a magistrate.

Malum in Se: Bad in itself; naturally evil, e.g., murder.

223

Malum Prohibitum: Bad or wrong because it is made unlawful by statute,. e.g., driving a vehicle on the wrong side of the street.

Mandamus Writ: A court order wherein the court orders a designated person (governmental official or corporate officer) to perform a designated act.

Mens Rea: A mental state required in criminal law; intention; criminal negligence (gross); reckless and/or knowing.

Misdemeanor: A class of criminal deviance which is usually punished by a maximum of $1,000 fine and/or up to one year in a country or city jail. It is less serious than a felony. Different jurisdictions classify misdemeanors and sanctions for violation thereof differently.

Mistrial: Where a prejudicial error occurs, a judge, on motion or sua sponte, may declare a mistrial. This has the effect of declaring the trial a nullity and does not preclude another trial of the same parties on the same facts. It is not a ground for a defense of double jeopardy.

Motion: An application to a judge or panel of judges requesting the relief desired, e.g., motion for a new trial.

Nisi Prius: In American law it has come to mean any court where a case is heard by a judge and jury for the first time. An appellate court is not a nisi prius court.

Nolo Contendere: From the Latin and common law courts where a defendant tells the court that he/she does not wish to interpose a defense or plea of not guilty in a criminal action. Some state courts do not permit a defendant to answer a charge in this way. The court must find a factual basis to accept this. It is not a confession of guilt. In criminal law it has the same effect as a plea of guilty.

N.O.V.: From the Latin—Non Obstante Verdicto. A motion for a judgment N.O.V., if granted, is one which reverses the conclusions reached by a jury because the court reasoned that based on the facts presented in the trial, the jury had no reasonable grounds to reach the conclusion indicated in its verdict.

Nunc pro Tunc: If a court order includes this phrase, it means that the action ordered to be taken reverts back to a specified time as if it had been taken at that time. It is frequently used to permit late filing of papers when it is in the interest of justice to permit such late filing.

Obiter Dicta: See dictum.

Opening Statement: This is a speech which the adversaries in a criminal trial make to the jury before any testimony is received in evidence. It is used to acquaint the jury with the facts and issues of a case which that litigant intends to prove. In criminal cases, many jurisdictions permit a defendant to waive a right to an opening statement.

Opinion: The reason that a judge gives for the court's conclusion. It differs from a decision which is the judgment of the court.

Oyer and Terminer: These were old English courts where the King would appoint a person to act as a judge to hear and determine a case forthwith, instead of waiting for the normal judicial procedure of the realm to prosecute, hear, and determine a criminal case.

Pardon: A power to forgive vested in the executive of the government, i.e., President, Governor. Its effect is to restore all rights to the defendant as if the defendant had never committed the criminal act for which s/he was pardoned.

Parole: This may be descriptive of a discretionary decision of an official or board of parole who has lawful authority to permit a prisoner to serve part of his/her sentence in the community. One who is on parole is serving part of the imposed sentence outside of confinement and in the community.

Perjury: A criminal offense where a person makes a false statement while under oath or affirmation.

Petition: A written request made to a court or governmental authority asking for an act to be done; sometimes referred to as a prayer for relief.

Plain View: This phrase is applied to items of evidence which a law enforcement officer sees without having violated a person's constitutional rights and which s/he came upon inadvertently while performing normal duties.

Plea: This is a formal answer to a charge against a defendant for a criminal offense, e.g., guilty, not guilty.

Plea Bargaining: This is a negotiation procedure where the criminal defendant's attorney discusses a possibility of the defendant's pleading guilty to a lesser included offense in return for the prosecutor's either not recommending a severs sanction or not proceeding to trial on the original charge.

Police Power: The power of the government to provide for the health, welfare, safety, morals, and general welfare of those persons within its territorial jurisdiction.

Preamble: A statement of purpose and intent which precedes the specific articles and sections of a constitution.

Preliminary Hearing: Usually a hearing held before a magistrate to determine if probable cause exists to hold a defendant for a trial or indictment. Bail conditions are sometimes set at the end of this hearing.

Presentment: An investigation and accusation of crime made by a Grand Jury, initiated by itself without the participation of the prosecutor. A prosecutor has the discretion not to sign a presentment and not to prosecute the accusation.

Prima Facie: If on the facts presented, unexplained, a defendant might be found guilty of a criminal offense in that all of the elements of a crime have been shown to exist, we say that the prosecution has proved a prima facie case.

Prison: This is a place where criminal defendants of the state or federal courts are incarcerated, usually after they have been found guilty. A jail is the term applied to City or County places of incarceration, usually used for detention while awaiting trial or incarceration for less serious offenses.

Probable Cause: The reasoning process that a reasonable person uses to conclude that (a) there is a good reason to make an arrest, and (b) there is a good reason to suspect that a person has contraband or evidence of crime in the suspect's possession.

Probation: A sanction imposed on those convicted of a crime wherein the offender is subject to conditions of behavior laid down by the judge. The defendant may be under the supervision of a probation officer to whom s/he must periodically report, or may be on a nonreporting status.

Pro Bono Publico: When attorneys represent a client without fee it is said that the representation is pro bono publico, i.e., for the public good.

Pro Se: For himself. Refers to a person arguing his/her own case instead of retaining an attorney.

Quasi: Almost; like; e.g., quasi-criminal proceeding which is almost like a criminal proceeding but not actually one; e.g., a parole revocation proceeding.

Question of Fact: An issue of what actually occurred at the time of the incident which brings the parties before the court. This issue is decided by a jury if the trial is one with a jury. If no jury is present, it is decided by the judge.

Question of Law: A dispute of what rule of law is applicable to the case at bar. The judge decides the issue of what rule of law is to determine the results in the instant case.

Quid pro Quo: Something in exchange for something, e.g., a witness may testify in behalf of the prosecution if the state will grant immunity from prosecution to the witness.

Quo Warranto: By what authority. This is an ancient common law writ.

Reasonable Doubt: Refers to the quantum of proof required to prove a defendant guilty in a criminal trial. The trier of the fact is required to come to the conclusion that a defendant is guilty beyond a reasonable doubt. This does not mean all doubt, but beyond the doubt that a reasonable person would have.

Reasonable Man (Person): This is a phrase which characterizes that a normal, average person with ordinary knowledge, intelligence, and judgment might do in a given set of circumstances. It is not necessarily what the particular judge hearing or reviewing the case might do but what a hypothetical normal person's actions might be, given the same factual situation.

Remand: To send back. Sometimes refers to a case being sent back to the court which decided it previously. Also refers to a prisoner being sent back to prison or detention facility.

Res Judicata (Res Adjudicata): The thing decided. The issue has previously been decided by a court of competent jurisdiction and thus is not to be relitigated.

Reversible Error: An error committed at the trial which substantially affected the outcome of the trial, that mandates either a new trial or a reversal of the outcome. Also known as "substantial error" or prejudicial error."

Revocation: Term used in connection with revocation of parole. It means that the parolee is returned to prison, usually to serve the remainder of his/her original sentence of incarceration.

Sanction: To permit one to do something. Also used to indicate punishment for violation of accepted behavior.

Search Warrant: A court order directing a law enforcement officer to search for and return to the court particular items of personal property to be used in the prosecution of a person for violation of a statute.

Selective Incorporation: This term has been used to indicate that the United States Supreme Court has absorbed most of the Bill of Rights into the minimum requirements that a state must afford to inhabitants but not every one of these rights. This has been done by the authority of the Fourteenth Amendment of the United States Constitution.

Show-up: This is to be distinguished from a lineup. In a show-up the suspect is exhibited singularly to a crime victim. This is usually done shortly after the crime has taken place where speed and the practicalities of the situation warrant this type of identification instead of a lineup.

Standing: A court's recognition of a party to a lawsuit that the party is properly before the court.

Star Chamber: An ancient English court whose jurisdiction and procedure became so onerous that it was abolished. The privilege against self-incrimination in America resulted from Star Chamber abuses.

Stare Decisis: To stand by decided cases; to decide cases based on precedent of what the courts have decided on similar issues in earlier cases.

Stop and Frisk: Refers to law enforcement's authority to stop a suspected person and pat that person's outer clothing to search for a concealed weapon. The officer must have reason to believe that the suspect is armed and dangerous.

Suppression of Evidence: When evidence is unconstitutionally obtained by law enforcement authorities, the defendant makes a motion to suppress this evidence. After a hearing before a judge, the judge will indicate that the motion is granted. This means that the prosecutor is not permitted to use the unconstitutionally obtained evidence in the trial of this defendant. Often the prosecutor is unable to proceed with the case without this evidence.

Trial: The legal proceeding where testimony is offered before a judge sitting without a jury, or a judge sitting with a jury, where issues of fact and law are determined.

True Bill: A Grand Jury finding that an indictment presented to it by the prosecutor is based on sufficient probable cause. The foreman then signs the indictment and it becomes a true bill.

Vacate: To make void; to set aside as though it never existed; to move out.

Verdict: The conclusion reached by a jury or judge deciding the facts as to the issues after the completion of other parts of a trial.

Waiver: A voluntary giving up of a known right, e.g., a waiver of jury trial wherein the defendant in a criminal action intentionally gives up his/her right to be tried by a jury.

Warrant (Criminal Law): A court order directing a law enforcement officer to perform an indicated act, e.g., search warrant, arrest warrant.

Writ: A court order directing a named person to perform a specifically indicated act.

Constitution of the United States of America - 1787[1]

[1]In May, 1785, a committee of congress made a report recommending an alteration in the Articles of Confederation, but no action was taken on it, and it was left to the State Legislatures to proceed in the matter. In January, 1786, the Legislature of Virginia passed a resolution providing for the appointment of five commissioners, who, or any three of them, should meet such commissioners as might be appointed in the other States of the Union, at a time and place to be agreed upon, to take into consideration the trade of the United States; to consider how far a uniform system in their commercial regulations may be necessary to their common interest and their permanent harmony; and to report to the several States such an act, relative to this great object, as, when ratified by them, will enable the United States in Congress effectually to provide for the same. The Virginia commissioners, after some correspondence, fixed the first Monday in September as the time, and the city of Annapolis as the place for the meeting, but only four other States were represented, viz: Delaware, New York, New Jersey, and Pennsylvania; the commissioners appointed by Massachusetts, New Hampshire, North Carolina, and Rhode Island failed to attend. Under the circumstances of so partial a representation, the commissioners present agreed upon a report, (drawn by Mr. Hamilton, of New York,) expressing their unanimous conviction that it might essentially tend to advance the interests of the Union if the States by which they were respectively delegated would concur, and use their endeavors to procure the concurrence of the other States, in the appointment of commissioners to meet at Philadelphia on the Second Monday of May following, to take into consideration the situation of the United States; to devise such further provisions as should appear to them necessary to render the Constitution of the Federal Government adequate to the exigencies of the Union; and to report such an act for that purpose to the United States in Congress assembled as, when agreed to by them and afterwards confirmed by the Legislatures of every State, would effectually provide for the same.

Congress, on the 21st of February, 1787, adopted a resolution in favor of a convention, and the Legislatures of those States which had not already done so (with the exception of Rhode Island) promptly appointed delegates. On the 25th of May, seven States having convened, George Washington, of Virginia, was unanimously elected President, and the consideration of the proposed constitution was commenced. On the 17th of September, 1787, the Constitution as engrossed and agreed upon was signed by all the members present, except Mr. Gerry of Massachusetts, and Messrs. Mason and Randolph, of Virginia. The president of the convention transmitted it to Congress, with a resolution stating September, 1787, directed the Constitution so framed, with the resolutions and letter concerning the same, to "be transmitted to the several Legislatures in order to be submitted to a convention of delegates chosen in each State by the people thereof, in conformity to the resolves of the convention."

On the 4th of March, 1789, the day which had been fixed for commencing the operations of Government under the new Constitution, it had been ratified by the conventions chosen in each State to consider it, as follows: Delaware, December 7, 1787; Pennsylvania, December 12, 1787; New Jersey, December 18, 1787; Georgia, January 2, 1788; Connecticut, January 9, 1788; Massachusetts, February 6 1788; Maryland, April 28, 1788; South Carolina, May 23, 1788; New Hampshire, June 21, 1788; Virginia, June 25, 1788; and New York, July 26, 1788.

The President informed Congress, on the 28th of January, 1790, that North Carolina had ratified the Constitution November 21, 1789; and he informed Congress on the 1st of June, 1790, that Rhode Island had ratified the Constitution May 29, 1790. Vermont, in convention, ratified the Constitution January 10, 1791, and was, by an act of Congress approved February 18, 1791, "received and admitted into this Union as a new and entire member of the United States."

WE THE PEOPLE of the United States, in Order to form a more perfect Union, establish Justice, insure domestic Tranquility, provide for the common defence, promote the general Welfare, and secure the Blessings of Liberty to ourselves and our posterity, do ordain and establish this Constitution for the United States of America.

Article I.

SECTION 1. All legislative Powers herein shall be vested in a Congress of the United States, which shall consist of a Senate and House of Representatives.

SECTION 2. The House of Representatives shall be composed of Members chosen every second Year by the People of the several States, and the Electors in each State shall have the Qualifications requisite for Electors of the most numerous Branch of the State Legislature.

No person shall be a Representative who shall not have attained to the Age of twenty five Years, and been seven Years a Citizen of the United States, and who shall not, when elected, be an Inhabitant of that State in which he shall be chosen.

[2]Representatives and direct Taxes shall be apportioned among the several States which may be included within this Union, according to their respective Numbers, which shall be determined by adding to the whole Number of free Persons, including those bound to Service for a Term of Years, and excluding Indians not taxes, three fifths of all other Persons. The actual Enumeration shall be made within three Years after the first Meeting of the Congress of the United States, and within every subsequent Term of ten Years, in such Manner as they shall be Law direct. The Number of Representatives shall not exceed one for every thirty Thousand, but each State shall have at Least one Representative; and until such enumeration shall be made, the State of New Hampshire shall be entitled to chuse three, Massachusetts eight, Rhode-Island and Providence Plantations one, Connecticut five, New-York six, New Jersey four, Pennsylvania eight, Delaware one, Maryland six, Virginia ten, North Carolina five, South Carolina five, and Georgia three.

When vacancies happen in the Representation from any

---

[2]This clause has been affected by the 14th and 16th amendments.

State, the Executive Authority thereof shall issue Writs of Election to fill such Vacancies.

The House of Representative shall chuse their Speaker and other Officers; and shall have the sole Power of Impeachment.

[3]SECTION 3. The Senate of the United States shall be composed of two Senators from each State, chosen by the Legislature thereof, for six Years; and each Senator shall have one Vote.

Immediately after they shall be assembled in Consequence of the first Election, they shall be divided as equally as may be into three Classes. The Seats of the Senators of the first Class shall be vacated at the Expiration of the second year, of the second Class at the Expiration of the fourth Year, and of the third Class at the Expiration of the sixth Year, so that one third may be chosen every second Year; and if Vacancies happen by Resignation, or otherwise, during the Recess of the Legislature of any State, the Executive thereof may make temporary Appointments until the next Meeting of the Legislature, which shall then fill such Vacancies.

No Person shall be a Senator who shall not have attained to the Age of thirty years, and been nine Years a Citizen of the United States, and who shall not, when elected, be an Inhabitant of that State for which he shall be chosen.

The Vice President of the United States shall be President of the Senate, but shall have no Vote, unless they be equally divided.

The Senate shall chuse their other Officers, and also a President pro tempore, in the Absence of the Vice President, or when he shall exercise the Office of President of the United States.

The Senate shall have the sole Power to try all impeachments. When sitting for that Purpose, they shall be on Oath or Affirmation. When the President of the United States is tried, the Chief Justice shall preside: And no Person shall be convicted without the Concurrence of two thirds of the Members present.

Judgment in Cases of Impeachment shall not extend further than to removal from Office, and disqualification to hold and enjoy any Office of honor, Trust or Profit under the United States: but the Party convicted shall

---

[3]This section has bee affected by the 17th amendment.

nevertheless be liable and subject to Indictment, Trial, Judgment and Punishment, according to Law.

[4]SECTION 4.   The Times, Places and Manner of holding Elections for Senators and Representatives, shall be prescribed in each State by the Legislature thereof; but the Congress may at any time by Law make or alter such Regulations, except as to the Places of chusing Senators.

The Congress shall assemble at least once in every Year, and such Meeting shall be on the first Monday in December, unless they shall by Law appoint a different Day.

SECTION 5.   Each House shall be the Judge of the Elections, Returns and Qualifications of its own Members, and a Majority of each shall constitute a Quorum to do Business; but a smaller Number may adjourn from day to day, and may be authorized to compel the Attendance of absent Members, in such Manner, and under such Penalties as each House may provide.

Each House may determine the Rules of its Proceedings, punish its Members for disorderly Behaviour, and, with the Concurrence of two thirds, expel a Member.

Each House shall keep a Journal of its Proceedings, and from time to time publish the same, excepting such Parts as may in their Judgment require Secrecy; and the Yeas and Nays of the Members of either House on any question shall, at the Desire of one fifth of those present, be entered on the Journal.

Neither House, during the Session of Congress, shall, without the consent of the other, adjourn for more than three days, nor to any other Place than that in which the two Houses shall be sitting.

SECTION 6.   The Senators and Representative shall receive a Compensation for their Services, to be ascertained by Law, and paid out of the Treasury of the United States.   They shall in all Cases, except Treason, Felony and Breach of the Peace, be privileged from Arrest during their Attendance at the Session of their respective Houses, and in going to and returning from the same; and for any Speech or Debate in either House, they shall not be questioned in any other Place.

No Senator or Representative shall, during the Time for which he was elected, be appointed to any civil

---

[4]This section has been affected by the 20th amendment.

Office under the Authority of the United States, which shall have been created, or the Emoluments whereof shall have been increased during such time; and no Person holding any Office under the United States, shall be a Member of either House during his Continuance in Office.

SECTION 7. All Bills for raising Revenue shall originate in the House of Representatives; but the Senate may propose or concur with Amendments as on other Bills.

Every Bill which shall have passed the House of Representatives and the Senate, shall, before it become a Law, be presented to the President of the United States; If he approves he shall sign it, but if not he shall return it, with his Objections to that House in which it shall have originated, who shall enter the Objections at large on their Journal, and proceed to reconsider it. If after such Reconsideration two thirds of that House shall agree to pass the Bill, it shall be sent, together with the Objections, to the other House, by which it shall likewise be reconsidered, and if approved by two thirds of that House, it shall become a Law. But in all such Cases the Votes of both Houses shall be determined by yeas and Nays, and the Names of the Persons voting for and against the Bill shall be entered on the Journal of each House respectively. If any Bill shall not be returned by the President within ten Days (Sundays excepted) after it shall have been presented to him, the Same shall be a Law, in like Manner as if he had signed it, unless the Congress by their Adjournment prevent its Return, in which Case it shall not be a Law.

Every Order, Resolution, or Vote to which the Concurrence of the Senate and House of Representative may be necessary (except on a question of Adjournment) shall be presented to the President of the United States; and before the Same shall take Effect, shall be approved by him, or being disapproved by him shall be repassed by two thirds of the Senate and House of Representatives, according to the Rules and Limitations prescribed in the Case of a Bill.

SECTION 8. The Congress shall have Power To lay and collect Taxes, Duties, Imposts and Excises, to pay the Debts and provide for the common Defence and general Welfare of the United States; but all Duties, Imposts and Excises shall be uniform throughout the United States;

To borrow Money on the credit of the United States;

To regulate Commerce with foreign Nations, and among

the several States, and with the Indian Tribes;

To establish a uniform Rule of Naturalization, and uniform Laws on the subject of Bankruptcies throughout the United States;

To coin Money, regulate the Value thereof, and of foreign Coin, and fix the Standard of Weights and Measures;

To provide for the Punishment of counterfeiting the Securities and current Coin of the United States;

To establish Post Offices and post Roads;

To promote the Progress of Science and useful Arts, by securing for limited Times to Authors and Inventors the exclusive Right to their respective writing and Discoveries;

To constitute Tribunals inferior to the supreme Court;

To define and punish Piracies and Felonies committed on the high Seas, and Offences against the law of Nations;

To declare War, grant Letters of Marque and Reprisal, and make Rules concerning Captures on Land and Water;

To raise and support Armies, but no Appropriation of Money to that Use shall be for a longer Term than two years;

To provide and maintain a Navy;

To make Rules for the Government and Regulation of the land and naval Forces; Insurrections and repel Invasions;

To provide for organizing, arming, and disciplining, the Militia, and for governing such Part of them as may be employed in the Service of the United States, reserving to the States respectively, the Appointment of the Officers, and the Authority of training the Militia according to the discipline prescribed by Congress;

To exercise exclusive Legislation in all Cases whatsoever, over such District (not exceeding ten Miles square) as may, by Cession of particular States, and the Acceptance of Congress, become the Seat of the Government of the United States, and to exercise like Authority over all Places purchased by the Consent of the Legislature of the State in which the Same shall be, for the Erection of Forts, Magazines, Arsenals, dock-Yards, and other needful Buildings; - And

To make all Laws which shall be necessary and proper for carrying into Execution the foregoing Powers, and all

other Powers
vested by this Constitution in the Government of the
United States, or in any Department or Officer thereof.

SECTION 9   The Migration or Importation of such
Persons as any of the Stats now existing shall think
proper to admit, shall not be prohibited by the Congress
prior to the Year one thousand eight hundred and eight,
but a Tax or duty may be imposed on such Importation, not
exceeding ten dollars for each Person.

The Privilege of the Writ of Habeas Corpus shall not
be suspended, unless when in Cases of Rebellion or
Invasion the public Safety may require it.

No bill of Attainder or ex post facto Law shall be
passed.

No Capitation, or other direct, Tax shall be laid,
unless in Proportion to the Census or Enumeration herein
before directed to be taken.[5]

No Tax or Duty shall be laid on Articles exported
from any State.

No preference shall be given by any Regulation of
Commerce or Revenue to the Ports of one State over those
of another: nor shall Vessels bound to, or from, one
State, be obliged to enter, clear, or pay Duties in
another.

No Money shall be drawn from the Treasury, but in
Consequence of Appropriations made by Law; and a regular
Statement and Account of the Receipts and Expenditures of
all public Money shall be published from time to time.

No Title of Nobility shall be granted by the United
States: And no Person holding any Office of Profit or
Trust under them, shall, without the Consent on the
Congress, accept of any present, Emolument, Office, or
Title, of any kind whatever, from any King, Prince, or
foreign State.

SECTION 10.   No State shall enter into any Treaty,
Alliance, or Confederation; grant Letters of Marque and
Reprisal;   coin Money;   emit Bills of Credit;   make any
Thing but gold and silver Coin a Tender in Payment of
Debts; pass any Bill of Attainder, ex post facto Law, or
Law impairing the Obligation of Contracts, or grant any
Title of Nobility.

No State shall, without the Consent of the Congress,
lay any Imposts or Duties on Imports or Exports, except

---

[5]This clause has been affected by the 16th amendment.

what may be absolutely necessary for executing it's inspection Laws: and the net Produce of all Duties and Imposts, laid by any State on Imports or Exports, shall be for the Use of the Treasure of the United States; and all such Laws shall be subject to the Revision and Controul of the Congress.

No State shall, without the Consent of Congress, lay any Duty of Tonnage, keep Troops, or Ships of War in time of Peace, enter into any Agreement or Compact with another State, or with a foreign Power, or engage in War, unless actually invaded, or in such imminent Danger as will not admit of delay.

Article II.

SECTION 1. The executive Power shall be vested in a President of the United States of America. He shall hold his Office during the Term of four Years, and, together with the Vice President, chosen for the Same Term, be elected as follows

Each State shall appoint, in such Manner as the Legislature thereof may direct, a Number of Electors, equal to the whole Number of Senators and Representatives to which the State may be entitled in the Congress: but no Senator or Representative, or Person holding an Office of Trust or Profit under the United States, shall be appointed an Elector.

[6]The Electors shall meet in their respective States, and vote by Ballot for two Persons of whom one at least shall not be an Inhabitant of the same State with themselves. And they shall make a List of all the Persons voted for, and of the number of Votes for each; which List they shall sign and certify, and transmit sealed to the Seat of the Government of the United States, directed to the president of the Senate. The President of the Senate shall, in the Presence of the Senate and House of Representatives, open all the Certificates, and the Votes shall then be counted. The Person having the greatest Number of Votes shall be the President, if such Number be a Majority of the whole Number of Electors appointed; and if there be more than one who have such Majority, and have an equal Number of Votes, then the House of Representatives shall immediately chuse by Ballot one of them for President;

---

[6]This clause has been affected by the 12th amendment.

and if no Person have a Majority, then from the five highest on the List the said House shall in like Manner chuse the President. But in chusing the President, the Votes shall be taken by States, the Representation from each State having one Vote; A quorum for this Purpose shall consist of a Member or Members from two thirds of the States, and a Majority of all the States shall be necessary to a Choice. In every Case, after the Choice of the President, the Person having the greatest Number of Votes of the Electors shall be the Vice President. But if there should remain two or more who have equal Votes, the Senate shall chuse from them by Ballot the Vice President.

The Congress may determine the Time of chusing the Electors, and the Day on which they shall give their Votes; which Day shall be the same throughout the United States.

No Person except a natural born Citizen, or a Citizen of the United States, at the time of the Adoption of this Constitution, shall be eligible to the Office of President; neither shall any Person be eligible to that Office who shall not have attained to the Age of thirty five Years, and been fourteen Years a Resident within the United States.

In Case of the Removal of the President from Office, or of his Death, Resignation, or Inability to discharge the Powers and Duties of the said Office, the same shall devolve on the Vice President, and the Congress may by Law provide for the Case of Removal, Death, Resignation or Inability, both of the President and Vice President, declaring what Officer shall then act as President, and such Officer shall act accordingly, until the Disability be removed, or a President shall be elected.

The President shall, at stated Times, receive for his Services, a Compensation, which shall neither be increased nor diminished during the Period for which he shall have been elected, and he shall not receive within that Period any other Emolument from the United States, or any of them.

Before he enter on the Execution of his Office, he shall take the following Oath or Affirmation: - "I do solemnly swear (or affirm) that I will faithfully execute the Office of President of the United States, and will to the best of my Ability, preserve, protect and defend the Constitution of the United States."

SECTION 2.   The President shall be Commander in

Chief of the Army and Navy of the United States, and of the Militia of the several States, when called into the actual Service of the United States; he may require the Opinion, in writing, of the principal Officer in each of the executive Departments, upon any Subject relating to the Duties of their respective Offices, and he shall have Power to grant Reprieves and Pardons for Offences against the United States, except in Cases of Impeachment.

He shall have Power, by and with the Advice and Consent of the Senate, to make Treaties, provided two thirds of the Senators present concur; and he shall nominate, and by and with the Advice and Consent of the Senate, shall appoint Ambassadors, other public Ministers and Consuls, Judges of the supreme Court, and all other Officers of the United States, whose Appointments are not herein otherwise provided for, and which shall be established by Law: but the Congress may by Law vest the Appointment of such inferior Officers, as they think proper, in the President alone, in the Courts of Law, or in the Heads of Departments.

The President shall have Power to fill up all Vacancies that may happen during the Recess of the Senate, by granting Commissions which shall expire at the End of their next Session.

SECTION 3. He shall from time to time give to the Congress Information of the State of the Union, and recommend to their Consideration such Measures as he shall judge necessary and expedient; he may, on extraordinary Occasions, convene both Houses, or either of them, and in Case of Disagreement between them, with Respect to the Time of Adjournment, he may adjourn them to such Time as he shall think proper; he shall receive Ambassadors and other public Ministers; he shall take Care that the Laws be faithfully executed, and shall Commission all the Officers of the United States.

SECTION 4. The President, Vice President and all civil Officers of the United States, shall be removed from Office on Impeachment for, and Conviction of, Treason, Bribery, or other high Crimes and Misdemeanors.

Article III.

SECTION 1. The judicial Power of the United States, shall be vested in one supreme Court, and in such inferior Courts as the Congress may from time to time ordain and establish. The Judges, both of the supreme and inferior Courts, shall hold their Offices during good

Behaviour, and shall, at stated Times, receive for their Services, a Compensation, which shall not be diminished during their Continuance in Office.

[7]SECTION 2. The judicial Power shall extend to all Cases, in Law and Equity, arising under this Constitution, the Laws of the United States, and Treaties made, or which shall be made, under their Authority; - to all cases affecting Ambassadors, other public Ministers and Consuls; - to all Cases of admiralty and maritime Jurisdiction; - to Controversies to which the United States shall be a party; - to Controversies between two or more States; - between a State and Citizens of another State; - between Citizens of different States, - between Citizens of the same State claiming Lands under Grants of different States, and between a State, or the Citizens thereof, and foreign States, Citizens or Subjects.

In all Cases affecting Ambassadors, other public ministers and Consuls, and those in which a State shall be Party, the supreme Court shall have original Jurisdiction. In all the other Cases before mentioned, the supreme Court shall have appellate Jurisdiction, both as to Law and Fact, with such Exceptions, and under such Regulations as the Congress shall make.

The Trial of all Crimes, except in Cases of Impeachment, shall be by Jury; and such Trial shall be held in the State where the said Crimes shall have been committed; but when not committed within any State, the Trial shall be at such Place or Places as the Congress may by Law have directed.

SECTION 3. Treason against the United States, shall consist only in levying War against them, or in adhering to their Enemies, giving them Aid and Comfort. No Person shall be convicted of Treason unless on the Testimony of two Witnesses to the same overt Act, or on Confession in open Court.

The Congress shall have power to declare the Punishment of Treason, but no Attainder of Treason shall work Corruption of Blood, or Forfeiture except during the Life of the Person attainted.

Article IV.

SECTION 1. Full Faith and Credit shall be given in each State to the public Acts, Records, and judicial

---

[7]This section has been affected by the 11th amendment.

Proceedings of every other State. And the Congress may by general Laws prescribe the Manner in which such Acts, Records and Proceedings shall be proved, and the Effect thereof.

SECTION 2. The Citizens of each State shall be entitled to all Privileges and Immunities of Citizens in the several States.

A Person charged in any State with Treason, Felony, or other Crime, who shall flee from Justice, and be found in another State, shall on Demand of the executive Authority of the State from which he fled, be delivered up, to be removed to the State having Jurisdiction of the Crime.

No Person held to Service or Labour in one State, under the Laws thereof, escaping into another, shall, in Consequence of any Law or Regulation therein, be discharged from such Service or Labour, but shall be delivered up on Claim of the Party to whom such Service or Labour may be due.[8]

SECTION 3. New States may be admitted by the Congress into this Union; but no new State shall be formed or erected within the Jurisdiction of any other State; nor any State be formed by the junction of two or more States, or Parts of States, without the Consent of the Legislatures of the States concerned as well as of the Congress.

The Congress shall have Power to dispose of and make all needful Rules and Regulations respecting the Territory or other Property belonging to the United States; and nothing in this Constitution shall be so construed as to Prejudice any Claims of the United States, or of any particular State.

SECTION 4. The United States shall guarantee to every State in this Union a Republican Form of Government, and shall protect each of them against Invasion; and on Application of the Legislature, or of the Executive (when the Legislature cannot be convened) against domestic Violence.

Article V.

The Congress, whenever two thirds of both Houses shall deem it necessary, shall propose Amendments to this Constitution, or on the Application of the Legislatures

---

[8]This clause was affected by the 13th amendment.

of two thirds of the several States, shall call a
Convention for proposing Amendments, which, in either
Case, shall be valid to all Intents and Purposes, as Part
of this Constitution, when ratified by the Legislatures
of three fourths of the several States, or by Conventions
in three fourths thereof, as the one or the other Mode of
Ratification may be proposed by the Congress; Provided
that no Amendment which may be made prior to the Year One
thousand eight hundred and eight shall in any Manner
affect the first and fourth Clauses in the ninth Section
of the first Article; and that no State, without its
Consent, shall be deprived of its equal Suffrage in the
Senate.

Article VI.
All Debts contracted and Engagements entered into,
before the Adoption of this Constitution, shall be as
valid against the United States under this Constitution,
as under the Confederation.

This Constitution, and the laws of the United States
which shall be made in Pursuance thereof; and all
Treaties made, or which shall be made, under the
Authority of the United States; shall be the supreme Law
of the Land; and the Judges in every State shall be bound
thereby, any Thing in the Constitution or Laws of any
State to the Contrary notwithstanding.

The Senators and Representatives before mentioned,
and the Members of the several State Legislatures, and
all executive and judicial officers, both of the United
States and of the several States, shall be bound by Oath
or Affirmation, to support this Constitution; but no
religious Test shall ever be required as a Qualification
to any Office or public Trust under the United States.

Article VII.
The Ratification of the Conventions of nine States,
shall be sufficient for the Establishment of this
Constitution between the States so ratifying the Same.

DONE in Convention by the Unanimous Consent of the States
present the Seventeenth Day of September in the Year of
our Lord one thousand seven hundred and Eighty seven and
of the Independence of the United States of America the
Twelfth. IN WITNESS whereof we have hereunto subscribed
our Names,

Go. WASHINGTON - *Presid't. and deputy from Virginia*

Attest WILLIAM JACKSON *Secretary*

New Hampshire

JOHN LANGDON   NICHOLAS GILMAN

Massachusetts

NATHANIEL GORHAM   RUFUS KING

Connecticut

WM. SAML. JOHNSON   ROGER SHERMAN

New York

ALEXANDER HAMILTON

New Jersey

WIL. LIVINGSTON   WM. PATERSON.
DAVID BREARLEY.   JONA. DAYTON

Pennsylvania

B. FRANKLIN   THOS. FITZSIMONS
THOMAS MIFFLIN   JARED INGERSOLL
ROBT. MORRIS   JAMES WILSON.
GEO. CLYMER   GOUV. MORRIS

Delaware

GEO. READ   RICHARD BASSETT
GUNNING BEDFORD jun   JACO. BROOM
JOHN DICKINSON

Maryland

JAMES MCHENRY   DANL. CARROLL
DAN OF ST. THOS. JENIFER

Virginia

JOHN BLAIR   JAMES MADISON Jr.

North Carolina

WM. BLOUNT   HU. WILLIAMSON
RICHD. DOBBS SPAIGHT.

South Carolina

J. RUTLEDGE   CHARLES PINCKNEY
CHARLES COTESWORTH   PIERCE BUTLER.
  PICKNEY

Georgia

WILLIAM FEW   ABR. BALDWIN

ARTICLES IN ADDITION TO, AND AMENDMENT OF THE CONSTITUTION OF THE UNITED STATES OF AMERICA, PROPOSED BY CONGRESS, AND RATIFIED BY THE LEGISLATURES OF THE SEVERAL STATES, PURSUANT TO THE FIFTH ARTICLE OF THE ORIGINAL CONSTITUTION.

Article [I.][9]

Congress shall make no law respecting an establishment of religion, or prohibiting the free exercise thereof; or abridging the freedom of speech, or of the press; or the right of the people peaceably to assemble, and to petition the Government for a redress of grievances.

Article [II.]

---

[9]The first ten amendments to the Constitution of the United States were proposed to the legislatures of the several States by the First Congress, on the 25th of September 1789. They were ratified by the following States, and the notifications of ratification by the governors thereof were successfully communicated by the President to Congress: New Jersey, November 20, 1789; Maryland, December 19, 1789; North Carolina, December 22, 1789; South Carolina, January 19, 1790; New Hampshire, January 25, 1790; Delaware, January 28, 1790; New York, February 24, 1790; Pennsylvania, March 10, 1790; Rhode Island, June 7, 1790; Vermont, November 3, 1791, and Virginia, December 15, 1791. The amendments were subsequently ratified by the legislatures of Massachusetts, March 2, 1939; Georgia, March 18, 1939; and Connecticut, April 19, 1939.

245

A well regulated militia, being necessary to the security of a free State, the right of the people to keep and bear arms, shall not be infringed.

Article [III.]

No Soldier shall, in time of peace be quartered in any house, without the consent of the owner, nor in time of war, but in a manner to be prescribed by law.

Article [IV.]

The right of the people to be secure in their persons, houses, papers, and effects, against unreasonable searches and seizures, shall not be violated, and no warrants shall issue, but upon probable cause, supported by oath or affirmation, and particularly describing the place to be searched, and the persons or things to be seized.

Article [V.]

No person shall be held to answer for a capital, or otherwise infamous crime, unless on a presentment or indictment of a Grand Jury, except in cases arising in the land or naval forces, or in the militia, when in actual service in time of war or public danger; nor shall any person be subject for the same offence to be twice put in jeopardy of life or limb; nor shall be compelled in any criminal case to be a witness against himself, nor be deprived of life, liberty, or property, without due process of law; nor shall private property be taken for public use, without just compensation.

Article [VI.]

In all criminal prosecutions, the accused shall enjoy the right to a speedy and public trial, by an impartial jury of the State and district wherein the crime shall have been committed, which district shall have been previously ascertained by law, and to be informed of the nature and cause of the accusation; to be confronted with the witnesses against him; to have compulsory process for obtaining witnesses in his favor, and to have the assistance of counsel for his defence.

Article [VII.]

In Suits at common law, where the value in controversy shall exceed twenty dollars, the right of trial by jury shall be preserved, and no fact tried by a jury, shall be otherwise reexamined in any Court of the United States, than according to the rules of the common law.

Article [VIII.]
Excessive bail shall not be required, nor excessive fines imposed, nor cruel and unusual punishment inflicted.

Article [IX.]
The enumeration in the Constitution, of certain rights, shall not be construed to deny or disparage others retained by the people.

Article [X.]
The powers not delegated to the United States by the Constitution, nor prohibited by it to the States, are reserved to the States respectively, or to the people.

Article [XI.]
The Judicial power of the United States shall not be construed to extend to any suit in law or equity, commenced or prosecuted against one of the United States by Citizens of another State, or by Citizens or Subjects of any Foreign State.

Proposal and Ratification
The eleventh amendment to the Constitution of the United States was proposed to the legislatures of the several States by the Third Congress, on the 4th of March 1794; and was declared in a message from the President to Congress, dated the 8th of January, 1798, to have been ratified by the legislatures of three-fourths of the States. The dates of ratification were: New York, March 27, 1794; Rhode Island, March 31, 1794; Connecticut, May 8, 1794; New Hampshire, June 16, 1794; Massachusetts, June 26, 1794; Vermont, between October 9, 1794 and November 9, 1794; Virginia, November 18, 1794; Georgia, November 29, 1794; Kentucky, December 7, 1794; Maryland, December 26, 1794; Delaware, January 23, 1795; North Carolina, February 7, 1795.
Ratification was completed on February 7, 1795.
The amendment was subsequently ratified by South Carolina on December 4, 1797. New Jersey and Pennsylvania did not take action on the amendment.

[Article XII.][10]

The Electors shall meet in their respective states, and vote by ballot for President and Vice-President, one of whom, at least, shall not be an inhabitant of the same state with themselves; they shall name in their ballots the person voted for as President, and in distinct ballots the person voted for as Vice-President, and they shall make distinct lists of all persons voted for as President, and of all persons voted for as Vice-President, and of the number of votes for each, which lists they shall sign and certify, and transmit sealed to the seat of the government of the United States, directed to the President of the Senate; - The President of the Senate shall, in the presence of the Senate and House of Representatives, open all the certificates and the votes shall then be counted; - The person having the greatest number of votes for President, shall be the President, if such number be a majority of the whole number of Electors appointed; and if no person have such majority, then from the persons having the highest numbers not exceeding three on the list of those voted for as President, the House of Representatives shall choose immediately, by ballot, the President. But in choosing the President, the votes shall be taken by states, the representation from each state having one vote; a quorum for this purpose shall consist of a member or embers from two-thirds of the states, and a majority of all the states shall be necessary to a choice. And if the House of Representative shall not choose a President whenever the right of choice shall devolve upon them, before the fourth day of March next following, then the Vice-President shall act as President, as in the case of the death or other constitutional disability of the President. - The person having the greatest number of votes as Vice-President, shall be the Vice-President, if such number be a majority of the whole number of Electors appointed, and if no person have a majority, then from the two highest numbers on the list, the Senate shall choose the Vice-President; a quorum for the purpose shall consist of two-thirds of the whole number of Senators, and a majority of the whole number shall be necessary to a choice. But no person constitutionally ineligible to the office of President shall be eligible to that of

---

[10]This amendment was affected by the 20th amendment, § 3.

248

Vice-President of the United States.

Proposal and Ratification
The twelfth amendment to the Constitution of the United States was proposed to the legislatures of the several States by the Eighth Congress, on the 9th of December, 1803, in lieu of the original third paragraph of the first section of the second article; and was declared in a proclamation of the Secretary of State, dated the 25th of September, 1804, to have been ratified by the legislatures of 13 of the 17 States. The dates of ratification were: North Carolina, December 21, 1803; Maryland, December 24, 1803; Kentucky, December 27, 1803; Ohio, December 30, 1803; Pennsylvania, January 5, 1804; Vermont, January 30, 1804; Virginia, February 3, 1804; New York, February 10, 1804; New Jersey, February 22, 1804; Rhode Island, March 12, 1804; South Carolina, May 15, 1804; Georgia, May 19, 1804; New Hampshire, June 15, 1804.

Ratification was completed on June 15, 1804.

The amendment was subsequently ratified by Tennessee, July 27, 1804.

The amendment was rejected by Delaware, January 18, 1804; Massachusetts, February 3, 1804; Connecticut, at its sessions begun May 10, 1804.

Article XIII.

SECTION 1. Neither slavery nor involuntary servitude, except as a punishment for crime whereof the party shall have been duly convicted, shall exist within the United States, or any place subject to their jurisdiction.

SECTION 2. Congress shall have power to enforce this article by appropriate legislation.

Proposal and Ratification
The thirteenth amendment to the Constitution of the United States was proposed to the legislatures of the several States by the Thirty-eighth Congress, on the 31st day of January, 1865, and was declared, in a proclamation of the Secretary of State, dated the 18th of December, 1865, to have been ratified by the legislatures of twenty-seven of the thirty-six States. The dates of ratification were: Illinois, February 1, 1865; Rhode Island, February 2, 1865; Michigan, February 2, 1865; Maryland, February 3, 1865; New York, February 3, 1865;

Pennsylvania, February 3, 1865; West Virginia, February 3, 1865; Missouri, February 6, 1865; Maine, February 7, 1865; Kansas, February 7, 1865; Massachusetts, February 7, 1865; Virginia, February 9, 1865; Ohio, February 10, 1865; Indiana, February 13, 1865; Nevada, February 16, 1865; Louisiana, February 17, 1865; Minnesota, February 23, 1865; Wisconsin, February 24, 1865; Vermont, March 9, 1865; Tennessee, April 7, 1865; Arkansas, April 14, 1865; Connecticut, May 4, 1865; New Hampshire, July 1, 1865; South Carolina, November 13, 1865; Alabama, December 2, 1865; North Carolina, December 4, 1865; Georgia, December 6, 1865.

Ratification was completed on December 6, 1865.

The amendment was subsequently ratified by Oregon, December 8, 1865; California, December 19, 1865; Florida, December 28, 1865; (Florida again ratified on June 9, 1868, upon its adoption of a new constitution); Iowa, January 15, 1866; New Jersey, January 23, 1866 (after having rejected the amendment on March 16, 1865); Texas, February 18, 1870; Delaware, February 2, 1901 (after having rejected the amendment on February 8, 1865); Kentucky, March 18, 1976 (after rejected on February 24, 1865).

The amendment was rejected (and not subsequently ratified) by Mississippi, December 4, 1865.

Article XIV.

SECTION 1. All persons born or naturalized in the United States, and subject to the jurisdiction thereof, are citizens of the United States and of the State wherein they reside. No State shall make or enforce any law which shall abridge the privileges or immunities of citizens of the United States; nor shall any State deprive any person of life, liberty, or property, without due process of law; nor deny to any person within its jurisdiction the equal protection of the laws.

SECTION 2. Representatives shall be appointed among the several States according to their respective numbers, counting the whole number of persons in each State, excluding Indians not taxed. But when the right to vote at any election for the choice of electors for President and Vice President of the United States, Representatives in Congress, the Executive and Judicial officers of a State, or the members of the Legislature thereof, is denied to any of the male inhabitants of such State, being twenty-one years of age, and citizens of the United

States, or in any was abridged, except for participation in rebellion, or other crime, the basis of representation therein shall be reduced in the proportion which the number of such male citizens shall bear to the whole number of male citizens twenty-one years of age in such State.

SECTION 3. No person shall be a Senator or Representative in Congress, or elector of President and Vice President, or hold any office, civil or military, under the United States, or under any State, who, having previously taken an oath, as a member of Congress, or as an officer of the United States, or as a member of any State legislature, or as an executive or judicial officer of any State, to support the Constitution of the United States, shall have engaged in insurrection or rebellion against the same, or given aid or comfort to the enemies thereof. But Congress may by a vote of two-thirds of each House, remove such disability.

SECTION 4. The validity of the public debt of the United States, authorized by law, including debts incurred for payment of pensions and bounties for services in suppressing insurrection or rebellion, shall not be questioned. But neither the United States nor any State shall assume or pay any debt or obligation incurred in aid of insurrection or rebellion against the United States, or any claim for the loss or emancipation of any slave; but all such debts, obligations and claims shall be held illegal and void.

SECTION 5. The Congress shall have power to enforce, by appropriate legislation, the provisions of this article.

Proposal and Ratification

The fourteenth amendment to the Constitution of the United States was proposed to the legislatures of the several States by the Thirty-ninth Congress, on the 13th of June, 1866. It was declared, in a certificate of the Secretary of State dated July 28, 1868 to have been ratified by the legislatures of 28 of the 37 States. The dates of ratification were: Connecticut, June 25, 1866; New Hampshire, July 6, 1866; Tennessee, July 19, 1866; New Jersey, September 11, 1866; (subsequently the legislature rescinded its ratification, and on March 5, 1868, readopted its resolution of rescission over the Governor's veto); Oregon, September 19, 1866; (and rescinded its ratification on October 15, 1868); Vermont,

October 30, 1866; Ohio, January 4, 1867 (and rescinded its ratification on January 15, 1868); New York, January 10, 1867; Kansas, January 11, 1867; Illinois, January 15, 1867; West Virginia, January 16, 1867; Michigan, January 16, 1867; Minnesota, January 16, 1867; Maine, January 19, 1867; Nevada, January 22, 1867; Indiana, January 23, 1867; Missouri, January 25, 1867; Rhode Island, February 7, 1867; Wisconsin, February 7, 1867; Pennsylvania, February 12, 1867; Massachusetts, March 20, 1867; Nebraska, June 15, 1867; Iowa, March 16, 1868; Arkansas, April 6, 1868; Florida, June 9, 1868; North Carolina, July 4, 1868 (after having rejected it on December 14, 1866); Louisiana, July 9, 1868 (after having rejected it on February 6, 1867); South Carolina, July 9, 1868 (after having rejected it on December 20, 1866).

Ratification was completed on July 9, 1868.

The amendment was subsequently ratified by Alabama, July 13, 1868; Georgia, July 21, 1868 (after having rejected it on November 9, 1866); Virginia, October 8, 1869 (after having rejected it on January 9, 1867); Mississippi, January 17, 1870; Texas, February 18, 1870 (after having rejected it on October 27, 1866); Delaware, February 12, 1902 (after having rejected it on February 8, 1867); Maryland, April 4, 1859 (after having rejected it on March 23, 1867); California, May 6, 1959; Kentucky, March 18, 1976 (after having rejected it on January 8, 1867).

Article XV.

SECTION 1. The right of citizens of the United States to vote shall not be denied or abridged by the United States or by any State on account of race, color, or previous condition of servitude.

SECTION 2. The Congress shall have power to enforce this article by appropriate legislation.

Proposal and Ratification

The fifteenth amendment to the Constitution of the United States was proposed to the legislatures of the several States by the Fortieth Congress, on the 26th of February, 1869, and was declared, in a proclamation of the Secretary of State, dated March 30, 1870, to have been ratified by the legislatures of twenty-nine of the thirty-seven States. The dates of ratification were: Nevada, March 1, 1869; West Virginia, March 3, 1869; Illinois, March 5, 1869; Louisiana, March 5, 1869; North

Carolina, March 5, 1869; Michigan, March 8, 1869; Wisconsin, March 9, 1869; Maine, March 11, 1869; Massachusetts, March 12, 1869; Arkansas, March 15, 1869; South Carolina, March 15, 1869; Pennsylvania, March 25, 1869; New York, April 14, 1869 (and the legislature of the same State passed a resolution January 5, 1870, to withdraw its consent to it, which action it rescinded on March 30, 1970); Indiana, May 14, 1869; Connecticut, May 19, 1869; Florida, June 14, 1869; New Hampshire, July 1, 1869; Virginia, October 8, 1869; Vermont, October 20, 1869; Missouri, January 7, 1870; Minnesota, January 13, 1870; Mississippi, January 17, 1870; Rhode Island, January 18, 1870; Kansas, January 19, 1870; Ohio, January 27, 1870 (after having rejected it on April 30, 1869); Georgia, February 2, 1870; Iowa, February 3, 1870.

Ratification was completed on February 3, 1870, unless the withdrawal of ratification by New York was effective; in which event ratification was completed on February 17, 1870, when Nebraska ratified.

The amendment was subsequently ratified by Texas, February 18, 1870; New Jersey, February 15, 1871 (after having rejected it on February 7, 1870); Delaware, February 12, 1901 (after having rejected it on January 28, 1870); Kentucky, March 18, 1976 (after having rejected it on March 12, 1869).

The amendment was approved by the Governor of Maryland, May 7, 1973; Maryland having previously rejected it on February 26, 1870.

The amendment was rejected (and not subsequently ratified) by Tennessee, November 16, 1869.

Article XVI.
The Congress shall have power to lay and collect taxes on incomes, from whatever source derived, without apportionment among the several States, and without regard to any census or enumeration.

Proposal and Ratification
The sixteenth amendment to the Constitution of the United States was proposed to the legislatures of the several States by the Sixty-first Congress on the 12th of July, 1909, and was declared, in a proclamation of the Secretary of State, dated the 25th of February, 1913, to have been ratified by 36 of the 48 States. The dates of ratification were: Alabama, August 10, 1909; Kentucky,

253

February 8, 1910; South Carolina, February 19, 1910; Illinois, March 1, 1910; Mississippi, March 7, 1910; Oklahoma, March 10, 1910; Maryland, April 8, 1910; Georgia, August 3, 1910; Texas, August 16, 1910; Ohio, January 19, 1911; Idaho, January 20, 1911; Oregon, January 23, 1911; Washington, January 26, 1911; Montana, January 30, 1911; Indiana, January 30, 1911; California, January 31, 1911; Nevada, January 31, 1911; South Dakota, February 3, 1911; Nebraska, February 9, 1911; North Carolina, February 11, 1911; Colorado, February 15, 1911; North Dakota, February 17, 1911; Kansas, February 18, 1911; Michigan, February 23, 1911; Iowa, February 24, 1911; Missouri, March 16, 1911; Maine, March 31, 1911; Tennessee, April 7, 1911; Arkansas, April 22, 1911 (after having rejected it earlier); Wisconsin, May 26, 1911; New York, July 12, 1911; Arizona, April 6, 1912; Minnesota; June 11, 1912; Louisiana, June 28, 1912; West Virginia; January 31, 1913; New Mexico, February 3, 1913.

Ratification was completed on February 3, 1913.

The amendment was subsequently ratified by Massachusetts, March 4, 1913; New Hampshire, March 7, 1913 (after having rejected it on March 2, 1911).

The amendment was rejected (and not subsequently ratified) by Connecticut, Rhode Island, and Utah.

Article [XVII.]

The Senate of the United States shall be composed of two Senators from each State, elected by the people thereof, for six years; and each Senator shall have one vote. The electors in each State shall have the qualifications requisite for electors of the most numerous branch of the State legislatures.

When vacancies happen in the representation of any State in the Senate, the executive authority of such State shall issue writs of election to fill such vacancies: *Provided*, That the legislature of any State may empower the executive thereof to make temporary appointments until the people fill the vacancies by election as the legislature may direct.

This amendment shall not be so construed as to affect the election or term of any Senator chosen before it becomes valid as part of the Constitution.

Proposal and Ratification

The seventeenth amendment to the Constitution of the United States was proposed to the legislatures of the several States by the Sixty-second Congress on the 13th of May, 1912, and was declared, in a proclamation of the Secretary of State, dated the 31st of May, 1913, to have been ratified by the legislatures of 36 of the 48 States. The dates of ratification were: Massachusetts, May 22, 1912; Arizona, June 3, 1912; Minnesota, June 10, 1912; New York, January 15, 1913; Kansas, January 17, 1913; Oregon, January 23, 1913; North Carolina, January 25, 1913; California, January 28, 1913; Michigan, January 28, 1913; Iowa, January 30, 1913; Montana, January 30, 1913; Idaho, January 31, 1913; West Virginia, February 4, 1913; Colorado, February, 5, 1913; Nevada, February 6, 1913; Texas, February 7, 1913; Washington, February 7, 1913; Wyoming, February 8, 1913; Arkansas, February 11, 1913; Maine, February 11, 1913; Illinois, February 13, 1913; North Dakota, February 14, 1913; Wisconsin, February 18, 1913; Indiana, February 19, 1913; New Hampshire, February 19, 1913; Vermont, February 19, 1913; South Dakota, February 19, 1913; Oklahoma, February 24, 1913; Ohio, February 25, 1913; Missouri, March 7, 1913; New Mexico, March 13, 1913; Nebraska, March 14, 1913; New Jersey, March 17, 1913; Tennessee, April 1, 1913; Pennsylvania, April 2, 1913; Connecticut, April 8, 1913.

Ratification was completed on April 8, 1913.

The amendment was subsequently ratified by Louisiana, June 11, 1914.

The amendment was rejected by Utah (and not subsequently ratified) on February 26, 1913.

Article [XVIII.] [11]

SECTION 1. After one year from the ratification of this article the manufacture, sale, or transportation of intoxicating liquors within, the importation thereof into, or the exportation thereof from the United States and all territory subject to the jurisdiction thereof for beverage purposes is hereby prohibited.

Sec. 2. The Congress and the several States shall have concurrent power to enforce this article by appropriate legislation.

Sec. 3. This article shall be inoperative unless it shall have been ratified as an amendment to the

---

[11]Repealed. See Article [XXI.]

Constitution by the legislatures of the several States, as provided in the Constitution, within seven years from the date of the submission hereof to the States by the Congress.

Proposal and Ratification
   The eighteenth amendment to the Constitution of the United States was proposed to the legislatures of the several States by the Sixth-fifth Congress, on the 18th of December, 1917, and was declared, in a proclamation of the Secretary of State, dated the 29th of January, 1919, to have been ratified by the legislatures of 36 of 48 States. The dates of ratification were: Mississippi, January 8, 1918; Virginia, January 11, 1918; Kentucky, January 14, 1918; North Dakota, January 25, 1918; South Carolina, January 29, 1918; Maryland, February 13, 1918; Montana, February 19, 1918; Texas, March 4, 1918; Delaware, March 18, 1918; South Dakota, March 20, 1918; Massachusetts, April 2, 1918; Arizona, May 24, 1918; Georgia, June 26, 1918; Louisiana, August 3, 1918; Florida, December 3, 1918; Michigan, January 2, 1919; Ohio, January 7, 1919; Oklahoma, January 7, 1919; Idaho, January 8, 1919; Maine, January 8, 1919; West Virginia, January 9, 1919; California, January 13, 1919; Tennessee, January 13, 1919; Washington, January 13, 1919; Arkansas, January 14, 1919; Kansas, January 14, 1919; Alabama, January, 15,1919; Colorado, January 15, 1919; Iowa, January 15, 1919 New Hampshire, January 15, 1919; Oregon, January 15, 1919; Nebraska, January 16, 1919; North Carolina, January 16, 1919; Utah, January 16, 1919; Missouri, January 16, 1919; Wyoming, January 16, 1919.
   Ratification was completed on January 16, 1919.
   The amendment was subsequently ratified by Minnesota on January 17, 1917; Wisconsin, January 17, 1919; New Mexico, January 20, 1919; Nevada, January 21, 1919; New York, January 29, 1919; Vermont, January 29, 1919; Pennsylvania, February 25, 1919; Connecticut, May 6, 1919; and New Jersey, March 9, 1922.
   The amendment was rejected (and not subsequently ratified) by Rhode Island.

Article [XIX].
   The right of citizens of the United States to vote shall not be denied or abridged by the United States or by any State on account of sex.

Congress shall have power to enforce this article by appropriate legislation.

Proposal and Ratification
The nineteenth amendment to the Constitution of the United States was proposed to the legislatures of the several States by the Sixty-sixth Congress, on the 4th of June, 1919, and was declared, in a proclamation of the Secretary of State, dated the 26th of August, 1920, to have been ratified by the legislatures of 36 of 48 States. The dates of ratification were: Illinois, June 10, 1919 (and that State readopted its resolution of ratification June 17, 1919); Michigan, June 10, 1919; Wisconsin, June 10, 1919; Kansas, June 16, 1919; New York, June 16, 1919; Ohio, June 16, 1919; Pennsylvania, June 24, 1919; Massachusetts, June 25, 1919; Texas, June 28, 1919; Iowa, July 2, 1919; Missouri, July 3, 1919; Arkansas, July 28, 1919; Montana, August 2, 1919; Nebraska, August 2, 1919; Minnesota, September 8, 1919; New Hampshire, September 10, 1919; Utah, October 2, 1919; California, November, 1, 1919; Maine, November 5, 1919; North Dakota, December 1, 1919; South Dakota, December 4, 1919; Colorado, December 15, 1919; Kentucky, January 6, 1920; Rhode Island, January 6, 1920; Oregon, January 13, 1920; Indiana, January 16, 1920; Wyoming, January 27, 1920; Nevada, February 7, 1920; New Jersey, February 9, 1920; Idaho, February 11, 1920; Arizona, February 12, 1920; New Mexico, February 21, 1920; Oklahoma, February 28, 1920; West Virginia, March 10, 1920; Washington, March 22, 1920; Tennessee, August 18, 1920.
Ratification was completed on August 18, 1920.
The amendment was subsequently ratified by Connecticut on September 14, 1920 (and that State reaffirmed on September 21, 1920); Vermont, February 8, 1921; Maryland, March 29, 1941 (after having rejected it on February 24, 1920); ratification certified on February 25, 1958); Virginia, February, 21, 1952 (after rejecting it on February 12, 1920); Alabama, September 8, 1953 (after rejecting it on September 22, 1919); Florida, May 13, 1969; South Carolina, July 1, 1969 (after rejecting it on January 28, 1920); ratification certified on August 22, 1973); Georgia, February 20, 1970 (after rejecting it on July 24, 1919); Louisiana, June 11, 1970 (after rejecting it on July 1, 1920); North Carolina, May 6, 1971.
The amendment was rejected (and not subsequently

ratified) by Mississippi, March 29, 1920; Delaware, June 2, 1920.

Article [XX.]

SECTION 1.   The terms of the President and Vice President shall end at noon on the 20th day of January, and the terms of Senators and Representatives at noon on the 3d day of January, of the years in which such terms would have ended if this article had not been ratified; and the terms of their successors shall then begin.

Sec. 2.   The Congress shall assemble at least once in every year, and such meeting shall begin at noon on the 3d day of January, unless they shall by law appoint a different day.

Sec. 3.   If, at the time fixed for the beginning of the term of the President, the President elect shall have died, the Vice President elect shall become President. If a President shall not have been chosen before the time fixed for the beginning of his term, or if the President elect shall have failed to qualify, then the Vice President elect shall act as President until a President shall have qualified; and the Congress may by law provide for the case wherein neither a President elect nor a Vice President elect shall have qualified, declaring who shall then act as President, or the manner in which one who is to act shall be selected, and such person shall act accordingly until a President or Vice President shall have qualified.

Sec. 4.   The Congress may by law provide for the case of the death of any of the persons from whom the House of Representatives may choose a President whenever the rights of choice shall have devolved upon them, and for the case of the death of any of the persons from whom the Senate may choose a Vice President whenever the right of choice shall have devolved upon them.

Sec. 5.   Sections 1 and 2 shall take effect on the 15th day of October following the ratification of this article.

Sec. 6.   This article shall be inoperative unless it shall have been ratified as an amendment to the Constitution by the legislatures of three-fourths of the several States within seven years from the date of its submission.

Proposal and Ratification
The twentieth amendment to the Constitution was

proposed to the legislatures of the several states by the Seventy-Second Congress, on the 2d day of March, 1932, and was declared, in a proclamation by the Secretary of State, dated on the 6th day of February, 1933, to have been ratified by the legislatures of 36 of the 48 States. The dates of ratification were: Virginia, March 4, 1932; New York, March 11, 1932; Mississippi, March 16, 1932; Arkansas, March 17, 1932; Kentucky, March 17, 1932; New Jersey, March 21, 1932; South Carolina, March 25, 1932; Michigan, March 31, 1932; Maine, April 1, 1932; Rhode Island, April 14, 1932; Illinois, April 21, 1932; Louisiana, June 22, 1932; West Virginia, July 30, 1932; Pennsylvania, August 11, 1932; Indiana, August 15, 1932; Texas, September 7, 1932; Alabama, September 13, 1932; California, January 4, 1933; North Carolina, January 5, 1933; North Dakota, January 9, 1933; Minnesota, January 13, 1933; Arizona, January 13, 1933; Montana, January 13, 1933; Nebraska, January 13, 1933; Oklahoma, January 13, 1933; Kansas, January 16, 1933;; Oregon, January 16, 1933; Delaware, January 19, 1933; Washington, January 19, 1933; Wyoming, January 19, 1933; Iowa, January 20, 1933; South Dakota, January 20, 1933; Tennessee, January 20, 1933; Idaho, January 21, 1933; New Mexico, January 21, 1933; Georgia, January 23, 1933; Missouri, January 23, 1933; Ohio, January 23, 1933; Utah, January 23, 1933. Ratification was completed on January 23, 1933.

The amendment was subsequently ratified by Massachusetts on January 24, 1933; Wisconsin, January 24, 1933; Colorado, January 24, 1933; Nevada, January 26, 1933; Connecticut, January 27, 1933; New Hampshire, January 31, 1933; Vermont, February 2, 1933; Maryland, March 24, 1933; Florida, April 26, 1933.

Article [XXI.]

SECTION 1. The eighteenth article of amendment to the Constitution of the United States is hereby repealed.

Sec. 2. The transportation or importation into any State, Territory, or possession of the United States for delivery or use therein of intoxicating liquors, in violation of the laws thereof, is hereby prohibited.

Sec. 3. This article shall be inoperative unless it shall have been ratified as an amendment to the Constitution by conventions in the several States, as provided in the Constitution, within seven years from the date of the submission hereof to the States by the Congress.

259

Proposal and Ratification
   The twenty-first amendment to the Constitution was proposed to the several states by the Seventy-Second Congress, on the 20th day of February, 1933, and was declared, in a proclamation by the Secretary of State, dated on the 5th day of December, 1933, to have been ratified by 36 of the 48 States. The dates of ratification were: Michigan, April 10, 1933; Wisconsin, April 25, 1933; Rhode Island, May 8, 1933; Wyoming, May 25, 1933; New Jersey, June 1, 1933; Delaware, June 24, 1933; Indiana, June 26, 1933; Massachusetts, June 26, 1933; New York, June 27, 1933; Illinois, July 10, 1933; Iowa, July 10, 1933; Connecticut, July 11, 1933; New Hampshire, July 11, 1933; California, July 24, 1933; West Virginia, July 25, 1933; Arkansas, August 1, 1933; Oregon, August 7, 1933; Alabama, August 8, 1933; Tennessee, August 11, 1933; Missouri, August 29, 1933; Arizona, September 5, 1933; Nevada, September 5, 1933; Vermont, September 23, 1933; Colorado, September 26, 1933; Washington, October 3, 1933; Minnesota, October 10, 1933; Idaho, October 17, 1933; Maryland, October 18, 1933; Virginia, October 25, 1933; New Mexico, November 2, 1933; Florida, November 14, 1933; Texas, November 24, 1933; Kentucky, November 27, 1933; Ohio, December 5, 1933; Pennsylvania, December 5, 1933; Utah, December 5, 1933.
   Ratification was completed on December 5, 1933.
   The amendment was subsequently ratified by Maine, on December 6, 1933, and by Montana, on August 6, 1934.
   The amendment was rejected (and not subsequently ratified) by South Carolina, on December 4, 1933.

Article [XXII.]
   SECTION 1. No person shall be elected to the office of the President more than twice, and no person who has held the office of President, or acted as President for more than two years of a term to which some other person was elected President shall be elected to the office of the President more than once. But this Article shall not apply to any person holding the office of President when this Article was proposed by the Congress, and shall not prevent any person who may be holding the office of President, or acting as President, during the term within which this Article becomes operative from holding the office of President or acting as President during the remainder of such term.

Sec. 2. This article shall be inoperative unless it shall have been ratified as an amendment to the Constitution by the legislatures of three-fourths of the several States within seven years from the date of its submission to the States by the Congress.

Proposal and Ratification
    This amendment was proposed to the legislatures of the several States by the Eightieth Congress on Mar. 21, 1974 by House Joint Res. No. 27, and was declared by the Administrator of General Services on Mar. 1, 1951, to have been ratified by the legislatures of 36 of the 48 States. The dates of ratification were: Maine, March 31, 1947; Michigan, March 31, 1947; Iowa, April 1, 1947; Kansas, April 1, 1947; New Hampshire, April 1, 1947; Delaware, April 2, 1947; Illinois, April 3, 1947; Oregon, April 3, 1947; Colorado, April 12, 1947, California, April 15, 1947; New Jersey, April 15, 1947; Vermont, April 15, 1947; Ohio, April 16, 1947; Wisconsin, April 16, 1947; Pennsylvania, April 29, 1947; Connecticut, May 21, 1947; Missouri, May 22, 1947; Nebraska, May 23, 1947; Virginia, January 28, 1948; Mississippi, February 12, 1948; New York, March 9, 1948; South Dakota, January 21, 1949; North Dakota, February 25, 1949; Louisiana, May 17, 1950; Montana, January 25, 1951; Indiana, January 29, 1951; Idaho, January 30, 1951; New Mexico, February 12, 1951; Wyoming, February 12, 1951; Arkansas, February 15, 1951; Georgia, February 17, 1951; Tennessee, February 20, 1951; Texas, February 22, 1951; Nevada, February 26, 1951; Utah, February 26, 1951; Minnesota, February 27, 1951.
    Ratification was completed on February 27, 1951.
    The amendment was subsequently ratified by North Carolina on February 28, 1951; South Carolina, March 13, 1951; Maryland, March 14, 1951; Florida, April 16, 1951; Alabama, May 4, 1951.
    The amendment was rejected (and not subsequently ratified) by Oklahoma in June 1947, and Massachusetts on June 9, 1949.

Certification of Validity
    Publication of the certifying statement of the Administrator of General Services that the Amendment had become valid was made on Mar. 1 1951, F.R. Doc.51-2940, 16 F.R. 2019.

Article [XXIII.]

SECTION 1. The District constituting the seat of Government of the United States shall appoint in such manner as the Congress may direct:

A number of electors of President and Vice President equal to the whole number of Senators and Representatives in Congress to which the District would be entitled if it were a State, but in no event more than the least populous State; they shall be in addition to those appointed by the States, but they shall be considered, for the purposes of the election of President and Vice President, to be electors appointed by a State; and they shall meet in the District and perform such duties as provided by the twelfth article of amendment.

Sec. 2. The Congress shall have power to enforce this article by appropriate legislation.

Proposal and Ratification

This amendment was proposed by the Eighty-sixth Congress on June 17, 1960 and was declared by the Administrator of General Services on Apr. 3, 1961, to have been ratified by 38 of the 50 States. The dates of ratification were: Hawaii, June 23, 1960 (and that State made a technical correction to its resolution on June 30, 1960); Massachusetts, August 22, 1960; New Jersey, December 19, 1960; New York, January 17, 1961; California, January 19, 1961; Oregon, January 27, 1961; Maryland, January 30, 1961; Idaho, January 31, 1961; Maine, January 31, 1961; Minnesota, January 31, 1961; New Mexico, February 1, 1961; Nevada, February 2, 1961; Montana, February 6, 1961; South Dakota, February 6, 1961; Colorado, February 8, 1961; Washington, February 9, 1961; West Virginia, February 9, 1961; Alaska, February 10, 1961; Wyoming, February 13, 1961; Delaware, February 20, 1961; Utah, February 21, 1961; Wisconsin, February 21, 1961; Pennsylvania, February 28, 1961; Indiana, March 3, 1961; North Dakota, March 3, 1961; Tennessee, March 6, 1961; Michigan, March 8, 1961; Connecticut, March 9, 1961; Arizona, March 10, 1961; Illinois, March 14, 1961; Nebraska, March 15, 1961; Vermont, March 15, 1961; Iowa, March 16, 1961; Missouri, March 20, 1961; Oklahoma, March 21, 1961; Rhode Island, March 22, 1961; Kansas, March 29, 1961; Ohio, March 29, 1961.

Ratification was completed on March 29, 1961.

The amendment was subsequently ratified by New Hampshire on March 30, 1961 (when that State annulled and then repeated its ratification of March 29, 1961).

The amendment was rejected (and not subsequently ratified) by Arkansas on January 24, 1961.

Certification of Validity
Publication of the certifying statement of the Administrator of General Services that the Amendment had become valid was made on Apr. 3, 1961, F.R. Doc 61-3017, 26 F.R. 2808.

Article [XXIV.]
SECTION 1. The right of citizens of the United States to vote in any primary or other election for President or Vice President, for electors for President or Vice President, or for Senator or Representative in Congress, shall not be denied or abridged by the United States or any State by reason of failure to pay any poll tax or other tax.
Sec. 2. The Congress shall have power to enforce this article by appropriate legislation.

Proposal and Ratification
This amendment was proposed by the Eighty-seventh Congress by Senate Joint Resolution No. 29, which was approved by the Senate on Mar. 27, 1962, and by the House of Representatives on Aug. 27, 1962. It was declared by the Administrator of General Services on Feb. 4, 1964, to have been ratified by the legislatures of 38 of the 50 States.
This amendment was ratified by the following States: Illinois, Nov. 14, 1962; New Jersey, Dec. 3, 1962; Oregon, Jan. 25, 1963; Montana, Jan. 28, 1963; West Virginia, Feb. 1, 1963; New York, Feb. 4, 1963; Maryland, Feb. 6, 1963; California, Feb. 7, 1963; Alaska, Feb. 11, 1963; Rhode Island, Feb. 14, 1963; Indiana, Feb. 19, 1963; Utah, Feb. 20, 1963; Michigan, Feb. 20, 1963; Colorado, Feb. 21, 1963; Ohio, Feb. 27, 1963; Minnesota, Feb. 27, 1963; New Mexico, Mar. 5, 1963; Hawaii, Mar. 6, 1963; North Dakota, Mar. 7, 1963; Idaho, Mar. 8, 1963; Washington, Mar. 14, 1963; Vermont, March. 15, 1963; Nevada, Mar. 19, 1963; Connecticut, Mar. 20, 1963; Tennessee, Mar. 21, 1963; Pennsylvania, Mar. 25, 1963; Wisconsin, Mar. 26, 1963; Kansas, Mar. 28, 1963; Massachusetts, Mar. 28, 1963; Nebraska, Apr. 4, 1963; Florida, Apr. 18, 1963; Iowa, Apr. 24, 1963; Delaware, May 1, 1963; Missouri, May 13, 1963; New Hampshire, June 12, 1963; Kentucky, June 27, 1963; Maine, Jan.16, 1964;

South Dakota, Jan. 23, 1964; Virginia, Feb. 25, 1977.
Ratification completed on January 23, 1964.
The amendment was rejected by Mississippi (and not subsequently ratified) on December 20, 1962.

Certification of Validity
Publication of the certifying statement of the Administrator of General Services that the Amendment had become valid was made on Feb. 5, 1964, F.R. Doc. 64-1229, 29 F.R. 1715.

Article [XXV.]
SECTION 1. In case of the removal of the President from office or of his death or resignation, the Vice President shall become President.
Sec. 2. Whenever there is a vacancy in the office of the Vice President, the President shall nominate a Vice President who shall take office upon confirmation by a majority vote of both Houses of Congress.
Sec. 3. Whenever the President transmit to the President pro tempore of the Senate and the Speaker of the House of Representatives his written declaration that he is unable to discharge the powers and duties of his office, and until he transmit to them a written declaration to the contrary, such powers and duties shall be discharged by the Vice President as Acting President.
Sec. 4. Whenever the Vice President and a majority of either the principal officers to the executive department or of such other body as Congress may by law provide, transmit to the President pro tempore of the Senate and the Speaker of the House of Representative their written declaration that the President is unable to discharge the powers and duties of his office, the Vice President shall immediately assume the powers and duties of the office as Acting President.
Thereafter, when the President transmits to the President pro tempore of the Senate and the Speaker of the House of Representatives his written declaration that no inability exists, he shall resume the powers and duties of his office unless the Vice President and a majority of either the principle officers of the executive department or of such other body as Congress may by law provide, transmit within four days to the President pro tempore of the Senate and the Speaker of the House of Representative their written declaration that the President is unable to discharge the powers and

duties of his office. Thereupon Congress shall decide the issue, assembling within forty-eight hours for that purpose if not in session. If the Congress, within twenty-one days after Congress is required to assemble, determines by two-thirds vote of both Houses that the President is unable to discharge the powers and duties of his office, the Vice President shall continue to discharge the same as Acting President; otherwise, the President shall resume the powers and duties of his office.

Proposal and Ratification
This amendment was proposed by the Eighth-ninth Congress by Senate Joint Resolution No. 1, which was approved by the Senate on Feb. 19, 1965, and by the House of Representatives, in amended form, on Apr. 13, 1965. The House of Representatives agreed to a Conference Report on June 30, 1965, and the Senate agreed to the Conference Report on July 6, 1965. It was declared by the Administrator of General Services, on Feb. 23, 1967, to have been ratified by the legislatures of 39 of the 50 States.
This amendment was ratified by the following States: Nebraska, July 12, 1965; Wisconsin, July 13, 1965; Oklahoma, July 16, 1965; Massachusetts, Aug. 9, 1965; Pennsylvania, Aug. 18, 1965; Kentucky, Sept. 15, 1965; Arizona, Sept. 22, 1965; Michigan, Oct. 5, 1965; Indiana, Oct. 20, 1965; California, Oct. 21, 1965; Arkansas, Nov. 4, 1965; New Jersey, Nov. 29, 1965; Delaware, Dec. 7, 1965; Utah, Jan. 17, 1966; West Virginia, Jan. 20, 1966; Maine, Jan. 24, 1966; Rhode Island, Jan. 28, 1966; Colorado, Feb. 1966; New Mexico, Feb. 3, 1966; Kansas, Feb. 8, 1966; Vermont, Feb. 10, 1966; Alaska, Feb. 18, 1966; Idaho, Mar. 2, 1966; Hawaii, Mar. 3, 1966; Virginia, Mar. 8, 1966; Mississippi, Mar. 10, 1966; New York, Mar. 14, 1966; Maryland, Mar. 23, 1966; Missouri, Mar. 30, 1966; New Hampshire, June 13, 1966; Louisiana, July 5, 1966; Tennessee, Jan. 12, 1967; Wyoming, Jan. 25, 1967; Washington, Jan. 26, 1967; Iowa, Jan. 26, 1967; Oregon, Feb. 2, 1967; Minnesota, Feb. 10, 1967; Nevada, Feb. 10, 1967.
Ratification was completed on Feb. 10, 1967.
The amendment was subsequently ratified by Connecticut, Feb. 14, 1967; Montana, Feb. 15, 1967; South Dakota, Mar. 6, 1967; Ohio, Mar. 7, 1967; Alabama, Mar. 14, 1967; North Carolina, Mar. 22, 1967; Illinois, Mar.

22, 1967; Texas, April 25, 1967; Florida, May 25, 1967.

Certification of Validity
Publication of the certifying statement of the Administrator of General Services that the Amendment had become valid was made on Feb. 25, 1967, F.R. Doc. 67-2208, 32 F.R. 3287.

Article [XXVI.]
SECTION 1. The right of citizens of the United States, who are eighteen years of age or older, to vote shall not be denied or abridged by the United States or by any State on account of age.
Sec. 2. The Congress shall have power to enforce this article by appropriate legislation.

Proposal and Ratification
This amendment was proposed by the Ninety-second Congress by Senate Joint Resolution No. 7, which was approved by the Senate on Mar. 10, 1971, and by the House of Representatives on Mar. 23, 1971. It was declared by the Administrator of General Services on July 5, 1971, to have been ratified by the legislatures of 39 of the 50 States.
This amendment was ratified by the following States: Connecticut, March 23, 1971; Delaware, March 23, 1971; Minnesota, March 23, 1971; Tennessee, March 23, 1971; Washington, March 23, 1971; Hawaii, March 24, 1971; Massachusetts, March 24, 1971; Montana, March 29, 1971; Arkansas, March 30, 1971; Idaho, March 30, 1971; Iowa, March 30, 1971; Nebraska, April 2, 1971; New Jersey, April 3, 1971; Kansas, April 7, 1971; Michigan, April 7, 1971; Alaska, April 8, 1971; Maryland, April 8, 1971; Indiana, April 8, 1971; Maine, April 9, 1971; Vermont, April 16, 1971; Louisiana, April 17, 1971; California, April 19, 1971; Colorado, April 27, 1971; Pennsylvania, April 27, 1971; Texas, April 27, 1971; South Carolina, April 28, 1971; West Virginia, April 28, 1971; New Hampshire, May 13, 1971; Arizona, May 14, 1971; Rhode Island, May 27, 1971; New York, June 2, 1971; Oregon, June 4, 1971; Missouri, June 14, 1971; Wisconsin, June 22, 1971; Illinois, June 29, 1971; Alabama, June 30, 1971; Ohio, June 30, 1971; North Carolina, July 1, 1971; Oklahoma, July 1, 1971.
Ratification was completed on July 1, 1971
The amendment was subsequently ratified by Virginia,

July 8, 1971; Wyoming, July 8, 1971; Georgia, October 4, 1971.

Certification of Validity
Publication of the certifying statement of the Administrator of General Services that the Amendment had become valid was made on July 7, 1971, F.R. Doc. 71-9691, 36 F.R. 12725.

TABLE OF CASES

Industrial Acceptance
Corporation v. Webb,
1.4
Irvine v. California,
2.1

Jenkins v Anderson
Warden, 2.55
Katz v. U.S., 2.45,
2.56
Kentucky v. Dennison,
1.54
Ker v. California, 1.44
Kimmelman v. Morrison,
2.28
Koldender v. Lawson,
1.45
Kretchmar v. Nebraska,
2.28
Kuhlmann v. Wilson,
2.50
Lee v. United States,
2.50
Leonel Torres Herrera,
Petitioner v. James
A. Collins, Director
Texas Department of
Criminal Justice,
Institutional
Division, 1.22
Lisenba v. California,
1.56
Lochner v. New York,
1.56
Lopez v. U.S., 2.50
Lux v. Haggin, 1.4, 1.6
Maine v. Moulton, 2.50
Mapp v. Ohio, 1.57,
2.1, 2.46
Marbelhead Land Co. v.
Los Angeles County,
1.25
Marbury v. Madison,
1.27, 1.32, 1.33
Martin v. Hunter's
Lessee, 1.33

Maryland v. Buie, 2.24,
2.34
Maryland v. Garrison,
2.9
Maryland v. Macon, 2.26
Massachusetts v.
Sheppard, 2.9
Massiah v. United
States, 1.21
McCleskey v. Zant, 1.21
McCray v. Illinois, 2.4
Miami v. Aronowitz,
1.45
Michigan v. Chesternut,
2.52
Michigan v. Clifford,
2.29
Michigan v. Long, 2.4,
2.9, 2.28
Michigan v. Summers,
2.10
Michigan Department of
State Police v.Setz,
1.50
Mills v. Rogers, 3.2
Minnesota v. Olson,
2.31
Miranda v. Arizona,
1.59
Monel v. Dept. of
Social Services, 3.2
Monroe v. Pape, 3.2
Murray v. United
States, 1.47
Nardone v. U.S., 2.41
National Treasury
Employees Union v.
Von Raab, 2.39
New Jersey v. T.L.O.,
2.32
New York v. Belton,
2.28
New York v. Burger,
2.29
New York v. Harris,
2.41

272

2.32
United States v.
  Watson, 2.1, 2.25
United States v.
  Williams, 2.9
Vignera v. New York,
  1.59
Warden v. Hayden, 2.31
Washington v. Chrisman,
  2.26
Weatherford v. Bursey,
  2.50
Weeks v. United States,
  1.44, 2.1, 2.24, 2.43
Welsh v. Wisconsin,
  2.31
West v. Atkins, 3.2
West Coast Hotel Co. v.
  Parrish, 1.56
Western Union Tel. Co.
  v. Call Pub. Co., 1.4
Westover v. United
  States, 1.59
Will v. Michigan Dept.
  of State Police, 3.2
Wilson v. Seiter, 3.4
Winston v. Lee, 2.47
Wolf v. Colorado, 1.44,
  2.1, 2.43
Wong Sun v. U.S., 2.41
Wyman v. James, 2.29

Index

References are made to section numbers, except where page number is indicated, thus: - page number -

INTERROGATION
Custodial, 1.59
Restrictions, 1.59

INTERSTATE COMPACTS
Constitutional basis for, 1.53

INVENTORY SEARCH
Probable cause search, 2.11

INVESTIGATIVE OFFICER
Authority to divulge
communications, -170-
Definition, -151-

JAY, JOHN
First Chief Justice, 1.32

JEFFERSON, THOMAS
Marbury v Madison decision, 1.27

JUDGE
Definition, of competent
jurisdiction, -152-
Immunity under title 42 Section
1983, 3.2

JUDICIAL REVIEW
James Otis, 1.29

JUDICIARY ART OF 1789
Constitutionality of, 1.27
Marbury v Madison decision, 1.27

JURY
Under early common law, 1.17

JUSTICES
Supreme Court, 1.37

**JUVENILE DELINQUENCY
PREVENTION AND
CONTROL**
Act of 1968, 2.49

KING
English King's accountability,
1.20

KU KLUX KLAN
Act of 1871, 1.55

LABOR, HOURS OF
Limitation on 1.55

LAW
Changes in, 1.5
Equality under, 1.19

**LAW ENFORCEMENT AND
ADMINISTRATION OF
JUSTICE**
Commission established, 2.49
Report published, 2.49

LAW ENFORCEMENT OFFICER
Authority to divulge
communication, -170-
Definition, -151-

LAW RULE OF
Albert V. Dicey, 1.19
Court interpretation, 1.19

LAWS OF NATIONS
Vattel, 1.28

LEGISLATIVE COURTS
Other than Article III, 1.38

MAGISTRATE
Issuance of search warrant, 1.46
Neutral and detached for search
warrant, 2.3

MAIL
Transportation of wiretap
device, -154-

MARBURY, WILLIAM
Midnight appointee, 1.27

MARSHALL, JOHN
Fifth Amendment decreed as
government limitation only, 1.56
Fourth Chief Justice, 2.16
Marbury v Madison decision, 1.27

MASSACHUSETTS
Close pursuit statute, 1.53

MILITARY
Appeals, 1.38

MILLER, SAMUEL F.
Slaughterhouse cases, 1.56

MIRANDA WARNING
Necessity in arrest, 1.59
Waiver of, by defendant, 1.59

281

TENTH AMENDMENT
Tenth Amendment Police power, 1.58
Reserved powers clause, 1.58

TESTIMONY
Accused under early common law, 1.17

THIRTEENTH AMENDMENT
Post war need, 1.56

TRAFFIC STOP
Information volunteered-no Miranda warning required, 1.59

TUDOR
Bill of attainder as weapon, 1.23

UNDERCOVER AGENTS
False friends of, 2.50

UNITED STATES GOVERNMENT
Early function of, 1.26

UNITED STATES SUPREME COURT
Methods for review by, 1.8

VATTEL, EMERICH de
Laws of Nations, 1.29

VIRGINIA
Bill of Rights, 1.16

WARRANT FOR ARREST
No authority to search third person, 2.25

WARRANT
Search Warrant Requires Independent Source, 1.47

WARRANTS
Arrests, 1.44
Common law, 1.43
Probable cause necessary, 1.43
Search, 1.44, 1.47

WARREN COURT
Individual rights orientation, 2.1

WIRE COMMUNICATION
Definition, -150-
Interception procedure, -172-

WIRE OR ORAL COMMUNICATIONS
Authorization to intercept, -166-

WIRETAPS
Identity of suspected persons, -166-, 2.45
Interception reports, -181-

WIRETAP DEVICES
Commercial use, -155-

WRITS
Assistance, 1.25
Certiorari, 1.39
Habeas Corpus, 1.21, 1.22

WRITS OF ASSISTANCE
James Otis, 1.29

Edited Judicial Decisions

JUDICIAL DECISIONS RELATING TO CHAPTERS ONE AND TWO

The following judicial decisions have been edited. If one reads and analyzes these decisions, I have no doubt that the contents of chapter one, two and three, will be more meaningful. It is suggested that the student be assigned to prepare a student brief in the format that the professor prefers, and be required to orally report on this brief in a classroom setting. The other members of the class can then have an opportunity to critique the presentation so that an enjoyable learning experience for all participants may result.

If the reader desires to read the full text of the decisions, this may easily be done by referring to the legal citations indicated, and locating the decision in a law school library, court house library, or some central city or county library.

* * * * *

DECISIONS FIRST REFERRED TO IN CHAPTER ONE

DECISIONS FIRST REFERRED TO IN CHAPTER TWO

283

COOLIDGE v. NEW HAMPSHIRE
403 U.S. 443, 91 S.Ct. 2022, 29 L.Ed. 2d. 564 (1971)
CERTIORARI TO THE SUPREME COURT OF NEW HAMPSHIRE

Argued January 12, 1971.-Decided June 21, 1971
. . .
MR. JUSTICE STEWART delivered the opinion of the Court.

We are called upon in this case to decide issues
under the Fourth and Fourteenth Amendments arising in the
context of a state criminal trial for the commission of
a particularly brutal murder. As in every case, our
single duty is to determine the issues presented in
accord with the Constitution and the law.

Pamela Mason, a 14-year-old girl, left her home in
Manchester, New Hampshire, on the evening of January 13,
1964, during a heavy snowstorm, apparently in response to
a man's telephone call for a babysitter. Eight days
later, after a thaw, her body was found by the side of a
major north-south highway several miles away. She had
been murdered. The event created great alarm in the area,
and the police immediately began a massive investigation.

On January 28, having learned from a neighbor that
the petitioner, Edward Coolidge, had been away from home
on the evening of the girl's disappearance, the police
went to his house to question him. They asked him, among
other things, if he owned any guns, and he produced
three, two shotguns and a rifle. They also asked whether
he would take a lie-detector test concerning his account
of his activities on the night of the disappearance. He
agreed to do so on the following Sunday, his day off. The
police later described his attitude on the occasion of
this visit as fully "cooperative." His wife was in the
house throughout the interview.

On the following Sunday, a policeman called Coolidge
early in the morning and asked him to come down to the
police station for the trip to Concord, New Hampshire,
where the lie-detector test was to be administered. That
evening, two plainclothes policemen arrived at the
Coolidge house, where Mrs. Coolidge was waiting with her
mother-in-law for her husband's return. These two
policemen were not the two who had visited the house
earlier in the week, and they apparently did not know
that Coolidge had displayed three guns for inspection
during the earlier visit. The plainclothesmen told Mrs.

Coolidge that her husband was in "serious trouble" and probably would not be home that night. They asked Coolidge's mother to leave, and proceeded to question Mrs. Coolidge. During the course of the interview they obtained from her four guns belonging to Coolidge, and some clothes that Mrs. Coolidge thought her husband might have been wearing on the evening of Pamela Mason's disappearance.

Coolidge was held in jail on an unrelated charge that night, but he was released the next day. During the ensuing two and a half weeks, the State accumulated a quantity of evidence to support the theory that it was he who had killed Pamela Mason. On February 19, the results of the investigation were presented at a meeting between the police officers working on the case and the State Attorney General, who had personally taken charge of all police activities relating to the murder, and was later to serve as chief prosecutor at the trial. At this meeting, it was decided that there was enough evidence to justify the arrest of Coolidge on the murder charge and a search of his house and two cars. At the conclusion of the meeting, the Manchester police chief made formal application, under oath, for the arrest and search warrants. The complaint supporting the warrant for a search of Coolidge's Pontiac automobile, the only warrant that concerns us here, stated that the affiant "has probable cause to suspect and believe, and does suspect and believe, and herewith offers satisfactory evidence, that there are certain objects and things used in the Commission of said offense, now kept, and concealed in or upon a certain vehicle, to wit: 1951 Pontiac two-door sedan...." The warrants were then signed and issued by the Attorney General himself, acting as a justice of the peace. Under New Hampshire law in force at that time, all justices of the peace were authorized to issue search warrants. N.H. Rev. Stat. Ann. § 595:1 (repealed 1969).

The police arrested Coolidge in his house on the day the warrant issued. Mrs. Coolidge asked whether she might remain in the house with her small child, but was told that she must stay elsewhere, apparently in part because the police believed that she would be harassed by reporters if she were accessible to them. When she asked whether she might take her car, she was told that both cars had been "impounded," and that the police would provide transportation for her. Some time later, the police called a towing company, and about two and a half hours after Coolidge had been taken into custody the cars were towed to the police station. It appears that at the time of the arrest the cars were parked in the Coolidge driveway, and that although dark had fallen they were plainly visible both from the street and from inside the house where Coolidge was actually arrested. The 1951 Pontiac was searched and vacuumed on February 21, two days after it was seized, again a year later, in January 1965, and a third time in April 1965.

At Coolidge's subsequent jury trial on the charge of murder, vacuum sweepings, including particles of gun powder, taken from the Pontiac were introduced in evidence against him, as part of an attempt by the State to show by microscopic analysis that it was highly probable that Pamela Mason had been in Coolidge's car. Also introduced in evidence was one of the guns taken by the police on their Sunday evening visit to the Coolidge house-a .22-caliber Mossberg rifle, which the prosecution claimed was the murder weapon. Conflicting ballistics testimony was offered on the question on whether the bullets found in Pamela Mason's body had been fired from this rifle. Finally, the prosecution introduced vacuum sweepings of the clothes taken from the Coolidge house that same Sunday evening, and attempted to show through microscopic analysis that there was a high probability that the clothes had been in contact with Pamela Mason's body. Pretrial motions to suppress all this evidence were referred to by the trial judge to the New Hampshire Supreme Court, which ruled the evidence admissible. 106 N.H. 186, 208 A.2d 322. The jury found Coolidge guilty and he was sentenced to life imprisonment. The New Hampshire Supreme Court affirmed the judgment of conviction, 109 N.H. 403, 206 A. 2d 547, and we granted certiorari to consider the constitutional questions raised by the admission of this evidence against Coolidge at his trial. 399 U.S. 926.

I

The petitioner's first claim is that the warrant authorizing the seizure and subsequent search of his 1951 Pontiac automobile was invalid because not issued by a "neutral and detached magistrate." Since we agree with the petitioner that the warrant was invalid for this reason, we need not consider his further argument that the allegations under oath supporting the issuance of the warrant were so conclusory as to violate relevant constitutional standards. Cf. **GIORDENELLO v. UNITED STATES**, 357 U.S. 480; **AGUILAR v. TEXAS**, 378 U.S. 108.

The classic statement of the policy underlying the warrant requirement of the Fourth Amendment is that of Mr Justice Jackson, writing for the Court in **JOHNSON v. UNITED STATES**, 333 U.S. 10, 13-14:

> "The point of the Fourth Amendment, which often is not grasped by zealous officers, is not that it denies law enforcement the support of the usual inferences which reasonable men draw from evidence. Its protection consists in requiring that those inferences be drawn by a neutral and detached magistrate instead of being judged by the officer engaged in the often competitive enterprise of ferreting out crime. Any assumption that evidence sufficient to support a magistrate's disinterested determination to issue a search warrant will justify the officers in making a search without a warrant would reduce the Amendment to a nullity and leave the people's homes secure only in the discretion of police officers.... When the right of privacy must reasonably yield to the right of search is, as a rule, to be decided by a judicial officer, not by a policeman or government enforcement agent."

Cf. **UNITED STATES v. LEFKOWITZ**, 285 U.S. 452, 464; **GIORDENELLO v. UNITED STATES**, supra, at 486; **WONG SUN v. UNITED STATES**, 371 U.S. 471, 481-482; **KATZ v. UNITED STATES**, 389 U.S. 347, 356-357.

In this case, the determination of probable cause was made by the chief "government enforcement agent" of the State-the Attorney General-who was actively in charge of the investigation and later was to be chief prosecutor at the trial. To be sure, the determination was formalized here by a writing bearing the title "search

Warrant," whereas in Johnson there was no piece of paper involved, but the State has not attempted to uphold the warrant on any such artificial basis. Rather, the State argues that the Attorney General, who was unquestionably authorized as a justice of the peace to issue warrants under then-existing state law, did in fact act as a "neutral and detached magistrate." Further, the State claims that *any* magistrate, confronted with the showing of probable cause made by the Manchester chief of police, would have issued the warrant in question. To the first proposition it is enough to answer that there could hardly be a more appropriate setting than this for a per se rule of disqualification rather than a case-by-case evaluation of all the circumstances. Without disrespect to the state law enforcement agent here involved, the whole point of the basic rule so well expressed by MR. JUSTICE JACKSON is that prosecutors and policemen simply cannot be asked to maintain the requisite neutrality with regard to their own investigations-the "competitive enterprise" that must rightly engage their single-minded attention. Cf. **MANCUSI v. DEFORTE**, 392 U.S. 364, 371. As for the proposition that the existence of probable cause renders noncompliance with the warrant procedure an irrelevance, it is enough to cite **AGNELLO v. UNITED STATES**, 269 U.S. 20, 33, decided in 1925:

> "Belief, however well founded, that an article sought is concealed in a dwelling house furnishes no justification for a search of that place without a warrant. And such searches are held unlawful notwithstanding facts unquestionably showing probable cause."

See also **JONES v. UNITED STATES**, 357 U.S. 493, 497-498; **SILVERTHORNE LUMBER CO. v. UNITED STATES**, 251 U.S. 385, 392. ("[T]he rights.... against unlawful search and seizure are to be protected even if the same result might have been achieved in a lawful way.")

But the New Hampshire Supreme Court, in upholding the conviction, relied upon the theory that even if the warrant procedure here in issue would clearly violate the standards imposed on the Federal Government by the Fourth Amendment, -it is not forbidden the States under the Fourteenth. This position was premised on a passage from the opinion of this Court in **KER v. CALIFORNIA**, 374 U.S. 23, 31:

"Preliminary to our examination of the search and seizures involved here, it might be helpful for us to indicate what was not decided in **MAPP [v. OHIO**, 367 U.S. 643]. First, it must be recognized that the 'principles governing the admissibility of evidence in federal criminal trials have not been restricted... to those derived solely from the Constitution. In the exercise of its supervisory authority over the administration of criminal justice in the federal courts... this Court has... formulated rules of evidence to be applied in federal criminal prosecutions.' **MCNABB v. UNITED STATES**, 318 U.S. 332, 341... Mapp, however, established no assumption by this Court of supervisory authority over state courts... and, consequently, it implied no total obliteration of state laws relating to arrests and searches in favor of federal law. Mapp sounded no death knell for our federalism; rather, it echoed the sentiment of **ELKINS v. UNITED STATES**, supra, at 221, that 'a healthy federalism depends upon the avoidance of needless conflict between state and federal courts' by itself urging that '[f]ederal-state cooperation in the solution of crime under constitutional standards will be promoted, if only by recognition of their now mutual obligation to respect *the same fundamental criterion* in their approaches.' 367 U.S., at 658." (Emphasis in Ker.)

It is urged that the New Hampshire statutes which at the time of the searches here involved permitted a law enforcement officer himself to issue a warrant was one of those "workable rules governing arrest, searches and seizures to meet 'the practical demands of effective criminal investigation and law enforcement' in the States," id., at 34, authorized by Ker.

That such a procedure was indeed workable from the point of view of the police is evident from testimony at the trial in this case:

"The Court: You mean that another police officer issues these [search warrants]?
"The Witness: Yes. Captain Couture and Captain Shea and Captain Loveren are J.P.'s.
"The Court: Well, let me ask you, Chief, your answer is to the effect that you never go out of the department for the Justice of the Peace?
"The Witness: It hasn't been our-policy to go out of the department.
"Question: Right. Your policy and experience, is to have a fellow police officer take the warrant in the capacity of Justice of the Peace?
"Answer: That has been our practice."

But it is too plain for extensive discussion that this now abandoned New Hampshire method of issuing "search warrants" violated a fundamental premise of both the Fourth and Fourteenth Amendments-a premise fully developed and articulated long before this Court's decisions in **KER v. CALIFORNIA**, supra, and **MAPP v. OHIO**, 367 U.S. 643. As MR. JUSTICE FRANKFURTER put it in **WOLF v. COLORADO**, 338 U.S. 25, 27-28:

"The security of one's privacy against arbitrary intrusion by the police-which is at the core of the Fourth Amendment-is basic to a free society. It is therefore implicit in 'the concept of ordered liberty' and as such enforceable against the States through the Due Process Clause. The knock at the door, whether by day or by night, as a prelude to a search, without authority of law but solely on the authority of the police, did not need the commentary of recent history to be condemned...."

We find no escape from the conclusion that the seizure and search of the Pontiac automobile cannot constitutionally rest upon the warrant issued by the state official who was the chief investigator and prosecutor in this case. Since he was not the neutral and detached magistrate required by the Constitution, the search stands on no firmer ground than if there had been no warrant at all. If the seizure and search are to be justified, they must, therefore, be justified on some other theory.

II

The state proposes three distinct theories to bring the facts of this case within one or another of the exceptions to the warrant requirement. In considering them, we must not lose sight of the Fourth Amendment's fundamental guarantee. MR. JUSTICE BRADLEY's admonition in his opinion for the Court almost a century ago in **BOYD v. UNITED STATES**, 116 U.S. 616, 635, is worth repeating here:

> "It may be that it is the obnoxious thing in its mildest and least repulsive form; but illegitimate and unconstitutional practices get their first footing in that way, namely, by silent approaches and slight deviations from legal modes of procedure. This can only be obviated by adhering to the rule that constitutional provisions for the security of person and property should be liberally construed. A close and literal construction deprives them of half their efficacy, and leads to gradual depreciation of the right, as if it consisted more in sound than in substance. It is the duty of courts to be watchful for the constitutional rights of the citizen, and against any stealthy encroachments thereon,"

Thus the most basic constitutional rule in this area is that "searches conducted outside the judicial process, without prior approval by judge or magistrate, are per se unreasonable under the Fourth Amendment-subject only to a few specifically established and well-delineated exceptions." The exceptions are "jealously and carefully drawn," and there must be "a showing by those who seek exemption.... that the exigencies of the situation made that course imperative." "[T]he burden is on those seeking the exemption to show the need for it." In times of unrest, whether caused by crime or racial conflict or fear of internal subversion, this basic law and the values that it represents may appear unrealistic or "extravagant" to some. But the values were those of the authors of our fundamental constitutional concepts. In times not altogether unlike our own they won-by legal and constitutional means in England, and by revolution on this continent-a right of personal security against arbitrary intrusions by official power. If times have changed, reducing everyman's scope to do as he pleases in an urban and industrial world, the changes have made the values served by the Fourth Amendment more, not less, important.

A

The State's first theory is that the seizure on February 19 and subsequent search of Coolidge's Pontiac were "incident" to a valid arrest. We assume that the arrest of Coolidge inside his house was valid, so that the first condition of a warrantless "search incident" is met. **WHITELEY v. WARDEN**, 401 U.S. 560, 567 n. 11. And since the events in issue took place in 1964, we assess the State's argument in terms of the law as it existed before **CHIMEL v. CALIFORNIA**, 395 U.S. 752, which substantially restricted the "search incident" exception to the warrant requirement, but did so only prospectively. **WILLIAMS v. UNITED STATES**, 401 U.S. 646. But even under pre-Chimel law, the State's position is untenable.

The leading case in the area before Chimel was **UNITED STATES v. RABINOWITZ**, 339 U.S. 56, which was taken to stand "for the proposition, inter alia, that a warrantless search 'incident to a lawful arrest' may generally extend to the area that is considered to be in the 'possession' or under the 'control' of the person arrested." Chimel, supra, at 760. In this case, Coolidge was arrested inside his house; his car was outside in the driveway. The car was not touched until Coolidge had been removed from the scene. It was then seized and taken to the station, but it was not actually searched until two days later.

First, it is doubtful whether the police could have carried out a contemporaneous search of the car under Rabinowitz standards. For this Court has repeatedly held that, even under Rabinowitz, "[a] search may be incident to an arrest "'only if it is substantially contemporaneous with the arrest and is confined to the immediate vicinity of the arrest.... ""' **VALE v. LOUISIANA**, 399 U.S. 30, 33, quoting from **SHIPLEY v. CALIFORNIA**, 395 U.S. 818, 819, quoting from **STONER v. CALIFORNIA**, 376 U.S. 483, 486. (Emphasis in Shipley.) Cf.

293

AGNELLO v. UNITED STATES, 269 U.S. at 30-31; **JAMES v. LOUISIANA**, 382 U.S. 36. These cases make it clear beyond any question that a lawful pre-Chimel arrest of a suspect outside his house could never by itself justify a warrantless search inside the house. There is nothing in search-incident doctrine (as opposed to the special rules for automobiles and evidence in "plain view," to be considered below) that suggests a different result where the arrest is made inside the house and the search outside and at some distance away.

Even assuming, *arguendo*, that the police might have searched the Pontiac in the driveway when they arrested Coolidge in the house, **PRESTON v. UNITED STATES**, 376 U.S. 364, makes plain that they could not legally seize the car, remove it, and search it at their leisure without a warrant. In circumstances virtually identical to those here, MR. JUSTICE BLACK's opinion for a unanimous Court held that "[o]nce an accused is under arrest and in custody, then a search [of his car] made at another place, without a warrant, is simply not incident to the arrest." Id., at 367. **DYKE v. TAYLOR IMPLEMENT MFG. CO.**, 391 U.S. 216. Cf. **CHAMBERS v. MARONEY**, 399 U.S. 42, 47. Search-incident doctrine, in short, has no applicability to this case.

B

The second theory put forward by the State to justify a warrantless seizure and search of the Pontiac car is that under **CARROLL v. UNITED STATES**, 267 U.S. 132, the police may make a warrantless search of an automobile whenever they have probable cause to do so, and, under our decision last Term in **CHAMBERS v. MARONEY**, 399 U.S. 42, whenever the police may make a legal contemporaneous search under Carroll, they may also seize the car, take it to the police station, and search it there. But even granting that the police had probable cause to search the car, the application of the Carroll case to these facts would extend it far beyond its original rationale.

Carroll did indeed hold that "contraband goods concealed and illegally transported in an automobile or other vehicle may be searched for without a warrant," provided that "the seizing officer shall have reasonable or probable cause for believing that the automobile which he stops and seizes has contraband liquor therein which is being illegally transported." Such searches had been explicitly authorized by Congress, and, as we have pointed out elsewhere, in the conditions of the time"[a]n automobile.... was an almost indispensable instrumentality in large scale violation of the National Prohibition Act, and the car itself therefore was treated somewhat as an offender and became contraband." In two later cases, each involving an occupied automobile stopped on the open highway and searched for contraband liquor, the Court followed and reaffirmed Carroll. And last Term in Chambers, supra, we did so again.

The underlying rationale of Carroll and of all the cases that have followed it is that there is

> "a necessary difference between a search of a store, dwelling house or other structure in respect of which a proper official warrant readily may be obtained, and a search of a shop, motor boat, wagon or automobile, for contraband goods, where *it is* not practicable to secure a warrant because the vehicle can be quickly moved out of the locality or jurisdiction in which the warrant must be sought." 267 U.S., at 153. (Emphasis supplied.)

As we said in Chambers, supra, at 51, "exigent circumstances" justify the warrantless search of "an automobile *stopped on the highway,*" where there is probable cause, because the car is "movable, the occupants are alerted, and the car's contents may never be found again if a warrant must be obtained." "[T]he opportunity to search is fleeting...." (Emphasis supplied.)

In this case, the police had known for some time of the probable role of the Pontiac car in the crime. Coolidge was aware that he was a suspect in the Mason murder, but he had been extremely cooperative throughout the investigation, and there was no indication that he meant to flee. He had already had ample opportunity to destroy any evidence he thought incriminating. There is no suggestion that, on the night in question, the car was being used for any illegal purpose, and it was regularly parked in the driveway of his house. The opportunity for search was thus hardly "fleeting." The objects that the

295

police are assumed to have had probable cause to search for in the car were neither stolen nor contraband nor dangerous.

When the police arrived at the Coolidge house to arrest him, two officers were sent to guard the back door while the main party approached from the front. Coolidge was arrested inside the house, without resistance of any kind on his part, after he had voluntarily admitted the officers at both the front and back doors. There was no way in which he could conceivably have gained access to the automobile after the police arrived on his property. When Coolidge had been taken away, the police informed Mrs. Coolidge, the only other adult occupant of the house, that she and her baby had to spend the night elsewhere and that she could not use either of the Coolidge cars. Two police officers then drove her in a police car to the house of a relative in another town, and they stayed with her there until around midnight, long after the police had the Pontiac towed to the station house. The Coolidge premises were guarded throughout the night by two policemen. T h e w o r d "automobile" is not a talisman in whose presence the Fourth Amendment fades away and disappears. And surely there is nothing in this case to invoke the meaning and purpose of the rule of **CARROLL v. UNITED STATES**—no alerted criminal bent on flight, no fleeting opportunity on an open highway after a hazardous chase, no contraband or stolen goods or weapons, no confederates waiting to move the evidence, not even the inconvenience of the special police detail to guard the immobilized automobile. In short, by no possible stretch of the legal imagination can this be made into a case where "it is not practicable to secure a warrant," Carroll, supra, at 153, and the "automobile exception," despite its label, is simply irrelevant.

Since Carroll would not have justified a warrantless search of the Pontiac at the time Coolidge was arrested, the later search at the station house was plainly illegal, at least so far as the automobile exception is concerned. Chambers, supra, is of no help to the State, since that case held only that, where the police may stop and search an automobile under Carroll, they may also seize or search it later at the police station. Rather this case is controlled by **DYKE v. TAYLOR IMPLEMENT MFG. CO.**, supra. There the police lacked probable cause to seize or search the defendant's automobile at the time of his arrest, and this was enough by itself to condemn the subsequent search at the station house. Here there was probable cause, but no exigent circumstances justified the police in proceeding without a warrant. As in Dyke, the later search at the station house was therefore illegal.

C

The State's third theory in support of the warrantless seizure and search of the Pontiac car is that the car itself was an "instrumentality of the crime," and as such might be seized by the police on Coolidge's property because it was in plain view. Supposing the seizure to be thus lawful, the case of **COOPER v. CALIFORNIA**, 386 U.S. 58, is said to support a subsequent warrantless search at the station house, with or without probable cause. Of course, the distinction between an "instrumentality of crime" and "mere evidence" was done away with by **WARDEN v. HAYDEN**, 387 U.S. 294, and we may assume that the police had probable cause to seize the automobile. But, for the reasons that follow, we hold that the "plain view" exception to the warrant requirement is inapplicable to this case. Since the seizure was therefore illegal, it is unnecessary to consider the applicability of Cooper, supra, to the subsequent search.

It is well established that under certain circumstances the police may seize evidence in plain view without a warrant. But it is important to keep in mind that, in the vast majority of cases, *any* evidence seized by the police will be in plain view, at least at the moment of seizure. The problem with the "plain view" doctrine has been to identify the circumstances in which plain view has legal significance rather than being simply the normal concomitant of any search, legal or illegal.

An example of the applicability of the "plain view" doctrine is the situation in which the police have a warrant to search a given area for specified objects, and in the course of the search come across some other article of incriminating character. Cf. **GO-BART IMPORTING CO. v. UNITED STATES**, 282 U.S. 344, 358; **UNITED STATES v. LEFKOWITZ**, 285 U.S. 452, 465; **STEELE v. UNITED STATES**,

267 U.S. 498; **STANLEY v. GEORGIA**, 394 U.S. 557, 571 (Stewart, J., concurring in result). Where the initial intrusion that brings the police within plain view of such an article is supported, not by a warrant, but by one of the recognized exceptions to the warrant requirement, the seizure is also legitimate. Thus the police may inadvertently come across evidence while in "hot pursuit" of a fleeing suspect; Warden v. Hayden, supra; cf. **HESTER v. UNITED STATES**, 265 U.S. 57. And an object that comes into view during a search incident to arrest that is appropriately limited in scope under existing law may be seized without a warrant. **CHIMEL v. CALIFORNIA**, 395 U.S., at 762-763. Finally, the "plain view" doctrine has been applied where a police officer is not searching for evidence against the accused, but nonetheless inadvertently comes across an incriminating object. **HARRIS v. UNITED STATES**, 390 U.S. 234; **FRAZIER v. CUPP**, 394 U.S. 731; **KER v. CALIFORNIA**, 374 U.S., at 43. Cf. **LEWIS v. UNITED STATES**, 385 U.S. 206.

What the "plain view" cases have in common is that the police officer in each of them had a prior justification for an intrusion in the course of which he came inadvertently across a piece of evidence incriminating the accused. The doctrine serves to supplement the prior justification-whether it be a warrant for another object, hot pursuit, search incident to lawful arrest, or some other legitimate reason for being present unconnected with a search directed against the accused-and permits the warrantless seizure. Of course, the extension of the original justification is legitimate only where it is immediately apparent to the police that they have evidence before them; the "plain view" doctrine may not be used to extend a general exploratory search from one object to another until something incriminating at last emerges. Cf. **STANLEY v. GEORGIA**, supra, at 571-572 (Stewart, J., concurring in result).

The rationale for the "plain view" exception is evident if we keep in mind the two distinct constitutional protections served by the warrant requirement. First, the magistrate's scrutiny is intended to eliminate altogether searches not based on probable cause. The premise here is that *any* intrusion in the way of search or seizure is an evil, so that no intrusion at all is justified without a careful prior determination of necessity. See, e.g., **MCDONALD v. UNITED STATES**, 335 U.S. 451; **WARDEN v. HAYDEN**, 387 U.S. 294; **KATZ v. UNITED STATES**, 389 U.S. 347; **CHIMEL v. CALIFORNIA**, 395 U.S., at 761-762. The second, distinct objective is that those searches deemed necessary should be as limited as possible. Here, the specific evil is the "general warrant" abhorred by the colonists, and the problem is not that of intrusion per se, but of general, exploratory rummaging in a person's belongings. See, e.g., **BOYD v. UNITED STATES**, 116 U.S., at 624-630; **MARRON v. UNITED STATES**, 275 U.S. 192, 195-196; **STANFORD v. TEXAS**, 379 U.S. 476. The warrant accomplishes this second objective by requiring a "particular description" of the things to be seized.

The "plain view" doctrine is not in conflict with the first objective because plain view does not occur until a search is in progress. In each case, this initial intrusion is justified by a warrant or by an exception such as "hot Pursuit" or search incident to a lawful arrest, or by an extraneous valid reason for the officer's presence. And, given the initial intrusion, the seizure of an object in plain view is consistent with the second objective, since it does not convert the search into a general or exploratory one. As against the minor peril to Fourth Amendment protections, there is a major gain in effective law enforcement. Where, once an otherwise lawful search is in progress, the police inadvertently come upon a piece of evidence, it would often be a needless inconvenience, and sometimes dangerous-to the evidence or to the police themselves-to require them to ignore it until they have obtained a warrant particularly describing it.

The limits on the doctrine are implicit in the statement of its rationale. The first of these is that plain view *alone* is never enough to justify the warrantless seizure of evidence. This is simply a corollary of the familiar principle discussed above, that no amount of probable cause can justify a warrantless search or seizure absent "exigent circumstances." Incontrovertible testimony of the senses that an incriminating object is on premises belonging to a criminal suspect may establish the fullest possible measure of probable cause. But even where the object is contraband, this Court has repeatedly stated and enforced

299

the basic rule that the police may not enter and make a
warrantless seizure. **TAYLOR v. UNITED STATES**, 286 U.S. 1;
JOHNSON v. UNITED STATES, 333 U.S. 10; **MCDONALD v. UNITED
STATES**, 335 U.S. 451; **JONES v. UNITED STATES**, 357 U.S.
493, 497-498; **CHAPMAN v. UNITED STATES**, 365 U.S. 610;
TRUPIANO v. UNITED STATES, 334 U.S. 699.

The second limitation is that the discovery of
evidence in plain view must be inadvertent. The rationale
of the exception to the warrant requirement, as just
stated, is that a plain-view seizure will not turn an
initially valid (and therefore limited) search into a
"general" one, while the inconvenience of procuring a
warrant to cover an inadvertent discovery is great. But
where the discovery is anticipated, where the police know
in advance the location of the evidence and intend to
seize it, the situation is altogether different. The
requirement of a warrant to seize imposes no
inconvenience whatever, or at least none which is
constitutionally cognizable in a legal system that regard
warrantless searches as "per se unreasonable" in absence
of "exigent circumstances."

If the initial intrusion is bottomed upon a warrant
that fails to mention a particular object, though the
police know its location and intend to seize it, then
there is a violation of the express constitutional
requirement of "Warrants.... particularly describing....
[the] things to be seized." The initial intrusion may, of
course, be legitimated not by a warrant but by one of the
exceptions to the warrant requirement, such as hot
pursuit or search incident to lawful arrest. But to
extend the scope of such an intrusion to the seizure of
objects-not contraband nor stolen nor dangerous in
themselves-which the police know in advance they will
find in plain view and intend to seize would fly in the
face of the basic rule that no amount of probable cause
can justify a warrantless seizure.

In the light of what has been said, it is apparent
that the "plain view" exception cannot justify the police
seizure of the Pontiac car in this case. The police had
ample opportunity to obtain a valid warrant; they knew
the automobile's exact description and location well in
advance; they intended to seize it when they came upon
Coolidge's property. And this is not a case involving

contraband or stolen goods or objects dangerous in themselves.

The seizure was therefore unconstitutional, and so was the subsequent search at the station house. Since evidence obtained in the course of the search was admitted at Coolidge's trial, the judgment must be reversed and the case remanded to the New Hampshire Supreme Court. **MAPP v. OHIO**, 367 U.S. 643.

. . .

Both sides to the controversy appear to recognize a distinction between searches and seizures that take place on a man's property-his home or office-and those carried out elsewhere. It is accepted, at least as a matter of principle, that a search or seizure carried out on a suspect's premises without a warrant is per se unreasonable, unless the police can show that it falls within one of a carefully defined set of exceptions based on the presence of "exigent circumstances." As to other kinds of intrusions, however, there has been disagreement about the basic rules to be applied, as our cases concerning automobile searches, electronic surveillance, street searches, and administrative searches make clear.

With respect to searches and seizures carried out on a suspect's premises, the conflict has been over the question of what qualifies as an "exigent circumstance." It might appear that the difficult inquiry would be when it is that the police can enter upon a person's property to seize his "person.... papers, and effects," without prior judicial approval. The question of the scope of search and seizure once the police are on the premises would appear to be subsidiary to the basic issue of when intrusion is permissible. But the law has not developed in this fashion.

The most common situation in which Fourth Amendment issues have arisen has been that in which the police enter the suspect's premises, arrest him, and then carry out a warrantless search of evidence. Where there is a warrant for the suspect's arrest, the evidence seized may later be challenged either on the ground that the warrant was improperly issued because there was not probable cause, or on the ground that the police search and seizure went beyond that which they could carry out as an incident to the execution of the arrest warrant. Where the police act without an arrest warrant, the suspect may argue that an arrest warrant was necessary, that there was no probable cause to arrest, or that even if the arrest was valid, the search and seizure went beyond permissible limits. Perhaps because each of these lines of attack offers a plethora of litigable issues, the more fundamental question of when the police may arrest a man in his house without a warrant has been little considered in the federal courts. This Court has chosen on a number of occasions to assume the validity of an arrest and decide the case before it on the issue of the scope of permissible warrantless search. E.g., **CHIMEL v. CALIFORNIA**, supra. The more common inquiry has therefore been: "Assuming a valid police entry for purposes of arrest, what searches and seizures may the police carry out without prior authorization by a magistrate?"

Two very broad, and sharply contrasting answers to this question have been assayed by this Court in the past. The answer of **TRUPIANO v. UNITED STATES**, supra, was that *no* searches and seizures could be legitimated by the mere fact of valid entry for purposes of arrest, so long as there was no showing of special difficulties in obtaining a warrant for search and seizure. The contrasting answer in **HARRIS v. UNITED STATES**, 331 U.S. 145, and **UNITED STATES v. RABINOWITZ**, supra, was that a valid entry for purposes of arrest served to legitimate warrantless searches and seizures throughout the premises where the arrest occurred, however spacious those premises might be.

The approach taken in Harris and Rabinowitz was open to the criticism that it made it so easy for the police to arrange to search a man's premises without a warrant that the Constitution's protection of a man's "effects" became a dead letter. The approach taken in Trupiano, on the other hand, was open to the criticism that it was absurd to permit the police to make an entry in the dead of night for purposes of seizing the "person" by main force, and then refuse them permission to seize objects lying around in plain sight. It is arguable that if the very substantial intrusion implied in the entry and arrest are "reasonable" in Fourth Amendment terms, then the less intrusive search incident to arrest must be reasonable.

This argument against the Trupiano approach is of little force so long as it is assumed that the police must, in the absence of one of a number of defined exceptions based on "exigent circumstances," obtain an arrest warrant before entering a man's house to seize his person. If the Fourth Amendment requires a warrant to enter and seize the person, then it makes sense as well to require a warrant to seize other items that may be on the premises. The situation is different, however, if the police are under no circumstances required to obtain an arrest warrant before entering to arrest a person they have probable cause to believe has committed a felony. If no warrant is ever required to legitimate the extremely serious intrusion of a midnight entry to seize the person, then it can be argued plausibly that a warrant should never be required to legitimate a very sweeping search incident to such an entry and arrest. If the arrest without a warrant is per se reasonable under the Fourth Amendment, then it is difficult to perceive why a search incident in the style of Harris and Rabinowitz is not per se reasonable as well.

It is clear, then, that the notion that the warrantless entry of a man's house in order to arrest him on probable cause is per se legitimate is in fundamental conflict with the basic principle of Fourth Amendment law that searches and seizures inside a man's house without warrant are per se unreasonable in the absence of some one of a number of well defined "exigent circumstances." This conflict came to the fore in **CHIMEL v. CALIFORNIA**, supra. The Court there applied the basic rule that the "search incident to arrest" is an exception to the warrant requirement and that its scope must therefore be strictly defined in terms of the justifying "exigent circumstances." The exigency in question arises from the dangers of harm to the arresting officer and of destruction of evidence within the reach of the arrestee. Neither exigency can conceivably justify the far-ranging searches authorized under Harris and Rabinowitz. The answer of the dissenting opinion of MR. JUSTICE WHITE in Chimel supported by no decision of this Court, was that a warrantless entry for the purpose of arrest on probable cause is legitimate and reasonable no matter what the circumstances. 395 U.S., at 776-780. From this it was said to follow that the full-scale search incident to arrest was also reasonable since it was a lesser intrusion. 395 U.S., at 772-775.

The same conflict arises in this case. Since the police knew of the presence of the automobile and planned all along to seize it, there was no "exigent circumstance" to justify their failure to obtain a warrant. The application of the basic rule of Fourth Amendment law therefore requires that the fruits of the warrantless seizure be suppressed. MR. JUSTICE WHITE's dissenting opinion, however, argues once again that so long as the police could reasonably make a warrantless nighttime entry onto Coolidge's property in order to arrest him, with no showing at all of an emergency, then it is absurd to prevent them from seizing his automobile as evidence of the crime.

MR. JUSTICE WHITE takes a basically similar approach to the question whether the search of the automobile in this case can be justified under **CARROLL v. UNITED STATES**, supra, and **CHAMBERS v. MARONEY**, supra. Carroll, on its face, appears to be a classic example of the doctrine that warrantless searches are per se unreasonable in the absence of exigent circumstances. Every word in the opinion indicates the Court's adherence to the underlying rule and its care in delineating a limited exception. Read thus, the case quite evidently does not extend to the situation at bar. Yet if we take the viewpoint of a judge called on only to decide in the abstract, after the fact, whether the police have behaved "reasonably" under all the circumstances-in short if we simply ignore the warrant requirement-Carroll comes to stand for something more. The stopping of a vehicle on the open highway and a subsequent search amount to a major interference in the lives of the occupants. Carroll held such an interference to be reasonable without a warrant, given probable cause. It may be thought to follow a fortiori that the seizure and search here-where there was no stopping and the vehicle was unoccupied-were also reasonable, since the intrusion was less substantial, although there were no exigent circumstances whatever. Using reasoning of this sort, it is but a short step to the position that it is *never* necessary for the police to obtain a warrant before searching and seizing an automobile, provided that they have probable cause.... The warrant- requirement has been a valued part of our constitutional law for decades, and it has determined the result in scores and scores of cases in courts all over this country. It is not an inconvenience to be somehow "weighed" against the claims of police efficiency. It is, or should be, an important working part of our machinery of government, operating as a matter of course to check the "well-intentioned but mistakenly over-zealous executive officers" who are part of any system of law enforcement. If it is to be a true guide to constitutional police action, rather than just a pious phrase, then "[t]he exceptions cannot be enthroned into the rule." **UNITED STATES v. RABINOWITZ**, supra, at 80 (Frankfurter, J., dissenting). The confinement of the exceptions to their appropriate scope was the function of **CHIMEL v. CALIFORNIA**, supra, where we dealt with the assumption that a search "incident" to a lawful arrest may encompass all of the premises where the arrest occurs, however spacious. The "plain view" exception is intimately linked with the search-incident exception, as the cases discussed in Part C above have repeatedly shown. To permit warrantless plain-view seizures without limit would be to undo much of what was decided in Chimel, as the similar arguments put forward in dissent in the two cases indicate clearly enough.

Finally, a word about **TRUPIANO v. UNITED STATES**, supra. Our discussion of "plain view" in Part C above corresponds with that given in Trupiano. Here, as in Trupiano, the determining factors are advance police knowledge of the existence and location of the evidence, police intention to seize it, and the ample opportunity for obtaining a warrant. See 334 U.S., at 707-708 and n. 27, supra. However, we do not "reinstate" Trupiano, since we cannot adopt all its implications. To begin with, in **CHIMEL v. CALIFORNIA**, supra, we held that a search of the person of an arrestee and of the area under his immediate control could be carried out without a warrant. We did not indicate there, and do not suggest here, that the police must obtain a warrant if they anticipate that they will find specific evidence during the course of such a search. See n. 24, supra. And as to the automobile exception, we do not question the decisions of the Court in **COOPER v. CALIFORNIA**, 386 U.S. 58, and **CHAMBERS v. MARONEY**, supra, although both are arguably inconsistent with Trupiano.

. . .

Of course, it would be nonsense to pretend that our decision today reduces Fourth Amendment law to complete order and harmony. The decisions of the Court over the

305

years point in differing directions and differ in emphasis. No trick of logic will make them all perfectly consistent. But it is no less nonsense to suggest, as does MR. JUSTICE WHITE., Post, at 521, 520, that we cease today "to strive for clarity and consistency of analysis," or that we have "abandoned any attempt" to find reasoned distinctions in this area. The time is long past when men believed that development of the law must always proceed by the smooth incorporation of new situations into a single coherent analytical framework. We need accept neither the "clarity and certainty" of a Fourth Amendment without a warrant requirement nor the facile consistency obtained by wholesale overruling of recently decided cases.... We are convinced that the result reached in this case is correct, and that the principle it reflects-that the police must obtain a warrant when they intend to seize an object outside the scope of a valid search incident to arrest-can be easily understood and applied by courts and law enforcement officers alike. It is a principle that should work to protect the citizen without overburdening the police, and a principle that preserves and protects the guarantees of the Fourth Amendment.

III

Because of the prospect of a new trial, the efficient administration of justice counsels consideration of the second substantial question under the Fourth and Fourteenth Amendments presented by this case. The petitioner contends that when the police obtained a rifle and articles of his clothing from his home on the night of Sunday, February 2, 1964, while he was being interrogated at the police station, they engaged in a search and seizure violative of the Constitution. In order to understand this contention, it is necessary to review in some detail the circumstances of the February 2 episode.

A

The lie-detector test administered to Coolidge in Concord on the afternoon of the 2d was inconclusive as to his activities on the night of Pamela Mason's disappearance, but during the course of the test Coolidge confessed to stealing $375 from his employer. After the group returned from Concord to Manchester, the interrogation about Coolidge's movements on the night of the disappearance continued, and apparently made a number of statements which the police immediately checked out as best they could. The decision to send two officers to the Coolidge house to speak with Mrs. Coolidge was apparently motivated in part by a desire to check his story against whatever she might say, and in part by the need for some corroboration of his admission to the theft from his employer. The trial judge found as a fact, and the record supports him, that at the time of the visit the police knew very little about the weapon that had killed Pamela Mason. The bullet that had been retrieved was of small caliber, but the police were unsure whether the weapon was a rifle or a pistol. During the extensive investigation following the discovery of the body, the police had made it a practice to ask all those questioned whether they owned any guns, and to ask the owners for permission to run tests on those that met the very general description of the murder weapon. The trial judge found as a fact that when the police visited Mrs. Coolidge on the night of the 2d, they were unaware of the previous visit during which Coolidge had shown other officers three guns, and that they were not motivated by a desire to find the murder weapon.

The two plainclothesmen asked Mrs. Coolidge whether her husband had been at home on the night of the murder victim's disappearance, and she replied that he had not. They then asked her if her husband owned any guns. According to her testimony at the pretrial suppression hearing, she replied, "Yes, I will get them in the bedroom." One of the officers replied, "We will come with you." The three men went into the bedroom where Mrs. Coolidge took all four guns out of the closet. Her account continued:

"*Answer:* I believe I asked if they wanted the guns. One gentleman said, 'No'; then the other turned around and said, 'We might as well take them.' I said, 'If you would like them, you may take them.'
"*Question:* Did you go further and say, 'We have nothing to hide.'?
"*Answer:* I can't recall if I said that then or before. I don't recall.
"*Question:* But at some time you indicated to them that as

307

far as you were concerned you had nothing to hide, and they might take what they wanted?
"*Answer:* That was it.
. . .

"*Question:* Did you feel at that time that you had something to hide?
"*Answer:* No."

    The two policemen also asked Mrs. Coolidge what her husband had been wearing on the night of the disappearance. She then produced four pairs of trousers and indicated that her husband had probably worn either of two of them on that evening. She also brought out a hunting jacket. The police gave her a receipt for the guns and the clothing, and, after a search of the Coolidge cars not here in issue, took the various articles to the police station.

B
    The first branch of the petitioner's argument is that when Mrs. Coolidge brought out the guns and clothing, and then handed them over to the police, she was acting as an "instrument" of the officials, complying with a "demand" made by them. Consequently, it is argued, Coolidge was the victim of a search and seizure within the constitutional meaning of those terms. Since we cannot accept this interpretation of the facts, we need not consider the petitioner's further argument that Mrs. Coolidge could not or did not "waive" her husband's constitutional protection against unreasonable searches and seizures.
    Had Mrs. Coolidge, wholly on her own initiative, sought out her husband's guns and clothing and then taken them to the police station to be used as evidence against him, there can be no doubt under existing law that the articles would later have been admissible in evidence. Cf. **BURDEAU v. MCDOWELL**, 256 U.S. 465. The question presented here is whether the conduct of the police officers at the Coolidge house was such as to make her actions their actions for purposes of the Fourth and Fourteenth Amendments and their attendant exclusionary rules. The test, as the petitioner's argument suggests,

is whether Mrs. Coolidge, in light of all the circumstances of the case, must be regarded as having acted as an "instrument" or agent of the state when she produced her husband's belongings. Cf. **UNITED STATES v. GOLDBERG**, 330 F. 2d 30 (CA3), cert. denied, 377 U.S. 953 (1964); **PEOPLE v. TARANTINO**, 45 Cal. 2d 590, 290 P. 2d 505 (1955); see **BYARS v. UNITED STATES**, 273 U.S. 28; **GAMBINO v. UNITED STATES**, 275 U.S. 310.

In a situation like the one before us there no doubt always exist forces pushing the spouse to cooperate with the police. Among these are the simple but often powerful convention of openness and honesty, the fear that secretive behavior will intensify suspicion, and uncertainty as to what course is most likely to be helpful to the absent spouse. But there is nothing constitutionally suspect in the existence, without more, of these incentives to full disclosure or active cooperation with the police. The exclusionary rules were fashioned "to prevent, not to repair," and their target is official misconduct. They are "to compel respect for the constitutional guaranty in the only effectively available way-by removing the incentive to disregard it." **ELKINS v. UNITED STATES**, 364 U.S. 206, 217. But it is no part of the policy underlying the Fourth and Fourteenth Amendments to discourage citizens from aiding to the utmost of their ability in the apprehension of criminals. If, then, the exclusionary rule is properly applicable to the evidence taken from the Coolidge house on the night of February 2, it must be upon the basis that some type of unconstitutional police conduct occurred.

Yet it cannot be said that the police should have obtained a warrant for the guns and clothing before they set out to visit Mrs. Coolidge, since they had no intention of rummaging around among Coolidge's effects or of dispossessing him of any of his property. Nor can it be said that they should have obtained Coolidge's permission for a seizure they did not intend to make. There was nothing to compel them to announce to the suspect that they intended to question his wife about his movements on the night of the disappearance or about the theft from his employer. Once Mrs. Coolidge had admitted them, the policemen were surely acting normally and properly when they asked her, as they had asked those questions earlier in the investigation, including Coolidge himself, about any guns there might be in the house. The question concerning the clothes Coolidge had been wearing on the night of the disappearance was logical and in no way coercive. Indeed, one might doubt the competence of the officers involved had they not asked exactly the questions they did ask. And surely when Mrs. Coolidge of her own accord produced the guns and clothes for inspection, rather than simply describing them, it was not incumbent on the police to stop her or avert their eyes.

The crux of the petitioner's argument must be that when Mrs. Coolidge asked the policemen whether they wanted the guns, they should have replied that they could not take them, or have first telephoned Coolidge at the police station and asked his permission to take them, or have asked her whether she had been authorized by her husband to release them. Instead, after one policeman had declined the offer, the other turned and said, "We might as well take them," to which Mrs. Coolidge replied, "If you would like them, you may take them."

In assessing the claim that this course of conduct amounted to a search and seizure, it is well to keep in mind that Mrs. Coolidge described her own motive as that of clearing her husband, and that she believed that she had nothing to hide. She had seen her husband himself produce his guns for two other policemen earlier in the week, and there is nothing to indicate that she realized that he had offered only three of them for inspection on that occasion. The two officers who questioned her behaved, as her own testimony shows, with perfect courtesy. There is not the slightest implication of an attempt on their part to coerce or dominate her, or, for that matter, to direct her actions by the more subtle techniques of suggestion that are available to officials in circumstances like these. To hold that the conduct of the police here was a search and seizure would be to hold, in effect, that a criminal suspect has constitutional protection against the adverse consequences of a spontaneous, good-faith effort by his wife to clear him of suspicion.

The judgment is reversed and the case is remanded to the Supreme Court of New Hampshire for further proceedings not inconsistent with this opinion.

It is so ordered.

W. T. STONE, Warden, Petitioner, v. LLOYD CHARLES POWELL; CHARLES L. WOLFF, Jr., Warden, Petitioners, v. DAVID L. RICE
428 US 465, 96 S Ct 3037, 49 L Ed 2d 1067 (1976)
Argued February 24, 1976.--Decided July 6, 1976
. . .

MR. Justice Powell delivered the opinion of the Court.

Respondents in these cases were convicted of criminal offenses in state courts, and their convictions were affirmed on appeal. The prosecution in each case relied upon evidence obtained by searches and seizures alleged by respondents to have been unlawful. Each respondent subsequently sought relief in a federal district court by filing a petition for a writ of federal habeas corpus under 28 USC § 2254 [28 USCS § 2254]. The question presented is whether a federal court should consider, in ruling on a petition for habeas corpus relief filed by a state prisoner, a claim that evidence obtained by an unconstitutional search or seizure was introduced at his trial, when he has previously been afforded an opportunity for full and fair litigation of his claim in the state courts. The issue is of considerable importance to the administration of criminal justice.

I

We summarize first the relevant facts and procedural history of these cases.

A

Respondent Lloyd Powell was convicted of murder in June 1968 after trial in a California state court. At about midnight on February 17, 1968, he and three companions entered the Bonanza Liquor Store in San Bernardino, Cal, where Powell became involved in an altercation with Gerald Parsons, the store manager, over the theft of a bottle of wine. In the scuffling that followed Powell shot and killed Parsons' wife. Ten hours later an officer of the Henderson, Nev., Police Department arrested Powell for violation of the Henderson vagrancy ordinance, and in the search incident to the arrest discovered a .38 caliber revolver with six expended cartridges in the cylinder.

311

Powell was extradited to California and convicted of second-degree murder in the Superior Court of San Bernardino County. Parsons and Powell's accomplices at the liquor store testified against him. A criminologist testified that the revolver found on Powell was the gun that killed Parsons' wife. The trial court rejected Powell's contention that testimony by the Henderson police officer as to the search and the discovery of the revolver should have been excluded because the vagrancy ordinance was unconstitutional. In October 1969, the conviction was affirmed by a California District Court of Appeal. Although the issue was duly presented, that court found it unnecessary to pass upon the legality of the arrest and search because it concluded that the error, if any, in admitting the testimony of the Henderson officer was harmless beyond a reasonable doubt under **CHAPMAN v. CALIFORNIA**, 386 US 18, 17 L Ed 2d 705, 87 S Ct 824, 24 ALR3d 1065 (1967). The Supreme Court of California denied Powell's petition for habeas corpus relief.

In August 1971 Powell filed an amended petition for a writ of federal habeas corpus under 28 USC § 2254 [28 USCS § 2254] in the United States District Court for the Northern District of California, contending that the testimony concerning the .38 caliber revolver should have been excluded as the fruit of an illegal search. He argued that his arrest had been unlawful because the Henderson vagrancy ordinance was unconstitutionally vague, and that the arresting officer lacked probable cause to believe that he was violating it. The District Court concluded that the arresting officer had probable cause and held that even if the vagrancy ordinance was unconstitutional, the deterrent purpose of the exclusionary rule does not require that it be applied to bar admission of the fruits of a search incident to an otherwise valid arrest. In the alternative, that court agreed with the California District Court of Appeal that the admission of the evidence concerning Powell's arrest, if error, was harmless beyond a reasonable doubt.

In December 1974, the Court of Appeals for the Ninth Circuit reversed. 507 F2d 93. The Court concluded that the vagrancy ordinance was unconstitutionally vague, that Powell's arrest was therefore illegal, and that although exclusion of the evidence would serve no deterrent purpose with regard to police officers who were enforcing statutes in good faith, exclusion would serve the public interest by deterring legislators from enacting unconstitutional statutes. Id., at 98. After an independent review of the evidence the court concluded that the admission of the evidence was not harmless error since it supported the testimony of Parsons and Powell's accomplices. Id., at 99.

B

Respondent David Rice was convicted of murder in April 1971 after trial in a Nebraska state court. At 2:05 a.m. on August 17, 1970, Omaha police received a telephone call that a woman had been heard screaming at 2867 Ohio Street. As one of the officers sent to that address examined a suitcase lying in the doorway, it exploded, killing him instantly. By August 22 the investigation of the murder centered on Duane Peak, a 15-year-old member of the National Committee to Combat Fascism ("NCCF"), and that afternoon a warrant was issued for Peak's arrest. The investigation also focused on other known members of the NCCF, including Rice, some of whom were believed to be planning to kill Peak before he could incriminate them. In their search for Peak, the police went to Rice's home at 10:30 that night and found lights and a television on, but there was no response to their repeated knocking. While some officers remained to watch the premises, a warrant was obtained to search for explosives and illegal weapons believed to be in Rice's possession. Peak was not in the house, but upon entering the police discovered, in plain view, dynamite, blasting caps, and other materials useful in the construction of explosive devices. Peak subsequently was arrested, and on August 27, Rice voluntarily surrendered. The clothes Rice was wearing at that time were subjected to chemical analysis, disclosing dynamite particles.

Rice was tried for first-degree murder in the District Court of Douglas County. At trial Peak admitted planting the suitcase and making the telephone call, and implicated Rice in the bombing plot. As corroborative evidence the State introduced items seized during the search, as well as the results of the chemical analysis of Rice's clothing. The court denied Rice's motion to suppress this evidence. On appeal the Supreme Court of Nebraska affirmed the conviction, holding that the search of Rice's home had been pursuant to a valid search warrant. **STATE v. RICE**, 188 Neb 728, 199 NW2d 480 (1972).

In September 1972 Rice filed a petition for a writ of habeas corpus in the United States District Court for Nebraska. Rice's sole contention was that his incarceration was unlawful because the evidence underlying his conviction had been discovered as the result of an illegal search of his home. The District Court concluded that the search warrant was invalid, as the supporting affidavit was defective under **SPINELLI v. UNITED STATES**, 393 US 410, 21 L Ed 2d 637, 89 S Ct 584 (1969), and **AGUILAR v. TEXAS**, 378 US 108, 12 L Ed 2d 723, 84 S Ct 1509 (1964). 388 F Supp 185, 190-194 (1974). The court also rejected the state's contention that even if the warrant was invalid the search was justified because of the valid arrest warrant for Peak and because of the exigent circumstances of the situation—danger to Peak and search for bombs and explosives believed in possession of NCCF. The court reasoned that the arrest warrant did not justify the entry as the police lacked probable cause to believe Peak was in the house, and further concluded that the circumstances were not sufficiently exigent to justify an immediate warrantless search. Id., at 194-202. The Court of Appeals for the Eighth Circuit affirmed, substantially for the reasons stated by the District Court. 513 F2d 1280 (1975).

Petitioners Stone and Wolff, the wardens of the respective state prisons where Powell and Rice are incarcerated, petitioned for review of these decisions, raising questions concerning the scope of federal habeas corpus and the role of the exclusionary rule upon collateral review of cases involving fourth Amendment claims. We granted their petitions for certiorari. 422 US 1055, 45 L Ed 2d 707, 95 S Ct 2676 (1975). We now reverse.

II

The authority of federal courts to issue the writ of habeas corpus ad subjiciendum was included in the first grant of federal court jurisdiction, made by the Judiciary Act of 1789, c20 § 14, 1 Stat 81, with the limitation that the writ extend only to prisoners held in custody by the United States. The original statutory authorization did not define the substantive reach of the writ. It merely stated that the courts of the United States "shall have power to issue writs of .... habeas corpus...." Ibid. The courts defined the scope of the writ in accordance with the common law and limited it to an inquiry as to the jurisdiction of the sentencing tribunal. See, e.g., Ex parte Watkins, 28 US (3 Pet) 193, 7 L Ed 650 (1830) (MARSHALL, C. J.).

In 1867 the writ was extended to state prisoners. Act of Feb. 5, 1867, c28, § 1, 14 Stat 385. Under the 1867 Act federal courts were authorized to give relief in "all cases where any person may be restrained of his or her liberty in violation of the constitution, or of any treaty or law of the United States ...." But the limitation of federal habeas corpus jurisdiction to consideration of the jurisdiction of the sentencing court persisted. See, e.g., In re Wood, 140 US 278, 35 L Ed 505, 11 S Ct 738 (1891); In re Rahrer, 140 US 545, 35 L Ed 572, 11 S Ct 865 (1891); **ANDREWS v. SWARTZ**, 156 US 272, 39 L Ed 422, 15 S Ct 389 (1895); **BERGEMANN v. BACKER**, 157 US 655, 39 L Ed 845, 15 S Ct 727 (1895); **PETTIBONE v. NICHOLS**, 203 US 192, 51 L Ed 148, 27 S Ct 111 (1906). And, although the concept of "jurisdiction" was subjected to considerable strain as the substantive scope of the writ was expanded, this expansion was limited to only a few classes of cases until **FRANK v. MANGUM**, 237 US 309, 59 L Ed 969, 35 S Ct 582, in 1915. In Frank, the prisoner had claimed in the state courts that the proceedings which resulted in his conviction for murder had been dominated by a mob. After the State Supreme Court rejected his contentions, Frank unsuccessfully sought habeas corpus relief in the Federal District Court. This Court affirmed the denial of relief because Frank's federal claims had been considered by a competent and unbiased state tribunal. The Court recognized, however that if a habeas corpus court found that the State had failed to provide adequate "corrective process" for the full and fair litigation of federal claims, whether or not "jurisdictional," the court could inquire into the merits to determine whether detention was lawful. Id., at 333-336. 59 L Ed 969, 35 S Ct 582.

In the landmark decision in **BROWN v. ALLEN**, 344 US 443, 482-487, 97 L Ed 469, 73 S Ct 397 (1953), the scope of the writ was expanded still further. In that case and its companion case, **DANIELS v. ALLEN**, state prisoners

315

applied for federal habeas corpus relief claiming that the trial courts had erred in failing to quash their indictments due to alleged discrimination in the selection of grand jurors and in ruling certain confessions admissible. In Brown, the highest court of the State had rejected these claims on direct appeal, **STATE v. BROWN**, 233 NC 202, 63 SE 2d 99, and this Court had denied certiorari, 341 US 943, 95 L Ed 1369, 71 S Ct 997 (1951). Despite the apparent adequacy of the state corrective process, the Court reviewed the denial of the writ of habeas corpus and held that Brown was entitled to a full reconsideration of these constitutional claims, including, if appropriate, a hearing in the Federal District Court. In Daniels, however, the state supreme court on direct review had refused to consider the appeal because the papers were filed out of time. This court held that since the state court judgment rested on a reasonable application of the State's legitimate procedural rules, a ground that would have barred direct review of his federal claims by this Court, the District Court lacked authority to grant habeas corpus relief. See 344 US at 458, 486, 97 L Ed 469, 73 S Ct 397.

This final barrier to broad collateral re-examination of state criminal convictions in federal habeas corpus proceedings was removed in **FAY v. GNAW**, 372 US 391, 9 L Ed 2d 837, 83 S Ct 822, 24 Ohio Ops 2d 12 (1963). Gnaw and two codefendants had been convicted of felony murder. The sole evidence against each defendant was a signed confession. Gnaw's codefendants, but not Gnaw himself, appealed their convictions. Although their appeals were unsuccessful, in subsequent state proceedings they were able to establish that their confessions had been coerced and their convictions therefore procured in violation of the Constitution. In a subsequent federal habeas corpus proceeding, it was stipulated that Gnaw's confession also had been coerced, but the District Court followed Daniels in holding that Gnaw's failure to appeal barred habeas corpus review. See 183 F Supp 222, 225 (1960). The Court of Appeals reversed, ordering that Gnaw's conviction be set aside and that he be released from custody or a new trial be granted. This Court affirmed the grant of the writ, narrowly restricting the circumstances in which a federal court may refuse to consider the merits of federal constitutional claims.

During the period in which the substantive scope of the writ was expanded, the Court did not consider whether exceptions to full review might exist with respect to particular categories of constitutional claims. Prior to the Court's decision in **KAUFMAN v. UNITED STATES**, 394 US 217, 22 L Ed 2d 227, 89 S Ct 1068 (1969), however, a substantial majority of the federal courts of appeals had concluded that collateral review of search-and-seizure claims was inappropriate on motions filed by federal prisoners under 28 USC § 2255 [28 USCS § 2255], the modern postconviction procedure available to federal prisoners in lieu of habeas corpus. The primary rationale advanced in support of those decisions was that Fourth Amendment violations are different in kind from denials of Fifth or Sixth Amendment rights in that claims of illegal search and seizure do not "impugn the integrity of the fact-finding process or challenge evidence as inherently unreliable; rather, the exclusion of illegally seized evidence is simply a prophylactic device intended generally to deter Fourth Amendment violations by law enforcement officers." Id., at 224, 22 L Ed 2d 227, 89 S Ct 1068. See **THORNTON v. UNITED STATES**, 125 US App DC 114, 368 F2d 822 (1966).

Kaufman rejected this rationale and held that search-and-seizure claims are cognizable in § 2255 proceedings. The Court noted that "the federal habeas remedy extends to state prisoners alleging that unconstitutionally obtained evidence was admitted against them at trial," 394 US, at 225, 22 L Ed 2d 227, 89 S Ct 1068, citing, e.g., **MANCUSI v. DEFORTE**, 392 US 364, 20 L Ed 2d 1154, 88 S Ct 2120 (1968); **CARAFAS v. LAVALLEE**, 391 US 234, 20 L Ed 2d 554, 88 S Ct 1556 (1968), and concluded, as a matter of statutory construction, that there was no basis for restricting "access by federal prisoners with illegal search-and-seizure claims to federal collateral remedies, while placing no similar restriction on access by state prisoners," 394 US, at 226, 22 L. Ed 2d 227, 89 S Ct 1068. Although in recent years the view has been expressed that the Court should re-examine the substantive scope of federal habeas jurisdiction and limit collateral review of search-and-seizure claims "solely to the question of whether the petitioner was provided with a fair opportunity to raise and have adjudicated the question in state courts,"

SCHNECKLOTH v. BUSTAMONTE, 412 US 218, 250, 36 L Ed 2d 854, 93 S Ct 2041 (1973) (POWELL, J., concurring, the court, without discussion or consideration of the issue, has continued to accept jurisdiction in cases raising such claims. See **LEFKOWITZ v. NEWSOME**, 420 US 283, 43 L Ed 2d 196, 95 S Ct 886 (1975); **CADY v. DOMBROWSKI**, 413 US 433, 37 L Ed 2d 706, 93 S Ct 2523 (1973); **CARDWELL v. LEWIS**, 417 US 583, 41 L Ed 2d 325, 94 S Ct 2464, 69 Ohio Ops 2d 69 (1974) (plurality opinion).

The discussion in Kaufman of the scope of federal habeas corpus rests on the view that the effectuation of the Fourth Amendment, as applied to the States through the Fourteenth Amendment, requires the granting of habeas corpus relief when a prisoner has been convicted in state court on the basis of evidence obtained in an illegal search or seizure since those Amendments were held in **MAPP v. OHIO**, 367 US 643, 6 L Ed 2d 1081, 81 S Ct 1684, 84 ALR2d 933, 16 Ohio Ops 2d 384, 86 Ohio L Abs 513 (1961), to require exclusion of such evidence at trial and reversal of conviction upon direct review. Until this case we have not had occasion fully to consider the validity of this view. See, e.g., **SCHNECKLOTH v. BLUSTAMONTE**, supra, at 249 n 38; 36 L Ed 2d 854, 93 S Ct 2041; **CARDWELL v. LEWIS**, supra at 596 and n 12, 41 L Ed 2d 325, 94 S Ct 2464, 69 Ohio Ops 2d 69. Upon examination, we conclude in light of the nature and purpose of the Fourth Amendment exclusionary rule, that this view is unjustified. We hold, therefore, that where the State has provided an opportunity for full and fair litigation of a Fourth Amendment claim, the Constitution does not require that a state prisoner be granted federal habeas corpus relief on the ground that evidence obtained in an unconstitutional search or seizure was introduced at his trial.

III

The Fourth Amendment assures the "right of the people to be secure in their persons, houses, papers, and effects, against unreasonable searches and seizures." The Amendment was primarily a reaction to the evils associated with the use of the general warrant in England and the writs of assistance in the Colonies, **STANFORD v. TEXAS**, 379 US 476, 481-485, 13 L Ed 2d 431, 85 S Ct 506

(1965); **FRANK v. MARYLAND**, 359 US 360, 363-365, 3 L Ed 2d 877, 79 S Ct 804 (1959), and was intended to protect the "sanctity of a man's home and the privacies of life," **BOYD v. UNITED STATES**, 116 US 616, 630, 29 L Ed 746, 6 S Ct 524 (1886), from searches under unchecked general authority.

The exclusionary rule was a judicially created means of effectuating the rights secured by the Fourth Amendment. Prior to the Court's decisions in **WEEKS v. UNITED STATES**, 232 US 383, 58 L Ed 652, 34 S Ct 341 (1914), and **GOULED v. UNITED STATES**, 255 US 298, 65 L Ed 647, 41 S Ct 261 (1921), there existed no barrier to the introduction in criminal trials of evidence obtained in violation of the Amendment. See **ADAMS v. NEW YORK**, 192 US 585, 48 L Ed 575, 24 S Ct 372 (1904). In Weeks the Court held that the defendant could petition before trial for the return of property secured through an illegal search or seizure conducted by federal authorities. In Gouled the Court held broadly that such evidence could not be introduced in a federal prosecution. See **WARDEN v. HAYDEN**, 387 US 294, 304-305, 18 L Ed 2d 782, 87 S Ct 1642 (1967). See also **SILVERTHORNE LUMBER CO. v. UNITED STATES**, 251 US 385, 64 L Ed 319, 40 S Ct 182, 24 ALR 1426 (1920) (fruits of illegally seized evidence). Thirty-five years after Weeks the Court held in **WOLF v. COLORADO**, 338 US 25, 93 L Ed 1782, 69 S Ct 1359 (1949), that the right to be free from arbitrary intrusion by the police that is protected by the Fourth Amendment is "implicit in 'the concept of ordered liberty' and as such enforceable against the States through the [Fourteenth Amendment] Due Process Clause." Id., at 27-28, 93 L Ed 1782, 69 S Ct 1359. The Court concluded, however, that the Weeks exclusionary rule would not be imposed upon the States as "an essential ingredient of that right." Id., at 29, 93 L Ed 1782, 69 S Ct 1359. The full force of Wolf was eroded in subsequent decisions, see **ELKINS v. UNITED STATES**, 364 US 206, 4 L Ed 1669, 80 S Ct 1437 (1960); **REA v. UNITED STATES**, 350 US 214, 100 L Ed 233, 76 S Ct 292 (1956), and a little more than a decade later the exclusionary rule was held applicable to the States in **MAPP v. OHIO**, 367 US 643, 6 L Ed 2d 1081, 81 S Ct 1684, 84 ALR2d 933, 16 Ohio Ops 2d 384, 86 Ohio L Abs 513 (1961).

Decisions prior to Mapp advanced two principal reasons for application of the rule in federal trials. The Court in Elkins, for example, in the context of its

319

special supervisory role over the lower federal courts, referred to the "imperative of judicial integrity," suggesting that exclusion of illegally seized evidence prevents contamination of the judicial process. 364 US, at 222, 4 L Ed 2d 1669, 80 S Ct 1437. But even in that context a more pragmatic ground was emphasized:

> "The rule is calculated to prevent, not to repair. Its purpose is to deter—to compel respect for the constitutional guaranty in the only effectively available way—by removing the incentive to disregard it." Id., at 217, 4 L Ed 2d 1669, 80 S Ct 1437.

The Mapp majority justified the application of the rule to the States on several grounds, but relied principally upon the belief that exclusion would deter future unlawful police conduct. 367 US, at 658, 6 L Ed 2d 1081, 81 S Ct 1684, 84 ALR2d 933, 16 Ohio Ops 2d 384, 86 Ohio L Abs 513.

Although our decisions often have alluded to the "imperative of judicial integrity," e.g., **UNITED STATES v. PELTIER**, 422 US 531, 536-539, 45 L Ed 2d 374, 95 S Ct 2313 (1975), they demonstrate the limited role of this justification in the determination whether to apply the rule in a particular context. Logically extended this justification would require that courts exclude unconstitutionally seized evidence despite lack of objection by the defendant, or even over his assent. Cf. **HENRY v. MISSISSIPPI**, 379 US 443, 13 L Ed 2d 408, 85 S Ct 564 (1965). It also would require abandonment of the standing limitations on who may object to the introduction of unconstitutionally seized evidence, **ALDERMAN v. UNITED STATES**, 394 US 165, 22 L Ed 2d 176, 89 S Ct 961 (1969), and retreat from the proposition that judicial proceedings need not abate when the defendant's person is unconstitutionally seized, **GERSTEIN v. PUGH**, 420 US 103, 119, 43 L Ed 2d 54, 95 S Ct 854 (1975); **FRISBIE v. COLLINS**, 342 US 519, 96 L Ed 541, 72 S Ct 509 (1952). Similarly, the interest in promoting judicial integrity does not prevent the use of illegally seized evidence in grand jury proceedings. **UNITED STATES v. CALANDRA**, 414 US 338, 38 L Ed 2d 561, 94 S Ct 613, 66

Ohio Ops 2d 320 (1974). Nor does it require that the trial court exclude such evidence from use for impeachment of a defendant, even though its introduction is certain to result in convictions in some cases. **WALDER v. UNITED STATES**, 347 US 62, 98 L Ed 503, 74 S Ct 354 (1954). The teaching of these cases is clear. While courts, of course, must ever be concerned with preserving the integrity of the judicial process this concern has limited force as a justification for the exclusion of highly probative evidence. The force of this justification becomes minimal where federal habeas corpus relief is sought by a prisoner who previously has been afforded the opportunity for full and fair consideration of his search-and-seizure claim at trial and on direct review.

The primary justification for the exclusionary rule then is the deterrence of police conduct that violates Fourth Amendment rights. Post-Mapp decisions have established that the rule is not a personal constitutional right. It is not calculated to redress the injury to the privacy of the victim of the search or seizure, for any "[r]eparation comes too late." **LINKLETTER v. WALKER**, 381 US 618, 637, 14 L Ed 2d 601, 85 S Ct 1731, 5 Ohio Misc 49, 33 Ohio Ops 2d 118 (1965). Instead

> "the rule is a judicially created remedy designed to safeguard Fourth Amendment rights generally through its deterrent effect. . . ." **UNITED STATES v. CALANDRA**, supra, at 348, 38 L Ed 2d 561, 94 S Ct 613, 66 Ohio Ops 2d 320.

Accord, **UNITED STATES v. PELTIER**, supra, at 538-539, 45 L Ed 2d 374 95 S Ct 2313; **TERRY v. OHIO**, 392 US 1, 28-29. 20 L Ed 2d 889, 88 S Ct 1868 (1968); **LINKLETTER v. WALKER** 381 US at 636-637, 14 L Ed 2d 601, 85 S Ct 1731, 5 Ohio Misc 49, 33 Ohio Ops 2d 118; **TEHAN v. SHOTT**, 382 US 406, 416, 15 L ed 2d 453, 86 S Ct 459 (1966).

Mapp involved the enforcement of the exclusionary rule at state trials and on direct review. The decision in **KAUFMAN**, as noted above, is premised on the view that implementation of the Fourth Amendment also requires the consideration of search-and-seizure claims upon collateral review of state convictions. But despite the broad deterrent purpose of the exclusionary rule, it has never been interpreted to proscribe the introduction of

321

illegally seized evidence in all proceedings or against
all persons. As in the case of any remedial device, "the
application of the rule has been restricted to those
areas where its remedial objectives are thought most
efficaciously served." **UNITED STATES v. CALANDRA**, supra,
at 348, 38 L Ed 2d 561, 94 S Ct 613, 66 Ohio Ops 2d 320.
Thus, our refusal to extend the exclusionary rule to
grand jury proceedings was based on a balancing of the
potential injury to the historic role and function of the
grand jury by such extension against the potential
contribution to the effectuation of the Fourth Amendment
through deterrence of police misconduct:

> "Any incremental deterrent effect which might be
> achieved by extending the rule to grand jury
> proceedings is uncertain at best. Whatever
> deterrence of police misconduct may result from the
> exclusion of illegally seized evidence from
> criminal trials, it is unrealistic to assume that
> the application of the rule to grand jury
> proceedings would significantly further that goal.
> Such an extension would deter only police
> investigation consciously directed toward the
> discovery of evidence solely for use in a grand
> jury investigation. . . .
> "We therefore decline to embrace a view that
> would achieve a speculative and undoubtedly minimal
> advance in the deterrence of police misconduct at
> the expense of substantially impeding the role of
> the grand jury." Id., at 351, 38 L Ed 2d 561, 94 S
> Ct 613, 66 Ohio Ops 2d 320 (footnote omitted).

The same pragmatic analysis of the exclusionary
rule's usefulness in a particular context was evident
earlier in **WALDER v. UNITED STATES**, supra, where the
Court permitted the Government to use unlawfully seized
evidence to impeach the credibility of a defendant who
had testified broadly in his own defense. The Court
held, in effect, that the interests safeguarded by the
exclusionary rule in that context were outweighed by the
need to prevent perjury and to assure the integrity of
the trial process. The judgment in Walder revealed most
clearly that the policies behind the exclusionary rule

are not absolute. Rather, they must be evaluated in light of competing policies. In that case, the public interest in determination of truth at trial was deemed to outweigh the incremental contribution that might have been made to the protection of Fourth Amendment values by application of the rule.

The balancing process at work in these cases also finds expression in the standing requirement. Standing to invoke the exclusionary rule has been found to exist only when the Government attempts to use illegally obtained evidence to incriminate the victim of the illegal search. **BROWN v. UNITED STATES**, 411 US 223, 36 L Ed 2d 208, 93 S Ct 1565 (1973); **ALDERMAN v. UNITED STATES**, 394 US 165, 22 L Ed 2d 176, 89 S Ct 961; **WONG SUN v. UNITED STATES**, 371 US 471, 491-492, 9 L Ed 2d 441, 83 S Ct 407 (1963). See **JONES v. UNITED STATES**, 362 US 257, 261, 4 L Ed 2d 697, 80 S Ct 725, 78 ALR2d 233 (1960). The standing requirement is premised on the view that the "additional benefits of extending the rule" to defendants other than the victim of the search or seizure are outweighed by the "further encroachment upon the public interest in prosecuting those accused of crime and having them acquitted or convicted on the basis of all the evidence which exposes the truth." **ALDERMAN v. UNITED STATES**, supra, at 174-175, 22 L Ed 2d 176, 89 S Ct 961.

IV

We turn now to the specific question presented by these cases. Respondents allege violations of Fourth Amendment rights guaranteed them through the Fourteenth Amendment. The question is whether state prisoners—who have been afforded the opportunity for full and fair consideration of their reliance upon the exclusionary rule with respect to seized evidence by the state courts at trial and on direct review—may invoke their claim again on federal habeas corpus review. The answer is to be found by weighing the utility of the exclusionary rule against the costs of extending it to collateral review of Fourth Amendment claims.

The costs of applying the exclusionary rule even at trial and on direct review are well known: the focus of the trial, and the attention of the participants therein, is diverted from the ultimate question of guilt or innocence that should be the central concern in a criminal proceeding. Moreover, the physical evidence sought to be excluded is typically reliable and often the most probative information bearing on the guilt or innocence of the defendant. As MR. JUSTICE BLACK emphasized in his dissent in **KAUFMAN**:

"A claim of illegal search and seizure under the Fourth Amendment is crucially different from many other constitutional rights; ordinarily the evidence seized can in no way have been rendered untrustworthy by the means of its seizure and indeed often this evidence alone establishes beyond virtually any shadow of a doubt that the defendant is guilty." 394 US at 237, 22 L Ed 2d 227, 89 S Ct 1068.

Application of the rule thus deflects the truthfinding process and often frees the guilty. The disparity in particular cases between the error committed by the police officer and the windfall afforded a guilty defendant by application of the rule is contrary to the idea of proportionality that is essential to the concept of justice. Thus, although the rule is thought to deter unlawful police activity in part through the nurturing of respect for Fourth Amendment values, if applied indiscriminately it may well have the opposite effect of generating disrespect for the law and administration of justice. These long-recognized costs of the rule persist when a criminal conviction is sought to be overturned on collateral review on the ground that a search-and-seizure claim was erroneously rejected by two or more tiers of state courts.

Evidence obtained by police officers in violation of the Fourth Amendment is excluded at trial in the hope that the frequency of future violations will decrease. Despite the absence of supportive empirical evidence, we have assumed that the immediate effect of exclusion will be to discourage law enforcement officials from violating the Fourth Amendment by removing the incentive to disregard it. More importantly, over the last term, this demonstration that our society attaches serious consequences to violation of constitutional rights is thought to encourage those who formulate law enforcement policies, and the officers who implement them, to incorporate Fourth Amendment ideals into their value system.

We adhere to the view that these considerations support the implementation of the exclusionary rule at trial and its enforcement on direct appeal of state court convictions. But the additional contribution, if any, of the consideration of search-and-seizure claims of state prisoners on collateral review is small in relation to the costs. To be sure, each case in which such claim is considered may add marginally to an awareness of the values protected by the Fourth Amendment. There is no reason to believe, however, that the overall educative effect of the exclusionary rule would be appreciably diminished if search-and-seizure claims could not be raised in federal habeas corpus review of state convictions. Nor is there reason to assume that any specific disincentive already created by the risk of exclusion of evidence at trial or the reversal of convictions on direct review would be enhanced if there were the further risk that a conviction obtained in state court and affirmed on direct review might be overturned in collateral proceedings often occurring years after the incarceration of the defendant. The view that the deterrence of Fourth Amendment violations would be furthered rests on the dubious assumption that law enforcement authorities would fear that federal habeas review might reveal flaws in a search or seizure that went undetected at trial and on appeal. Even if one rationally could assume that some additional incremental effect would be present in isolated cases, the resulting advance of the legitimate goal of furthering Fourth Amendment rights would be outweighed by the acknowledged costs to other values vital to a rational system of criminal justice.

In sum, we conclude that where the State has provided an opportunity for full and fair litigation of a Fourth Amendment claim, a state prisoner may not be granted federal habeas corpus relief on the ground that evidence obtained in an unconstitutional search or seizure was introduced at his trial. In this context the contribution of the exclusionary rule, if any, to the effectuation to the Fourth Amendment is minimal and the substantial societal costs of application of the rule persist with special force.

Accordingly, the judgments of the Court of Appeals are

Reversed.

TERRY v. OHIO

392 U.S. 1, 88 S.Ct. 1868,20 L.Ed. 2d. 889 (1968)
CERTIORARI TO THE SUPREME COURT OF OHIO
Argued December 12, 1967.-Decided June 10, 1968.

. . .

MR. Chief Justice Warren, delivered the opinion of the Court.

This case presents serious questions concerning the role of the Fourth Amendment in the confrontation on the street between the citizen and the policeman investigating suspicious circumstances.

Petitioner Terry was convicted of carrying a concealed weapon and sentenced to the statutory prescribed term of one to three years in the penitentiary. Following the denial of a pretrial motion to suppress, the prosecution introduced in evidence two revolvers and a number of bullets seized from Terry and a codefendant, Richard Chilton, by Cleveland Police Detective Martin McFadden. At the hearing on the motion to suppress this evidence, Officer McFadden testified that while he was patrolling in plain clothes in downtown Cleveland at approximately 2:30 in the afternoon of October 31, 1963, his attention was attracted by two men, Chilton and Terry, standing on the corner of Huron Road and Euclid Avenue. He had never seen the two men before, and he was unable to say precisely what first drew his eye to them. However, he testified that he had been a policeman for 39 years and a detective for 35 and that he had been assigned to patrol this vicinity of downtown Cleveland for shoplifters and pickpockets for 30 years. He explained that he had developed routine habits of observation over the years and that he would "stand and watch people or walk and watch people at many intervals of the day." He added: "Now, in this case when I looked over they didn't look right to me at the time."

His interest aroused, Officer McFadden took up a post of observation in the entrance to a store 300 to 400 feet away from the two men. "I get more purpose to watch them when L seen their movements, "he testified. He saw one of the men leave the other one and walk southwest on Huron Road, past some stores. The man paused for a moment and looked in a store window, then walked on a short

326

distance, turned around and walked back toward the corner, pausing once again to look in the same store window. He rejoined his companion at the corner, and the two conferred briefly. Then the second man went through the same series of motions, strolling down Huron Road, looking in the same window, walking on a short distance, turning back, peering in the store window again, and returning to confer with the first man at the corner. The two men repeated this ritual alternately between five and six times apiece-in all, roughly a dozen trips. At one point, while the two were standing together on the corner, a third man approached them and engaged them briefly in conversation. This man then left the two others and walked west on Euclid Avenue. Chilton and Terry resumed their measured pacing, peering, and conferring. After this had gone on for 10 to 12 minutes, the two men walked off together, heading west on Euclid Avenue, following the path earlier by the third man.

By this time Officer McFadden had become thoroughly suspicious. He testified that after observing their elaborately casual and oft-repeated reconnaissance of the store window on Huron Road, he suspected the two men of "casing a job, a stick-up," and that he considered it his duty as a police officer to investigate further. He added that he feared "they may have a gun." Thus, Officer McFadden followed Chilton and Terry and saw them stop in front of Zucker's store to talk to the same man who had conferred with them earlier on the street corner. Deciding that the situation was ripe for direct action, Officer McFadden approached the three men, identified himself as a police officer and asked for their names. At this point his knowledge was confined to what he had observed. He was not acquainted with any of the three men by name or by sight, and he had received no information concerning them from any other source. When the men "mumbled something" in response to his inquiries, Officer McFadden grabbed petitioner Terry, spun him around so that they were facing the other two, with Terry between McFadden and the others, and patted down the outside of his clothing. In the left breast pocket of Terry's overcoat Officer McFadden felt a pistol. He reached inside the overcoat pocket, but was unable to remove the gun. At this point, keeping Terry between himself and the others, the officer ordered all three men to enter Zucker's store. As they went in, he removed Terry's overcoat completely, removed a .38-caliber revolver from

327

the pocket and ordered all three men to face the wall with their hands raised. Officer McFadden proceeded to pat down the outer clothing of Chilton and the third man, Katz. He discovered another revolver in the outer pocket of Chilton's overcoat, but no weapons were found on Katz. The officer testified that he only patted the men down to see whether they had weapons, and that he did not put his hands beneath the outer garments of either Terry or Chilton until he felt their guns. So far as appears from the record, he never placed his hands beneath Katz' outer garments. Officer McFadden seized Chilton's gun, asked the proprietor of the store to call a police wagon, and took all three men to the station, where Chilton and Terry were formally charged with carrying concealed weapons.

On the motion to suppress the guns the prosecution took the position that they had been seized following a search incident to a lawful arrest. The trial court rejected this theory, stating that it "would be stretching the facts beyond reasonable comprehension" to find that Officer McFadden had probable cause to arrest the men before he patted them down for weapons. However, the court denied the defendants' motion on the ground that Officer McFadden, on the basis of his experience, "had reasonable cause to believe.... that the defendants were conducting themselves suspiciously, and some interrogation should be made of their action." Purely for his own protection, the court held, the officer had the right to pat down the outer clothing of these men, who he had reasonable cause to believe might be armed. The court distinguished between an investigatory "stop" and an arrest, and between a "frisk" of the outer clothing for weapons and a full-blown search for evidence of crime. The frisk, it held, was essential to the proper performance of the officer's investigatory duties, for without it "the answer to the police officer may be a bullet, and a loaded pistol discovered during the frisk is admissible,"

After the court denied their motion to suppress, Chilton and Terry waived jury trial and pleaded not guilty. The court adjudged them guilty, and the Court of Appeals for the Eighth Judicial District, Cuyahoga County, affirmed. **STATE v. TERRY**, 5 Ohio App. 2d 122, 214

N.E. 2d 114 (1966). The Supreme Court of Ohio dismissed their appeal on the ground that no "substantial constitutional question" was involved. We granted certiorari, 387 U.S. 929 (1967), to determine whether the admission of the revolvers in evidence violated petitioner's rights under the Fourth Amendment, made applicable to the States by the Fourteenth. **MAPP v. OHIO**, 367 U.S. 643 (1961). We affirm the conviction.

I

The Fourth Amendment provides that "the right of the people to be secure in their persons, houses, papers, and effects, against unreasonable searches and seizures, shall not be violated.... " This inestimable right of personal security belongs as much to the citizen on the streets of our cities as to the homeowner closeted in his study to dispose of his secret affairs. For, as this Court has always recognized,

> "No right is held more sacred, or is more carefully guarded, by the common law, than the right of every individual to the possession and control of his own person, free from all restraint or interference of others, unless by clear and unquestionable authority of law." **UNION PAC. R. CO. v. BOTSFORD**, 141 U.S. 250, 251 (1891).

We have recently held that "the Fourth Amendment protects people, not places," **KATZ v. UNITED STATES**, 389 U.S. 347, 351 (1967), and wherever an individual may harbor a reasonable "expectation of privacy," id., at 361 (MR. JUSTICE HARLAN, concurring), he is entitled to be free from unreasonable governmental intrusion. Of course, the specific content and incidents of this right must be shaped by the context in which it is asserted. For "what the Constitution forbids is not all searches and seizures, but unreasonable searches and seizures," **ELKINS v. UNITED STATES**, 364 U.S. 206, 222 (1960). Unquestionably petitioner was entitled to the protection of the Fourth Amendment as he walked down the street in Cleveland. **BECK v. OHIO**, 379 U.S. 89 (1964); **RIOS v. UNITED STATES**, 364 U.S. 253 (1960); **HENRY v. UNITED STATES**, 361 U.S. 98 (1959); **UNITED STATES v. DI RE**, 332 U.S. 581 (1948); **CARROLL v. UNITED STATES**, 267 U.S. 132 (1925). The question is whether in all the circumstances of this on-the-street encounter, his right to personal security was violated by an unreasonable search and seizure.

We would be less than candid if we did not acknowledge that this question thrusts to the fore difficult and troublesome issues regarding a sensitive area of police activity-issues which have never before been squarely presented to this Court. Reflective of the tensions involved are the practical and constitutional arguments pressed with great vigor on both sides of the pubic debate over the power of the police to "stop and frisk"-as it is sometimes euphemistically termed-suspicious persons.

On the one hand, it is frequently argued that in dealing with the rapidly unfolding and often dangerous situations on city streets the police are in need of an escalating set of flexible responses, graduated in relation to the amount of information they possess. For this purpose it is urged that distinctions should be made between a "stop" and an "arrest" (or a "seizure" of a person), and between a "frisk" and a "search." Thus, it is argued, the police should be allowed to "stop" a person and detain him briefly for questioning upon suspicion that he may be connected with criminal activity. Upon suspicion that the person may be armed, the police should have the power to "frisk" him for weapons. If the "stop" and the "frisk" give rise to probable cause to believe that the suspect has committed a crime then the police should be empowered to make a formal "arrest," and a full incident "search" of the person. This scheme is justified in part upon the notion that a "stop" and a "frisk" amount to a mere "minor inconvenience and petty indignity," which can properly be imposed upon the citizen in the interest of effective law enforcement on the basis of a police officer's suspicion.

On the other side the argument is made that the authority of the police must be strictly circumscribed by the law of arrest and search as it has developed to date in the traditional jurisprudence of the Fourth Amendment. It is contended with some force that there is not-and cannot be-a variety of police activity which does not depend solely upon the voluntary cooperation of the citizen and yet which stops short of an arrest based upon probable cause to make such an arrest. The heart of the Fourth Amendment, the argument runs, is a severe requirement of specific justification for any intrusion upon protected personal security, coupled with a highly developed system of judicial controls to enforce upon the agents of the State and commands of the Constitution. Acquiescence by the courts in the compulsion inherent in the field interrogation practices at issue here, it is urged, would constitute an abdication of judicial control over, and indeed an encouragement of, substantial interference with liberty and personal security by police officers whose judgment is necessarily colored by their primary involvement in "the often competitive enterprise of ferreting out crime." **JOHNSON v. UNITED STATES**, 333 U.S. 10, 14 (1948). This, it is argued, can only serve to exacerbate police-community tensions in the crowded centers of our Nation's cities.

In this context we approach the issues in this case mindful of the limitations of the judicial function in controlling the myriad daily situations in which policemen and citizens confront each other on the street. The State has characterized the issue here as "the right of a police officer... to make an on-the-street stop, interrogate and pat down for weapons (known in street vernacular as 'stop and frisk')." But this is only partly accurate. For the issue is not the abstract propriety of the police conduct, but the admissibility against petitioner of the evidence uncovered by the search and seizure. Ever since its inception, the rule excluding evidence seized in violation of the Fourth Amendment has been recognized as a principal mode of discouraging lawless police conduct. See **WEEKS v. UNITED STATES**, 232 U.S. 383, 391-393 (1914). Thus its major thrust is a deterrent one, see **LINKLETTER v. WALKER**, 381 U.S. 618, 629-635 (1965), and experience has taught that it is the only effective deterrent to police misconduct in the criminal context, and that without it the constitutional guarantee against unreasonable searches and seizures would be a mere "form of words." **MAPP v. OHIO**, 367 U.S. 643, 655 (1961). The rule also serves another vital function-"the imperative of judicial integrity." **ELKINS v. UNITED STATES**, 364 U.S. 206, 222 (1960). Courts which sit under our Constitution cannot and will not be made party to lawless invasions of the constitutional rights of citizens by permitting unhindered governmental use of the fruits of such invasions. Thus in our system evidentiary rulings provide the context in which the judicial process of inclusion and exclusion approves some conduct as comporting with constitutional guarantees and disapproves other actions by state agents. A ruling admitting evidence in a criminal trial, we recognize has the necessary effect of legitimizing the conduct which produced the evidence, while an application of the exclusionary rule withholds the constitutional imprimatur.

The exclusionary rule has its limitations, however, as a tool of judicial control. It cannot properly be invoked to exclude the products of legitimate police investigative techniques on the ground that much conduct which is closely similar involves unwarranted intrusions upon constitutional protections. Moreover, in some contexts the rule is ineffective as a deterrent. Street encounters between citizens and police officers are incredibly rich in diversity. They range from wholly friendly exchanges of pleasantries or mutually useful information to hostile confrontations of armed men involving arrest, or injuries, or loss of life. Moreover, hostile confrontations are not all of a piece. Some of them begin in a friendly enough manner, only to take a different turn upon the injection of some unexpected element into the conversation. Encounters are initiated by the police for a wide variety of purposes, some of which are wholly unrelated to a desire to prosecute for crime. Doubtless some police "field interrogation" conduct violates the Fourth Amendment. But a stern refusal by this Court to condone such activity does not necessarily render it responsive to the exclusionary rule. Regardless of how effective the rule may be where obtaining convictions is an important objective of the police either have no interest in prosecuting or are willing to forgo successful prosecution in the interest of serving some other goal.

Proper adjudication of cases in which the exclusionary rule is invoked demands a constant awareness of these limitations. The wholesale harassment by certain elements of the police community, of which minority groups, particularly Negroes, frequently complain, will not be stopped by the exclusion of any evidence from any criminal trial. Yet a rigid and unthinking application of the exclusionary rule, in futile protest against practices which it can never be used effectively to control, may exact a high toll in human injury and frustration of efforts to prevent crime. No judicial opinion can comprehend the protean variety of the street encounter, and we can only judge the facts of the case before us. Nothing we say today is to be taken as indicating approval of police conduct outside the legitimate investigative sphere. Under our decision, courts still retain their traditional responsibility to guard against police conduct which is overbearing or harassing, or which trenches upon personal security without the objective evidentiary justification which the Constitution requires. When such conduct is identified, it must be condemned by the judiciary and its fruits must be excluded from evidence in criminal trials. And, of course, our approval of legitimate and restrained investigative conduct undertaken on the basis of ample factual justification should in no way discourage the employment of other remedies than the exclusionary rule to curtail abuses for which that sanction may prove inappropriate.

Having thus roughly sketched the perimeters of the constitutional debate over the limits on police investigative conduct in general and the background against which this case presents itself, we turn our attention to the quite narrow question posed by the facts before us: whether it is always unreasonable for a policeman to seize a person and subject him to a limited search for weapons unless there is probable cause for an arrest. Given the narrowness of this question, we have no occasion to canvass in detail the constitutional limitations upon the scope of a policeman's power when he confronts a citizen without probable cause to arrest him.

II

Our first task is to establish at that point in this encounter the Fourth Amendment becomes relevant. That is, we must decide whether and when Officer McFadden "seized" Terry and whether and when he conducted a "search." There is some suggestion in the use of such terms as "stop" and "frisk" that such police conduct is outside the purview of the Fourth Amendment because neither action rises to the level of a "search" or seizure" within the meaning of the Constitution. We emphatically reject this notion. It is quite plain that the Fourth Amendment governs "seizures" of the person which do not eventuate in a trip to the station house and prosecution for crime-"arrests" in traditional terminology. It must be recognized that whenever a police officer accosts an individual and restrains his freedom to walk away, he has "seized" that person. And it is nothing less than sheer torture of the English language to suggest that a careful exploration of the outer surfaces of a person's clothing all over his or her body in an attempt to find weapons is not a "search." Moreover, it is simply fantastic to urge that such a procedure performed in public by a policeman while the citizen stands helpless, perhaps facing the wall with his hands raised, is a "petty indignity." It is a serious intrusion upon the sanctity of the person, which may inflict great indignity and arouse strong resentment, and it is not to be undertaken lightly.

The danger in the logic which proceeds upon distinctions between a "stop" and an "arrest," or "seizure"of the person, and between a "frisk" and a "search" is twofold. It seeks to isolate from constitutional scrutiny the initial stages of the contact between the policeman and the citizen. And by suggesting a rigid all-or-nothing model of justification and regulation under the Amendment, it obscures the utility of limitations upon the scope, as well as the initiation, of police action as a means of constitutional regulation. This Court has held in the past that a search which is reasonable at its inception may violate the Fourth Amendment by virtue of its intolerable intensity and scope. **KREMEN v. UNITED STATES**, 353 U.S. 346 (1957); **GO-BART IMPORTING CO. v. UNITED STATES**, 282 U.S. 344, 356-358 (1931); see **UNITED STATES v. DI RE**, 332 U.S. 581, 586-587 (1948). The scope of the search must be "strictly tied to and justified by" the circumstances which rendered its initiation permissible. **WARDEN v. HAYDEN**, 387 U.S. 294, 310 (1967) (MR. JUSTICE FORTAS, concurring); see, e.g., **PRESTON V. UNITED STATES**, 376 U.S. 364, 367-368 (1964); **AGNELLO v. UNITED STATES**, 269 U.S. 20, 30-31 (1925).

The distinctions of classical "stop-and-frisk" theory thus serve to divert attention from the central inquiry under the Fourth Amendment-the reasonableness in all the circumstances of the particular governmental invasion of a citizen's personal security. "Search" and "Seizure" are not talismans. We therefore reject the notions that the Fourth Amendment does not come into play at all as a limitation upon police conduct if the officers stop short of something called a "technical arrest" or a "full-blown search."

In this case there can be no question, then, that Officer McFadden "seized" petitioner and subjected him to a "search" when he took hold of him and patted down the outer surfaces of his clothing. We must decide whether at that point it was reasonable for Officer McFadden to have interfered with petitioner's personal security as he did. And in determining whether the seizure and search were "unreasonable" our inquiry is a dual one-whether the officer's action was justified at its inception, and whether it was reasonably related in scope to the circumstances which justified the interference in the first place.

III

If this case involved police conduct subject to the Warrant Clause of the Fourth Amendment, we would have to ascertain whether "probable cause" existed to justify the search and seizure which took place. However, that is not the case. We do not retreat from our holdings that the police must, whenever practicable, obtain advance judicial approval of searches and seizures through the warrant procedure, see, e.g., **KATZ v. UNITED STATES**, 389 U.S. 347 (1967); **BECK v. OHIO**, 379 U.S. 89, 96 (1964); **CHAPMAN v. UNITED STATES**, 365 U.S. 610 (1961), or that in most instances failure to comply with the warrant requirement can only be excused by exigent circumstances, see, e.g., **WARDEN v. HAYDEN**, 387 U.S. 294 (1967) (hot pursuit); cf. **PRESTON v. UNITED STATES**, 376 U.S. 364, 367-368 (1964). But we deal here with an entire rubric of police conduct-necessarily swift action predicated upon the on-the-spot observations of the officer on the beat-which historically has not been, and as a practical matter could not be, subjected to the warrant procedure. Instead, the conduct involved in this case must be tested by the Fourth Amendment's general proscription against unreasonable searches and seizures.

Nonetheless, the notions which underlie both the warrant procedure and the requirement of probable cause remain fully relevant in this context. In order to assess the reasonableness of Officer McFadden's conduct as a general proposition, it is necessary "first to focus upon the constitutionally protected interests of the private citizen," for there is "no ready test for determining reasonableness other than by balancing the need to search [or seize] against the invasion which the search [or seizure] entails." **CAMARA v. MUNICIPAL COURT**, 387 U.S. 523, 534-535, 536-537 (1967). And in justifying the particular intrusion the police officer must be able to point to specific and articulable facts which, taken together with rational inferences from those facts, reasonably warrant that intrusion. The scheme of the Fourth Amendment becomes meaningful only when it is assured that at some point the conduct of those charged with enforcing the laws can be subjected to the more detached, neutral scrutiny of a judge who must evaluate the reasonableness of a particular search or seizure in light of the particular circumstances. And in making that assessment it is imperative that the facts be judged against an objective standard: would the facts available to the officer at the moment of the seizure or the search "warrant a man of reasonable caution in the belief" that the action taken was appropriate? Cf. **CARROLL v. UNITED STATES**, 267 U.S. 132 (1925); **BECK v. OHIO**, 379 U.S. 89, 96-97 (1964). Anything less would invite intrusions upon constitutionally guaranteed rights based on nothing more substantial than inarticulate hunches, a result this Court has consistently refused to sanction. See, e.g., **BECK v. OHIO**, supra; **RIOS v. UNITED STATES**, 364 U.S. 253 (1960); **HENRY v. UNITED STATES**, 361 U.S. 98 (1959). And simple '"good faith on the part of the arresting officer is not enough.'.... If subjective good faith alone were the test, the protections of the Fourth Amendment would evaporate, and the people would be 'secure in their persons, houses, papers, and effects,' only in the discretion of the police." **BECK v. OHIO**, supra, at 97.

Applying these principles to this case, we consider first the nature and extent of the governmental interests involved. One general interest is of course that of effective crime prevention and detection; it is this interest which underlies the recognition that a police officer may in appropriate circumstances and in an appropriate manner approach a person for purposes of investigating possibly criminal behavior even though there is no probable cause to make an arrest. It was this legitimate investigative function Officer McFadden was discharging when he decided to approach the petitioner and his companions. He had observed Terry, Chilton, and Katz go through a series of acts, each of them perhaps innocent in itself, but which taken together warranted further investigation. There is nothing unusual in two men standing together on a street corner, perhaps waiting for someone. Nor is there anything suspicious about people in such circumstances strolling up and down the street, singly or in pairs. Store windows, moreover, are made to be looked in. But the story is quite different where, as here, two men hover about a street corner for an extended period of time, at the end of which it becomes apparent they are not waiting for someone or anything; where these men pace alternately along an identical route, pausing to stare in the same store window roughly 24 times; where each completion of this route is followed immediately by a conference between the two men on the corner; where they are joined in one of these conferences by a third man who leaves swiftly; and where the two men finally follow the third and rejoin him a couple of blocks away. It would have been poor police work indeed for an officer of 30 years' experience in the detection of thievery from stores in this same neighborhood to have failed to investigate this behavior further.

The crux of this case, however, is not the propriety of Officer McFadden's taking steps to investigate petitioner's suspicious behavior, but rather, whether there was justification for McFadden's invasion of Terry's personal security by searching him for weapons in the course of that investigation. We are now concerned with more than the governmental interest in investigating crime; in addition, there is the more immediate interest of the police officer in taking steps to assure himself that the person with whom he is dealing is not armed with a weapon that could unexpectedly and fatally be used against him. Certainly it would be unreasonable to require that police officers take unnecessary risks in the performance of their duties. American criminals have a long tradition of armed violence, and every year in this country many law enforcement officers are killed in the line of duty, and thousands more are wounded. Virtually all of these deaths and a substantial portion of the injuries are inflicted with guns and knives.

337

In view of these facts, we cannot blind ourselves to the need for law enforcement officers to protect themselves and other prospective victims of violence in situations where they may lack probable cause for an arrest. When an officer is justified in believing that the individual whose suspicious behavior he is investigating at close range is armed and presently dangerous to the officer or to others, it would appear to be clearly unreasonable to deny the officer the power to take necessary measures to determine whether the person is in fact carrying a weapon and to neutralize the threat of physical harm.

We must still consider, however, the nature and quality of the intrusion on individual rights which must be accepted if police officers are to be conceded the right to search for weapons in situations where probable cause to arrest for crime is lacking. Even a limited search of the outer clothing for weapons constitutes severe, though brief, intrusion upon cherished personal security, and it must surely be an annoying, frightening, and perhaps humiliating experience. Petitioner contends that such an intrusion is permissible only incident to a lawful arrest, either for a crime involving the possession of weapons or for a crime the commission of which led the officer to investigate in the first place. However, this argument must be closely examined.

Petitioner does not argue that a police officer should refrain from making any investigation of suspicious circumstances until such time as he has probable cause to make an arrest; nor does he deny that police officers in properly discharging their investigative function may find themselves confronting persons who might well be armed and dangerous. Moreover, he does not say that an officer is always unjustified in searching a suspect to discover weapons. Rather, he says, it is unreasonable for the policeman to take that step until such time as the situation evolves to a point where there is probable cause to make an arrest. When that point has been reached, petitioner would concede the officer's right to conduct a search of the suspect for weapons, fruits or instrumentalities of the crime, or "mere" evidence, incident to the arrest.

There are two weaknesses in this line of reasoning,

however. First, it fails to take account of traditional limitations upon the scope of searches, and thus recognizes no distinction in purpose, character, and extent between a search incident to an arrest and a limited search for weapons. The former, although justified in part by the acknowledged necessity to protect the arresting officer from assault with a concealed weapon, **PRESTON v. UNITED STATES**, 376 U.S. 364, 367 (1964), is also justified on other grounds, ibid., and can therefore involve a relatively extensive exploration of the person. A search for weapons in the absence of probable cause to arrest, however, must, like any other search, be strictly circumscribed by the exigencies which justify its initiation. **WARDEN v. HAYDEN**, 387 U.S. 294, 310 (1967) (MR. JUSTICE FORTAS, concurring). Thus it must be limited to that which is necessary for the discovery of weapons which might be used to harm the officer or others nearby, and may realistically be characterized as something less than a "full" search, even though it remains a serious intrusion.

A second, and related, objection to petitioner's argument is that it assumes that the law of arrest has already worked out the balance between the particular interests involved here-the neutralization of danger to the policeman in the investigative circumstance and the sanctity of the individual. But this is not so. An arrest is a wholly different kind of intrusion upon individual freedom from a limited search for weapons, and the interests each is designed to serve are likewise quite different. An arrest is the initial stage of a criminal prosecution. It is intended to vindicate society's interest in having its laws obeyed, and it is inevitably accompanied by future interference with the individual's freedom of movement, whether or not trial or conviction ultimately follows. The protective search for weapons, on the other hand, constitutes a brief, though far from inconsiderable, intrusion upon the sanctity of the person. It does not follow that because an officer may lawfully arrest a person only when he is apprised of facts sufficient to warrant a belief that the person has committed or is committing a crime, the officer is equally unjustified, absent that kind of evidence, in making any intrusions short of an arrest. Moreover, a perfectly reasonable apprehension of danger may arise long before the officer is possessed of adequate information to justify taking a person into custody for the purpose of prosecuting him for a crime. Petitioner's reliance on cases which have worked out standards of reasonableness with regard to "seizures" constituting arrests and searches incident thereto is thus misplaced. It assumes that the interests sought to be vindicated and the invasions of personal security may be equated in the two cases, and thereby ignores a vital aspect of the analysis of the reasonableness of particular types of conduct under the Fourth Amendment. See **CAMARA v. MUNICIPAL COURT**, supra.

Our evaluation of the proper balance that has to be struck in this type of case leads us to conclude that there must be a narrowly drawn authority to permit a reasonable search for weapons for the protection of the police officer, where he has reason to believe that he is dealing with an armed and dangerous individual, regardless of whether he has probable cause to arrest the individual for a crime. The officer need not be absolutely certain that the individual is armed; the issue is whether a reasonably prudent man in the circumstances would be warranted in the belief that his safety or that of others was in danger. Cf. **BECK v. OHIO**, 379 U.S. 89, 91 (1964); **BRINEGAR v. UNITED STATES**, 338 U.S. 160, 174-176 (1949); **STACEY v. EMERY**, 97 U.S. 642, 645 (1878). And in determining whether the officer acted reasonably in such circumstances, due weight must be given, not to his inchoate and unparticularized suspicion or "hunch," but to the specific reasonable inferences which he is entitled to draw from the facts in light of his experience. Cf. **BRINEGAR v. UNITED STATES**, supra.

IV

We must now examine the conduct of Officer McFadden in this case to determine whether his search and seizure of petitioner were reasonable, both at their inception and as conducted. He had observed Terry, together with Chilton and another man, acting in the manner he took to be preface to a "stick-up." We think on the facts and circumstances Officer McFadden detailed before the trial judge a reasonably prudent man would have been warranted in believing petitioner was armed and thus presented a threat to the officer's safety while he was investigating his suspicious behavior. The actions of Terry and Chilton were consistent with McFadden's hypothesis that these men were contemplating a daylight robbery-which, it is reasonable to assume, would be likely to involve the use of weapons-and nothing in their conduct from the time he first noticed them until the time he confronted them and identified himself as a police officer gave him sufficient reason to negate that hypothesis. Although the trio had departed the original scene, there was nothing to indicate abandonment of an intent to commit a robbery at some point. Thus, when Officer McFadden approached the three men gathered before the display window at Zucker's store he had observed enough to make it quite reasonable to fear that they were armed; and nothing in their response to his hailing them, identifying himself as a police officer, and asking their names served to dispel that reasonable belief. We cannot say his decision at that point to seize Terry and pat his clothing for weapons was the product of a volatile or inventive imagination, or was undertaken simply as an act of harassment; the record evidences the tempered act of a policeman who in the course of an investigation had to make a quick decision as to how to protect himself and others from possible danger, and took limited steps to do so.

The manner in which the seizure and search were conducted is, of course, as vital a part of the inquiry as whether they were warranted at all. The Fourth Amendment proceeds as much by limitations upon the scope of governmental action as by imposing preconditions upon its initiation. Compare **KATZ v. UNITED STATES**, 389 U.S. 347, 354-356 (1967). The entire deterrent purpose of the rule excluding evidence seized in violation of the Fourth Amendment rests on the assumption that "limitations upon the fruit to be gathered tend to limit the quest itself." **UNITED STATES v. POLLER**, 43 F. 2d 911, 914 (C.A. 2d Cir. 1930); see, e.g., **LINKLETTER v. WALKER**, 381 U.S. 618, 629-635 (1965); **MAPP v. OHIO**, 367 U.S. 643 (1961); **ELKINS v. UNITED STATES**, 364 U.S. 206, 216-221 (1960). Thus, evidence may not be introduced if it was discovered by means of a seizure and search which were not reasonably related in scope to the justification for their initiation. **WARDEN v. HAYDEN**, 387 U.S. 294, 310 (1967) (MR. JUSTICE FORTAS, Concurring).

We need not develop at length in this case, however,

the limitations which the Fourth Amendment places upon a protective seizure and search for weapons. These limitations will have to be developed in the concrete factual circumstances of individual cases. See **SIBRON v. NEW YORK**, post, p. 40, decided today. Suffice it to note that such a search, unlike a search without a warrant incident to a lawful arrest, is not justified by any need to prevent the disappearance or destruction of evidence of crime. See **PRESTON v. UNITED STATES**, 376 U.S. 364, 367 (1964). The sole justification of the search in the present situation is the protection of the police officer and others nearby, and it must therefore be confined in scope to an intrusion reasonably designed to discover guns, knives, clubs, or other hidden instruments for the assault of the police officer.

The scope of the search in this case presents no serious problem in light of these standards. Officer McFadden patted down the outer clothing of petitioner and his two companions. He did not place his hands in their pockets or under the outer surface of their garments until he had felt weapons, and then he merely reached for and removed the guns. He never did invade Katz' person beyond the outer surfaces of his clothes, since he discovered nothing in his pat-down which might have been a weapon. Officer McFadden confined his search strictly to what was minimally necessary to learn whether the men were armed and to disarm them once he discovered the weapons. He did not conduct a general exploratory search for whatever evidence of criminal activity he might find.

V

We conclude that the revolver seized from Terry was properly admitted in evidence against him. At the time he seized petitioner and searched him for weapons, Officer McFadden had reasonable grounds to believe that petitioner was armed and dangerous, and it was necessary for the protection of himself and others to take swift measures to discover the true facts and neutralize the threat of harm if it materialized. The policeman carefully restricted his search to what was appropriate to the discovery of the particular items which he sought. Each case of this sort will, of course, have to be decided on its own facts. We merely hold today that where a police officer observes unusual conduct which leads him reasonably to conclude in light of his experience that criminal activity may be afoot and that the persons with whom he is dealing may be armed and presently dangerous, where in the course of investigating this behavior he identifies himself as a policeman and makes reasonable inquiries, and where nothing in the initial stages of the encounter serves to dispel his reasonable fear for his own or others' safety, he is entitled for the protection of himself and others in the area to conduct a carefully limited search of the outer clothing of such persons in an attempt to discover weapons which might be used to assault him. Such a search is a reasonable search under the Fourth Amendment, and any weapons seized may properly be introduced in evidence against the person from whom they were taken.

Affirmed.

MIRANDA v. ARIZONA
384 U.S. 436, 86 S.Ct. 1602, 16 L.Ed.2d 694 (1966)
· · ·

On March 13, 1963, petitioner, Ernesto Miranda, was arrested at his home and taken in custody to a Phoenix police station. He was there identified by the complaining witness. The police then took him to "Interrogation Room NO.2" of the detective bureau. There he was questioned by two police officers. The officers admitted at trial that Miranda was not advised that he had a right to have an attorney present. Two hours later, the officers emerged from the interrogation room with a written confession signed by Miranda. At the top of the statement was a typed paragraph stating the confession was made voluntarily, without threats or promises of immunity and "with full knowledge of my legal rights, understanding any statement I make may be used against me."

At his trial before a jury, the written confession was admitted into evidence over the objection of defense counsel, and the officers testified to the prior oral confession made by Miranda during the interrogation. Miranda was found guilty of kidnapping and rape. He was sentenced to 20 to 30 years' imprisonment on each count, the sentences to run concurrently. On appeal, the Supreme Court of Arizona held that Miranda's constitutional rights were not violated in obtaining the confession and affirmed the conviction. 98 Ariz. 18, 401 P.2d 721. In reaching its decision, the court emphasized heavily the fact that Miranda did not specifically request counsel.

We reverse. From the testimony of the officers and by the admission of respondent, it is clear that Miranda was not in any way apprised of his right to consult with an attorney and to have one present during the interrogation, nor was his right not to be compelled to incriminate himself effectively protected in any other manner. Without these warnings the statements were inadmissible. The mere fact that he signed a statement which contained a typed-in clause stating that he had "full knowledge" of his "legal rights" does not approach the knowing and intelligent waiver required to relinquish constitutional rights.   Cf. **HAYNES v. WASHINGTON**, 373 U.S. 503, 512-513 (1963); **HALEY v. OHIO**, 332 U.S. 596, 601 (1948)(opinion of MR. JUSTICE DOUGLAS).

. . .

ELKINS, ET AL. v. UNITED STATES
364 U.S. 206, 80 S.Ct. 1437, 4 L.Ed.2d 1669 (1960)
CERTIORARI TO THE UNITED STATES COURT OF APPEALS FOR
THE NINTH CIRCUIT
No. 126 Argued March 28-29, 1960.-Decided June 27, 1960.

MR. JUSTICE STEWART delivered the opinion of the Court.
The petitioners were indicted in the United States District Court in Oregon for the offense of intercepting and divulging telephone communications and of conspiracy to do so. 47 U.S.C. §§ 501, 605; 18 U.S.C § 371. Before trial the petitioners made a motion to suppress as evidence several tape and wire recordings and a recording machine, which had originally been seized by state law enforcement officers in the home of the petitioner Clark under circumstances which, two Oregon courts had found, had rendered the search and seizure unlawful. At the hearing on the motion the district judge assumed without deciding that the articles had been obtained as the result of an unreasonable search and seizure, but denied the motion to suppress because there was no evidence that any "agent of the United States had any knowledge or information or suspicion of any kind that this search was being contemplated or was eventually made by the State officers until they read about it in the newspaper." At the trial the articles in question were admitted in evidence against the petitioners, and they were convicted.
The convictions were affirmed by the Court of Appeals for the Ninth Circuit, 266 F.2d 588. That court agreed with the district judge that it was unnecessary to determine whether or not the original state search and seizure had been lawful, because there had been no participation by federal officers. "Hence the unlawfulness of the State search and seizure, if indeed they were unlawful, did not entitle defendants to an order of the District Court suppressing the property seized." 266 F.2d, at 594.
We granted certiorari, 361 U.S. 810, to consider a question of importance in the administration of federal justice. The question is this" May articles obtained as the result of an unreasonable search and seizure by state

346

officers, without involvement of federal officers, be introduced in evidence against a defendant over his timely objection in a federal criminal trial? In a word, we re-examine here the validity of what has come to be called the silver platter doctrine. For the reasons that follow we conclude that this doctrine is no longer accepted.

To put the issue in historic perspective, the appropriate starting point must be **WEEKS v. UNITED STATES**, 232 U.S. 383, decided in 1914. It was there that the Court established the rule which excludes in a federal criminal prosecution evidence obtained by federal agents in violation of the defendant's Fourth Amendment rights. The foundation for that decision was set out in forthright words:

> "The effect of the Fourth Amendment is to put the courts of the United States and Federal officials, in the exercise of their power and authority, under limitations and restraints as to the exercise of such power and authority, and to forever secure the people, their persons, houses, papers and effects against all unreasonable searches and seizures under the guise of law. This protection reaches all alike, whether accused of crime or not, and the duty of giving to it force and effect is obligatory upon all entrusted under our Federal system with the enforcement of the laws. The tendency of those who execute the criminal laws of the country to obtain conviction by means of unlawful seizures and enforced confessions, the latter often obtained after subjecting accused persons to unwarranted practices destructive of rights secured by the Federal Constitution, should find no sanction in the judgments of the courts which are charged at all times with the support of the Constitution and to which people of all conditions have a right to appeal for the maintenance of such fundamental rights.

> .   .   .   .   .

> ". . . .If letters and private documents can thus be seized and held used in evidence against a citizen accused of an offense, the protection of the Fourth Amendment declaring his right to be secure against such searches and seizures is of no

347

value, and, so far as those placed are concerned, might as well be stricken from the Constitution. The efforts of the courts and their officials to bring the guilty to punishment, praiseworthy as they are, are not to be aided by the sacrifice of those great principles established by years of endeavor and suffering which have resulted in their embodiment in the fundamental law of the land." 232 U.S. 383, 391-393.

To the exlusionary rule of **WEEKS v. UNITED STATES** there has been unquestioning adherence for now almost half a century. See **SILVERTHORNE LUMBER CO. v. UNITED STATES**, 251 U.S. 385; **GOULED v. UNITED STATES**, 255 U.S. 298; **AMOS v. UNITED STATES**, 255 U.S. 313; **AGNELLO v. UNITED STATES**, 269 U.S. 20; **GO-BART CO. v. UNITED STATES**, 282 U.S. 344; **GRAU v. UNITED STATES**, 287 U.S. 124; **McDONALD v. UNITED STATES**, 335 U.S. 451; **UNITED STATES v. JEFFERS**, 342 U.S. 48.

But the WEEKS case also announced, unobtrusively but nonetheless definitely, another evidentiary rule. Some of the articles used as evidence against WEEKS had been unlawfully seized by local police officers acting on their own account. The Court held that the admission of this evidence was not error for the reason that "the Fourth amendment is not directed to individual misconduct of such officials. Its limitations reach the Federal Government and its agencies." 232 U.S., at 398. Despite the limited discussion of this second ruling in the WEEKS opinion, the right of the prosecutor in a federal criminal trial to avail himself of evidence unlawfully seized by state officers apparently went unquestioned for the next thirty-five years. See, e.g., **BYARS v. UNITED STATES**, 273 U.S. 28, 33; **FELDMAN v. UNITED STATES**, 322 U.S. 487, 492.

That such a rule would engender practical difficulties in an era of expanding federal criminal jurisdiction could not, perhaps, have been foreseen. In any event the difficulties soon appeared. They arose from the entirely commendable practice of state and federal agents to cooperate with each other in the investigation and detection of criminal activity. When in a federal criminal prosecution evidence which had been illegally seized by state officers was thought to be introduced, the question inevitably arose whether there had been such participation by federal agents in the search and seizure as to make applicable the exlusionary rule of WEEKS. Se **FLAGG v. UNITED STATES**, 233 Fed. 481, 483; **UNITED STATES v. SLUSSER**, 270 Fed. 818, 820; **UNITED STATES v. FALLOCO**, 277 Fed. 75, 82; **LEGMAN v. UNITED STATES**, 295 Fed. 474, 476-478; **MARRON v. UNITED STATES**, 8 F.2d 251, 259; **UNITED STATES v. BROWN**, 8 F.2d 630, 631.

This Court first came to grips with the problem in **BYARS v. UNITED STATES**, 273 U.S. 28. There it was held that when the participation of the federal agent in the search was "under color of his federal office" and the search "in substance and effect was a joint operation of the local and federal officers," then the evidence must be excluded, because "the effect is the same as though [the federal agent] had engaged in the undertaking as one exclusively his own." 273 U.S., at 33. In **GAMBINO v. UNITED STATES**, 275 U.S., at 310, the Court went further. There state officers had seized liquor from the defendant's automobile after an unlawful search in which no federal officers had participated. The liquor was admitted in evidence against the defendants in their subsequent federal trial for violation of the National Prohibition Act. This Court reversed the judgments of conviction, holding that the illegally seized evidence should have been excluded. Pointing out that there was "no suggestion that the defendants were committing, at the time of the arrest, search and seizure, any state offense; or that they had done so in the past; or that the [state] troopers believed that they had," the Court found that "[t]he wrongful arrest, search and seizure were made solely on behalf of the United States." 275 U.S., at 314, 316.

Despite these decisions, or perhaps because of them, cases kept arising in which the federal courts were faced with determining whether there had been such participation by federal officers in a lawless state search as to make inadmissible in evidence that which had been seized. And it is fair to say that in their approach to this recurring question, no less than in their disposition of concrete cases, the federal courts did not find themselves in complete harmony, nor even internally self-consistent. No less difficulty was experienced by the courts in determining whether, even in the absence of actual participation by federal agents, the state officers' illegal search and seizure had nevertheless been made "solely on behalf of the United States."

But difficult and unpredictable as may have been their application to concrete cases, the controlling principles seemed clear up to 1949. Evidence which had been seized by federal officers in violation of the Fourth Amendment could not be used in a federal criminal prosecution. Evidence which had been obtained by state agents in an unreasonable search and seizure was admissible, because, as WEEKS had pointed out, the Fourth Amendment was not "directed to" the "misconduct of such officials." But if federal agents had participated in an unreasonable search and seizure by state officers, or if the state officers had acted solely on behalf of the United States, the evidence was not admissible in a federal prosecution.

Then came **WOLF v. COLORADO**, 338 U.S. 25. With the ultimate determination in WOLF - that the Due Process Clause of the Fourteenth Amendment does not itself require state courts to adopt the exclusionary rule with respect to evidence illegally seized by state agents - we are not here directly concerned. But nothing could be of greater relevance to the present inquiry than the underlying constitutional doctrine which WOLF established. For there it was unequivocally determined by a unanimous Court that the Federal Constitution, by virtue of the Fourteenth Amendment, prohibits unreasonable searches and seizures by state officers. "The security of one's privacy against arbitrary intrusion by the police . . .is . . .implicit in 'the concept of ordered liberty' and as such enforceable against the States through the Due Process Clause." 338 U.S. 25, 27-28. The Court had subsequently found frequent occasion to reiterate this statement from Wolf. See **STEFANELLI v. MINARD**, 342 U.S. 117, 119; **IRVINE v. CALIFORNIA**, 347 U.S. 128, 132; **FRANK v. MARYLAND**, 359 U.S. 360, 362-363.

The foundation upon which the admissibility of state-seized evidence in a federal trial originally rested - that unreasonable state searches did not violate the Federal Constitution - thus disappeared in 1949. This removal of the doctrinal underpinning for the admissibility rule has apparently escaped the attention of most of the federal courts, which have continued to approve the admission of evidence illegally seized by state officers without so much as even discussing the impact of WOLF. only two of the courts of appeals which have adhered to the admissibility rule appear to have recognized that WOLF casts doubt upon its continuing validity. **JONES v. UNITED STATES**, 217 F.2d 381 (C.A. 8th Cir); **UNITED STATES v. BENANTI**, 224 F.2d 389 (C.A. 2d Cir), reversed on other grounds, 355 U.S. 96. Cf. **KENDALL v. UNITED STATES**, 272 F.2d 163, 165 (C.A. 5th Cir). The Court of Appeals for the District of Columbia had been alone in aurally holding "that the WEEKS and the WOLF decision, considered together, make all evidence obtained by unconstitutional search and seizure unacceptable in federal courts." **HANNA v. UNITED STATES**, 104 U.S. App D.C. 205, 209, 260 F.2d 723, 727.

Yet this Court's awareness that the constitutional doctrine of WOLF operated to undermine the logical foundation of the WEEKS admissibility rule has been manifest from the very day that WOLF was decided. In **LUSTIG v. UNITED STATES**, 338 U.S. 74, decided that day, the prevailing opinion carefully left open the question of the continuing validity of the admissibility rule. "Where there is participation on the part of federal officers," the opinion said, "it is not necessary to consider what would be the result if the search had been conducted entirely by State officers." 338 U.S. at 79. And in **BENNANTI v. UNITED STATES**, 355 U.S. 96, the Court was at pains to point out that "[i]t has remained an open question in this Court whether evidence obtained solely by state agents in an illegal search may be admissible in federal court . . . ." 355 U.S., at 102, note 10. There the question has stood for 11 years.

If resolution of the issue were to be dictated solely by principles of logic, it is clear what our decision would have to be. For surely no distinction can logically be drawn between evidence obtained in violation of the Fourth Amendment and that obtained in violation of Fourteenth. The Constitution is flouted equally in either case. To the victim it matters not whether his constitutional right has been invaded by a federal agent or by a state officer. It would be a curiously ambivalent rule that would require that courts of the United States to differentiate between unconstitutionally seized evidence upon so arbitrary a basis. Such a distinction indeed would appear to reflect an indefensibly selective evaluation of the provisions of the Constitution. Moreover, it would seem logically impossible to justify a policy that would bar from a federal trial what state officers had obtained in violation of a federal statute, yet would admit that which they had seized in violation of Constitution itself. Cf. **BENANTI v. UNITED STATES**, 355 U.S. 96.

Mere logical symmetry and abstract reasoning are perhaps not enough, however, to support a doctrine that would exclude relevant evidence from the trial of a federal criminal case. It is true that there is not involved here an absolute or qualified testimonial privilege such as that accorded a spouse, a patient, or a penitent, which irrevocably bars otherwise admissible evidence because of the status of the witness or his relationship to the defendant. Cf. **HAWKINS v. UNITED STATES**, 358 U.S 74. A rule which would exclude evidence if , and only if, government officials in a particular case had chosen to engage in unlawful conduct is of a different order. Yet, any apparent limitation upon the process of discovering truth in a federal trial ought to be imposed only upon the basis of considerations which outweigh the general need for untrammeled disclosure of competent and relevant evidence in a court of justice.

What is here invoked is the Court's supervisory power over the administration of criminal justice in the federal courts, under which the Court has "from the very beginning of its history, formulated rules of evidence to be applied in federal criminal prosecutions." **MCNABB v. UNITED STATES**, 318 U.S. 332, 341. In devising such evidentiary rules, we are to be governed by "principles of the common law as they may be interpreted . . . in the light of reason and experience." Rule 26, Fed. Rules Crim. Proc. Determination of the issue before us must ultimately depend , therefore, upon evaluation of the exclusionary rule itself in the context here presented.

The exclusionary rule has for decades been the subject of ardent controversy. The arguments of its antagonists and of its proponents have been so many times marshalled as to require no lengthy elaboration here. Most of what has been said in opposition to the rule was distilled in a single Cardozo sentence - "The criminal is to go free because the constable has blundered." **PEOPLE v. DEFORE** 242 N.Y. 13, 21, 150 N.E. 585, 587. The same point was made at somewhat greater length in the often quoted words of Professor Wigmore: "Titus, you have been found guilty of conducting a lottery; Flavius, you have confessedly violated the constitution. Titus ought to suffer imprisonment for crime, and Flavius for contempt. But no! We shall let you both go free. We shall not punish Flavius directly, but shall do so by reversing Titus' conviction. This is our way of teaching people like Flavius to behave, and of teaching people like Titus to behave, and incidentally of securing respect for the Constitution. Our way of upholding the Constitution is not to strike at the man who breaks it, but to let off somebody else who broke something else." 8 Wigmore, Evidence (3d ed. 1940), § 2184.

Yet, however felicitous their phrasing, these objections hardly answer the basic postulate of the exclusionary rule itself. The rule is calculated to prevent, not to repair. Its purpose is to deter - to compel respect for the constitutional guaranty in the only effectively available way - by removing the incentive to disregard it. See **ELEUTERI v. RICHMAN**, 26 N.J. 506, 513, 141 A.2d 46, 50. MR. JUSTICE JACKSON summed it up well"

"Only occasional and more flagrant abuses come to the attention of the courts, and then only those where the search and seizure yields incriminating evidence and the defendant is at least sufficiently compromised to be indicted. If the officers raid a home, an office, or stop and search an automobile but find nothing incriminating, this invasion of the personal liberty of the innocent too often finds no practical redress. There may be, and I am convinced that there are, many unlawful searches of homes and automobiles of innocent people which turn up nothing incriminating, in which no arrest is made, about which courts do nothing, and about which we never hear.

"Courts can protect the innocent against such invasions only indirectly and through the medium of excluding evidence obtained against those who frequently are guilty." **BRINEGAR v. UNITED STATES**, 338 U.S. 160, 181 (dissenting opinion).

Empirical statistics are not available to show that

the inhabitants of states which follow the exclusionary rule suffer less from lawless searches and seizures than do those of states which admit evidence unlawfully obtained. Since as a practical matter it is never easy to prove a negative, it is hardly likely that conclusive factual data could ever be assembled. For much the same reason, it cannot positively be demonstrated that enforcement of the criminal law is either more or less effective under either rule.

But pragmatic evidence of a sort is not wanting. The federal courts themselves have operated under the exclusionary rule of WEEKS for almost half a century; yet it has not been suggested either that the Federal Bureau of Investigation has thereby been rendered ineffective, or that the administration of criminal justice in the federal courts has thereby been disrupted. Moreover, the experience of the states is impressive. Not more than half the states continue totally to adhere to the rule that evidence is freely admissible no matter how it was obtained. Most of the others have adopted the exlusionary rule in its entirely; the rest have adopted it in part. The movement toward the rule of exclusion has been halting but seemingly inexorable. Since the WOLF decision one state has switched its position in that direction by legislation, and two others by judicial decision. Another state, uncommitted until 1955, in that year adopted the rule of exclusion. Significantly, most of the exclusionary states which have had to consider the issue have held that evidence obtained by federal officers in a search and seizure unlawful under the Fourth Amendment must be suppressed in a prosecution in the state courts. **STATE v. ARREGUI**, 44 Idaho 43, 254 P. 788; **WALTERS v. COMMONWEALTH**, 199 Ky. 182, 250 S.W. 839; **LITTLE v. STATE**, 171 Miss. 818, 159 So. 103; **STATE v. REBASTI**, 306 Mo. 336, 267 S.W. 858; **STATE v. HITESHEW**, 42 Wyo. 147, 292 P.2; see **RAMIREZ v. STATE**, 123 Tex. Cr.R. 254, 58 S.W.2d 829. Compare **REA v. UNITED STATES**, 350 U.S. 214.

The experience in California has been most illuminating. In 1955 the Supreme Court of that State resolutely turned its back on many years of precedent and adopted the exclusionary rule. **PEOPLE v. CAHAN**, 44 Cal. 2d 43, 282 P.2d 905. "We have been compelled to reach that conclusion because other remedies have completely failed to secure compliance with the constitutional provisons on that part of police officers with the attendant result that the courts under the old rule have been constantly required to participate in, and in effect condone, the lawless activities of law enforcement officers . . . Experience has demonstrated, however, that neither administrative, criminal nor civil remedies are effective in suppressing lawless searches and seizures. The innocent suffer with the guilty, and we cannot close our eyes to the effect the rule we adopt will have on the rights of those not before the court." 44 Cal.2d 434, at 445, 447, 282 P.2d 905, at 911-912, 913.

The chief law enforcement officer of California was quoted as having made this practical evaluation of the Cahan decision less than two years later:

"The over-all effects of the Cahan decision , particularly in view of the rules now worked out by the Supreme Court, have been excellent. A much greater education is called for on the part of all peace officers of California. As a result, I am confident they will be much better police officers. I think there is more cooperation with the District Attorneys and this will make for better administration of criminal justice."

Impressive as is this experience of individual states, even more is to be said for adoption of the exclusionary rule in the particular context here presented - a context which brings into focus considerations of federalism. The very essence of a healthy federalism depends upon the avoidance of needless conflict between state and federal courts. Yet when a federal court sitting in an exclusionary state admits evidence lawlessly seized by state agents, it not only frustrates state policy, but frustrates that policy in a particularly inappropriate and ironic way. For by admitting the unlawfully seized evidence the federal court serves to defeat the state's effort to assure obedience to the Federal constitution. In states which have not adopted the exclusionary rule, on the other hand, it would work no conflict with local policy for a federal court to decline to receive evidence unlawfully seized by state officers. The question with which we deal today affects not all the freedom of the states to develop and apply their own sanctions in their own way.

Cf. **WOLF v. COLORADO**, 338 U.S. 25.

Free and open cooperation between state and federal law enforcement officers is to be commended and encouraged. Yet that kind of cooperation is hardly promoted by a rule that implicitly invites federal officers to withdraw from such association and at least tacitly to encourage state officers in the disregard of constitutionally protected freedom. If, on the other hand, it is understood that the fruit of an unlawful search by state agents will be inadmissible in a federal trial, there can be no inducement to subterfuge and evasion with respect to federal-state cooperation in criminal investigation. Instead, forthright cooperation under constitutional standards will be promoted and fostered.

It must always be remembered that what the Constitution forbids is not all searches and seizures, but unreasonable searches and seizures. Without pausing to analyze individual decisions, it can fairly be said that in applying the Fourth Amendment this Court has seldom shown itself unaware of the practical demands of effective criminal investigation and law enforcement. Indeed, there are those who think that some of the court's decisions have tipped the balance too heavily against the protection of that individual privacy which it was the purpose of the Fourth Amendment to guarantee. See **HARRIS v. UNITED STATES**, 331 U.S. 145, 155, 183, 195 (dissenting opinions); **UNITED STATES v. RABINOWITZ**, 339 U.S. 56, 66, 68 (dissenting opinions). In any event, while individual cases have sometimes evoked "fluctuating differences of view," **ABEL v. UNITED STATES**, 362 U.S. 217, 235, it can hardly be said that in the over-all pattern of Fourth Amendment decisions this Court has been either unrealistic or visionary.

These, then, are the considerations of reason and experience which point to the rejection of a doctrine that would freely admit in a federal criminal trial evidence seized by state agents in violation of the defendant's constitutional rights. But there is another consideration - the imperative of judicial integrity. It was of this that MR. JUSTICE HOMES and MR. JUSTICE BRANDEIS so eloquently spoke in **OLMSTEAD v. UNITED STATES**, 277 U.S. 438, at 469, 471, more than 30 years ago. "For those who agree with me," said MR. JUSTICE HOLMES, " no distinction can be taken between the Government as prosecutor and the Government as judge." 277 U.S., at 470. (Dissenting opinion.) "In a government of laws," said MR. JUSTICE BRANDEIS, "existence of the government will be imperilled if it fails to observe the law scrupulously. Our Government is the potent, the omnipresent teacher. For good or for ill, it teaches the whole people by its example. Crime is contagious. If the Government becomes a lawbreaker, it breeds contempt for law; it invites every man to become a law unto himself; it invites anarchy. To declare that in the administration of the criminal law the end justifies the means - to declare that the Government may commit crimes in order to secure the conviction of a private criminal - would bring terrible retribution . Against that pernicious doctrine this Court should resolutely set its face." 277 U.S., at 485. (Dissenting opinion).

This basic principle was accepted by the Court in **McNABB v. UNITED STATES**, 38 U.S.332. There it was held that "a conviction resting on evidence secured through such a flagrant disregard of the procedure which Congress has commanded cannot be allowed to stand without making the courts themselves accomplices in willful disobedience of law." 318 U.S., at 345. Even less should the federal courts be accomplices in the willful disobedience of a Constitution they are sworn to uphold.

For these reasons we hold that evidence obtained by state officers during a search which, if conducted by federal officers, would have violated the defendant's immunity from unreasonable searches and seizures under the Fourth Amendment is inadmissible over the defendant's timely objection in a federal criminal trial. In determining whether there has been an unreasonable search and seizure by state officers, a federal court must make an independent inquiry, whether or not there has been such an inquiry by a state court, and irrespective of how any such inquiry may have turned out. The test is one of federal law, neither enlarged by what one state court may have countenanced, nor diminished by what another may have colorably suppressed.

The judgment of the Court of Appeals is set aside, and the case is remanded to the District Court for further proceedings consistent with this opinion.

Vacated and remanded.

MAPP v. OHIO
367 U.S. 643, 81 S.Ct. 1680, 6 L.Ed.2d. 1081 (1961)
APPEAL FROM THE SUPREME COURT OF OHIO.
Argued March 29, 1961.—Decided June 19, 1961.
. . .
MR. JUSTICE CLARK delivered the opinion of the Court.

Appellant stands convicted of knowingly having had in her possession and under her control certain lewd and lascivious books, pictures, and photographs in violation of § 2905.34 of Ohio's Revised Code. As officially stated in the syllabus to its opinion, the Supreme Court of Ohio found that her conviction was valid though "based primarily upon the introduction in evidence of lewd and lascivious books and pictures unlawfully seized during an unlawful search of defendant's home ...." 170 Ohio St. 427-428, 166 N.E. 2d 387, 388.

On May 23, 1957, three Cleveland police officers arrived at appellant's residence in that city pursuant to information that "a person [was] hiding out in the home, who was wanted for questioning in connection with a recent bombing, and that there was a large amount of policy paraphernalia being hidden in the home." Miss Mapp and her daughter by a former marriage lived on the top floor of the two-family dwelling. Upon their arrival at the house, the officers knocked on the door and demanded entrance but appellant, after telephoning her attorney, refused to admit them without a search warrant. They advised their headquarters of the situation and undertook a surveillance of the house.

The officers again sought entrance some three hours later when four or more additional officers arrived on the scene. When Miss Mapp did not come to the door immediately, at least one of the several doors to the house was forcibly opened and the policemen gained admittance. Meanwhile Miss Mapp's attorney arrived, but the officers, having secured their own entry, and continuing in their defiance of the law, would permit him neither to see Miss Mapp nor to enter the house. It appears that Miss Mapp was halfway down the stairs from the upper floor to the front door when the officers, in this highhanded manner, broke into the hall. She demanded to see the search warrant. A paper, claimed to be a warrant, was held up by one of the officers. She grabbed the "warrant" and placed it in her bosom. A struggle ensued in which the officers recovered the piece of paper and as a result of which they handcuffed appellant because she had been "belligerent" in resisting their official rescue of the "warrant" from her person. Running roughshod over appellant, a policeman "grabbed" her, "twisted [her] hand," and she "yelled [and] pleaded with him" because "it was hurting." Appellant, in handcuffs, was then forcibly taken upstairs to her bedroom where the officers searched a dresser, a chest of drawers, a closet and some suitcases. They also looked into a photo album and through personal papers belonging to the appellant. The search spread to the rest of the second floor including the child's bedroom, the living room, the kitchen and a dinette. The basement of the building and a trunk found therein were also searched. The obscene materials for possession of which she was ultimately convicted were discovered in the course of that widespread search.

At the trial no search warrant was produced by the prosecution, nor was the failure to produce one explained or accounted for. At best, "There is, in the record, considerable doubt as to whether there ever was any warrant for the search of defendant's home." 170 Ohio St., at 430, 166 N.E. 2d, at 389. The Ohio Supreme Court believed a "reasonable argument" could be made that the conviction should be reversed "because the 'methods' employed to obtain the [evidence] .... were such as to 'offend "a sense of justice,"'" but the court found determinative the fact that the evidence had not been taken "from defendant's person by the use of a brutal or offensive physical force against defendant." 170 Ohio St., at 431, 166 N.E.2d, at 389-390.

The State says that even if the search were made without authority, or otherwise unreasonably, it is not prevented from using the unconstitutionally seized evidence at trial, citing **WOLF v. COLORADO**, 338 U.S. 25 (1949), in which this Court did indeed hold "that in a prosecution in a State court for a State crime the Fourteenth Amendment does not forbid the admission of evidence obtained by an unreasonable search and seizure." At p. 33. On this appeal, of which we have noted probable jurisdiction, 364 U.S. 868, it is urged once again that we review that holding.

359

I

Seventy-five years ago, in **BOYD v. UNITED STATES**, 116 U.S. 616, 630 (1886), considering the Fourth and Fifth Amendments as running "almost into each other" on the facts before it, this Court held that the doctrines of those Amendments

> "apply to all invasions on the part of the government and its employees of the sanctity of a man's home and the privacies of life. It is not the breaking of his doors, and the rummaging of his drawers, that constitutes the essence of the offence; but it is the invasion of his indefeasible right of personal security, personal liberty and private property .... Breaking into a house and opening boxes and drawers are circumstances of aggravation, but any forcible and compulsory extortion of a man's own testimony or of his private papers to be used as evidence to convict him of crime or to forfeit his goods, is within the condemnation .... [of those Amendments]."

The Court noted that

> "constitutional provisions for the security of person and property should be liberally construed .... It is the duty of courts to be watchful for the constitutional rights of the citizen, and against any stealthy encroachments thereon." At p. 635

In this jealous regard for maintaining the integrity of individual rights, the Court gave life to Madison's prediction that "independent tribunals of justice .... will be naturally led to resist every encroachment upon rights expressly stipulated for in the Constitution by the declaration of rights." I Annals of Cong. 439 (1789). Concluding, the Court specifically referred to the use of the evidence there seized as "unconstitutional." At p. 638.

Less than 30 years after Boyd, this Court, in **WEEKS v. UNITED STATES**, 232 U.S. 383 (1914), stated that "the Fourth Amendment .... put the courts of the United States and Federal officials, in the exercise of their power and authority, under limitations and restraints [and] .... forever secure[d] the people, their persons, houses, papers and effects against all unreasonable searches and seizures under the guise of law .... and the duty of giving to it force and effect is obligatory upon all entrusted under our Federal system with the enforcement of the laws." At pp. 391-392.

Specifically dealing with the use of the evidence unconstitutionally seized, the Court concluded:

"If letters and private documents can thus be seized and held and used in evidence against a citizen accused of an offense, the protection of the Fourth Amendment declaring his right to be secure against such searches and seizures is of no value, and, so far as those thus placed are concerned, might as well be stricken from the Constitution. The efforts of the courts and their officials to bring the guilty to punishment, praiseworthy as they are, are not to be aided by the sacrifice of those great principles established by years of endeavor and suffering which have resulted in their embodiment in the fundamental law of the land." At p. 393.

Finally, the Court in that case clearly stated that use of the seized evidence involved "a denial of the constitutional rights of the accused." At p. 398. Thus, in the year 1914, in the Weeks case, this court "for the first time" held that "in a federal prosecution the Fourth Amendment barred the use of evidence secured through an illegal search and seizure." **WOLF v. COLORADO**, supra, at 28. This Court has ever since required of federal law officers a strict adherence to that command which this Court has held to be a clear, specific, and constitutionally required—even if judicially implied—deterrent safeguard without insistence upon which the Fourth Amendment would have been reduced to "a form of words." HOLMES, J., **SILVERTHORNE LUMBER CO. v. UNITED STATES**, 251 U.S. 385, 392 (1920). It meant, quite simply, that "conviction by means of unlawful seizures and enforced confessions .... should find no sanction in

361

the judgments of the courts ...." **WEEKS v. UNITED STATES**, supra, at 392, and that such evidence "shall not be used at all." **SILVERTHORNE LUMBER CO. v. UNITED STATES**, supra, at 392.

There are in the cases of this Court some passing references to the Weeks rule as being one of evidence. But the plain and unequivocal language of Weeks—and its later paraphrase in Wolf—to the effect that the Weeks rule is of constitutional origin, remains entirely undisturbed. In **BYARS v. UNITED STATES**, 273 U.S. 28 (1927), a unanimous Court declared that "the doctrine [cannot] .... be tolerated *under our constitutional system,* that evidences of crime discovered by a federal officer in making a search without lawful warrant may be used against the victim of the unlawful search where a timely challenge has been interposed." At pp. 29-30 (emphasis added). The Court, in **OLMSTEAD v. UNITED STATES**, 277 U.S. 438 (1928), in unmistakable language restated the Weeks rule:

> "The striking outcome of the Weeks case and those which followed it was the sweeping declaration that the Fourth Amendment, although not referring to or limiting the use of evidence in courts, really forbade its introduction if obtained by government officers through a violation of the Amendment." At p. 462.

In **MCNABB v. UNITED STATES**, 318 U.S. 332 (1943), we note this statement:

> "[A] conviction in the federal courts, the foundation of which is evidence obtained in disregard of liberties deemed fundamental by the Constitution, cannot stand. **BOYD v. UNITED STATES** .... **WEEKS v. UNITED STATES** .... And this court has, on Constitutional grounds, set aside convictions, both in the federal and state courts, which were based upon confessions 'secured by protracted and repeated questioning of ignorant and untutored persons, in whose minds the power of officers was greatly magnified'... or 'who have been unlawfully held incommunicado without advice

of friends or counsel'.... " At pp. 339-340.

Significantly, in McNabb, the Court did then pass on to formulate a rule of evidence, saying, "[i]n the view we take of the case, however, it becomes unnecessary to reach the Constitutional issue [for] .... [t]he principles governing the admissibility of evidence in federal criminal trials have not been restricted .... to those derived solely from the Constitution." At pp. 340-341.

II

In 1949, 35 years after *Weeks* was announced, this Court, in **WOLF v. COLORADO**, supra, again for the first time, discussed the effect of the Fourth Amendment upon the States through the operation of the Due Process Clause of the Fourteenth Amendment. It said:

"[W]e have no hesitation in saying that were a State affirmatively to sanction such police incursion into privacy it would run counter to the guaranty of the Fourteenth Amendment." At p. 28.

Nevertheless, after declaring that the "security of one's privacy against arbitrary intrusion by the police" is "implicit in 'the concept of ordered liberty' and as such enforceable against the States through the Due Process Clause," cf. **PALKO v. CONNECTICUT**, 302 U.S. 319 (1937), and announcing that it "stoutly adhere[d]" to the Weeks decision, the Court decided that the Weeks exclusionary rule would not then be imposed upon the States as "an essential ingredient of the right." 338 U.S., at 27-29. The Court's reasons for not considering essential to the right to privacy, as a curb imposed upon the States by the Due Process Clause, that which decades before had been posited as part and parcel of the Fourth Amendment's limitation upon federal encroachment of individual privacy, were bottomed on factual considerations.

While they are not basically relevant to a decision that the exclusionary rule is an essential ingredient of the Fourth Amendment as the right it embodies is vouchsafed against the States by the Due Process Clause, we will consider the current validity of the factual grounds upon which Wolf was based.

The Court in Wolf first stated that "[t]he

contrariety of views of the States" on the adoption of
the exclusionary rule of Weeks was "particularly
impressive" (at p. 29); and, in this connection, that it
could not "brush aside the experience of States which
deem the incidence of such conduct by the police too
slight to call for a deterrent remedy .... by overriding
the [States'] relevant rules of evidence." At pp. 31-32.
While in 1949, prior to the Wolf case, almost two-thirds
of the States were opposed to the use of the exclusionary
rule, now, despite the Wolf case, more than half of those
since passing upon it, by their own legislative or
judicial decision, have wholly or partly adopted or
adhered to the Weeks rule. See **ELKINS v. UNITED STATES**,
364 U.S. 206, Appendix, pp. 224-232 (1960).
Significantly, among those now following the rule is
California, which, according to its highest court, was
"compelled to reach that conclusion because other
remedies have completely failed to secure compliance with
the constitutional provisions...." **PEOPLE v. CAHAN**, 44
Cal.2d 434, 445, 282 P.2d 905, 911 (1955). In connection
with this California case, we note that the second basis
elaborated in Wolf in support of its failure to enforce
the exclusionary doctrine against the States was that
"other means of protection" have been afforded "the right
to privacy." 338 U.S., at 30. The experience of
California that such other remedies have been worthless
and futile is buttressed by the experience of other
States. The obvious futility of relegating the Fourth
Amendment to the protection of other remedies has,
moreover, been recognized by this Court since Wolf. See
IRVINE v. CALIFORNIA, 347 U.S. 128, 137 (1954).

Likewise, time has set its face against what Wolf
called the "weighty testimony" of **PEOPLE v. DEFORE**, 242
N.Y. 13, 150 N.E. 585 (1926). There JUSTICE "(then
Judge) CARDOZA, rejecting adoption of the Weeks
exclusionary rule in New York, had said that "[t]he
Federal rule as it stands is either too strict or too
lax." 242 N.Y., at 22, 150 N.E., at 588. However, the
force of that reasoning has been largely vitiated by
later decisions of this Court. These include the recent
discarding of the "silver platter" doctrine which allowed
federal judicial use of evidence seized in violation of
the Constitution by state agents, **ELKINS v. UNITED**

STATES, supra; the relaxation of the formerly strict requirements as to standing to challenge the use of evidence thus seized, so that now the procedure of exclusion, "ultimately referable to constitutional safeguards," is available to anyone even "legitimately on [the] premises" unlawfully searched, **JONES v. UNITED STATES**, 362 U.S. 257, 266-267 (1960); and, finally, the formulation of a method to prevent state use of evidence unconstitutionally seized by federal agents, **REA v. UNITED STATES**, 350 U.S. 214 (1956). Because there can be no fixed formula, we are admittedly met with "recurring questions of the reasonableness of searches," but less is not to be expected when dealing with a Constitution, and, at any rate, "[r]easonableness is in the first instance for the [trial court] .... to determine." **UNITED STATES v. RABINOWITZ**, 339 U.S. 56, 63 (1950).

It, therefore, plainly appears that the factual considerations supporting the failure of the Wolf Court to include the Weeks exclusionary rule when it recognized the enforceability of the right to privacy against the States in 1949, while not basically relevant to the constitutional consideration, could not, in any analysis, now be deemed controlling.

III

Some five years after Wolf, in answer to a plea made here Term after Term that we overturn its doctrine on applicability of the Weeks exclusionary rule, this Court indicated that such should not be done until the States had "adequate opportunity to adopt or reject the [Weeks] rule." **IRVINE v. CALIFORNIA**, supra, at 134. There again it was said:

"Never until June of 1949 did this Court hold the basic search-and-seizure prohibition in any way applicable to the states under the Fourteenth Amendment." Ibid.

And only last Term, after again carefully re-examining the Wolf doctrine in **ELKINS v. UNITED STATES**, supra, the Court pointed out that "the controlling principles" as to search and seizure and the problem of admissibility "seemed clear" (at p. 212) until the announcement in Wolf "that the Due Process Clause of the Fourteenth Amendment does not itself require state courts to adopt the exclusionary rule" of the Weeks case. At p.

213. At the same time, the Court pointed out, "the
underlying constitutional doctrine which Wolf established
.... that the Federal Constitution .... prohibits
unreasonable searches and seizures by state officers" had
undermined the "foundation upon which the admissibility
of state-seized evidence in a federal trial originally
rested. ...." Ibid. The Court concluded that it was
therefore obliged to hold, although it chose the narrower
ground on which to do so, that all evidence obtained by
an unconstitutional search and seizure was inadmissible
in a federal court regardless of its source. Today we
once again examine Wolf's constitutional documentation of
the right to privacy free from unreasonable state
intrusion, and, after its dozen years on our books, are
led by it to close the only courtroom door remaining open
to evidence secured by official lawlessness in flagrant
abuse of that basic right, reserved to all persons as a
specific guarantee against that very same unlawful
conduct. We hold that all evidence obtained by searches
and seizures in violation of the Constitution is, by that
same authority, inadmissible in a state court.

IV
Since the Fourth Amendment's right of privacy has
been declared enforceable against the States through the
Due Process Clause of the Fourteenth, it is enforceable
against them by the same sanction of exclusion as is used
against the Federal Government. Were it otherwise, then
just as without the Weeks rule the assurance against
unreasonable federal searches and seizures would be "a
form of words," valueless and undeserving of mention in
a perpetual charter of inestimable human liberties, so
too, without that rule the freedom from state invasions
of privacy would be so ephemeral and so neatly severed
from its conceptual nexus with the freedom from all
brutish means of coercing evidence as not to merit this
Court's high regard as a freedom "implicit in the concept
of ordered liberty." At the time that the Court held in
Wolf that the Amendment was applicable to the States
through the Due Process Clause, the cases of this Court,
as we have seen, has steadfastly held that as to federal
officers the Fourth Amendment included the exclusion of
the evidence seized in violation of its provisions. Even

366

Wolf "stoutly adhered" to that proposition. The right to privacy, when conceded operatively enforceable against the States, was not susceptible of destruction by avulsion of the sanction upon which its protection and enjoyment had always been deemed dependent under the Boyd, Weeks and Silverthorne cases. Therefore, in extending the substantive protections of due process to all constitutionally unreasonable searches—state or federal—it was logically and constitutionally necessary that the exclusion doctrine—an essential part of the right to privacy—be also insisted upon as an essential ingredient of the right newly recognized by the Wolf case. In short, the admission of the new constitutional right by Wolf could not consistently tolerate denial of its most important constitutional privilege, namely, the exclusion of the evidence which an accused had been forced to give by reason of the unlawful seizure. To hold otherwise is to grant the right but in reality to withhold its privilege and enjoyment. Only last year the Court itself recognized that the purpose of the exclusionary rule "is to deter—to compel respect for the constitutional guaranty in the only effectively available way—by removing the incentive to disregard it." **ELKINS v. UNITED STATES**, supra, at 217.

Indeed, we are aware of no restraint, similar to that rejected today, conditioning the enforcement of any other basic constitutional right. The right to privacy, no less important than any other right carefully and particularly reserved to the people, would stand in marked contrast to all other rights declared as "basic to a free society." **WOLF v. COLORADO**, supra, at 27. This Court has not hesitated to enforce as strictly against the States as it does against the Federal Government the rights of free speech and of a free press, the rights to notice and to a fair, public trial, including, as it does, the right not to be convicted by use of a coerced confession, however logically relevant it be, and without regard to its reliability. **ROGERS v. RICHMOND**, 365 U.S. 534 (1961). And nothing could be more certain than that when a coerced confession is involved, "the relevant rules of evidence" are overridden without regard to "the incidence of such conduct by the police," slight or frequent. Why should not the same rule apply to what is tantamount to coerced testimony by way of unconstitutional seizure of goods, papers, effects, documents, etc.? We find that as to the Federal

Government, the Fourth and Fifth Amendments and, as to the states, the freedom from unconscionable invasions of privacy and the freedom from convictions based upon coerced confessions do enjoy an "intimate relation" in their perpetuation of "principles of humanity and civil liberty [secured] .... only after years of struggle." **BRAM v. UNITED STATES**, 168 U.S. 532, 543-544 (1897). They express "supplementing phases of the same constitutional purpose—to maintain inviolate large areas of personal privacy." **FELDMAN v. UNITED STATES**, 322 U.S. 487, 480-490 (1944). The philosophy of each Amendment and of each freedom is complementary to, although not dependent upon, that of the other in its sphere of influence—the very least that together they assure in either sphere is that no man is to be convicted on unconstitutional evidence. Cf. **ROCHIN v. CALIFORNIA**, 342 U.S. 165, 173 (1952).

V

Moreover, our holding that the exclusionary rule is an essential part of both the Fourth and Fourteenth Amendments is not only the logical dictate of prior cases, but it also makes very good sense. There is no war between the Constitution and common sense. Presently, a federal prosecutor may make no use of evidence illegally seized, but a State's attorney across the street may, although he supposedly is operating under the enforceable prohibitions of the same Amendment. Thus the State, by admitting evidence unlawfully seized serves to encourage disobedience to the Federal Constitution which it is bound to uphold. Moreover, as was said in Elkins, "[t]he very essence of a healthy federalism depends upon the avoidance of needless conflict between state and federal courts." 364 U.S., at 221. Such a conflict, hereafter needless, arose this very Term, in **WILSON v. SCHNETTLER**, 365 U.S. 381 (1961), in which, and in spite of the promise made by Rea, we gave full recognition to our practice in this regard by refusing to restrain a federal officer from testifying in a state court as to evidence unconstitutionally seized by him in the performance of his duties. Yet the double standard recognized until today hardly put such a thesis into practice. In nonexclusionary States, federal officers, being human, were by it invited to and did, as our cases indicate, step across the street to the State's attorney with their unconstitutionally seized evidence. Prosecution on the basis of that evidence was then had in a state court in utter disregard of the enforceable Fourth Amendment. If the fruits of an unconstitutional search had been inadmissible in both state and federal courts, this inducement to evasion would have been sooner eliminated. There would be no need to reconcile such cases as Rea and Schnettler, each pointing up the hazardous uncertainties of our heretofore ambivalent approach.

Federal-state cooperation in the solution of crime under constitutional standards will be promoted, if only by recognition of their now mutual obligation to respect the same fundamental criteria in their approaches. "However much in a particular case insistence upon such rules may appear as a technicality that inures to the benefit of a guilty person, the history of the criminal law proves that tolerance of shortcut methods in law enforcement impairs it enduring effectiveness." **MILLER v. UNITED STATES**, 357 U.S. 301, 313 (1958). Denying shortcuts to only one of two cooperating law enforcement agencies tends naturally to breed legitimate suspicion of "working arrangements" whose results are equally tainted. **BYARS v. UNITED STATES**, 273 U.S. 28 (1927); **LUSTIG v. UNITED STATES**, 338 U.S. 74 (1949).

There are those who say, as did JUSTICE (then Judge) CARDOZO, that under our constitutional exclusionary doctrine "[t]he criminal is to go free because the constable has blundered." **PEOPLE v. DEFORE**, 242 N.Y., at 21, 150 N.E., at 587. In some cases this will undoubtedly be the result. But, as was said in Elkins, "there is another consideration—the imperative of judicial integrity." 364 U.S., at 222. The criminal goes free, if he must, but it is the law that sets him free. Nothing can destroy a government more quickly than its failure to observe its own laws, or worse, its disregard of the charter of its own existence. As MR. JUSTICE BRANDEIS, dissenting, said in **OLMSTEAD v. UNITED STATES**, 277 U.S. 438, 485 (1928): "Our Government is the potent, the omnipresent teacher. For good or for ill, it teaches the whole people by its example.... If the Government becomes a lawbreaker, it breeds contempt for law; it invites every man to become a law unto himself; it invites anarchy." Nor can it lightly be assumed that, as a practical matter, adoption of the exclusionary rule fetters law enforcement. Only last year this Court expressly considered that contention and found that "pragmatic evidence of a sort" to the contrary was not wanting. **ELKINS v. UNITED STATES**, supra, at 218. The Court noted that

> "The federal courts themselves have operated under the exclusionary rule of Weeks for almost half a century; yet it has not been suggested either that the Federal Bureau of Investigation has thereby been rendered ineffective, or that the administration of criminal justice in the federal courts has thereby been disrupted. Moreover, the experience of the states is impressive.... The movement towards the rule of exclusion has been halting but seemingly inexorable." Id., at 218-219.

The ignoble shortcut to conviction left open to the State tends to destroy the entire system of constitutional restraints on which the liberties of the people rest. Having once recognized that the right to privacy embodied in the Fourth Amendment is enforceable against the States, and that the right to be secure against rude invasions of privacy by state officers is, therefore, constitutional in origin, we can no longer permit that right to remain an empty promise. Because it is enforceable in the same manner and to like effect as other basic rights secured by the Due Process Clause, we can no longer permit it to be revocable at the whim of any police officer who, in the name of law enforcement itself, chooses to suspend its enjoyment. Our decision, founded on reason and truth, gives to the individual no more than that which the Constitution guarantees him, to the police officer no less than that to which honest law enforcement is entitled, and, to the courts, that judicial integrity so necessary in the true administration of justice.

The judgment of the Supreme Court of Ohio is reversed and the cause remanded for further proceedings not inconsistent with this opinion.

Reversed and Remanded.

ROCHIN v. CALIFORNIA
342 U.S. 165, 72 S.Ct. 205, 96 L.Ed. 183 (1952)
CERTIORARI TO THE DISTRICT OF APPEAL FOR
THE SECOND APPELLATE DISTRICT OF CALIFORNIA
Argued October 16, 1951.—Decided January 2, 1952.
. . .

MR. JUSTICE FRANKFURTER delivered the opinion of the
Court.

Having "some information that [the petitioner here]
was selling narcotics," three deputy sheriffs of the
County of Los Angeles, on the morning of July 1, 1949,
made for the two-story dwelling house in which Rochin
lived with his mother, common-law wife, brothers and
sisters. Finding the outside door open, they entered and
then forced open the door to Rochin's room on the second
floor. Inside they found petitioner sitting partly
dressed on the side of the bed, upon which his wife was
lying. On a "night stand" beside the bed the deputies
spied two capsules. When asked "Whose stuff is this?"
Rochin seized the capsules and put them in his mouth. A
struggle ensued, in the course of which the three
officers "jumped upon him" and attempted to extract the
capsules. The force they applied proved unavailing
against Rochin's resistance. He was handcuffed and taken
to a hospital. At the direction of one of the officers
a doctor forced an emetic solution through a tube into
Rochin's stomach against his will. This "stomach
pumping" produced vomiting. In the vomited matter were
found two capsules which proved to contain morphine.

Rochin was brought to trial before a California
Superior Court, sitting without a jury, on the charge of
possessing "a preparation of morphine" in violation of
the California Health and Safety Code, 1947, § 11,500.
Rochin was convicted and sentenced to sixty days'
imprisonment. The chief evidence against was the two
capsules. They were admitted over petitioner's
objection, although the means of obtaining them was
frankly set forth in the testimony by one of the
deputies, substantially as here narrated.

On appeal, the District Court of Appeal affirmed the
conviction, despite the finding that the officers "were
guilty of unlawfully breaking into and entering
defendant's room and were guilty of unlawfully assaulting
and battering defendant while in the room," and "were
guilty of unlawfully assaulting, battering, torturing and

371

falsely imprisoning the defendant at the alleged hospital." 101 Cal. App. 2d 140, 143, 225 P.2d 1, 3. One of the three judges, while finding that "the record in this case reveals a shocking series of violations of constitutional rights," concurred only because he felt bound by decisions of his Supreme Court. These, he asserted, "have been looked upon by law enforcement officers as an encouragement, if not an invitation, to the commission of such lawless acts." Ibid. The Supreme Court of California denied without opinion Rochin's petition for a hearing. Two justices dissented from this denial, and in doing so expressed themselves thus: ".... a conviction which rests upon evidence of incriminating objects obtained from the body of the accused by physical abuse is as invalid as a conviction which rests upon a verbal confession extracted from him by such abuse. .... Had the evidence forced from the defendant's lips consisted of an oral confession that he illegally possessed a drug .... he would have the protection of the rule of law which excludes coerced confessions from evidence. But because the evidence forced from his lips consisted of real objects the People of this state are permitted to base a conviction upon it. [We] find no valid ground of distinction between a verbal confession extracted by physical abuse and a confession wrested from defendant's body by physical abuse." 101 Cal. App. 2d 143, 149-150, 225 P.2d 913, 917-918.

This Court granted certiorari, 341 U.S. 939, because a serious question is raised as to the limitations which the Due Process Clause of the Fourteenth Amendment imposes on the conduct of criminal proceedings by the States.

In our federal system the administration of criminal justice is predominantly committed to the case of the States. The power to define crimes belongs to Congress only as an appropriate means of carrying into execution its limited grant of legislative powers. U.S. Const., Art. I, § 8, cl. 18. Broadly speaking, crimes in the United States are what the laws of the individual States make them, subject to the limitations of Art. I, § 10, cl. 1, in the original Constitution, prohibiting bills of attainer and ex post facto laws, and of the Thirteenth and Fourteenth Amendments.

These limitations, in the main, concern not restrictions upon the powers of the States to define crime, except in the restricted area where federal authority has preempted the field, but restrictions upon the manner in which the States may enforce their penal codes. Accordingly, in reviewing a State criminal conviction under a claim of right guaranteed by the Due Process Clause of the Fourteenth Amendment, from which is derived the most far-reaching and most frequent federal basis of challenging State criminal justice, "we must be deeply mindful of the responsibilities of the States for the enforcement of criminal laws, and exercise with due humility our merely negative function in subjecting convictions from state courts to the very narrow scrutiny which the Due Process Clause of the Fourteenth Amendment authorizes." **MALINSKI v. NEW YORK**, 324 U.S. 401, 412, 418. Due process of law, "itself a historical product," **JACKMAN v. ROSENBAUM CO.**, 260 U.S. 22, 31 is not to be turned into a destructive dogma against the States in the administration of their systems of criminal justice.

However, this Court too has its responsibility. Regard for the requirements of the Due Process Clause "inescapably imposes upon this Court an exercise of judgment upon the whole course of the proceedings [resulting in a conviction] in order to ascertain whether they offend those canons of decency and fairness which express the notions of justice of English-speaking peoples even toward those charged with the most heinous offenses." **MALINSKI V. NEW YORK**, supra, at 416-417. These standards of justice are not authoritatively formulated anywhere as though they were specifics. Due process of law is a summarized constitutional guarantee of respect for those personal immunities which, as MR. JUSTICE CARDOZO twice wrote for the Court are "so rooted in the traditions and conscience of our people as to be ranked as fundamental." **SNYDER v. MASSACHUSETTS**, 291 U.S. 97, 105, or are "implicit in the concept of ordered liberty." **PALKO v. CONNECTICUT**, 302 U.S. 319, 325.

The Court's function in the observance of this settled conception of the Due Process Clause does not leave us without adequate guides in subjecting State criminal procedures to constitutional judgment. In dealing not with the machinery of government but with human rights, the absence of formal exactitude, or want of fixity of meaning, is not an unusual or even regrettable attribute of constitutional provisions.

Words being symbols do not speak without a gloss. On the one hand the gloss may be the deposit of history, whereby a term gains technical content. Thus the requirements of the Sixth and Seventh Amendments for trial by jury in the federal courts have a rigid meaning. No charges or chances can alter the content of the verbal symbol of "jury"—a body of twelve men who must reach a unanimous conclusion if the verdict is to go against the defendant. On the other hand, the gloss of some of the verbal symbols of the Constitution does not give them a fixed technical content. It exacts a continuing process of application.

When the gloss has thus not been fixed but is a function of the process of judgment, the judgment is bound to fall differently at different times and differently at the same time through different judges. Even more specific provisions, such as the guaranty of freedom of speech and the detailed protection against unreasonable searches and seizures, have inevitably evoked as sharp divisions in this Court as the least specific and most comprehensive protection of liberties, the Due Process Clause.

The vague contours of the Due Process Clause do not leave judges at large. We may not draw on our merely personal and private notions and disregard the limits that bind judges in their judicial function. Even though the concept of due process of law is not final and fixed, these limits are derived from considerations that are fused in the whole nature of our judicial process. See Cardozo, The Nature of the Judicial Process; The growth of the Law; The Paradoxes of Legal Science. These are considerations deeply rooted in reason and in the compelling traditions of the legal profession. The Due Process Clause places upon this Court the duty of exercising a judgment, within the narrow confines of judicial power in reviewing State convictions, upon interests of society pushing in opposite directions.

Due process of law thus conceived is not to be derided as resort to a revival of "natural law." To believe that this judicial exercise of judgment could be avoided by freezing "due process of law" at some fixed stage of time or thought is to suggest that the most important aspect of constitutional adjudication is a

374

function for inanimate machines and not for judges, for whom the independence safeguarded by Article III of the Constitution was designed and who are presumably guided by established standards of judicial behavior. Even cybernetics has not yet made that haughty claim. To practice the requisite detachment and to achieve sufficient objectivity no doubt demands of judges the habit of self-discipline and self-criticism, incertitude that one's own views are incontestable and alert tolerance toward views not shared. But these are precisely the presuppositions of our judicial process. They are precisely the qualities society has a right to expect from those entrusted with ultimate judicial power.

Restraints on our jurisdiction are self-imposed only in the sense that there is from our decisions no immediate appeal short to impeachment or constitutional amendment. But that does not make due process of law a matter of judicial caprice. The faculties of the Due Process Clause may be indefinite and vague, but the mode of their ascertainment is not self-willed. In each case "due process of law" requires an evaluation based on a disinterested inquiry pursued in the spirit of science, on a balanced order of facts exactly and fairly stated, on the detached consideration of conflicting claims, see **HUDSON COUNTY WATER CO. v. McCARTER**, 209 U.S. 349, 355, on a judgment not ad hoc and episodic but duly mindful of reconciling the needs both of continuity and of change in a progressive society.

Applying these general considerations to the circumstances of the present case, we are compelled to conclude that the proceedings by which this conviction was obtained do more than offend some fastidious squeamishness or private sentimentalism about combatting crime too energetically. This is conduct that shocks the conscience. Illegally breaking into the privacy of the petitioner, the struggle to open his mouth and remove what was there, the forcible extraction of his stomach's contents—this course of proceeding by agents of government to obtain evidence is bound to offend even hardened sensibilities. They are methods too close to the rack and the screw to permit of constitutional differentiation.

It has long since ceased to be true that due process of law is heedless of the means by which otherwise relevant and credible evidence is obtained. This was not true even before the series of recent cases enforced the

375

constitutional principle that the States may not base convictions upon confessions, however much verified, obtained by coercion. These decisions are not arbitrary exceptions to the comprehensive right of States to fashion their own rules of evidence for criminal trials. They are not sports in our constitutional law but applications of a general principle. They are only instances of the general requirement that States in their prosecutions respect certain decencies of civilized conduct. Due process of law, as a historic and generative principle, precludes defining, and thereby confining, these standards of conduct more precisely than to say that convictions cannot be brought about by methods that offend "a sense of justice." See MR. CHIEF JUSTICE HUGHES, speaking for a unanimous Court in **BROWN v. MISSISSIPPI**, 297 U.S. 278, 285-286. It would be a stultification of the responsibility which the course of constitutional history has cast upon this Court to hold that in order to convict a man the police cannot extract by force what is in his mind but can extract what is in his stomach.

To attempt in this case to distinguish what lawyers call "real evidence" from verbal evidence is to ignore the reasons for excluding coerced confessions. Use of involuntary verbal confessions in State criminal trials is constitutionally obnoxious not only because of their unreliability. They are inadmissible under the Due Process Clause even though statements contained in them may be independently established as true. Coerced confessions offend the community's sense of fair play and decency. So here, to sanction the brutal conduct which naturally enough was condemned by the court whose judgment is before us, would be to afford brutality the cloak of law. Nothing would be more calculated to discredit law and thereby to brutalize the temper of a society.

In deciding this case we do not heedlessly bring into question decisions in many States dealing with essentially different, even if related, problems. We therefore put to one side cases which have arisen in the State courts through use of modern methods and devices for discovering wrongdoers and bringing them to book. It does not fairly represent these decisions to suggest that they legalize force so brutal and so offensive to human dignity in securing evidence from a suspect as is revealed by this record. Indeed the California Supreme Court has not sanctioned this mode of securing a conviction. It merely exercised its discretion to decline a review of the conviction. All the California judges who have expressed themselves in this case have condemned the conduct in the strongest language.

We are not unmindful that hypothetical situations can be conjured up, shading imperceptibly from the circumstances of this case and by gradations producing practical differences despite seemingly logical extensions. But the Constitution is "intended to preserve practical and substantial rights, not to maintain theories." **DAVIS v. MILLS**, 194 U.S. 451, 457.

Reversed

UNITED STATES v. SANTANA, et al.
427 U.S. 38, 96 S.Ct. 2406, 49 L.Ed.2d. 300 (1976)
CERTIORARI TO THE UNITED STATES COURT OF APPEALS
FOR THE THIRD CIRCUIT
Argued April 27, 1976--Decided June 24, 1976.
. . .
Mr. Justice Rehniquist delivered the opinion of the Court.

I

On August 16, 1974, Michael Gilletti, an undercover officer with the Philadelphia Narcotics Squad arranged a heroin "buy" with one Patricia McCafferty (from whom he had purchased narcotics before). McCafferty told him it would cost $115 "and we will go down to Mom Santana's for the dope."

Gilletti notified his superiors of the impending transaction, recorded the serial numbers of $110 [sic] in marked bills, and went to meet McCafferty at a prearranged location. She got in his car and directed him to drive to 2311 North Fifth Street, which, as she had previously informed him, was respondent Santana's residence.

McCafferty took the money and went inside the house, stopping briefly to speak to respondent Alejandro who was sitting on the front steps. She came out shortly afterwards and got into the car. Gilletti asked for the heroin; she thereupon extracted from her bra several glassine envelopes containing a brownish-white powder and gave them to him.

Gilletti then stopped the car, displayed his badge and placed McCafferty under arrest. He told her that the police were going back to 2311 North Fifth Street and that he wanted to know where the money was. She said, "Mom has the money." At this point Sergeant Pruitt and other officers came up to the car. Gilletti showed them the envelope and said "Mom Santana has the money." Gilletti then took McCafferty to the police station.

Pruitt and the others then drove approximately two blocks back to 2311 North Fifth Street. They saw Santana standing in the doorway of the house with a brown paper bag in her hand. They pulled up to within 15 feet of Santana and got out of their van, shouting "police," and displaying their identification. As the officers approached, Santana retreated into the vestibule of her house.

The officers followed through the open door, catching her in the vestibule. As she tried to pull away, the bag tilted and "two bundles of glazed paper packets with a white powder" fell to the floor. Respondent Alejandro tried to make off with the dropped envelopes but was forcibly restrained. When Santana was told to empty her pockets she produced $135, $70 of which could be identified as Gilletti's marked money. The white powder in the bag was later determined to be heroin.

An indictment was filed in the United States District Court for the Eastern District of Pennsylvania charging McCafferty with distribution of heroin, in violation of 21 U.S.C. § 841, and respondents with possession of heroin with intent to distribute in violation of the same section. McCafferty pleaded guilty. Santana and Alejandro moved to suppress the heroin and money found during and after their arrests.

The District Court granted respondents' motion. In an oral opinion the court found that "[t]here was strong probable cause that Defendant Santana had participated in the transaction with Defendant McCafferty." However, the court continued:

> "One of the police officers .... testified that the mission was to arrest Defendant Santana. Another police officer testified that the mission was to recover the bait money. Either one would require a warrant, one a warrant of arrest under ordinary circumstances and one a search warrant."

The court further held that Santana's "reentry from the doorway into the house" did not support allowing the police to make a warrantless entry into the house on the grounds of "hot pursuit," because it took "hot pursuit" to mean "a chase in and about public streets." The court did find, however, that the police acted under "extreme emergency" conditions. The Court of Appeals affirmed this decision without opinion.

II

In **UNITED STATES v. WATSON**, 423 U.S. 411 (1976), we held that the warrantless arrest of an individual in a public place upon probable cause did not violate the Fourth Amendment. Thus the first question we must decide is whether, when the police first sought to arrest Santana, she was in a public place.

While it may be true that under the common law of property the threshold of one's dwelling is "private," as is the yard surrounding the house, it is nonetheless clear that under the cases interpreting the Fourth Amendment Santana was in a "public" place. She was not in an area where she had any expectation of privacy. "What a person knowingly exposes to the public, even in his own house or office, is not a subject of Fourth Amendment protection." **KATZ v. UNITED STATES**, 389 U.S. 347, 351 (1967). She was not merely visible to the public but was as exposed to public view, speech, hearing, and touch as if she had been standing completely outside her house. **HESTER v. UNITED STATES**, 265 U.S. 57, 59 (1924). Thus, when the police, who concededly had probable cause to do so, sought to arrest her, they merely intended to perform a function that we have approved in Watson.

The only remaining question is whether her act of retreating into her house could thwart an otherwise proper arrest. We hold that it could not. In **WARDEN v. HAYDEN**, 387 U.S. 294 (1967), we recognized the right of police, who had probable cause to believe that an armed robber had entered a house a few minutes before, to make a warrantless entry to arrest the robber and to search for weapons. This case, involving a true "hot pursuit," is clearly governed by Warden; the need to act quickly here is even greater than in that case while the intrusion is much less. The District Court was correct in concluding that "hot pursuit" means some sort of a chase, but it need not be an extended hue and cry "in and about [the] public streets." The fact that the pursuit here ended almost as soon as it began did not render it any the less a "hot pursuit" sufficient to justify the warrantless entry into Santana's house. Once Santana saw the police, there was likewise a realistic expectation that any delay would result in destruction of evidence. See **VALE v. LOUISIANA**, 399 U.S. 30, 35 (1970). Once she had been arrested the search, incident to that arrest, which produced the drugs and money was clearly justified.

UNITED STATES v. ROBINSON, 414 U.S. 218 (1973); **CHIMEL v. CALIFORNIA,** 395 U.S. 752, 762-763 (1969).

We thus conclude that a suspect may not defeat an arrest which has been set in motion in a public place, and is therefore proper under Watson, by the expedient of escaping to a private place. The judgment of the Court of Appeals is

Reversed.

UNITED STATES v. WATSON
423 US 411, 96 S Ct 820, 46 L Ed 2d 598, (1976)
. . .

MR. JUSTICE WHITE delivered the opinion of the Court.

This case presents questions under the Fourth Amendment as to the legality of a warrantless arrest and of an ensuing search of the arrestee's automobile carried out with his purported consent.

I

The relevant events began on August 17, 1972, when an informant, one Khoury, telephoned a postal inspector informing him that respondent Watson was in possession of a stolen credit card and had asked Khoury to cooperate in using the card to their mutual advantage. On five to 10 previous occasions Khoury had provided the inspector with reliable information on postal inspection matters, some involving Watson. Later that day Khoury delivered the card to the inspector. On learning that Watson had agreed to furnish additional cards, the inspector asked Khoury to arrange to meet with Watson. Khoury did so, a meeting being scheduled for August 22. Watson canceled that engagement, but at noon on August 23, Khoury met with Watson at a restaurant designated by the latter. Khoury had been instructed that if Watson had additional stolen credit cards, Khoury was to give a designated signal. The signal was given, the officers closed in, and Watson was forthwith arrested. He was removed from the restaurant to the street where he was given the warnings required by **MIRANDA v. ARIZONA**, 384 US 436, 16 L Ed 2d 694, 86 S Ct 1602, 10 Ohio Misc 9, 36 Ohio Ops 2d 237, 10 ALR3d 974 (1966). A search having revealed that Watson had no credit cards on his person, the inspector asked if he could look inside Watson's car, which was standing within view. Watson said, "Go ahead," and repeated these words when the inspector cautioned that [i]f I find anything, it is going to go against you." Using keys furnished by Watson, the inspector entered the car and found under the floor mat an envelope containing two credit cards in the names of other persons. These cards were the basis for two counts of four-count indictment charging Watson with possessing stolen mail in violation of 18 USC § 1708 [18 USCS § 1708].

Prior to trial, Watson moved to suppress the cards, claiming that his arrest was illegal for want of probable cause and an arrest warrant and that his consent to search the car was involuntary and ineffective because he had not been told that he could withhold consent. The motion was denied, and Watson was convicted of illegally possessing the two cards seized from his car.

A divided panel of the Court of Appeals for the Ninth Circuit reversed, 504 F2d 849 (1974), ruling that the admission in evidence of the two credit cards found in the car was prohibited by the Fourth Amendment. In reaching this judgment, the court decided two issues in Watson's favor. First, notwithstanding its agreement with the District Court that Khoury was reliable and that there was probable cause for arresting Watson, the court held the arrest unconstitutional because the postal inspector had failed to secure an arrest warrant although he concededly had time to do so. Second, based on the totality of the circumstances, one of which was the illegality of the arrest, the court held Watson's consent to search had been coerced and hence was not a valid ground for the warrantless search of the automobile. We granted certiorari. 420 US 924, 43 L Ed 2d 392, 95 S Ct 1117 (1975).

II

A major part of the court of Appeals' opinion was its holding that Watson's warrantless arrest violated the Fourth Amendment. Although it did not expressly do so, it may have intended to overturn the conviction on the independent ground that the two credit cards were the inadmissible fruits of an unconstitutional arrest. Cf. **BROWN v. ILLINOIS**, 422 US 590, 45 L Ed 2d 416, 95 S Ct 2254 (1975). However that may be, the Court of Appeals treated the illegality of Watson's arrest as an important factor in determining the voluntariness of his consent to search his car. We therefore deal first with the arrest.

Contrary to the Court of Appeals' view, Watson's arrest was not invalid because executed without a warrant. § 3061(a)(3) Title 18 USC [18 USCS § 306(a)] expressly empowers the Board of Governors of the Postal Service to authorize Postal Service officers and employees "performing duties related to the inspection of

383

postal matters" to

> "make arrests without warrant for felonies
> cognizable under the laws of the United States if they
> have reasonable grounds to believe that the person to be
> arrested has committed or is committing such a felony."

By regulation, 39 CFR § 232.5(a)(3)(1975), and in
identical language, the Board of Governors has exercised
that power and authorized warrantless arrests. Because
there was probable cause in this case to believe that
Watson had violated § 1708, the inspector and his
subordinates, in arresting Watson, were acting strictly
in accordance with the governing statute and regulations.
The effect of the judgment of the Court of Appeals was to
invalidate the statute as applied in this case and as
applied to all the situations where a court fails to find
exigent circumstances justifying a warrantless arrest.
We reverse that judgment.

Under the Fourth Amendment, the people are to be
"secure in their persons, houses, papers, and effects,
against unreasonable searches and seizures, ... and no
Warrants shall issue, but upon probable cause...."
Section 3061 represents a judgment by Congress that it is
not unreasonable under the Fourth Amendment for postal
inspectors to arrest without a warrant provided they have
probable cause to do so. This was not an isolated or
quixotic judgment of the legislative branch. Other
federal law enforcement officers have been expressly
authorized by statute for many years to make felony
arrests on probably cause but without a warrant. This is
true of United States marshals, 18 USC § 3053 [18 USCS §
3053], and of agents of the Federal Bureau of
Investigation, 18 USC § 3052 [18 USCS § 3052]; the Drug
Enforcement Administration, 84 Stat 1273, 21 USC § 878
[21 USCS § 878]; the Secret Service, 18 USC § 3056(a) [18
USCS § 3056(a)]; and the Customs Service, 26 USC § 7607
[26 USCS § 7607].

Because there is a "strong presumption of
constitutionality due to an Act of Congress, especially
when it turns on what is 'reasonable,'" "[o]bviously the
court should be reluctant to decide that a search thus
authorized by Congress was unreasonable and that the Act

384

was therefore unconstitutional." **UNITED STATES v. DI RE**, 332 US 581, 585, 92 L Ed 210, 68 S Ct 222 (1948). Moreover, there is nothing in the Court's prior cases indicating that under the Fourth Amendment a warrant is required to make a valid arrest for a felony. Indeed, the relevant prior decisions are uniformly to the contrary.

"The usual rule is that a police officer may arrest without warrant one believed by the officer upon reasonable cause to have been guilty of a felony. . . ." **CARROLL v. UNITED STATES**, 267 US 132, 156, 69 L Ed 543, 45 S Ct 280, 39 ALR 790 (1925). In **HENRY v. UNITED STATES**, 361 US 98, 4 L Ed 2d 134, 80 S Ct 168 (1959), the Court dealt with an FBI agent's warrantless arrest under 18 USC § 3052 [18 USCS § 3052], which authorizes a warrantless arrest where there are reasonable grounds to believe that the person to be arrested has committed a felony. The Court declared that "[t]he statute states the constitutional standard . . . ." 361 US, at 100, 4 L Ed 2d 134, 80 S Ct 168. The necessary inquiry, therefore, was not whether there was a warrant or whether there was time to get one, but whether there was probable cause for the arrest. In **ABEL v. UNITED STATES**, 362 US 217, 232, 4 L Ed 2d 668, 80 S Ct 683 (1960), the Court sustained an administrative arrest made without "a judicial warrant within the scope of the Fourth Amendment." The crucial question in **DRAPER v. UNITED STATES**, 358 US 307, 3 L Ed 2d 327, 79 S Ct 329 (1959), was whether there was probable cause for the warrantless arrest. If there was, the Court said, "the arrest, though without a warrant, was lawful. . . ." Id., at 310, 3 L Ed 2d 327, 790 S Ct 329, **KER v. CALIFORNIA**, 374 US 23, 34–35, 10 L Ed 2d 726, 83 S Ct 1623, 24 Ohio Ops 3d 201 (1963) (opinion of CLARK, J.) reiterated the rule that "[t]he lawfulness of the arrest without warrant in turn, must be based upon probable cause . . . ." and went on to sustain the warrantless arrest over other claims going to the mode of entry. Just last Term, while recognizing that maximum protection of individual rights could be assured by requiring a magistrate's review of the factual justification prior to any arrest, we stated that "such a requirement would constitute an intolerable handicap for legitimate law enforcement" and noted that the Court "has never invalidated an arrest supported by probable cause solely because the officers failed to secure a warrant." **GERSTEIN v. PUGH**, 420 US 103, 113, 43 L Ed 2d

54, 95 S Ct 854 (1975).

The cases construing the Fourth Amendment thus reflect the ancient common-law rule that a peace officer was permitted to arrest without a warrant for a misdemeanor or felony committed in his presence as well as for a felony not committed in his presence if there was reasonable grounds for making the arrest. 10 Halsbury's Laws of England 344-345 (3d ed 1955); 4 W. Blackstone, Commentaries 292; 1 J. Stephen, A History of the Criminal Law of England 193 (1883); 2 M. Hale, Plea of the Crown 72-74; Wilgus, Arrest Without a Warrant, 22 Mich L Rev 541, 547-550, 686-688 (1924); **SAMUEL v. PAYNE**, 1 Doug 359, 99 Eng Rep 230 (KB 1780); **BECKWITH v. PHILBY**, 6 Barn & Cress, 635, 108 Eng Rep 585 (KB 1827). This has also been the prevailing rule under state constitutions and statutes. "The rule of the common law, that a peace officer or a private citizen may arrest a felon without a warrant, has been generally held by the courts of the several States to be in force in cases of felony punishable by the civil tribunals." **KURTZ v. MOFFITT**, 115 US 487, 504, 29 L Ed 458, 6 S Ct 148 (1885).

In **ROHAN v. SAWIN**, 59 Mass 281 (1850), a false-arrest case, the Supreme Judicial Court of Massachusetts held that the common-law rule obtained in that State. Given probable cause to arrest, "[t]he authority of a constable, to arrest without warrant, in cases of felony, is most fully established by the elementary books, and adjudicated cases." Id., at 284. In reaching this judgment the court observed:

> "It has been sometimes contended, that an arrest of this character, without a warrant, was a violation of the great fundamental principles of our national and state constitutions, forbidding unreasonable searches and arrests, except by warrant founded upon a complaint made under oath. Those provisions doubtless had another and different purpose, being in restraint of general warrants to make searches, and requiring warrants to issue only upon a complaint made under oath. They do not conflict with the authority of constables or other peace-officers, or private persons under proper limitations, to arrest without warrant those who

have committed felonies. The public safety, and the due apprehension of criminals, charged with heinous offenses, imperiously require that such arrests should be made without warrant by officers of the law." Id., at 284-285.

Also rejected, id., at 285-286, was the trial court's view that to justify a warrantless arrest, the State must show "an immediate necessity therefor, arising from the danger, that the plaintiff would otherwise escape, or secrete the stolen property, before a warrant could be procured against him." The Supreme Judicial Court ruled that there was no "authority for thus restricting a constable in the exercise of his authority to arrest for a felony without a warrant." Id., at 286. Other early cases to similar effect were **WAKELY v. HART**, 6 Binn 316 (Pa 1814); **HOLLEY v. MIX**, 3 Wend 350 (NY Sup Ct 1829); **STATE v. BROWN**, 5 Del 505 (Ct Gen Sess 1853); **JOHNSON v. STATE**, 30 Ga 426 (1860); **WADE v. CHAFFEE**, 8 RI 224 (1865). See **REUCK v. MCGREGOR**, 32 NJL 70, 74 (Sup Ct 1866); **BALTIMORE & O.R. CO. v. CAIN**, 81 Md 87, 100, 102, 31 A 801, 803, 804 (1895).

Because the common-law rule authorizing arrests without a warrant generally prevailed in the States, it is important for present purposes to note that in 1792 Congress invested United States marshals and their deputies with "the same powers in executing the laws of the United States, as sheriffs and their deputies in the several states have by law, in executing the laws of their respective states." Act of May 2, 1972, c28, § 9, 1 Stat 265. The Second Congress thus saw no inconsistency between the Fourth Amendment and legislation giving United States marshals the same power as local peace officers to arrest for a felony without a warrant. This provision equating the power of federal marshals to those of local sheriffs was several times reenacted and is today § 570 of Title 28 of the United States Code. That provision, however, was supplemented in 1935 by § 504a of the Judicial Code, which in its essential elements is now 18 USC § 3053 [18 USCS § 3053] and which expressly empowered marshals to make felony arrests without warrant and on probable cause. It was enacted to furnish a federal standard independent of the vagaries of state laws, the Committee Report remarking that under existing law, a "marshal or deputy marshal may make an arrest without a warrant within his district in all cases where the sheriff might do so under the State statutes." HR Rep No. 283, 74th Cong. 1st Sess, 1 (1935). See **UNITED STATES v. RIGGS**, 474 F2d 699, 702-703, n2 (CA2), cert denied, 414 US 820, 38 L Ed 2d 53, 94 S Ct 115 (1973).

This balance struck by the common law in generally authorizing felony arrests on probable cause, but without a warrant, has survived substantially intact. It appears in almost all the States in the form of express statutory authorization. In 1963, the American Law Institute undertook the task of formulating a model statute governing police powers and practice in criminal law enforcement and related aspects of pretrial procedure. In 1975, after years of discussion, A Model Code of Prearraignment Procedure was proposed. Among its provisions was §120.1 which authorizes an officer to take a person into custody if the officer has reasonable cause to believe that the person to be arrested has committed a felony, or has committed a misdemeanor or petty misdemeanor in his presence. The commentary to this section said: "The Code thus adopts the traditional and almost universal standard for arrest without a warrant."

This is the rule Congress has long directed its principal law enforcement officers to follow. Congress has plainly decided against conditioning warrantless arrest power on proof of exigent circumstances. Law enforcement officers may find it wise to seek arrest warrants where practicable to do so, and their judgments about probable cause may be more readily accepted where backed by a warrant issued by a magistrate. See **UNITED STATES v. VENTRESCA**, 380 US 102, 106, 13 L Ed 2d 684, 85 S Ct 741 (1965); **AGUILAR v. TEXAS**, 378 US 108, 111, 12 L Ed 2d 723, 84 S Ct 1509 (1964); **WONG SUN v. UNITED STATES**, 371 US 471, 479-480, 9 L Ed 2d 441, 83 S Ct 497 (1963). But we decline to transform this judicial preference into a constitutional rule when the judgment of the Nation and Congress has for so long been to authorize warrantless public arrests on probable cause rather than to encumber criminal prosecutions with endless litigation with respect to the existence of exigent circumstances, whether it was practicable to get a warrant, whether the suspect was about to flee, and the like.

Watson's arrest did not violate the Fourth

Amendment, and the Court of Appeals erred in holding to the contrary.

III

Because our judgment is that Watson's arrest comported with the Fourth Amendment, Watson's consent to the search of his car was not the product of an illegal arrest. To the extent that the issue of the voluntariness of Watson's consent was resolved on the premise that his arrest was illegal, the Court of Appeals was also in error.

We are satisfied in addition that the remaining factors relied upon by the Court of Appeals to invalidate Watson's consent are inadequate to demonstrate that, in the totality of the circumstances, Watson's consent was not his own "essentially free and unconstrained choice" because his "will ha[d] been overborne and his capacity for self-determination critically impaired." **SCHNECKLOTH v. BUSTAMONTE**, 412 US 218, 225, 36 L Ed 2d 854, 93 S Ct 2041 (1973). There was no overt act or threat of force against Watson proved or claimed. There were no promises made to him and no indication of more subtle forms of coercion that might flaw his judgment. He had been arrested and was in custody, but his consent was given while on a public street, not in the confines of the police station. Moreover, the fact of custody alone has never been enough in itself to demonstrate a coerced confession or consent to search. Similarly, under Schneckloth, the absence of proof that Watson knew he could withhold his consent, though it may be a factor in the overall judgment, is not to be given controlling significance. There is no indication in this record that Watson was a newcomer to the law, mentally deficient, or unable in the fact of custodial arrest to exercise a free choice. He was given Miranda warnings and was further cautioned that the results of the search of his car could be used against him. He persisted in his consent.

In these circumstances, to hold that illegal coercion is made out from the fact of arrest and the failure to inform the arrestee that he could withhold consent would not be consistent with Schneckloth and would distort the voluntariness standard that we reaffirmed in that case.

In consequence, we reverse the judgment of the Court of Appeals.

So ordered.

BREITHAUPT v. ABRAM. Warden.
352 U.S. 432, 77 S.Ct. 408, 1 L.Ed.2d. 448 (1957)
CERTIORARI TO THE SUPREME COURT OF NEW MEXICO

MR. JUSTICE CLARK delivered the opinion of the Court.

Petitioner, while driving a pickup truck on the highways of New Mexico, was involved in a collision with a passenger car. Three occupants of the car were killed and petitioner was seriously injured. A pint whiskey bottle, almost empty, was found in the glove compartment of the pickup truck. Petitioner was taken to a hospital and while he was lying unconscious in the emergency room the smell of liquor was detected on his breath. A state patrolman requested that a sample of petitioner's blood be taken. An attending physician, while petitioner was unconscious, withdrew a sample of about 20 cubic centimeters of blood by use os a hyperdermic needle. This sample was delivered to the patrolman and subsequent laboratory analysis showed this blood to contain about .17% alcohol.

Petitioner was thereafter charged with involuntary manslaughter. Testimony regarding the blood test and its result was admitted into evidence at trial over petitioner's objection. This included testimony of an expert that a person with .17% alcohol in his blood was under the influence of intoxicating liquor. Petitioner was convicted and sentenced for involuntary manslaughter. he did not appeal the conviction. Subsequently, however, he sought release from his imprisonment by a petition for a writ of habeas corpus to the Supreme Court of New Mexico. That court, after argument, denied the writ. 58 N.M. 385, 271 P.2d 827 (1954). Petitioner contends that his conviction, based on the result of the involuntary blood test, deprived him of his liberty without that due process of law guaranteed him by the Fourteenth Amendment to the Constitution. We granted certiorari, 351 U.S. 906, to determine whether the requirements of the Due Process Clause, as it concerns state criminal proceedings, necessitate the invalidation of the conviction.

It has been clear since **WEEKS v. UNITED STATES**, 232 U.S. 383 (1914), that evidence obtained in violation of rights protected by the Fourth Amendment to the Federal Constitution must be excluded in federal criminal prosecutions. There is argument on behalf of petitioner that the evidence used here, the result of the blood test, was obtained in violation of the Due Process Clause of the Fourteenth Amendment in that the taking was the result of an unreasonable search and seizure violative of the Fourth Amendment. Likewise, he argues that by way of the Fourteenth Amendment there has been a violation of the Fifth Amendment in that introduction of the test result compelled him to be a witness against himself. Petitioner relies on the proposition that "the generative principle" of the Bill of Rights should extend the protection of the Fourth and Fifth Amendment to his case through the Due Process Clause of the Fourteenth Amendment. But **WOLF v. COLORADO**, 338 U.S. 25 (1949), answers this contention in the negative. See also **TWINING v. NEW JERSEY**, 211 U.S. 78 (1908); **PALKO v. CONNECTICUT**, 302 U.S. 319 (1937); **IRVINE v. CALIFORNIA**. 347 U.S. 128 (1954). New Mexico has rejected, as it may, the exclusionary rule set forth in Weeks, supra. **STATE v. DILLON**, 34 N.M. 366, 281 P. 474 (1929). Therefore, the rights petitioner claims afford no aid to him here for the fruits of the violations, if any, are admissible in the State's prosecution.

Petitioner's remaining and primary assault on his conviction is not so easily unhorsed. He urges that the conduct of the state officers here offends that "sense of justice" of which we spoke in **ROCHIN v. CALIFORNIA**, 342 U.S. 165 (1952). In that case state officers broke into the home of the accused and observed him place something in his mouth. The officers forced open his mouth after considerable struggle in an unsuccessful attempt to retrieve whatever was there. A stomach pump was later forcibly used and among the matter extracted from his stomach were found narcotic pills. As we said there, " this course of proceeding by agents of government to obtain evidence is bound to offend even hardened sensibilities." Id., at 172. We set aside the conviction because such conduct "shocked the conscience" and was so "brutal" and "offensive" that it did not comport with traditional ideas of fair play and decency. We therefore found that the conduct was offensive to due process. But we see nothing comparable here to the facts in Rochin.

Basically the distinction rests on the fact that

there is nothing "brutal" or "offensive" in the taking of
a sample of blood when done, as in this case, under the
protective eye of a physician. To be sure, the driver
here was unconscious when the blood was taken, but the
absence of conscious consent,, without more, does not
necessarily render the taking a violation of a
constitutional right; and certainly the test as
administered here would not be considered offensive by
even the most delicate. Further more, due process is not
measured by the yardstick of personal reaction or the
sphygmogram of the most sensitive person, but by that
whole community sense of "decency and fairness" that has
been woven by common experience into the fabric of
acceptable conduct. It is on this bedrock that this Court
has established the concept of due process. The blood
test procedure has become routine in our everyday life.
It is a ritual for those going into the military serviced
as well as those applying for marriage licenses. Many
colleges require such tests before permitting entrance
and literally millions of us have voluntarily gone
through the same, though a longer, routine in becoming
blood donors. Likewise, we note that a majority of our
States have either enacted statutes in some form
authorizing tests of this nature or permit findings so
obtained to be admitted in evidence. We therefore
conclude that a blood test taken by a skilled technician
is not such "conduct that shocks the conscience,"
Rochin, supra, at 172, nor such a method of obtaining
evidence that it offends a "sense of justice," **BROWN v.
MISSISSIPPI**, 297 U.S. 278, 285-286 (1936). This is not to
say that the indiscriminate taking of blood under
different conditions or by those not competent to do so
may not amount to such "brutality" as would come under
the Rochin rule. The chief law-enforcement officer of
New Mexico, while at the Bar of this Court, assured us
that every proper medical precaution is afforded an
accused from whom blood is taken.
　　The test upheld here is not attacked on the ground
of any basic deficiency or of injudicious application,
but admittedly is a scientifically accurate method of
detecting alcoholic content in the blood, thus furnishing
an exact measure upon which to base a decision as to
intoxication. Modern community living requires modern

scientific methods of crime detection lest the public go unprotected. The increasing slaughter on our highways, most of which should be avoidable, now reaches the astounding figures only heard of on the battlefield. The States, through safety measures, modern scientific methods, and strict enforcement of traffic laws, are using all reasonable means to make automobile driving less dangerous.

As against the right of an individual that his person be held inviolable, even against so slight an intrusion as is involved in applying a blood test of the kind to which millions of Americans submit as a matter of course nearly every day, must be set the interest of society in the scientific determination of intoxication, one of the great causes of the mortal hazards of the road. And the more so since the test likewise may establish innocence, thus affording protection against the treachery of judgment based on one or more of the senses. Furthermore, since our criminal law is to no small extent justified by the assumption of deterrence, the individual's rights to immunity from such invasion of the body as is involved in a properly safeguarded blood test is far outweighed by the value of its deterrent effect due to public realization that the issue of driving while under the influence of alcohol can often by this method be taken out of the confusion of conflicting contentions.

For these reasons the judgment is

Affirmed.

MR. CHIEF JUSTICE WARREN, with whom MR. JUSTICE BLACK and MR. JUSTICE DOUGLAS join, dissenting.

The judgment in this case should be reversed if ROCHIN v. CALIFORNIA, 342 U.S. 165, is to retain its vitality and stand as more than an instance of personal revulsion against particular police methods. I cannot agree with the Court when it says, "we see nothing comparable here to the facts in Rochin." It seems to me the essential elements of the cases are the same and the same result should follow.

There is much in the Court's opinion concerning the hazards on our nation's highways, the efforts of the States to enforce the traffic laws and the necessity for the use of modern scientific methods in the detection of

crime. Everybody can agree with these sentiments, and
yet they do not help us particularly in determining
whether this case can be distinguished from Rochin. That
case grew out of police efforts to curb the narcotics
traffic, in which there is surely a state interest of at
least as great magnitude as the interest in highway law
enforcement. Nor does the fact that many States sanction
the use of blood test evidence differentiate the cases.
At the time Rochin was decided illegally obtained
evidence was admissible in the vast majority of States.
In both Rochin and this case the officers had probable
cause to suspect the defendant of the offense of which
they sought evidence. In Rochin the defendant was known
as a narcotics law violator, was arrested under
suspicious circumstances and was seen by the officers to
swallow narcotics. In neither case, of course, are we
concerned with the defendant's guilt or innocence.

* * *

Apart from the irrelevant factor of physical
resistance, the techniques used in this case and in
Rochin are comparable. In each the operation was
performed by a doctor in a hospital. In each there was
an extraction of body fluids. Neither operation normally
causes any lasting ill effects. The Court denominates a
blood test as a scientific method for detecting crime and
cites the frequency of such tests in our everyday life.
The stomach pump too is a common and accepted way of
making tests and relieving distress. But it does not
follow from the fact that a technique is a product of
science or is in common, consensual use for other
purposes that it can be used to extract evidence from a
criminal defendant without his consent. Would the taking
of spinal fluid from an unconscious person be condoned
because such tests are commonly made and might be used as
a scientific aid to law enforcement?

Only personal reaction to the stomach pump and the
blood test can distinguish them. To base the restriction
which the Due Process Clause imposes on state criminal
procedures upon such reactions is to build on shifting
sands. We should, in my opinion, hold that due process
means at least that law-enforcement officers in their
efforts to obtain evidence from persons suspected of
crime must stop short of bruising the body, breaking

skin, puncturing tissue or extracting body fluids, whether they contemplate doing it by force or by stealth.

Viewed according to this standard, the judgment should be reversed.

MR. JUSTICE DOUGLAS, with whom MR. JUSTICE BLACK joins, dissenting.

The Court seems to sanction in the name of law enforcement the assault made by the police on this unconscious man. If law enforcement were the chief value in our constitutional scheme, then due process would shrivel and become of little value

* * *

Yet, there is compulsion here, following the violation by the police of the sanctity of the body of an unconscious man.

And if the decencies of a civilized state are the test, it is repulsive to me for the police to insert needles into an unconscious person in order to get the evidence necessary to convict him, whether they find the person unconscious, give him a pill which puts him to sleep, or use force to subdue him. The indignity to the individual is the same in one case as in the other, for in each is his body invaded and assaulted by the police who are supposed to be the citizen's protector.

I would reverse this judgment of conviction.

UNITED STATES, Petitioner,
v.
GIACOMO VENTRESCA
380 U.S. 102, 13 L.Ed.2d 684, 85 S.Ct. 741 (1965)
Argued January 18 and 19, 1965. Decided March 1, 1965.

MR. JUSTICE GOLDBERG delivered the opinion of the Court.

Respondent, Ventresca, was convicted in the United States District Court for the District of Massachusetts of possessing and operating an illegal distillery. The conviction was reversed by the Court of Appeals (one judge dissenting) on the ground that the affidavit for a search warrant pursuant to which the still was found was insufficient to establish probable cause. 324 F2d 864.

The affidavit upon which the warrant was issued was made and submitted to a United States Commissioner on August 31, 1961, by Walter Mazaka, an Investigator for the Alcohol and Tobacco Tax Division of the Internal Revenue Service. He stated that he had reason to believe that an illegal distillery was in operation in respondent, Ventresca's house at 148 1/2 Coburn Avenue in Worcester, Massachusetts. The grounds for this belief were set forth in detail in the affidavit, prefaced with the following statement:

> "Based upon observation made by me, and based upon information received officially from other Investigators attached to the Alcohol and Tobacco Tax Division assigned to this investigation, and reports orally made to me describing the results of their observations and investigation, this request for the issuance of a search warrant is made."

The affidavit then described seven different occasions between July 28 and August 30, 1961, when a Pontiac car was driven into the yard to the rear of Ventresca's house. On four occasions the car carried loads of sugar in 60-pound bags; it made two trips loaded with empty tin cans; and once it was merely observed as being heavily laden. Garry, the car's owner, and Incardone, a passenger, were seen on several occasions loading the car at Ventresca's house and later unloading apparently full five-gallon cans at Garry's house late in the evening. On August 28, after a delivery of empty tin cans to Ventresca's house, Garry and Incardone were observed carrying from the house cans which appeared to be filled and placing them in the trunk of Garry's car. The affidavit went on to state that at about 4 a.m. on August 18, and at about 4 a.m on August 30, "Investigators smelled the odor of fermenting mash as they walked along the sidewalk in front of Ventresca's house. On August 18 they heard, "[a]t or about the same time, . . . certain metallic noises." On August 30, the day before the warrant was applied for, they heard (as they smelled the mash) "sounds similar to that of a motor or a pump coming from the direction of" Ventresca's house. The affidavit concluded : "The foregoing information is based upon personal knowledge and information which has been obtained from Investigators of the Alcohol and Tobacco Tax Division, Internal Revenue Service, who have been assigned to this investigation."

The District Court upheld the validity of the warrant on a motion to suppress. The divided Court of Appeals held the warrant insufficient because it read the affidavit as not specifically stating in so many words that the information it contained was based upon the personal knowledge of Mazaka or other reliable investigators. The court of Appeals reasoned that all of the information recited in the affidavit might conceivably have been obtained by investigators other than Mazaka, and it could not be certain that the information of these other investigators was not in turn based upon hearsay received from unreliable informants rather than their own personal observations. For this reason the court found that probable cause had not been established. 324 F2d, at 868-870. We granted certiorari to consider the standards by which a reviewing court should approach the interpretation of affidavits supporting warrants which have been duly issued by examining magistrates. 377 U.S. 989, 12 L.Ed.2d 1043, 84 S.Ct. 1910. For the reasons stated below, we reverse the judgment of the Court of Appeals.

I

[1] The Fourth Amendment states:

"The right of the people to be secure in their persons, houses, papers, and effects, against unreasonable searches and seizures, shall not be violated, and no Warrants shall issue, but upon probable cause, supported by Oath or affirmation, and particularly describing the place to be searched, and the persons or things to be seized."

We begin our analysis of this constitutional rule mindful of the fact that in this case a search was made pursuant to a search warrant. In discussing the Fourth Amendment policy against unnecessary invasions of privacy, we stated in **AGUILAR v. TEXAS**, 378 U.S. 108, 12 L.Ed.2d 723, 84 S.Ct. 1509:

"An evaluation of the constitutionality of a search warrant should begin with the rule that 'the informed and deliberate determinations of magistrates empowered to issue warrants . . .are to be preferred over the hurried action of officers . . . who may happen to make arrests.' **UNITED STATES v. LEFKOWITZ**, 285 U.S. 452, 464 [76 L.Ed. 877, 882, 52 S.Ct. 420, 82 ALR 775]. The reasons for this rule go to the foundations of the Fourth Amendment." 378 U.S., at 110-111, 12 L.Ed.2d at 726.

In **JONES v. UNITED STATES**, 362 U.S. 257, 270, 4 L.Ed.2d. 697, 707, 80 S.Ct. 725, 78 ALR2d 233, this Court, strongly supporting the preference to be accorded searches under a warrant, indicated that in a doubtful or marginal case a search under a warrant may be sustainable where without one it would fall. In **JOHNSON v. UNITED STATES**, 333 U.S. 10, 92 L.Ed 436, 68 S.Ct. 367, and **CHAPMAN v. UNITED STATES**, 365 U.S. 610, 5 L.Ed.2d 828, 81 S.Ct. 776, the Court, in condemning searches by officers who invaded premises without a warrant, plainly intimated that had the proper course of obtaining a warrant from a magistrate been followed and had the magistrate been followed and had the magistrate on the same evidence available to the police made a finding of probable cause,

398

the search under the warrant would have been sustained.
MR. JUSTICE JACKSON stated for the Court in Johnson:

> "The point of the Fourth Amendment, which often is
> not grasped by zealous officers, is not that it
> denies law enforcement the support of the usual
> inferences which reasonable men draw from evidence.
> Its protection consists in requiring that those
> inferences be drawn by a neutral and detached
> magistrate instead of being judged by the officer
> engaged in the often competitive enterprise of
> ferreting out crime. Any assumption that evidence
> sufficient to support a magistrate's disinterested
> determination to issue a search warrant will
> justify the officers in making a search without a
> warrant would reduce the Amendment to a nullity and
> leave the people's homes secure only in the
> discretion of police officers." **JOHNSON v. UNITED
> STATES**, supra, 333 U.S. at 13-14, 92 L.Ed at 440.

The fact that exceptions to the requirement that searches
and seizures be undertaken only after obtaining a warrant
are limited underscores the preference accorded police
action taken under a warrant as against searches and
seizures without one.

[2-5] While a warrant may issue only upon a finding
of "probable cause," this Court has long held that "the
term 'probable cause' . . .means less than evidence which
justify condemnation," **LOCKE v. UNITED STATES**, 7 Cranch
339, 348, 3 L.Ed. 364, 367, and that a finding of
"probable cause" may rest upon evidence which is not
legally competent in a criminal trial. **DRAPER v. UNITED
STATES**, 358 U.S. 307, 311 3 L.Ed.2d 327, 331, 79 S.Ct.
329. As the Court stated in **BRINEGAR v. UNITED STATES**,
338 U.S. 160, 173, 93 L.Ed. 1879, 1889, 69 S.Ct. 1302,
"There is a large difference between two things to be
proved [guilt and probable cause], as well as between the
tribunals which determine them, and therefore a like
difference in the quanta and modes of proof required to
establish them." Thus hearsay may be the basis for
issuance of the warrant "so long as there [is] a
substantial- basis for crediting the hearsay." **JONES v.
UNITED STATES**, supra, 362 U.S. at 272, 4 L.Ed.2d at 708,
78 ALR2d 233. And, in Aguilar we recognized that "an
affidavit may be based on hearsay information and need

not reflect the direct personal observations of the affiant," so long as the magistrate is "informed of some of the underlying circumstances" supporting the affiant's conclusions and his belief that any informant involved "whose identity need not be disclosed . . . was 'credible' or his information 'reliable.'" **AGUILAR v. TEXAS,** supra 378 U.S. at 114, 12 L.Ed.2d at 729.

[6,7] These decisions reflect the recognition that the Fourth Amendment's commands, like all constitutional requirements, are practical and not abstract. If the teaching of the Court's cases are to be followed and the constitutional policy served, affidavits for search warrants, such as the one involved here, must be tested and interpreted by magistrates and courts in a common sense and realistic fashion. They are normally drafted by nonlawyers in the midst and haste of a criminal investigation. Technical requirements of elaborate specificity once exacted under common law pleadings have no proper place in this area. A grudging or negative attitude by reviewing courts toward warrants will tend to discourage police officers from submitting their evidence to a judicial officer before acting.

[8,9] This is not to say that probable cause can be made out by affidavits which are purely conclusory, stating only the affiant's or an informer's belief that probable cause exists without detailing any of the "underlying circumstances" upon which that belief is based. See **AGUILAR v. TEXAS,** supra. Recital of some of the underlying circumstances in the affidavit is essential if the magistrate is to perform his detached function and not serve merely as a rubber stamp for the police. However, where these circumstances are detailed, where reason for crediting the source of the information is given, and when a magistrate has found probable cause, the courts should not invalidate the warrant by interpreting the affidavit in a hypertechnical, rather than a commonsense, manner. Although in a particular case it may not be easy to determine when an affidavit demonstrates the existence of probable cause, the resolution of doubtful or marginal cases in this area should be largely determined by the preference to be accorded to warrants. **JONES v. UNITED STATES,** supra 362 U.S. at 270, 4 L.Ed.2d. at 707, 78 ALR2d 233.

II

The application of the principles stated above leads us to reverse the Court of Appeals. The affidavit in this case, if read in a commonsense way rather than technically, shows ample facts to establish probable cause and allow the Commissioner to issue the search warrant. The affidavit at issue here, unlike the affidavit held insufficient in Aguilar, is detailed and specific. It sets forth not merely "some of the underlying circumstances" supporting the officer's belief, but a good many of them. This is apparent from the summary of the affidavit already recited and from its text which is reproduced in the Appendix.

The Court of Appeals did not question the specificity of the affidavit. It rested its holding that the affidavit was insufficient on the ground that "[t]he affidavit failed to clearly indicate which of the facts alleged therein were hearsay or which were within the affiant's own knowledge," and therefore "[t]he Commissioner could only conclude that the entire affidavit was based on hearsay." 324 F2d, at 868. While the Court of Appeals recognized that an affidavit based on hearsay will be sufficient, "so long as a substantial basis for crediting the hearsay is presented," **JONES v. UNITED STATES**, supra 362 U.S. at 269, 4 L.Ed.2d at 707, 78 ALR2d 233, it felt that no such basis existed here because the hearsay consisted of reports by "Investigators," and the affidavit did not recite how the Investigators obtained their information. The Court of Appeals conceded that the affidavit stated that the Investigators themselves smelled the odor of fermenting mash, but argued that the rest of their information might itself have been based upon hearsay thus raising "the distinct possibility of hearsay-upon-hearsay." 324 F2d, at 869. For this reason, it held that the affidavit did not establish probable cause.

[10,11] We disagree with the conclusion of the Court of Appeals. Its determination that the affidavit might have been based wholly upon hearsay cannot be supported in light of the fact that Mazaka, a Government Investigator , swore under oath that the relevant information was in part based "upon observations made by me" and "upon personal knowledge' as well as upon "information which has been obtained from Investigators of the Alcohol and Tobacco Tax Division, Internal Revenue Service, who have been assigned to this investigation."

It also seems to us that the assumption of the Court of Appeals that all of the information in Mazaka's affidavit may in fact have come from unreliable anonymous informers, passed on to Government Investigators, who in turn related this information to Mazaka is without foundation. Mazaka swore that, insofar as the affidavit was not based upon his own observations, it was "based upon information received officially from other Investigators attached to the Alcohol and Tobacco Tax Division assigned to this investigation, and reports orally made to me describing the results of their *observations* and investigations." (Emphasis added.) The Court of Appeals itself recognized that the affidavit stated that "'Investigators' [employees of the Service] smelled the odor of fermenting mash in the vicinity of the suspected dwelling." 324 F2d, at 869. A qualified officer's detection of the smell of mash has often been held a very strong factor in determining that probable cause exists so as to allow issuance of a warrant. Moreover, upon reading the affidavit as a whole, it becomes clear that the detailed observations recounted in the affidavit cannot fairly be regarded as having been made in any significant part by persons other than full-time Investigators of the Alcohol and Tobacco Tax Division of the Internal Revenue Service. Observations of fellow officers of the Government engaged in a common investigation are plainly a reliable basis for a warrant applied for by one of their number. We conclude that the affidavit showed probable cause and that the Court of Appeals misapprehended its judicial function in reviewing this affidavit by giving it an unduly technical and restrictive reading.

This Court is alert to invalidate unconstitutional searches and seizures whether with or without a warrant. See **AGUILAR v TEXAS**, supra; **STANFORD v. TEXAS**, 379 U.S. 476, 13 L.Ed.2d 431, 85 S.Ct. 506; **PRESTON v. UNITED STATES**, 376 U.S. 364, 11 L.Ed.2d 777, 84 S.Ct. 881; **BECK v. OHIO**, 379 U.S. 89, 13 L.Ed.2d 142, 85 S.Ct. 223. By doing so, it vindicates individual liberties and strengthens the administration of justice by promoting respect for law and order. This Court is equally concerned to uphold the actions of law enforcement officers consistently following the proper constitutional course. This is no less important to the administration of justice than the invalidation of convictions because of disregard of individual rights or official overreaching. In our view the officers in this case did what the Constitution requires. They obtained a warrant from a judicial officer "upon probable cause, supported by Oath or affirmation, and particularly describing the place to be searched, and the . . . things to be seized." It is vital that having done so their actions should be sustained under a system of justice responsive both to the needs of individual liberty and to the rights of the community.

Reversed.

APPENDIX

AFFIDAVIT FOR SEARCH WARRANT

BEFORE W. ARTHUR GARRITY, Worcester, Massachusetts

The undersigned being duly sworn deposes and says:

That he has reason to believe that on the premises known as a one-family light green wooden frame dwelling house located at 148 1/2 Coburn Avenue, Worcester, occupied by Giacomo Ventresca and his family, together with all approaches and appurtenances thereto, in the District of Massachusetts, there is now being concealed certain property, namely an unknown quantity of material and certain apparatus, articles and devices, including a still and distilling apparatus setup with all attachments thereto, in the District of Massachusetts, there is now being concealed certain property, namely an unknown quantity of material and certain apparatus, articles and devices, including a still and distilling apparatus setup with all attachments thereto, together with an unknown quantity of distilled spirits, and other material used in the manufacture of non-tax-paid liquors; which are being held and possessed, and which have been used and are intended for use, in the distillation, manufacture, possession, and distribution of non-tax-paid liquors, in violation of the provisions of 26 USC 5171 (a), 5173,

5178, 5179 (a), 5222 (a), 5602, and 5686.

And that the facts tending to establish the foregoing grounds for issuance of a Search Warrant are as follows:

SEE ATTACHED SHEET

/s/ WALTER a. MAZAKA
     Investigator, Alcohol and Tobacco Tax Div.,
     Internal Revenue Service

Sworn to before me, and subscribed in my presence, August 31st, 1961

/s/ W. ARTHUR GARRITY
     United States Commissioner

Based upon observation made by me, and based upon information received officially from other Investigators attached to the Alcohol and Tobacco Tax Division assigned to this investigation, and reports orally made to me describing the results of their observations and investigation, this request for the issuance of a search warrant is made.

On or about July 28, 1961, about 6:45 P.M., an observation was made covering a Pontiac automobile owned by one Joseph Garry. Garry and one Joseph Incardone put thirteen bags of sugar into the car. These bags of sugar weighed sixty pounds each. Ten such bags were put into the trunk, and three were placed in the rear seat. Those in the rear seat were marked "Domino." The others appeared to have similar markings. After the sugar was loaded into the car, Garry together with Incardone drove it to the vicinity of 148 Coburn Avenue, Worcester, Massachusetts, where the car was parked. Sometime later, the car with its contents was driven into the yard to the rear of 148 1/2 Coburn Avenue. After remaining there about twenty-five minutes, the same two men drove in the direction of Boston.

On August 2, 1961 a Pontiac car owned by Garry, and driven by Garry with Incardone as a passenger, was followed from Boston to Worcester. The car appeared heavily laden. The car was again driven into the

404

driveway at 148 and 148 1/2 Coburn Avenue to the rear of the yard and between the above-numbered houses

On August 7, 1961 at least six sixty-pound bags of Domino Sugar were loaded into the Pontiac owned by Garry. The loading was done by Garry and Incardone. The car traveled from Boston to Worcester, then to Holden, and returned with its contents and entered the driveway at 148 and 148 1/2 Coburn Avenue, where the car was parked at the rear between the two houses.

On August 11, 1961 new empty metal or tin cans were transferred from a car owned by Incardone to the Pontiac owned by Garry on Highland Street in Hyde Park. The Pontiac was driven by Garry with Incardone as a passenger to Worcester, and into the yard at 148 and 148 1/2 Coburn Avenue to the rear and between the two numbered premises.

On August 16, 1961 the Pontiac was observed. In the back seat bags of sugar were observed covered with a cloth or tarpaulin. A sixty-pound bag of sugar was on the front seat. Garry was observed after loading the above-described sugar into the car placing a carton with various five-pound bags of sugar on the top of the tarpaulin. The car was then driven by Garry with Incardone as a passenger to Worcester together with its contents into the yard at 148 and 148 1/2 Coburn Avenue to the rear of and between the two houses. About Midnight on the same night, the Pontiac driven by Garry with Incardone as a passenger was seen pulling up to the premises at 59 Highland Street, Hyde Park, where Garry lives. Garry opened the trunk of his car, and removed the five-gallon cans therefrom, and placed them on the sidewalk. He then entered the house, and opened a door on the side. Incardone made five trips from the sidewalk to the side of the house carrying two five-gallon cans on each such trip. It appeared that the cans were filled. On each of these trips, Incardone passed the two cans to someone standing in the doorway. Immediately after the fifth such trip, Garry came out of the door and joined Incardone. They walked to the sidewalk, and talked for a few moments. Incardone then drove away, and Garry went into his home.

On August 18, 1961 Investigators smelled an odor of fermenting mash on two occasions between 4:00 A.M. and 5:00 A.M. The first such odor was detected as they walked along the sidewalk in front of 148 Coburn Avenue, and the second such odor was detected from the side of 148 Coburn Avenue. At or about the same time, the Investigators

405

heard certain metallic noises which cannot be further identified by source or sound.

On August 24, 1961 the Pontiac was observed parked at a bowling alley and coffee shop off Route 9. The back of the car contained what appeared to be boxes covered by a cloth or tarpaulin, but which cannot be more specifically identified. On the front seat of the car was observed a sixty-pound bag of Revere Sugar. Garry and Incardone were observed in the restaurant or coffee shop eating. Later the car was seen driven to the rear of 148 between 148 and 148 1/2 Coburn Avenue, Worcester.

About Midnight the Pontiac was observed pulling up in front of Garry's house at 59 Highland Street, Hyde Park. Garry was driving, and Incardone was a passenger. They both got out of the car. Garry opened the trunk, and then entered his house. From the trunk of the car there was removed eleven five-gallon cans which appeared to be filled. Incardone made six trips to a door on the side of the house. He carried two five-gallon cans on each trip, except the sixth trip. On that trip he carried one can, having passed the others to somebody in the doorway, and one (S.I.C) the last trip he entered the house. He remained there at least forty-five minutes, and was not observed to leave.

On August 28, 1961 Garry drove Incardone in his car to Worcester. On Lake Ave. they met Giacomo Ventresca, who lives at 148 1/2 Coburn Avenue, Worcester. Ventresca entered the car driven by Garry. The car was then driven into the yard to the rear of 148 and between 148 and 148 1/2 Coburn Avenue. An observation was made that empty metal cans, five-gallon size, were being taken from the car owned by Garry, and brought into the premises at 148 1/2 Coburn Avenue, which was occupied by Ventresca. Later, new cans similar in size, shape and appearance were observed being placed into the trunk of Garry's car while parked at the rear of 148 and in front of 148 1/2 Coburn Avenue. The manner in which the cans were handled, and the sounds which were heard during the handling of these cans, were consistent with that of cans containing liquid.

On August 30, 1961, at about 4:00 A.M., an odor of fermenting mash was detected while Investigators were walking on the sidewalk in front of 148 Coburn Avenue.

406

At the same time, they heard sounds similar to that of a
motor or a pump coming from the direction of 148 1/2
Coburn Avenue.

The foregoing information is based upon personal
knowledge and information which has been obtained from
Investigators of the Alcohol and Tobacco Tax Division,
Internal Revenue Service, who have been assigned to this
investigation.

/s/ WALTER A. MAZAKA

MR. JUSTICE DOUGLAS, with whom THE CHIEF JUSTICE
concurs, dissenting.

With all deference, the present affidavit seems
hopelessly inadequate to me as a basis for a magistrate's
informed determination that a search warrant should
issue.

We deal with the constitutional right of privacy
that can be invaded only on a showing of "probable cause"
as provided by the Fourth Amendment. That is a strict
standard; what the police say does not necessarily carry
the day; "probable cause" is in the keeping of the
magistrate. **GIORDENELLO v. UNITED STATES**, 357 U.S. 480,
486-487, 2 L.Ed.2d 1503, 1509, 1520, 78 S.Ct. 1245;
JOHNSON v. UNITED STATES, 333 U.S. 10, 14, 92 L.Ed 436,
440, 68 S.Ct. 367. Yet anything he says does not
necessarily go either. He too is bound by the
Constitution. His discretion is reviewable. **AGUILAR v.
TEXAS**, 378 U.S. 108, 111, 12 L.Ed.2d 723, 726, 84 S.Ct.
1509. But unless the constitutional standard of "probable
cause" is defined in meticulous ways, the discretion of
police and of magistrates alike will become absolute.
The present case, illustrates how the mere weight of
lengthy and vague recitals takes the place of reasonably
probative evidence of the existence of crime.

I

Investigator Mazaka sought a warrant for the purpose
of searching the premises at 148 1/2 Coburn Avenue,
occupied by respondent and his family, because, he
averred, he had reason to believe that there was
concealed on the premises an illegal still and other
material connected with the manufacture of non-tax-paid
liquors. The ground for this belief were recited in 12
paragraphs on an attached sheet, as reproduced in the
Appendix to the Court's opinion, ante, pp. 691-693.

The factual recitals comprise 10 paragraphs, each paragraph setting forth the alleged events of a single day, except that August 24, 1961, is dealt with in two paragraphs. Of these factual recitals more will be said in a moment. The first and last paragraph of the 12 describe the sources from which the affiant has gained the information set forth in the factual paragraphs. These sources are, according to the first paragraph, three in number: (1) "observations made by me"; (2) "information received officially from other Investigators"; and (3) "reports orally made to me [by other investigators] describing the results of their observations and investigation." In the last paragraph the affiant describes the sources of his information slightly differently: "The foregoing information is based upon personal knowledge and information which has been obtained from Investigators . . . ."

Of the 10 factual paragraphs eight describe trips said to have been made to and from the vicinity of 148 1/2 Coburn Avenue by one Garry and one Incardone. On these trips, it is said, there were delivered to the vicinity of 148 1/2 Coburn Avenue large quantities of sugar (four deliveries) and empty metal cans (two deliveries, on one of which respondent himself is said to have been a passenger in the car); on one occasion it was observed only that the car was "heavily laden." It is said that on two occasions Garry and Incardone were seen taking apparently filled cans into Garry's house, 59 Highland Street, from the Pontiac; on one such occasion the Pontiac, it is said, had been at Coburn Avenue earlier in the day, apparently making a sugar delivery. And, finally, it is averred that on one occasion seemingly filled cans were loaded into the Pontiac near 148 1/2 Coburn Avenue, shortly after a delivery of empties to that address.

The "facts" recited in these eight paragraphs, it is said, permit the inference that a still was being operated on respondent's premises. But are these "facts" really facts? A statement of "fact" is only as credible as its source. Investigator Mazaka evidently believes these statements to be correct; but the magistrate must, of course, know something of the basis of that belief. **NATHANSON v. UNITED STATES**, 290 U.S. 41, 78 L.Ed 159, 54

S.Ct. 11. Is the belief of this affiant based on personal observation, or on hearsay, or on hearsay on hearsay? Nowhere in the affidavit is the source of these eight paragraphs of information revealed. In each paragraph the alleged events are simply described directly, or else it is said that certain events "were observed." Scarcely a clue is given as to who the observer might have been. It might have been the affiant, though one would not expect that he would so studiously refrain from revealing that he himself witnessed these events. The observers might have been some other investigators, though the affiant does not say so; yet in the two paragraphs next to be discussed the observers are prominently identified as investigators. Perhaps the ultimate source of most of these statements was one or more private citizens, who were interviewed by investigators, whose reports on these interviews came in due course to Investigator Mazaka, who then composed the affidavit. Perhaps many of the "facts" recited in the affidavit were supplied by an unknown informant over the telephone.

In most instances the language of the affidavit suggests that some investigator witnessed the alleged events. For example, the second paragraph begins: " On or about July 28, 1961, about 6:45 P.M., an observation was made covering a Pontiac automobile owned by one Joseph Garry." But the presumed investigator who may have been "covering" this automobile is in no way identified. There is no way of knowing whether the report of this alleged observation was made directly to the affiant or whether it went through one or more intermediaries.

Turning now to the remaining two "factual" paragraphs, we find it averred that "Investigators" smelled fermenting mash and heard metallic and other noises in the vicinity of 148 1/2 Coburn Avenue. On August 18, it is said, investigators twice smelled mash between 4 and 5 a.m. as they walked on the sidewalk in front of and beside the house at 148 Coburn Avenue, which is apparently the house next to respondent's. The "Investigators" are not further identified. On August 30 at about 4 a.m., it is averred, unidentified investigators detected the odor of fermenting mash while they were "walking on the sidewalk in front of 148 Coburn Avenue." The source of the odor is again not specified; but sounds heard at the same time, similar to the sounds

409

made by "a motor or a pump," are stated to have come "from the direction of 148 1/2 Coburn Avenue."

Such is the substance of the affidavit. No particular item of information is identified as within the first-hand knowledge of the affiant. Certain smells and sounds are explicitly described as having been directly perceived by unnamed investigators. The sources of all the other information are left to speculation.

The Court's unconcern over the failure of the affidavit to identify the sources of the information recited seems based in part on the detailed, lengthy nature of the factual recitals. The Court seems to say that even if we assume that only some small part of the information is trustworthy, still enough remains to establish probable cause. But I would direct attention to the fact that only one of the 12 paragraphs in this affidavit definitely points the finger of suspicion at 148 1/2 Coburn Avenue: that is the paragraph describing the alleged events of August 28, 1961. In every other paragraph the recitals point no more to 148 1/2 Coburn Avenue than they do to 148 Coburn Avenue. The August 28 paragraph is critical to the finding of the existence of probable cause for the search of 148 1/2 Coburn Avenue. Yet the source of the information contained in that paragraph is in no way identified and it is therefore impossible to determine the trustworthiness of that crucial information.

II

A discussion of the legal principles governing the sufficiency of this affidavit must, unhappily, begin with **DRAPER v. UNITED STATES**, 358 U.S. 307, L.Ed.2d 327, 79 S.Ct. 329. There an officer had been told by an informer, known to the officer to be reliable, that a man of a certain description would get off a certain train with heroin in his possession. The officer met the train, observed a man of that description getting off, and arrested him. The Court held that there was probable cause for the arrest. In **JONES v. UNITED STATES**, 362 U.S. 257, 4 L.Ed.2d 697, 80 S.Ct. 725, 78 ALR2d 233, the Court applied the holding in Draper to find an affidavit sufficient to establish probable cause for the issuance of a search warrant, even though the facts stated in the affidavit did not rest on the affiant's personal observations but rather on the observation of another. The Court held that an affidavit could rest on hearsay, "so long as a substantial basis for crediting the hearsay is presented." Id., at 269, 4 L.Ed.2d at 707, 78 ALR2d 233. (Emphasis supplied.) In Jones the basis for crediting the informant's hearsay was: (1) the affiant swore that the informant had previously given information to him which was correct; (2) the affiant had been given corroborating information by other informants; and (3) the affiant was independently familiar with the persons claimed by the informants to be concealing narcotics in their apartment, and he knew them to have admitted to the use of narcotics.

I dissented from the decisions of the Court in these two cases, for the reasons which I set forth most fully in Draper, supra, 358 U.S. at 314, et seq., 3 L.Ed.2d at 333, et seq. But though I regard these decisions as taking a view destructive of the guarantes of the Fourth Amendment, they are in any event clearly not dispositive of the present case. As I have already shown, the affidavit here does not set forth a single corroborating fact that is sworn to be within the personal knowledge of the affiant. Moreover, there is not a single statement in the affidavit that could not well be hearsay on hearsay or some other multiple form of hearsay.

We are told, however, that it is at least clear that "Investigators" detected the smell of mash in the vicinity of 148 1/2 Coburn Avenue. And the Court says: "Observations of fellow officers of the Government engaged in a common investigation are plainly a reliable basis for a warrant applied for by one of their number," ante, p 690. But I would make **TAYLOR v. UNITED STATES**, 286 U.S. 1, 6, 76 L.Ed 951, 953, 52 S.Ct. 466, my starting point, where the Court stated: "Prohibition officers may rely on a distinctive odor as a physical fact indicative of possible crime; but its presence alone does not strip the owner of a building of constitutional guarantees against unreasonable search." In **JOHNSON v. UNITED STATES**, 333 U.S. 10, 13, 92 L.Ed. 436, 440, 68 S.Ct 367, the Court explained what the decision in Taylor meant: "That decision held only that odors alone do not authorize a search without warrant. If the presence of odors is testified to before a magistrate and he finds the affiant qualified to know the odor, and it is one

411

sufficiently distinctive to identify a forbidden substance, this Court has never held such a basis insufficient to justify issuance of a search warrant." (Emphasis supplied.) It is hardly necessary to point that a magistrate cannot begin to assess the odor-identifying qualifications of persons whose identity is unknown to him. Nor is it necessary to belabor the point that these odors of mash are not ever stated in the affidavit to have emanated from 148 1/2 Coburn Avenue.

III

The Court of Appeals was surely correct when it observed that "the affidavit leaves as a complete mystery the manner in which the Investigators discovered their information." 324 F2d 864, 869. Such being the case, I see no way to avoid the conclusion of the majority below: "If hearsay evidence is to be relied upon in the preparation of an affidavit for a search warrant, the officer or attorney preparing such an affidavit should keep in mind that hearsay statements are only as credible as their source and only as strong as their corroboration. And where the source of the information is in doubt and the corroboration by the affiant is unclear, the affidavit is insufficient." Id., at 869-870. That conclusion states a relatively clear standard of probable cause and is in sharp contrast to the amorphous one upon which today's decision rests.

In **JONES v. UNITED STATES**, supra, this Court forgot, as it forgets again today, that the duty of the magistrate is not delegable to the police. **NATHANSON v. UNITED STATES**, 290 U.S. 41, 78 L.Ed 159, 54 S.Ct. 11. It is for the magistrate, not the police, to decide whether there is probable cause for the issuance of the warrant. That function cannot be discharged by the magistrate unless the police first discharge their own, different responsibility: "to evidence what is reliable and why, and not to introduce a hodge-podge under some general formalistic coverall." 324 F2d, at 870. And see **MASIELLO v. UNITED STATES**, 304 F2d 399, 401-402. That is the duty of the police - the rest is not for them.

I would affirm the decision below.

McCRAY v. ILLINOIS
386 U.S. 300, 87 S.Ct. 1056, 18 L.Ed.2d 782 (1967)
CERTIORARI TO THE SUPREME COURT OF ILLINOIS

MR. JUSTICE STEWART delivered the opinion {of} the Court.

The petitioner was arrested in Chicago, Illinois, on the morning of January 6, 1964, for possession of narcotics. The Chicago police officers who made the arrest found a package containing heroin on his person and he was indicted for its unlawful possession. Prior to trial he filed a motion to suppress the heroin as evidence against him, claiming that the police had acquired it in an unlawful search and seizure in violation of the Fourth and Fourteenth Amendments. See **MAPP v. OHIO**, 367 U.S. 643. After hearing, the court denied the motion, and the petitioner was subsequently convicted upon the evidence of heroin the arresting officers had found in his possession. The judgment of conviction was affirmed by the Supreme Court of Illinois, and we granted certiorari to consider the petitioner's claim that the hearing on his motion to suppress was constitutionally defective.

The petitioner's arrest occurred near the intersection of 49th Street and Calumet Avenue at about seven in the morning. After the hearing on the motion to suppress, he testified that up until a half hour before he was arrested he had been at "a friends's house" about a block away, that after leaving the friend's house he had "walked with a lady from 48th to 48th and South Park," and that, as he approached 49th Street and Calumet Avenue, "[t]he Officers stopped me going through the alley." "The officers," he said, "did not show me a search warrant for my person or an arrest warrant for my arrest." He said the officers then searched him and found the narcotics in question. The petitioner did not identify the "friend" or the "lady," and neither of them appeared as a witness.

The arresting officers then testified. Officer Jackson states that he and two fellow officers had had a conversation with an informant on the morning of January 16 in their unmarked police car. The officer said that the informant had told them that the petitioner, with whom Jackson was acquainted, "was selling narcotics and had narcotics on his person and that he could be found in

413

the vicinity of 47th and Calumet at this particular
time." Jackson said that he and his fellow officers drove
to that vicinity in the police car and that when they
spotted the petitioner, the informant pointed him out and
then departed on foot. Jackson stated that the officers
observed the petitioner walking with a woman, then
separating from her and meeting briefly with a man, then
proceeding alone, and finally, after seeing the police
car, "hurriedly walk[ing] between two buildings." "At
this point," Jackson testified, "my partner and myself
got out of the car and informed him we had information he
had narcotics on his person, placed him in the police
vehicle at this point." Jackson stated that the officers
then searched the petitioner and found the heroin in a
cigarette package.

Jackson testified that he had been acquainted with
the informant for approximately a year, that during this
period the informant had supplied him with information
about narcotics activities "fifteen, sixteen times at
least," that the information had proved to be accurate
and had resulted in numerous arrests and convictions. On
cross-examination, Jackson was even more specific as to
the informant's previous reliability, giving the names of
people who had been convicted of narcotics violations as
the result of information the informant had supplied.
When Jackson was asked for the informant's name and
address, counsel for the State objected, and the
objection was sustained by the court.

Officer Arnold gave substantially the same account
of the circumstances of the petitioner's arrest and
search, stating that the informant had told the officers
that the petitioner "was selling narcotics and had
narcotics on his person now in the vicinity of 47th and
Calumet." The informant, Arnold testified, "said he had
observed [the petitioner] selling narcotics to various
people, meaning various addicts, in the area of 47th and
Calumet." Arnold testified that he had known the
informant "roughly two years," that the informant had
given him information concerning narcotics "20 or 25
times," and that the information had resulted in
convictions. Arnold too was asked on cross-examination
for the informant's name and address, and objections to
these questions were sustained by the court.

414

There can no doubt, upon the basis of the circumstances related by Officers Jackson and Arnold, that there was probable cause to sustain the arrest and incidental search in this case. **DRAPER v. UNITED STATES**, 358 U.S. 307. Unlike the situation in **BECK v. OHIO**, 379 U.S. 89, each of the officers in this case described with specificity "what the informer actually said, and why the officer thought the information was credible." 379 U.S., at 97. The testimony of each of the officers informed the court of the "underlying circumstances from which the informant concluded that the narcotics were where he claimed they were, and some of the underlying circumstances from which the officer concluded that the informant . . . was 'credible' or his information 'reliable'." **AGUILAR v. TEXAS**, 378 U.S. 108, 114. See **UNITED STATES v. VENTRESCA**, 380 U.S. 102. Upon the basis of those circumstances, along with the officers' personal observations of the petitioner, the court was fully justified in holding that at the time the officers made the arrest "the facts and circumstances within their knowledge and of which they had reasonably trustworthy information were sufficient to warrant a prudent man in believing that the petitioner had committed or was committing an offense. **BRINEGAR v. UNITED STATES**, 338 U.S. 160, 175-176; **HENRY v. UNITED STATES**, 361 U.S. 98, 102." **BECK v. OHIO**, supra, at 91. It is the petitioner's claim, however, that even though the officers' sworn testimony fully supported a finding of probable cause for the arrest and search, the state court nonetheless violated the Constitution when it sustained objections to the petitioner's questions as to the identity of the informant. We cannot agree.

In permitting the officers to withhold the informant's identity, the court was following well-settled Illinois law. When the issue is not guilt or innocence, but, as here, the question of probable cause for an arrest or search, the Illinois Supreme Court has held that police officers need not invariably be required to disclose an informant's identity if the trial judge is convinced, by evidence submitted in open court and subject to cross-examination, that the officers did rely in good faith upon credible information supplied by a reliable informant. This Illinois evidentiary rule is consistent with the law of many other States. In California, the State Legislature in 1965 enacted a statute adopting just such a rule for cases like the one before us:

"[I]n any preliminary hearing, criminal trial, or other criminal proceeding, for violation of any provision of Division 10 (commencing with Section 11000) of the Health and Safety Code, evidence of information communicated to a peace officer by a confidential informant, who is not a material witness to the guilt or innocence of the accused of the offense charged, shall be admissible on the issue of reasonable cause to make an arrest or search without requiring that the name or identity of the informant be disclosed if the judge or magistrate is satisfied, based upon evidence produced in open court, out of the presence of the jury, that such information was received from a reliable informant and in his discretion does not require such disclosure." California Evid. Code § 1042 (c).

The reasoning of the Supreme Court of New Jersey in judicially adopting the same basic evidentiary rule was instructively expressed by Chief Justice Weintraub in **STATE v. BURNETT**, 42 N.J. 377, 201 A.2d 39:

"If a defendant may insist upon disclosure of the informant in order to test the truth of the officer's statement that there is an informant or as to what the informant related or as to the informant's reliability, we can be sure that every defendant will demand disclosure. He has nothing to lose and the prize may be the suppression of damaging evidence if the State cannot afford to reveal its source, as is so often the case. And since there is no way to test the good faith of a defendant who presses the demand, we must assume the routine demand would have to be routinely granted. The result would be that the State could use the informant's information only as a lead and could search only if it could gather adequate evidence of probable cause apart from the informant's data. Perhaps that approach would sharpen investigatorial techniques, but we doubt that there would be enough talent and time to cope

416

with crime upon that basis. Rather we accept the premise that the informer is a vital part of society's defensive arsenal. The basic rule protecting his identity rests upon that belief.

"We must remember also that we are not dealing with the trial of the criminal charge itself. There the need for a truthful verdict outweighs society's need for the informer privilege. Here, however, the accused seeks to avoid the truth. The very purpose of a motion to suppress is to escape the inculpatory thrust of evidence in hand, not because its probative force is diluted in the least by the mode of seizure, but rather as a sanction to compel enforcement officers to respect the constitutional security of all of us under the Fourth Amendment. **STATE v. SMITH**, 37 N.J. 481, 486 (1962). If the motion to suppress is denied, defendant will still be judged upon the untarnished truth.

"The Fourth Amendment is served if a judicial mind passes upon the existence of probable cause. Where the issue is submitted upon an application for a warrant, the magistrate is trusted to evaluate the credibility of the affiant in an ex parte proceeding. As we have said, the magistrate is concerned, not with whether the informant lied, but with whether the affiant is truthful in his recitation what he was told. If the magistrate doubts the credibility of the affiant, he may require that the informant be identified or even produced. It seems to us that the same approach is equally sufficient where the search was without a warrant, that is to say, that it should rest entirely with the judge who hears the motion to suppress to decide whether he needs such disclosure as to the informant in order to decide whether the officer is a believable witness." 42 N.J., at 385-388, 201 A.2d, at 43-45.

What Illinois and her sister States have done is no more than recognize a well-established testimonial privilege, long familiar to the law of evidence. Professor Wigmore, not known as an enthusiastic advocate of testimonial privileges generally, has described that privilege in these words:

417

"A genuine privilege, on . . .fundamental principle
. . ., must be recognized for the identity of
persons supplying the government with information
concerning the commission of crimes.
Communications of this kind ought to receive
encouragement. They are discouraged if the
informer's identity is disclosed. Whether an
informer is motivated by good citizenship, promise
of leniency or prospect of pecuniary reward, he
will usually condition his cooperation on an
assurance of anonymity - to protect himself and his
family from harm, to preclude adverse social
reactions to avoid the risk of defamation or
malicious prosecution actions against him. The
government also has an interest in nondisclosure of
the identity of its informers. Law enforcement
officers often depend upon professional informers
to furnish them with a flow of information about
criminal activities. Revelation of the dual role
played by such persons ends their usefulness to the
government and discourages others from entering
into a like relationship.
    "That the government has this privilege is well
established ,and its soundness cannot be
questioned." (footnotes omitted.) 8 Wigmore,
Evidence § 2374 (McNaughton rev. 1961).

    In the federal courts the rules of evidence in
criminal trials are governed "by the principles of the
common law as they may be interpreted by the courts of
the United States in the light of reason and experience."
This Court, therefore, has the ultimate task of defining
the scope to be accorded to various common law
evidentiary privileges in the trial of federal criminal
cases. See **HAWKINS v. UNITED STATES**, 358 U.S. 74. This
is a task which is quite different, of course, from the
responsibility of constitutional adjudication. In the
exercise of this supervisory jurisdiction the Court had
occasion 10- years ago, in **ROVIARO v. UNITED STATES**, 353
U.S. 53, to give thorough consideration to one aspect of
the informer's privilege, the privilege itself having
long been recognized in the federal judicial system.

The Roviaro case involved the informer's privilege, not at a preliminary hearing to determine probable cause for an arrest or search, but at the trial itself where the issue was the fundamental one of innocence or guilt. The petitioner there had been brought to trial upon a two-count federal indictment charging sale and transportation of narcotics. According to the prosecution's evidence, the informer had been an active participant in the crime. He "had taken a material part in bringing about the possession of certain drugs by the accused, had been present with the accused at the occurrence of the alleged crime, and might be a material witness as to whether the accused knowingly transported the drugs as charged." 353 U.S., at 55. The trial court nonetheless denied a defense motion to compel the prosecution to disclose the informer's identity.

This Court held that where, in an actual trial of a federal criminal case,

> "the disclosure of an informer's identity . . .is relevant and helpful to the defense of an accused, or is essential to a fair determination of a cause, the privilege must give way. In these situations the trial court may require disclosure and, if the Government withholds the information, dismiss the action . . .

> "We believe that no fixed rule with respect to disclosure is justifiable. The problem is one that calls for balancing the public interest in protecting the flow of information against the individual's right to prepare his defense. Whether a proper balance renders nondisclosure erroneous must depend on the particular circumstances of each case, taking into consideration the crime charged, the possible defenses, the possible significance of the informer's testimony, and other relevant factors." 353 U.S., at 60-61, 62 (footnotes omitted.)

The Court's opinion then carefully reviewed the particular circumstances of Roviaro's trial, pointing out that the informer's "possible testimony was highly relevant . . .," that he "might have disclosed an entrapment . . ., " "might have thrown doubt upon petitioner's identity or on the identity of the package

419

. . ., " might have testified to petitioner's possible lack of knowledge of the contents of the package that he 'transported' . . ., " and that the "informer was the sole participant, other than the accused, in the transaction charged." 353 U.S., at 63-64.   The Court concluded "that, under these circumstances, the trial court committed prejudicial error in permitting the Government to withhold the identity of its undercover employee in the face of repeated demands by the accused for his disclosure." 353 U.S., at 65.

What Roviaro thus makes clear is that this Court was unwilling to impose any absolute rule requiring disclosure of an informer's identity even in formulating evidentiary rules for federal criminal trials. Much less has the Court ever approached the formulation of a federal evidentiary rule of compulsory disclosure where the issue is the preliminary one of probable cause, and guilt or innocence is not at stake.   Indeed, we have repeatedly made clear that federal officers need not disclose an informer's identity in applying for an arrest or search warrant.   As was said in **UNITED STATES v. VENTRESCA**, 380 U.S. 102, 108, we have "recognized that 'an affidavit may be based upon hearsay information and need not reelect the direct personal observations of the affiant,' so long as the magistrate is 'informed of some of the underlying circumstances' supporting the affiant's conclusions and his belief that any informant involved *'whose identity need not be disclosed. . .*was "credible" or his information "reliable." '**AGUILAR v. TEXAS, supra**, at 114."   (emphasis added.) See also **JONES v. UNITED STATES**, 362 U.S. 257, 271-272; **RUGENDORF v. UNITED STATES**, 376 U.S. 528, 533. And just this Term we have taken occasion to point out that a rule virtually prohibiting the use of informers would "severely hamper the Government" in enforcement of the narcotics law. **LEWIS v. UNITED STATES**, 385 U.S. 206, 210.

In sum, the Court in the exercise of its power to formulate evidentiary rules for federal criminal cases has consistently declined to hold that an informer's identity need always be disclosed in a federal criminal trial, let alone in a preliminary hearing to determine probable cause for an arrest or search.   Yet we are now asked to hold that the Constitution somehow compels

Illinois to abolish the informer's privilege from its law of evidence, and to require disclosure of the informer's identity in every such preliminary hearing where it appears that the officers made the arrest or search in reliance upon facts supplied by an informer they had reason to trust. The argument is based upon the Due Process Clause of the Fourteenth Amendment, and upon the Sixth Amendment right of confrontation, applicable to the States through the Fourteenth Amendment. **POINTER v. TEXAS**, 380 U.S. 400. We find no support for the petitioner's position in either of those constitutional provisions.

The arresting officers in this case testified, in open court, fully and in precise detail as to what the informer told them and as to why they had reason to believe his information was trustworthy. Each officer was under oath. Each was subjected to searching cross-examination. The judge was obviously satisfied that each was telling the truth, and for that reason he exercised the discretion conferred upon him by the established law of Illinois to respect the informer's privilege.

Nothing in the Due Process Clause of the Fourteenth Amendment requires a state court judge in every such hearing to assume the arresting officers are committing perjury. "To take such a step would be quite beyond the pale of this Court's proper function in our federal system. It would be a wholly unjustifiable encroachment by this Court upon the constitutional power of States to promulgate their own rules of evidence . . .in their own state courts . . . ." **SPENCER v. TEXAS**, 385 U.S. 554, 568-569.

The petitioner does not explain precisely how he thinks his Sixth Amendment right to confrontation and cross-examination was violated by Illinois' recognition of the informer's privilege in this case. If the claim is that the State violated the Sixth Amendment by not producing the informer to testify against the petitioner, then we need no more than repeat the Court's answer to that claim a few weeks ago in **COOPER v. CALIFORNIA:**

"Petitioner also presents the contention here that he was unconstitutionally deprived of the right to confront a witness against him, because the State did not produce the informant to testify against him. This contention we consider absolutely devoid of merit." Ante, p. 58, at 62, n.2.

On the other hand, the claim may be that the petitioner was deprived of his Sixth Amendment right to cross-examine the arresting officers themselves, because their refusal to reveal the informer's identity was upheld. But it would follow from this argument that no witness on cross-examination could ever constitutionally assert a testimonial privilege, including the privilege against compulsory self-incrimination guaranteed by the Constitution itself. We have never given the Sixth Amendment such a construction, and we decline to do so now.

Affirmed.

MR. JUSTICE DOUGLAS, with whom THE CHIEF JUSTICE, MR. JUSTICE BRENNAN and MR. JUSTICE FORTAS concur, dissenting.

We have here a Fourth Amendment question concerning the validity of an arrest. If the police see a crime being committed they can of course seize the culprit. If a person is fleeing the scene of a crime, the police can make an arrest. But normally an arrest should be made only on a warrant issued by a magistrate on a showing of "probable cause, supported by oath or affirmation," as required by the Fourth Amendment. At least since **MAPP v. OHIO**, 367 U.S. 643, the States are as much bound by those provisions as is the Federal Government. But for the Fourth Amendment they could fashion the rule for arrests that the Court now approves. With all deference, the requirements of the Fourth Amendment now make that conclusion unconstitutional.

No warrant for the arrest of petitioner was obtained in this case. The police, instead of going to a magistrate and making a showing of "probable cause" based on their informant's tip-off, acted on their own. They, rather than the magistrate, became the arbiters of "probable cause." The Court's approval of that process effectively rewrites the Fourth Amendment.

In **ROVIARO v. UNITED STATES**, 353 U.S. 53, 61, we held that where a search without a warrant is made on the basis of communications of an informer and the Government claims the police had "probable cause," disclosure of the identity of the informant is normally required. In no other way can the defense show an absence of "probable cause." By reason of **MAPP v. OHIO**, supra, that rule is now applicable to the states.

In **BECK v. OHIO**, 379 U.S. 89, 96, we said:

"An arrest without a warrant bypasses the safeguards provided by an objective predetermination of probable cause, and substitutes instead the far less reliable procedure of an after-the-event justification for the arrest or search, too likely to be subtly influenced by the familiar shortcoming of hindsight judgment."

For that reason we have weighted arrests with warrants more heavily than arrests without warrants. See UNITED STATES v. VENTRESCA, 380 U.S. 102, 106. Only through the informer's testimony can anyone other than the arresting officers determine "the persuasiveness of the facts relied on . . .to show probable cause." **AGUILAR v. TEXAS**, 378 U.S. 108, 113. Without that disclosure neither we nor the lower courts can ever know whether there was "probable cause" for the arrest. Under the present decision we leave the Fourth Amendment exclusively in the custody of the police. As stated by Mr. Justice Schaefer dissenting in **PEOPLE v. DURR**, 28 ILL. 2d 308, 318, 192 N.E. 2d 379, 384, unless the identity of the informer is disclosed "the policeman himself conclusively determines the validity of his own arrest." That was the view of the Supreme Court of California in **PRESTLY v. SUPERIOR COURT**, 50 Cal. 2d 812, 818, 330 P.2d 39, 43:

"Only by requiring disclosure and giving the defendant an opportunity to present contrary or impeaching evidence as to the truth of the officer's testimony and the reasonableness of his reliance on the informer can the court make a fair determination of the issue. Such a requirement does not unreasonably discourage the free flow of information to law enforcement officers or otherwise impede law enforcement. Actually its effect is to compel independent investigations to verify information given by an informer or to uncover other facts that establish reasonable cause to make an arrest or search."

There is no way to determine the reliability of Old

Reliable, the informer , unless he is produced at the
trial and cross-examined.   Unless he is produced, the
Fourth Amendment is entrusted to the tender mercies of
the police. What we do today is to encourage arrests and
searches without warrants.   The whole momentum of
criminal law administration should be in precisely the
opposite direction, if the Fourth Amendment is to remain
a vital force.   Except in rare and emergency cases, it
requires magistrates to make the findings of "probable
cause."   We should be mindful that "disclosure, rather
than suppression, of relevant materials ordinarily
promotes the proper administration of criminal justice."
DENNIS v. UNITED STATES, 384 U.S. 855, 870.

MICHIGAN v. LONG
463 U.S. 1033, 103 S.Ct. 3469, 77 L.Ed.2d 1201 (1983)
CERTIORARI TO THE SUPREME COURT OF MICHIGAN
No. 82-256. Argued February 23, 1983 -
Decided July 6, 1983

JUSTICE O'CONNOR delivered the opinion of the Court.
In **TERRY v. OHIO**, 392 U.S. 1 (1968), we upheld the
validity of a protective search for weapons in the
absence of probable cause to arrest because it is
unreasonable to deny a police officer the right "to
neutralize the threat of physical harm," id., at 24, when
he possesses an articulable suspicion that an individual
is armed and dangerous. We did not, however, expressly
address whether such a protective search for weapons
could extend to an area beyond the person in the absence
of probable cause to arrest. In the present case,
respondent David Long was convicted for possession of
marihuana found by police in the passenger compartment
and trunk of the automobile that he was driving. The
police searched the passenger compartment because they
had reason to believe that the vehicle contained weapons
potentially dangerous to the officers. We hold that the
protective search of the passenger compartment was
reasonable under the principles articulated in TERRY and
other decisions of this Court. We also examine Long's
argument that the decision below rests upon an adequate
and independent state ground, and we decide in favor of
our jurisdiction.

I

Deputies Howell and Lewis were on patrol in a rural
area one evening when, shortly after midnight, they
observed a car traveling erratically and at excessive
speed. The officers observed the car turning down a side
road, where it swerved off into a shallow ditch. The
officers stopped to investigate. Long, the only occupant
of the automobile, met the deputies at the rear of the
car, which was protruding from the ditch onto the road.
The door on the driver's side of the vehicle was left
open.

Deputy Howell requested Long to produce his
operator's license, but he did not respond. After the
request was repeated, Long produced his license. Long
again failed to respond when Howell requested him to

425

produce the vehicle registration. After another repeated request, Long, who Howell thought "appeared to be under the influence of something," 413 Mich. 461, 469, 320 N.W. 2d 866, 868 (1982), turned from the officers and began walking toward the open door of the vehicle. The officers followed Long and both observed a large hunting knife on the floorboard of the driver's side of the car. The officers then stopped Long's progress and subjected him to a Terry protective patdown, which revealed no weapons.

Long and Deputy Lewis stood by the rear of the vehicle while Deputy Howell shined his flashlight into the interior of the vehicle, but did not actually enter it. The purpose of Howell's action was "to search for other weapons." 413 Mich., at 469, 320 N.W.2d, at 868. The officer noticed that something was protruding from under the armrest on the front sear. He knelt in the vehicle and lifted the armrest. He saw an open pouch on the front seat, and upon flashing his light on the pouch, determined that it contained what appeared to be marihuana. After Deputy Howell showed the pouch and its contents to Deputy Lewis, Long was arrested for possession of marihuana. A further search of the interior of the vehicle, including the glovebox, revealed neither more contraband nor the vehicle registration. The officers decided to impound the vehicle. Deputy Howell opened the trunk, which did not have a lock, and discovered inside it approximately 75 pounds of marihuana.

The Barry County Circuit Court denied Long's motion to suppress the marihuana taken from both the interior of the car and its trunk. He was subsequently convicted of possession of marihuana. The Michigan Court of Appeals affirmed Long's conviction, holding that the search of the passenger compartment was valid as a protective search under Terry, supra, and that the search of the trunk was valid as an inventory search under **SOUTH DAKOTA v. OPPERMAN**, 428 U.S. 364 (1976). See 94 Mich. App. 338, 288 N.W. 2d 629 (1979). The Michigan Supreme Court reversed. The court held that "the sole justification of the TERRY search, protection of the police officers and others nearby, cannot justify the search in this case." 413 Mich., at 472, 320 N.W. 2d, at 869. The marihuana

426

found in Long's trunk was considered by the court below to be the "fruit" of the illegal search of the interior, and was also suppressed.

We granted certiorari in this case to consider the important question of the authority of a police officer to protect himself by conducting a TERRY type search of the passenger compartment of a motor vehicle during the lawful investigatory stop of the occupant of the vehicle. 459 U.S. 904 (1982).

II

Before reaching the merits, we must consider Long's argument that we are without jurisdiction to decide this case because the decision below rests on an adequate and independent state ground. The court below referred twice to the State Constitution in its opinion, but otherwise relied exclusively on federal law. Long argues that the Michigan courts have provided greater protection from searches and seizures under the State Constitution than is afforded under the Fourth Amendment, and the references to the State Constitution therefore establish an adequate and independent ground for the decision below.

It is, of course, "incumbent upon this Court . . .to ascertain for itself . . .whether the asserted non-federal ground independently and adequately supports the judgment." **ABIE STATE BANK v. BRYAN**, 282 U.S. 765, 773 (1931). Although we have announced a number of principles in order to help us determine whether various forms of references to state law constitute adequate and independent state grounds, we openly admit that we have thus far not developed a satisfying and consistent approach for resolving this vexing issue. In some instances, we have taken the strict view that if the ground of decision was at all unclear, we would dismiss the case. See, e.g., **LYNCH v. NEW YORK EX REL. PIERSON**, 293 U.S. 52 (1934). In other instances, we have vacated see. e.g., **MINNESOTA v. NATIONAL TEA CO**, 309 U.S. 51 (1940), or continued a case, see, e.g., **HERB v. PITCAIRN**, 324 U.S.S. 117 (1945), in order to obtain clarification about the nature of a state court decision. See also **CALIFORNIA v. KRIVDA**, 409 U.S. 33 (1972). In more recent cases, we have ourselves examined state law to determine whether state courts have used federal law to guide their application of state law or to provide the actual basis

427

for the decision that was reached. See **TEXAS v. BROWN,** 460 U.S. 730, 732-733, n.1 (1983) (plurality opinion). Cf. **SOUTH DAKOTA v. NEVILLE,** 459 U.S. 553, 569 (1983) (STEVENS, J., dissenting). In **OREGON v. KENNEDY,** 456 U.S. 667, 670-671 (1982), we rejected an invitation to remand to the state court for clarification even when the decision rested in part on a case from the state court, because we determined that the state case itself rested upon federal grounds. We added that "[e]ven if the case admitted of more doubts as to whether federal and state grounds for decision were intermixed, the fact that the state court relied to the extent it did on federal grounds requires us to reach the merits." Id., at 671.

This ad hoc method of dealing with cases that involve possible adequate and independent state grounds is antithetical to the doctrinal consistency that is required when sensitive issues of federal-state relations are involved. Moreover, none of the various methods of disposition that we have employed thus far recommends itself as the preferred method that we should apply to the exclusion of others, and we therefore determine that it is appropriate to reexamine our treatment of this jurisdictional issue in order to achieve the consistency that is necessary.

The process of examining state law is unsatisfactory because it requires us to interpret state laws with which we are generally unfamiliar, and which often, as in this case, have not been discussed at length by the parties. Vacation and continuance for clarification have also been unsatisfactory both because of the delay and decrease in efficiency of judicial administration, see **DIXON v. DUFFY,** 344 U.S. 143 (1952), and, more important, because these methods of disposition place significant burdens on state courts to demonstrate the presence or absence of our jurisdiction. See **PHILADELPHIA NEWSPAPERS, INC. v. JEROME,** 434 U.S. 241, 244 (1978)(REHNQUIST, J., dissenting); **DEPARTMENT OF MOTOR VEHICLES v. RIOS,** 410 U.S. 425, 427 (1973) (Douglas, J., dissenting). Finally, outright dismissal of cases is clearly not a panacea because it cannot be doubted that there is an important need for uniformity in federal law, and that this need goes unsatisfied when we fail to review an opinion that rests primarily upon federal grounds and where the independence of an alleged state ground is not apparent from the four corners of the opinion. We have long recognized that dismissal is inappropriate "where there is strong indication . . .that the federal constitution as judicially construed controlled the decision below." **NATIONAL TEA CO.**, supra, at 556.

Respect for the independence of state courts, as well as avoidance of rendering advisory opinions, have been the cornerstones of this Court's refusal to decide cases where there is an adequate and independent state ground. It is precisely because of this respect for state courts, and this desire to avoid advisory opinions, that we do not wish to continue to decide issues of state law that go beyond the opinion that we review, or to require state courts to reconsider cases to clarify the grounds of their decisions. Accordingly, when, as in this case, a state court decision fairly appears to rest primarily on federal law, or to be interwoven with the federal law, and when the adequacy and independence of any possible state law ground is not clear from the face of the opinion, we will accept as the most reasonable explanation that the state court decided the case the way it did because it believed that federal law required it to do so. If a state court chooses merely to rely on federal precedents as it would on the precedents of all other jurisdictions, then it need only make clear by a plain statement in its judgment or opinion that the federal cases are being used only for the purpose of guidance, and do not themselves compel the result that the court has reached. In this way, both justice and judicial administration will be greatly improved. If the state court decision indicates clearly and expressly that it is alternatively based on bona fide separate, adequate, and independent grounds, we, of course, will not undertake to review the decision.

This approach obviates in most instances the need to examine state law in order to decide the nature of the state court decision, and will at the same time avoid the danger of our rendering advisory opinions. It also avoids the unsatisfactory and intrusive practice of requiring state courts to clarify their decisions to the satisfaction of this Court. We believe that such an approach will provide state judges with a clearer opportunity to develop state jurisprudence unimpeded by federal interference, and yet will preserve the integrity of federal law. "It is fundamental that state courts be

429

left free and unfettered by us in interpreting their state constitutions. But it is equally important that ambiguous or obscure adjudications by state courts do not stand as barriers to a determination by this Court of the validity under the federal constitution of state action." **NATIONAL TEA CO.**, supra, at 557.

The principle that we will not review judgments of state courts that rest on adequate and independent state grounds is based, in part, on "the limitations of our own jurisdiction." **HERB v. PITCAIRAN**, 324 U.S. 117, 125 (1945). The jurisdictional concern is that we not "render an advisory opinion, and if the same judgment would be rendered by the state court after we corrected its views of federal laws, our review could amount to nothing more than an advisory opinion." Id., at 126. Our requirement of a "plain statement" that a decision rests upon adequate and independent state grounds does not in any way authorize the rendering of advisory opinions. Rather, in determining, as we must, whether we have jurisdiction to review a case that is alleged to rest on adequate and independent state grounds, see **ABIE STATE BANK v. BRYAN**, 282 U.S., at 773, we merely assume that there are no such grounds when it is not clear from the opinion itself that the state court relied upon an adequate and independent state ground and when it fairly appears that the state court rested its decision primarily on federal law.

Our review of the decision below under this framework leaves us unconvinced that it rest upon an independent state ground. Apart from its two citations to the State Constitution, the court below relied exclusively on its understanding of TERRY and other federal cases. Not a single state case was cited to support the state court's holding that the search of the passenger compartment was unconstitutional. Indeed, the court declared that the search in this case was unconstitutional because "[t]he Court of Appeals erroneously applied the principles of **TERRY v. OHIO** . . . to the search of the interior of the vehicle in this case. 413 Mich., at 471, 320 N.W. 2d, at 869. The references to the State Constitution in no way indicate that the decision below rested on grounds in any way independent from the state court's interpretation of federal law. Even if we accept that the Michigan Constitution has been interpreted to provide independent protection for certain rights also secured under the Fourth Amendment, it fairly appears in this case that the Michigan Supreme Court rested its decision primarily on federal law.

Rather than dismissing the case, or requiring that the state court reconsider its decision on our behalf solely because of a mere possibility that an adequate and independent ground supports the judgment, we find that we have jurisdiction in the absence of a plain statement that the decision below rested on an adequate and independent state ground. It appears to us that the state court "felt compelled by what it understood to be federal constitutional considerations to construe . . . its own law in the manner it did." **ZACCHINI v. SCRIPPS-HOWARD BROADCASTING CO.,** 433 U.S. 562, 568 (1977).

III

The court below held, and respondent Long contends, that Deputy Howell's entry into the vehicle cannot be justified under the principles set forth in TERRY because "TERRY authorized only a limited pat-down search of a person suspected of criminal activity" rather than a search of an area. 413 Mich., at 472, 320 N.W. 2d, at 869 (footnote omitted). Brief for Respondent 10. Although TERRY did involve the protective frisk of a person, we believe that the police action in this case justified by the principles that we have already established in TERRY and other cases.

In TERRY, the Court examined the validity of a "stop and frisk" in the absence of probable cause and a warrant. The police officer in TERRY detained several suspects to ascertain their identities after the officer had observed the suspects for a brief period of time and formed the conclusion that they were about to engage in criminal activity. Because the officer feared that the suspects were armed he patted down the outside of the suspects' clothing and discovered two revolvers.

Examining the reasonableness of the officer's conduct in TERRY, we held that there is "'no ready test for determining reasonableness other than by balancing the need to search [or seize] against the invasion which the search [or seizure] entails.'" 392 U.S., at 21 (quoting **CAMARA v. MUNICIPAL COURT**, 387 U.S. 523, 536-537

(1967)). Although the conduct of the officer in TERRY involved a "severe, though brief, intrusion upon cherished personal security," 392 U.S., at 24-25, we found that the conduct was reasonable when we weighed the interest of the individual against the legitimate interest in "crime prevention and detention," id., at 22, and the "need for law enforcement officers to protect themselves and other prospective victims of violence in situations where they may lack probable cause for an arrest." Id., at 24. When the officer has a reasonable belief "that the individual whose suspicious behavior he is investigating at close range is armed and presently dangerous to the officer or to others, it would appear to be clearly unreasonable to deny the officer the power to take necessary measure to determine whether the person is in fact carrying a weapon and to neutralize the threat of physical harm." Ibid.

Although TERRY itself involved the stop and subsequent patdown search of a person, we were careful to note that "[w]e need not develop at length in this case, however, the limitations which the Fourth Amendment places upon a protective search and seizure for weapons. These limitations will have to be developed in the concrete factual circumstances of individual cases." Id., at 29. Contrary to Long's view, TERRY need not be read as restricting the preventive search to the person of the detained suspect.

In two cases in which we applied TERRY to specific factual situations, we recognized that investigative detentions involving suspects in vehicles are especially fraught with danger to police officers. In **PENNSYLVANIA v. MIMMS**, 434 U.S. 106 (1977), we held that police may order persons out of an automobile during a stop for a traffic violation, and may frisk those persons for weapons if there is a reasonable belief that they are armed and dangerous. Our decision rested in part on the "inordinate risk confronting an officer as he approaches a person seated in an automobile." Id., at 110. In **ADAMS v. WILLIAMS**, 407 U.S. 143 (172), we held that the police, acting on an informant's tip, may reach into the passenger compartment of an automobile to remove a gun from a driver's waistband even where the gun was not apparent to police from the outside of the car and the police knew of its existence only because of the tip. Again, our decision rested in part on our view of the danger presented to police officers in "traffic stop" and automobile situations.

Finally, we have also expressly recognized that suspects may injure police officers and others by virtue of their access to weapons, even though they may not themselves be armed. In the Term following TERRY, we decided **CHIMEL v. CALIFORNIA**, 395 U.S. 752 (1969), which involved the limitations imposed on police authority to conduct a search incident to a valid arrest. Relying explicitly on TERRY, we held that when an arrest is made, it is reasonable for the arresting officer to search "the arrestee's person and the area 'within his immediate control' - construing that phrase to mean the area from within which he might gain possession of a weapon or destructible evidence." 395 U.S., at 763. We reasoned that "[a] gun on a table or in a drawer in front of one who is arrested can be as dangerous to the arresting officer as one concealed in the clothing of the person arrested." Ibid. In **NEW YORK v. BELTON**, 453 U.S. 454 (1981), we determined that the lower courts "have found no workable definition of 'the area within the immediate control of the arrestee' when that area arguably includes the interior of an automobile and the arrestee is its recent occupant." Id., at 460. In order to provide a "workable rule," ibid., we held that "articles inside the relatively narrow compass of the passenger compartment of an automobile are in fact generally, even if not inevitably, within 'the area into which an arrestee might reach in order to grab a weapon' . . . ." Ibid. (quoting CHIMEL, supra, at 763). We also held that the police may examine the contents of any open or closed container found within the passenger compartment, "for if the passenger compartment is within the reach of the arrestee, so will containers in it be within his reach." 453 U.S., at 460 (footnote omitted). See also **MICHIGAN v. SUMMERS**. 452 U.S. 692, 702 (1981).

Our past cases indicate then that protection of police and others can justify protective searches when police have a reasonable belief that the suspect poses a danger, that roadside encounters between police and suspects are especially hazardous, and that danger may arise from the possible presence of weapons in the area surrounding a suspect. These principles compel our conclusion that the search of the passenger compartment

433

of an automobile, limited to those areas in which a weapon may be placed or hidden, is permissible if the police officer possesses a reasonable belief based on "specific and articulable facts which, taken together with the rational inferences from those facts, reasonably warrant" the officer in believing that the suspect is dangerous and the suspect may gain immediate control of weapons. See TERRY, 392 U.S., at 21. "[T]he issue is whether a reasonably prudent man in the circumstances would be warranted in the belief that his safety or that of others was in danger." Id., at 27. If a suspect is "dangerous," he is no less dangerous simply because he is not arrested. If, while conducting a legitimate TERRY search of the interior of the automobile, the officer should, as here, discover contraband other than weapons, he clearly cannot be required to ignore the contraband, and the Fourth Amendment does not require its suppression in such circumstances. **COOLIDGE v. NEW HAMPSHIRE**, 403 U.S. 443, 465 (1971); **MICHIGAN v. TYLER**, 436 U.S. 499, 509 (1978); **TEXAS v. BROWN**, 460 U.S., at 739 (plurality opinion by REHNQUIST, J.); id., at 746 (POWELL, J., concurring in judgment).

The circumstances of this case clearly justified Deputies Howell and Lewis in their reasonable belief that Long posed a danger if he were permitted to reenter his vehicle. The hour was late and the area rural. Long was driving his automobile at excessive speed, and his car swerved into a ditch. The officers had to repeat their questions to Long, who appeared to be "under the influence" of some intoxicant. Long was not frisked until the officers observed that there was a large knife in the interior of the car into which Long was about to reenter. The subsequent search of the car was restricted to those areas to which Long would generally have immediate control, and that could contain a weapon. The trial court determined that the leather pouch containing marihuana could have contained a weapon. App. 64a. It is clear that the intrusion was "strictly circumscribed by the exigencies which justifi[ed] its initiation." TERRY, supra at 26.

In evaluating the validity of an officers' investigative or protective conduct under TERRY, the "[t]ouchstone of our analysis . . .is always 'the

434

reasonableness in all the circumstances of the particular governmental invasion of a citizen's personal security.'" **PENNSYLVANIA v. MIMMS**, 434 U.S., at 108-109 (quoting TERRY, supra, at 19). In this case, the officers did not act unreasonably in taking preventive measures to ensure that there were no other weapons within Long's immediate grasp before permitting him to enter his automobile. Therefore, the balancing required by TERRY clearly weighs in favor of allowing the police to conduct an area search of the passenger compartment to uncover weapons, as long as they possess an articulable and objectively reasonable belief that the suspect is potentially dangerous.

The Michigan Supreme Court appeared to believe that it was not reasonable for the officers to fear that Long could injure them, because he was effectively under their control during the investigative stop and could not get access to any weapons that might have been located in the automobile. See 413 Mich., at 472, 320 N.W. 2d, at 869. This reasoning is mistaken in several respects. During any investigative detention, the suspect is "in the control" of the officers in the sense that he may be briefly detained against his will . . . ." TERRY, supra, at 34 (WHITE, J., concurring). Just as a TERRY suspect on the street may, despite being under the brief control of a police officer, reach into his clothing and retrieve a weapon, so might a TERRY suspect in Long's position break away from police control and retrieve a weapon from his automobile. See **UNITED STATES v. RAINONE**, 586 F.2D 1132, 1134 (CA7 1978), cert. denied, 440 U.S. 980 (1979). In addition, if the suspect is not placed under arrest, he will be permitted to reenter his automobile, and he will then have access to any weapon inside. **UNITED STATES v. POWLESS**, 546 F.2d 792, 795-796 (CA8), cert. denied, 430 U.S. 910 (1977). Or, as here, the suspect may be permitted to reenter the vehicle before the TERRY investigation is over, and again, may have access to weapons. In any event, we stress that a TERRY investigation, such as the one that occurred here, involves police investigation "at close range," TERRY, 392 U.S., at 24, when the officer remains particularly vulnerable in part because a full custodial arrest has not been effected, and the officer must make a "quick decision as to how to protect himself and others from possible danger . . . ." Id., at 28. In such circumstances, we have not required that officers adopt alternative means to ensure their safety in order to avoid the intrusion involved in a TERRY encounter.

IV

The trial court and the Court of Appeals upheld the search of the trunk as a valid inventory search under this Court's decision in **SOUTH DAKOTA v. OPPERMAN**, 428 U.S. 364 (1976). The Michigan Supreme Court did not address this holding, and instead suppressed the marihuana taken from the trunk as a fruit of the illegal search of the interior of the automobile. Our holding that the initial search was justified under TERRY makes it necessary to determine whether the trunk search was permissible under the Fourth Amendment. However, we decline to address this question because it was not passed upon by the Michigan Supreme Court, whose decision we review in this case. See **CARDINALE v. LOUISIANA**, 394 U.S. 437, 438 (1969). We remand this issue to the court below, to enable it to determine whether the trunk search was permissible under OPPERMAN, supra, or other decisions of this Court. See, e.g., **UNITED STATES v. ROSS**, 456 U.S. 798 (1982).

V

The judgment of the Michigan Supreme court is reversed, and the case is remanded for further proceedings not inconsistent with this opinion.

It is so ordered.

JUSTICE BLACKMUN, concurring in part and concurring in the judgment.
I join Parts I, III, IV, and V of the Court's opinion. While I am satisfied that the Court has jurisdiction in this particular case, I do not join the Court, in Part II of its opinion, in fashioning a new presumption of jurisdiction over cases coming here from state courts. Although I agree with the Court that uniformity -in federal criminal law is desirable, I see little efficiency and an increased danger of advisory opinions in the Court's new approach.

CHIMEL v. CALIFORNIA
395 U.S. 752, 89 S.Ct. 2034, 23 L.Ed.2d 685 (1969)
CERTIORARI TO THE SUPREME COURT OF CALIFORNIA
Argued March 27, 1969.——Decided June 23, 1969.
. . .
MR. Justice Stewart delivered the opinion of the court.

This case raises basic questions concerning the permissible scope under the Fourth Amendment of a search incident to a lawful arrest.

The relevant facts are essentially undisputed. Late in the afternoon of September 13, 1965, three police officers arrived at the Santa Ana, California, home of the petitioner with a warrant authorizing his arrest for the burglary of a coin shop. The officers knocked on the door, identified themselves to the petitioner's wife, and asked if they might come inside. She ushered them into the house, where they waited 10 or 15 minutes until the petitioner returned home from work. When the petitioner entered the house, one of the officers handed him the arrest warrant and asked for permission to "look around." The petitioner objected, but was advised that "on the basis of the lawful arrest," the officers would nonetheless conduct a search. No search warrant had been issued.

Accompanied by the petitioner's wife, the officers then looked through the entire three-bedroom house, including the attic, the garage, and a small workshop. In some rooms the search was relatively cursory. In the master bedroom and sewing room, however, the officers directed the petitioner's wife to open drawers and "to physically move contents of the drawers from side to side so that [they] might view any items that would have come from [the] burglary." After completing the search, they seized numerous items—primarily coins, but also several medals, tokens, and a few other objects. The entire search took between 45 minutes and an hour.

At the petitioner's subsequent state trial on two charges of burglary, the items taken from his house were admitted into evidence against him, over his objection that they had been unconstitutionally seized. He was convicted, and the judgments of conviction were affirmed by both the California Court of Appeal, 61 Cal. Rptr. 714, and the California Supreme Court, 68 Cal.2d 436, 439 P.2d 333. Both courts accepted the petitioner's contention that the arrest warrant was invalid because

437

the supporting affidavit was set out in conclusory terms, but held that since the arresting officers had procured the warrant "in good faith," and since in any event they had had sufficient information to constitute probable cause for the petitioner's arrest, that arrest had been lawful. From this conclusion the appellate courts went on to hold that the search of the petitioner's home had been justified, despite the absence of a search warrant, on the ground that it had been incident to a valid arrest. We granted certiorari in order to consider the petitioner's substantial constitutional claims. 393 U.S. 958.

Without deciding the question, we proceed on the hypothesis that the California courts were correct in holding that the arrest of the petitioner was valid under the Constitution. This brings us directly to the question whether the warrantless search of the petitioner's entire house can be constitutionally justified as incident to that arrest. The decisions of this Court bearing upon that question have been far from consistent, as even the most cursory review makes evident.

Approval of a warrantless search incident to a lawful arrest seems first to have been articulated by the Court in 1914 as dictum in **WEEKS v. UNITED STATES** 232 U.S. 383, in which the Court stated:

> "What then is the present case? Before answering that inquiry specifically, it may be well by a process of exclusion to state what it is not. It is not an assertion of the right on the part of the Government, always recognized under English and American law, to search the person of the accused when legally arrested to discover and seize the fruits or evidences of crime." Id., at 392.

That statement made no reference to any right to search the *place* where an arrest occurs, but was limited to a right to search the "person." Eleven years later the case of **CARROLL v. UNITED STATES**, 267 U.S. 132, brought the following embellishment of the Weeks statement:

> "When a man is legally arrested for an offense, whatever is found upon his person *or in his control*

438

which it is unlawful for him to have and which may
be used to prove the offense may be seized and held
as evidence in the prosecution." Id., at 158.
(Emphasis added.)

Still, that assertion too was far from a claim that
the "place" where one is arrested may be searched so long
as the arrest is valid. Without explanation, however,
the principle emerged in expanded form a few months later
in **AGNELLO v. UNITED STATES**, 269 U.S. 20—although still
by way of dictum:

"The right without a search warrant
contemporaneously to search persons lawfully
arrested while committing crime and to search the
place where the arrest is made in order to find and
seize things connected with the crime as its fruits
or as the means by which it was committed, as well
as weapons and other things to effect an escape
from custody, is not to be doubted. See **CARROLL v.
UNITED STATES**, 267 U.S. 132, 158; **WEEKS v. UNITED
STATES**, 232 U.S. 383, 392." 269 U.S., at 30.

And in **MARRON v. UNITED STATES**, 275 U.S. 192, two
years later, the dictum of Agnello appeared to be the
foundation of the Court's decision. In that case federal
agents had secured a search warrant authorizing the
seizure of liquor and certain articles used in its
manufacture. When they arrived at the premises to be
searched, they saw "that the place was used for retailing
and drinking intoxicating liquors." Id., at 194. They
proceeded to arrest the person in charge and to execute
the warrant. In searching a closet for the items listed
in the warrant they came across an incriminating ledger,
concededly not covered by the warrant, which they also
seized. The Court upheld the seizure of the ledger by
holding that since the agents had made a lawful arrest,
"[t]hey had a right without a warrant contemporaneously
to search the place in order to find and seize the things
used to carry on the criminal enterprise." Id., at 199.
That the Marron opinion did not mean all that it
seemed to say became evident, however, a few years later
in **GO-BART IMPORTING CO. v. UNITED STATES**, 282 U.S. 344,
and **UNITED STATES v. LEFKOWITZ**, 285 U.S. 452. In each of
those cases the opinion of the Court was written by MR.
JUSTICE BUTLER, the author of the opinion in Marron. In

Go-Bart, agents had searched the office of persons whom
they had lawfully arrested, and had taken several papers
from a desk, a safe, and other parts of the office. The
court noted that no crime had been committed in the
agents' presence, and that although the agent in charge
"had an abundance of information and time to swear out a
valid [search] warrant, he failed to do so." 282 U.S., at
358. In holding the search and seizure unlawful, the
Court stated:

> "Plainly the case before us is essentially
> different from **MARRON v. UNITED STATES**, 275 U.S.
> 192. There officers executing a valid search
> warrant for intoxicating liquors found and arrested
> one Birdsall who in pursuance of a conspiracy was
> actually engaged in running a saloon. As an
> incident to the arrest they seized a ledger in a
> closet where the liquor or some of it was kept and
> some bills beside the cash register. These things
> were visible and accessible and in the offender's
> immediate custody. There was no threat of force or
> general search or rummaging of the place." 282
> U.S., at 358.

This limited characterization of Marron was
reiterated in Lefkowitz, a case in which the Court held
unlawful a search of desk drawers and a cabinet despite
the fact that the search had accompanied a lawful arrest.
285 U.S., at 465.

The limiting views expressed in Go-Bart and
Lefkowitz were thrown to the winds, however, in **HARRIS v.
UNITED STATES**, 331 U.S. 145, decided in 1947. In that
case, officers had obtained a warrant for Harris' arrest
on the basis of his alleged involvement with the cashing
and interstate transportation of a forged check. He was
arrested in the living room of his four-room apartment,
and in an attempt to recover two canceled checks thought
to have been used in effecting the forgery, the officers
undertook a thorough search of the entire apartment.
Inside a desk drawer they found a sealed envelope marked
"George Harris, personal papers." The envelope, which
was then torn open, was found to contain altered
Selective Service documents, and those documents were

440

used to secure Harris' conviction for violating the Selective Training and Service Act of 1940. The Court rejected Harris' Fourth Amendment claim, sustaining the search as "incident to arrest." Id., at 151.

Only a year after Harris, however, the pendulum swung again. In **TRUPIANO v. UNITED STATES**, 334 U.S. 699, agents raided the site of an illicit distillery, saw one of several conspirators operating the still, and arrested him, contemporaneously "seiz[ing] the illicit distillery." Id., at 702. The Court held that the arrest and others made subsequently had been valid, but that the unexplained failure of the agents to procure a search warrant—in spite of the fact that they had had more than enough time before the raid to do so—rendered the search unlawful. The opinion stated.

> "It is a cardinal rule that, in seizing goods and articles, law enforcement agents must secure and use search warrants wherever reasonably practicable.... This rule rests upon the desirability of having magistrates rather than police officers determine when searches and seizures are permissible and what limitations should be placed upon such activities.... To provide the necessary security against unreasonable intrusions upon the private lives of individuals, the framers of the Fourth Amendment required adherence to judicial processes wherever possible. And subsequent history has confirmed the wisdom of that requirement.
>
> . . .
>
> "A search or seizure without a warrant as an incident to a lawful arrest has always been considered to be a strictly limited right. It grows out of the inherent necessities of the situation at the time of the arrest. But there must be something more in the way of necessity than merely a lawful arrest." Id., at 705, 708.

In 1950, two years after Trupiano, came **UNITED STATES V. RABINOWITZ**, 339 U.S. 56, the decision upon which California primarily relies in the case now before us. In Rabinowitz, federal authorities had been informed that the defendant was dealing in stamps bearing forged overprints. On the basis of that information they secured a warrant for his arrest, which they executed at his one-room business office. At the time of the arrest, the officers "searched the desk, safe, and file cabinets in the office for about an hour and a half," Id., at 59, and seized 573 stamps with forged overprints. The stamps were admitted into evidence at the defendant's trial, and this Court affirmed his conviction, rejecting the contention that the warrantless search had been unlawful. The Court held that the search in its entirety fell within the principle giving law enforcement authorities "[t]he right 'to search the place where the arrest is made in order to find and seize things connected with the crime....'" Id., at 61. Harris was regarded as "ample authority" for that conclusion. Id., at 63. The opinion rejected the rule of Trupiano that "in seizing goods and articles, law enforcement agents must secure and use search warrants wherever reasonably practicable." The test, said the court, "is not whether it is reasonable to procure a search warrant, but whether the search was reasonable." Id., at 66.

Rabinowitz has come to stand for the proposition, inter alia, that a warrantless search "incident to a lawful arrest" may generally extend to the area that is considered to be in the "possession" or under the "control" of the person arrested. And it was on the basis of that proposition that the California courts upheld the search of the petitioner's entire house in this case. That doctrine, however, at least in the broad sense in which it was applied by the California courts in this case, can withstand neither historical nor rational analysis.

Even limited to its own facts, the Rabinowitz decision was, as we have seen, hardly founded on an unimpeachable line of authority. As MR. Justice Frankfurter commented in dissent in that case, the "hint" contained in Weeks was, without persuasive justification, "loosely turned into dictum and finally elevated to a decision," 339 U.S., at 75. And the approach taken in cases such as Go-Bart, Lefkowitz, and Trupiano was essentially disregarded by the Rabinowitz Court.

Nor is the rationale by which the State seeks here to sustain the search of the petitioner's house supported by a reasoned view of the background and purpose of the

Fourth Amendment. MR. JUSTICE FRANKFURTER wisely pointed out in his Rabinowitz dissent that the Amendment's proscription of "unreasonable searches and seizures" must be read in light of "the history that gave rise to the words"—a history of "abuses so deeply felt by the Colonies as to be one of the potent causes of the Revolution...." 339 U.S., at 69. The Amendment was in large part a reaction to the general warrants and warrantless searches that had so alienated the colonists and had helped speed the movement for independence. In the scheme of the Amendment, therefore, the requirement that "no Warrants shall issue, but upon probable cause," plays a crucial part. As the Court put it in **MCDONALD v. UNITED STATES**, 335 U.S. 451:

> "We are not dealing with formalities. The presence of a search warrant serves a high function. Absent some grave emergency, the Fourth Amendment has interposed a magistrate between the citizen and the police. This was done not to shield criminals nor to make the home a safe haven for illegal activities. It was done so that an objective mind might weigh the need to invade that privacy in order to enforce the law. The right of privacy was deemed too precious to entrust to the discretion of those whose job is the detection of crime and the arrest of criminals.... And so the Constitution requires a magistrate to pass on the desires of the police before they violate the privacy of the home. We cannot be true to that constitutional requirement and excuse the absence of a search warrant without a showing by those who seek exemption from the constitutional mandate that the exigencies of the situation made that course imperative." Id., at 455-456.

Even in the Agnello case the Court relied upon the rule that "[b]elief, however well founded, that an article sought is concealed in a dwelling house furnishes no justification for a search of that place without a warrant. And such searches are held unlawful notwithstanding facts unquestionably showing probable cause." 269 U.S., at 33. Clearly, the general requirement that a search warrant be obtained is not lightly to be dispenses with, and "the burden is on those seeking [an] exemption [from the requirement] to show the

443

need for it...." **UNITED STATES v. JEFFERS**, 342 U.S. 48, 51.

Only last Term in **TERRY v. OHIO**, 392 U.S. 1, we emphasized that "the police must, whenever practicable, obtain advance judicial approval of searches and seizures through the warrant procedure," Id., at 20, and that "[t]he scope of [a] search must be 'strictly tied to and justified by' the circumstances which rendered its imitation permissible." Id., at 19. The search undertaken by the officer in that "stop and frisk" case was sustained under that test, because it was no more than a "protective ....search for weapons." Id., at 29. But in a companion case, **SIBRON v. NEW YORK**, 392 U.S. 40, we applied the same standard to another set of facts and reached a contrary result, holding that a policeman's action in thrusting his hand into a suspect's pocket had been neither motivated by nor limited to the objective of protection. Rather, the search had been made in order to find narcotics, which were in fact found.

A similar analysis underlies the "search incident to arrest" principle, and marks its proper extent. When an arrest is made, it is reasonable for the arresting officer to search the person arrested in order to remove any weapons that the latter might seek to use in order to resist arrest or effect his escape. Otherwise, the officer's safety might well be endangered, and the arrest itself frustrated. In addition, it is entirely reasonable for the arresting officer to search for and seize any evidence on the arrestee's person in order to prevent its concealment or destruction. And the area into which an arrestee might reach in order to grab a weapon or evidentiary items must, of course, be governed by a like rule. A gun on a table or in a drawer in front of one who is arrested can be as dangerous to the arresting officer as one concealed in the clothing of the person arrested. There is ample justification, therefore, for a search of the arrestee's person and the area "within his immediate control"—construing that phrase to mean the area from within which he might gain possession of a weapon or destructible evidence.

There is no comparable justification, however, for routinely searching any room other than that in which an arrest occurs—or, for that matter, for searching through all the desk drawers or other closed or concealed areas in that room itself. Such searches, in the absence of well recognized exceptions, may be made only under the authority of a search warrant. The "adherence to judicial processes" mandated by the Fourth Amendment requires no less.

This is the principle that underlay our decision in **PRESTON v. UNITED STATES**, 376 U.S. 364. In that case three men had been arrested in a parked car, which had later been towed to a garage and searched by police. We held the search to have been unlawful under the Fourth Amendment, despite the contention that it had been incidental to a valid arrest. Our reasoning was straightforward:

> "The rule allowing contemporaneous searches is justified, for example, by the need to seize weapons and other things which might be used to assault an officer or effect an escape, as well as by the need to prevent the destruction of evidence of the crime—things which might easily happen where the weapon or evidence is on the accused's person or under his immediate control. But these justifications are absent where a search is remote in time or place from the arrest." Id., at 367.

The same basic principle was reflected in our opinion last Term in Sibron. That opinion dealt with **PETERS v. NEW YORK**, No. 74, as well as with Sibron's case, and Peters involved a search that we upheld as incident to a proper arrest. We sustained the search, however, only because its scope had been "reasonably limited" by the "need to seize weapons" and "to prevent the destruction of evidence," to which Preston had referred. We emphasized that the arresting officer "did not engage in an unrestrained and thoroughgoing examination of Peters and his personal effects. He seized him to cut short his flight, and he searched him primarily for weapons." 392 U.S., at 67.

It is argued in the present case that it is "reasonable" to search a man's house when he is arrested in it. But that argument is founded on little more than a subjectivē view regarding the acceptability of certain sorts of police conduct, and not on considerations relevant to Fourth Amendment interests. Under such an unconfined analysis, Fourth Amendment protection in this

445

area would approach the evaporation point. It is not easy
to explain why, for instance, it is less subjectively
"reasonable" to search a man's house when he is arrested
on his front lawn—or just down the street—than it is
when he happens to be in the house at the time of arrest.
As MR. Justice Frankfurter put it:

> "To say that the search must be reasonable is to
> require some criterion of reason. It is no guide at
> all either for a jury or for district judges or the
> police to say that an 'unreasonable search' is
> forbidden—that the search must be reasonable.
> What is the test of reason which makes a search
> reasonable? The test is the reason underlying and
> expressed by the Fourth Amendment: the history and
> the experience which it embodies and the safeguards
> afforded by it against the evils to which it was a
> response." **UNITED STATES v. RABINOWITZ,** 339 U.S.,
> at 83 (dissenting opinion).

Thus, although "[t]he recurring questions of the
reasonableness of searches" depend upon "the facts and
circumstances—the total atmosphere of the case," Id., at
63, 66 (opinion of the Court), those facts and
circumstances must be viewed in the light of established
Fourth Amendment principles.

It would be possible, of course, to draw a line
between Rabinowitz and Harris on the one hand, and this
case on the other. For Rabinowitz involved a single room,
and Harris a four-room apartment, while in the case
before us an entire house was searched. But such a
distinction would be highly artificial. The rationale
that allowed the searches and seizures in Rabinowitz and
Harris would allow the searches and seizures in this
case. No consideration relevant to the Fourth Amendment
suggests any point of rational limitation, once the
search is allowed to go beyond the area from which the
person arrested might obtain weapons or evidentiary
items. The only reasoned distinction is one between a
search of the person arrested and the area within his
reach on the one hand, and more extensive searches on the
other.

The petitioner correctly points out that one result

446

of decisions such as Rabinowitz and Harris is to give law
enforcement officials the opportunity to engage in
searches not justified by probable cause, by the simple
expedient of arranging to arrest suspects at home rather
than elsewhere. We do not suggest that the petitioner is
necessarily correct in his assertion that such a strategy
was utilized here, but the fact remains that had he been
arrested earlier in the day, at his place of employment
rather than at home, no search of his house could have
been made without a search warrant. In any event, even
apart from the possibility of such police tactics, the
general point so forcefully made by Judge Learned Hand in
UNITED STATES v. KIRSCHENBLATT, 16 F.2d 202, remains:

> "After arresting a man in his house, to rummage at
> will among his papers in search of whatever will
> convict him, appears to us to be indistinguishable
> from what might be done under a general warrant;
> indeed, the warrant would give more protection, for
> presumably it must be issued by a magistrate.
> True, by hypothesis the power would not exist, if
> the supposed offender were not found on the
> premises; but it is small consolation to know that
> one's papers are safe only so long as one is not at
> home." Id., at 203.

Rabinowitz and Harris have been the subject of
critical commentary for many years, and have been relied
upon less and less in our own decisions. It is time, for
the reasons we have stated, to hold that on their own
facts, and insofar as the principles they stand for are
inconsistent with those that we have endorsed today, they
are no longer to be followed.

Application of sound Fourth Amendment principles to
the facts of this case produces a clear result. The
search here went far beyond the petitioner's person and
the area from within which he might have obtained either
a weapon or something that could have been used as
evidence against him. There was no constitutional
justification, in the absence of a search warrant, for
extending the search beyond that area. The scope of the
search was, therefore, "unreasonable" under the Fourth
and Fourteenth Amendments, and the petitioner's
conviction cannot stand.

Reversed.

MASSACHUSETTS, Petitioner v. OSBORNE SHEPPARD.
468 U.S. 981, 104 S.Ct. 3424, 82 L.Ed.2d 737 (1984)

. . .

Justice WHITE delivered the opinion of the Court.

This case involves the application of the rules articulated today in **UNITED STATES v. LEON,** ante. to a situation in which police officers seize items pursuant to a warrant subsequently invalidated because of a technical error on the part of the issuing judge.

I

The badly burned body of Sandra Boulware was discovered in a vacant lot in the Roxbury section of Boston at approximately 5 a.m., Saturday, May 5, 1979. An autopsy revealed that Boulware had died of multiple compound skull fractures caused by blows to the head. After a brief investigation the police decided to question one of the victim's boyfriends, Osborne Sheppard. Sheppard told the police that he had last seen the victim on Tuesday night and that he had been at a local gaming house (where cards games were played) from 9 p.m. Friday until 5 a.m. Saturday. He identified several people who would be willing to substantiate the latter claim.

By interviewing the people Sheppard had said were at the gaming house on Friday night, the police learned that although Sheppard was at the gaming house that night, he had borrowed an automobile at about 3 a.m. Saturday morning in order to give two men a ride home. Even though the trip normally took only fifteen minutes, Sheppard did not return with the car until nearly 5 a.m.

On Sunday morning, police officers visited the owner of the car Sheppard had borrowed. He consented to an inspection of the vehicle. Bloodstains and pieces of hair were found on the rear bumper and within the trunk compartment. In addition, the officers noticed strands of wire in the trunk similar to wire strands found on and near the body of the victim. The owner of the car told the officers that when he last used the car on Friday night, shortly before Sheppard borrowed it, he placed articles in the trunk and had not noticed any stains on the bumper or in the trunk.

448

On the basis of the evidence gathered thus far in the investigation, Detective Peter O'Malley drafted an affidavit designed to support an application for an arrest warrant and a search warrant authorizing a search of Sheppard's residence. The affidavit set forth the results of the investigation and stated that the police wished to search for

> "[a] fifth bottle of amaretto liquor, 2 nickel bags of marijuana, a woman's jacket that had been described as black-grey (charcoal), any possessions of Sandra D. Boulware, similar type wire and rope that match those on the body of Sandra D. Boulware, or in the above Thunderbird. A blunt instrument that might have been used on the victim, men's or women's clothing that may have blood, gasoline burns on them. Items that may have fingerprints of the victim ."

Detective O'Malley showed the affidavit to the district attorney, the district attorney's first assistant, and a sergeant, who all concluded that it set forth probable cause for the search and the arrest. 387 Mass. 488, 492, 441 N.E.2d 725, 727 (1982).

Because it was Sunday, the local court was closed, and the police had a difficult time finding a warrant application form. Detective O'Malley finally found a warrant form previously in use in the Dorchester District. The form was entitled "Search Warrant-- Controlled Substance G.L. c. 276 §§ 1 through 3A." Realizing that some changes had to be made before the form could be used to authorize the search requested in the affidavit, Detective O'Malley deleted the subtitle "controlled substance" with a typewriter. He also substituted "Roxbury" for the printed "Dorchester" and typed Sheppard's name and address into blank spaces provided for that information. However, the reference to "controlled substance" was not deleted in the portion of the form that constituted the warrant application and that, when signed, would constitute the warrant itself.

Detective O'Malley then took the affidavit and the warrant form to the residence of a judge who had consented to consider the warrant application. The judge examined the affidavit and stated that he would authorize the search as requested. Detective O'Malley offered the warrant form and stated that he knew the form as presented dealt with controlled substances. He showed the judge where he had crossed out the subtitles. After unsuccessfully searching for a more suitable form, the judge informed O'Malley that he would make the necessary changes so as to provide a proper search warrant. The judge then took the form, made some changes on it, and dated and signed the warrant. However, he did not change the substantive portion of the warrant, which continued to authorize a search for controlled substances; nor did he alter the form so as to incorporate the affidavit. The judge returned the affidavit and the warrant to O'Malley, informing him that the warrant was sufficient authority in form and content to carry out the search as requested. O'Malley took the two documents and, accompanied by other officers, proceeded to Sheppard's residence. The scope of the ensuing search was limited to the items listed in the affidavit, and several incriminating pieces of evidence were discovered. Sheppard was then charged with first degree murder.

At a pretrial suppression hearing, the trial judge concluded that the warrant failed to conform to the commands of the Fourth Amendment because it did not particularly describe the items to be seized. The judge ruled, however, that the evidence could be admitted notwithstanding the defect in the warrant because the police had acted in good faith in executing what they reasonably thought was a valid warrant. App. 35a. At the subsequent trial, Sheppard was convicted.

On appeal, Sheppard argued that the evidence obtained pursuant to the defective warrant should have been suppressed. The Supreme Judicial Court of Massachusetts agreed. A plurality of the justices concluded that although "the police conducted the search in a good faith belief, reasonably held, that the search was lawful and authorized by the warrant issued by the judge," 387 Mass., at 503, 441 N.E.2d, at 733, the evidence had to be excluded because this Court had not recognized a good-faith exception to the exclusionary rule. Two justices combined in a separate concurrence to stress their rejection of the good-faith exception, and one justice dissented, contending that since exclusion of the evidence in this case would not serve to deter any police misconduct, the evidence should be admitted. We

450

granted certiorari and set the case for argument in conjunction with **UNITED STATES v. LEON**, ante.

II

[1] Having already decided that the exclusionary rule should not be applied when the officer conducting the search acted in objectively reasonable reliance on a warrant issued by a detached and neutral magistrate that subsequently is determined to be invalid, *id.*, at ——, the sole issue before us in this case is whether the officers reasonably believed that the search they conducted was authorized by a valid warrant. There is no dispute that the officers believed that the warrant authorized the search that they conducted. Thus, the only question is whether there was an objectively reasonable basis for the officers' mistaken belief. Both the trial court, App,. 35a, and a majority of the Supreme Judicial Court, 387 Mass., at 503, 441 N.E.2d, at 733; *id.*, at 524-525, 441 N.E.2d, at 745 (Lynch, J., dissenting), concluded that there was. We agree.

The officers in this case took every step that could reasonably be expected of them. Detective O'Malley prepared an affidavit which was reviewed and approved by the District Attorney. He presented that affidavit to a neutral judge. The judge concluded that the affidavit established probable cause to search Sheppard's residence, App. 26a, and informed O'Malley that he would authorize the search as requested. O'Malley then produced the warrant form and informed the judge that it might need to be changed. He was told by the judge that the necessary changes would be made. He then observed the judge make some changes and received the warrant and the affidavit. At this point, a reasonable police officer would have concluded, as O'Malley did, that the warrant authorized a search for the materials outlined in the affidavit.

[2] Sheppard contends that since O'Malley knew the warrant form was defective, he should have examined it to make sure that the necessary changes had been made. However, that argument is based on the premise that O'Malley had a duty to disregard the judge's assurances that the requested search would be authorized and the necessary changes would be made. Whatever an officer may be required to do when he executes a warrant without knowing beforehand what items are to be seized, we refuse to rule that an officer is required to disbelieve a judge

451

who has just advised him, by word and by action, that the
warrant he possesses authorizes him to conduct the search
he has requested. In Massachusetts, as in most
jurisdictions, the determinations of a judge acting
within his jurisdiction, even if erroneous, are valid and
binding until they are set aside under some recognized
procedure. **STREETER v. CITY OF WORCHESTER**, 336 Mass.
469, 472, 146 N.E.2d 514, 517 (1957); **MOLL v. TOWNSHIP OF
WAKEFIELD**, 274 Mass. 505, 507, 175 N.E. 81, 82 (1931).
If an officer is required to accept at face value the
judge's conclusion that a warrant form is invalid, there
is little reason why he should be expected to disregard
assurances that everything is all right, especially when
he has alerted the judge to the potential problems.

In sum, the police conduct in this case clearly was
objectively reasonable and largely error-free. An error
of constitutional dimensions may have been committed with
respect to the issuance of the warrant, but it was the
judge, not the police officers, who made the critical
mistake. "[T]he exclusionary rule was adopted to deter
unlawful searches by police, not to punish the errors of
magistrates and judges." **ILLINOIS v. GATES**, 462 U.S.——,
103 S.Ct. 2317, 2345, 76 L.Ed.2d 527 (1983) (WHITE, J.,
concurring in the judgment) Suppressing evidence because
the judge failed to make all the necessary clerical
corrections despite his assurances that such changes
would be made will not serve the deterrent function that
the exclusionary rule was designed to achieve.
Accordingly, federal law does not require the exclusion
of the disputed evidence in this case. The judgement of
the Supreme Judicial Court is therefore reversed, and the
case is remanded for further proceedings not inconsistent
with this opinion.

It is so ordered

MARYLAND v. GARRISON
480 U.S. 79, 107 S.Ct. 1013, 94 L.Ed.2d. 72 (1987)
CERTIORARI TO THE COURT OF APPEALS OF MARYLAND

JUSTICE STEVENS delivered the opinion of the Court. Baltimore police officers obtained and executed a warrant to search the person of Lawrence McWebb and "the premises known as 2036 Park Avenue third floor apartment." When the police applied for the warrant and when they conducted the search pursuant to the warrant, they reasonably believed that there was only one apartment on the premises described in the warrant. In fact, the third floor was divided into two apartments, one occupied by McWebb and one by respondent Garrison. Before the officers executing the warrant became aware that they were in a separate apartment occupied by respondent, they had discovered the contraband that provided the basis for respondent's conviction for violating Maryland's Controlled Substances Act. The question presented is whether the seizure of that contraband was prohibited by the Fourth Amendment.

The trial court denied respondent's motion to suppress the evidence seized from his apartment, App. 46, and the Maryland Court of Special Appeals affirmed. 58 Md. App. 417, 473 A.2d 514 (1984). The Court of Appeals of Maryland reversed and remanded with instructions to remand the case for a new trial. 303 Md 385, 494 A.2d 193 (1985).

There is no question that the warrant was valid and was supported by probable cause. Id., at 392, 494 A.2d, at 9. The trial court found, and the two appellate courts did not dispute, that after making a reasonable investigation, including a verification of information obtained from a reliable informant, an exterior examination of the three-story building at 2036 Park Avenue, and an inquiry of the utility company, the officer who obtained the warrant reasonably concluded that there was only one apartment on the third floor and that it was occupied by McWebb. App. 41;58 Md. App., at 433, 473 A.2d, at 522;303 Md., at 387-390, 494 A.2d, at 194-195. When six Baltimore police officers executed the warrant, they fortuitously encountered McWebb in front of the building and used his key to gain admittance to the first-floor hallway and to the locked floor at the top of the stairs to the third floor. As they entered the vestibule on the third floor, they encountered respondent, who was standing in the hallway area. The police could see into the interior of both McWebb's apartment to the left and respondent's to the right, for the doors to both were open. Only after respondent's apartment had been entered and heroin, cash, and drug paraphernalia had been found did any of the officers realize that the third floor contained two apartments. App. 41-46. As soon as they became aware of that fact, the search was discontinued. Id., at 32, 39. All of the officers reasonably believed that they were searching McWebb's apartment. No further search of respondents apartment was made.

The matter on which there is a difference of opinion concerns the proper interpretation of the warrant. A literal reading of its plain language, as well as the language used in the application for the warrant, indicates that it was intended to authorize a search of the entire third floor. This is the construction adopted by the intermediate appellate court, see 58 Md. App., at 419, 473 A.2d, at 515, and it also appears to be the construction adopted by the trial judge. See App. 41. One sentence in the trial judge's oral opinion, however, lends support to the construction adopted by the Court of Appeals, namely, that the warrant authorized a search of McWebb's apartment only. Under that interpretation, the Court of Appeals concluded that the warrant did not authorize the search of respondent's apartment and the police had no justification for making a warrantless entry into his premises.

The opinion of the Maryland Court of Appeals relies on Article 26 of the Maryland Declaration of Rights and Maryland cases as well as the Fourth Amendment to the Federal Constitution and federal cases. Rather than containing any "plain statement" that the decision rests upon adequate and independent state grounds, see **MICHIGAN v. LONG**, 463 U.S. 1032, 1042 (1983), the opinion indicates that the Maryland constitutional provision is construed in pari materia with the Fourth Amendment. We therefore have jurisdiction. Because the result that the Court of Appeals reached did not appear to be required by the Fourth Amendment, we granted certiorari. 475 U.S. 1009 (1986). We reverse.

In our view, the case presents two separate

454

constitutional issues, one concerning the validity of the warrant and the other concerning the reasonableness of the manner in which it was executed. See **DALIA v. UNITED STATES**, 441 U.S. 238, 258 (1979). We shall discuss the questions separately.

I

The Warrant Clause of the Fourth Amendment categorically prohibits the issuance of any warrant except one "particularly describing the place to be searched and the persons or things to be seized." The manifest purpose of this particularity requirement was to prevent general searches. By limiting the authorization to search to the specific areas and things for which there is probable cause to search, the requirement ensures that the search will be carefully tailored to its justifications, and will not take on the character of the wide-ranging exploratory searches the Framers intended to prohibit. Thus, the scope of a lawful search is "defined by the object of the search and the places in which there is probable cause to believe that it may be found. Just as probable cause to believe that a stolen lawnmower may be found in a garage will not support a warrant to search an upstairs bedroom, probable cause to believe that undocumented aliens are being transported in a van will not justify a warrantless search of a suitcase." **UNITED STATES v. ROSS**, 456 U.S. 798, 824 (1982).

In this case there is no claim that the "persons or things to be seized" were inadequately described or that there was no probable cause to believe that those things might be found in "the place to be searched" as it was described in the warrant. With the benefit of hindsight, however, we now know that the description of that place was broader than appropriate because it was based on the mistaken belief that there was only one apartment on the third floor of the building at 2036 Park Avenue. The question is whether that factual mistake invalidated a warrant that undoubtedly would have been valid if it had reflected a completely accurate understanding of the building's floor plan.

Plainly, if the officers had known, or even if they should have known, that there were two separate dwelling units on the third floor of 2036 Park Avenue, they would have been obligated to exclude respondent's apartment from the scope of the requested warrant. But we must judge the constitutionality of their conduct in light of the information available to them at the time they acted. Those items of evidence that emerge after the warrant is issued have no bearing on whether or not a warrant was validly issued. Just as the discovery of contraband cannot validate a warrant invalid when issued, so is it equally clear that the discovery of facts demonstrating that a valid warrant was unnecessarily broad does not retroactively invalidate the warrant. The validity of the warrant must be assessed on the basis of the information that the officers disclosed, or had a duty to discover and to disclose, to the issuing Magistrate. On the basis of that information, we agree with the conclusion of all three Maryland courts that the warrant, insofar as it authorized a search that turned out to be ambiguous in scope, was valid when it issued.

II

The question whether the execution of the warrant violated respondent's constitutional right to be secure in his home is somewhat less clear. We have no difficulty concluding that the officers' entry into the third-floor common area was legal; they carried a warrant for those premises, and they were accompanied by McWebb, who provided the key that they used to open the door giving access to the third-floor common area. If the officers had known, or should have known, that the third floor contained two apartments before they entered the living quarters on the third floor, and thus had been aware of the error in the warrant, they would have been obligated to limit their search to McWebb's apartment. Moreover, as the officers recognized, they were required to discontinue the search of respondent's apartment as soon as they discovered that there were two separate units on the third floor and therefore were put on notice of the risk that they might be in a unit erroneously included within the terms of the warrant. The officers' conduct and the limits of the search were based on the information available as the search proceeded. While the purposes justifying a police search strictly limit the permissible extent of the search, the Court has also recognized the need to allow some latitude for honest

456

mistakes that are made by officers in the dangerous and difficult process of making arrests and executing search warrants.

In **HILL v. CALIFORNIA**, 401 U.S. 797 (1971), we considered the validity of the arrest of a man named Miller based on the mistaken belief that he was Hill. The police had probable cause to arrest Hill and they in good faith believed that Miller was Hill when they found him in Hill's apartment. As we explained:

> "The upshot was that the officers in good faith believed Miller was Hill and arrested him. They were quite wrong as it turned out, and subjective good-faith belief would not in itself justify either the arrest or the subsequent search. But sufficient probability, not certainly, is the touchstone of reasonableness under the Fourth Amendment and on the record before us the officers' mistake was understandable and the arrest a reasonable response to the situation facing them at the time." Id., at 803-804.

While Hill involved an arrest without a warrant, its underlying rationale that an officer's reasonable misidentification of a person does not invalidate a valid arrest is equally applicable to an officer's reasonable failure to appreciate that a valid warrant describes too broadly the premises to be searched. Under the reasoning in Hill, the validity of the search of respondent's apartment pursuant to a warrant authorizing the search of the entire third floor depends on whether the officers' failure to realize the overbreadth of the warrant was objectively understandable and reasonable. Here it unquestionably was. The objective facts available to the officers at the time suggested no distinction between McWebb's apartment and the third-floor premises.

For that reason, the officers properly responded to the command contained in a valid warrant even if the warrant is interpreted as authorizing a search limited to McWebb's apartment rather than the entire third floor. Prior to the officers' discovery of the factual mistake, they perceived McWebb's apartment and the third-floor premises as one and the same; therefore their execution of the warrant reasonably included the entire third floor. Under either interpretation of the warrant, the officers' conduct was consistent with a reasonable effort to ascertain and identify the place intended to be searched within the meaning of the Fourth Amendment. Cf. **STEELE v. UNITED STATES**, 267 U.S. 498, 503 (1925).

The judgment of the Court of Appeals is reversed, and the case is remanded for further proceedings not inconsistent with this opinion.

It is so ordered.

JUSTICE BLACKMUN, with whom JUSTICE BRENNAN and JUSTICE MARSHALL join, dissenting.

Under this Court's precedents, the search of respondent Garrison's apartment violated the Fourth Amendment. While executing a warrant specifically limited to McWebb's residence, the officers expanded their search to include respondent's adjacent apartment, an expansion made without a warrant and in the absence of exigent circumstances. In my view, Maryland's highest court correctly concluded that the trial judge should have granted respondent's motion to suppress the evidence seized as a result of this warrantless search of his apartment. Moreover, even if I were to accept the majority's analysis of this case as one involving a mistake on the part of the police officers, I would find that the officers' error, either in obtaining or in executing the warrant, was not reasonable under the circumstances.

I

The home always has received special protection in analysis under the Fourth Amendment, which protects the "right of the people to be secure in their persons, houses, papers, and effects, against unreasonable searches and seizures"(emphasis added). See **SILVERMAN v. UNITED STATES**, 365 U.S. 505, 511 (1961)("At the very core [of the Fourth Amendment] stands the right of a man to retreat into his own home and there be free from unreasonable governmental intrusion"). The Fourth Amendment, in fact, was a direct response to the colonists' objection to searches of homes under general warrants or without warrants. See **CHIMEL v. CALIFORNIA**,

395 U.S. 752, 761 (1969); **HARRIS v. UNITED STATES**, 331
U.S. 145, 157-163 (1947) (Frankfurter, J., dissenting).
In today's society, the protection of the Amendment of
course is extended to the equivalent of the traditional
single family house, such as an apartment. See, e.g.,
KER v. CALIFORNIA, 374 U.S. 23, 42 (1963).

The Court has observed that, in determining whether
one has an interest protected by the Fourth Amendment, it
is appropriate not to limit the analysis to the place in
question, for "the Fourth Amendment protects people - and
not simply 'areas.'" **KATZ v. UNITED STATES**, 389 U.S.
347, 353 (1967). As articulated by Justice Harlan in his
Katz concurrence, the proper test under the Amendment is
whether "a person [has] exhibited an actual (subjective)
expectation of privacy . . .that society is prepared to
recognize as 'reasonable.'" Id., at 361. Justice Harlan
noted, however, that an answer to the question
concerning what protection the Fourth Amendment gave to
a particular person always "requires reference to a
'place.'" Ibid. In his view, the home would meet this
test in virtually all situations. "[A] man's home," he
stated "is, for most purposes, a place where he expects
privacy." Ibid. The home thus has continued to occupy
its special role in Fourth Amendment analysis in the
post-Katz era. See **PAYTON v. NEW YORK**, 445 U.S. 573, 585
(1980)("[T]he 'physical entry of the home is the chief
evil against which the wording of the Fourth Amendment is
directed,'" quoting **UNITED STATES v. UNITED STATES
DISTRICT COURT**, 407 U.S. 297, 313 (1972)); **UNITED STATES
v. KARO**, 468 u.s. 705, 714-715 (1984)("Searches and
seizures inside a home without a warrant are
presumptively unreasonable absent exigent
circumstances"); **CALIFORNIA v. CARNEY**, 471 U.S. 386, 407-
408 (1985) (STEVENS, J., dissenting)("These places
[mobile homes] may be as spartan as a humble cottage when
compared to the most majestic mansion . . . but the
highest and most legitimate expectations of privacy
associated with these temporary abodes should command the
respect of this Court"); see also **STEAGOLD v. UNTIED
STATES**, 451 U.S. 204, 211 (1981); **COOLIDGE v. NEW
HAMPSHIRE**, 403 U.S. 443, 477-478 (1971).

The Fourth Amendment also states that "no Warrants
shall issue, but upon probable cause, supported by Oath
or affirmation, and *particularly describing* the place to
be searched, and the persons or things to be seized"
(emphasis added). The particularity-of-description

requirement is satisfied where "the description is such that the officer with a search warrant can with reasonable effort ascertain and identify the place intended." **STEELE v. UNITED STATES**, 267 U.S. 498, 503 (1925). In applying this requirement to searches aimed at residences within multi-unit buildings, such as the search in the present case, courts have declared invalid those warrants that fail to describe the targeted unit with enough specificity to prevent a search of all the units. See, e.g., **UNITED STATES v. HIGGINS**, 428 F.2d 232 (CA7 9170); **UNITED STATES v. VOTTELLER**, 544 F.2d 1355, 1362-1363 (CA6 1976). Courts have used different criteria to determine whether a warrant has identified a unit with sufficient particularity. See, e.g., **UNITED STATES v. BEDFORD** 519 F.2d 650, 655 (CA3 1975)(by name of cooccupant of apartment), cert. denied, 424 U.S. 917 (1976); **HAYNES v. STATE**, 475 S.W. 2d 739, 741 (Tex Crim. App. 1971)(by directions on how to reach a particular room); see generally 2 W. LaFave, Search and Seizure § 4.5, p.79 (1978); Crais, Sufficiency of Description of Apartment or Room to be Searched in Multiple-Occupancy Structure, 11 A.L.R. 3d 1330, 1340-1341, § 5 (1967 and Supp. 1986).

Applying the above principles to this case, I conclude that the search of respondent's apartment was improper. The words of the warrant were plain and distinctive: the warrant directed the officers to seize marijuana and drug paraphernalia on the person of McWebb and in McWebb's apartment, i.e., "on the premises known as 2036 Park Avenue third floor apartment." App. 9. As the Court of Appeals observed, this warrant specifically authorized a search only of McWebb's -not respondent's- residence. 303 Md.. 385, 392, 494 A.2d 193, 196 (1985). In its interpretation of the warrant, the majority suggests that the language of this document, as well as that in the supporting affidavit, permitted a search of the entire third floor. Ante, at 82, and n.4. It escapes me why the language in question, "third floor apartment," when used with reference to a single unite in a multiple occupancy building and in the context of a person's residence, plainly has the meaning the majority discerns, rather than its apparent and, indeed, obvious signification - one apartment located on the third floor.

Accordingly, if, as appears to be the case, the warrant was limited in its description to the third-floor apartment of McWebb, then the search of an additional apartment -respondent's- was warrantless and is presumed unreasonable "in the absence of some of a number of well defined 'exigent circumstances.'"**COOLIDGE v. NEW HAMPSHIRE**, 403 U.S., at 478. Because the State has not advanced any such exception to the warrant requirement, the evidence obtained as a result of this search should have been excluded.

II

Because the Court cannot justify the officers' search under the "exceptional circumstances" rubric, it analyzes the police conduct here in terms of "mistake." According to the Court, hindsight makes it clear that the officers were mistaken, first, in not describing McWebb's apartment with greater specificity in the warrant, ante, at 85, and, second, in including respondent's apartment within the scope of the execution of the warrant, ante, at 86-86. The Court's inquiry focuses on what the officers knew or should have known at these particular junctures. The Court reasons that if, in light of the officers' actual or imputed knowledge, their behavior was reasonable, then their mistakes did not constitute an infringement on respondents Fourth Amendment rights. In this case, the Court finds no Fourth Amendment violation because the officers could not reasonably have drawn the warrant with any greater particularity and because, until the moment when the officers realized that they were in fact searching two different apartments, they had no reason to believe that McWebb's residence did not cover the entire third floor.

The majority relies upon **HILL v. CALIFORNIA**, 401 U.S. 797 (1971), for its conclusion that "honest mistakes" in arrests or searches may obviate Fourth Amendment problems. Ante, at 87-88. It is doubtful whether Hill carries the precedential weight that the majority would ascribe to it. Decided after **CHIMEL v. CALIFORNIA**, 395 U.S. 752 (1969), but involving a pre-Chimel incident, Hill presented a situation where officers, who had probable cause but no warrant to arrest Hill went to Hill's apartment and found Miller instead. 401 U.S., at 799. They mistook Miller for Hill, despite the former's protestations to the contrary, and conducted

461

a search of Hill's apartment, which produced the only substantial evidence later used to convict Hill for robbery. Id., at 801. In deciding that neither the arrest nor the ensuing search constituted a Fourth Amendment violation, the Court was entertaining a challenge made by Hill. The Court here, however, is faced with a Fourth Amendment claim brought by respondent, whose position is comparable to that of Miller. It may make some sense to excuse a reasonable mistake by police that produces evidence against the intended target of an investigation or warrant if the officers had probable cause for arresting that individual or searching his residence. Similar reasoning does not apply with respect to one whom probable cause has not singled out and who is the victim of the officers' error. See **BRINEGAR v. UNITED STATES**, 338 U.S. 160, Q76 (1949)("These long-prevailing standards [of probable cause] seek to safeguard citizens from rash and unreasonable interferences with privacy and from unfounded charges of crime"); cf. **YBARRA v. ILLINOIS**, 444 U.S. 85, 91 (1979)("But, a person's mere propinquity to others independently suspected of criminal activity does not, without more, give rise to probable cause to search that person.... This requirement [of probable cause] cannot be undercut or avoided by simply pointing to the fact that coincidentally there exists probable cause to search or seize another or to search the premises where the person may happen to be").

Even if one accepts the majority's view that there is no Fourth Amendment violation where the officers' mistake is reasonable, it is questionable whether that standard was met in this case. To repeat Justice Harlan's observation, although the proper question in Fourth Amendment analysis is "what protection it affords to . . .people requires reference to a place.'" **KATZ v. UNITED STATES**, 389 U.S., at 361 (concurring opinion). The "place" at issue here is a small multiple-occupancy building. Such forms of habitation are now common in this country, particularly in neighborhoods with changing populations and of declining affluence. Accordingly, any analysis of the "reasonableness" of the officers' behavior here must be done with this context in mind.

The efforts of Detective Marcus, the officer who procured the search warrant, do not meet a standard of reasonableness, particularly considering that the detective knew the search concerned a unit in a multiple-occupancy building. See App. 34. Upon learning from his informant that McWebb was selling marijuana in his third-floor apartment, Marcus inspected the outside of the building. Id., at 35. He did not approach it, however, to gather information about the configuration of the apartments. Ibid. Had he done so, he would have discovered, as did another officer on the day of executing the warrant, id., at 13, that there were seven separate mailboxes and bells on the porch outside the main entrance to the house. Although there is some dispute over whether names were affixed near the boxes and bells, id., at 13-14; Suppression Hearing Tr. M2-96 to M2-97, their existence alone puts a reasonable observer on notice that the three-story structure (with, possibly, a basement) had seven individual units. The detective, therefore, should have been aware that further investigation was necessary to eliminate the possibility of more than one unit's being located on the third floor. Moreover, when Detective Marcus' informant told him that he had purchased drugs in McWebb's apartment, App. 6, it appears that the detective never thought to ask the informant whether McWebb's apartment was the only one on the third floor. These efforts, which would have placed a slight burden upon the detective, are necessary in order to render reasonable the officer's behavior in seeking the warrant.

Moreover, even if one believed that Marcus' efforts in providing information for issuance of the warrant were reasonable, I doubt whether the officers' execution of the warrant could meet such a standard. In the Court's view, the "objective facts" did not put the officers on notice that they were dealing with two separate apartments on the third floor until the moment, considerably into the search after they had rummaged though a dresser and a closet in respondent's apartment and had discovered evidence incriminating him, when they realized their "mistake." Ante, at 80, 88-89. The Court appears to base its conclusion that the officers' error here was reasonable on the fact that neither McWebb nor respondent ever told the officers during the search that they lived in separate apartments. See ante, at 88, n. 12.

In my view, however, the "objective facts" should have made the officers aware that there were two

463

different apartments on the third floor well before they discovered the incriminating evidence in respondent;s apartment. Before McWebb happened to drive up while the search party was preparing to execute the warrant, one of the officers, Detective Shea, somewhat disguised as a constriction worker, was already on the porch of the row house and was seeking to gain access to the locked first-floor door that permitted entrance into the building. App. 13. From this vantage point he had time to observe the seven mailboxes and bells; indeed, he rang all seven bells, apparently in an effort to summon some resident to open the front door to the search party. Id., at 13, 15. A reasonable officer in Detective Shea's position, already aware that this was a multiunit building and now armed with further knowledge of the number of units in the structure, would have conducted at that time more investigation to specify the exact location of McWebb's apartment before proceeding further. For example, he might have questioned another resident of the building.

It is surprising, moreover, that the Court places so much emphasis on the failure of McWebb to volunteer information about the exact location of his apartment. When McWebb drove up, one of the police vehicles blocked his car and the officers surrounded him and his passenger as they got out. Suppression Hearing Tr. M2-15, M2-56, M2-130 to M2-131. Although the officers had no arrest warrant for McWebb, but only a search warrant for his person and apartment, and although they testified that they did not arrest him at that time, id., at M2-14, M2-60, it was clear that neither McWebb nor his passenger was free to leave. See App. 42, Suppression Hearing Tr. M2-157 to M2-158. In such circumstances, which strongly suggest that McWebb was already in custody, it was proper for the officers to administer to him warnings pursuant to **MIRANDA v. ARIZONA**, 384 U.S. 436 (1966). It would then have been reasonable for the officers, aware of the problem, from Detective Shea's discovery, in the specificity of their warrant, to ask McWebb whether his apartment was the only one on the third floor. As it is, the officers made several requests of and questioned McWebb, without giving him Miranda warnings, and yet failed to ask him the question, obvious in the circumstances, concerning the exact location of his apartment. Suppression Hearing Tr. M2-60, M2-131, M2-157.

Moreover, a reasonable officer would have realized the mistake in the warrant during the moments following the officers'entrance to the third floor. The officers gained access to the vestibule separating McWebb's and respondent's apartment through a locked door for which McWebb supplied the key. App. 17. There, in the open doorway to his apartment, they encountered respondent, clad in pajamas and wearing a half-body cast as a result of a recent spinal operation. Id.,m at 16; Suppression Hearing Tr. M2-104 to M2-105. Although the facts concerning what next occurred are somewhat in dispute, see id., at M2-108, M2-167, it appears that respondent, together with McWebb and the passenger from McWebb's car, were shepherded into McWebb's apartment across the vestibule form his own. Once again, the officers were curiously silent. The informant had not led the officers to believe that anyone other than McWebb, the person targeted by the search warrant, in custody when it gained access to the vestibule; yet when they met respondent on the third floor, they simply asked him who he was but never where he lived. Id., at M2-165. Had they done so, it is likely that they would have discovered the mistake in the warrant before they began their search.

Finally and most importantly, even if the officers had learned nothing form respondent, they should have realized the error in the warrant from their initial security sweep. Once on the third floor, the officers first fanned out throughout the rooms to conduct a preliminary check for other occupants who might pose a danger to them. Id., at M2-63. M2-74, M2-87, M2-167. As the map of the third floor demonstrates, see 303 Md., at 396, 494 A.2d, at 199, the two apartments were almost a mirror image of each other - each had a bathroom, a kitchen, a living room, and a bedroom. Given the somewhat symmetrical layout of the apartment, it is difficult to imagine that, in the initial security sweep, a reasonable officer would not have discerned that two apartments were on the third floor, realized his mistake, and then confined the ensuing search to McWebb's residence.

Accordingly, even if a reasonable error on the part of the police officers prevents a Fourth Amendment violation, the mistakes here, both with respect to obtaining and executing the warrant, are not reasonable and could easily have been avoided.

I respectfully dissent.

ANDERSON v. CREIGHTON, ET AL.
483 U.S. 635, 17 S.Ct. 3034, 97 L.Ed.2d 523 (1987)
CERTIORARI TO THE UNITED STATES COURT OF APPEALS
FOR THE EIGHTH CIRCUIT

JUSTICE SCALIA delivered the opinion of the Court. The question presented is whether a federal law enforcement officer who participates in a search that violates the Fourth Amendment may be held personally liable for money damages if a reasonable officer could have believed that the search comported with the Fourth Amendment.

I

Petitioner Russell Anderson is an agent of the Federal Bureau of Investigation. On November 11, 1983, Anderson and other state and federal law enforcement officers conducted a warrantless search of the home of respondents, the Creighton family. The search was conducted because Anderson believed that Vadaain Dixon, a man suspected of a bank robbery committed earlier that day, might be found there. He was not.

The Creightons later filed suit against Anderson in a Minnesota state court, asserting among other things a claim for money damages under the Fourth Amendment, see **BIVENS v. SIX UNKNOWN FED. NARCOTICS AGENTS**, 403 U.S. 388 (1971). After removing the suit to Federal District Court, Anderson filed a motion to dismiss or for summary judgment, arguing that the Bivens claim was barred by Anderson's qualified immunity from civil damages liability. See **HARLOW v. FITZGERALD**, 457 U.S. 800 (1982). Before any discovery took place, the District Court granted summary judgment on the ground that the search was lawful, holding that the undisputed facts revealed that Anderson had had probable cause to search the Creighton's home and that his failure to obtain a warrant was justified by the presence of exigent circumstances. App. to Pet. for Cert. 23a-25a.

The Creightons appealed to the Court of Appeals for the Eight Circuit, which reversed. **CREIGHTON v. ST.PAUL**, 766 F.2d 1269 (1985). The Court of Appeals held that the issue of the lawfulness of the search could not properly

466

be decided on summary judgment, because unresolved factual disputes made it impossible to determine as a matter of law that the warrantless search had been supported by probable cause and exigent circumstances. Id., at 1272-1276. The Court of Appeals also held that Anderson was not entitled to summary judgment on qualified immunity grounds, since the right of Anderson was alleged to have violated - the right of person to be protected from warrantless searches of their home unless the searching officers have probable cause and there are exigent circumstances - was clearly established. Ibid

Anderson filed a petition for certiorari, arguing that the Court of Appeals erred by refusing to consider his argument that he was entitled to summary judgment on qualified immunity grounds if he could establish as a matter of law that a reasonable officer could have believed the search to be lawful. We granted the petition, 478 U.S. 1003 (1986), to consider that important question.

II

When government officials abuse their offices, "action[s] for damages may offer the only realistic avenue for vindication of constitutional guarantees." **HARLOW v. FITZGERALD**, 457 U.S., at 814. On the other hand, permitting damages suits against government officials can entail substantial social costs, including the risk that fear of personal monetary liability and harassing litigation will unduly inhibit officials in the discharge of their duties. Ibid. Our cases have accommodated these conflicting concerns by generally providing government officials performing discretionary functions with a qualified immunity, shielding them from civil damages liability as long as their actions could reasonably have been thought consistent with the rights they are alleged to have violated. See, e.g., **MALLEY v. BRIGGS**, 475 U.S. 335, 341 (1986) (qualified immunity protects "all but the plainly incompetent or those who knowingly violate the law"); id., at 344-345 (police officers applying for warrants are immune if a reasonable officer could have believed that there was probable cause to support the application); **MITCHELL v. FORSYTH**, 472 U.S. 511, 528 (1985) (officials are immune unless "the law clearly proscribed the actions" they took); **DAVIS v. SHERER**, 486 U.S. 183, 191 (1984); id., at 198 (BRENNAN,

467

J., concurring in part and dissenting in part); **HARLOW v. FITZGERALD**, supra, at 819. Cf., e.g., **PROCUNIER v. NAVARETTE**, 434 U.S. 555, 562 (1978). Somewhat more concretely, whether an official protected by qualified immunity may be held personally liable for an allegedly unlawful official action generally turns on the "objective legal reasonableness" of the action, HARLOW, 457 U.S., at 819, assessed in light of the legal rules that were "clearly established" at the time it was taken, id., at 818.

The operation of this standard, however, depends substantially upon the level of generality at which the relevant "legal rule" is to be identified. For example, the right to due process of law is quite clearly established by the Due Process Clause, and thus there is a sense in which any action that violates that Clause (no matter how unclear it may be that the particular action is a violation) violates a clearly established right. Much the same could be said of any other constitutional or statutory violation. But if the test of "clearly established law" were to be applied at this level of generality, it would bear no relationship to the "objective legal reasonableness" that is the touchstone of HARLOW. Plaintiffs would be able to convert the rule of qualified immunity that our cases plainly establish into a rule of virtually unqualified liability simply by alleging violation of extremely abstract rights. HARLOW would be transformed from a guarantee of immunity into a rule of pleading. Such an approach, in sum, would bestow "the balance that our cases strike between the interests in vindication of citizens' constitutional rights and in public officials' effective performance of their duties," by making it impossible for officials "reasonably [to] anticipate when their conduct may give rise to liability for damages." DAVIS, supra at 195. It should not be surprising, therefore, that our cases establish that the right the official is alleged to have violated must have been "clearly established" in a more particularized, and hence more relevant, sense: The contours of the right must be sufficiently clear that a reasonable official would understand that what he is doing violates that right. This is not to say that an official action is protected by qualified immunity unless the very action in question has previously been held unlawful, see MITCHELL, supra, at 535, n. 12; but it is to say that in the light of pre-existing law the unlawfulness must be apparent. See, e.g., MALLEY, supra, at 344-345; MITCHELL, supra, at 528; DAVIS, supra, at 195.

Anderson contends that the Court of Appeals misapplied these principles. We agree. The Court of Appeals' brief discussion of qualified immunity consisted of little more than an assertion that a general right Anderson was alleged to have violated - the right to be free from warrantless searches of one's home unless the searching officers have probable cause and there are exigent circumstances - was clearly established. The Court of Appeals specifically refused to consider the argument that it was not clearly established that the circumstances with which Anderson was confronted did not constitute probable cause and exigent circumstances. The previous discussion should make clear that this refusal was erroneous. It simply does not follow immediately from the conclusion that it was firmly established that warrantless searches not supported by probable cause and exigent circumstances violate the Fourth Amendment that Anderson's search was objectively legally unreasonable. We have recognized that it is inevitable that law enforcement officials will in some cases reasonably but mistakenly conclude that probable cause is present, and we have indicated that in such cases those officials - like other officials who act in ways they reasonably believe to be lawful - should not be held personally liable. See MALLEY, supra, at 344-345. The same is true of their conclusions regarding exigent circumstances.

It follows from what we have said that the determination whether it was objectively legally reasonable to conclude that a given search was supported by probable cause or exigent circumstances will often require examination of the information possessed by the searching officials. But contrary to the Creightons' assertion, this does not reintroduce into qualified immunity analysis the inquiry into officials' subjective intent that HARLOW sought to minimize. See HARLOW, 457 U.S., at 815-82. The relevant question in this case, for example, is the objective (albeit fact-specific) question whether a - reasonable officer could have believed Anderson's warrantless search to be lawful, in light of clearly established law and the information the searching officers possessed. Anderson's subjective beliefs about the search are irrelevant.

The principles of qualified immunity that we reaffirm today require that Anderson be permitted to argue that he is entitled to summary judgment on the ground that, in light of the clearly established principles governing warrantless searches, he could, as a matter of law, reasonably have believed that the search of the Creightons' home was lawful.

III

In addition to relying on the reasoning of the Court of Appeals, the Creightons advance three alternative grounds for affirmance. All of these take the same form, i.e., that even if Anderson is entitled to qualified immunity under the usual principles of qualified immunity law we have just described, an exception should be made to those principles in the circumstances of this case. We note at the outset the heavy burden this argument must sustain to be successful. We have emphasized that the doctrine of qualified immunity reflects a balance that has been struck "across the board," HARLOW, supra, at 821 (BRENNAN, J., concurring). See also MALLEY, 475 U.S., at 340 ("'For executive officers in general, . . . qualified immunity represents the norm'" (quoting HARLOW, supra, at 807)). Although we have in narrow circumstances provided officials with an absolute immunity, see, e.g., NIXON v. FITZGERALD, 457 U.S. 731 (1982), we have been unwilling to complicate qualified immunity analysis by making the scope or extent of immunity turn on the precise nature of various officials' duties or the precise character of the particular rights alleged to have been violated. An immunity that has as many variants as there are modes of official action and types of rights would not give conscientious officials that assurance of protection that it is the object of the doctrine to provide. With that observation in mind, we turn to the particular arguments advanced by the Creightons.

First, and most broadly, the Creightons argue that it is inappropriate to give officials alleged to have violated the Fourth Amendment - and thus necessarily to have *unreasonably* searched or seized - the protection of a qualified immunity intended only to protect reasonable official action. It is not possible, that is, to say that one "reasonably" acted unreasonably. The short answer to this argument is that it is foreclosed by the fact that we have previously extended qualified immunity to officials who were alleged to have violated the Fourth Amendment. See MALLEY, supra (police officers alleged to have caused an unconstitutional arrest); **MITCHELL v. FORSYTH**, 472 U.S. 511 (1985) (officials alleged to have conducted warrantless wiretaps). Even if that were not so, however, we would still find the argument unpersuasive. Its surface appeal is attributable to the circumstance that the Fourth Amendment's guarantees have been expressed in terms of "unreasonable" searches and seizures. Had an equally serviceable term, such as "undue" searches and seizures been employed, what might be termed the "reasonably unreasonable" argument against application of HARLOW to the Fourth Amendment would not be available - just as it would be available against application of HARLOW to the Fifth Amendment if the term "reasonable process of law" had been employed there. The fact is that, regardless of the terminology used, the precise content of most of the Constitution's civil liberties guarantees rests upon an assessment of what accommodation between governmental need and individual freedom is reasonable, so that the Creighton's objection, if it has any substance, applies to the application of HARLOW generally. We have frequently observed, and our many cases on the point amply demonstrate, the difficulty of determining whether particular searches or seizures comport with the Fourth Amendment. See, e.g., MALLEY, supra, at 341. Law enforcement officers whose judgments in making these difficult determinations are objectively legally reasonable should no more be held personally liable in damages than should officials making analogous determinations in other areas of law.

For the same reasons, we also reject the Creightons' narrower suggestion that we overrule MITCHELL, supra (extending qualified immunity to officials who conducted warrantless wiretaps), by holding that qualified immunity may never be extended to officials who conduct unlawful warrantless searches.

Finally, we reject the Creightons' narrowest and most procrustean proposal: that no immunity should be provided to police officers who conduct unlawful warrantless searches of innocent third parties' homes in search of fugitives. They rest this proposal on the assertion that officers conducting such searches were strictly liable at English common law if the fugitive was not present. See, e.g., **ENTICK v. CARRINGTON**, 19 How. St.Tr. 1029, 95 Eng.Rep. 807 (K.B. 1765). Although it is true we have observed that our determinations as to the scope of official immunity are made in the light of the "common-law tradition," MALLEY, supra, at 342, we have never suggested that the precise contours of official immunity can and should be slavishly derived from the often arcane rules of the common law. That notion is plainly contradicted by HARLOW, where the Court completely reformulated qualified immunity along principles not at all embodied in the common law, replacing the inquiry into subjective malice so frequently required at common law with an objective inquiry into the legal reasonableness of the official action. See HARLOW, 457 U.S., at 815-820. As we noted before, HARLOW clearly expressed the understanding that the general principle of qualified immunity it established would be applied "across the board."

The approach suggested by the Creightons would introduce into qualified immunity analysis a complexity rivaling that which we found sufficiently daunting to deter us from tailoring the doctrine to the nature of officials' duties or of the rights allegedly violated. See supra, at 642-643. Just in the field of unlawful arrests, for example, a cursory examination of the Restatement (Second) of Torts (1965) suggests that special exceptions from the general rule of qualified immunity would have to be made for arrests pursuant to a warrant but outside the jurisdiction of the issuing authority, §§ 122, 129(a), arrests after the warrant had lapsed, §§ 122, 130(a), and arrests without a warrant, § 121. Both the complexity and the unsuitability of this approach are betrayed by the fact that the Creightons' proposal itself does not actually apply the musty rule that is purportedly its justification but instead suggests an exception to qualified immunity for all fugitive searches of third parties' dwellings, and not merely (as the English rule appears to have provided) for all unsuccessful fugitive searches of third parties' dwellings. Moreover, from the sources cited by the Creightons it appears to have been a corollary of the

English rule that where the search was successful, no civil action would lie, whether or not probable cause for the search existed. That also is (quite prudently but quite illogically) not urged upon us in the Creightons' selective use of the common law.

The general rule of qualified immunity is intended to provide government officials with the ability "reasonably [to] anticipate when their conduct may give rise to liability for damages." DAVIS, 468 U.S., at 195. Where that rule is applicable, officials can know that they will not be held personally liable as long as their actions are reasonable in light of current American law. That security would be utterly defeated if officials were unable to determine whether they were protected by the rule without entangling themselves in the vagaries of the English and American common law. We are unwilling to Balkanize the rule of qualified immunity by carving exceptions at the level of detail the Creightons propose. We therefore decline to make an exception to the general rule of qualified immunity for cases involving allegedly unlawful warrantless searches of innocent third parties' homes in search of fugitives.

For the reasons stated, we vacate the judgment of the Court of Appeals and remand the case for further proceedings consistent with this opinion.

It is so ordered.

JUSTICE STEVENS, with whom JUSTICE BRENNAN and JUSTICE MARSHALL join, dissenting.

This case is beguiling in its apparent simplicity. The Court accordingly represents its task as the clarification of the settled principles of qualified immunity that apply in damages suits brought against federal officials. Its opinion, however, announces a new rule of law that protects federal agents who make forcible nighttime entries into the homes of innocent citizens without probable cause, without a warrant, and without any valid emergency justification for their warrantless search. The Court stunningly restricts the constitutional accountability of the police by creating a false dichotomy between police entitlement to summary judgment on immunity grounds and damages liability for every police misstep, by responding to this dichotomy with an uncritical application of the precedents of qualified immunity that we have developed for a quite different group of high public office holders, and by displaying remarkably little fidelity to the countervailing principles of individual liberty and privacy that infuse the Fourth Amendment. Before I turn to the Court's opinion, it is appropriate to identify the issue confronted by the Court of Appeals. It is now apparent that it was correct in vacating the District Court's award of summary judgment to petitioner in advance of discovery.

I

The Court of Appeals understood the principle of qualified immunity as implemented in **HARLOW v. FITZGERALD**, 457 U.S. 800 (1982), to shield government officials performing discretionary functions from exposure to damages liability unless their conduct violated clearly established statutory or constitutional rights of which a reasonable person would have known. Applying this principle, the Court of Appeals held that respondents' Fourth Amendment rights and the "exigent circumstances" doctrine were "clearly established" at the time of the search. **CREIGHTON v. ST. PAUL**, 766 F.2d 1269, 1277 (CA 1985). Moreover, apparently referring to the "extraordinary circumstances" defense left open in HARLOW for a defendant who "can prove that he neither knew nor should have known of the relevant legal standard,: 457 U.S., at 819, the Court determined that petitioner could not reasonably have been unaware of these clearly established principles of law. Thus, in reviewing the Court of Appeals' judgment rejecting petitioner Anderson's claim to immunity, the first question to be decided is whether **HARLOW v. FITZGERALD** requires immunity for a federal law enforcement agent who advances the fact-specific claim that a reasonable person in his position could have believed that his particular conduct would not violate rights that he concedes are clearly established. A negative answer to that question is required, both because HARLOW provided an inappropriate measure of immunity when police acts that violate the Fourth Amendment are challenged, and also because petitioner cannot make the showing required for HARLOW immunity. Second, apart from the particular

474

requirements of the HARLOW doctrine, a full review of the Court of Appeals' judgment raises the question whether this Court should approve a double standard for reasonableness - the constitutional standard already embodied in the Fourth Amendment and an even more generous standard that protects any officer who reasonably could have believed that his conduct was constitutionally reasonable. Because a careful analysis of the HARLOW-related set of questions will be helpful in assessing the Court's continuing embrace of a double standard of reasonableness, I begin with a discussion of petitioner's claim of entitlement to HARLOW immunity.

II

Accepting for the moment the Court's double standard of reasonableness, I would affirm the judgment of the Court of Appeals because it correctly concluded that petitioner has not satisfied the HARLOW standard for immunity. The inquiry upon which the immunity determination hinges in this case illustrates an important limitation on the reach of the Court's opinion in HARLOW. The defendant's claims to immunity at the summary judgment stage in HARLOW and in **MITCHELL v. FORSYTH**, 472 U.S. 511 (1985), were bolstered by two policy concerns that are attenuated in suits against law enforcement agents in the field based on the Fourth Amendment. One was the substantial public interest in allowing government officials to devote their time and energy to the press of public business without the burden and distractions that invariably accompany the defense of a lawsuit. HARLOW, 457 U.S., at 816-817; MITCHELL, 472 U.S., at 524. The second underpinning of HARLOW was the special unfairness associated with charging government officials with knowledge of a rule of law that had not yet been clearly recognized. HARLOW, 457 U.S., at 818; MITCHELL, 472 U.S., at 535. Thus, if the plaintiff's claim was predicated on a principle of law that was not clearly established at the time of the alleged wrong, both of those concerns would favor a determination of immunity not only in advance of trial, but of equal importance, before the time-consuming pretrial discovery process commenced. Concern for the depletion and diversion of public officials' energies led the Court in HARLOW to abolish the doctrine that an official would be deprived of immunity on summary judgment if the plaintiff

475

alleged that the official had acted with malicious intent to deprive his constitutional rights. See, e.g., **WOOD v. STRICKLAND**, 420 U.S. 308, 322 (1975).

The Court's decision today, however, fails to recognize that HARLOW'S removal of one arrow from the plaintiff's arsenal at the summary judgment stage did not also preclude the official from advancing a good-faith reasonableness claim at trial if the character of his conduct as established by the evidence warranted this strategy. The rule of the HARLOW case, in contrast, focuses on the character of the plaintiff's legal claim and, when properly invoked, protects the government executive from spending his time in depositions, document review, and conferences about litigation strategy. Consistently with this overriding concern to avoid "the litigation of the subjective good faith of government officials," 457 U.S., at 816, HARLOW does not allow discovery until the issue whether the official's alleged conduct violated a clearly established constitutional right has been determined on a motion for summary judgment. Id., at 818. HARLOW implicitly assumed that many immunity issues could be determined as a matter of law before the parties had exchanged depositions, answers to interrogatories, and admissions.

The considerations underlying the formulation of the immunity rule in HARLOW for Executive Branch officials, however, are quite distinct from those that led the Court to its prior recognition of immunity for federal law enforcement officials in suits against them founded on the Constitution. This observation is hardly surprising, for the question of immunity only acquires importance once a cause of action is created; the "practical consequences of a holding that no remedy has been authorized against a public official are essentially the same as those flowing from a conclusion that the official has absolute immunity." **MITCHELL v. FORSYTH**, 472 U.S., at 538 (STEVENS, J., concurring in judgment). Probing the question of immunity raised in this case therefore must begin, not with a rote recitation of the HARLOW standard, but with an examination of the cause of action that brought the immunity question now before us into play in the first instance.

As every student of federal jurisdiction quickly

learns, the Court in **BIVENS v. SIX UNKNOWN FED. NARCOTICS AGENTS**, 403 U.S. 388, 397 (1971), held that BIVENS had a cause of action against federal agents "to recover money damages for any injuries he has suffered as a result of the agents' violation of the [Fourth] Amendment." In addition to finding that no cause of action was available, the District Court in that case had relied on the alternative holding that respondents were immune from liability because of their position. Because the Court of Appeals for the Second Circuit had not passed on this immunity ruling, we did not consider it. Id., at 397-398. On remand, in **BIVENS v. SIX UNKNOWN NAMED AGENTS OF FEDERAL BUREAU OF NARCOTICS**, 456 F.2d 1339, 1348 (1972), the Court of Appeals articulated a dual standard of reasonableness. As an initial matter, the Court rejected the agents' claim under **BARR v. MATTEO**, 360 U.S. 564 (1959), which had recognized immunity for an official who performs "discretionary acts at those levels of government where the concept of duty encompasses the sound exercise of discretionary authority." Id., at 575. The Second Circuit wisely noted that it "would be a sorry state of affairs if an officer had the 'discretion' to enter a dwelling at 6:30 A.M, without a warrant or probable cause . . . ." 456 F.2d, at 1346. That court nevertheless recognized the need to balance protection of the police from "the demands of every person who manages to escape from the toils of the criminal law" against the "right of citizens to be free from unlawful arrests and searches." Id., at 1347. According to this Second Circuit, the officer "must not be held to act at his peril": to obtain immunity, he need not allege and prove probable cause in the constitutional sense." Id., at 1848. Instead, an agent should prevail if he could prove "not only that he believed in good faith, that his conduct was lawful, but also that his belief was reasonable." Ibid. Thus, an affirmative defense of reasonable good faith was available at trial. In contrast, an immunity claim of the HARLOW type that would foreclose any trial at all was not available and, in my view, was not appropriate. The strength of the reasonable good-faith defense in any specific case would, of course, vary with the trial evidence about the facts upon which the officer had relied when he made the challenged search or arrest.

As the Court of Appeals recognized, assuring police officers the discretion to act in illegal ways would not be advantageous to society. While executives such as the Attorney General of the United States or a senior assistant to the President of the United States must have the latitude to take action in legally uncharted areas without constant exposure to damages suits, and are therefore entitled to a rule of qualified immunity from many pretrial and trial proceedings, quire different considerations led the Second Circuit to recognize the affirmative defense of reasonable good faith in the BIVENS case. Today this Court nevertheless makes the fundamental error of simply assuming that HARLOW immunity is just as appropriate for federal law enforcement officers such as petitioner as it is for high government officials. The doctrinal reach and precedential sweep of this moment of forgetfulness are multiplied because of the interchangeability of immunity precedents between § 1983 suits against state officials and BIVENS action against federal officials. Moreover, for the moment restricting my criticism of the Court's analysis to the four corners of the HARLOW framework, the Court errs by treating a denial of immunity for failure to satisfy the HARLOW standard as necessarily tantamount to a ruling that the defendants are exposed to damages liability for their every violation of the Fourth Amendment. Such a denial would not necessarily foreclose an affirmative defense based on the Second Circuit's thesis in BIVENS that an officer may not be liable if his conduct complied whit a lesser standard of reasonableness than the constitutional standard which it violated. The Court's failure to recognize that federal agents may retain a partial shield from damages liability, although not necessarily from pretrial and trail proceedings, leads it to the erroneous conclusion that petitioner must have HARLOW immunity or else none at all save the Fourth Amendment itself.

In Part III, I explain why the latter alternative is appropriate. For now, I assert the more limited proposition that the Court of Appeals quite correctly rejected Anderson's claim that he entitled to immunity under HARLQW. HARLOW does not speak to the extent, if any, of an official's insulation from monetary liability when the official concedes that the constitutional right he is charged with violating was deeply etched in our jurisprudence, but argues that he reasonably believed that his particular actions comported with the constitutional command. In this case the District Judge granted Anderson's motion for summary judgment because she was convinced that the agent had probable cause to enter the Creightons' home and that the absence of a search warrant was justified by exigent circumstances. In other words, the District Judge concluded as a matter of law that there was no substantive constitutional violation. When respondent appealed, petitioner argued that even if the Constitution was violated, he was entitled to immunity because the law defining exigent circumstances was not clearly established when he searched the Creightons' home. In setting aside the order granting summary judgment, the Court of Appeals concluded that many essential factual matters were sharply disputed and that if the Creightons' version of the incident were accepted, there was neither probable cause nor an exigent circumstances justification for the search. It was therefore necessary to try the case to find out whether the Fourth Amendment had been violated. CREIGHTON v. ST. PAUL, 766 F.2d, at 1277. The Court of Appeals' conclusion that summary judgment on the probable-cause and exigent-circumstances issues was not appropriate in advance of discovery was unquestionably correct.

The Court of Appeals also was correct in rejecting petitioner's argument based on the holding in HARLOW that the qualified-immunity issue ought to be resolved on a motion for summary judgment before any discovery has taken place. 457 U.S., at 818-819. The Court of Appeals rejected this argument because it was convinced that the rule of law was clear. It also could have rejected the argument on an equally persuasive ground - namely, that the HARLOW requirement concerning clearly established law applied to the rule on which the plaintiff relies, and that there was no doubt about the proposition that a warrantless entry into a home without probable cause is always unlawful. The court does not even reach the exigent-circumstances inquiry unless and until the defendant has shown probable cause and is trying to establish that the search was legal notwithstanding the failure of the police to obtain a warrant. Thus, if we assume that the Court of Appeals was correct in its conclusion that probable cause had not been established it was also correct in rejecting petitioner's claim to

HARLOW immunity, either because the exigent-circumstances exception to the warrant requirement was clearly established, or because a warrantless entry into a home without probable cause is always unlawful whether or not exigent circumstances are present.

In this Court, Anderson has not argued that any relevant rule of law - whether the probable-cause requirement or the exigent-circumstances exception to the warrant requirement- was not "clearly established" in November 1983. Rather, he argues that a competent officer might have concluded that the particular set of facts he faced did constitute "probable cause' and "exigent circumstances," and that his own reasonable belief that the conduct engaged in was within the law suffices to establish immunity. But the factual predicate for Anderson's argument is not found in the Creightons' complaint, but rather in the affidavits that he has filed in support of his motion for summary judgment. Obviously, the respondents must be given an opportunity to have discovery to test the accuracy and completeness of the factual basis for the immunity claim. Neither this Court, nor petitioner, disagrees with this proposition. It is therefore pellucidly clear that the Court of Appeals was correct in its conclusion that the record before it did not support the summary judgment.

The Court's decision today represents a departure from the view we expressed two years ago in **MITCHELL v. FORSYTH**, 472 U.S. 511 (1985). We held that petitioner was entitled to qualified immunity for authorizing an unconstitutional wiretap because it was clearly established that warrantless domestic security wiretapping violated the Fourth Amendment. We added in a footnote:

> "We do not intend to suggest that an official is always immune from liability or suit for a warrantless search merely because the warrant requirement has never explicitly been held to apply to a search conducted in identical circumstances. But in cases where there is a legitimate question whether an exception to the warrant requirement exists, it cannot be said that a warrantless search violates clearly established law." Id., at 535, n.

12.

Of course, the probable-cause requirement for an officer
who faces the situation petitioner did was clearly
established. In addition, an officer's belief that his
particular warrantless search was justified (by exigent
circumstances, in this case) is analytically no different
from a situation in which the warrant requirement has not
been explicitly held to apply to the particular search
undertaken by the officer - the precise situation in
which, as the Court recognized in **MITCHELL v. FORSYTH**,
there would certainly be no immunity. The good-faith
argument advanced by petitioner might support a judgment
in his favor after there has been a full examination of
the facts, but it is not the kind of claim to immunity,
based on the tentativeness or nonexistence of the
constitutional rule allegedly violated by the officer,
that we accepted in HARLOW or in MITCHELL.

III

Although the question does not appear to have been
argued in, or decided by, the Court of Appeals, this
Court has decided to apply a double standard of
reasonableness in damages actions against federal agents
who are alleged to have violated an innocent citizen's
Fourth Amendment rights. By double standard I mean a
standard that affords a law enforcement official two
layers of insulation from liability or other adverse
consequences, such as suppression of evidence. Having
already adopted such a soluble standard in applying the
exclusionary rule to searches authorized by an invalid
warrant, **UNITED STATES v. LEON**, 486 U.S. 897 91984), the
Court seems prepared and even anxious in this case to
remove any requirement that the officer must obey the
fourth Amendment when entering a private home. I remain
convinced that in a suite for damages as well as in a
hearing on a motion to suppress evidence, "an official
search and seizure cannot be both 'unreasonable' and
'reasonable' at the same time." Id., at 960 (STEVENS,
J., dissenting).

A "federal official may not with impunity ignore the
limitations which the controlling law has placed on his
powers." **BUTZ v. ENONOMOU**, 438 U.S. 478, 489 (1978). The
effect of the Court's (literally unwarranted) extension
of qualified immunity, I fear, is that it allows federal

agents to ignore the limitations of the probable-cause and warrant requirements with impunity. The Court does so in the name of avoiding interference with legitimate law enforcement activities even though the probable-cause requirement, which limits the police's exercise of coercive authority, is itself a form of immunity that frees them to exercise that power without fear of strict liability. See **PIERSON v. RAY**, 386 U.S. 547 (1967).

The Court advances four arguments in support of the position that even though an entry into a private home is constitutionally unreasonable, it will not give rise to monetary liability if a reasonable officer could have believed it was reasonable: First, the probable-cause standard is so vague that it is unfair to expect law enforcement officers to comply with it; second, the reasons for not saddling high government officials with the burdens of litigation apply equally to law enforcement officers; third, there is nothing new in the Court's decision today because "we have previously extended qualified immunity to officials who were alleged to have violated the Fourth Amendment," ante, at 643, and finally, holding police officers to the constitutional standard of reasonableness would "unduly inhibit officials in the discharge of their duties," ante, at 638. None of these arguments on behalf of a double standard of reasonableness is persuasive to me.

Unquestionably, there is, and always has been, some uncertainty in the application of the probable-cause standard to particular cases. It is nevertheless a standard that has survived the test of time both in England and in America. See 2 M.Hale, History of the Pleas of the Crown 150 (1847); J. Jolowicz & T. Lewis, Winfield on Tort 579-580 (8th ed. 1967); Weber, The Birth of Probable Cause, 11 Anglo-Am. L. Rev. 155, 166 (1982). Except in cases in which an officer relies on the fact that a magistrate has issued a warrant, there is no reason to believe that the Court's newly minted standard will provide any more certainty than the constitutional standard. Indeed, it is worth emphasizing that the probable-cause standard itself recognized the fair leeway that law enforcement officers must have in carrying out their dangerous work. The concept of probable cause leaves room for mistake, provided always that they are

482

mistakes that could have been made by a reasonable officer. See 1 W. LaFave, Search and Seizure 567 (2 ed. 1987). I find nothing in this Court's new standard that provides the officer with any more guidance than the statement in our opinion in **BRINEGAR v. UNITED STATES**, 338 U.S. 160 (1949), almost four decades ago:

"These long-prevailing standards seek to safeguard citizens from rash and unreasonable interferences with privacy and from unfounded charges of crime. They also seek to give fair leeway for enforcing the law in the community's protection. Because many situations which confront officers in the course of executing their duties are more or less ambiguous, room must be allowed for some mistakes on their part. But the mistakes must be those of reasonable men, acting on facts leading sensibly to their conclusions of probability. The rule of probable cause is a practical, nontechnical conception affording the best compromise that has been found for accommodating these often opposing interests. Requiring more would unduly hamper law enforcement. To allow less would be to leave law-abiding citizens at the mercy of the officers' whim or caprice." Id., at 176.

The suggestion that every law enforcement officer should be given the same measure of immunity as a Cabinet officer or a senior aide to the President of the United States is not compelling. Testifying in court is a routine part of an officer's job; his or her participation in litigation does not occasion nearly as great a disruption of everyday duties as it would with those of a senior government official. Moreover, the political constraints that deter high government officials from violating the Constitution have only slight, if any, application to police officers, and may actually lead to more, rather than less, vigorous enforcement activity. It is thus quite wrong simply to assume that the considerations that justified the decision in **HARLOW v. FITZGERALD** also justify an equally broad rule of immunity for police officers. As we reasoned in **SCHEUER v. RHODES**, 416 U.S. 232, 245-247 (1974):

"When a court evaluates police conduct relating to

an arrest its guideline is 'good faith and probable
cause.' . . . In the case of higher officers of
the executive branch, however, the inquiry is far
more complex since the range of decisions and
choices - whether the formulation of policy, of
legislation, or budgets, or of day-to-day decisions
- is virtually infinite . . . .[S]ince the options
which a chief executive and his principal
subordinates must consider are far broader and far
more subtle than those made by officials with less
responsibility, the range of discretion must be
comparably broad."

The Court supports its assertion that we have
previously extended qualified immunity to officials who
are alleged to have violated the Fourth Amendment, ante,
at 643, by reference to two cases: **MALLEY v. BRIGGS**, 475
U.S. 335 (1986), which involved a search pursuant to a
warrant, and **MITCHELL v. FORSYTH**, 472 U.S. 515 (1985), in
which the plaintiff relied on a rule of law that was not
clearly established at the time of the alleged wrong.
Neither of these cases supports the proposition that a
warrantless search should be evaluated under a standard
less strict than the constitutional standard of
reasonableness. Despite its protestations to the
contrary, the Court makes new law today.
    The argument that police officers need special
immunity to encourage them to take vigorous enforcement
action when they are uncertain about their right to make
a forcible entry into a private home has already been
accepted in our jurisprudence. We have held that the
police act reasonably in entering a house when they have
probable cause to believe a fugitive is in the house and
exigent circumstances make it impracticable to obtain a
warrant. This interpretation of the Fourth Amendment
allows room for police intrusion, without a warrant, on
the privacy of even innocent citizens. In **PIERSON v.
RAY**, 386 U.S., at 555, we held that police officers would
not be liable in an action brought under 42 U.S.C. § 1983
"if they acted in good faith and with probable cause . .
. ." We explained: "Under the prevailing view in this
country a peace officer who arrests someone with probable
cause is not liable for false arrest simply because the

innocence of the suspect is later proved. Restatement, Second, Torts § 121 (1965); 1 Harper & James, The Law of Torts § 3.18, at 277-278 (1956); **WARD v. FIDELITY & DEPOSIT CO. OF MARYLAND**, 179 F.2d 327 (CA 8th Cir. 1950). A policeman's lot is not so unhappy that he must choose between being charged with dereliction of duty if he does not arrest when he has probable cause, and being mulcted in damages if he does." Ibid.

Thus, until now the Court has not found intolerable the use of a probable-cause standard to protect the police officer from exposure to liability simply because his reasonable conduct is subsequently shown to have been mistaken. Today, however, the Court counts the law enforcement interest twice and the individual's privacy interest only once.

The Court's double-counting approach reflects understandable sympathy for the plight of the officer and an overriding interest in unfettered law enforcement. It ascribes a far lesser importance to the privacy interest of innocent citizens than did the Framers of the Fourth Amendment. The importance of that interest and the possible magnitude of its invasion are both illustrated by the facts of this case. The home of an innocent family was invaded by several officers without a warrant, without the owner's consent, with a substantial show of force, and with blunt expressions of disrespect for the law and for the rights of the family members. As the case comes to us, we must assume that the intrusion violated the Fourth Amendment. See **STEAGALD v. UNITED STATES**, 451 U.S. 204, 211 (1981). Proceeding on that assumption, I see no reason why the family's interest in the security of its own home should be accorded a lesser weight than the Government's interest in a carrying out an invasion that was unlawful. Arguably, if the Government considers it important not to discourage such conduct, it should provide indemnity to its officers. preferably, however, it should furnish the kind of training for its law enforcement agents that would entirely eliminate the necessity for the Court to distinguish between the conduct that a competent officer considers reasonable and the conduct that the Constitution deems reasonable. "Federal officials will not be liable for mere mistakes in judgment, whether the mistake is one of fact or one of law." **BUTZ v. ECONOMOU**, 438 U.S., at 507. On the other hand, surely an innocent family should not bear the entire risk that a trial court, with the benefit of hindsight, will find that a federal agent reasonably believed that he could break into their home equipped with force and arms but without probable cause or a warrant.

IV

The Court was entirely faithful to the traditions that have been embedded in our law since the adoption of the Bill of Rights when it wrote:

> "The Fourth Amendment protects the individual's privacy in a variety of settings. In none is the zone of privacy more clearly defined that when bounded by the unambiguous physical dimensions of an individual's home - a zone that finds its roots in clear and specific constitutional terms: 'The right of the people to be secure in their. . . . houses . . . shall not be violated.' That language unequivocally established the proposition that '[a]t the very core [of the Fourth Amendment] stands the right of a man to retreat into his own home and there be free from unreasonable governmental intrusion.' **SILVERMAN v. UNITED STATES**, 365 U.S. 505, 511 [1961]. In terms that apply equally to seizures of property and to seizures of persons, the Fourth Amendment has drawn a firm line at the entrance to the house. Absent exigent circumstances, that threshold may not reasonably be crossed without a warrant." **PAYTON v. NEW YORK**, 445 U.S.

The warrant requirement safeguards this bedrock principle of the Fourth Amendment, while the immunity bestowed on a police officer who acts with probable cause permits him to do his job free of constant fear of monetary liability. The Court rests its doctrinally flawed opinion upon a double standard of reasonableness which unjustifiably and unnecessarily upsets the delicate balance between respect for individual privacy and protection of the public servants who enforce our laws.

I respectfully dissent.

FLORIDA, Petitioner
v.
TERRANCE BOSTICK
501 U.S ___, 115 L.Ed.2d. 389, 111 S.Ct. 2382 (1991)

O'Connor, J., delivered the opinion of the Court, in which Rehnquist, C.J., and White, Scalia, Kennedy, and Souter, JJ., joined. Marshall, J., filed a dissenting opinion, in which Blackmun and Stevens, JJ., joined.

OPINION OF THE COURT

Justice O'Connor delivered the opinion of the Court.

[1a, 2a] We have held that the Fourth Amendment permits police officers to approach individuals at random in airport lobbies and other public places to ask them questions and to request consent to search their luggage, so long as a reasonable person would understand that he or she could refuse to cooperate. This case requires us to determine whether the same rule applies to police encounters that take place on a bus.

I

Drug interdiction efforts have led to the use of police surveillance at airports, train stations, and bus depots. Law enforcement officers stationed at such locations routinely approach individuals, either randomly or because they suspect in some vague way that the individuals may be engaged in criminal activity, and ask them potentially incriminating questions. Broward County has adopted such a program. County Sheriff's Department officers routinely board buses at scheduled stops and ask passengers for permission to search their luggage.

In this case, two officers discovered cocaine when they searched a suitcase belonging to Terrance Bostick. The underlying facts of the search are in dispute, but the Florida Supreme Court, whose decision we review here, stated explicitly the factual premise for its decision:

"'Two officers, complete with badges, insignia and one of them holding a recognizable zipper pouch, containing a pistol, boarded a bus bound from Miami to Atlanta during a stopover in Fort Lauderdale. Eyeing the passengers, the officers admittedly,

without articulable suspicion, picked out the
defendant passenger and asked to inspect his ticket
and identification. The ticket, from Miami to
Atlanta, matched the defendant's identification and
both were immediately returned to him as
unremarkable. However, the two police officers
persisted and explained their presence as narcotics
agents on the lookout for illegal drugs. In
pursuit of that aim, they then requested the
defendant's consent to search his luggage.
Needless to say, there is a conflict in the
evidence about whether the defendant consented to
the search of the second bag in which the
contraband was found and as to whether he was
informed of his right to refuse consent. However,
any conflict must be resolved in favor of the
state, it being a question of fact decided by the
trial judge.'" 554 So 2d 1153, 1154-1155 (1989),
quoting 510 So 2d 321, 322 (Fla App 1987) (Letts,
J. dissenting in part).

Two facts are particularly worth noting. First, the
police specifically advised Bostick that he had the right
to refuse consent. Bostick appears to have disputed the
point, but, as the Florida Supreme Court noted
explicitly, the trial court resolved this evidentiary
conflict in the State's favor. Second, at no time did
the officers threaten Bostick with a gun. The Florida
Supreme Court indicated that one officer carried a zipper
pouch containing a pistol - the equivalent of carrying a
gun in a holster - but the court did not suggest that the
gun was ever removed from its pouch, pointed at Bostick,
or otherwise used in a threatening manner. The dissent's
characterization of the officers as "gun-wielding
inquisitor[s]," ... ___, 115 L.Ed.2d, at 407, is
colorful, but lacks any basis in fact.
Bostick was arrested and charged with trafficking in
cocaine. He moved to suppress the cocaine on the grounds
that it had been seized in violation of his Fourth
Amendment rights. The trial court denied the motion but
made no factual findings. Bostick subsequently entered
a plea of guilty, but reserved the right to appeal the
denial of the motion to suppress.

The Florida District Court of Appeal affirmed, but considered the issue sufficiently important that it certified a question to the Florida Supreme Court. 510 So 2d, at 322. The Supreme Court reasoned that Bostick had been seized because a reasonable passenger in his situation would not have felt free to leave the bus to avoid questioning by the police. 554 So 2d, at 1154. It rephrased and answered the certified question so as to make the bus setting dispositive in every case. It ruled categorically that "'an impermissible seizure result[s] when police mount a drug search on buses during scheduled stops and question boarded passengers without articulable reason for doing so, thereby obtaining consent to search the passengers' luggage.'" Ibid. The Florida Supreme Court thus adopted a per se rule that the Broward County Sheriff's practice of "working the buses" is unconstitutional. The result of this decision is that police in Florida, as elsewhere, may approach persons at random in most public places, ask them questions and seek consent to search, see id., at 1156; but they may not engage in the same behavior on a bus. Id., at 1157. We granted certiorari, 498 US ___, 112 L.Ed.2d. 201, 111 S.Ct. 241 (1990), to determine whether the Florida Supreme Court's per se rule is consistent with our Fourth Amendment jurisprudence.

II

[1b] The sole issue presented for our review is whether a police encounter on a bus of the type described above necessarily constitutes a "seizure" within the meaning of the Fourth Amendment. The State concedes, and we accept for purposes of this decision, that the officers lacked the reasonable suspicion required to justify a seizure and that, if a seizure took place, the drugs found in Bostick's suitcase must be suppressed as tainted fruit.

[3a] Our cases make it clear that a seizure does not occur simply because a police officer approaches an individual and asks a few questions. So long as a reasonable person would feel free "to disregard the police and go about his business," **CALIFORNIA v. HODARI D.**,499 US -___, ___, 113 L.Ed.2d. 690, 111 S.Ct. 1547 (1991), the encounter is consensual and no reasonable suspicion is required. The encounter will not trigger Fourth Amendment scrutiny unless it loses its consensual

489

nature. The Court made precisely this point in **TERRY v. OHIO**, 392 U.S. 1, 19, N 16, 20 L.Ed.2d 889, 88 S.Ct. 1868 (1968): "Obviously, not all personal intercourse between policemen and citizens involves 'seizure' of persons. Only when the officer, by means of physical force or show of authority, has in some way restrained the liberty of a citizen may we conclude that a 'seizure' has occurred."

Since Terry, we have held repeatedly that mere police questioning does not constitute a seizure. In **FLORIDA v. ROYER**, 460 U.S. 491, 75 L.Ed.2d 229, 103 S.Ct. 1319 (1983) (plurality opinion), for example, we explained that "law enforcement officers do not violate the Fourth Amendment by merely approaching an individual on the street or in another public place, by asking him if he is willing to answer some questions, by putting questions to him if the person is willing to listen, or by offering in evidence in a criminal prosecution his voluntary answers to such questions." Id., at 497, 75 L.Ed.2d 229, 103 S.Ct. 1319; see id., at 523, n 3, 75 L.Ed.2d 229, 103 S.Ct. 1319 (Rehnquist, J., dissenting).

[1c] There is no doubt that if this same encounter had taken place before Bostick boarded the bus or in the lobby of the bus terminal, it would not rise to the level of a seizure. The Court has dealt with similar encounters in airports and has found them to be "the sort of consensual encounter[s] that implicat[e] no Fourth Amendment interest." **FLORIDA v. RODRIGUEZ**, 469 U.S. 1, 5-6, 83 L.Ed.2d. 165, 105 S.Ct. 308 (1984). We have stated that even when officers have no basis for suspecting a particular individual, they may generally ask question of that individual, see **INS v. DELGADO**, 466 U.S. 210, 216, 80 L.Ed.2d. 247, 104 S.Ct. 1758 (1984); Rodriguez, supra, at 5-6, 83 L.Ed.2d. 165, 105 S.Ct. 308; ask to examine the individual's identification, see Delgado, supra, at 216, 80 L.Ed.2d 247, 104 S.Ct. 1758; Royer, supra, at 501, 75 L.Ed.2d 229, 103 S.Ct. 1319 (plurality opinion); **UNITED STATES v. MENDENHALL**, 446 U.S. 544, 557-558, 64 L.Ed.2d 497, 100 S.Ct. 1870 (1980); and request consent to search his or her luggage, see Royer, supra, at 501, 75 L.Ed.2d 229, 103 S.Ct. 1319 (plurality opinion) - as long as the police do not convey a message that compliance with their requests is

required.

Bostick insists that this case is different because it took place in the cramped confines of a bus. A police encounter is much more intimidating in this setting, he argues, because police tower over a seated passenger and there is little room to move around. Bostick claims to find support in language from **MICHIGAN v. CHERTERNUT**, 486 U.S. 567, 573, 100 L.Ed.2d 565, 108 S.Ct. 1975 (1988), and other cases, indicating that a seizure occurs when a reasonable person would believe that he or she is not "free to leave." Bostick maintains that a reasonable bus passenger would not have felt free to leave under the circumstances of this case because there is nowhere to go on a bus. Also, the bus was about to depart. Had Bostick disembarked he would have risked being stranded and losing whatever baggage he had locked away in the luggage compartment.

The Florida Supreme Court found this argument persuasive, so much so that it adopted a per se rule prohibiting the police from randomly boarding buses as a means of drug interdiction. The state court erred, however, in focusing on whether Bostick was "free to leave" rather than on the principle that those words were intended to capture. When police attempt to question a person who is walking down the street or through an airport lobby, it makes sense to inquire whether a reasonable person would feel free to continue walking. But when the person is seated on a bus and has no desire to leave, the degree to which a reasonable person would feel that he or she could leave is not an accurate measure of the coercive effect of the encounter.

Here, for example, the mere fact that Bostick did not feel free to leave the bus does not mean that the police seized him. Bostick was a passenger on a bus that was scheduled to depart. he would not have felt free to leave the bus even if the police had not been present. Bostick's movements were "confined" in a sense, but this was the natural result of his decision to take the bus; it says nothing about whether or not the police conduct at issue was coercive.

In this respect, the Court's decision in **INS v. DELGADO**, supra, is dispositive. At issue there was the INS' practice of visiting factories at random and questioning employees to determine whether any were illegal aliens. Several INS agents would stand near the building's exits, while other agents walked through the factory questioning workers. The Court acknowledged that the workers may not have been free to leave their worksite, but explained that this was not the result of police activity: "Ordinarily, when people are at work their freedom to move about has been meaningfully restricted, not by the actions of law enforcement officials, but by the workers' voluntary obligations to their employers." Id., at 218, 80 L.Ed.2d. 247, 104 S.Ct. 1758. We concluded that there was no seizure because, even though the workers were not free to leave the building without being questioned, the agents' conduct should have given employees "no reason to believe that they would be detained if they gave truthful answers to the questions put to them or if they simply refused to answer." Ibid.

[1d, 4, 5]   The present case is analytically indistinguishable from Delgado. Like the workers in that case, Bostick's freedom of movement was restricted by a factor independent of police conduct - i.e., by his being a passenger on a bus. Accordingly, the "free to leave" analysis on which Bostick relies is an applicable. In such a situation, the appropriate inquiry is whether a reasonable person would feel free to decline the officers' requests or otherwise terminate the encounter. This formulation follows logically from prior cases and breaks no new ground. We have said before that the crucial test is whether, taking into account all of the circumstances surrounding the encounter, the police conduct would "have communicated to a reasonable person that he was not at liberty to ignore the police presence and go about his business." Chesternut, supra, at 569, 100 L.Ed.2d. 565, 108 S.Ct. 1975. See also Hodari D., supra, at ___, 113 L.Ed.2d. 690, 111 S.Ct. 1547. Where the encounter takes place is one factor, but it is not the only one. And, as the Solicitor General correctly observes, an individual may decline an officer's request without fearing prosecution. See Brief for the United States as Amicus Curiae 25. We have consistently held that a refusal to cooperate, without more, does not furnish the minimal level of objective justification needed for a detention or seizure. See Delgado, 466 U.S., at 216-217, 80 L.Ed.2d. 247, 104 S.Ct. 1758; Royer, 460 U.S, at 498, 75 L.Ed.2d 229, 103 S.Ct. 1319 (plurality opinion); **BROWN v. TEXAS**, 443 U.S. 47, 52-53, 61 L.Ed.2d 357, 99 S.Ct. 2637 (1979).

[3b, 6a] The facts of this case, as described by the Florida Supreme Court, leave some doubt whether a seizure occurred. Two officers walked up to Bostick on the bus, asked him a few questions, and asked if they could search his bags. As we have explained, no seizure occurs when police ask questions of an individual, ask to examine the individual's identification, and request consent to search his or her luggage - so long as the officers do not convey a message that compliance with their requests is required. Here, the facts recited by the Florida Supreme Court indicate that the officers did not point guns at Bostick or otherwise threaten him and that they specifically advised Bostick that he could refuse consent.

[6b, 7] Nevertheless, we refrain from deciding whether or not a seizure occurred in this case. The trial court made no express findings of fact, and the Florida Supreme Court rested its decision on a single fact - that the encounter took place on a bus - rather than on the totality of the circumstances. We remand so that the Florida courts may evaluate the seizure question under the correct legal standard. We do reject, however, Bostick's argument that he must have been seized because no reasonable person would freely consent to a search of luggage that he or she knows contains drugs. This argument cannot prevail because the "reasonable person" test presupposes an innocent person. See Royer, supra, at 519, n 4, 75 L.Ed.2d 229, 103 S.Ct. 1319 (Blackmun, J., dissenting)("The fact that [respondent] knew the search was likely to turn up contraband is of course irrelevant; the potential intrusiveness of the officers' conduct must be judged from the viewpoint of an innocent person in [his] position"). Accord Chesternut, 486 U.S. 574, 100 L.Ed.2d. 565, 108 S.Ct. 1975("This 'reasonable person' standard . . .ensures that the scope of Fourth Amendment protection does not vary with the state of mind of the particular individual being approached").

[6c, 8] The dissent characterizes our decision as holding that police may board buses and by an " intimidating show of authority," post, at ___, 115 L.Ed.2d, at 406 (emphasis added), demand of passengers their "voluntary" cooperation. That characterization is correct. Clearly, a bus passenger's decision to cooperate with law enforcement officers authorizes the

493

police to conduct a search without first obtaining a warrant only if the cooperation is voluntary. "Consent" that is the product of official intimidation or harassment is not consent at all. Citizens do not forfeit their constitutional rights when they are coerced to comply with a request that they would prefer to refuse. The question to be decided by the Florida courts on remand is whether Bostick chose to permit the search of his luggage.

The dissent also attempts to characterize our decision as applying a lesser degree of constitutional protection to those individuals who travel by bus, rather than by other forms of transportation. This, too, is an erroneous characterization. Our Fourth Amendment inquiry in this case - whether a reasonable person would have felt free to decline the officers' request or otherwise terminate the encounter - applies equally to police encounters that take place on trains, planes, and city streets. It is the dissent that would single out this particular mode of travel for differential treatment by adopting a per se rule that random bus searches are unconstitutional.

The dissent reserves its strongest criticism for the proposition that police officers can approach individuals as to whom they have no reasonable suspicion and ask them potentially incriminating questions. But this proposition is by no means novel; it has been endorsed by the Court any number if times. Terry, Royer, Rodriguez, and Delgado are just a few examples. As we have explained, today's decision follows logically from those decisions and breaks no new ground. Unless the dissent advocates overruling a long unbroken line of decisions dating back more than 20 years, its criticism is not well taken.

[9, 10] This Court, as the dissent correctly observes, is not empowered to suspend constitutional guarantees so that the Government may more effectively wage a "war on drugs." See post, ___, ___ _ ___, 115 L.Ed.2d., at 402, 409. If that war is to be fought, those who - fight it must respect the rights of individuals, whether or not those individuals are suspected of having committed a crime. By the same token, this Court is not empowered to forbid law

enforcement practices simply because it considers them distasteful. The Fourth Amendment proscribes unreasonable searches and seizures; it does not proscribe voluntary cooperation. The cramped confines of a bus are one relevant factor that should be considered in evaluating whether a passenger's consent is voluntary. We cannot agree, however, with the Florida Supreme Court that this single factor will be dispositive in every case.

[2b] We adhere to the rule that, in order to determine whether a particular encounter constitutes a seizure, a court must consider all the circumstances surrounding the encounter to determine whether the police conduct would have communicated to a reasonable person that the person was not free to decline the officers' requests or otherwise terminate the encounter. That rule applies to encounters that take place on a city street or in an airport lobby, and it applies equally to encounters on bus. The Florida Supreme Court erred in adopting a per se rule.

The judgment of the Supreme Court is reversed, and the case remanded for further proceedings not inconsistent with this opinion.

It is so ordered.

SEPARATE OPINION

Justice Marshall, with whom Justice Blackmun and Justice Stevens join, dissenting.

Our Nation, we are told, is engaged in a "war on drugs." No one disputes that it is the job of law enforcement officials to devise effective weapons for fighting this war. But the effectiveness of a law-enforcement technique is not proof of its constitutionality. The general warrant, for example, was certainly an effective means of law enforcement. Yet it was one of the primary aims of the Fourth Amendment to protect citizens from the tyranny of being singled out for search and seizure without particularized suspicion notwithstanding the effectiveness of this method. See **BOYD v. UNITED STATES**, 116 U.S. 616, 625-630, 29 L.Ed.2d. 746, 6 S.Ct. 524 (1886); see also **HARRIS v. UNITED STATES**, 331 U.S. 145, 171, 91 L.Ed.2d. 1399, 67 S.Ct. 1098 (1947) (Frankfurter, J., dissenting). In my view,

the law-enforcement technique with which we are
confronted in this case - the suspicionless police sweep
of buses in intrastate or interstate travel - bears all
of the indicia of coercion and unjustified intrusion
associated with the general warrant. Because I believe
that the bus sweep at issue in this case violates the
core values of the Fourth Amendment, I dissent.

I

     At issue in this case is a "new and increasingly
common tactic in the war on drugs": the suspicionless
police sweep of buses in interstate or intrastate travel.
UNITED STATES v. LEWIS, ___ U.S. App DC ___, ___, 921 F2d
1294, 1295 (1990); see **UNITED STATES v. FLOWERS**, 912 F2d
707, 710 (CA4 1990)(describing technique in Charlotte,
North Carolina); **UNITED STATES v. MADISON**, ___ F2d ___,
___ (CA2 1991) (describing technique in Port Authority
terminal in New York City); **UNITED STATES v. CHANDLER**,
744 F Supp 333, 335 (DC 1990) ("[I]t has become routine
to subject interstate travelers to warrantless searches
and intimidating interviews while sitting aboard a bus
stopped for a short layover in the Capital"); 554 So 2d
153, 1156-57 (Fla 1989) (describing Florida police of
"'working the buses'"); see also ante, at ___, 115
L.Ed.2d., at 396. Typically under this technique, a
group of state or federal officers will board a bus while
it is stopped at an intermediate point on its route.
Often displaying badges, weapons or other indicia of
authority, the officers identify themselves and announce
their purpose to intercept drug traffickers. They
proceed to approach individual passengers, requesting
them to show identification, produce their tickets, and
explain the purpose of their travels. Never do the
officers advise the passengers that they are free not to
speak with the officers. An "interview" of this type
ordinarily culminates in a request for consent to search
the passenger's luggage. See generally **UNITED STATES v.
LEWIS**, supra, at ___, 921 F2d, at 1296; **UNITED STATES v.
MADISON**, supra, at ___; 554 So 2d, at 1154.
     These sweeps are conducted in "dragnet" style. The

496

police admittedly act without an "articulable suspicion" in deciding which buses to board and which passengers to approach for interviewing. By proceeding systematically in this fashion, the police are able to engage in a tremendously high volume of searches. See, e.g., **FLORIDA v. KERWICK**, 512 So 2d 347, 348-349 (Fla App 1987) (single officer employing sweep technique able to search over 3,000 bags in nine-month period). The percentage of successful drug interdiction is low. See **UNITED STATES v. FLOWERS**, SUPRA, at 710 (sweep of 100 buses resulted in seven arrests).

To put it mildly, these sweeps "are inconvenient, intrusive, and intimidating." **UNITED STATES v. CHANDLER**, 744 F Supp, at 335. They occur within cramped confines, with officers typically placing themselves in between the passenger selected for an interview and the exit of the bus. See, e.g., id., at 336. Because the bus is only temporarily stationed at a point short of its destination, the passengers are in no position to leave as a means of evading the officers' questioning. Undoubtedly, such a sweep holds up the progress of the bus. See **UNITED STATES v. REMBERT**, 694 F Supp 163, 175 (WDNC 1988)(reporting testimony of officer that he makes "'every effort in the world not to delay the bus'" but that the driver does not leave terminal until sweep is completed). Thus, this "new and increasingly common tactic, " **UNITED STATES v. LEWIS**, supra, at ___, 921 F2d, at 1295, burdens the experience of traveling by bus with a degree of governmental interference to which, until now, our society has been proudly unaccustomed. See, e.g., **STATE EX REL. EKSTROM v. JUSTICE COURT**, 136 Ariz 1, 6, 663 P2d 992, 997 (1983) (Feldman, J., concurring) ("The thought that an American can be compelled to 'show his papers' before exercising his right to walk the streets, drive the highways or board the trains is repugnant to American institutions and ideals").

This aspect of the suspicionless sweep has not been lost on many of the lower courts called upon to review the constitutionality of this practice. Remarkably, the courts located at the heart of the "drug war" have been the most adamant in condemning this technique. As one Florida court put it:

> "'[T]he evidence in this cause has evoked images of other days, under other flags, when no man traveled his nation's roads or railways without fear of

unwarranted interruption, by individuals who held temporary power in the Government. The spectre of American citizens being asked, by badge-wielding police, for identification, travel papers - in short a raison d'etre - is foreign to any fair reading of the Constitution, and its guarantee of human liberties. This is not Hitler's Berlin, nor Stalin's Moscow, nor is it white supremacist South Africa. Yet in Broward County, Florida, these police officers approach every person on board buses and trains ("that time permits") and check identification [and] tickers, [and] ask to search luggage - all in the name of "voluntary cooperation" with law enforcement . . . .'" 554 So 2d , at 1158, quoting **STATE v. KERWICK**, supra, at 348-349 (quoting trial court order).

The District Court for the District of Columbia spoke in equally pointed words:

"It seems rather incongruous at this point in the world's history that we find totalitarian states becoming more like our free society while we in this nation are taking on their former trappings of suppressed liberties and freedoms."

"The random indiscriminate stopping and questioning of individuals on interstate busses seems to have gone too far. If this Court approves such 'bus stops' and allows prosecutions to be based on evidence seized as a result of such 'stops', then we will have stripped our citizens of basic Constitutional protections. Such action would be inconsistent with what this nation has stood for during its 200 years of existence. If passengers on a bus passing through the Capital of this great nation cannot be free from police interference where there is absolutely no basis for the police officers to stop and question them, then the police will be free to accost people on our streets without any reason or cause. In this 'anything goes' war on drugs, random knocks on the doors of our citizens' homes seeking 'consent' to search for

drugs cannot be far away. This is not America."
UNITED STATES v. LEWIS, 728 F Supp 784, 788-789,
rev'd, ___ U.S. App DC ___, 921 F2d 1294 (1990).

See also **UNITED STATES v. ALEXANDER**, 755 F Supp 448, 453
(DC 1991); **UNITED STATES v. MADISON**, 744 F Supp 490, 495-
497 (SDNY 1990), revd, ___ F2d ___ (CA2 1991); **UNITED
STATES v. CHANDLER**, supra, at, 335-336; **UNITED STATES v.
MARK**, 742 F Supp 17, 18-19 (DC 1990; **UNITED STATES v.
ALSTON**, 742 F Supp 13, 15 (DC 1990); **UNITED STATES v.
COTHRAN**, 729 F Supp 153, 156-158 (DC 1990), rev'd, ___ US
App DC ___, 921 F2d 1294 (1990); **UNITED STATES v. FELDER**,
732 F Supp 204, 209 (DC 1990).
The question for this Court, then, is whether the
suspicionless, drag-net-style sweep of buses in
intrastate and interstate travel is consistent with the
Fourth Amendment. The majority suggests that this latest
tactic in the drug war is perfectly compatible with the
Constitution. I disagree.

II

I have no objection to the manner in which the
majority frames the test for determining whether a
suspicionless bus sweep amounts to a Fourth Amendment
"seizure." I agree that the appropriate question is
whether a passenger who is approached during such a sweep
"would feel free to decline the officers' requests or
otherwise terminate the encounter." Ante, at ___, 115
L.Ed.2d, at 400. What I cannot understand is how the
majority can possibly suggest an affirmative answer to
this question.
The majority reverses what it characterizes as the
Florida Supreme Court's "per se rule" against
suspicionless encounters between the police and bus
passengers, see ante, at ___ _ ___, ___ _ ___, ___, 115
L.Ed.2d, at 397 399, 402, suggesting only in dictum its
"doubt" that a seizure occurred on the facts of this
case, see ante, at ___, 115 L.Ed.2d, at 400. However,
the notion that the Florida Supreme Court decided this
case on the basis of any "per se rule" independent of
the facts of this case is wholly a product of the
majority's imagination. As the majority acknowledges,
the Florida Supreme Court "stated explicitly the factual
premise for its decision." Ante, at ___, 115 L.Ed.2d, at
396. This factual premise contained all of the details

of the encounter between respondent and the police. See
554 So 2d, at 1154; ante, at ___, 115 L.Ed.2d, at 396-
399. The lower court's analysis of whether respondent
was seized drew heavily on these facts, and the court
repeatedly emphasized that its conclusion was based on
all the circumstances of this case. 554 So 2d, at 1157
(emphasis added); see ibid. ("Here the circumstances
indicate that the officers effectively `seized'
[respondent]" (emphasis added).
    The majority's conclusion that the Florida Supreme
Court, contrary to all appearances, ignored these facts
is based solely on the failure of the lower court to
expressly incorporate all of the facts into its
reformulation of the certified question on which
respondent took his appeal. See ante, at ___, 115
L.Ed.2d, at 397. The majority never explains the basis
of its implausible assumption that the Florida Supreme
Court intended its phrasing of the certified question to
trump its opinion's careful treatment of the facts in
this case. Certainly, when this Court issues an opinion,
it does not intend lower courts and parties to treat as
irrelevant the analysis of facts that the parties
neglected to cram into the question presented in the
petition for certiorari. But in any case, because the
issue whether a seizure has occurred in any given factual
setting is a question of law, see **UNITED STATES v.
MENDENHALL**, 446 U.S 544, 554-555, 64 L.Ed.2d. 497, 100
S.Ct. 1870 (1980) (opinion of Stewart, J.); **UNITED STATES
v. MARAGH**, 282 U.S. App DC 256, 258-259, 894 F2d 415,
417-418 (CADC), cert denied, 498 U.S. ___, 112 L.Ed.2d
174, 111 S.Ct. 214 (1990), nothing prevents this Court
from deciding on its own whether a seizure occurred based
on all of the facts of this case as they appear in the
opinion of the Florida Supreme Court.
    These facts exhibit all of the elements of coercion
associated with a typical bus sweep. Two officers
boarded the Greyhound bus on which respondent was a
passenger while the bus, en route from Miami to Atlanta,
was on brief stop to pick up passengers in Fort
Lauderdale. The officers made a visible display of their
badges and wore bright green "raid" jackets bearing the
insignia of the Broward County Sheriff's Department; one
held a gun in a recognizable weapons pouch. See 554 So

2d, at 1154, 1157. These facts alone constitute an intimidating "show of authority." See **MICHIGAN v. CHESTERNUT**, 486 U.S 567, 575, 100 L.Ed.2d 565, 108 S.Ct. 1975 (1988)(display of weapon contributes to coercive environment); **UNITED STATES v. MENDENHALL**, supra, at 554, 64 L.Ed.2d 497, 100 S.Ct. 1870 (opinion of Stewart, J.) ("threatening presence of several officers' and "display of a weapon"); id., at 555, 64 L.Ed.2d 497, 100 S.Ct. 1870 (uniformed attire). Once on board, the officers approached respondent, who was sitting in the back of the bus, identified themselves as narcotics officers and began to question him. See 554 So 2d, at 1154. One officer stood in front of respondent's seat, partially blocking the narrow aisle through which respondent would have been required to pass to reach the exit of the bus. See id., at 1157.

As far as is revealed by facts on which the Florida Supreme Court premised its decision, the officers did not advise respondent that he was free to break off this "interview." In explicabley, the majority repeatedly stresses the trial court's implicit finding that the police officers advised respondent that he was free to refuse permission to search his travel bag. See ante, at ___, ___ _ ___, 115 L.Ed.2d, at 397, 400. This aspect of the exchange between respondent and the police is completely irrelevant to the issue before us. For as the State concedes, and as the majority purports to "accept," id., at ___, 115 L.Ed.2d, at 398, if respondent was unlawfully seized when the officers approached him and initiated questioning, the resulting search was likewise unlawful no matter how well advised respondent was of his right to refuse it. See **FLORIDA v. ROYER**, 460 US 491, 501, 507-508, 75 L Ed 2d 229, 103 S.Ct. 1319 (1983) (plurality opinion); **WONG v. UNITED STATES**, 371 US 471, 9 L Ed 2d 441, 83 S.Ct. 407 (1963). Consequently, the issue is not whether a passenger in respondent's position would have felt free to deny consent to the search of his bag, but whether a passenger in respondent's position would have felt free to deny consent to the search of his bag, but whether such a passenger - without being apprised of his rights - would have felt free to terminate the antecedent encounter with the police.

Unlike the majority, I have no doubt that the answer to this question is no. Apart from trying to accommodate the officers, respondent had only two options. First, he could have remained seated while obstinately refusing to

respond to the officers' questioning. But in light of the
intimidating show of authority that the officers made
upon boarding the bus, respondent reasonably could have
believed that such behavior would only arouse the
officers' suspicions and intensify their interrogation.
Indeed, officers who carry out bus sweeps like the one at
issue here frequently admit that this is the effect of a
passenger's refusal to cooperate. See, e.g., **UNITED
STATES v. COTHRAN**, 729 F Supp, at 156; **UNITED STATES v.
FELDER**, 732 F Supp, at 205. The majority's observation
that a mere refusal to answer questions, "without more,"
does not give rise to a reasonable basis for seizing a
passenger, ante , at ___, 115 L.Ed.2d, at 400, is utterly
beside the point, because a passenger unadvised of his
rights and otherwise unversed in constitutional law has
no reason to know that the police cannot hold his
refusal to cooperate against him.

Second, respondent could have tried to escape the
officers' presence by leaving the bus altogether. But
because doing so would have required respondent to
squeeze past the gunweilding inquisitor who was blocking
the aisle of the bus, this hardly seems like a course
that respondent reasonably would have viewed as available
to him. The majority lamely protests that nothing in
the stipulated facts shows that the questioning officer
"point[ed] [his] gu[n] at [respondent] or otherwise
threatened him" with the weapon. Ante, at ___, 115 L Ed
2d, at 397, 400 (emphasis added). Our decisions
recognize the obvious point, however, that the choice of
the police to "display" their weapons during an encounter
exerts significant coercive pressure on the confronted
citizen. E.g., **MICHIGAN v. CHESTERNUT**, supra at 575, 100
L.Ed.2d 565, 108 S.Ct. 1975; **UNITED STATES v. MENDENHALL**,
supra, at 554, 64 L.Ed.2d. 497, 100 S.Ct. 1870. We have
never suggested that the police must go so far as to put
a citizen in immediate apprehension of being shot before
a court can take account of the intimidating effect of
being questioned by an officer with weapon in hand.

Even if respondent had perceived that the officers
would let him leave the bus, moreover, he could not
reasonably have been expected to resort to this means of
evading their intrusive questioning. For so far as
respondent knew, the bus departure from the terminal was

imminènt. Unlike a person approached by the police on the street, see **MICHIGAN v. CHESTERNUT**, supra or at a bus or airport terminal after reaching his destination, see **UNITED STATES v. MENDENHALL**, supra, a passenger approached by the police at an intermediate point in a long bus journey cannot simply leave the scene and repair to a safe haven to avoid unwanted probing by law-enforcement officials. The vulnerability that an intrastate or interstate traveler experiences when confronted by the police outside of his "own familiar territory" surely aggravates the coercive quality of such an encounter. See **SCHNECKLOTH v. BUSTAMONTE**, 412 US 218, 247, 36 L.Ed.2d 854, 93 S.Ct. 2401 (1973).

The case on which the majority primarily relies, INS v DELGADO, 466 US 210, 80 L.Ed.2d 247, 104 S.CT. 1758 (1984), is distinguishable in every relevant respect. In Delgado, this Court held that workers approached by law-enforcement officials inside of a factory were not "seized" for purposes of the Fourth Amendment. The Court was careful to point out, however, that the presence of the agents did not furnish the workers with a reasonable basis for believing that they were not free to leave the factory, as at least some of them did. See id., at 218-219, and n 7 80 L.Ed.2d 247, 104 S.Ct. 1758. Unlike passengers confronted by law-enforcement officials on a bus stopped temporarily at an intermediate point in its journey, workers approached by law-enforcement officials at their workplace need not abandon personal belongings and venture into unfamiliar environs in order to avoid unwanted questioning. Moreover, the workers who did not leave the building in Delgado remained free to move about the entire factory, see id., at 218, 80 L.Ed.2d 247, 104 S.CT. 1758, a considerably less confining environment than a bus. Finally, contrary to the officer who confronted respondent, the law-enforcement officials in Delgado did not conduct their interviews with guns in hand. See id., at 212, 80 L.Ed.2d 247, 104 S.Ct. 1758.

Rather than requiring the police to justify the coercive tactics employed here, the majority blames respondent for his own sensation of constraint. The majority concedes that respondent "did not feel free to leave the bus" as a means of breaking off the interrogation by the Broward County officers. Ante, at ___, 115 L.Ed.2d., at 399. But this experience of confinement the majority explains, "was the natural result of his decision to take the bus." Ibid (emphasis

503

added). Thus in the majority's view, because respondent's "freedom of movement was restricted by a factor independent of police conduct - i.e., by his being a passenger on a bus," ante, at ___, 115 L.Ed.2d, at 400, respondent was not seized for purposes of the Fourth Amendment.

This reasoning borders on sophism and trivialized the values that underlie the Fourth Amendment. Obviously, a person's "voluntary decision" to place himself in a room with only one exit does not authorize the police to force an encounter upon him by placing themselves in front of the exit. It is no more acceptable for the police to force an encounter on a person by exploiting his "voluntary decision" to expose himself to perfectly legitimate personal or social constraints. By consciously deciding to single out persons who have undertaken interstate or intrastate travel, officers who conduct suspicionless, dragnet-style sweeps puts passengers to the choice of cooperating or of exiting their buses and possibly being stranded in unfamiliar locations. It is exactly because this "choice" is no "choice" at all that police engage this technique.

In my view, the Fourth Amendment clearly condemns the suspicionless, dragnet-style sweep of intrastate or interstate buses. Withdrawing this particular weapon from the government's drug-war arsenal would hardly leave the police without any means of combatting the use of buses as instrumentalities of the drug trade. The police would remain free, for example, to approach passengers whom they have a reasonable, articulable basis to suspect of criminal wrongdoing. Alternatively, they could continue to confront passengers without suspicion so long as they took simple steps, like advising the passengers confronted of their right to decline to be questioned, to dispel the aura of coercion and intimidation that pervades such encounters. There is no reason to expect that such requirements would render the Nation's buses law-enforcement -free zones.

III

    The majority attempts to gloss over the violence that today's decision does to the Fourth Amendment with empty admonitions. "If the[e] [war on drugs] is to be fought," the majority intones, "those who fight it must respect the rights of individuals, whether or not those individuals are suspected of having committed a crime." Ante, at ___, 115 L.Ed.2d., at 401. The majority's action, however, speak louder than its words.

I dissent.

ILLINOIS v. RODRIGUEZ
497 U.S. 127, 110 S.Ct. 2793, 110 L.Ed.2d. 148 (1990)
CERTIORARI TO THE APPELLATE COURT OF ILLINOIS,
FIRST DISTRICT

SCALIA,J., delivered the opinion of the court, in which REHNQUIST, C.J., and WHITE, BLACKMUN, O'CONNOR, and KENNEDY, JJ., joined. MARSHALL, J., filed a dissenting opinion, in which BRENNAN and STEVENS, JJ., joined, post, p.189.

JUSTICE SCALIA delivered the opinion of the Court.

In **UNITED STATES v. MATLOCK**, 415 U.S. 164 (1974), this Court reaffirmed that a warrantless entry and search by law enforcement officers does not violate the Fourth Amendment's proscription of "unreasonable searches and seizures" if the officers have obtained the consent of a third party who possesses common authority over the premises. The present case presents an issue we expressly reserved in Matlock, see id., at 177, n.14: Whether a warrantless entry is valid when based upon the consent of a third party whom the police, at the time of the entry, reasonably believe to possess common authority over the premises, but who in fact does not do so.

I

Respondent Edward Rodriguez was Arrested in his apartment by law enforcement officers and charged with possession of illegal drugs. The police gained entry to the apartment with the consent and assistance of Gail Fischer, who had lived there with respondents for several months. The relevant facts leading to the arrest are as follows.

On July 26, 1985, police were summoned to the residence of Dorothy Jackson on South Wolcott in Chicago. They were met by Ms. Jackson's daughter, Gail Fischer, who showed signs of a severe beating. She told the officers that she had been assaulted by respondent Edward Rodriguez earlier that day in an apartment on South California Avenue. Fischer stated that Rodriguez was then asleep in the apartment, and she consented to travel

506

there with the police in order to unlock the door with her key so that the officers could enter and arrest him. During this conversation, Fischer several times referred to the apartment on South California as "our" apartment, and said that she had clothes and furniture there. It is unclear whether she indicated that she currently lived at the apartment, or only that she used to live there.

The police officers drove to the apartment on South California, accompanied by Fischer. They did not obtain an arrest warrant for Rodriguez, nor did they seek a search warrant for the apartment. At the apartment, Fischer unlocked the door with her key and gave the officers permission to enter. They moved through the door into the living room, where they observed in plain view drug paraphernalia and containers filled with white powder that they believed (correctly, as later analysis showed) to be cocaine. They proceeded to the bedroom, where they found Rodriguez asleep and discovered additional containers of white powder in two open attache cases. The officers arrested Rodriguez and seized the drugs and related paraphernalia.

Rodriguez was charged with possession of a controlled substance with intent to deliver. He moved to suppress all evidence seized at the time of his arrest, claiming that Fischer had vacated the apartment several weeks earlier and had no authority to consent to the entry. The Cook County Circuit Court granted the motion, holding that at the time she consented to the entry Fischer did not have common authority over the apartment. The Court concluded that Fischer was not a "usual resident" but rather an "infrequent visitor" at the apartment on South California, based upon its findings that Fischer's name was not on the lease, that she did not contribute to rent, that she did not have access to the apartment when respondent was away, and that she had moved some of her possessions from the apartment. The Circuit Court also rejected the State's contention that, even if Fischer did not possess common authority over the premises, there was no Fourth Amendment violation if the police reasonably believed at the time that Fischer possessed the authority to consent.

The Appellate Court of Illinois affirmed the Circuit Court in all respects. The Illinois Supreme Court denied the State's Petition for Leave to Appeal, 125 Ill, 2d 572, 537 N.E.2d 816 (1989), and we granted certiorari. 493 U.S. 932 (1989).

II

The Fourth Amendment generally prohibits the warrantless entry of a person's home whether to make an arrest or to search for specific objects. **PAYTON v. NEW YORK**, 445 U.S. 573 (1980); **JOHNSON v. UNITED STATES**, 333 U.S. 10 (1948). The prohibition does not apply, however, to situations in which voluntary consent has been obtained, either from the individual whose property is searched, see **SCHNECKLOTH v. BUSTAMONTE**, 412 U.S. 218 (1973), or from a third party who possesses common authority over the premises, see **UNITED STATES v. MATLOCK**, supra, at 171. The State of Illinois contends that the exception applies in the present case.

As we stated in MATLOCK, supra, at 171, n.7, "[c]ommon authority" rests "on mutual use of the property by persons generally having joint access or control for most purposes . . ." The burden was not sustained. The evidence showed that although Fischer, with her two small children, had lived with Rodriguez beginning in December 1984, she had moved out July 1, 1985, almost a month before the search at issue here, and had gone to live with her mother. She took her and her children's clothing with her, though leaving behind some furniture and household effects. During the period after July 1 she sometimes spent the night at Rodriguez's apartment, but never invited her friends there, and never went there herself when he was not home. Her name was not on the lease nor did she contribute to the rent. She had a key to the apartment, which she said at trial she had taken without Rodriguez's knowledge (though she testified at the preliminary hearing that Rodriguez had given her the key). On these facts the State has established that, with respect to the South California apartment, Fischer had "joint access or control for most purposes." To the contrary, the Appellate Court's determination of no common authority over the apartment was obviously correct.

III
A

The State contends that, even if Fischer did not in

fact have authority to give consent, it suffices to validate the entry that the law enforcement officers reasonably believed she did. Before reaching the merits of that contention, we must consider a jurisdictional objection: that the decision below rests on an adequate and independent state ground. Respondent asserts that the Illinois Constitution provides greater protection that is afforded under the Fourth Amendment, and that the Appellate Court relied upon this when it determined that a reasonable belief by the police officers was insufficient.

When a state-court decision is clearly based on state law that is both adequate and independent, we will not review the decision. **MICHIGAN v. LONG**, 463 U.S. 1032, 1041 (1983). But when "a state court decision fairly appears to rest primarily on federal law, or to be interwoven with the federal law," we require that it contain a "'plain statement' that [it] rests upon adequate and independent state grounds," id., at 1040, 1042; otherwise, "we will accept as the most reasonable explanation that the state court decided the case the way it did because it believed that federal law required it to do so." Id., at 1041. Here, the Appellate Court's opinion contains no "plain statement" that its decision rests on state law. The opinion does not rely on (or even mention) any specific provision of the Illinois Constitution, nor even the Illinois Constitution generally. Even the Illinois cases cited by the opinion rely upon no constitutional provisions other than the Fourth and Fourteenth Amendments of the United States Constitution. We conclude that the Appellate Court of Illinois rested its decision on federal law.

B

On the merits of the issue, respondent asserts that permitting a reasonable belief of common authority to validate an entry would cause a defendant's Fourth Amendment rights to be "vicariously waived." Brief for Respondent 32. We disagree.

We have been unyielding in our insistence that a defendant's waiver of his trial rights cannot be given effect unless it is "knowing" and "intelligent." **COLORADO v. SPRING**, 479 U.S. 564, 574-575 (1987)' **JOHNSON v. ZERBST**, 304 U.S 458 (1938). We would assuredly not permit, therefore, evidence seized in violation of the

509

Fourth Amendment to be introduced on the basis of a trial court's mere "reasonable belief"- derived from statements by unauthorized persons - that the defendant has waived his objection. But one must make a distinction between, on the one hand, trial rights that derive from the violation of constitutional guarantees and, on the other hand, the nature of those constitutional guarantees themselves. As we said in Schneckloth:

> "There is a vast difference between those rights that protect a fair criminal trial and the rights guaranteed under the Fourth Amendment. Nothing, either in the purposes behind requiring a 'knowing' and 'intelligent' waiver of trial rights, or in the practical application of such a requirement suggests that it ought to be extended to the constitutional guarantee against unreasonable searches and seizures." 412 U.S., at 241.

What Rodriguez is assured by the trial right of the exclusionary rule, where it applies, is that no evidence seized in violation of the Fourth Amendment will be introduced at his trial unless he consents. What he is assured by the Fourth Amendment itself, however, is not that no government search of his house will occur unless he consents; but that no such search will occur that is "unreasonable." U.S. Const., Amdt. 4. There are various elements, of course, that can make a search of a person's house "reasonable" - one of which is the consent of the person or his cotenant. The essence of respondent's argument is that we should impose upon this element a requirement that we have not imposed upon other elements that regularly compel government officers to exercise judgment regarding the facts: namely, the requirement that their judgment be not only responsible but correct.

The fundamental objective that alone validates all unconsented government searches is, of course, the seizure of persons who have committed or are about to commit crimes, or of evidence related to crimes. But "reasonableness," with respect to this necessary element, does not demand that the government be factually correct in its assessment that that is what a search will

510

produce. Warrants need only be supported by "probable cause," which demands no more than a proper "assessment of probabilities in particular factual contexts . . ." **ILLINOIS v. GATES**, 462 U.S. 213, 232 (1983). If a magistrate, based upon seemingly reliable but factually inaccurate information, issues a warrant for the search of a house in which the sought-after felon is not present, has never been present, and was never likely to have been present, the owner of that house suffers one of the inconveniences we all expose ourselves to as the cost of living in a safe society; he does not suffer a violation of the Fourth Amendment.

Another element often, though not invariably, required in order to render an unconsented search "reasonable" is, of course, that the officer be authorized by a valid warrant. Here also we have not held that "reasonableness" precludes error with respect to those factual judgments that law enforcement officials are expected to make. In **MARYLAND v. GARRISON**, 480 U.S. 79 (1987), a warrant supported by probable cause with respect to one apartment was erroneously issued for an entire floor that was divided (though not clearly) into two apartments. We upheld the search of the apartment not properly covered by the warrant. We said:

> "[T]he validity of the search of respondent's apartment pursuant to a warrant authorizing the search of the entire third floor depends on whether the officers' failure to realize the overbreadth of the warrant was objectively understandable and reasonable. Here it unquestionably was. The objective facts available to the officers at the time suggested no distinction between {the suspect's] apartment and the third-floor premises." Id., at 88.

The ordinary requirement of a warrant is sometimes supplanted by other elements that render the unconsented search "reasonable." Here also we have not held that the Fourth Amendment requires factual accuracy. A warrant is not needed, for example, where the search is incident to an arrest. In **HILL v. CALIFORNIA**, 401 U.S. 797 (1971), we upheld a search incident to an arrest, even though the arrest was made of the wrong person. We said:

> " The upshot was that the officers in good

faith believed Miller was Hill and arrested him. They were quite wrong as it turned out, and subjective good-faith belief would not in itself justify either the arrest or the subsequent search. But sufficient probability, not certainty, is the touchstone of reasonableness under the Fourth Amendment and on the record before us the officers' mistake was understandable and the arrest a reasonable response to the situation facing them at the time." Id., at 803-804.

It would be superfluous to multiply these examples. It is apparent that in order to satisfy the "reasonableness" requirement of the Fourth Amendment, what is generally demanded of the many factual determinations that must regularly be made by agents of the government - whether the magistrate issuing a warrant, the police officer executing a warrant, or the police officer conducting a search or seizure under one of the exceptions to the warrant requirement - is not that they always be correct, but that they always be reasonable. As we put it in **BRINEGAR v. UNITED STATES**, 338 U.S. 160, 176 (1949):

"Because many situation which confront officers in the course of executing their duties are more or less ambiguous, room must be allowed for some mistakes on their part. But the mistake must be those of reasonable men, acting on facts leading sensibly to their conclusions of probability."

We see no reason to depart from this general rule with respect to facts bearing upon the authority to consent to a search. Whether the basis for such authority exists is the sort of recurring factual question to which law enforcement officials must be expected to apply their judgment; and all the Fourth Amendment requires is that they answer it reasonably. The Constitution is no more violated when officers enter without a warrant because they reasonably (though erroneously) believe that the person who has consented to their entry is a resident of the premises, than it is

512

violated when they enter without a warrant because they reasonably (though erroneously) believe they are in pursuit of a violent felon who is about to escape. See **ARCHIBALD v. MOSEL**, 677 F. 2s 5 (CA1 1982).

STONER v. CALIFORNIA, 376 U.S. 483 (1964), is in our view not to the contrary. There, in holding that police had improperly entered the defendant's hotel room based on the consent of a hotel clerk, we stated that "the rights protected by the Fourth Amendment are not to be eroded ... by unrealistic doctrines of 'apparent authority'." Id., at 488. It is ambiguous, of course, whether the word "unrealistic" is descriptive or limiting – that is, whether we were condemning as unrealistic all reliance upon apparent authority, or whether we were condemning only such reliance upon apparent authority as is unrealistic. Similarly ambiguous is the opinion's earlier statement that "there [is no] substance to the claim that the search was reasonable because the police, relying upon the night clerk's expressions of consent, had a reasonable basis for the belief that the clerk had authority to consent to the search." Ibid. Was there no substance to it because it failed as a matter of law, or because the facts could not possibly support it? At one point the opinion does seem to speak clearly:

> "It is important to bear in mind that it was the petitioner's constitutional right which was at stake here, and not the night clerk's not the hotel's. It was a right, therefore, which only the petitioner could waive by word or deed, either directly or through an agent." Id., at 489.

But as we have discussed, what is at issue when a claim of apparent consent is raised is not whether the right to be free of searches has been waived, but whether the right to be free of unreasonable searches has been violated. Even if one does not think the Stoner opinion had this subtlety in mind, the supposed clarity of its foregoing statement is immediately compromised, as follows:

> "It is true that the night clerk clearly and unambiguously consented to the search. But there is nothing in the record to indicate that *the police had any basis whatsoever to believe that* the

513

night clerk had been authorized by the petitioner to permit the police to search the petitioner's room." Ibid. (emphasis added).

The italicized language should have been deleted, of course, if the statement two sentences earlier meant that an appearance of authority could never validate a search. In the last analysis, one must admit that the rationale of Stoner was ambiguous - and perhaps deliberately so. It is at least a reasonable reading of the case, and perhaps a preferable one, that the police could not rely upon the obtained consent because they knew it came from a hotel clerk, knew that the room was rented and exclusively occupied by the defendant, and could not reasonably have believed that the former had general access to or control over the latter. Similarly ambiguous in its implications (the Court's opinion does not even allude to, much less discuss the effects of, "reasonable belief") is **CHAPMAN v. UNITED STATES**, 365 U.S. 610 (1961). In sum, we were correct in Matlock, 415 U.S., at 177, n. 14, when we regarded the present issue as unresolved.

As Stoner demonstrates, what we hold today does not suggest that law enforcement officers may always accept a person's invitation to enter premises. Even when the invitation is accompanied by an explicit assertion that the person lives there, the surrounding circumstances could conceivably be such that a reasonable person would doubt its truth and not act upon it without further inquiry. As with other factual determinations bearing upon search and seizure, determination of consent to enter must "be judged against an objective standard: would the facts available to the officer at the moment ... 'warrant a man of reasonable caution in the belief'" that the consenting party had authority over the premises? **TERRY v. OHIO**, 392 U.S. 1, 21-22 (1968). If not, then warrantless entry without further inquiry is unlawful unless authority actually exists. But if so, the search is valid.

*   *   *

In the present case, the Appellate Court found it

unnecessary to determine whether the officers reasonably believed that Fischer had the authority to consent, because it ruled as a matter of law that a reasonable belief could not validate the entry. Since we find that ruling to be in error, we remand for consideration of that question. The judgment of the Illinois Appellate Court is reversed, and the case is remanded for further proceedings not inconsistent with this opinion.

So ordered.

JUSTICE MARSHALL, with whom JUSTICE BRENNAN and JUSTICE STEVENS join, dissenting.

Dorothy Jackson summoned police officers to her house to report that her daughter Gail Fischer had been beaten. Fischer told police that Ed Rodriguez, her boyfriend, was her assaulter. During an interview with Fischer, one of the officers asked if Rodriguez dealt in narcotics. Fischer did not respond. Fischer did agree, however, to the officers' request to let them into Rodriguez's apartment so that they could arrest him for battery. The police, without a warrant and despite the absence of an exigency, entered Rodriguez's home to arrest him. As a result of their entry, the police discovered narcotics that the State subsequently sought to introduce in a drug prosecution against Rodriguez.

The majority agrees with the Illinois Appellate Court's determination that Fischer did not have authority to consent to the officers' entry of Rodriguez's apartment. Ante, at 181-182. The Court holds that the warrantless entry into Rodriguez's home was nonetheless valid if the officers reasonably believed that Fischer had authority to consent. Ante this page. The majority's defense of this position rests on a misconception of the basis for third-party consent searches. That such searches do not give rise to claims of constitutional violations rests not on the premise that they are "reasonable" under the Fourth Amendment, see ante, at 183-184, but on the premise that a person may voluntarily limit his expectation of privacy by allowing others to exercise authority over his possessions. Cf. **KATZ v. UNITED STATES**, 389 U.s. 347, 351 (1967)("What a person knowingly exposes to the public, even in his own home or office, is not a subject of Fourth Amendment protection"). Thus, an individual's decision to permit another "joint access [to] or control [over the property] for most purposes," **UNITED STATES v. MATLOCK**, 415 U.S. 164, 171, n. 7 (1974), limits that individual's reasonable expectation of privacy and to that extent limits his Fourth Amendment protection. Cf. **RAKAS v. ILLINOIS**, 439 U.S. 128, 148 (1978) (because passenger in car lacked "legitimate expectation of privacy in the glove compartment," Court did not decide whether search would violate Fourth Amendment rights of someone who had such expectation). If an individual has not so limited his expectation of privacy, the police may not dispense with the safeguards established by the Fourth Amendment.

The baseline for the reasonableness of a search or seizure in the home is the presence of a warrant. **SKINNER v. RAILWAY LABOR EXECUTIVES' ASSN**, 489 U.S. 602 (1989). Indeed, "searches and seizures inside a home without a warrant requirement must therefore serve "compelling" law enforcement goals. **MINCEY v. ARIZONA**, 437 U.S. 385, 394 (1978). Because the sole law enforcement purpose underlying third party consent searches is avoiding the inconvenience of securing a warrant, a departure from the warrant requirement is not justified simply because an officer reasonably believes a third party has consented to a search of the defendant's home. In holding otherwise, the majority ignores our longstanding view that "the informed and deliberate determinations of magistrates . . . as to what searches and seizures are permissible under the Constitution are to be preferred over the hurried action of officers and others who may happen to make arrests." **UNITED STATES v. LEFKOWITZ**, 285 U.S 452, 464 (1932).

I

The Fourth Amendment provides that "[t]he right of the people to be secure in their . . . houses . . . shall not be violated." We have recognized that the "physical entry of the home is the chief evil against which the wording of the Fourth Amendment is directed." **UNITED STATES v. UNITED STATES DISTRICT COURT, EASTERN DISTRICT OF MICHIGAN**, 407 U.S. 297, 313 (1972). We have further held that "a search or seizure carried out on a suspect's premises without a warrant is per se unreasonable, unless the police can show that it falls within one of a carefully defined set of exceptions." **COOLIDGE v. NEW HAMPSHIRE**, 403 U.S. 443, 474 (1971). Those exceptions must be crafted in light of the warrant requirement's purposes. As this Court stated in **MCDONALD v. UNITED STATES**, 335 U.S. 451 (1948):

"The presence of a search warrant serves a high function. Absent some grave emergency, the Fourth Amendment has interposed a magistrate between the citizen and the police. This was done not to shield criminals nor to make the home a safe haven for illegal activities. It was done so that an objective mind might weigh the need to invade that privacy in order to enforce the law. The right of privacy was deemed too precious to entrust to the discretion of those whose job is the detection of crime and the arrest of criminals." Id., at 455-456.

The Court has tolerated departures from the warrant requirement only when an exigency makes a warrantless search imperative to the safety of the police and of the community. See, e.g., id., at 456 ("We cannot be true to that constitutional requirement and excuse the absence of a search warrant without a showing by those who seek exemption from the constitutional mandate that the exigencies of the situation made that course imperative"); **WARDEN v. HAYDEN**, 387 U.S. 294 (1967) (hot pursuit); **CHIMEL v. CALIFORNIA**, 395 U.S. 752 (1969) (interest in officers' safety justifies search incident to an arrest); **MICHIGAN v. TYLER**, 436 U.S. 499, 509 (1978) ("compelling need for official action and no time to secure a warrant" justifies warrantless entry of burning building). The Court has often heard, and steadfastly rejected, the invitation to carve out further exceptions to the warrant requirement for searches of the home because of the burdens on police investigation and prosecution of crime. Our rejection of such claims is not due to lack of appreciation of the difficulty and importance of effective law enforcement, but rather to our firm commitment to "the view of those who wrote the bill of Rights that the privacy of a person's home and property may not be totally sacrificed in the name of maximum simplicity in enforcement of the criminal law."

MINCEY, supra, at 393 (citing **UNITED STATES v. CHADWICK,** 433 U.S. 1, 6-11 (1977).

In the absence of an exigency, then, warrantless home searches and seizure are unreasonable under the Fourth Amendment. The weighty constitutional interest in preventing unauthorized intrusions into the home overrides any law enforcement interest in relying on the reasonable but potentially mistaken belief that a third party has authority to consent to such a search or seizure. Indeed, as the present case illustrates, only the minimal interest in avoiding the inconvenience of obtaining a warrant weighs in on the law enforcement side.

Against this enforcement interest in expediting arrests is "the right of a man to retreat into his own home and there be free from unreasonable governmental intrusion." **SILVERMAN v. UNITED STATES**, 365 U.S. 505, 511 (1961). To be sure, in some cases in which police officers reasonably rely on a third party's consent, the consent will prove valid, no intrusion will result, and the police will have been spared the inconvenience of securing a warrant. But in other cases, such as this one, the authority claimed by the third party will be false. The reasonableness of police conduct must be measured in light of the possibility that the target has not consented. Where"[n]o reason is offered for not obtaining a search warrant except the inconvenience to the officers and some slight delay necessary to prepare papers and present the evidence to a magistrate," the Constitution demands that the warrant procedure be observed. **JOHNSON v. UNITED STATES**, 333 U.S. 10, 15 (1948). The concerns of expediting police work and avoiding paperwork "are never very convincing reasons and, in these circumstances, certainly are not enough to by-pass the constitutional requirement." Ibid. In this case, as in Johnson, "[n]o suspect was fleeing or likely to take flight. The search was of permanent premises, not of a movable vehicle. No evidence or contraband was threatened with removal or destruction .... If the officers in this case were excused from the constitutional duty of presenting their evidence to a magistrate, it is difficult to think of a case in which it should be required." Ibid.

Unlike searches conducted pursuant to the recognized exceptions to the warrant requirement, see supra, at 191-192, third-party consent searches are not based on an exigency and therefore serve no compelling social goal. Police officers, when faced with the choice of relying on consent by a third party or securing a warrant, should secure a warrant and must therefore accept the risk of error should they instead choose to rely on consent.

II

Our prior cases discussing searches based on third-party consent have never suggested that such searches are "reasonable." In **UNITED STATES v. MATLOCK**, this Court upheld a warrantless search conducted pursuant to the consent of a third party who was living with the defendant. The Court rejected the defendant's challenge to the search, stating that a person who permits others to have "joint access or control for most purposes ... assume[s] the risk that [such persons] might permit the common area to be searched." 415 U.S., at 171, n.7; see also **FRAZIER v. CUPP**, 394 U.S. 731, 740 (1969)(holding that defendant who left a duffel bag at another's house and allowed joint use of the bag "assumed the risk that [the person] would allow someone else to look inside"). As the Court's assumption-of-risk analysis makes clear, third-party consent limits a person's ability to challenge the reasonableness of the search only because that person voluntarily has relinquished some of his expectation of privacy by sharing access or control over his property with another person.

A search conducted pursuant to an officer's reasonable but mistaken belief that a third party had authority to consent is thus on an entirely different constitutional footing from one based on the consent of a third party who in fact has such authority. Even if the officers reasonably believed that Fischer had authority to consent, she did not, and Rodriguez's expectation of privacy was therefore undiminished. Rodriguez accordingly can challenge the warrantless intrusion into his home as a violation of the Fourth Amendment. This conclusion flows directly from **STONER v. CALIFORNIA**, 376 U.S. 483 (1964). There , the Court required the suppression of evidence seized in reliance on a hotel clerk's consent to a warrantless search of a guest's room. The Court reasoned that the guest's right

519

to be free of unwarranted intrusion "was a right ... which only [he] could waive by word or deed, either directly or through an agent." Id., at 489. Accordingly, the Court rejected resort to "unrealistic doctrines of 'apparent authority'" as means of upholding the search to which the guest had not consented. Id., at 488.

III

Acknowledging that the third party in this case lacked authority to consent, the majority seeks to rely on cases suggesting the reasonable but mistaken factual judgments by police will not invalidate otherwise reasonable searches. The majority reads these cases as establishing a "general rule" that "what is generally demanded of the many factual determinations that must regularly be made by agents of the government - whether the magistrate issuing a warrant, the police officer executing a warrant, or the police officer conducting a search or seizure under one of the exception to the warrant requirement- is not that they always be correct, but that they always be reasonable." Ante, at 185-186.

The majority's assertion, however, is premised on the erroneous assumption that third-party consent searches are generally reasonable. The cases the majority cites thus provide no support for its holding. In **BRINEGAR v. UNITED STATES**, 338 U.S. 160 (1949), for example, the Court confirmed the unremarkable proposition that police need only probable cause, not absolute certainty, to justify the arrest of a suspect on a highway. As Brinegar makes clear, the possibility of factual error is built into the probable cause standard, and such a standard, by its very definition, will in some cases result in the arrest of a suspect who has not actually committed a crime. Because probable cause defines the reasonableness of searches and seizures outside of the home, a search is reasonable under the Fourth Amendment whenever that standard is met, notwithstanding the possibility of "mistakes" on the part of police. Id., at 176. In contrast, our cases have already struck the balance against warrantless home intrusions in the absence of an exigency. See supra, at 191-192. Because reasonable factual errors by law enforcement officers will not validate unreasonable searches, the reasonableness of the officer's mistaken belief that the third party had authority to consent is irrelevant.

The majority's reliance on **MARYLAND v. GARRISON**, 480 U.S. 79 (1987), is also misplaced. In Garrison, the police obtained a valid warrant for the search of the "third floor apartment" of a building whose third floor in fact housed two apartments. Id., 80. Although the police had probable cause to search only one of the apartments, they entered both apartments because "[t]he objective facts available to the officers at the time suggested no distinction between [the apartment for which they legitimately had the warrant and the entire third floor]." Id., at 88. The Court held that the officers' reasonable mistake of fact did not render the search unconstitutional. Id., at 88-89. As in Brinegar, the Court's decision was premised on the general reasonableness of the type of police action involved. Because searches based on warrants are generally reasonable, the officers' reasonable mistake of fact did not render their search "unreasonable." This reasoning is evident in the Court's conclusion that little would be gained by adopting additional burdens "over and above the bedrock requirement that, with the exceptions we have traced in our cases, the police may conduct searches only pursuant to a reasonably detailed warrant." Garrison, supra, at 89, n.14.

Garrison, like Brinegar, thus tells us nothing about the reasonableness under the Fourth Amendment of a warrantless arrest in the home based on an officer's reasonable but mistaken belief that the third party consenting to the arrest was empowered to do so. The majority's glib assertion that "[i]t would be superfluous to multiply" its citations to cases like Brinegar, Hill, and Garrison, ante, at 185, is thus correct, but for a reason entirely different than the majority suggests. Those cases provide no illumination of the issue raised in this case, and further citation to like cases would be as superfluous as the discussion on which the majority's conclusion presently depends.

IV

Our cases demonstrate that third-party consent searches are free from constitutional challenge only to

the extent that they rest on consent by a party empowered
to do so. The majority's conclusion to the contrary
ignores the legitimate expectations of privacy on which
individuals are entitled to rely. That a person who
allows another joint access to his property thereby
limits his expectation of privacy does not justify
trampling the rights of a person who has not similarly
relinquished any of his privacy expectation.

Instead of judging the validity of consent searches,
as we have in the past, based on whether a defendant has
in fact limited his expectation of privacy, the Court
today carves out an additional exception to the warrant
requirement for third party consent searches without
pausing to consider whether "'the exigencies of the
situation' make the needs of law enforcement so
compelling that the warrantless search is objectively
reasonable under the Fourth Amendment," Mincey, 437
U.S., at 394 (citations omitted). Where this free-
floating creation of "reasonable" exception to the
warrant requirement will end, now that the Court has
departed from the balancing approach that has long been
part of our Fourth Amendment jurisprudence, is unclear.
But by allowing a person to be subjected to a warrantless
search in his home without his consent and without
exigency, the majority has taken away some of the liberty
that the Fourth Amendment was designed to protect.

MARYLAND v. BUIE
494 U.S. 325, 110 S.Ct. 1093, 10 L.Ed.2d 276, (1990)
CERTIORARI TO THE COURT OF APPEALS OF MARYLAND
No. 88-1389. Argued December 4, 1889 -
Decided February 28, 1990

WHITE, J., delivered the opinion of the Court, in which REHNQUIST, C.J., and BLACKMUN, STEVENS, O'CONNOR, SCALIA, and KENNEDY, JJ., joined. STEVENS, J., post, p.334, and KENNEDY, J., post, p.339, filed concurring opinions. BRENNAN, J., filed a dissenting opinion, in which MARSHALL, J., joined, post, p 339.

JUSTICE WHITE delivered the opinion of the Court.

A "protective sweep" is a quick and limited search of premises, incident to an arrest and conducted to protect the safety of police officers or others. It is narrowly confined to a cursory visual inspection of those places in which a person might be hiding. In this case we must decide what level of justification is required by the Fourth and Fourteenth Amendments before police officers, while effecting the arrest of a suspect in his home pursuant to an arrest warrant, may conduct a warrantless protective sweep of all or part of the premises The Court of Appeals of Maryland held that a running suit seized in plain view during such a protective sweep should have been suppressed at respondent's armed robbery trial because the officer who conducted the sweep did not have probable cause to believe that a serious and demonstrable potentiality for danger existed. 314 Md. 151, 166, 500 A. 2d 79, 86 (1988). We conclude that the Fourth Amendment would permit the protective sweep undertaken here if the searching officer "possesse[d] a reasonable belief based on 'specific and articuable facts which, taken together with the rational interferences from those facts, reasonably warrant[ed]' the officer in believing," **MICHIGAN v. LONG,**463 U.S. 1032, 1049-1050 (1983) (quoting **TERRY v. OHIO,** 392 U.S. 1, 21 (1968)), that the area swept harbored an individual posing a danger to the officer or others. We accordingly vacate the judgment below and remand for application of this standard.

I

On February 3, 1986, two men committed an armed robbery of a Godfather's Pizza restaurant in Prince George's County, Maryland. One of the robbers was wearing a red running suit. That same day, Prince George's County police obtained arrest warrants for respondent Jerome Edward Buie and his suspected accomplice in the robbery, Lloyd Allen. Buie's house was placed under police surveillance.

On February 5, the police executed the arrest warrant for Buie. They first had a police department secretary telephone Buie's house to verify that he was home. The secretary spoke to a female first, then to Buie himself. Six or seven officers proceeded to Buie's house. Once inside, the officers fanned out through the first and second floors. Corporal James Rozar announced that he would "freeze the basement so that no one could come up and surprise the officers. With his service revolver drawn, Rozar twice shouted into the basement, ordering anyone down there to come out. When a voice asked who was calling, Rozar announced three times: "this is the police, show me your hands." App.5 Eventually, a pair of hands appeared around the bottom of the stairwell and Buie emerged from the basement. He was arrested, searched and handcuffed by Rozar. Thereafter, Detective Joseph Frolich entered the basement "in case there was someone else" down there. Id., at 14. He noticed a red running suit lying in plain view on a stack of clothing and seized it.

The trial court denied Buie's motion to suppress the running suit, stating in part: "The man comes out from a basement, the police don't know how many other people are down there. He is charged with a serious offense." Id., at 19. The State introduced the running suit into evidence at Buie's trial. A jury convicted Buie of robbery with a deadly weapon and using a handgun in the commission of felony. The Court of Special Appeals of Maryland affirmed the trial court's denial of the suppression motion. The court stated that Detective Frolich did not go into the basement to search for evidence, but to look for the suspected accomplice or anyone else who might pose a threat to the officers on the scene. 72 Md. App. 562, 571-572, 531 A.d 1290, 1295 (1987).

"Traditionally, the sanctity of a person's home - his castle - requires that the police may not invade it without a warrant except under the most exigent circumstances. But once the police are lawfully within the home, their conduct is measured by a standard of reasonableness....[I]f there is reason to believe that the arrestee had accomplices who are still at large, something less than probable cause - reasonable suspicion - should be sufficient to justify a limited additional intrusion to investigate the possibility of their presence." Id., at 575-576, 531 A.2d, at 1297 (emphasis in original).

The Court of Appeals of Maryland reversed by a 4-to-3 vote. 314 Md. 151, 550 A.2d 79 (1988). The court acknowledged that "when the intrusion is slight, as in the case of a brief stop and frisk on a public street, and the public interest in prevention of crime is substantial, reasonable articulable suspicion may be enough to pass constitutional muster," id., at 159, 550 A.2d, at 83. The court, however, stated that when the sanctity of the home is involved, the exceptions to the warrant requirement are few, and held: "[T]o justify a protective sweep of a home, the government must show that there is probable cause to believe that '"a serious and demonstrable potentiality for danger"' exists." Id., at 159-160, 550 A.2d, at 83 (citation omitted). The court went on to find that the State had not satisfied that probable-cause requirement. Id., at 165-166, 550 A.2d, at 86. We granted certiorari, 490 U.S. 1097 (1989).

II

It is not disputed that until the point of Buie's arrest the police had the right, based on the authority of the arrest warrant, to search anywhere in the house that Buie might have been found, including the basement. "If there is sufficient evidence of a citizen's participation in a felony to persuade a judicial officer that his arrest is justified, it is constitutionally reasonable to require him to open his door to the officers of the law." **PAYTON v. NEW YORK**, 445 U.S. 573,

525

602-603 (1980). There is also no dispute that if Detective Frolich's entry into the basement was lawful, the seizure of the red running suit, which was in plain view and which the officer had probable cause to believe was evidence of a crime, was also lawful under the Fourth Amendment. See **ARIZONA v. HICKS**, 480 U.S. 321, 326 (1987). The issue in this case is what level of justification the Fourth Amendment required before Detective Frolich could legally enter the basement to see if someone else was there.

Petitioner, the State of Maryland, argues that, under a general reasonableness balancing test, police should be permitted to conduct a protective sweep whenever they make an in-home arrest for a violent crime. As an alternative to this suggested bright-line rule, the State contends that protective sweeps fall within the ambit of the doctrine announced in **TERRY v. OHIO**, 392 U.S. 1 (1968), and that such sweeps may be conducted in conjunction with a valid in-home arrest whenever the police reasonably suspect a risk of danger to the officers or others at the arrest scene. The United States, as amicus curiae supporting the State, also argues for a Terry-type standard of reasonable articulable suspicion of risk to the officer, and contends that that standard is met here. Respondent argues that a protective sweep may not be undertaken without a warrant unless the exigencies of the situation render such warrantless search objectively reasonable. According to Buie, because the State has shown neither exigent circumstances to immediately enter Buie's house nor an unforeseen danger that arose once the officers were in the house, there is no excuse for the failure to obtain a search warrant to search for dangerous persons believed to be on the premises. Buie further contends that, even if the warrant requirement is inapplicable, there is no justification for relaxing the probable-cause standard. If something less than probable cause is sufficient, respondent argues that it is no less than individualized suspicion - specific, articulable facts supporting a reasonable belief that there are persons on the premises who are a threat to the officers. According to Buie, there were no such specific, articulable facts to justify the search of his basement.

III

It goes without saying that the Fourth Amendment bars only unreasonable searches and seizures, **SKINNER v. RAILWAY LABOR EXECUTIVES' ASSN.**, 489 U.S. 602 (1989). Our cases show that in determining reasonableness, we have balanced the intrusion on the individual's Fourth Amendment interests against its promotion of legitimate governmental interests. **UNITED STATES v. VILLAMONTE-MARQUEZ**, 462 U.S. 579, 588 (1983); **DELAWARE v. PROUSE**, 440 U.S. 648, 654 (1979). Under this test, a search of the house or office is generally not reasonable without a warrant issued on probable cause. There are other contexts, however, where the public interest is such that neither a warrant nor probable cause is required. **SKINNER, SUPRA**, at 619-620; **GRIFFIN v. WISCONSIN**, 483 U.S. 868, 873 (1987); **NEW JERSEY v. T.L.O.**, 469 u.s. 325, 340-341 (1985); **TERRY V. OHIO**, 392 U.S., at 20.

The **TERRY** case is most instructive for present purposes. There we held that an on-the-street "frisk" for weapons must be tested by the Fourth Amendment's general proscription against unreasonable searches because such a frisk involves "an entire rubric of police conduct - necessarily swift action predicated upon the on-the-spot observations of the officer on the beat - which historically has not been and as a practical matter could not be, subjected to the warrant procedure." Ibid. We stated that there is "no ready test for determining reasonableness other than by balancing the need to search ... against the invasion which the search ... entails'" Id., at 21 (quoting **CAMARA v. MUNICIPAL COURT OF SAN FRANCISCO**, 387 U.S. 523, 536-537 (1967). Applying that balancing test, it was held that although a frisk for weapons "constitutes a severe, though brief, intrusion upon cherished personal security," 392 U.S., at 24-25, such a frisk is reasonable when weighed against the "need for law enforcement officers to protect themselves and other prospective victims of violence in situations where they may lack probable cause for an arrest." Id., at 24. We therefore authorized a limited patdown for weapons where a reasonably prudent officer would be warranted in the belief, based on "specific and articulable facts," id., at 21, and not on a mere "inchoate and unparticularized suspicion or'hunch,'" id., at 27, "that he is dealing with an armed and dangerous individual," ibid.

In **MICHIGAN v. LONG**, 463 U.S. 1032 (1983), the principles of Terry were applied in the context of a roadside encounter: "[T]he search of the passenger compartment of an automobile, limited to those areas in which a weapon may be placed or hidden, is permissible if the police officer possesses a reasonable belief based on ʻspecific and articulable facts which, taken together with the rational inferences from those facts, reasonably warrant; the officer in believing that the suspect is dangerous and the suspect may gain immediate control of weapons." Id., at 1049-1050 (quoting Terry, supra, at 21). The Long Court expressly rejected the contention that Terry restricted preventative searches to the person of a detained suspect. 463 U.S., at 1047. In a sense, Long authorized a "frisk" of an automobile for weapons.

The ingredients to apply the balance struck in Terry and Long are present in this case. Possessing an arrest warrant and probable cause to believe Buie was in his home, the officers were entitled to enter and to search anywhere in the house in which Buie might be found. Once he was found, however, the search for him was over, and there was no longer that particular justification for entering any rooms that had not yet been searched.

That Buie had an expectation of privacy in those remaining areas of his house, however, does not mean such rooms were immune from entry. In Terry and Long we were concerned with the immediate interest of the police officers in taking steps to assure themselves that the persons with whom they were dealing were not armed with, or able to gain immediate control of, a weapon that could unexpectedly and fatally be used against them. In the instant case, there is an analogous interest of the officers in taking steps to assure themselves that the house in which a suspect is being, or has just been, arrested is not harboring other persons who are dangerous and who could unexpectedly launch an attack. The risk of danger in the context of an arrest in the home is as great as, if not greater than, it is in an on-the-street or roadside investigatory encounter. A Terry or Long frisk occurs before a police-citizen confrontation has escalated to the point of arrest. A protective sweep, in contrast , occurs as an adjunct to the serious step of taking a person into custody for the purpose of prosecuting him for a crime. Moreover, unlike an encounter on the street or along a highway, an in-home arrest puts the officer at the disadvantage of being on his adversary's "turf." An ambush in a confined setting of unknown configuration is more to be feared than it is in open, more familiar surroundings.

We recognized in Terry that "[e]ven a limited search of the outer clothing for weapons constitutes a severe, though brief, intrusion upon cherished personal security, and it must surely be an annoying, frightening, and perhaps humiliating experience." Terry, supra, at 24-25. But we permitted the intrusion, which was no more than necessary to protect the officer from harm. Nor do we here suggest, as the State does, that entering rooms not examined prior to the arrest is a de minimis intrusion that may be disregarded. We are quite sure, however, that the arresting officers are permitted in such circumstances to take reasonable steps to ensure their safety after, and while making, the arrest. That interest is sufficient to outweigh the intrusion such procedures may entail.

We agree with the State, as did the court below, that a warrant was not required. We also hold that as an incident to the arrest the officers could , as a precautionary matter and without probable cause or reasonable suspicion, look in closets and other spaces immediately adjoining the place of arrest from which an attack could be immediately launched. Beyond that, however, we hold that there must be articulable facts which, taken together with the rational inferences from those facts, would warrant a reasonably prudent officer in believing that area to be swept harbors an individual posing a danger to those on the arrest scene. This is no more and no less than we required in Terry and Long as in those cases, we think this balance is the proper one.

We should emphasize that such a protective sweep, aimed at protecting the arresting officers, if justified by the circumstances, is nevertheless not a full search of the premises, but may extend only to a cursory inspection of those spaces where a person may be found. The sweep lasts no longer than is necessary to dispel the reasonable suspicion of danger and in any event no longer than it takes to complete the arrest and depart the premises.

IV

Affirmance is not required by **CHIMEL v. CALIFORNIA**, 395 U.S. 752 (1969), where it was held that in the absence of a search warrant, the justifiable search incident to an in-home arrest could not extend beyond the arrestee's person and the area from within which the arrestee might have obtained a weapon. First, Chimel was concerned with a full-blown search of the entire house for evidence of the crime for which the arrest was made, see id., at 754, 763, not the more limited intrusion contemplated by a protective sweep. Second, the justification for the search incident to arrest considered in Chimel was the threat posed by the arrestee, not the safety threat posed by the house, or more properly by unseen third parties in the house. To reach our conclusion today, therefore, we need not disagree with the Court's statement in Chimel, id., at 766-767, n. 12, that "the invasion of privacy that results from a top-to-bottom search of a man's house [cannot be characterized] as 'minor," nor hold that "simply because some interference with an individual's privacy and freedom of movement has lawfully taken place, further intrusions should automatically be allowed despite the absence of a warrant that the Fourth Amendment would otherwise require," ibid. The type of search we authorize today is far removed from the "top-to-bottom" search involved in Chimel; moreover, it is decidedly not "automati[c]," but may be conducted only when justified by a reasonable, articulable suspicion that the house is harboring a person posing a danger to those on the arrest scene.

V

We conclude that by requiring a protective sweep to be justified by probable cause to believe that a serious and demonstrable potentiality for danger existed, the Court of Appeals of Maryland applied an unnecessarily strict Fourth Amendment standard. The Fourth Amendment permits a properly limited protective sweep in conjunction with an in-home arrest when the searching officer possesses a reasonable belief based on specific and articulable facts that the area to be swept harbors an individual posing a danger to those on the arrest scene. We therefore vacate the judgment below and remand this case to the Court of Appeals of Maryland for further proceedings not inconsistent with this opinion.

It is so ordered.

JUSTICE STEVENS, concurring.

Today the Court holds that reasonable suspicion, rather than probable cause, is necessary to support a protective sweep while an arrest is in progress. I agree with that holding and with the Court's opinion, but I believe it is important to emphasize that the standard applied only to protective sweeps. Officers conducting such a sweep must have a reasonable basis for believing that their search will reduce the danger of harm to themselves or of violent interference with their mission; in short, the search must be protective.

In this case, to justify Officer Frolich's entry into the basement, it is the State's burden to demonstrate that the officers had a reasonable basis for believing not only that someone in the basement might attack them or otherwise try to interfere with the arrest, but also that it would be safer to go down the stairs instead of simply guarding them from above until respondent had been removed from the house. The fact that respondent offered no resistance when he emerged from the basement is somewhat inconsistent with the hypothesis that the danger of an attack by a hidden confederate persisted after the arrest. Moreover, Officer Rozar testified that he was not worried about any possible danger when he arrested Buie. App. 9. Officer Frolich, who conducted the search, supplied no explanation for why he might have thought another person was in the basement. He said only that he "had no idea who lived there." Id., at 15. This admission is made telling by Officer Frolich's participation the 3-day pre-arrest surveillance of Buie's home. Id., at 4. The Maryland Court of Appeals was under the impression that the search took place after "Buie was safely outside the house, handcuffed and unarmed." 314 Md. 151, 166, 550 A.2d 79, 86 (1988). All of this suggests that no reasonable suspicion of danger justified the entry into the basement.

Indeed, were the officers concerned about safety, one would expect them to do what Officer Rozar did before

531

the arrest: guard the basement door to prevent surprise attacks. App. 5. As the Court indicates, Officer Frolich might, at the time of arrest, reasonably have "look[ed] in" the already open basement door, ante, at 334, to ensure that no accomplice had followed Buie to the stairwell. But Officer Frolich did not merely "look in" the basement; he entered it. That strategy is sensible if one wishes to search the basement. It is a surprising choice for an officer, worried about safety, who need not risk entering the stairwell at all.

The State may thus face a formidable task on remand. However, the Maryland courts are better equipped than are we to review the record. See, e.g., 314 Md., at 155, n.2, 550 A.2d, at 81, n.2 (discussing state-law rules restricting review of the record on appeal of suppression decisions); cf. **UNITED STATES v. HASTING**, 461 U.S. 499, 516-518 (1983) (STEVENS, J., dissenting) (This Court should avoid undertaking record review function that can "better be performed by other judges"). Moreover, the Maryland Court of Special Appeals suggested that Officer Frolich's search could survive a "reasonable suspicion" test, 72 Md. App. 562, 576, 531 A.2s 1290, 1297 (1987), and the Maryland Court of Appeals has not reviewed this conclusion. I therefore agree that a remand is appropriate.

JUSTICE KENNEDY, concurring.

The Court adopts the prudent course of explaining the general rule and permitting the state court to apply it in the first instance. The concurrence by JUSTICE STEVENS, however, makes the gratuitous observation that the State has a formidable task on remand. My view is quite to the contrary. Based on my present understanding of the record, I should think the officers' conduct here was in full accord with standard police safety procedure, and that the officers would have been remiss if they had not taken these precautions. This comment is necessary, lest by acquiescence the impression be left that JUSTICE STEVENS' views can be interpreted as authoritative guidance for application of our ruling to the facts of the case.

JUSTICE BRENNAN, with whom JUSTICE MARSHALL joins,

dissenting.

Today the Court for the first time extends **TERRY v. OHIO**, 392 U.S. 1 (1968), into the home, dispensing with the Fourth Amendment's general requirements of a warrant and probable cause and carving a "reasonable suspicion" exception for protective sweeps in private dwellings. In Terry, supra, the Court held that a police officer may briefly detain a suspect based on a reasonable suspicion of criminal activity and may conduct a limited "frisk" of the suspect for concealed weapons in order to protect herself [himself] from personal danger. The Court deemed such a frisk "reasonable" under the Fourth Amendment in light of the special "need for law enforcement officers to protect themselves and other prospective victims of violence" during investigative detention, id., at 24, and the "brief, though far from inconsiderable, intrusion upon the sanctity of the person." Id., at 26.

Terry and its early progeny "permit[ted] only brief investigative stops and extremely limited searches based on reasonable suspicion." **UNITED STATE v. PLACE**, 462 U.S. 696, 714 (1983) (BRENNAN, J., concurring in result). But this Court more recently has applied the rationale underlying Terry to a wide variety of more intrusive searches and seizures, prompting my continued criticism of the "'emerging tendency on the part of the Court to convert the Terry decision'" from a narrow exception into one that "'swallow[s] the general rule that [searches] are "reasonable' only if based on probable cause.'" Place, supra at 719 (BRENNAN, J., concurring in result) (citations omitted).

The Court today holds that Terry's "reasonable suspicion" standard "strikes the proper balance between officer safety and citizen privacy" for protective sweeps in private dwellings. Ante, at 335, n.2. I agree with the majority that officers executing an arrest warrant within a private dwelling have an interest in protecting themselves against potential ambush by third parties, see ante, at 333, but the majority offers no support for its assumption that the danger of ambush during planned home arrests approaches the danger of unavoidable "on-the-beat' confrontations in "the myriad daily situations in which policemen and citizens confront each other on the street." Terry, supra, at 12. In any event, the Court's implicit judgment that a protective sweep constitutes a "minimally intrusive" search akin to that involved in Terry markedly undervalues the nature and scope of the

533

privacy interests involved.

While the Fourth Amendment protects a person's privacy interests in a variety of settings, "physical entry of the home is the chief evil against which the wording of the Fourth Amendment is directed." **UNITED STATES v. UNITED STATES DISTRICT COURT, EASTERN DISTRICT OF MICHIGAN**, 407 U.S. 297, 313 (1972). The Court discounts the nature of the intrusion because it believes that the scope of the intrusion is limited. The Court explains that a protective sweep's scope is "narrowly confined to a cursory visual inspection of those places in which a person might be hiding," ante, at 327, and confined in duration to a period "no longer than is necessary to dispel the reasonable suspicion of danger and in any event no longer than it takes to complete the arrest and depart the premises." Ante, at 335-336. But these spatial and temporal restrictions are not particularly limiting. A protective sweep would bring within police purview virtually all personal possessions within the house not hidden from view in a small enclosed space. Police officers searching for potential ambushers might enter every room including basements and attics; open up closets, lockers, chests, wardrobes, and cars; and peer under beds and behind furniture. The officers will view letters, documents, and personal effects that are on tables or desks or are visible inside open drawers; books, records, tapes, and pictures on shelves; and clothing, medicines , toiletries and other paraphernalia not carefully stored in dresser drawers or bathroom cupboards. While perhaps not a "full-blown" or "top-to-bottom" search, ante, at 336, a protective sweep is much closer to it than to a "limited patdown for weapons" or a "'frisk' of an automobile." Ante at 332. Because the nature and scope of the intrusion sanctioned here are far greater than those upheld in Terry and Long, the Court's conclusion that "[t]he ingredients to apply the balance struck in Terry and Long are present in this case," ibid., is unwarranted. The "ingredient' of a minimally intrusive search is absent, and the Court's holding today therefore unpalatably deviates from Terry and its progeny.

In light of the special sanctity of a private residence and the highly intrusive nature of a protective sweep, I firmly believe that police officers must have probable cause to fear that their personal safety is threatened by a hidden confederate of an arrestee before they may sweep through the entire home. Given the state-court determination that the officers searching Buie's home lacked probable cause to perceive such a danger and therefore were not lawfully present in the basement, I would affirm the state court's decision to suppress the incriminating evidence. I respectfully dissent.

STEAGALD v. UNITED STATES
CERTIORARI TO THE UNITED STATES COURT OF APPEALS
FOR THE FIFTH CIRCUIT
No. 79-6777 Argued January 14, 1981 -
Decided April 21, 1981

JUSTICE MARSHALL delivered the opinion of the Court. The issue in this case is whether, under the Fourth Amendment, a law enforcement officer may legally search for the subject of an arrest warrant in the home of a third party without first obtaining a search warrant. Concluding that a search warrant must be obtained absent exigent circumstances or consent, we reverse the judgment of the United States Court of Appeals for the Fifth Circuit affirming petitioner's conviction.

I

In early January 1978, an agent of the Drug Enforcement Administration (DEA) was contacted in Detroit, Mich., by a confidential informant who suggested that he might be able to locate Ricky Lyons, a federal fugitive wanted on drug charges. On January 14, 1978, the informant called the agent again, and gave him a telephone number in the Atlanta, Ga., area where, according to the informant, Ricky Lyons could be reached during the next 24 hours. On January 16, 1978, the agent called fellow DEA Agent Kelly Goodowens in Atlanta and relayed the information he had obtained from the informant. Goodowens contacted Southern Bell Telephone Co., and secured the address corresponding to the telephone number obtained by the informant. Goodowens also discovered that Lyons was the subject of a 6-month-old arrest warrant.

Two days later, Goodowens and 11 other officers drove to the address supplied by the telephone company to search for Lyons. The officers observed two men standing outside the house to be searched. These men were Hoyt Gaultney and petitioner Gary Steagald. The officers approached with guns drawn, frisked both men, and after demanding identification, determined that neither man was Lyons. Several agents proceeded to the house. Gaultney's wife answered the door, and informed the

536

agents that she was alone in the house. She was told to place her hands against the wall and was guarded in that position while one agent searched the house. Ricky Lyons was not found, but during the search of the house the agent observed what he believed to be cocaine. Upon being informed of this discovery, Agent Goodowens sent an officer to obtain a search warrant and in the meantime conducted a search of the house, which uncovered additional incriminating evidence. During a third search conducted pursuant to a search warrant, the agents uncovered 43 pounds of cocaine. Petitioner was arrested and indicted on federal drug charges.

Prior to trial, petitioner moved to suppress all evidence uncovered during the various searches on the ground that it was illegally obtained because the agents had failed to secure a search warrant before entering the house. Agent Goodowens testified at the suppression hearing that there had been no "physical hinderance" preventing him from obtaining a search warrant and that he did not do so because he believed that the arrest warrant for Ricky Lyons was sufficient to justify the entry and search. The District Court agreed with this view, and denied the suppression motion. Petitioner was convicted, and renewed his challenge to the search in his appeal. A divided Court of Appeals for the Fifth Circuit affirmed the District Court's denial of petitioner's suppression motion. **UNITED STATES v. GAULTNEY**, 606 F.2 540 (1979). Because the issue presented by this case is an important one that has divided the Circuits , we granted certiorari.

II

The Government initially seeks to avert our consideration of the Fifth Circuit's decision by suggesting that petitioner may, regardless of the merits of that decision, lack an expectation of privacy in the house sufficient to prevail on his Fourth Amendment claim. This argument was never raised by the Government in the courts below. Moreover, in its brief in opposition to certiorari the Government represented to this court that the house in question was "petitioner's residence" and was "occupied by petitioner, Gaultney, and Gaultney's wife." Brief in Opposition 1,3. However, the Government now contends that the record does not clearly show that petitioner had a reasonable expectation of privacy in the house, and hence urges us to remand the case to the District Court for re-examination of this factual question.

We decline to follow the suggested disposition. Aside from arguing that a search warrant was not constitutionally required, the Government was initially entitled to defend against petitioner's charge of an unlawful search by asserting that petitioner lacked a reasonable expectation of privacy in the searched home, or that he consented to the search, or that exigent circumstances justified the entry. The Government, however, may lose its right to raise factual issues of this sort before this Court when it has made contrary assertions in the courts below, when it has acquiesced in contrary findings by those courts, or when it has failed to raise such questions in a timely fashion during the litigation.

We conclude that this is such a case. The Magistrate's report on petitioner's suppression motion, which was adopted by the District Court, characterized the issue as whether an arrest warrant was sufficient to justify the search of "the home of a third person" for the subject of the warrant. App. 12. The Government never sought to correct this characterization on appeal, and instead acquiesced in the District Court's view of petitioner's Fourth Amendment claim. Moreover, during both the trial and the appeal in this case the Government argued successfully that petitioner's connection with the searched home was sufficient to establish his constructive possession of the cocaine found in a suitcase in the closet of the house. Moreover, the Court of Appeals concluded, as had the Magistrate and the District Court, that petitioner's Fourth Amendment claim involved the type of warrant necessary to search "premises belonging to a third party." 606 F.2d, at 544. Again, the Government declined to disturb this characterization. When petitioner sought review in this Court, the Government could have filed a cross-petition for certiorari suggesting, as it does now, that the case be remanded to the District Court for further proceedings. Instead, the Government argued that further review was unnecessary. Finally, the Government in its opposition to certiorari expressly represented that the searched home was petitioner's residence.

Thus, during the course of these proceedings the Government has directly sought to connect petitioner with the house, has acquiesced in statements by the courts below characterizing the search as one of petitioner's residence, and has made similar concessions of its own. Now, two years after petitioner's trial, the Government seeks to return the case to the District Court for a re-examination of this factual issue. The tactical advantages to the Government of this disposition are obvious, for if the Government prevailed on this claim upon a remand, it would be relieved of the task of defending the judgment of the Court of Appeals before this Court. We conclude, however, that the Government, through its assertions, concessions, and acquiescence, has lost its right to challenge petitioner's assertion that he possessed a legitimate expectation of privacy in the searched home. We therefore turn to the merits of petitioner's claim.

III

The question before us is a narrow one. The search at issue here took place in the absence of consent or exigent circumstances. Except in such special situations, we have consistently held that the entry into a home to conduct a search or make an arrest is unreasonable under the Fourth Amendment unless done pursuant to a warrant. See **PAYTON v. NEW YORK**, 445 U.S. 573 (1980); **JOHNSON v. UNITED STATES**, 333 U.S. 10, 13-15 (1948). Thus, as we recently observed: "[I]n terms that apply equally to seizures of property and to seizures of persons, the Fourth Amendment has drawn a firm line at the entrance to the house. Absent exigent circumstances, that threshold may not reasonably be crossed without a warrant." **PAYTON v. NEW YORK**, supra, at 590. See **COOLIDGE v. NEW HAMPSHIRE**, 403 U.S. 443, 474-475, 477-478 (1971); **JONES v. UNITED STATES**, 357 U.S. 493, 497-498 (1958); **AGNELLO v. UNITED STATES**, 269 U.S. 20, 32-33 (1925). Here, of course, the agents had a warrant - one authorizing the arrest of Ricky Lyons. However, the Fourth Amendment claim here is not being raised by Ricky Lyons. Instead, the challenge to the search is asserted by a person not named in the warrant who was convicted on the basis of evidence uncovered during a search of his residence for Ricky Lyons. Thus, the narrow issue before

539

us is whether an arrest warrant - as opposed to a search warrant - is adequate to protect the Fourth Amendment interests of persons not named in the warrant, when their homes are searched without their consent and in the absence of exigent circumstances.

The purpose of a warrant is to allow a neutral judicial officer to assess whether the police have probable cause to make an arrest or conduct a search. As we have often explained, the placement of this checkpoint between the Government and the citizen implicitly acknowledges that an "officer engaged in the often competitive enterprise of ferreting out crime," **JOHNSON v. UNITED STATES**, supra, at 14, may lack sufficient objectivity to weigh correctly the strength of the evidence supporting the contemplated action against the individual's interests in protecting his own liberty and the privacy of his home. **COOLIDGE v. NEW HAMPSHIRE**, supra, at 449-451; **McDONALD v. UNITED STATES**, 335 U.S. 451, 455-456 (1948). However, while an arrest warrant and a search warrant both serve to subject the probable-cause determination of the police to judicial review, the interests protected by the two warrants differ. An arrest warrant is issued by a magistrate upon a showing that probable cause exists to believe that the subject of the warrant has committed an offense and thus the warrant primarily serves to protect an individual from an unreasonable seizure. A search warrant, in contrast, is issued upon a showing of probable cause to believe that the legitimate object of a search is located in a particular place, and therefore safeguards an individual's interest in the privacy of his home and possessions against the unjustified intrusion of the police.

Thus, whether the arrest warrant issued in this case adequately safeguarded the interests protected by the Fourth Amendment depends upon what the warrant authorized the agents to do. To be sure, the warrant embodied a judicial finding that there was probable cause to believe that Ricky Lyons had committed a felony, and the warrant therefore authorized the officers to seize Lyons. However, the agents sought to do more than use the warrant to arrest Lyons in a public place or in his home; instead, they relied on the warrant as legal authority to enter the home of a third person based on their belief that Ricky Lyons might be a guest there. Regardless of how reasonable this belief might have been, it was never subjected to the detached scrutiny of a judicial officer. Thus, while the warrant in this case may have protected Lyons from an unreasonable seizure, it did absolutely nothing to protect petitioner's privacy interest in being free from an unreasonable invasion and search of his home. Instead, petitioner's only protection from an illegal entry and search was the agent's personal determination of probable cause. In the absence of exigent circumstances, we have consistently held that such judicially untested determinations are not reliable enough to justify an entry into a person's home to arrest him without a warrant, or a search of a home for objects in the absence of a search warrant. **PAYTON v. NEW YORK**, supra; **JOHNSON v. UNITED STATES**, supra. We see no reason to depart from this settled course when the search of a home is for a person rather than an object.

A contrary conclusion - that the police, acting alone and in the absence of exigent circumstances, may decide when there is sufficient justification for searching the home of a third party for the subject of an arrest warrant - would create a significant potential for abuse. Armed solely with an arrest warrant for a single person, the police could search all the homes of that individual's friends and acquaintances. See, e.g., **LANKFORD v. GELSTON**, 364 F.2d 197 (CA4 1966) (enjoining police practice under which 300 homes were searched pursuant to arrest warrants for two fugitives). Moreover, an arrest warrant may serve as the pretext for entering a home in which the police have a suspicion, but not probable cause to believe, that illegal activity is taking place. Cf. **CHIMEL v. CALIFORNIA**, 395 U.S. 752, 767 (1969). The Government recognized the potential for such abuses, but contends that existing remedies - such as motions to suppress illegally procured evidence and damages actions for Fourth Amendment violations - provide adequate means of redress. We do not agree. As we observed on a previous occasion, "[t]he [Fourth] Amendment is designed to prevent, not simply to redress, unlawful police action." **CHIMEL v. CALIFORNIA**, supra, at 766, n.12. Indeed, if suppression motions and damages actions were sufficient to implement the Fourth Amendment's prohibition against unreasonable searches and seizures, there would be no need for the constitutional requirement that in the absence of exigent circumstances a warrant must be obtained for a home arrest or a search of a home for objects. We have instead concluded that in such cases the participation of a detached magistrate in the probable-cause determination is an essential element of a reasonable search or seizure, and we believe that the same conclusion should apply here.

In sum, two distinct interests were implicated by the search at issue here - Ricky Lyons' interest in being free from an unreasonable seizure and petitioner's interest in being free from an unreasonable search of his home. Because the arrest warrant for Lyons addressed only the former interest, the search of petitioner's home was no more reasonable from petitioner's perspective than it would have been if conducted in the absence of any warrant. Since warrantless searches of a home are impermissible absent consent or exigent circumstances, we conclude that the instant search violated the Fourth Amendment.

IV

The Government concedes that this view is "apparently logical," that it furthers the general policies underlying the Fourth Amendment, and that it "has the virtue of producing symmetry between the law of entry to conduct a search for things to be seized and the law of entry to conduct a search for persons to be seized." Brief for United States 36. Yet we are informed that this conclusion is "not without its flaws" in that it is contrary to common-law precedent and creates some practical problems of law enforcement. We treat these contentions in turn.

A

The common law may, within limits, be instructive in determining what sorts of searches the Framers of the Fourth Amendment regarded as reasonable. See, e.g. **PAYTON v. NEW YORK**, 445 U.S., at 591. The Government contends that at common law an officer could forcibly enter the home of a third party to execute an arrest warrant. To be secure, several commentators do suggest that a constable could "break open doors" to effect such an arrest. See 1 J. Chitty, Criminal Law *57 (Chitty); M. Foster, Crown Law 320 (1972)(Foster); 2M. Hale, Pleas of the Crown 116-117 (ast Am.ed. 1847) (Hale). But see 4#. Coke, Instituters *177. As support for this proposition, these commentators all rely on a single decision, Semayne's Case, 5 Co. Rep. 91a, 92b-93a. 77 Eng. Rep. 194, 198 (K.B. 1603). See 1 Chitty *57; Foster 320; 2 Hale 116. Although that case involved only the authority of a sheriff to effect civil service on a person within his own home, the court noted in dictum that a person could not "escape the ordinary process of law" by seeking refuge in the home of a third party. 5 Co.Rep., at 93a, 77 Eng. Rep., at 198. However, the language of the decision, while not free from ambiguity suggests that forcible entry into a third party's house was permissible only when the person to be arrested was pursued to the house. The decision refers to a person who "flies" to another's home, ibid., and the annotation notes that "in order to justify the breaking of the outer door; after denial on request to take a person ... in the house of a stranger, it must be understood ... that the person upon a pursuit taketh refuge in the house of another." Id., at 93a, n. (I), 77 Eng. Rep., at 198, n. (I) (emphasis in original). The common-law commentators appear to have adopted this limitation. See 1 Chitty *57 (sheriff may enter third parties' home "if the offender fly to it for refuge"); Foster 320 ("For if a Stranger whose ordinary Residence is elsewhere, upon a Pursuit taketh Refuge in the House of another, this is not his Castle, He cannot claim the Benefit of Sanctuary in it"); 2 Hale 116, n.20 (forcible entry permissible "only upon strong necessity"). We have long recognized that such "hot pursuit" cases fall within the exigent-circumstances exception the warrant requirement, see **WARDEN v. HAYDEN**, 387 U.S. 294 (1967), and therefore are distinguishable from the routine search situation presented here.

More important the general question addressed by the common-law commentators was very different from the issue presented by this case. The authorities on which the Government relies were concerned with whether the subject of the arrest warrant could claim sanctuary from arrest by hiding in the home of a third party. See 1 Chitty *57; Foster 320; 2 Hale 116-117. Thus, in Semayne's Case it was observed:

"[T}he house of any one is not a castle or privilege but for himself, and shall not extend to protect any person who flies to his house, or the goods of any other which are brought and conveyed into his house, to prevent a lawful execution, and to escape the ordinary process of law; for the privilege of his house extends only to him and his family, and to his own proper goods." 5 Co.Rep., at 93a, 77 Eng.Rep., at 128.

The common law thus recognized, as have our recent decisions, that rights such as those conferred by the Fourth Amendment are personal in nature, and cannot bestow vicarious protection on those who do not have a reasonable expectation of privacy in the place to be searched. See **UNITED STATES v. SALVUCCI**, 448 U.S. 83 (1980); **RAKAS v. ILLINOIS**, 439 U.S 128 (1978). The issue here, however, is not whether the subject of an arrest warrant can object to the absence of a search warrant when he is apprehended in another person's home, but rather whether the residents of that home can complain of the search. Because the authorities relied on by the Government focus on the former question without addressing the latter, we find their usefulness limited. Indeed, if anything, the little guidance that can be gleaned from common-law authorities undercuts the Government's position. The language of Semayne's Case quoted above, for example, suggests that although the subject of an arrest warrant could not find sanctuary in the home of the third party, the home remained a "castle or privilege" for its residents. Similarly, several commentators suggested that a search warrant, rather than an arrest warrant, was necessary to fully insulate a constable from an action for trespass brought by a party whose home was searched. See, e.g., 1 Chitty *57; 2 Hale 116-117, 151.

While the common law thus sheds relatively little light on the narrow question before us, the history of the Fourth Amendment strongly suggests that its Framers would not have sanctioned the instant search. The Fourth Amendment was intended partly to protect against the abuses of the general warrants that had occurred in England and of the writs of assistance used in the

544

Colonies.   See **PAYTON v. NEW YORK**, 445 U.S., at 608-609
(WHITE, J., dissenting); **BOYD v. UNITED STATES**, 116 U.S.
616,   624-629   (1886);   N.   Lasson,   The   History   and
Development of the Fourth Amendment to the United States
Constitution 13-78 (1937). The general warrant specified
only an offense - typically seditious libel - and left to
the discretion of the executing officials the decision as
to which persons should be arrested and which places
should be searched.   Similarly, the writs of assistance
used in the Colonies noted only the object of the search
- any uncustomed goods - and thus left customs officials
completely free to search any place where they believed
such goods might be.   The central objectionable feature
of both warrants was that they provided no judicial check
on the determination of the executing officials that the
evidence available justified an intrusion into any
particular home.   **STANFORD v. TEXAS**, 379 U.S. 476, 481-
485 (1965). An arrest warrant, to the extent that it is
invoked as authority to enter the homes of third parties,
suffers   from   the   same   infirmity.   Like   a   writ   of
assistance, it specified only the object of a search - in
this case, Ricky Lyons -and leaves to the unfettered
discretion of the police the decision as to which
particular homes should be searched.   we do not believe
that the Framers of the Fourth Amendment would have
condoned such a result.

B

    The Government also suggests that practical problems
might arise if law enforcement officers are required to
obtain a search warrant before entering the home of a
third party to made an arrest.   The basis of this concern
is that persons, as opposed to objects, are inherently
mobile, and thus officers seeking to effect an arrest may
be forced to return to the magistrate several times as
the subject of the arrest warrant moves from place to
place.   We are convinced, however, that a search warrant
requirement will not significantly impede effective law
enforcement efforts.
    First, the situation in which a search warrant will
be necessary are few.   As noted in **PAYTON v. NEW YORK**,
supra, at 602-603, an arrest warrant alone will suffice
to enter a suspect's own residence to effect his arrest.
Furthermore, if probable cause exists, no warrant is
required to apprehend a suspected felon in a public

place. **UNITED STATES v. WATSON**, 423 U.S. 411 (1976).
Thus, the subject of an arrest warrant can be readily
seized before entering or after leaving the home of a
third party. Finally, the exigent-circumstances doctrine
significantly limits the situation in which a search
warrant would be needed. For example, a warrantless
entry of a home would be justified if the police were in
"hot pursuit" of a fugitive. See **UNITED STATES v.
SANTANA**, 427 U.S 38, 42-43 (1976); **WARDEN v. HAYDEN**, 387
U.S. 294 (1967). Thus, to the extent that searches for
persons pose special problems, we believe that the
exigent-circumstances doctrine is adequate to accommodate
legitimate law enforcement needs.

Moreover, in those situations in which a search
warrant is necessary, the inconvenience incurred by the
police is simply not that significant. First, if the
police know of the location of the felon when they obtain
an arrest warrant, the additional burden of obtaining a
search warrant at the same time is minuscule. The
inconvenience of obtaining such a warrant does not
increase significantly when an outstanding arrest warrant
already exists. In this case, for example, Agent
Goodowens knew the address of the house to be searched
two days in advance, and planned the raid from the
federal courthouse in Atlanta where, we are informed,
three full-time magistrates were on duty. In routine
search cases such as this, the short time required to
obtain a search warrant from a magistrate will seldom
hinder efforts to apprehend a felon. Finally, if a
magistrate is not nearby, a telephonic search warrant can
usually be obtained. See Fed.Rule Crim. Proc. 41 (c)(1).
(2).

Whatever practical problems remain, however, cannot
out-weigh the constitutional interest at stake. Any
warrant requirement impedes to some extent the vigor with
which the Government can seek to enforce its laws, yet
the Fourth Amendment recognized that this restraint is
necessary in some cases to protect against unreasonable
searches and seizures. We conclude that this is such a
case. The additional burden imposed on the police by a
warrant requirement is minimal. In contrast, the right
protected - that of presumptively innocent people to be
secure in their homes from unjustified, forcible

intrusion by the Government - is weighty. Thus, in order to render the instant search reasonable under the Fourth Amendment, a search warrant was required.

Accordingly, the judgment of the Court of Appeals is reversed, and the case is remanded to that court for further proceedings consistent with this opinion.

So ordered.

THE CHIEF JUSTICE concurs in the judgment.

JUSTICE REHNQUIST, with whom JUSTICE WHITE joins dissenting.

The Courts opinion reversing petitioner's conviction proceeds in a pristinely simple manner: Steagald had a Fourth Amendment privacy interest in the dwelling entered by the police, and even though the police entered the premises for the sole purpose of executing a valid arrest warrant for Lyons, a fugitive from justice, whom they had probable cause to believe was within, the arrest warrant was not sufficient absent exigent circumstances to justify invading Steagald's privacy interest in the dwelling. Petitioner Steagald's privacy interest is different from Lyons' interest in being free from an unreasonable seizure, according to the Court, and the arrest warrant only validated the invasion of the latter. In the words of the Court:

> "[T]he search of petitioner's home was no more reasonable from petitioner's perspective than it would have been if conducted in the absence of any warrant. Since warrantless searches of a home are impermissible absent consent or exigent circumstances, we conclude that the instant search violated the Fourth Amendment." Ante, at 216.

This "reasoning" not only assumes the answer to the question presented - whether the search of petitioner's dwelling could be undertaken without a search warrant - but also conveniently ignores the critical fact in this case, the existence of an arrest warrant for a fugitive believed on the basis of probable cause to be in the dwelling. The Court assumes that because the arrest warrant did not specifically address petitioner's privacy interest it is of no further relevance to the case. Incidental infringements of distinct Fourth Amendment

547

interests may, however, be reasonable when they occur in the course of executing a valid warrant addressed to other interests. In **DALIA v. UNITED STATES**, 441 U.S. 238 (1979), the Court rejected the argument that a separate search warrant was required before police could enter a business office to install an eavesdropping device when a warrant authorizing the eavesdropping itself had already been obtained. As the Court put it: "This view of the Warrant Clause parses too finely the interests protected by the Fourth Amendment. Often in executing a warrant the police may find it necessary to interfere with privacy rights not explicitly considered by the judge who issued the warrant." Id., at 257 (emphasis supplied). In **PAYTON v. NEW YORK**, 445 U.S. 573 (1980), the Court rejected the suggestion that a separate search warrant was required before police could execute an arrest warrant by entering the home of the subject of the warrant. Although the subject of the warrant had a Fourth Amendment interest in the privacy of his dwelling quite distinct from the interest in being free from unreasonable seizures addressed by the arrest warrant, the Court concluded that it was "constitutionally reasonable to require him to open his doors to the officers of the law." Id., at 602-603.

This case, therefore, cannot be resolved by the simple Aristotelian syllogism which the Court employs. concluding as it does that the arrest warrant did not address the privacy interest affected by the search by no means ends the matter; it is simply presents the issue for decision. Resolution of that issue depends upon a balancing of the "need to search against the invasion which the search entails." **CAMARA v. MUNICIPAL COURT OF SAN FRANCISCO**, 387 U.S. 523, 537 (1967). Here, as in all Fourth Amendment cases, "reasonableness is still the ultimate standard." Id., at 539. See **WAMAN v. JAMES**, 400 U.S. 309, 318 (1971); **MARSHALL v. BARLOW'S INC.**, 436 U.S. 307, 315-316 (1978). In determining the reasonableness of dispensing with the requirement of a separate search warrant in this case, I believe that the existence of a valid arrest warrant is highly relevant.

The government's interest in the warrantless entry of a third-party dwelling to execute an arrest warrant are compelling. The basic problem confronting police in such situation is the inherent mobility of the fugitive. By definition, the police have probable cause to believe that the fugitive is in a dwelling which is not his home. He may stay there for a week, a day, or 10 minutes. fugitives from justice tend to be mobile, and police officers will generally have no way of knowing whether the subject of an arrest will be at the dwelling when they return from seeking a search warrant. See **UNITED STATES v. MCKINNEY**, 379 F.2d 259, 263 (CA6 1967);**STATE v. JORDAN**, 288 Ore. 391, 400-401, 605 P.2d 646, 651 (1980) (en banc). Imposition of a search warrant requirement in such circumstances will frustrate the compelling interests of the government and indeed the public in the apprehension of those subject to outstanding arrest warrants.

The Court's responses to these very real concerns are singularly unpersuasive. It first downplays them by stating that "the situation in which a search warrant will be necessary are few," ante, at 221, because no search warrant is necessary to arrest a suspect at his home and, if the suspect is at another's home, the police need only wait until he leaves, since no search warrant is needed to arrest him in a public place. Ibid. These beguiling simple answers to a serious law enforcement problem simply will not wash. Criminals who know or suspect they are subject to arrest warrants would not be likely to return to their homes, and while "[t]he police could reduce the likelihood of escape by staking out all possible exits . . . the costs of such a stakeout seem excessive in an era of rising crime and scarce police resources." **PAYTON v. NEW YORK**, supra, at 619 (WHITE, J., dissenting). The Court's ivory tower misconception of the realities of the apprehension of fugitives from justice reaches its apogee when it states: "In routine search cases such as this, the short time required to obtain a search warrant from a magistrate will seldom hinder efforts to apprehend a felon." Ante, at 222. The cases we are considering are not "routine search cases." They are cases of attempted arrest, pursuant to a warrant, when the object of the arrest may flee at any time - including the "short time" during which the police are endeavoring to obtain a search warrant.

At the same time of the interference with the Fourth Amendment privacy interests of those whose homes are entered to apprehend the felon is not nearly as significant as suggested by the Court. The arrest

549

warrant serves some of the functions a separate search warrant would. It assures the occupants that the police officer is present on official business. The arrest warrant also limits the scope of the search, specifying what the police may search for - i.e., the subject of the arrest warrant. No general search is permitted, but only a search of those areas in which the object of the search might hide. See **FISHER v. VOLZ**, 496 F.2d 333, 343 (CA3 1974); **STATE v. JORDAN**, supra, at 400-401, 605 P.2d, at 651; **UNITED STATES v. CRAVERO**, 545 F.2d 406, 421, nn. 1, 2 (CA5 1976), cert. denied, 429 U.S. 1100 and 430 U.S. 983 (1977). Indeed there may be no intrusion on the occupant's privacy at all, since if present the suspect will have the opportunity to voluntarily surrender at the door. Even if the suspect does not surrender but secretes himself within the house, the occupant can limit the search by pointing him out to the police. It is important to remember that contraband discovered during the entry and search for Lyons was in plain view, and was discovered during a "sweep search" for Lyons, not a probing of drawers or cabinets for contraband. **UNITED STATES v. GAULTNEY**, 606 F.2d 540, 544 (1979).

Because the burden on law enforcement officers to obtain a separate search warrant before entering the dwelling of a third party to execute a concededly valid arrest warrant is great, and carries with it a high possibility that the fugitive named in the arrest warrant will escape apprehension, I would conclude that the application of the traditional "reasonableness" standard of the Fourth Amendment does not require a separate search warrant in a case such as this.

This conclusion is supported by the common law as it existed at the time of the framing of the Fourth Amendment, which incorporated the standard of "reasonableness." As the Court noted last Term in Payton: "An examination of the common-law understanding of an officer's authority to arrest sheds light on the obviously relevant, if not entirely dispositive, consideration of what the Framers of the Amendment might have thought to be reasonable." 445 U.S., at 591; see also id., at 604 (WHITE, J., dissenting). The duty of the populace to aid in the apprehension of felons was well established at common law, see **ROBERTS v. UNITED STATES**,

445 U.S. 552, 557 (1980), and in light of the overriding interest in apprehension, the common law permitted officers to enter the dwelling of third parties when executing an arrest warrant. Chitty wrote that "[t]he house of a third person, if the offender fly to it for refuge, is not privileged, but may be broken open after the usual demand; for it may even be so upon civil process." 1 J. Chitty Criminal Law (*57 (hereafter Chitty). Gabbett agreed: "Neither is the house of a third person, if the offender fly to it for refuge, privileged but it may be broken open, after the usual demand; for it may be even so upon civil process." 2 J. Gabbett. Criminal Law 142 (1843) (hereafter Gabbett). Hale noted that an officer could forcibly enter the house of the subject of an arrest warrant, '[a]nd so much more may he break open the house of another person to take him, for so the sheriff may do upon a civil process." 2 M. Hale Pleas of the Crown 117 (1936) (hereafter Hale). See also M. Foster, Crown Law 320 (1762). A 17th century work on constables noted:

> "[I]t is the chief part of their office to represse fellony, and albeit to be a man's house he doth dwell in, which they doe suspect the fellon to be in, yet they may enter in there to search; and if the owner of the house, upon request, will not open his dores, it seems the officer may break open the dores upon him to come in to search." W. Sheppard, The Offices of Constables, ch. 8, § 2, no. 4 (c. 1650) (quoted in T. Taylor, Two Studies in Constitutional Interpretation 28-29 (1969)).

The leading authority, Semayne's Case, 5 Co.Rep. 91a, 93a, 77 Eng. Rep. 194, 198 (K.B. 1603), recognized that "[t]he house of any one is not a castle or privilege but for himself, and shall not extend to protect any person who flies to his house . . . to prevent a lawful execution, and to escape the ordinary process of law . . . and therefore in such cases after denial on request made, the sheriff may break the house." In **RATCLIFFE v. BURTON**, 3 Bos. & Pul. 223, 230, 127 Eng. Rep. 123, 126-127 (C.P. 1802), Judge Heath ruled that before breaking doors, officers must announce their authority, because a contrary rule "must equally hold good in cases of process upon escape, where the party has taken refuge in the house of a stranger. Shall it be said that in such case

---

the officer may break open the outer door of a stranger's house without declaring the authority under which he acts . . .?" Thus no distinction was recognized between authority to enter the suspect's home and that of a stranger. See also **COMMONWEALTH v. REYNOLDS**, 120 Mass. 190, 196-197 91876); ef. **STATE v. BROWN**, Del, 505 (1854).

The basic error in the Court's treatment of the common law is its reliance on the adage that "a man's home is his castle." Though there is undoubtedly early case support for this in the common law, it cannot be accepted as an uncritical statement of black letter law which answers all questions in this area. William Pitt, when he was Prime Minister of England, used it with telling effect in a speech on the floor of the House of Commons; but parliamentary speaking ability and analytical legal ability ought not to be equated with one another. It is clear that the privilege of the home did not extend when the King was a party, i.e., when a warrant in a criminal case had been issued. See 1 Russell 520; 2 Gabbett 141; **BURDETT v. ABBOTT**, 14 East, 1, 79, 104 Eng. Rep. 501, 531 (K.B. 1811); **COMMONWEALTH v. REYNOLDS**, supra, at 196. That a man's home may be his castle in civil cases, but not in criminal cases, was recognized as far back as the Year Books. See Y.B. 13 Ewd.IV,f.9a (quoted Burdett, supra, at 79, 104 Eng. Rep., at 531). The suggestion in the Court's opinion, ante, at 219, that "[t]he language of Semayne's Case . . . suggest that although the subject of an arrest warrant could not find sanctuary in the home of the third party, the home remained a 'castle or privilege' for its residents," is thus completely unfounded in the present context.

An officer could break into one's own home to execute an arrest warrant for the owner, and "so much more may he break open the house of another person to take him," 2 Hale 117. Entry into the house of a third party to effect arrest was considered to follow a fortiori from the accepted entry into the home of the subject of the arrest warrant himself. This was because those in the home of a third party had no protection against civil process, let alone criminal process. See 1 Chitty *57; 2 Gabbett 142; 2 Hale 117. See generally Wilgus, Arrest Without a Warrant, 22 Mich. L.. Rev. 798, 800-801 (1924). At common law the Sovereign's key -

criminal process - unlocked all doors, whether to apprehend the owner or someone else.

While I cannot subscribe to the Court's decision today. I will not falsely cry "wolf" in this dissent. The decision rests on a very special set of facts, and with a change in one or more of them it is clear that no separate search warrant would be required even under the reasoning of the Court.

On the one side Payton makes clear that an arrest warrant is all that is needed to enter the suspect's "home" to effect the arrest. 445 U.S., at 602-603. If a suspect has been living in a particular dwelling for any significant period, say a few days, it can certainly be considered his "home" for Fourth Amendment purposes, even if the premises are owned by a third party and others are living there, and even if the suspect concurrently maintains a residence elsewhere as well. In such a case the police could enter the premises with only an arrest warrant. On the other side, the more fleeting a suspect's connection with the premises, such as when he is a mere visitor, the more likely that exigent circumstances will exist justifying immediate police action without departing to obtain a search warrant. The practical damage done to effective law enforcement by today's decision, without any basis in the Constitution, may well be minimal if courts carefully consider the various congeries of facts in the actual case before them.

The genuinely unfortunate aspect of today's ruling is not that fewer fugitives will be brought to book, or fewer criminals apprehended, though both of these consequences will undoubtedly occur; the greater misfortune is the increased uncertainty imposed on police officers in the field, committing magistrates, and trial judges, who must confront variations and permutations of this factual situation on a day-to-day basis. They will, in their various capacities, have to weigh the time during which a suspect from whom there is an outstanding arrest warrant has been in the building, whether the dwelling is the suspect's home, how long he has lived there, whether he is likely to leave immediately, and a number of related and equally imponderable questions. Certainty and repose, as Justice Holmes said, may not be the destiny of man, but one might have hoped for a higher degree of certainty in this one narrow but important area of the, law than is offered by today's decision.

TEXAS v. BROWN
CERTIORARI TO THE COURT OF CRIMINAL APPEALS OF TEXAS
No. 81-419. Argued January 12, 1983 -
Decided April 19, 1983

JUSTICE REHNQUIST announced the judgment of the
Court and delivered an opinion, in which THE CHIEF
JUSTICE, JUSTICE WHITE, and JUSTICE O'CONNOR joined.

Respondent Clifford James Brown was convicted in the
District Court of Tarrant County, Tex., for possession of
heroin in violation of state law. The Texas Court of
Criminal Appeals reversed his conviction, holding that
certain evidence should have been suppressed because it
was obtained in violation of the Fourth Amendment to the
United States Constitution. 617 S.W. 2d 196. That court
rejected the State's contention that the so-called
"plain view" doctrine justified the police seizure.
Because of apparent uncertainty concerning the scope and
applicability of this doctrine, we granted certiorari,
457 U.S. 1116, and now reverse the judgment of the Court
of Criminal Appeals.
On a summer evening in June 1979, Tom Maples, an
officer of the Fort Worth police force, assisted in
setting up a routine driver's license checkpoint on East
Allen Street in that city. Shortly before midnight Maples
stopped an automobile driven by respondent Brown, who was
alone. Standing alongside the driver's window of Brown's
car, Maples asked him for his driver's license. At
roughly the same time, Maples shined his flashlight into
the car and saw Brown withdraw his right hand from his
right pants pocket. Caught between the two middle finger
of the hand was an opaque, green party balloon, knotted
about one-half inch from the tip. Brown let the balloon
fall to the seat beside his leg, and then reached across
the passenger seat and opened the glove compartment.
Because of his previous experience in arrests for
drug offenses, Maples testified that he was aware that
narcotics frequently were packaged in balloons like the
one in Brown's hand. When he saw the balloon, Maples
shifted his position in order to obtain a better view of
the interior of the glove compartment. He noticed that
it contained several small plastic vials, quantities of

loose white powder, and an open bag of party balloons. After rummaging briefly through the glove compartment, Brown told Maples that he had no driver's license in his possession. Maples then instructed him to get out of the car and stand at its rear. Brown complied, and, before following him to the rear of the car, Maples reached into the car and picked up the green balloon; there seemed to be a sort of powdery substance within the tied-off portion of the balloon.

Maples then displayed the balloon to a fellow officer who indicated that he "understood the situation." The two officers then advised Brown that he was under arrest. They also conducted an on-the-scene inventory of Brown's car, discovering several plastic bags containing a green leafy substance and a large bottle of milk sugar. These items, like the balloon, were seized by the officers. At the suppression hearing conducted by the District Court, a police department chemist testified that he had examined the substance in the balloon seized by Maples and determined that it was heroin. He also testified that narcotics frequently were packaged in ordinary party balloons.

The Court of Criminal Appeals, discussing the Fourth Amendment issue, observed that "'plain view alone is never enough to justify the warrantless seizure of evidence.'" 617 S.W. 2d, at 200 quoting **COOLIDGE v. NEW HAMPSHIRE**, 403 U.S. 443, 468 (1971) (opinion of Stewart, J., joined by Douglas, BRENNAN, and MARSHALL, JJ.) It further concluded that "Officer Maples had to know that 'incriminatory evidence was before him when he seized the balloon.'" 617 S.W. 2d, at 200 (emphasis supplied), quoting **DELAO v. STATE**, 550 S.W. 2d 289, 291 (Tex. Crim. App. 1977). On the State's petition for rehearing, three judges dissented, stating their view that "[t]he issue turns on whether an officer, relying on years of practical experience and knowledge commonly accepted, has probable cause to seize the balloon in plain view." 617 S.W. 2d, at 210.

Because the "plain view" doctrine generally is invoked in conjunction with other Fourth Amendment principles, such as those relating to warrants, probable cause, and search incident to arrest, we rehearse briefly these better understood principles of Fourth Amendment law. That Amendment secures the persons, houses, papers, and effects of the people against unreasonable searches and seizures, and requires the existence of probable

cause before a warrant shall issue. Our cases hold that
procedure by way of a warrant is preferred, although in
a wide range of diverse situations we have recognized
flexible, common-sense exceptions to this requirement.
See, e.g., **WARDEN v. HAYDEN**, 387 U.S. 294 (1967) (hot
pursuit); **UNITED STATES v. JEFFERS**, 342 U.S. 48, 51-52
(1951) (exigent circumstances); **UNITED STATES v. ROSS**,
456 U.S. 798 (1982) (automobile search); **CHIMEL v.
CALIFORNIA**, 395 U.S. 752 (1969), **UNITED STATES v.
ROBINSON**, 441 U.S. 218 (1973), and **NEW YORK v. BELTON**,
453 U.S. 454 (1981)(search of person and surrounding area
incident to arrest); **ALMEIDA-SANCHEZ v. UNITED STATES**,
413 U.S. 266 (1973)(search at border or "functional
equivalent"); **ZAP v. UNITED STATES**, 328 U.S. 624, 630
(1946) (consent). We have also held to be permissible
intrusions less severe than full-scale searches or
seizures without the necessity of a warrant. See, e.g.,
TERRY v. OHIO, 392 U.S. 1 (1968) (stop and frisk); **UNITED
STATES v. BRIGNONI-PONCE**, 422 U.S. 873 (1975) (seizure
for questioning); **DELAWARE v. PROUSE**, 440 U.S. 648 (1979)
(roadblock). One frequently mentioned "exception to the
warrant requirement," **COOLIDGE v. NEW HAMPSHIRE**, supra,
at 456, is the so-called "plain view" doctrine, relied
upon by the State in this case.

While conceding that the green balloon seized by
Officer Maples was clearly visible to him, the Court of
Criminal Appeals held that the State might not avail
itself of the "plain view" doctrine. That court said:

> "For the plain view doctrine to apply, not only
> must the officer be legitimately in a position to
> view the object, but it must be immediately
> apparent to the police that they have evidence
> before them. This 'immediately apparent' aspect is
> central to the plain view exception and is here
> relied upon by appellant. [Citation omitted.] In
> this case then, Officer Maples had to know that
> 'incriminatory evidence was before him when he
> seized the balloon.'" 617 S.W. 2d, at 200.

The Court of Criminal Appeals based its conclusion
primarily on the plurality portion of the opinion of this
Court in **COOLIDGE V. NEW HAMPSHIRE**, supra. In the

556

Coolidge plurality's view, the "plain view" doctrine permits the warrantless seizure by police of private possessions where three requirements are satisfied. First, the police officer must lawfully make an "initial intrusion" or otherwise properly be in a position from which he can view a particular area. Id., at 465-468. Second, the officer must discover incriminating evidence "inadvertently," which is to say, he may not "know in advance the location of [certain] evidence and intend to seize it," relying on the plain-view doctrine only as a pretext. Id., at 470. Finally, it must be "immediately apparent" to the police that the items they observe may be evidence of a crime, contraband, or otherwise subject to seizure. Id., at 466. While the lower courts generally have applied the Coolidge plurality's discussion of "plain view, " it has never been expressly adopted by a majority of this Court. On the contrary, the plurality's formulation was sharply criticized at the time, see, **COOLIDGE v. NEW HAMPSHIRE**, 403 U.S., at 506 (Black, J., dissenting); id., at 516-521 (White, J., dissenting). While not a binding precedent, as the considered opinion of four Members of this Court it should obviously be the point of reference for further discussion of the issue.

The Coolidge plurality observed: "it is important to keep in mind that, in the vast majority of cases, any evidence seized by the police will be in plain view, at least at the moment of seizure," simply as 'the normal concomitant of any search, legal or illegal." Id., at 465. The question whether property in plain view of the police may be seized therefore must turn on the legality of the intrusion that enables them to perceive and physically seize the property in question. The Coolidge plurality, while following this approach to "plain view," characterized it as an independent exception to the warrant requirement. At least from an analytical perspective, this description may be somewhat inaccurate. We recognized in **PAYTON v. NEW YORK**, 445 U.S. 573, 587 (1980), the well-settled rule that "objects such as weapons or contraband found in a public place may be seized by the police without a warrant. The seizure of property in plain view involves no invasion of privacy and is presumptively reasonable, assuming that there is probable cause to associate the property with criminal activity." A different situation is presented, however, when the property in open view is "situated on private premises to which access is not otherwise available for the seizing officer." Ibid, quoting **G.M. LEASING CORP v. UNITED STATES**, 429 U.S. 338, 354 (1977). as these cases indicate, "plain view" provides grounds for seizure of an item when an officer's access to an object has some prior justification under the Fourth Amendment. "Plain view" is perhaps better understood, therefore, not as an independent "exception" to the Warrant Clause, but simply as an extension of whatever the prior justification for an officer's access to an object" may be.

The principle is grounded on the recognition that when a police officer has observed an object in "plain view," the owner's remaining interests in the object are merely those of possession and ownership, see **COOLIDGE v. NEW HAMPSHIRE**, supra, at 515 (WHITE,J., dissenting). Likewise, it reflects the fact that requiring police to obtain a warrant once they have obtained a first-hand perception of contraband, stolen property, or incriminating evidence generally would be a "needless inconvenience," 403 U.S., at 468, that might involve danger to the police and public. Ibid. We have said previously that "the permissibility of a particular law enforcement practice is judged by balancing its intrusion on... Fourth Amendment interest against its promotion of legitimate governmental interests." **DELAWARE v. PROUSE**, 440 U.S., at 654. In light of the private and governmental interests just outlined, our decisions have come to reflect the rule that if, while lawfully engaged in an activity in a particular place, police officers perceive a suspicious object , they may seize it immediately. See **MARRON v. UNITED STATES**, 275 u.s. 192 (1927); **GO-BART IMPORTING CO. v. UNITED STATES**, 282 U.S. 344, 358 (1931); **UNITED STATES v. LEFKOWITZ**, 285 U.S. 452, 465 (1932); **HARRIS v. UNITED STATES**, 390 U.S. 234, 236 (1968); **FRAZIER v. CUPP**, 394 U.S. 731 (1969). This rule merely reflects an application of the Fourth Amendment's central requirement of reasonableness to the law governing seizures of property.

Applying these principles, we conclude that Officer Maples properly seized the green balloon from Brown's automobile. The Court of Criminal Appeals stated that it did not "question ... the validity of the officer's initial stop of appellant's vehicle as a part of a license check." 617 S.W. 2d, at 200, and we agree. **DELAWARE v. PROUSE**, supra, at 654-655. It is likewise beyond dispute that Maples' action in shining his flashlight to illuminate the interior of Brown's car trenched upon no right secured to the latter by the Fourth Amendment. The Court said in **UNITED STATES v. LEE**, 274 U.S. 559, 563 (1927): "[The] use of a searchlight is comparable to the use of a marine glass or a field glass. It is not prohibited by the Constitution." Numerous other courts have agreed that the use of artificial means to illuminate a darkened area simply does not constitute a search, and thus triggers no Fourth Amendment protection.

Likewise, the fact that Maples "changed [his] position" and "bent down at an angle so [he] could see what was inside " Brown's car, App. 16, is irrelevant to Fourth Amendment analysis. The general public could peer into the interior of Brown's automobile from any number of angles; there is no reason Maples should be precluded from observing as an officer what would be entirely visible to him as a private citizen. There is no legitimate expectation of privacy, **KATZ v. UNITED STATES**, 389 U.S. 347, 361 (1967) (Harlan, J., concurring); **SMITH v. MARYLAND**, 442 U.S. 735, 739-745 (1979), shielding that portion of the interior of an automobile which may be viewed from outside the vehicle by either inquisitive passerby or diligent police officers. In short, the conduct that enabled Maples to observe the interior of Brown's car and of his open glove compartment was not a search within the meaning of the Fourth Amendment.

Thus there can be no dispute here as to the presence of the first of the three requirements held necessary by the Coolidge plurality to invoke the "plain view" doctrine. But the Court of Criminal Appeals, as we have noted, felt the State's case ran aground on the requirement that the incriminating nature of the items be "immediately apparent" to the police officer. To the Court of Criminal Appeals, this apparently meant that the officer must be possessed of near certainty as to the sizable nature of the items. Decisions by this Court since Coolidge indicate that the use of the phrase "immediately apparent" was very likely an unhappy choice of words, since it can be taken to imply that an unduly high degree of certainty as to the incriminatory character of evidence is necessary for an application of the "plain view" doctrine.

In **COLORADO v. BANNISTER**, 449 U.S. 1, 3-4 (1980), we applied what was in substance the plain-view doctrine to an officer's seizure of evidence from an automobile. Id., at 4, n.4. The officer noticed that the occupants of the automobile matched a description of persons suspected of a theft and that auto parts in the open glove compartment of the car similarly resembled ones reported stolen. The Court held that these facts supplied the officer with "probable cause," id., at 4, and therefore, that he could seize the incriminating items from the car without a warrant. Plainly, the Court did not view the "immediately apparent" language of Coolidge as establishing any requirement that a police officer "know" that certain items are contraband or evidence of a crime. Indeed, **COLORADO v. BANNISTER**, supra, was merely an application of the rule, set forth in **PAYTON v. NEW YORK**, 445 U.S. 573 (1980), that "[t]he seizure of property in plain view involves no invasion of privacy and is presumptively reasonable, assuming that there is probable cause to associate the property with criminal activity." Id., at 587 (emphasis added). We think this statement of the rule from Payton, supra, requiring probable cause for seizure in the ordinary case, is consistent with the Fourth Amendment and we reaffirm it here.

As the Court frequently remarked, probable cause is a flexible, common-sense standard. It merely requires that the facts available to the officer would 'warrant a man of reasonable caution in the belief," **CARROLL v. UNITED STATES**, 267 U.S. 132, 162 (1925), that certain items may be contraband or stolen property or useful as evidence of a crime; it does not demand any showing that such a belief be correct or more likely true than false. A "practical, nontechnical" probability that incriminating evidence is involved is all that is required. **BRINEGAR v. UNITED STATES**, 338 U.S 160, 176 (1949). Moreover, our observation in **UNITED STATES v. CORTEZ**, 449 U.S. 411, 418 (1981), regarding "particularized suspicion," is equally applicable to the probable-cause requirement:

"The process does not deal with hard certainties, but with probabilities. Long before the law of probabilities was articulated as such, practical people formulated certain common-sense conclusions about human behavior; jurors as fact finders are permitted to do the same - and so are law enforcement officers. Finally, the evidence thus collected must be seen and weighed not in terms of library analysis by scholars, but as understood by those versed in the field of law enforcement."

With these considerations in mind it is plain that Officer Maples possessed probable cause to believe that the balloon in Brown's hand contained an illicit substance. Maples testified that he was aware, both from his participation in previous narcotics arrests and from discussions with other officers, that balloons tied in the manner of the one possessed by Brown were frequently used to carry narcotics. This testimony was corroborated by that of a police department chemist who noted that it was "common" for balloons to be used in packaging narcotics. In addition, maples was able to observe the contents of the glove compartment of Brown's car, which revealed further suggestions that Brown was engaged in activities that might involve possession of illicit substances. The fact that Maples could not see throughout the opaque fabric of the balloon is all but irrelevant: the distinctive character of the balloon itself spoke volumes as to its contents - particularly to the trained eye of the officer.

In addition to its statement that for seizure of objects in plain view to be justified the basis upon which they might be seized had to be "immediately apparent," and the requirement that the initial intrusion be lawful, both of which requirements we hold were satisfied here, the Coolidge plurality also stated that the police must discover incriminating evidence "inadvertently," which is to say, they may not "know in advance the location of [certain] evidence and intend to seize it," relying on the plain-view doctrine only as a pretense. 430 U.S., at 470. Whatever may be the final disposition of the "inadvertence" element of "plain view," it clearly was no bar to the seizure here. The circumstances of this meeting between Maples and Brown give no suggestion that the roadblock was a pretext whereby evidence of narcotics violation might be uncovered in "plain view" in the course of a check for driver's licenses. Here, although the officers no doubt had an expectation that some of the cars they halted on

East Allen Street - which was part of a "medium" area of narcotics traffic, App. 33 - would contain narcotics or paraphernalia, there is no indication in the record that they had anything beyond this generalized expectation. Likewise, there is no indication that Maples had any reason to believe that any particular object would be in Brown's glove compartment or elsewhere in his automobile. The "inadvertence" requirement of "plain view," properly understood, was no bar to the seizure her.

Maples lawfully viewed the green balloon in the interior of Brown's car, and had probable cause to believe that it was subject to seizure under the Fourth Amendment. The judgment of the Texas Court of Criminal Appeals is accordingly reversed, and the case is remanded for further proceedings.

It is so ordered.

JUSTICE WHITE, concurring.
While joining JUSTICE REHNQUIST'S plurality opinion, I continue to disagree with the view of four Justices in **COOLIDGE v. NEW HAMPSHIRE**, 403 U.S. 433, 469 (1971), that plain-view seizures are valid only if the viewing is "inadvertent." Nor does the Court purport to endorse that views in its opinion today.

JUSTICE POWELL, with whom JUSTICE BLACKMUN joins concurring in the judgment.
I concur in the judgment, and also agree with much of the plurality's opinion relating to the application in this case of the plain-view exception to the Warrant Clause. But I do not join the plurality's opinion because it goes well beyond the application of the exception. As I read the opinion, it appears to accord less significance to the Warrant Clause of the Fourth Amendment that is justified by the language and purpose of that Amendment. In dissent in **UNITED STATES v. RABINOWITZ**, 339 U.S. 56 (1950), Justice Frankfurter wrote eloquently:

"One cannot wrench 'unreasonable searches' from the text and context and historic content of the Fourth Amendment ... When [that] Amendment outlawed

562

'unreasonable searches' and then went on to define the very restricted authority that even a search warrant issued by a magistrate could give, the framers said with all the clarity of the gloss of history that a search is 'unreasonable' unless a warrant authorized it, barring only exceptions justified by absolute necessity." Id., at 70.

To be sure, the opinions of this Court in Warrant Clause cases have not always been consistent. They have reflected disagreement among Justices as to the extent to which the Clause defines the reasonableness standard of the Amendment. In one of my earliest opinions, **UNITED STATES v. UNITED STATES DISTRICT COURT**, 407 U.S. 297 (1972), I cited Justice Frankfurter's Rabinowitz dissent in emphasizing the importance of the Warrant Clause. 407 U.S., at 316. Although I would not say that exceptions can be justified only by "absolute necessity," I stated that they were "few in number and carefully delineated." Id., at 318. This has continued to be my view,as expressed recently in **ARKANSAS v. SANDERS**, 442 U.S. 753, 759 (1979). It is a view frequently repeated by this Court. See, e.g., **UNITED STATES v. ROSS**, 456 U.S. 798, 825 (1982); **MINCEY v. ARIZONA**, 437 U.S. 385, 390 (1978) (unanimous decision); **VALE v. LOUISIANA**, 399 U.S. 30, 34 (1970); **KATZ v. UNITED STATES**, 389 U.S. 347, 357 (1967); **CAMARA v. MUNICIPAL COURT**, 387 U.S. 523, 528-529 (1967); **JONES v. UNITED STATES,**357 U.S. 493, 499 (1958).

This case involves an application of the plain-view exception, first addressed at some length by the plurality portion of the opinion in **COOLIDGE v. NEW HAMPSHIRE**, 403 U.S. 443 (1971). The plurality today states that this opinion "has never been expressly adopted by a majority of this Court." Ante, at 737. Whatever my view might have been when Coolidge was decided, I see no reason at this late date to imply criticism of its articulation of this exception. It has been accepted generally for over a decade. Moreover, it seems unnecessary to cast doubt on Coolidge in this case. Its plurality formulation is dispositive of the questions before us.

Respondent Brown does not dispute that Officer Maples' initial intrusion was lawful. Brown also concedes that the discovery of the tied-off balloon was inadvertent in that it was observed in the course of a lawful inspection of the front seat area of the automobile. If probable cause must be shown, as the Payton dicta suggest, see **PAYTON v. NEW YORK**, 445 U.S. 573, 587 (1980), I think it is clear that it existed here. Officer Maples testified that he previously had made an arrest in a case where narcotics were carried in tied-off balloons similar to the one at issue here. Other officers had told him of such cases. Even if it were not generally known that a balloon is a common container for carrying illegal narcotics, we have recognized that a law enforcement officer may rely on his training and experience to draw inferences and make deduction that might well elude an untrained person. **UNITED STATES v. CORTEZ**, 449 U.S. 411, 418 (1981). We are not advised of any innocent item that is commonly carried in an inflated, tied-off balloons such as the one Officer Maples seized.

Accordingly, I concur in the judgment as it is consistent with principles established by our prior decisions.

JUSTICE STEVENS, with whom JUSTICE BRENNAN and JUSTICE MARSHALL join, concurring in the judgment.

The Texas Court of Criminal Appeals held that the warrantless seizure of respondent's balloon could not be justified under the plain-view doctrine because incriminating evidence was not immediately apparent. This Court reverses, holding that even though the contents of the balloon were not visible to the officer, incriminating evidence was immediately apparent because he had probable cause to believe the balloon contained an illicit substance. I agree with the Court that contraband need not be visible in order for a plain-view seizure to be justified. I therefore concur in the conclusion that the Texas Court interpreted the Fourth Amendment more strictly than is required.

The plurality's explanation of our disposition of this case is, however, incomplete. It gives inadequate consideration to our cases holding that a closed container may not be opened without a warrant, even when the container is in plain view and the officer has probable cause to believe contraband is concealed within. **UNITED STATES v. CHADWICK**, 433 U.S. 1 (1977); **ARKANSAS v.**

SANDERS, 442 U.S. 753 (1979); **UNITED STATES v. ROSS**, 456 U.S. 798, 811-812 (1982). Final determination of whether the trial court properly denied the suppression motion requires a more complete understanding of the plain-view doctrine, as well as the answer to a factual inquiry that remains open to the state court on remand.

Although our Fourth Amendment cases sometimes refer indiscriminately to searches and seizures, there are important differences between the two that are relevant to the plain-view doctrine. The Amendment protects two different interests of the citizen - the interest in retaining possession of property and the interest in maintaining personal privacy. A seizure threatens the former, a search the latter. As a matter of timing, a seizure is usually preceded by a search, but when a container is involved the converse is often true. Significantly, the two protected interests are not always present to the same extent; for example, the seizure of a locked suitcase does not necessarily compromise the secrecy of its contents, and the search of a stopped vehicle does not necessarily deprive its owner of possession.

An object may be considered to be "in plain view" if it can be seized without compromising any interest in privacy. Since seizure of such an object threatens only the interest in possession, circumstances diminishing that interest may justify exceptions to the Fourth Amendment's usual requirements. Thus, if an item has been abandoned, neither Fourth Amendment interest is implicated, and neither probable cause nor a warrant is necessary to justify seizure. See, e.g., **ABEL v. UNITED STATES**, 362 U.S. 217, 241 (1960); cf. **UNITED STATES v. LISK**, 522 F.2d 228, 230 (CA7 1975). And if an officer has probable cause to believe that a publicly situated item is associated with criminal activity, the interest in possession is outweighed by the risk that such an item might disappear or be put to its intended use before a warrant could be obtained. The officer may therefore seize it without a warrant. See **G.M. LEASING CORP. v. UNITED STATES**, 429 U.S. 338, 354 (1975); **PAYTON v. NEW YORK**, 445 U.S. 573, 587 (1980). The "plain view" exception to the warrant requirement is easy to understand and to apply in cases in which no search is made and no intrusion on privacy occurs.

The Court's more difficult plain-view cases, however, have regularly arisen in two contexts that link the seizure with a prior or subsequent search. The first is the situation in which an officer who is executing a valid search for one item seizes a different item. The Court has been sensitive to the danger inherent in such a situation that officers will enlarge a specific authorization, furnished by a warrant or an exigency, into the equivalent of a general warrant to rummage and seize at will. That danger is averted by strict attention to two of the core requirements of plain view: seizing the item must entail no significant additional invasion of privacy, and at the time of seizure the officer must have probable cause to connect the item with criminal behavior. See **UNITED STATES v. LEFKOWITZ** 285 U.S. 452, 465 (1932); cf. **COOLIDGE v. NEW HAMPSHIRE**, 403 U.S. 443, 465-466 (1971).

The second familiar context is the situation in which an officer comes upon a container in plain view and wants both to seize it and to examine its contents. In recent years, the Court has spoken at some length about the latter act, e.g., Ross, supra; Chadwick, supra; Sanders, supra, emphasizing the Fourth Amendment privacy values implicated whenever a container is opened. In this case, however, both the search of a container (the balloon) and the antecedent seizure are open to challenge. In that regard, it more closely resembles Coolidge, supra. All of these cases, however, demonstrate that the constitutionality of a container search is not automatically determined by the constitutionality of the prior seizure. See Chadwick, 433 U.S., at 13-14, n. 8; Sanders, 442 U.S., at 761-762. Separate inquires are necessary, taking into account the separate interests at stake.

If a movable container is in plain view, seizure does not implicate any privacy interests. Therefore, if there is probable cause to believe it contains contraband, the owner's possessory interest in the container yield to society's interest in making sure that the contraband does not vanish during the time it would take to obtain a warrant. The item may be seized temporarily. It does not follow, however, that the container may be opened on the spot. Once the container is in custody, there is no risk that evidence will be destroyed. Some inconvenience to the officer is entailed

566

by requiring him to obtain a warrant before opening the container, but that alone does not excuse the duty to go before a neutral magistrate.**JOHNSON v. UNITED STATES**, 333 U.S. 10, 15 (1948); **McDONALD v. UNITED STATES**, 335 U.S. 451, 455 (1948). As JUSTICE POWELL emphasizes, ante, at 744-745, the Warrant Clause embodies our government's historical commitment to bear the burden of inconvenience. Exigent circumstances must be shown before the Constitution will entrust and individual's privacy to the judgment of a single police officer.

In this case, I have no doubt concerning the propriety of the officer's warrantless seizure of the balloon. For the reasons stated by JUSTICE POWELL and REHNQUIST, I agree that the police officer invaded no privacy interest in order to see the balloon, and that when he saw it he had probable cause to believe it contained drugs. But before the balloon's contents could be used as evidence against the respondent, the State also had to justify opening it without a warrant. I can perceive two potential justifications. First, it is entirely possible that what the officer saw in the car's glove compartment coupled with his observation of respondent and the contents of his pockets, provided probable cause to believe that contraband was located somewhere in the car - and not merely in the one balloon at issue. If so, then under **UNITED STATES v. ROSS**, 456 U.S. 7998 (1982), which was not decided until after the Texas Court of Criminal Appeals reviewed this case, it was permissible to examine the contents of any container in the car, including this balloon.

Alternatively, the balloon could be one of those rare single purpose containers which " by their very nature cannot support any reasonable expectation of privacy because their contents can be inferred from their outward appearance." Sanders, supra, at 764-765, n. 13. Whereas a suitcase or a paper bag may contain an almost infinite variety of items, a balloon of this kind might be used only to transport drugs. Viewing it where he did could have given the officer a degree of certainty that is equivalent to the plain view of the heroin itself. If that be true, I would conclude that the plain-view doctrine supports the search as well as the seizure even though the contents of the balloon were not actually visible to the officer.

This reasoning leads me to the conclusion that the Fourth Amendment would not require exclusion of the balloon's contents in this case if, but only if, there was probable cause to search the entire vehicle or there was virtual certainty that the balloon contained a controlled substance. Neither of these fact-bound inquires was made by the Texas courts, and neither should be made by this Court in the first instance. Moreover, it may be that on remand the Texas Court of Criminal Appeals will find those inquiries unnecessary because the respondent may have waived his right to demand them. See n. 3, supra. I therefore concur in the judgment.

HORTON v. CALIFORNIA
495 U.S 128, 110 S.Ct. 2301, 110 L.Ed.2d 112, (1990)
CERTIORARI TO THE COURT OF APPEAL OF CALIFORNIA,
SIXTH APPELLATE DISTRICT
No. 88-7164. Argued February 21,1990.
Decided June 4, 1990.

STEVENS, J., delivered the opinion of the Court, in which
REHNQUIST, C.J., and WHITE, BLACKMUN, O'CONNOR, SCALIA,
and KENNEDY, JJ., joined. BRENNAN, J., filed a
dissenting opinion, in which MARSHALL, J., joined.

JUSTICE STEVENS delivered the opinion of the Court.

In this case we revisit an issue that was
considered, but not conclusively resolved, in **COOLIDGE v.
NEW HAMPSHIRE**, 403 U.S. 443 (1971): Whether the
warrantless seizure of evidence of crime in plain view is
prohibited by the Fourth Amendment if the discovery of
the evidence was not inadvertent. We conclude that even
though inadvertence is a characteristic of most
legitimate "plain-view" seizures, it is not a necessary
condition.

I

Petitioner was convicted of the armed robbery of
Erwin Wallaker, the treasurer of the San Jose Coin Club.
When Wallaker returned to his home after the Club's
annual show, he entered his garage and was accosted by
two masked men, one armed with a machine gun and the
other with an electrical shocking device, sometimes
referred to as a "stun gun." The two men shocked
Wallaker, bound and handcuffed him, and robbed him of
jewelry and cash. During the encounter sufficient
conversation took place to enable Wallaker subsequently
to identify petitioner's distinctive voice. His
identification was partially corroborated by a witness
who saw the robbers leaving the scene and by evidence
that petitioner had attended the coin show.
Sergeant LaRault, an experienced police officer,
investigated the crime and determined that there was
probable cause to search petitioner's home for the
proceeds of the robbery and for the weapons used by the
robbers. His affidavit for a search warrant referred to
police reports that described the weapons as well as the
proceeds, but the warrant issued by the Magistrate only

authorized a search for the proceeds, including three
specifically described rings.

Pursuant to the warrant, LaRault searched
petitioner's residence, but he did not find the stolen
property. During the course of the search, however, he
discovered the weapons in plain view and seized them.
Specifically, he seized an Uzi machine gun, a .38-caliber
revolver, two stun guns, a handcuff key, a San Jose Coin
Club advertising brochure, and a few items of clothing
identified by the victim. LaRault testified that while he
was searching for the rings, he also was interested in
finding other evidence connecting petitioner to the
robbery. Thus, the seized evidence was not discovered
"inadvertently."

The trial court refused to suppress the evidence
found in petitioner's home and, after a jury trial,
petitioner was found guilty and sentenced to prison. The
California Court of Appeal affirmed. App. 43. It rejected
petitioner's argument that our decision in Coolidge
required suppression of the seized evidence that had not
been listed in the warrant because its discovery was not
inadvertent. App. 52-53. The court relied on the
California Supreme Court's decision in **NORTH v. SUPERIOR
COURT**, 8 Cal. 3d301, 502P.2d.1305 (1972). In that case
the court noted that the discussion of the inadvertence
limitation on the "plain-view" doctrine in Justice
Stewart's opinion in Coolidge had been joined by only
three other Members of this Court and therefore was not
binding on it. The California Supreme Court denied
petitioner's request for review. App 78.

Because the California courts' interpretation of the
"plain-view" doctrine conflicts with the view of other
courts, and because the unresolved issue is important, we
granted certiorari, 493 U.S. 889 (1989).

II

The Fourth Amendment provides:

"The right of the people to be secure in their
persons, houses, papers, and effects, against
unreasonable searches and seizures, shall not
be violated, and no Warrants shall issue, but

upon probable cause, supported by Oath or affirmation, and particularly describing the place to be searched, and the persons or things to be seized."

The right to security in person and property protected by the Fourth Amendment may be invaded in quite different ways by searches and seizures. A search compromises the individual interest in privacy; a seizure deprives the individual of dominion over his or her person or property. **UNITED STATES v. JACOBSEN**, 466 U.S. 109, 113 (1984). The "plain-view" doctrine is often considered an exception to the general rule that warrantless searches are presumptively unreasonable, but this characterization overlooks the important difference between searches and seizures. If an article is already in plain view, neither its observation nor its seizure would involve any invasion of privacy. **ARIZONA v. HICKS**, 480 U.S. 321, 325 (1987); **ILLINOIS v. ANDREAS**, 463 U.S. 765, 771 (1983). A seizure of the article, however, would obviously invade the owner's possessory interest. **MARYLAND v. MACON**, 472 U.S. 463, 469 (1985); **JACOBSEN**, 466 U.S., at 113. If "plain view" justifies an exception from an otherwise applicable warrant requirement, therefore, it must be an exception that is addressed to the concerns that are implicated by seizures rather than by searches.

The criteria that generally guide " plain-view" seizures were set forth in **COOLIDGE v. NEW HAMPSHIRE**, 403 U.S. 443 (1971). The Court held that the police, in seizing two automobiles parked in plain view on the defendant's driveway in the course of arresting the defendant, violated the Fourth Amendment. Accordingly, particles of gun powder that had been subsequently found in vacuum sweepings from one of the cars could not be introduced in evidence against the defendant. The State endeavored to justify the seizure of the automobiles, and their subsequent search at the police station, on four different grounds, including the "plain-view" doctrine. The scope of that doctrine as it had developed in earlier cases was fairly summarized in these three paragraphs from Justice Stewart's opinion:

"It is well established that under certain circumstances the police may seize evidence in plain view with out a warrant. But it is important

571

to keep in mind that, in the vast majority of cases, any evidence seized by the police will be in plain view, at least at the moment of seizure. The problem with the 'plain-view'doctrine has been to identify the circumstances in which plain view has legal significance rather than being simply the normal concomitant of any search, legal or illegal. "An example of the applicablilty of the 'plain-view' doctrine is the situation in which the police have a warrant to search a given area for specified objects, and in the course of the search come across some other article of incriminating character. Cf. **GO-BART IMPORTING CO. v. UNITED STATES**, 282 U.S. 344,358 [(1931)]; **UNITED STATES v. LEFKOWITZ**, 285 U.S. 452, 465 [(1932)]; **STEELE v. UNITED STATES**, 267 U.S. [(1925)]; **STANLEY v. GEORGIA**, 394 U.S. 557, 571 [(1969)] (Stewart, J., concurring in result). Where the initial intrusion that brings the police within plain view of such an article is supported, not by a warrant, but by one of the recognized exceptions to the warrant requirement, the seizure is also legitimate. Thus the police may inadvertently come across evidence while in 'hot pursuit' of a fleeing suspect. **WARDEN v. HAYDEN**, [387 U.S. 294 (1967)]; cf. **HESTER v. UNITED STATES**, 265 U.S. 57 [(1924)]. And an object that comes into view during a search incident to arrest that is appropriately limited in scope under existing law may be seized without a warrant. **CHIMEL v. CALIFORNIA**, 395 U.S. [752,] 762-763 [(1969)]. Finally, the 'plain-view' doctrine has been applied where a police officer is not searching for evidence against the accused, but nonetheless inadvertently comes across an incriminating object. **HARRIS v. UNITED STATES**, 390 U.S. 234 [(1968)]; **FRAZIER v. CUPP**, 394 U.S. 731 [(1969)]; **KER v. CALIFORNIA**, 374 U.S. [23,] 43 [(1963)]. Cf. **LEWIS v. UNITED STATES**, 385 U.S. 206 [(1966)].

"What the 'plain-view' cases have in common is that the police officer in each of them had a prior justification for an intrusion in the course of which he came inadvertently across a piece of

572

evidence incriminating the accused. The doctrine serves to supplement the prior justification - whether it be a warrant for another object, hot pursuit, search incident to lawful arrest, or some other legitimate reason for being present unconnected with a search directed against the accused - and permits the warrantless seizure. Of course, the extension of the original justification is legitimate only where it is immediately apparent to the police that they have evidence before them; the 'plain-view' doctrine may not be used to extend a general exploratory search from one object to another until something incriminating at last emerges."

Justice Stewart then described the two limitations on the doctrine that he found implicit in its rationale: First, that "plain view alone is never enough to justify the warrantless seizure of evidence," id., at 468; and second, that "the discovery of evidence in plain view must be inadvertent." id., at 469.

Justice Stewart's analysis of the "plain-view" doctrine did not command a majority, and a plurality of the Court has since made clear that the discussion is "not a binding precedent." **TEXAS v. BROWN**, 460 U.S. 730,737 (1983)(opinion of REHNQUIST, J.). Justice Harlan, who concurred in the Court's judgment and in its response to the dissenting opinions, 403 U.S., at 473-484, 490-493, did not join the plurality's discussion of the 'plain-view' doctrine. See id., at 464-473. The decision nonetheless is a binding precedent. Before discussing the second limitation, which is implicated in this case, it is therefore necessary to explain why the first adequately supports the Court's judgment.

It is, of course, an essential predicate to any valid warrantless seizure of incriminating evidence that the officer did not violate the Fourth Amendment in arriving at the place from which the evidence could be plainly viewed. There are, moreover, two additional conditions that must be satisfied to justify the warrantless seizure. First, not only must the item be in plain view; its incriminating character must also be "immediately apparent." Id., at 466; see also **ARIZONA v. HICKS**, 480 U.S., at 326-327. Thus, in Coolidge, the cars were obviously in plain view, but their probative value remained uncertain until after the interiors were swept

573

and examined microscopically. Second, not only must the officer be lawfully located in a place from which the object can be plainly seen, but he or she must also have a lawful right of access to the object itself. As the United States has suggested, Justice Harlan's vote in Coolidge may have rested on the fact that the seizure of the cars was accomplished by means of a warrantless trespass on the defendant's property. In all events, we are satisfied that the absence of inadvertence was not essential to the Court's rejection of the State's "plain-view" argument in Coolidge.

III

Justice Stewart concluded that the inadvertence requirement was necessary to avoid a violation of the express constitutional requirement that a valid warrant must particularly describe the things to be seized. He explained:

> "The rationale of the exception to the warrant requirement, as just stated, is that a plain-view seizure will not turn an initially valid (and therefore limited) search into a 'general' one, while the inconvenience of procuring a warrant to cover an inadvertent discovery is great. But where the discovery is anticipated, where the police know in advance the location of the evidence and intend to seize it, the situation is altogether different. The requirement of warrant to seize imposes no inconvenience whatever, or at least none which is constitutionally cognizable in a legal system that regards warrantless searches as 'per se unreasonable' in the absence of 'exigent circumstances.'
> "If the initial intrusion is bottomed upon a warrant that fails to mention a particular object, though the police know its location and intend to seize it, then there is a violation of the express constitutional requirement of 'Warrants ... particularly describing ... [the] things to be seized.'" 403 U.S., at 469-471.

We find two flaws in this reasoning. First, evenhanded law enforcement is best achieved by the application of objective standards of conduct, rather that standards that depend upon the subjective state of mind of the officer. The fact that an officer is interested in an item of evidence and fully expects to find it in the course of a search should not invalidate its seizure if the search is confined in area and duration by the terms of a warrant or a valid exception to the warrant requirement. If the officer has knowledge approaching certainly that the item will be found, we see no reason why he or she would deliberately omit a particular description of the item to be seized from the application for a search warrant. Specification of the additional item could only permit the officers to expand the scope of the search. On the other hand, if he or she has a valid warrant to search for one item and merely a suspicion concerning the second, whether or not it amounts to probable cause, we fail to see why that suspicion should immunize the second item from seizure if it is found during a lawful search for the first. The hypothetical case put by JUSTICE WHITE in his concurring and dissenting opinion in Coolidge is instructive:

> "Let us suppose officers secure a warrant to search a house for a rifle. While staying well within the range of a rifle search, they discover two photographs of the murder victim, both in plain sight in the bedroom. Assume also that the discovery of the one photograph was inadvertent but finding the other was anticipated. The Court would permit the seizure of only one of the photographs. But in terms of the 'minor' peril to Fourth Amendment values there is surely no difference between these two photographs: the interference with possession is the same in each case and the officers' appraisal of the photograph they expected to see is no less reliable than their judgment about the other. And in both situations the actual inconvenience and danger to evidence remain identical if the officers must depart and secure a warrant." Id., at 516.

Second, the suggestion that the inadvertence requirement is necessary to prevent the police from conducting general searches, or from converting specific warrants

575

into general warrants, is not persuasive because that
interest is already served by the requirements that no
warrant issue unless it " particularly describ[es] the
place to be searched and the persons or things to be
seized," see **MARYLAND v. GARRISON,** 480 U.S. 79, 84
(1987); **STEELE v. UNITED STATES** No. 1, 267 U.S. 498, 503
(1925), and that a warrantless search be circumscribed by
the exigencies which justify its initiation. See, e.g.,
MARYLAND v. BUIE, 494 U.S. 325, 332-334 (1990); **MINCEY v.
ARIZONA,** 437 U.S. 385, 393 (1978). Scrupulous adherence
to these requirements serves the interests in limiting
the area and duration of the search that inadvertence
requirement inadequately protects. Once those commands
have been satisfied and the officer has a lawful right of
access, however, no additional Fourth Amendment interest
is furthered by requiring that discovery of evidence be
inadvertent. If the scope of the search exceeds that
permitted by the terms of a validly issued warrant or the
character of the relevant exception from the warrant
requirement, the subsequent seizure is unconstitutional
without more. Thus, in the case of a search incident to
a lawful arrest, "[i]f the police stray outside the scope
of an authorized Chimel search they are already in
violation of the Fourth Amendment, and evidence so seized
will be excluded; adding a second reason for excluding
evidence hardly seems worth the candle." Coolidge, 403
U.S., at 517 (WHITE, J., concurring and dissenting).
Similarly, the object of a warrantless search of an
automobile also defines its scope:

> " The scope of a warrantless search of an
> automobile thus is not defined by the nature of the
> container in which the contraband is secreted.
> Rather, it is defined by the object of the search
> and the places in which there is probable cause to
> believe that it may be found. Just as probable
> cause to believe that a stolen lawn mower may be
> found in a garage will not support a warrant to
> search an upstairs bedroom, probable cause to
> believe that undocumented aliens are being
> transported in a van will not justify a warrantless
> search of a suitcase. Probable cause to believe
> that a container placed in the trunk of a taxi

576

contains contraband or evidence does not justify a search of the entire cab." **UNITED STATES v. ROSS**, 456 U.S. 798, 824 (1982).

In this case, the scope of the search was not enlarged in the slightest by the omission of any reference to the weapons in the warrant. Indeed, if the three rings and other items named in the warrant had been found at the outset - or if petitioner had them in his possession and had responded to the warrant by producing them immediately - no search for weapons could have taken place. Again, JUSTICE WHITE's concurring and dissenting opinion in Coolidge is instructive:

> "Police with a warrant for a rifle may search only places where rifles might be and must terminate the search once the rifle is found; the inadvertence rule will in no way reduce the number of places into which they may lawfully look." 403 U.S., at 517.

As we have already suggested, by hypothesis the seizure of an object in plain view does not involve an intrusion on privacy. If the interest in privacy has been invaded, the violation must have occurred before the object came into plain view and there is no need for an inadvertence limitation on seizures to condemn it. The prohibition against general searches and general warrants serves primarily as a protection against unjustified intrusions on privacy. But reliance on privacy concerns that support that prohibition is misplaced when the inquiry concerns the scope of an exception that merely authorizes an officer with a lawful right of access to an item to seize it without a warrant.

In this case the items seized from petitioner's home were discovered during a lawful search authorized by a valid warrant. When they were discovered, it was immediately apparent to the officer that they constituted incriminating evidence. He had probable cause, not only to obtain a warrant to search for the stolen property, but also to believe that the weapons and handguns had been used in the crime he was investigating. The search was authorized by the warrant; the seizure was authorized by the "plain-view" doctrine. The judgment is affirmed.

It is so ordered.

577

JUSTICE BRENNAN, with whom JUSTICE MARSHALL joins, dissenting.

I remain convinced that Justice Stewart correctly articulated the plain view doctrine in **COOLIDGE v. NEW HAMPSHIRE**, 403 U.S. 443 (1971). The Fourth Amendment permits law enforcement officers to seize items for which they do not have a warrant when those items are found in plain view and (1) the officers are lawfully in a position to observe the items, (2) the discovery of the items is "inadvertent", and (3) it is immediately apparent to the officers that the items are evidence of a crime, contraband, or otherwise subject to seizure. In eschewing the inadvertent discovery requirement, the majority ignores the Fourth Amendment's express command that warrants particularly describe no only the places to be searched, but also the things to be seized. I respectfully dissent from this rewriting of the Fourth Amendment.

I

The Fourth Amendment states:

"The right of the people to be secure in their persons, houses, papers, and effects, against unreasonable searches and seizures, shall not be violated, and no Warrants shall issue, but upon probable cause, supported by Oath or affirmation, and particularly describing the place to be searched, and the persons or things to be seized."

The Amendment protects two distinct interests. The prohibition against unreasonable searches and the requirement that a warrant "particularly describ[e] the place to be searched" protect an interest in privacy. The prohibition against unreasonable seizures and the requirement that a warrant "particularly describ[e] ... the ... things to be seized" protect a possessory interest in property. See ante, at 133; **TEXAS v. BROWN**, 460 U.S. 730, 747 (1983) (STEVENS, J., concurring in judgment). The Fourth Amendment, by its terms, declares the privacy and possessory interests to be equally

578

important. As this Court recently stated: "Although the interest protected by the Fourth Amendment injunction against unreasonable searches is quite different from that protected by its injunction against unreasonable seizures, neither the one nor the other is of inferior worth or necessarily requires only lesser protection." **ARIZONA v. HICKS**, 480 U.S. 321, 328 (1987)(citation omitted).

The Amendment protects these equally important interests in precisely the same manner: by requiring a neutral and detached magistrate to evaluate, before the search or seizure, the government's showing of probable cause and its particular description of the place to be searched and the items to be seized. Accordingly, just as a warrantless search is per se unreasonable absent exigent circumstances, so too a seizure of personal property is "per se unreasonable within the meaning of the Fourth Amendment unless it is accomplished pursuant to a judicial warrant issued upon probable cause and particularly describing the items to be seized." **UNITED STATES v. PLACE**, 462 U.S. 696, 701 (1983)(footnote omitted)(citing **MARRON v. UNITED STATES**, 275 U.S. 192, 196 (1927)). "Prior review by a neutral and detached magistrate is the time-tested means of effectuating Fourth Amendment rights." **UNITED STATES v. UNITED STATES DISTRICT COURT, EASTERN DISTRICT OF MICHIGAN**, 407 U.S. 297, 318 (1972). A decision to invade a possessory interest in property is too important to be left to the discretion of zealous officers "engaged in the often competitive enterprise of ferreting out crime." **JOHNSON v. UNITED STATES**, 333 U.s. 10,14 (1948). "The requirement that warrants shall particularly describe the things to be seized makes general searches under them impossible and prevents the seizure of one thing under a warrant describing another. As to what is to be taken, nothing is left to the discretion of the officer executing the warrant." Marron, supra, at 196.

The plain-view doctrine is an exception to the general rule that a seizure of personal property must be authorized by a warrant. As Justice Stewart explained in Coolidge, 403 U.S., at 470, we accept a warrantless seizure when an officer is lawfully in a location and inadvertently sees evidence of a crime because of "the inconvenience of procuring a warrant" to seize this newly discovered piece of evidence. But "where the discovery is anticipated, where the police know in advance the

579

location of the evidence and intend to seize it," the argument that procuring a warrant would be "inconvenient" loses much, if not all, of its force. Ibid. Barring an exigency, there is no reason why the police officers could not have obtained a warrant to seize this evidence before entering the premises. The rationale behind the inadvertent discovery requirement is simply that we will not excuse officers from the general requirement of a warrant to seize if the officers know the location of evidence, have probable cause to seize it, intend to seize it, and yet do not bother to obtain a warrant particularly describing that evidence. To do so would violate "the express constitutional requirement of 'Warrants ... particularly describing ... [the] things to be seized,'" and would "fly in the face of the basic rule that no amount of probable cause can justify a warrantless seizure." Id., at 471.

Although joined by only three other Members of the Court, Justice Stewart's discussion of the inadvertent discovery requirement has become widely accepted. See **TEXAS v. BROWN**, supra, at 746 (Powell, J., concurring in judgment)("What ever my view might have been when Coolidge was decided, I see no reason at this late date to imply criticism of its articulation of this exception. It has been accepted generally for over a decade"). Forty-six States and the District of columbia and twelve United States Courts of Appeals now require plain-view seizures to be inadvertent. There has been accepted no outcry from law enforcement officials that the inadvertent discovery requirement unduly burdens their efforts. Given that the requirement is inescapably rooted in the plain language of the Fourth Amendment, I cannot fathom the Court's enthusiasm for discarding this element of the plain-view doctrine.

The Court posits two "flaws" in Justice Stewart's reasoning that it believes demonstrate the inappropriateness of the inadvertent discovery requirement. But these flaws are illusory. First, the majority explains that it can see no reason why an officer who "has knowledge approaching certainty" that an item will be found in a particular location "would deliberately omit a particular description of the item to be seized from the application for a search warrant."

Ante, at 138. But to the individual whose possessory interest has been invaded, it matters not why the police officer decided to omit a particular item from his application for a search warrant. When an officer with probable cause to seize an item fails to mention that item in his application for a search warrant. When an officer with probable cause to seize an item fails to mention that item in his application for a search warrant- for whatever reason- and then seized the item anyway, his conduct is per se unreasonable. Suppression of the evidence so seized will encourage officers to be more precise and complete in future warrant applications.

Furthermore, there are a number of instances in which a law enforcement officer might deliberately choose to omit certain items from a warrant application even though he has probable cause to seize them, knows they are on the premises, and intends to seize them when they are discovered in plain view. For example, the warrant application process can often be time consuming, especially when the police attempt to seize a large number of items. An officer interested in conducting a search as soon as possible might decide to save time by listing only one or two hard-to-find items, such as the stolen rings in this case, confident that he will find in plain view all of the other evidence is looking for before he discovers the listed items. Because rings could be located almost anywhere inside or outside a house, it is unlikely that a warrant to search for a seize the rings would restrict the scope of the search. An officer might rationally find the risk of immediately discovering the items listed in the warrant - thereby forcing him to conclude the search immediately - outweighed by the time saved in the application process.

The majority also contends that, once an officer is lawfully in a house and the scope of his search is adequately circumscribed by a warrant, "no additional Fourth Amendment interest is furthered by requiring that the discovery of evidence be inadvertent." Ante, at 140. Put another way, "'the inadvertent rule will in no way reduce the number of places into which [law enforcement officers] may lawfully look.'" Ante, at 141 (quoting Coolidge, 403 U.S., at 517(WHITE, J., concurring and dissenting)). The majority is correct, but it has asked the wrong question. It is true that the inadvertent discovery requirement furthers no privacy interests. The requirement in no way reduced the scope of a search or

581

the number of places into which officers may look. But it does protect possessory interest. Cf. **ILLINOIS v. ANDREAS**, 463 U.S. 765, 771 (1983)("The plain-view doctrine is grounded on the proposition that once police are lawfully in a position to observe an item first-hand, its owner's privacy interest in that item is lost; the owner may retain the incidents of title and possession but not privacy")(emphasis added). The inadvertent discovery requirement is essential if we are to take seriously the Fourth Amendment's protection of possessory interests as well as privacy interests. See supra, at 143. The Court today eliminates a rule designed to further possessory interests on the ground that it fails to further privacy interests. I cannot countenance such constitutional legerdemain.

II

Fortunately, this decision should have only a limited impact, for the Court is not confronted today with what were courts have described as a "pre-textual" search. See, e.g., **STATE v. LAIR**, 95 Wash. 2d 706, 717-718, 630 P.2d 427, 434 (1981)(en banc)(holding pre-textual searches invalid). For example, if an officer enters a house pursuant to a warrant to search for evidence of one crime when he is really interested only in seizing evidence relating to another crime, for which he does not have a warrant, his search is "pre-textual" and the fruits of that search should be suppressed. See, e.g., **STATE v. KELSEY**, 592 S.W. 2d 509 (Mo. App. 1979) (evidence suppressed because officers, who had ample opportunity to obtain [a] warrant relating to [a] murder investigation, entered the premises instead pursuant to a warrant relating to a drug investigation, and searched only the hiding place of the murder weapon, rather than conducting a "top to bottom" search for drugs). Similarly, an officer might use an exception to the generally applicable warrant requirement, such as "hot pursuit," as a pretext to enter a home to seize items he knows he will find in plain view. Such conduct would be a deliberate attempt to circumvent the constitutional requirement of a warrant "particularly describing the place to be searched, and the persons or things to be seized," and cannot be condoned.

The discovery of evidence in pre-textual searches is not "inadvertent" and should be suppressed for that reason. But even state courts that have rejected the inadvertent discovery requirement have held that the Fourth Amendment prohibits pre-textual searches. See **STATE v. BUSSARD**, 114 Idaho 781, 788, n. 2, 760 P. 2d 1197, 1204, n. 2 (1988); **STATE v. KELLY**, 718 P. 2d 385, 389, n. 1 (Utah 1986). The Court's opinion today does not address pre-textual searches, but I have no doubt that such searches violate the Fourth Amendment.

III

The Fourth Amendment demands that an individual's possessory interest in property be protected from unreasonable governmental seizures, not just by requiring a showing of probable cause, but also by requiring a neutral and detached magistrate to authorize the seizure in advance. The Court today ignores the explicit language of the Fourth Amendment, which protects possessory interests in the same manner as it protects privacy interests, in order to eliminate a generally accepted element of the plain-view doctrine that has caused no apparent difficulties for law enforcement officers. I am confident, however, that when confronted with more egregious police conduct than that found in this case, ante, at 130-131, such as pretextual searches, the Court's interpretation of the Constitution will be less parsimonious than it is today. I respectfully dissent.

APPENDIX A

STATES THAT HAVE ADOPTED THE
INADVERTENT DISCOVERY REQUIREMENT

Ala.   **Taylor v. State**, 399 So. 2d 881, 892
           (Ala. 1981)

Alaska   **Deal v. State**, 626 P.2d 1073, 1079 (Alaska
           1980)

Ariz   **State v. Ault**, 150 Ariz. 459, 464, 724 P.2d
           545, 550 (1986)

Ark.   **Johnson v. State**, 291 Ark. 260, 263, 724 S. W.
           2d 160, 162 (1987)

Colo.   **People v. Cummings**, 706 P.2d 766, 771 (Colo.
           1985)

Conn.   **State v. Hamilton**, 214 Conn. 692, 701, 573 A.2d
           1197, 1201 (1990)

D.C.   **Gant v. United States**, 518 A.2d 103, 107 (DC
           App. 1986)

Fla.   **Hurt v. State**, 388 So.2d 281, 282-283 (Fla.
           App. 1980), review denied, 399 So.2d 1146 (Fla.
           1981)

Ga.   **Mooney v. State**, 243 Ga. 373, 383-384, 254
           S.E.2d 337, 346, cert. denied, 444 U.S. 886
           (1979)

Haw.   **State v. Barnett**, 68 Haw. 32, 35, 703 P.2d 680,
           683 (1985)

Ill.   **People v. Madison**, 121 Ill.2d 195, 208, 520
           N.E.2d 374, 380-381, cert. denied, 488 U.S. 907
           (1988)

Ind.   **Clark v. State**, 498 N.E.2d 918, 921 (Ind. 1986)

Iowa   **State v. Emerson**, 375 N.W.2d 256, 259 (Iowa
           1985)

Kan.   **State v. Doile, 244 Kan. 493, 497, 769 P.2d
           666, 669 (1989)**

Ky.   **Patrick v. Commonwealth**, 535 S.W.2d 88, 89 (Ky.
           1976)

La.   **State v. Stott**, 395 So.2d 714, 716 (La. 1981)

Me.   **State v. Cloutier**, 544 A.2d 1277, 1281, n.4
           (Me. 1988)

584

Md.	**Wiggins v. State**, 315 Md. 232, 251-252, 554 A.2d 356, 365 (1989)
Mass.	**Commonwealth v. Cefalo**, 381 Mass. 319, 330-331, 409 N.E. 2d 719, 727 (1980)
Mich.	**People v. Dugan**, 102 Mich. App. 497, 503-505, 302 N.W.2d 209, 211-212 (1980), cert. denied, 455 U.S. 927 (1982)
Minn.	**State v. Buschkopf**, 373 N.W.2d 756, 768 (Minn. 1985)
Miss.	**Smith v. State**, 419 So.2d 563, 571 (Miss. 1982), cert. denied, 460 U.S. 1047 (1983)
Mo.	**State v. Clark**, 592 S.W.2d 709, 713 (Mo. 1979), cert. denied, 449 U.S. 847 (1980)
Mont.	**State v. Hembd**, 235 Mont. 361, 368-369, 767 P.2d 864, 869 (1989)
Neb.	**State v. Hansen**, 221 Neb. 103, 108-109, 375 N.W.2d 605, 609 (1985)
Nev.	**Johnson v. State**, 97 Nev. 621, 624, 637 P.2d 1209, 1211 (1981)
N.H.	**State v. Cote**, 126 N.H. 514, 525, 526, 493 A.2d 1170, 1177-1178 (1985)
N.J.	**State v. Bruzzese**, 94 N.J. 210, 237-238, 463 A.2d 320, 334-335 (1983), cert. denied, 465 U.S. 1030 (1984)
N.M.	**State v. Luna**, 93 N.M. 773, 779, 606 P.2d 183, 188 (1980)
N.Y.	**People v. Jackson**, 41 N.Y.2d 146, 150-151, 359 N.E.2d 677, 681 (1976)
N.C.	**State v. White**, 322 N.C. 770, 773, 370 S.E.2d 390, 392, cert. denied, 488 U.S. 958 (1988)
N.D.	**State v. Riedinger**, 374 N.W.2d 866, 874 (N.D. 1985)

Ohio	**State v. Benner**, 40 Ohio St.3d 301, 308 533 N.E.2d 701, 709-710 (1988), cert. denied, 494 U.S. 1090 (1990)
Okla.	**Farmer v. State**, 759 P.2d 1031, 1033 (Okla. Cr. App. 1988)
Ore.	**State v. Handran**, 97 Ore. App. 546, 550-551, 777 P. 2d 981, 983, review denied, 308 Ore. 405, 781 P.2d 855 (1989)
Pa.	**Commonwealth v. Davidson**, 389 Pa. Super. 166, 175, 566 A.2d 897, 901 (1989)
R.I.	**State v. Robalewski**, 418 A.2d 817, 824 (R.I. 1980)
S.C.	**State v. Culbreath**, 300 S.C. 232, 237, 387 S.E.2d 255, 257 (1990)
S.D.	**State v. Albright**, 418 N.W.2d 292, 295 (S.D. 1988)
Tenn.	**State v. Byerley**, 635 S.W. 2d 511, 513 (Tenn. 1982)
Tex.	**Stoker v. State**, 788 S.W.2d 1, 9 (Tex.Crim.App. 1989)(en banc)
Vt.	**State v. Dorn,**145 Vt. 606, 620-621, 496 A.2d 451, 459-460 (1985)
Va.	**Holloman v. Commonwealth**, 221 Va. 947, 949, 275 S.E.2d 620, 621-622 (1981)
Wash.	**State v. Bell**, 108 Wash.2d 193, 196, 737 P.2d 254, 257 (1987)
W.Va.	**State v. Moore**, 165 W.Va. 837, 852-853, 272 S.E.2d 804, 813-814 (1980)
Wis.	**State v. Washington**, 134 Wis.2d 108, 119-121, 396 N.W.2d 156, 161 (1986)

Wyo.   **Jessee v. State**, 640 P.2d 56, 63 (Wyo. 1982)

APPENDIX B

UNITED STATES COURTS OF APPEALS
THAT HAVE ADOPTED THE
INADVERTENT DISCOVERY REQUIREMENT

CA1:   **United·States v. Caggiano**, 899 F.2d 99, 103 (1990)

CA2:   **United States v. Barrios-Moriera**, 872 F.2d 12, 16, cert. denied, 493 U.S. 953 (1989)

CA3:   **United States v. Meyer**, 827 F.2d 943, 945 (1987)

CA4:   **Tarantino v. Baker**, 825 F.2d 772, 777, n.3 (1987)

CA5:   **Crowder v. Sinyard**, 884 F.2d 804, 826, n.30 (1989), cert. pending, No. 89-1326

CA6:   **United States v. Poulos**, 895 F.2d 1113, 1121 (1990)

CA7:   **United States v. Perry**, 815 F.2d 1100, 1105 (1987)

CA8:   **United States v. Peterson**, 867 F.2d 1110, 1113 (1989)

CA9:   **United States v. Holzman, 871 F.2d 1496, 1512 (1989)**

CA10:   **Wolfenbarger v. Williams**, 826 F.2d 930, 935 (1987)

CA11:   **United States v. Bent-Santana**, 774 F.2d 1545, 1551 (1985)

CADC: **In re Search Warrant Dated July 4, 1977, for Premises at 2125 S Street, Northwest, Washington**, D.C., 215 U.S. App. D.C. 74, 102, 667 F.2d 117, 145 (1981), cert. denied, 455 U.S. 926 (1982)

FLORIDA, PETITIONER v. ENIO JIMENO, ET AL.
___U.S___, 111 S.Ct. 1801, 114 L.ED.2d 297 (1991)
ON WRIT OF CERTIORARI TO THE SUPREME COURT
OF FLORIDA

CHIEF JUSTICE REHNQUIST delivered the opinion of the Court.

In this case we decide whether a criminal suspect's Fourth Amendment right to be free from unreasonable searches is violated when, after he gives a police officer permission to search his automobile, the officer opens a closed container found within the car that might reasonably hold the object of the search. We find that it is not. The Fourth Amendment is satisfied when, under the circumstances, it is objectively reasonable for the officer to believe that the scope of the suspect's consent permitted him to open a particular container within the automobile.

This case began when a Dade County police officer, Frank Trujillo, overheard respondent, Enio Jimeno, arranging what appeared to be a drug transaction over a public telephone. Believing that Jimeno might be involved in illegal drug trafficking, Officer Trujillo followed his car. The officer observed respondents make a right turn at a red light without stopping. He then pulled Jimeno over to the side of the road in order to issue him a traffic citation. Officer Trujillo told Jimeno that he had been stopped for committing a traffic infraction. The officer went on to say that he had reason to believe that Jimeno was carrying narcotics in his car, and asked permission to search the car. He explained that Jimeno did not have to consent to a search of the car. Jimeno stated that he had nothing to hide, and gave Trujillo permission to search the automobile. After Jimeno's spouse, respondent Luz Jimeno, stepped out of the car, Officer Trujillo went to the passenger side, opened the door, and saw a folded, brown paper bag on the floorboard. The officer picked up the bag, opened it, and found a kilogram of cocaine inside.

The Jimenos were charged with possession with intent to distribute cocaine in violation of Florida law. Before trial, they moved to suppress the cocaine found in the bag on the ground that Jimeno's consent to search the car did not extend to the closed paper bag inside the car. The trial court granted the motion. It found that although Jimeno "could have assumed that the officer would have searched the bag" at the time he gave his consent, his mere consent to search the car did not carry with it specific consent to open the bag and examine its contents. No. 88-23967 (Cir. Ct. Dade Cty, Fla., Mar 21, 1989); App. to Pet. for Cert. A-6.

The Florida District Court of Appeal affirmed the trial court's decision to suppress the evidence of the cocaine. 550 So.12d 1176 (Fla. 3d DCA 1989). In doing so, the court established a per se rule that "consent to a general search for narcotics does not extend to 'sealed containers within the general area agreed to by the defendant.'" Ibid. (citation omitted). The Florida Supreme Court affirmed, relying upon its decision in **STATE v. WELLS**, 539 So.2d 464 (1989 aff'd on other grounds, 495 U.S. ___ (1990). 564 So.2d 1083(1990). We granted certiorari to determine whether consent to search a vehicle may extend to closed containers found inside the vehicle. 498 U.S. ___ (1990), and we now reverse the judgment of the Supreme Court of Florida.

The touchstone of the Fourth Amendment is reasonableness. **KATZ v. UNITED STATES**, 389 U.S. 347, 360 (1967). The Fourth Amendment does not proscribe all state-initiated searches and seizures; it merely proscribes those which are unreasonable. **ILLINOIS v. RODRIGUEZ**, 497 U.S. ___ (1990). Thus, we have long approved consensual searches because it is no doubt reasonable for the police to conduct a search once they have been permitted to do so. **SCHNECKLOTH v. BUSTAMONTE**, 412 U.S. 218, 219 (1973). The standard for measuring the scope of a suspect's consent under the Fourth Amendment is that of "objective" reasonableness - what would the typical reasonable person have understood by the exchange between the officer and the suspect? **ILLINOIS v. RODRIGUEZ**, supra, at ___ ___ (slip op., at 5-11); **FLORIDA v. ROYER**, 460 U.S. 49, 501-502 (1983) (opinion of WHITE, J.); id., at 514 (BLACKMUN, J., dissenting). The question before us, then, is whether it is reasonable for an officer to consider a suspect's general consent to a search of his car to include consent to examine a paper bag lying on the floor of the car. We think that it is.

The scope of a search is generally defined by its expressed object. **UNITED STATES v. ROSS**, 456 U.S. 798 (1982). In this case, the terms of the search's authorization were simple. Respondent granted Officer Trujillo permission to search his car, and did not place any explicit limitation on the scope of the search. Trujillo had informed Jimeno that he believed Jimeno was carrying narcotics, and that he would be looking for narcotics in the car. We think that it was objectively reasonable for the police to conclude that the general consent to search respondent's car included consent to search containers within that car which might bear drugs. A reasonable person may be expected to know that narcotics are generally carried in some form of a container. "Contraband goods rarely are strewn across the trunk or floor of a car." Id., at 820. The authorization to search in this case, therefore extended beyond the surfaces of the car's interior to the paper bag lying on the car's floor.

The facts of this case are therefore different from those in **STATE v. WELLS**, supra, on which the Supreme Court of Florida relied in affirming the suppression order in this case. There the Supreme Court of Florida held that consent to search the trunk of a car did not include authorization to pry open a locked briefcase found inside the trunk. It is very likely unreasonable to think that a suspect, by consenting to the search of his trunk, has agreed to the breaking open of a locked briefcase within the trunk, but it is otherwise with respect to a closed paper bag.

Respondents argue, and the Florida trial court agreed, that if the police wish to search closed containers within a car they must separately request permission to search each container. But we see no basis for adding this sort of superstructure to the Fourth Amendment's basic test of objective reasonableness. Cf. **ILLINOIS v. GATES**, 462 U.S. 213 (1983). A suspect may of course delimit as he chooses the scope of the search to which he consents. But if his consent would reasonably be understood to extend to a particular container, the Fourth Amendment provides no grounds for requiring a more explicit authorization. "[T]he community has a real interest in encouraging consent, for the resulting search may yield necessary evidence for the solution and prosecution of crime, evidence that may ensure that a wholly innocent person is not wrongly charged with a criminal offense." **SCHNECKLOTH v. BUSTAMONTE**, supra at 243.

The judgment of the Supreme Court of Florida is accordingly reversed, and the case remanded for further proceedings not inconsistent with this opinion.

It is so ordered

JUSTICE MARSHALL, with whom JUSTICE STEVENS joins, dissenting.

The question in this case is whether an individual's general consent to search of the interior of his car for narcotics should reasonably be understood as consent to a search of closed containers inside the car. Nothing in today's opinion dispels my belief that the two are not one and the same from the consenting individual's standpoint. Consequently, an individual's consent to a search of the interior of his car should not be understood to authorize a search of closed containers inside the car. I dissent.

In my view, analysis of this question must start by identifying the differing expectations of privacy that attach to cars and closed containers. It is well established that an individual has but a limited expectation of privacy in the interior of his car. A car ordinarily is not used as a residence or repository for one's personal effects, and its passengers and contents are generally exposed to public view. See **CARDWELL v. LEWIS**, 417 U.S. 583, 590 (1974) (plurality opinion). Moreover, cars "are subjected to pervasive and continuing governmental regulation and controls," **SOUTH DAKOTA v. OPPERMAN**, 428 U.S. 364, 368 (1976), and may be seized by the police when necessary to protect public safety or to facilitate the flow of traffic, see id., at 368-369.

In contrast, it is equally well established that an individual has a heightened expectation of privacy in the contents of a closed container. See, e.g. **UNITED STATES v. CHADWICK**, 433 U.S. 1, 13 (1977). Luggage, handbags, paper bags, and other containers are common repositories for one's papers and effects, and the protection of these items from state intrusion lies at the heart of the Fourth Amendment. U.S. Const., Amdt. 4 ("The rights of the people⁻ to be secure in their . . .papers, and effects, against unreasonable searches and seizures, shall not be violated"). By placing his possessions inside a container, an individual manifests an intent

591

that his possessions be "preserve[d] as private," **UNITED STATES v. KATZ**, 389 U.S. 347, 351 (1967), and thus kept "free from public examination," **UNITED STATES v. CHADWICK**, supra, at 11.

The distinct privacy expectations that a person has in a car as opposed to a closed container do not merge when the individual uses his car to transport the container. In this situation, the individual still retains a heightened expectation of privacy in the container. See **ROBBINS v. CALIFORNIA**, 453 U.S. 420, 425 (1981) (plurality opinion); **ARKANSAS v. SANDERS**, 442 U.S. 753, 763-764 (1979). Nor does an individual's heightened expectation of privacy turn on the type of container in which he stores his possessions. Notwithstanding the majority's suggestion to the contrary, see ante, at 3-4, this Court has soundly rejected any distinction between "worthy" containers, like locked briefcases, and "unworthy" containers, like paper bags.

> "Even though such a distinction perhaps could evolve in a series of cases in which paper bags, locked trunks, lunch buckets, and orange crates were placed on one side of the line or the other, the central purpose of the Fourth Amendment forecloses such a distinction. For just as the most frail cottage in the kingdom is absolutely entitled to the same guarantees of privacy as the most majestic mansion, so also may a traveler who carries a toothbrush and a few articles of clothing in a paper bag or knotted scarf claim an equal right to conceal his possessions from official inspection as the sophisticated executive with the locked attache case." **UNITED STATES v. ROSS**, 456 U.S. 798, 822 (1982)(footnotes omitted).

Because an individual's expectation of privacy in a container is distinct from, and far greater than, his expectation of privacy in the interior of his car, it follows that an individual's consent to a search of the interior of his car cannot necessarily be understood as extending to containers in the car. At the very least, general consent to search the car is ambiguous with respect to containers mandates that a police officer who wishes to search a suspicious container found during a consensual automobile search obtain additional consent to search the container. If the driver intended to authorize search of the container, he will say so; if not, then he will say no. The only objection that the police could have to such a rule is that it would prevent them from exploiting the ignorance of a citizen who simply did not anticipate that his consent to search the car would be understood to authorize the police to rummage through his packages.

According to the majority, it nonetheless is reasonable for a police officer to construe generalized consent to search an automobile for narcotics as extending to closed containers, because "[a] reasonable person may be expected to know that narcotics are generally carried in some form of a container." Ante, at 3. This is an interesting contention. By the same logic a person who consents to a search of the car from the driver's seat could also be deemed to consent to a search of his person or indeed of his body cavities, since a reasonable person may be expected to know that drug couriers frequently store their contraband on their persons or in their body cavities. I suppose (and hope) that even the majority would reject this conclusion, for a person who consents to the search of his car for drugs certainly does not consent to a search of things other than his car for drugs. But this example illustrates that if there is a reason for not treating a closed container as something "other than the car in which it sits, the reason cannot be based on intuition about where people carry drugs. The majority, however, never identifies a reason for conflating the distinct privacy expectations that a person has in a car and in closed containers.

The majority also argues that the police should not be required to secure specific consent to search a closed container, because "'[t]he community has a real interest in encouraging consent.'" Ante, at 4, quoting **SCHNECKLOTH v. BUSTAMONTE**, 412 U.S. 218, 243 (1973). I find this rationalization equally unsatisfactory. If anything, a rule that permits the police to construe a consent to search more broadly than it may have been intended would discourage individuals from consenting to searches of their cars. Apparently, the majority's real concern is that if the police were required to ask for additional consent to search a closed container found during the consensual search of an automobile, an individual who did not mean to authorize such additional searching would have an opportunity to say no. In essence, then, the majority is claiming that "the community has a real interest" not in encouraging citizens to consent to investigatory efforts of their law enforcement agents, but rather in encouraging individuals to be duped by them. This is not the community that the Fourth Amendment contemplates.

Almost 20 years ago, this Court held that an individual could validly "consent" to a search - or, in other words, waive his right to be free from an otherwise unlawful search - without being told that he had the right to withhold his consent. See **SCHNECKLOTH v. BUSTAMONTE**, supra. In Schneckloth, as in this case, the Court cited the practical interests in efficacious law enforcement as the basis of an individual's consent. I dissented in Schneckloth, and what I wrote in that case applies with equal force here.

> "I must conclude, with some reluctance, that when the Court speaks of practicality, what it really is talking of is the continued ability of the police to capitalize on the ignorance of citizens so as to accomplish by subterfuge what they could not achieve by relying only on the knowing relinquishment of constitutional rights. Of course it would be "practical" for the police to ignore the commands of the Fourth Amendment, if by practicality we mean that more criminals will be apprehended, even though the constitutional rights of innocent people go by the board. But such a practical advantage is achieved only at the cost of permitting the police to disregard the limitations that the Constitution places on their behavior, a cost that a constitutional democracy cannot long absorb." 412 U.S., at 288.

I dissent.

UNITED STATES, Petitioner v. WILLIAM HARRIS SHARPE and
DONALD DAVIS SAVAGE
470 U.S. 675, 84 L.Ed.2d 605, 105 S.Ct. 1568 (1985)

Chief Justice Burger delivered the opinion of the Court.

[1a] We granted certiorari to decide whether an individual reasonably suspected of engaging in criminal activity may be detained for a period of 20 minutes, when the detention is necessary for law enforcement officers to conduct a limited investigation of the suspected criminal activity.

I
A
On the morning of June 9, 1978, Agent Cooke of the Drug Enforcement Administration (DEA) was on patrol in an unmarked vehicle on a coastal road near Sunset Beach, North Carolina, an area under surveillance for suspected drug trafficking. At approximately 6:30 a.m., Cooke noticed a blue pickup truck with an attached camper shell traveling on the highway in tandem with a blue Pontiac Bonneville. Respondent Savage was driving the pickup, and respondent Sharpe was driving the Pontiac. The Pontiac also carried a passenger, Davis, the charges against whom were later dropped. Observing that the truck was riding low in the rear and that the camper did not bounce or sway appreciably when the truck drove over bumps or around curves, Agent Cooke concluded that it was heavily loaded. A quilted material covered the rear and side windows of the camper.

Cooke's suspicions were sufficiently aroused to follow the two vehicles for approximately 20 miles as they proceeded south into South Carolina. He then decided to make an "investigative stop" and radioed the State Highway Patrol for assistance. Officer Thrasher, driving a marked patrol car, responded to the call. Almost immediately after Thrasher caught up with the procession, the Pontiac and the pickup turned off the highway and onto a campground road. Cooke and Thrasher followed the two vehicles as the latter drove along the road at 55 to 60 miles an hour, exceeding the speed limit of 35 miles an hour. The road eventually looped back to the highway, onto which Savage and Sharpe turned and continued to drive south.

At this point, all four vehicles were in the middle

595

lane of the three righthand lanes of the highway. Agent Cooke asked Officer Thrasher to signal both vehicles to stop. Thrasher pulled alongside the Pontiac, which was in the lead, turned on his flashing light, and motioned for the driver of the Pontiac to stop. As Sharpe moved the Pontiac into the right lane, the pickup truck cut between the Pontiac and Thrasher's patrol car, nearly hitting the patrol car, and continued down the highway. Thrasher pursued the truck while Cooke pulled up behind the Pontiac.

Cooke approached the Pontiac and identified himself. He requested identification, and Sharpe produced a Georgia driver's license bearing the name of Raymond J. Pavlovich. Cooke then attempted to radio Thrasher to determine whether he had been successful in stopping the pickup truck, but he was unable to make contact for several minutes, apparently because Thrasher was not in his patrol car. Cooke radioed the local police for assistance, and two officers from the Myrtle Beach Police Department arrived about 10 minutes later. Asking the two officers to "maintain the situation," Cooke left to join Thrasher.

In the meantime, Thrasher had stopped the pickup truck about one-half mile down the road. After stopping the truck, Thrasher had approached it with his revolver drawn, ordered the driver, Savage, to get out and assume a "spread eagled" position against the side of the truck, and patted him down. Thrasher then holstered his gun and asked Savage for his driver's license and the truck's vehicle registration. Savage produced his own Florida driver's license and a bill of sale for the truck bearing the name of Pavlovich. In response to questions from Thrasher concerning the ownership of the truck, Savage said that the truck belonged to a friend and that he was taking it to have its shock absorbers repaired. When Thrasher told Savage that he would be held until the arrival of Cooke, whom Thrasher identified as a DEA agent, Savage became nervous, said that he wanted to leave, and requested the return of his driver's license. Thrasher replied that Savage was not free to leave at that time.

Agent Cooke arrived at the scene approximately 15 minutes after the truck had stopped. Thrasher handed

Cooke Savage's license and the bill of sale for the truck; Cooke noted that the bill of sale bore the same name as Sharpe's license. Cooke identified himself to Savage as a DEA agent and said that he thought the truck was loaded with marihuana. Cooke twice sought permission to search the camper, but Savage declined to give it, explaining that he was not the owner of the truck. Cooke then stepped on the rear of the truck and, observing that it did not sink any lower, confirmed his suspicion that it was probably overloaded. He put his nose against the rear window, which was covered from the inside, and reported that he could smell marihuana. Without seeking Savage's permission, Cooke removed the keys from the ignition, opened the rear of the camper, and observed a large number of burlap-wrapped bales resembling bales of marihuana that Cooke had seen in previous investigations. Agent Cooke then placed Savage under arrest and left him with Thrasher.

Cooke returned to the Pontiac and arrested Sharpe and Davis. Approximately 30 to 40 minutes had elapsed between the time Cooke stopped the Pontiac and the time he returned to arrest Sharpe and Davis. Cooke Assembled the various parties and vehicles and led them to the Myrtle Beach police station. That evening, DEA agents took the truck to the Federal Building in Charleston, South Carolina. Several days later, Cooke supervised the unloading of the truck, which contained 43 bales weighing a total of 2,629 pounds. Acting without a search warrant, Cooke had eight randomly selected bales opened and sampled. Chemical tests showed that the samples were marihuana.

B

Sharpe and Savage were charged with possession of a controlled substance with intent to distribute it in violation of 21 USC § 841 (a)(1) and 18 USC § 2 [21 § 841 (a)(1) and 18 USCS § 2]. The United States District Court for the District of South Carolina denied respondents' motion to suppress the contraband, and respondents were convicted.

A divided panel of the Court of Appeals for the Fourth Circuit reversed the convictions. **SHARPE v. UNITED STATES**, 660 F2d 967 (1981). The majority assumed that Cooke "had an articulable and reasonable suspicion that Sharpe and Savage were engaged in marijuana trafficking when he and Thrasher stopped the Pontiac and the truck." Id., at 970. But the court held the investigative stops unlawful because they "failed to meet the requirement of brevity" thought to govern detentions on less than probable cause. Ibid. Basing its decision solely on the duration of the respondents' detentions, the majority concluded that "the length of the detentions effectively transformed them into de facto arrests without bases in probable cause, unreasonable seizures under the Fourth Amendment." Ibid. The majority then determined that the samples of marihuana should have been suppressed as the fruit of respondents' unlawful seizures. Id., at 971. As an alternative basis for its decision, the majority held that the warrantless search of the bales taken from the pickup violated **ROBBINS v. CALIFORNIA**, 453 US 420, 69 L Ed 2d 744, 101 S Ct 2841 (1981). Judge Russell dissented as to both grounds of the majority's decision.

The Government petitioned for certiorari, asking this Court to review both of the alternative grounds held by the Court of Appeals to justify suppression. We granted the petition, vacated the judgment of the Court of Appeals, and remanded the case for further consideration in the light of the intervening decision in **UNITED STATES v. ROSS**, 456 US 798, 72 L Ed 2d 572, 102 S Ct 2157 (1982). **UNITED STATES v. SHARPE**, 457 US 1127, 73 L Ed 2d 1345, 102 S Ct 2951 (1982).

On remand, a divided panel of the court of Appeals again reversed the convictions. 712 F2d 65 (1933). The majority concluded that, in the light of Ross, it was required to "disavow" its alternative holding disapproving the warrantless search of the marihuana bales. But, "[f]inding that Ross does not adversely affect our primary holding" that the detentions of the two defendants constituted illegal seizures, the court readopted the prior opinion as modified. Ibid. The majority declined "to reexamine our principal holding or to reargue the same issues that were addressed in detail in the original majority and dissenting opinions," reasoning that its action complied with this Court's mandate. The panel assumed that "[h]ad [this] Court felt that a reversal was in order, it could and would have said so." Id., at 65, n 1. Judge Russel again dissented.

We granted certiorari, 467 US ——, 82 L Ed 2d 837, 104 S Ct 3531 (1984), and we reverse.

II

A

The Fourth Amendment is not, of course, a guarantee against *all* searches and seizures, but only against *unreasonable* searches and seizures. The authority and limits of the Amendment apply to investigative stops of vehicles such as occurred here. **UNITED STATES v. HENSLEY**, 469 US 1, 83 L Ed 2d 604, 105 S.Ct. 675 (1985); **UNITED STATES v. CORTEZ**, 449 US 411, 417, 66 L Ed 2d 621, 101 S Ct 690 (1981); **DELAWARE v. PROUSE**, 440 US 648, 663, 59 L Ed 2d 660, 99 S Ct 1391 (1979); **UNITED STATES v. BRIGNONI-PONCE**, 422 US 873, 878, 880, 45 L Ed 2d 607, 95 S Ct 2574 (1975). In **TERRY v. OHIO**, 392 US 1, 20 L Ed 2d 889, 88 S Ct 1868, 44 Ohio Ops 2d 383 (1968), we adopted a dual inquiry for evaluating the reasonableness of an investigative stop. Under this approach, we examine

"whether the officer's action was justified at its inception, and whether it was reasonable related in scope to the circumstances which justified the interference in the first place." Id., at 20, 20 L Ed 2d 889, 88 S Ct 1868, 44 Ohio Ops 2d 383.

[4a] As to the first part of this inquiry, the Court of Appeals assumed that the police had an articulable and reasonable suspicion that Sharpe and Savage were engaged in marihuana trafficking, given the setting and all the circumstances when the police attempted to stop the Pontiac and the pickup. 660 F2d, at 970. That assumption is abundantly supported by the record. As to the second part of the inquiry, however, the court concluded that the 30-to 40-minute detention of Sharpe and the 20-minute detention of Savage "failed to meet the [Fourth Amendment's] requirement of brevity." Ibid.

[1b] It is not necessary for us to decide whether the length of Sharpe's detention was unreasonable, because that detention bears no causal relation to Agent Cooke's discovery of the marihuana. The marihuana was in Savage's pickup, not in Sharpe's Pontiac; the contraband introduced at respondents' trial cannot logically be considered the "fruit" of Sharpe's detention. The only issue in this case, then, is whether it was reasonable

under the circumstances facing Agent Cooke and Officer
Thrasher to detain Savage, whose vehicle contained the
challenged evidence, for approximately 20 minutes. We
conclude that the detention of Savage clearly meets the
Fourth Amendment's standard of reasonableness.

The Court of Appeals did not question the
reasonableness of Officer Thrasher's or Agent Cooke's
conduct during their detention of Savage. Rather, the
court concluded that the length of the detention alone
transformed it from a Terry stop into a de facto arrest.
Counsel for respondents, as amicus curiae, assert that
conclusion as their principal argument before this Court,
relying particularly upon our decisions in **DUNAWAY v. NEW
YORK**, 442 US 200, 60 L Ed 2d 824, 99 S Ct 2248 (1979);
FLORIDA v. ROYER, 460 US 491, 75 L Ed 2d 229, 103 S Ct
1319 (1983); and **UNITED STATES v. PLACE**, 462 US 696, 77
L Ed 2d 110, 103 S Ct 2637 (1983). That reliance is
misplaced.

In Dunaway, the police picked up a murder suspect
from a neighbor's home and brought him to the police
station, where, after being interrogated for an hour, he
confessed. The state conceded that the police lacked
probable cause when they picked up the suspect, but
sought to justify the warrantless detention and
interrogation as an investigative stop. The Court
rejected this argument, concluding that the defendant's
detention was "in important respects indistinguishable
from a traditional arrest." 442 US, at 212, 60 L Ed 2d
824, 99 S Ct 2248. Dunaway is simply inapposite here:
the Court was not concerned with the length of the
defendant's detention, but with events occurring during
the detention.

In Royer, government agents stopped the defendant in
an airport, seized his luggage, and took him to a small
room used for questioning, where a search of the luggage
revealed narcotics. The Court held that the defendant's
detention constituted an arrest. See 460 US, at 503, 75
L Ed 2d 229, 103 S Ct 1319 (plurality opinion); id., at
509, 75 L Ed 2d 229, 103 S Ct 1319 (Powell, J.,
concurring); ibid. (Brennan, J., concurring in the
result). As in Dunaway, though, the focus was primarily
on facts other than the duration of the defendant's
detention—particularly the fact that the police confined

the defendant in a small airport room for questioning.
The plurality in Royer did note that "an investigative detention must be temporary and last no longer than is necessary to effectuate the purpose of the stop." 460 US,. at 500, 75 L Ed 2d 229, 103 S Ct 1319. The Court followed a similar approach in Place. In that case, law enforcement agents stopped the defendant after his arrival in an airport and seized his luggage for 90 minutes to take it to a narcotics detection dog for a "sniff test." We decided that an investigative seizure of personal property could be justified under the Terry doctrine, but that "[t]he length of the detention of respondent's luggage alone precludes the conclusion that the seizure was reasonable in the absence of probable cause." 462 US, at 709, 77 L Ed 2d 110, 103 S Ct 2637. However, the rationale underlying that conclusion was premised on the fact that the police knew of respondent's arrival time for several hours beforehand, and the Court assumed that the police could have arranged for a trained narcotics dog in advance and thus avoided the necessity of holding respondent's luggage for 90 minutes. "[I]n assessing the effect of the length of the detention, we take into account whether the police diligently pursue their investigation." Ibid; see also Royer, supra, at 500, 75 L Ed 2d 229, 103 S Ct 1319.

Here, the Court of Appeals did not conclude that the police acted less than diligently, or that they unnecessarily prolonged Savage's detention. Place and Royer thus provide no support for the Court of Appeals' analysis.

[3b] Admittedly, Terry, Dunaway, Royer, and Place, considered together, may in some instances create difficult line-drawing problems in distinguishing an investigative stop from a de facto arrest. Obviously, if an investigative stop continues indefinitely, at some point it can no longer be justified as an investigative stop. But our cases impose no rigid time limitation on Terry stops. While it is clear that "the brevity of the invasion of the individual's Fourth Amendment interests is an important factor in determining whether the seizure is so minimally intrusive as to be justifiable on reasonable suspicion," **UNITED STATES v. PLACE**, supra, at 709, 77 L Ed 2d 110, 103 S Ct 2637, we have emphasized the need to consider the law enforcement purposes to be served by the stop as well as the time reasonably needed to effectuate those purposes. **UNITED STATES v. HENSLEY,**

469 US -1, 83 L Ed 2d 604, 105 S.Ct. 675 (1985); Place, supra, at 703-704, 709, 77 L Ed 2d 110, 103 S.Ct. 2637; **MICHIGAN v. SUMMERS**, 452 US 692, 700, and n 12, 69 L Ed 2d 340, 101 S.Ct. 2587 (1981) (quoting 3 W. LaFave, Search and Seizure § 9.2, at 36-37 (1978). Much as a "bright line" rule would be desirable, in evaluating whether an investigative detention is unreasonable, common sense and ordinary human experience must govern over rigid criteria.

We sought to make this clear in **MICHIGAN v. SUMMERS**, supra:

> "If the purpose underlying a Terry stop—investigating possible criminal activity—is to be served, the police must under certain circumstances be able to detain the individual for longer than the brief time period involved in Terry and Adams [v Williams, 407 US 143 [32 L Ed 2d 612, 92 S Ct 1921] (1972)." 452 US, at 700, n 12, 69 L Ed 2d 340, 101 S Ct 2587.

Later, in Place, we expressly rejected the suggestion that we adopt a hard-and-fast time limit for permissible Terry stop:

> "We understand the desirability of providing law enforcement authorities with a clear rule to guide their conduct. Nevertheless, we question the wisdom of a rigid time limitation. Such a limit would undermine the equally important need to allow authorities to graduate their responses to the demands of any particular situation." 462 US, at 709, n 10, 77 L Ed 2d 110, 103 S Ct 2637.

The Court of Appeals' decision would effectively establish a per se rule that a 20-minute detention is too long to be justified under the Terry doctrine. Such a result is clearly and fundamentally at odds with our approach in this area.

B

[5]   In assessing whether a detention is too long in duration to be justified as an investigative stop, we consider it appropriate to examine whether the police diligently pursued a means of investigation that was likely to confirm or dispel their suspicions quickly, during which time it was necessary to detain the defendant. See **MICHIGAN v. SUMMERS**, 452 US, at 701, n 14, 69 L Ed 2d 340, 101 S Ct 2587 (quoting 3 W. Lafave, Search and Seizure § 9.2, at 40 (1978); see also Place, 462 US, at 709, 77 L Ed 2d 110, 103 S Ct 2637; Royer, 460 US,. at 500, 75 L Ed 2d 229, 103 S Ct 1319.   A court making this assessment should take care to consider whether the police are acting in a swiftly developing situation, and in such cases the court should not indulge in unrealistic second-guessing. See generally post, at —— U.S. ——, 84 L Ed 2d 632-635 (Brennan, J., dissenting).   A creative judge engaged in post hoc evaluation of police conduct can almost always imagine some alternative means by which the objectives of the police might have been accomplished.   But "[t]he fact that the protection of the public might, in the abstract, have been accomplished by 'less intrusive' means does not, in itself, render the search unreasonable." **CALDY v. DOMBROWSKI**, 413 US 433, 447, 37 L Ed 2d 706, 93 S Ct 2523 (1973); see also **UNITED STATES v. MARTINEZ-FUERTE**, 428 US 543, 557, n 12, 49 L Ed 2d 1116, 96 S Ct 3074 (1976).   The question is not simply whether some other alternative was available, but whether the police acted unreasonably in failing to recognize or to pursue it.

[1c]   We readily conclude that, given the circumstances facing him, Agent Cooke pursued his investigation in a diligent and reasonable manner. During most of Savage's 20-minute detention, Cooke was attempting to contact Thrasher and enlisting the help of the local police who remained with Sharpe while Cooke left to pursue Officer Thrasher and the pickup.   Once Cooke reached Officer Thrasher and Savage, he proceeded expeditiously: within the space of a few minutes, he examined Savage's driver's license and the truck's bill of sale, requested (and was denied) permission to search the truck, stepped on the rear bumper and noted that the truck did not move, confirming his suspicion that it was probably overloaded.   He then detected the odor of marihuana.

[1d]   Clearly this case does not involve any delay unnecessary to the legitimate investigation of the law

enforcement officers. Respondents presented no evidence that the officers were dilatory in their investigation. The delay in this case was attributable almost entirely to the evasive actions of Savage, who sought to elude the police as Sharpe moved his Pontiac to the side of the road. Except for Savage's maneuvers, only a short and certainly permissible pre-arrest detention would likely have taken place. The somewhat longer detention was simply the result of a "graduate[d] .... respons[e] to the demands of [the] particular situation," Place, supra, at 709, n 10, 77 L Ed 2d 110, 103 S Ct 2637.

We reject the contention that a 20-minute stop is unreasonable when the police have acted diligently and a suspect's actions contribute to the added delay about which he complains. The judgment of the Court of Appeals is reversed, and the case is remanded for further proceedings consistent with this opinion.

Reversed and remanded.

GEORGE K. WYMANN, Individually and
as Commissioner of the State of New York,
Department of Social Services, Appellant,
v. BARBARA JAMES, etc,
400 U.S. 309, 91 S.Ct. 381, 21 L.Ed.2d. 408 (1971)
Argued October 20, 1970.—Decided January 12, 1971.
. . .
MR. JUSTICE BLACKMUN delivered the opinion of the Court.

This appeal presents the issue whether a beneficiary
of the program for Aid to Families with Dependent
Children (AFDC) may refuse a home visit by the caseworker
without risking the termination of benefits.
The New York State and City social services
commissioners appeal from a judgment and decree of a
divided three-judge District Court holding invalid and
unconstitutional in application § 134 of the New York
Social Services Law, § 175 of the New York Policies
Governing the Administration of Public Assistance, and §§
351.10 and 351.21 of Title 18 of the New York Code of
Rules and Regulations, and granting injunctive relief.
JAMES v. GOLDBERG, 303 F Supp 935 (SDNY 1969). This
Court noted probable jurisdiction but, by a divided vote,
denied a requested stay. 397 US 904, 25 L Ed 2d 85, 90 S
Ct 921.
The District Court majority held that a mother
receiving AFDC relief may refuse, without forfeiting her
right to that relief, the periodic home visit which the
cited New York statutes and regulations prescribe as a
condition for the continuance of assistance under the
program. The beneficiary's thesis, and that of the
District Court majority is that home visitation is a
search and, when not consented to or when not supported
by a warrant based on probable cause, violates the
beneficiary's Fourth and Fourteenth Amendment rights.
Judge McLean, in dissent, thought it unrealistic to
regard the home visit as a search; felt that the
requirement of search warrant to issue only upon a
showing of probable cause would make the AFDC program "in
effect another criminal statute" and would "introduce a
hostile arm's length element into the relationship"
between worker and mother, "a relationship which can be
effective only when it is based upon mutual confidence
and trust"; and concluded that the majority's holding
struck "a damaging blow" to an important social welfare

program. 303 F Supp, at 946.

I

The case comes to us on the pleading and supporting affidavits and without the benefit of testimony which an extended hearing would have provided. The pertinent facts, however, are not in dispute.

Plaintiff Barbara James is the mother of a son, Maurice, who was born in May 1967. They reside in New York City. Mrs. James first applied for AFDC assistance shortly before Maurice's birth. A caseworker made a visit to her apartment at that time without objection. The assistance was authorized.

Two years later, on May 8, 1969, a caseworker wrote Mrs. James that she would visit her home on May 14. Upon receipt of this advice, Mrs. James telephoned the worker that, although she was willing to supply information "reasonable and relevant" to her need for public assistance, any discussion was not to take place at her home. The worker told Mrs. James that she was required by law to visit in her home and that refusal to permit the visit would result in the termination of assistance. Permission was still denied.

On May 13 the City Department of Social Services sent Mrs. James a notice of intent to discontinue assistance because of the visitation refusal. The notice advised the beneficiary of her right to a hearing before a review officer. The hearing was requested and was held on May 27. Mrs. James appeared with an attorney at that hearing. They continued to refuse permission for a worker to visit the James home, but again expressed willingness to cooperate and to permit visits elsewhere. The review officer ruled that the refusal was a proper ground for the termination of assistance. His written decision stated:

> "The home visit which Mrs. James refuses to permit is for the purpose of determining if there are any changes in her situation that might affect her eligibility to continue to receive Public Assistance, or that might affect the amount of such assistance, and to see if there are any social services which the Department of Social Services

606

can provide to the family."

A notice of termination issued on June 2.
Thereupon, without seeking a hearing at the state level, Mrs. James, individually and on behalf of Maurice, and purporting to act on behalf of all other persons similarly situated, instituted the present civil rights suit under 42 USC § 1983. She alleged the denial of rights guaranteed to her under the First, Third, Fourth, Fifth, Sixth, Ninth, Tenth, and Fourteenth Amendments, and under Subchapters IV and XVI of the Social Security Act and regulations issued thereunder. She further alleged that she and her son have no income, resources, or support other than the benefits received under the AFDC program. She asked for declaratory and injunctive relief. A temporary restraining order was issued on June 13, **JAMES v. GOLDBERG**, 302 F Supp 478 (SDNY 1969), and the three-judge District Court was convened.

II
The federal aspects of the AFDC program deserve mention. They are provided for in Subchapter IV, Part A, of the Social Security Act of 1935, 49 Stat 627, as amended, 42 USC §§ 601-610 (1964 ed. and Supp V). Section 401 of the Act, 42 USC § 601 (1964 ed., Supp V), specifies its purpose, namely, "encouraging the care of dependent children in their own homes or in the homes of relatives by enabling each State to furnish financial assistance and rehabilitation and other services .... to needy dependent children and the parents or relatives with whom they are living to help maintain and strengthen family life...." The same section authorizes the federal appropriation for payments to States that qualify. Section 402, 42 USC § 602 (1964 ed., Supp V), provides that a state plan, among other things, must "provide for granting an opportunity for a fair hearing before the State agency to any individual whose claim for aid to families with dependent children is denied or is not acted upon with reasonable promptness"; must "provide that the State agency will make such reports .... as the Secretary [of Health, Education, and Welfare] may from time to time require"; must "provide that the State agency shall, in determining need, take into consideration any other income and resources of any child or relative claiming aid"; and must "provide that where

607

the State agency has reason to believe that the home in which a relative and child receiving aid reside is unsuitable for the child because of the neglect, abuse, or exploitation of such child it shall bring such condition to the attention of the appropriate court or law enforcement agencies in the State...." Section 405, 42 USC § 605, provides that

> "Whenever the State agency has reason to believe that any payments of aid .... made with respect to a child are not being or may not be used in the best interests of the child, the State agency may provide for such counseling and guidance services with respect to the use of such payments and the management of other funds by the relative .... in order to assure use of such payments in the best interest of such child, and may provide for advising such relative that continued failure to so use such payments will result in substitution therefor of protective payments .... or in seeking the appointment of a guardian .... or in the imposition of criminal or civil penalties...."

III

When a case involves a home and some type of official intrusion into that home, as this case appears to do, an immediate and natural reaction is one of concern about Fourth Amendment rights and the protection which that Amendment is intended to afford. Its emphasis indeed is upon one of the most precious aspects of personal aspects of personal security in the home: "The right of the people to be secure in their persons, houses, papers, and effects...." This Court has characterized that right as "basic to a free society." **WOLF v. COLORADO**, 338 US 25, 27, 93 L Ed 1782, 1785, 69 S Ct 1359 (1949); **CAMARA v. MUNICIPAL COURT** 387 US 523, 528, 18 L Ed 2d 930, 985, 87 S Ct 1727 (1967). And over the years the Court consistently has been most protective of the privacy of the dwelling. See, for example, **BOYD v. UNITED STATES**, 116 US 616-630, 29 L Ed 746, 749, 751, 6 S Ct 538 (1886); **MAPP v. OHIO**, 367 US 643, 6 L Ed 2d 1081, 81 S Ct 1684, 84 ALR 2d 933 (1961); **CHIMEL v. CALIFORNIA**, 395 US 752, 23 L Ed 2d 685, 89 S Ct 2034

(1969); **VALE v. LOUISIANA**, 399 US 30, 26 L Ed 2d 409, 90 S Ct 1969 (1970). In Camara MR. JUSTICE WHITE, after noting that the "translation of the abstract prohibition against 'unreasonable searches and seizures' into workable guidelines for the decision of particular cases is a difficult task," went on to observe,

> "Nevertheless, one governing principle, justified by history and by current experience, has consistently been followed: except in certain carefully defined classes of cases, a search of private property without proper consent is 'unreasonable' unless it has been authorized by a valid search warrant." 387 US, at 528-529, 18 L Ed 2d at 935.

He pointed out, too, that one's Fourth Amendment protection subsists apart from his being suspected of criminal behavior. 387 US, at 530, 18 L Ed 2d at 936.

IV
This natural and quite proper protective attitude, however, is not a factor in this case, for the seemingly obvious and simple reasons that we are not concerned here with any search by the New York social service agency in the Fourth Amendment meaning of that term. It is true that the governing statute and regulations appear to make mandatory the initial home visit and the subsequent periodic "contacts" (which may include home visits) for the inception and continuance of aid. It is also true that the caseworker's posture in the home visit is perhaps, in a sense, both rehabilitative and investigative. But this latter aspect, we think, is given too broad a character and far more emphasis than it deserves if it is equated with a search in the traditional criminal law context. We note, too, that the visitation in itself is not forced or compelled, and that the beneficiary's denial of permission is not a criminal act. If consent to the visitation is withheld, no visitation takes place. The aid then never begins or merely ceases, as the case may be. There is no entry of the home and there is no search.

V
If however, we were to assume that a caseworker's home visit, before or subsequent to the beneficiary's

initial qualification for benefits, somehow (perhaps because the average beneficiary might feel she is in no position to refuse consent to the visit), and despite its interview nature, does possess some of the characteristics of a search in the traditional sense, we nevertheless conclude that the visit not fall within the Fourth Amendment's proscription. This is because it does not descend to the level of unreasonableness. It is unreasonableness which is the Fourth Amendment's standard. **TERRY v. OHIO**, 392 US 1, 9, 20 L Ed 2d 889, 898, 88 S Ct 1868 (1968); **ELKINS v. UNITED STATES**, 364 US 206, 222, 4 L Ed 2d 1669, 1689, 80 S Ct 1437 (1960). And MR. CHIEF JUSTICE WARREN observed in Terry that "the specific content and incidents of this right must be shaped by the context in which it is asserted." 392 US, at 9, 20 L Ed 2d at 898.

There are a number of factors that compel us to conclude that the home visit proposed for Mrs. James is not unreasonable.:

1. The public's interest in this particular segment of the area of assistance to the unfortunate is protection and aid for the dependent child whose family requires such aid for that child. The focus is on the *child* and, further, it is on the child who is *dependent*. There is no more worthy object of the public's concern. The dependent child's needs are paramount, and only with hesitancy would we relegate those needs, in the scale of comparative values, to a position secondary to what the mother claims as her rights.

2. The agency, with tax funds provided from federal as well as from state sources, is fulfilling a public trust. The state, working through its qualified welfare agency, has appropriate and paramount interest and concern in seeing and assuring that the intended and proper objects of that tax produced assistance are the ones who benefit from the aid it dispenses. Surely it is not unreasonable, in the Fourth Amendment sense or in any other sense of that term, that the State have as its command a gentle means, of limited extent and of practical and considerate application, of achieving the assurance.

3. One who dispenses purely private charity naturally has an interest in and expects to know how his

charitable funds are utilized and put to work. The public, when it is the provider, rightly expects the same. It might well expect more, because of the trust aspect of public funds, and the recipient, as well as the caseworker, has not only an interest but an obligation.

4. The emphasis of the New York statutes and regulations is upon the home, upon "close contract" with the beneficiary, upon restoring the aid recipient "to a condition of self-support," and upon the relief of his distress. The federal emphasis is no different. It is upon "assistance and rehabilitation," upon maintaining and strengthening family life and upon "maximum self-support and personal independence consistent with the maintenance of continuing parental care and protection. . . ." 42 USC § 601 (1964 ed., Supp V); **DANDRIDGE v. WILLIAMS**, 397 US 471, 479, 25 L Ed 2d 491, 498, 90 S Ct 1153 (1970), and id., at 510, 25 L Ed 2d at 516 (MARSHALL, J., dissenting). It requires cooperation from the state agency upon specified standards and in specified ways. And it is concerned about any possible exploitation of the child.

5. The home visit it is true, is not required by federal statute or regulation. But it has been noted that the visit is "the heart of welfare administration"; that it affords "a personal, rehabilitative orientation, unlike that of most federal programs"; and that the "more pronounced service orientation" effected by Congress with the 1956 amendments to the Social Security Act "gave redoubled importance to the practice of home visiting." Note, Rehabilitation, Investigation and the Welfare Home Visit, 79 Yale LJ 746, 748 (1970). The home visit is an established routine in States besides New York.

6. The means employed by the New York agency are significant. Mrs. James received written notice several days in advance of the intended home visit. The date was specified. Section 134-a of the New York Social Services Law, effective April 1, 1967 and set forth in n.2, supra, sets the tone. Privacy is emphasized. The applicant-recipient is made the primary source of information as to eligibility-. Outside informational source, other than public records, are to be consulted only with the beneficiary's consent. Forcibly entry or entry under false pretenses or visitation outside working hours or

611

snooping in the home are forbidden. HEW Handbook of Public Assistance Administration pt. IV, §§ 2200(a) and 2300; 18 NYCRR §§ 351.1, 351.6, and 351.7. All this minimizes any "burden" upon the homeowner's right against unreasonable intrusion.

7. Mrs. James, in fact, on this record presents no specific complaint of any unreasonable intrusion of her home and nothing that supports an inference that the desired home visit had as its purpose the obtaining of information as to criminal activity. She complains of no proposed visitation at an awkward or retirement hour. She suggests no forcible entry. She refers to no snooping. She describes no impolite or reprehensible conduct of any kind. She alleges only, in general and nonspecific terms, that on previous visits and, on information and belief, on visitation at the home of other aid recipients, "questions concerning personal relationships, beliefs and behavior are raised and pressed which are unnecessary for a determination of continuing eligibility." Paradoxically, this same complaint could be made of a conference held elsewhere than in the home, and yet this is what is sought by Mrs. James. The same complaint could be made of the census taker's questions. See MR. JUSTICE MARSHALL's opinion, as United States Circuit Judge, in **UNITED STATES v. RIKENBACKER**, 309 F2d 462 (CA2 1962), cert denied, 371 US 962, 9 L Ed 2d 509, 83 S Ct 542. What Mrs. James appears to want from the agency that provides her and her infant son with the necessities for life is the right to receive those necessities upon her own informational terms, to utilize the Fourth Amendment as a wedge for imposing those terms, and to avoid questions of any kind.

8. We are not persuaded, as Mrs. James would have us be, that all information pertinent to the issue of eligibility can be obtained by the agency through an interview at a place other than the home, or, as the District Court majority suggested, by examining a lease or a birth certificate, or by periodic medical examinations, or by interviews with school personnel. 33 F Supp, at 943. Although these secondary sources might be helpful, they would not always assure verification of actual residence or of actual physical presence in the home, which are requisites for AFDC benefits, or of impending medical needs. And, of course, little

children, such as Maurice James, are not yet registered in school.

9. The visit is not one by police or uniformed authority. It is made by a caseworker of some training whose primary objective is, or should be, the welfare, not the prosecution, of the aid recipient for whom the worker has profound responsibility. As has already been stressed, the program concerns dependent children and the needy families of those children. It does not deal with crime or with the actual or suspected perpetrators of crime. The caseworker is not a sleuth but rather we trust, is a friend to one in need.

10. The home visit is not a criminal investigation, does not equate with a criminal investigation, and despite the announced fears of Mrs. James and those who would join her, is not in aid of any criminal proceeding. If the visitation serves to discourage misrepresentation or fraud, such a byproduct of that visit does not impress upon the visit itself a dominant criminal investigative aspect. And if the visit should, by chance, lead to the discovery of fraud and a criminal prosecution should follow, then, even assuming that the evidence discovered upon the home visitation is admissible, an issue upon which we express no opinion, that is a routine and expected fact of life and a consequence no greater than that which necessarily ensues upon any other discovery by a citizen of criminal conduct.

11. The warrant procedure, which the plaintiff appears to claim to be so precious to her, even if civil in nature, is not without its seriously objectionable features in welfare context. If a warrant could be obtained (the plaintiff affords us little help as to how it would be obtained), it presumably could be applied for ex parte, its execution would require no notice, it would justify entry by force, and its hours for execution would not be so limited as those prescribed for home visitation. The warrant necessarily would imply conduct either criminal or out of compliance with an asserted governing standard. Of course, the force behind the warrant argument, welcome to the one asserting it, is the fact that it would have to rest upon probable cause, the probable cause in the welfare context, as Mrs. James concedes, requires more than the mere need of the

caseworker to see the child in the home and to have assurance that the child is there and is receiving the benefit of the aid that has been authorized for it.   In this setting the warrant argument is out of place.

It seems to us that the situation is akin to that where an Internal Revenue Service agent, in making a routine civil audit of a taxpayer's income tax return, asks that the taxpayer produce for the agent's review some proof of a deduction the taxpayer has asserted to his benefit in the computation of his tax.   If the taxpayer refuses, there is, absent fraud, only a disallowance of the claimed deduction and a consequent additional tax.   The taxpayer is fully within his "rights" in refusing to produce the proof, but in maintaining and asserting those rights a tax detriment results and it is a detriment of the taxpayer's own making.   So here Mrs. James has the "right" to refuse the home visit, but a consequence in the form of cessation of aid, similar to the taxpayer's resultant additional tax, flows from that refusal.   The choice is entirely hers, and nothing of constitutional magnitude is involved.

VI

CAMARA v. MUNICIPAL COURT, 387 US 523, 18 L Ed 2d 930, 87 S Ct 1727 (1967), and its companion case, **SEE v. CITY OF SEATTLE**, 387 US 541, 18 L Ed 2d 943, 87 S Ct 1727 (1967), both by a divided Court, are not inconsistent with our result here.   Those cases concerned, respectively, a refusal of entry to city housing inspectors checking for a violation of a building's occupancy permit, and a refusal of entry to a fire department representative interested in compliance with a city's fire code.   In each case a majority of this Court held that the Fourth Amendment barred prosecution for refusal to permit the desired warrantless inspection. **FRANK v. MARYLAND**, 359 US 360, 3 L Ed 2d 377, 79 S Ct 804 (1959), a case that reached an opposing result and that concerned a request by a health officer for entry in order to check the source of a rat infestation, was pro tanto overruled.   Both Frank and Camara involved dwelling quarters.   See had to do with a commercial warehouse.

But the facts of the three cases are significantly different from those before us.   Each concerned a true search for violations.   Frank was a criminal prosecution for the owner's refusal to permit entry.   So, too, was

See.   Camara had to do with a writ of prohibition sought
to prevent an already pending criminal prosecution.   The
community welfare aspects, of course, were highly
important, but each case arose in a criminal context
where a genuine search was denied and prosecution
followed.
        In contrast, Mrs. James is not being prosecuted for
her refusal to permit the home visit and is not about to
be so prosecuted.   Her wishes in that respect are fully
honored.   We have not been told, and have not found, that
her refusal is made a criminal act by any applicable New
York or federal statute.   The only consequence of her
refusal is that the payment of benefits ceases.
Important and serious as this is, the situation is no
different than if she had exercised a similar negative
choice initially and refrained from applying for AFDC
benefits.   If a statute made her refusal a criminal
offense, and if this case were one concerning her
prosecution under that statute, Camara and See would have
conceivable pertinency.

        VII
        Our holding today does not mean, of course, that a
termination of benefits upon refusal of a home visit is
to be upheld against constitutional challenge under all
conceivable circumstances.   The early morning mass raid
upon homes of the welfare recipients is not unknown.   See
PARRISH v. CIVIL SERVICE COMM'N, 66 Cal 2d 260, 425 P2d
223 (1967); Reich, Midnight Welfare Searches and the
Social Security Act, 72 Yale LJ 1347 (1963).   But that is
not this case.   Facts of that kind present another case
for another day.
        We therefore conclude that the home visitation as
structured by the New York statutes and regulations is a
reasonable administrative tool; that it serves a valid
and proper administrative purpose for the dispensation of
the AFDC program; that it is not an unwarranted invasion
of personal privacy; and that it violates no right
guaranteed by the Fourth Amendment.

        Reversed and remanded with directions to enter a
judgment of dismissal.

                                It is so ordered.

NEW JERSEY v. T.L.O
469 U.S. 325, 105 U.S. 733, 83 L.Ed.2d. 720 (1990)
CERTIORARI TO THE SUPREME COURT OF NEW JERSEY

JUSTICE WHITE delivered the opinion of the Court.

We granted certiorari in this case to examine the appropriateness of the exclusionary rule as a remedy for searches carried out in violation of the Fourth Amendment by public school authorities. Our consideration of the proper application of the Fourth Amendment to the public schools, however, has led us to conclude that the search that gave rise to the case now before us did not violate the Fourth Amendment. Accordingly, we here address only the questions of the proper standard for assessing the legality of searches conducted by public school officials and the application of that standard to the facts of this case.

I

On March 7, 1980, a teacher at Piscataway High School in Middlesex County, N.J., discovered two girls smoking in a lavatory. One of the two girls was the respondent T.L.O., who at that time was a 14-year-old high school freshman. Because smoking in the lavatory was a violation of a school rule, the teacher took the two girls to the Principal's office, where they met with Assistant Vice Principal Theodore Choplick. In response to questioning by Mr. Choplick, T.L.O's companion admitted that she had violated the rule. T.L.O., however, denied that she had been smoking in the lavatory and claimed that she did not smoke at all.

Mr. Choplick asked T.L.O. to come into his private office and demanded to see her purse. Opening the purse, he found a pack of cigarettes, which he removed from the purse and held before T.L.O. as he accused her of having lied to him. As he reached into the purse for the cigarettes, Mr. Choplick also noticed a package of cigarette rolling papers. In his experience, possession of rolling papers by high school students was closely associated with the use of marihuana. Suspecting that a closer examination of the purse might yield further evidence of drug use, Mr. Choplick proceeded to search the purse thoroughly. The search revealed a small amount of marihuana, a pipe, a number of empty plastic bags, a substantial quantity of money in one-dollar bills, an index card that appeared to be a list of students who owed T.L.O. money, and two letters that implicated T.L.O. in marihuana dealing.

Mr. Choplick notified T.L.O.'s mother and the police, and turned the evidence of drug dealing over to the police. At the request of the police, T.L.O.'s mother took her daughter to police headquarters, where T.L.O.confessed that she had been selling marihuana at the high school. On the basis of the confession and the evidence seized by Mr. Choplick, the State brought delinquency charges against T.L.O. in the Juvenile and Domestic Relations Court of Middlesex County. Contending that Mr. Choplick's search of her purse violated the Fourth Amendment, T.L.O. moved to suppress the evidence found in her purse as well as her confession, which she argued, was tainted by the allegedly unlawful search. The Juvenile Court denied the motion to suppress. State ex rel. T.L.O., 78 N.J. Super. 329, 428 A.2d 1327 (1980). Although the court concluded that the Fourth Amendment did apply to searches carried out by school officials, it held that

"a school official may properly conduct a search of a student's person if the official has a reasonable suspicion that a crime has been or is in the process of being committed, or reasonable cause to believe that the search is necessary to maintain school discipline or enforce school policies." Id., at 341, 428 A.2d, at 1333 (emphasis in original).

Applying this standard, the court concluded that the search conducted by Mr. Choplick was a reasonable one. The initial decision to open the purse was justified by Mr. Choplick's well-founded suspicion that T.L.O. had violated the rule forbidding smoking in the lavatory. Once the purse was open, evidence of marihuana violations was in plain view, and Mr. Choplick was entitled to conduct a thorough search to determine the nature and extent of T.L.O's drug-related activities. Id., at 343, 428 A.2d, at 1334. Having denied the motion to suppress, the court on March 23, 1981, found T.L.O. to be a delinquent and on January 8, 1982, sentenced her to a year's probation.

On appeal from the final judgment of the Juvenile Court, a divided Appellate Division affirmed the trial court's finding that there had been no Fourth Amendment violation, but vacated the adjudication of delinquency and remanded for a determination whether T.L.O had knowingly and voluntarily waived her Fifth Amendment rights before confessing. State ex rel. T.L.O., 185 N.J. Super. 279, 448 A.2d 493 (1982). T.L.O. appealed the Fourth Amendment ruling, and the Supreme Court of New Jersey reversed the judgment of the Appellate Division and ordered the suppression of the evidence found in T.L.O's purse. State ex rel. T.L.O., 94 N.J. 331, 463 A.2d 934 (1983).

The New Jersey Supreme Court agreed with the lower courts that the Fourth Amendment applies to searches conducted by school officials. The court also rejected the State of New Jersey's argument that the exclusionary rule should not be employed to prevent the use in juvenile proceedings of evidence unlawfully seized by school officials. Declining to consider whether applying the rule to the fruits of searches by school official would have any deterrent value, the court held simply that the precedents of this Court establish that "if an official search violates constitutional rights, the evidence is not admissible in criminal proceedings." Id., at 341, 463 A.2d, at 939 (footnote omitted).

With respect to the question of the legality of the search before it, the court agreed with the Juvenile Court that a warrantless search by a school official does not violate the Fourth Amendment so long as the official "has reasonable grounds to believe that a student possesses evidence of illegal activity or activity that would interfere with school discipline and order." Id., at 346, 463 A.2d, at 941-942. However, the court, with two justices dissenting, sharply disagreed with the Juvenile Court's conclusion that the search of the purse was reasonable. According to the majority, the contents of T.L.O.'s purse had no bearing on the accusation against T.L.O., for possession of cigarettes (as opposed to smoking them in the lavatory) did not violate school rules, and a mere desire for evidence that would impeach

T.L.O.'s claim that she did not smoke cigarettes could not justify the search. Moreover, even if a reasonable suspicion that T.L.O had cigarettes in her purse would justify a search, Mr. Choplick had no such suspicion, as no one had furnished him with any specific information that there were cigarettes in the purse. Finally, leaving aside the question whether Mr. Choplick was justified in opening the purse, the court held that the evidence of drug use that he saw inside did not justify the extensive "rummaging" through T.L.O.'s papers and effects that followed. Id., at 347, 463 A.2d, at 942-943.

We granted the State of New Jersey's petition for certiorari. 464 U.S. 991 (1983). Although the State had argued in the Supreme Court of New Jersey that the search of T.L.O.'s purse did not violate the Fourth Amendment, the petition for certiorari raised only the question whether the exclusionary rule should operate to bar consideration in juvenile delinquency proceedings of evidence unlawfully seized by a school official without the involvement of law enforcement officers. When this case was first argued last Term, the State conceded for the purpose of argument that the standard devised by the New Jersey Supreme Court for determining the legality of school searches was appropriate and that the court had correctly applied that standard; the State contended only that the remedial purposes of the exclusionary rule were not well served by applying it to searches conducted by public authorities not primarily engaged in law enforcement.

Although we originally granted certiorari to decide the issue of the appropriate remedy in juvenile court proceedings for unlawful school searches, our doubts regarding the wisdom of deciding that question in isolation from the broader question of what limits, if any, the Fourth Amendment places on the activities of school authorities prompted us to order reargument on that question. Having heard argument on the legality of the search of T.L.O.'s purse, we are satisfied that the search did not violate the Fourth Amendment.

II

In determining whether the search at issue in this case violated the Fourth Amendment, we are faced initially with the question whether that Amendment's

619

prohibition on unreasonable searches and seizures applies to searches conducted by public school officials. We hold that it does.

It is now beyond dispute that "the Federal Constitution, by virtue of the Fourteenth Amendment, prohibits unreasonable searches and seizures by state officers." **ELKINS v. UNITED STATES**, 364 U.S. 206, 213 (1960); accord, **MAPP v. OHIO**, 367 U.S. 643 (1961); **WOLF v. COLORADO**, 338 U.S. 25 (1949). Equally indisputable is the proposition that the Fourteenth Amendment protects the rights of students against encroachment by public school officials:

> "The Fourteenth Amendment, as now applied to the States, protects the citizen against the State itself and all of its creatures - Boards of Education not excepted. These have, of course, important, delicate, and highly discretionary functions, but none that they may not perform within the limits of the Bill of Rights. That they are educating the young for citizenship is reason for scrupulous protection of Constitutional freedoms of the individual, if we are not to strangle the free mind at its source and teach youth to discount important principles of our government as mere platitudes." **WEST VIRGINIA STATE BD. OF EDUCATION v. BARNETTE**, 319 U.S. 624, 637 (1943).

These two propositions-- that the Fourth Amendment applies to the States through the Fourteenth Amendment, and that the actions of public school officials are subject to the limits places on state action by the Fourteenth Amendment--might appear sufficient to answer the suggestion that the Fourth Amendment does not proscribe unreasonable searches by school officials. On reargument, however, the State of New Jersey has argued that the history of the Fourth Amendment indicates that the Amendment was intended to regulate only searches and seizures carried out by law enforcement officers; accordingly, although public school officials are concededly state agents for purposes of the Fourteenth Amendment, the Fourth Amendment creates no rights enforceable against them.

It may well be true that the evil toward which the Fourth Amendment was primarily directed was the resurrection of the pre-Revolutionary practice of using general warrants or "writs of assistance" to authorize searches for contraband by officers of the Crown. See **UNITED STATES v. CHADWICK**, 433 U.S. 1, 7-8 (1977); **BOYD v. UNITED STATES**, 116 U.S. 616, 624-629 (1886). But this Court has never limited the Amendment's prohibition on unreasonable searches and seizures to operations conducted by the police. Rather the Court has long spoken of the Fourth Amendment's strictures as restraints imposed upon "governmental action"--that is, "upon the activities of sovereign authority." **BURDEAU v. McDOWELL**, 256 U.S. 465, 475 (1921). Accordingly, we have held the Fourth Amendment applicable to the activities of civil as well as criminal authorities: building inspectors, see **CAMARA v. MUNICIPAL COURT**, 387 U.S. 523, 528 91967), Occupational Safety and Health Act inspectors, see **MARSHALL v. BARLOW'S INC.**, 436 U.S. 307, 312-313 (1978), and even firemen entering privately owned premises to battle a fire, see **MICHIGAN v. TYLER**, 436 U.S. 499, 506 (1978), are all subject to the restraints imposed by the Fourth Amendment. As we observed in **CAMARA v. MUNICIPAL COURT, supra,** "[t]he basic purpose of this Amendment, as recognized in countless decisions of this Court, is to safeguard the privacy and security of individuals against arbitrary invasions by governmental officials." 387 U.S., at 528. Because the individual's interest in privacy and personal security "suffers whether the government's motivation is to investigate violations of criminal laws or breaches of other statutory or regulatory standards," **MARSHALL v. BARLOW'S INC., supra**, at 312-313, it would be "anomalous to say that the individual and his private property are fully protected by the Fourth Amendment only when the individual is suspected of criminal behavior." **CAMARA v. MUNICIPAL COURT, supra,**a at 530.

Notwithstanding the general applicability of the Fourth Amendment to the activities of civil authorities, a few courts have concluded that school officials are exempt from the dictates of the Fourth Amendment by virtue of the special nature of their authority over schoolchildren. See, e.g., **R.C.M v. STATE**, 660 S.W. 2d 552 (Tex. App. 1983). Teachers and school administrators, it is said, act in loco parentis in their dealings with students: their authority is that of the parent, not the

State, and is therefore not subject to the limits of the Fourth Amendment. Ibid.

Such reasoning is in tension with contemporary reality and the teachings of this Court. We have held school officials subject to the commands of the First Amendment, see **TINKER v. DES MOINES INDEPENDENT COMMUNITY SCHOOL DISTRICT**, 393 U.S. 503 (1969), and the Due Process Clause of the Fourteenth Amendment, see **GOSS v. LOPEZ**, 419 U.S. 565 (1975). If school authorities are state actors for purposes of the constitutional guarantees of freedom of expression and due process, it is difficult to understand why they should be deemed to be exercising parental rather than public authority when conducting searches of their students. More generally, the Court has recognized that "the concept of parental delegation" as a source of school authority is not entirely "consonant with compulsory education laws." **INGRAHAM v. WRIGHT**, 430 U.S. 651, 662 (1977). Today's public school officials do not merely exercise authority voluntarily conferred on them by individual parents; rather, they act in furtherance of publicly mandated educational and disciplinary policies. See, e.g., the opinion in State ex rel. T.L.O., 94 N.J., at 343, 463 A.2d, at 934, 940, describing the New Jersey statutes regulating school disciplinary policies and establishing the authority of school officials over their students. In carrying out searches and other disciplinary policies and establishing the authority of school officials over their students. In carrying out searches and other disciplinary functions pursuant to such policies, school officials act as representatives of the State, not merely as surrogates for the parents, and they cannot claim the parent's immunity from the strictures of the Fourth Amendment.

III

To hold that the Fourth Amendment applies to searches conducted by school authorities is only to begin the inquiry into the standards governing such searches. Although the underlying command of the Fourth Amendment is always that searches and seizures be reasonable, what is reasonable depends on the context within which a search takes place. The determination of the standard of reasonableness governing any specific class of searches requires "balancing the need to search against the invasion which the search entails." **CAMARA v. MUNICIPAL COURT, supra,** at 536-537. On one side of the balance are arrayed the individual's legitimate expectations of privacy and personal security; on the other, the government's need for effective methods to deal with breaches of public order.

We have recognized that even a limited search of the person is a substantial invasion of privacy. **TERRY v. OHIO,** 392 U.S. 1, 24-25 (1967). We have also recognized that searches of closed items of personal luggage are intrusions on protected privacy interests, for "the Fourth Amendment provides protection to the owner of every container that conceals its contents from plain view." **UNITED STATES v. ROSS,** 456 U.S. 798, 822-823 (1982). A search of a child's person or of a closed purse or other bag carried on her person, no less than a similar search carried out on an adult, is undoubtedly a severe violation of subjective expectations of privacy.

Of course, the Fourth Amendment does not protect subjective expectations of privacy that are unreasonable or otherwise "illegitimate." See, e.g., **HUDSON v. PALMER,** 468 U.S. 517 91984); **RAWLINGS v. KENTUCKY,** 448 U.S. 98 (1980). To receive the protection of the Fourth Amendment, an expectation of privacy must be one that society is "prepared to recognize as legitimate." **HUDSON v. PALMER,** supra, at 526. The State of New Jersey has argued that because of the pervasive supervision to which children in the schools are necessarily subject, a child has virtually no legitimate expectation of privacy in articles of personal property "unnecessarily" carried into a school. This argument has two factual premises: (1) the fundamental incompatibility of expectations of privacy with the maintenance of a sound educational environment; and (2) the minimal interest of the child bringing any items of personal property into the school. Both premises are severely flawed.

Although this Court may take notice of the difficulty of maintaining discipline in the public schools today, the situation is not so dire that students in the schools may claim no legitimate expectations of privacy. We have recently recognized that the need to maintain order in a prison is such that prisoners retain no legitimate expectations of privacy in their cells, but it goes almost without saying that "[t]he prisoner and

623

the schoolchild stand in wholly different circumstances, separated by the harsh facts of criminal conviction and incarceration." **INGRAHAM v. WRIGHT, supra**, at 669. We are not yet ready to hold that the schools and the prisons need be equated for purposes of the Fourth Amendment.

Nor does the State's suggestion that children have no legitimate need to bring personal property into the schools seem well anchored in reality. Students at a minimum must bring to school not only the supplies needed for their studies but also keys, money, and necessaries of personal hygiene and grooming. In addition, students may carry on their persons or in purses or wallets such nondisruptive yet highly personal items as photographs, letters and diaries. Finally, students may have perfectly legitimate reasons to carry with them articles of property needed in connection with extracurricular or recreational activities. In short, schoolchildren may find it necessary to carry with them a variety of legitimate, noncontraband items, and there is no reason to conclude that they have necessarily waived all rights to privacy in such items merely by bringing them onto school grounds.

Against the child's interest in privacy must be set the substantial interest of teachers and administrators in maintaining discipline in the classroom and on school grounds. Maintaining order in the classroom has never been easy, but in recent years, school disorder has often taken particularly ugly forms: drug use and violent crime in the schools have become major social problems. See generally 1 NIE, U.S. Dept. of Health, Education and Welfare, Violent Schools--Safe Schools: The Safe School Study Report to the Congress (1978). Even in schools that have been spared the most severe disciplinary problems, the preservation of order and a proper educational environment requires close supervision of schoolchildren, as well as the enforcement of rules against conduct that would be perfectly permissible if undertaken by an adult. "Events calling for discipline are frequent occurrences and sometimes require immediate, effective action." **GOSS v. LOPEZ**, 419 U.S., at 580. Accordingly, we have recognized that maintaining security and order in the schools requires a certain degree of flexibility in school disciplinary procedures, and we have respected the value of preserving the informality of the student-teacher relationship. See id., at 582-583; **INGRAHAM v. WRIGHT**, 430 U.S., AT 680-682.

How, then, should we strike the balance between the schoolchild's legitimate expectations of privacy and the school's equally legitimate need to maintain an environment in which learning can take place? It is evident that the school setting requires some easing of the restrictions to which searches by public authorities are ordinarily subject. The warrant requirement, in particular, is unsuited to the school environment: requiring a teacher to obtain a warrant before searching a child suspected on an infraction of school rules (or of the criminal law) would unduly interfere with the maintenance of the swift and informal disciplinary procedures needed in the schools. Just as we have in other cases dispensed with the warrant requirement when "the burden of obtaining a warrant is likely to frustrate the governmental purpose behind the search," **CAMARA v. MUNICIPAL COURT**, 387 U.S., at 532-533, we hold today that school officials need not obtain a warrant before searching a student who is under their authority.

The school setting also requires some modification of the level of suspicion of illicit activity needed to justify a search. Ordinarily, a search--even one that may permissibly be carried out without a warrant--must be based upon "probable cause" to believe that a violation of the law has occurred. See, e.g., **ALMEIDA-SANCHEZ v. UNITED STATES**, 413 U.S. 266, 273 (1973); **SIBRON v. NEW YORK**, 392 U.S. 40, 2-66 (1968). However, "probable cause" is not an irreducible requirement of a valid search. The fundamental command of the Fourth Amendment is that searches and seizures be reasonable, and although "both the concept of probable cause and the requirement of a warrant bear on the reasonableness of a search, . . . in certain limited circumstances neither is required." **ALMEIDA-SANCHEZ v. UNITED STATES, supra**, at 277 (POWELL, J., concurring). Thus, we have in a number of cases recognized the legality of searches and seizures based on suspicions that, although "reasonable," do not rise to the level of probable cause. See, e.g., **TERRY v. OHIO**, 392 U.S. 1 ¯(1968); **UNITED STATES v. BRIGNONI-PONCE**, 422 U.S. 873, 881 (1975); **DELAWARE v. PROUSE**, 440 U.S. 648, 654-655 (1979); **UNITED STATES v. MARTINEZ-FUERTE**, 428 U.S. 543 91976); cf. **CAMARA v. MUNICIPAL COURT, supra**, at

534-539. Where a careful balancing of governmental and private interests suggests that the public interest is best served by a Fourth Amendment standard of reasonableness that stops short of probable cause, we have not hesitated to adopt such a standard.

We join the majority of courts that have examined this issue in concluding that the accommodation of the privacy interests of schoolchildren with the substantial need of teachers and administrators for freedom to maintain order in the schools does not require strict adherence to the requirement that searches be based on probable cause to believe that the subject of the search has violated or is violating the law. Rather, the legality of a search of a student should depend simply on the reasonableness, under all the circumstances, of the search. Determining the reasonableness of any search involves a two fold inquiry: first, one must consider "whether the . . . action was justified at its inception," **TERRY v. OHIO**, 392 U.S., at 20; second, one must determine whether the search as actually conducted "was reasonably related in scope to the circumstances which justified the interference in the first place," ibid. Under ordinary circumstances, a search of a student by a teacher or other school official will be "justified at its inception" when there are reasonable grounds for suspecting that the search will turn up evidence that the student has violated or is violating either the law or the rules of the school. Such a search will be permissible in its scope when the measures adopted are reasonably related to the objectives of the search and not excessively intrusive in light of the age and sex of the student and the nature of the infraction.

This standard will, we trust, neither unduly burden the efforts of school authorities to maintain order in their schools nor authorize unrestrained intrusions upon the privacy of schoolchildren. By focusing attention on the question of reasonableness, the standard will spare teachers and school administrators the necessity of schooling themselves in the niceties of probable cause and permit them to regulate their conduct according to the dictates of reason and common sense. At the same time, the reasonableness standard should ensure that the interests of students will be invaded no more than is necessary to achieve the legitimate end of preserving order in the schools.

IV

There remains the question of the legality of the search in this case. We recognize that the "reasonable grounds" standard applied by the New Jersey Supreme Court in its consideration of this question is not substantially different from the standard that we have adopted today. Nonetheless, we believe that the New Jersey court's application of that standard to strike down the search of T.L.O.'s purse reflects a somewhat crabbed notion of reasonableness. Our review of the facts surrounding the search leads us to conclude that the search was in no sense unreasonable for Fourth Amendment purposes.

The incident that gave rise to this case actually involved two separate searches, with the first-the search for cigarettes--providing the suspicion that gave rise to the second--the search for marihuana. Although it is the fruits of the second search that are at issue here, the validity of the search for marihuana must depend on the reasonableness of the initial search for cigarettes, as there would have been no reason to suspect that T.L.O. possessed marihuana had the first search not taken place. Accordingly, it is to the search for cigarettes that we first turn our attention.

The New Jersey Supreme Court pointed to two grounds for its holding that the search for cigarettes was unreasonable. First, the court observed that possession of cigarettes was not in itself illegal or a violation of school rules. Because the contents of T.L.O.'s purse would therefore have "no direct bearing on the infraction" of which she was accused (smoking in a lavatory where smoking was prohibited), there was no reason to search her purse. Second, even assuming that a search of T.L.O.'s purse might under some circumstances be reasonable in light of the accusation made against T.L.O., the New Jersey court concluded that Mr. Choplick in this particular case had no reasonable grounds to suspect that T.L.O. had cigarettes in her purse. At best, according to the court, Mr. Choplick had "a good hunch." 94 N.J., at 347, 463 A.2d, at 942.

Both these conclusions are implausible. T.L.O. had been accused of smoking, and had denied the accusation in the strongest possible terms when she states that she said she did not smoke at all. Surely it cannot be said that under these circumstances, T.L.O.'s possession of cigarettes would be irrelevant to the charges against her or to her response to those charges. T.L.O.'s possession of cigarettes, once it was discovered, would both corroborate the report that she had been smoking and undermine the credibility of her defense to the charge of smoking. To be sure, the discovery of the cigarettes would not prove that T.L.O. had been smoking in the lavatory; nor would it, strictly speaking, necessarily be inconsistent with her claim that she did not smoke at all. But it is universally recognized that evidence to be relevant to an inquiry, need not conclusively prove the ultimate fact in issue, but only have "any tendency to make the existence of any fact that is of consequence to the determination of the action more probable or less probable than it would be without the evidence." Fed. Rule Evid. 401. The relevance of T.L.O.'s possession of cigarettes to the question whether she had been smoking and to the credibility of her denial that she smoked supplied the necessary "nexus" between the item searched for and the infraction under investigation. See **WARDEN v. HAYDEN**, 387 U.S. 294, 306-307 (1967). Thus, if Mr. Choplick in fact had a reasonable suspicion that T.L.O. had cigarettes in her purse, the search was justified despite the fact that the cigarettes, if found, would constitute "mere evidence" of a violation. Ibid.

Of course, the New Jersey Supreme Court also held that Mr. Choplick had no reasonable suspicion that the purse would contain cigarettes. This conclusion is puzzling. A teacher had reported that T.L.O. was smoking in the lavatory. Certainly this report gave Mr. Choplick reason to suspect that T.L.O. was carrying cigarettes with her; and if she did have cigarettes, her purse was the obvious place in which to find them. Mr. Choplick's suspicion that there were cigarettes in the purse was not an "inchoate and unparticularized suspicion or 'hunch,'" **TERRY v. OHIO** 392 U.S., at 27; rather, it was the sort of "common-sense conclusio[n] about human behavior" upon which "practical people"--including governmental officials--are entitled to rely. **UNITED STATES v. CORTEZ**, 449 U.S. 411, 418 (1981). Of course, even if the teacher's report were true, T.L.O. might not have had a pack of cigarettes with her; she might have borrowed a cigarette from someone else or have been sharing a cigarette with another student. But the requirement of reasonable suspicion is not a requirement of absolute certainty: "sufficient probability, not certainty, is the touchstone of reasonableness under the Fourth Amendment ...." **HILL v. CALIFORNIA**, 401 U.S. 797, 804 (1971). Because the hypothesis that T.L.O. was carrying cigarettes in her purse was itself not unreasonable, it is irrelevant that other hypotheses were also consistent with the teacher's accusation. Accordingly, it cannot be said that Mr. Choplick acted unreasonably when he examined T.L.O.'s purse to see if it contained cigarettes.

Our conclusion that Mr. Choplick's decision to open T.L.O.'s purse was reasonable brings us to the question of the further search for marihuana once the pack of cigarettes was located. The suspicion upon which the search for marihuana was founded provided when Mr. Choplick observed a package of rolling papers in the purse as he removed the pack of cigarettes. Although T.L.O. does not dispute the reasonableness of Mr. Choplick's belief that the rolling papers indicated the presence of marihuana, she does contend that the scope of the search Mr. Choplick conducted exceeded permissible bounds when he seized and read certain letters that implicated T.L.O in drug dealing. This argument, too, is unpersuasive. The discovery of the rolling papers concededly gave rise to a reasonable suspicion that T.L.O was carrying marihuana as well as cigarettes in her purse. This suspicion justified further exploration of T.L.O.'s purse, which turned up more evidence of drug-related activities: a pipe, a number of plastic bags of the type commonly used to store marihuana, a small quantity of marihuana, and a fairly substantial amount of money. Under these circumstances it was not unreasonable to extend the search to a separate zippered compartment of the purse; and when a search of that compartment revealed an index card containing a list of "people who owe me money" as well as two letters, the inference that T.L.O. was involved in marihuana trafficking was substantial‾ enough to justify Mr. Choplick in examining the letters to determine whether they contained any further evidence. In short, we cannot conclude that the search for marihuana was unreasonable in any respect.

Because the search resulting in the discovery of the evidence of marihuana dealing by T.L.O. was reasonable, the New Jersey Supreme Court's decision to exclude that evidence from T.L.O.'s juvenile delinquency proceedings on Fourth Amendment grounds was erroneous. Accordingly, the judgment of the Supreme Court of New Jersey is

Reversed.

JUSTICE POWELL, with whom JUSTICE O'CONNOR joins, concurring.

I agree with the Court's decision, and generally with its opinion. I would place greater emphasis, however, on the special characteristics of elementary and secondary schools that make it unnecessary to afford students the same constitutional protection granted adults and juveniles in a nonschool setting.

In any realistic sense, students within the school environment have a lesser expectation of privacy than members of the population generally. They spend the school hours in close association with each other, both in the classroom and during recreation periods. The students in a particular class often know each other and their teachers quite well. Of necessity, teachers have a degree of familiarity with, and authority over, their students that is unparalleled except perhaps in the relationship between parent and child. It is simply unrealistic to think that students have the same subjective expectation of privacy as the population generally. But for purposes of deciding this case, I can assume that children in school—no less than adults—have privacy interests that society is prepared to recognize as legitimate.

However one may characterize their privacy expectations, students properly are afforded some constitutional protection. In an often quoted statement, the Court said that students do not "shed their constitutional rights . . . at the schoolhouse gate." **TINKER v. DES MOINES INDEPENDENT COMMUNITY SCHOOL DISTRICT**, 393 U.S. 503, 506 (1969). The Court also has "emphasized the need for affirming the comprehensive authority of the state and of school officials to prescribe and control conduct in the schools." Id., at 507. See also **EPPERSON v. ARKANSAS**, 393 U.S. 97, 104

(1968). The Court has balanced the interests of the student against the school officials' need to maintain discipline by recognizing qualitative differences between the constitutional remedies to which students and adults are entitled.

In **GOSS v. LOPEZ**, 419 U.S. 565 (1975), the Court recognized a constitutional right to due process , and yet was careful to limit the exercise of this right by a student who challenged a disciplinary suspension. The only process found to be "due" was notice and a hearing described as "rudimentary"; it amounted to no more than "the disciplinarian . . . informally discuss[ing] the alleged misconduct with the student minutes after it has occurred." Id., at 581-582. In **INGRAHAM v. WRIGHT**, 430 U.S. 651 (1977), we declined to extend the Eighth Amendment to prohibit the use of corporal punishment of schoolchildren as authorized by Florida law. We emphasized in that opinion that familiar constraints in the school and also in the community, provide substantial protection against the violation of constitutional rights by school authorities. "[A]t the end of the school day, the child is invariably free to return home. Even while at school, the child brings with him the support of family and friends and is rarely apart from teachers and other pupils who may witness and protest any instances of mistreatment." Id., at 670. The INGRAHAM Court further pointed out that the openness of the public school and its supervision by the community afford significant safeguard" against the violation of constitutional rights. Ibid.

The special relationship between teacher and student also distinguishes the setting within which school children operate. Law enforcement officers function as adversaries of criminal suspects. These officers have the responsibility to investigate criminal activity, to locate and arrest those who violate our laws, and to facilitate the charging and bringing of such persons to trial. Rarely does this type of adversarial relationship exist between school authorities and pupils. Instead, there is a commonality of interest between teachers and their pupils. The attitude of the typical teacher is one of personal responsibility for the student's welfare as well as for his education.

The primary duty of school officials and teachers, as the Court states, is the education and training of young people. A State has a compelling interest in assuring that the schools meet this responsibility. Without first establishing discipline and maintaining order, teachers cannot begin to educate their students. And apart from education, the school has the obligation to protect pupils from mistreatment by other children, and also to protect teachers themselves from violence by the few students whose conduct in recent years has prompted national concern. For me, it would be unreasonable and at odds with history to argue that the full panoply of constitutional rules applies with the same force and effect in the schoolhouse as it does in the enforcement of criminal laws.

In sum, although I join the Court's opinion and its holding, my emphasis is somewhat different.

JUSTICE BLACKMUN, concurring in the judgment.

I join the judgment of the Court and agree with much that is said in its opinion. I write separately, however, because I believe the Court omits a crucial step in its analysis of whether a school search must be based upon probable cause. The Court correctly states that we have recognized limited exceptions to the probable-cause requirement "[w]here a careful balancing of governmental and private interests suggests that the public interest is best served" by a lesser standard. Ante, at 341. I believe that we have used such a balancing test, rather than strictly applying the Fourth Amendment's Warrant and Probable-Cause Clause, only when we were confronted with "a special law enforcement need for greater flexibility." **FLORIDA v. ROYER**, 460 U.S. 491, 514 (1983) (BLACKMUN, J., dissenting). I pointed out in **UNITED STATES v. PLACE**, 462 U.S. 696 (1983):

"While the Fourth Amendment speaks in terms of freedom from unreasonable [searches], the Amendment does not leave the reasonableness of most [searches] to the judgment of courts or government officers; the Framers of the Amendment balanced the interests involved and decided that a [search] is reasonable only if supported by a judicial warrant based on probable cause. See **TEXAS v. BROWN**, 460 U.S. 730, 744-745 (1983) (POWELL, J., concurring); **UNITED STATES v. RABINOWITZ**, 339 U.S. 56, 70 (1950)

632

(Frankfurter, J., dissenting)."   Id., at 722
(opinion concurring in judgment).

See also **DUNAWAY v. NEW YORK**, 442 U.S. 200, 213-214
(1979); **UNITED STATES v. UNITED STATES DISTRICT COURT**,
407 U.S. 297, 315-316 (1972). Only in those exceptional
circumstances in which special needs beyond the normal
need for law enforcement, make the warrant and probable -
cause requirement impracticable, is a court entitled to
substitute its balancing of interests for that of the
Framers.

Thus, for example, in determining that police can
conduct a limited "stop and frisk" upon less than
probable cause, this Court relied upon the fact that "as
a practical matter" the stop and frisk could not be
subjected to a warrant and probable-cause requirement,
because a law enforcement officer must be able to take
immediate steps to assure himself that the person he has
stopped to question is not armed with a weapon that could
be used against him. **TERRY v. OHIO**, 392 U.S. 1, 20-21,
23-24 (1968). Similarly, this Court's holding that a
roving Border Patrol may stop a car and briefly question
its occupants upon less than probable cause was based in
part upon "the absence of practical alternatives for
policing the border." **UNITED STATES v. BRIGNONI-PONCE**,
422 U.S. 873, 881 (1975). See also **MICHIGAN v. LONG**, 463
U.S. 1032, 1049, n. 14 (1983); **UNITED STATES v. MARTINEZ-
FUERTE**, 428 U.S. 543, 557 (1976); **CAMARA v. MUNICIPAL
COURT**, 387 U.S. 523, 537 (1967).

The Court's implication that the balancing test is
the rule rather than the exception is troubling for me
because it is unnecessary in this case . The elementary
and secondary school setting presents a special need for
flexibility justifying a departure from the balance
struck by the Framers. As JUSTICE POWELL notes,
"[w]ithout first establishing discipline and maintaining
order, teachers cannot begin to educate their students."
Ante, at 350. Maintaining order in the classroom can be
a difficult task. A single teacher often must watch over
a large number of students, and, as any parent knows,
children at ceratin ages are inclined to test the outer
boundaries of acceptable conduct and to imitate the
misbehavior⁻ of a peer if that misbehavior is not dealt
with quickly. Every adult remembers their own schooldays
the havoc a water pistol or peashooter can wreak until it
is taken away. Thus, the Court recognized that "[e]vents

calling for discipline are frequent occurrences and sometimes require immediate, effective action." **GOSS v. LOPEZ**, 419 U.S. 565, 580 (1975). Indeed, because drug use and possession of weapons have become increasingly common among young people, an immediate response frequently is required not just to maintain an environment conducive to learning, but to protect the very safety of students and school personnel.

Such immediate action obviously would not be possible if a teacher were required to secure a warrant before searching a student. Nor would it be possible if a teacher could not conduct a necessary search until the teacher thought there was probable cause for the search. A teacher has neither the training nor the day-to-day experience in the complexities of probable cause that a law enforcement officer possesses, and is ill-equipped to make a quick judgment about the existence of probable cause. The time required for a teacher to ask the questions or make the observations that are necessary to turn reasonable grounds into probable cause is time during which the teacher, and other students, are diverted from the essential task of education. A teacher's focus is, and should be, on teaching and helping students, rather than on developing evidence against a particular troublemaker.

Education "is perhaps the most important function" of government, **BROWN v. BOARD OF EDUCATION**, 347 U.S. 483, 493 (1954), and government has a heightened obligation to safeguard students whom it compels to attend school. The special need for an immediate response to behavior that threatens either the safety of schoolchildren and teachers or the educational process itself justifies the Court in excepting school searches from the warrant and probable-cause requirement, and in applying a standard determined by balancing the relevant interests. I agree with the standard the Court has announced, and with its application of the standard to the facts of this case. I therefore concur in its judgment.

JUSTICE BRENNAN, with whom JUSTICE MARSHALL joins, concurring in part and dissenting in part.

I fully agree with Part II of the Court's opinion. Teachers, like all other government officials, must conform their conduct to the Fourth Amendment's protection of personal privacy and personal security. As JUSTICE STEVENS points out, post, at 373-374, 385-386, this principle is of particular importance when applied to schoolteachers, for children learn as much by example as by exposition. It would be incongruous and futile to charge teachers with the task of embuing their students with an understanding of our system of constitutional democracy, while at the same time immunizing those same teachers from the need to respect constitutional protection. See **BOARD OF EDUCATION v. PICO**, 457 U.S. 853, 864-865, (1982) (plurality opinion); **WEST VIRGINIA STATE BOARD OF EDUCATION v. BARNETTE**, 319 U.S. 624, 637 (1943).

I do not, however, otherwise join the Court's opinion. Today's decision sanctions school officials to conduct full-scale searches on a "reasonable" standard whose only definite content is that it is to the same test as the "probable cause" standard found in the text of the Fourth Amendment. In adopting this unclear, unprecedented, and unnecessary departure from generally applicable Fourth Amendment standard, the Court carves out a broad exception to standards, the Court carves out a broad exception to standards that this Court has developed over years of considering Fourth Amendment problems. Its decision is supported neither by precedent nor even by a fair application of the "balancing test" it proclaims in this very opinion.

I

Three basic principles underly this Court's Fourth Amendment jurisprudence. First, warrantless searches are per se unreasonable, subject only to a few specifically delineated and well-recognized exceptions. See, e.g., **KATZ v. UNITED STATES**, 389 U.S. 347, 357 (1967); accord, **WELSH v. WISCONSIN**, 466 U.S. 740, 748-749 (1984); **UNITED STATES v. PLACE**, 462 U.S. 696, 701 (1983); **STEAGALD v. UNITED STATES**, 451 U.S. 204, 211-212 (1981); **MINCEY v. ARIZONA**, 437 U.S. 385 (1978); **TERRY v. OHIO**, 392 U.S. 1, 20 (1968); **JOHNSON v. UNITED STATES**, 333 U.S. 10, 13-14 (1948). Second, full-scale searches-whether conducted in accordance with the warrant requirement or pursuant to one of its exceptions - are "reasonable" in Fourth Amendment terms only on a showing of probable cause to believe that a crime has been committed and that evidence of the crime will be found in the place to be searched. **BECK v. OHIO**, 379 U.S. 89, 91 (1946); **WONG SUN v. UNITED STATES**, 371 U.S. 471, 479 (1963); **BRINEGAR v. UNITED STATES**, 338 U.S. 160, 175-176 (1949). Third, categories of intrusions that are substantially less intrusive than full-scale searches or seizures may be justifiable in accordance with a balancing test even absent a warrant or probable cause, provided that the balancing test used gives sufficient weight to the privacy interests that will be infringed. **DUNAWAY v. NEW YORK**, 442 U.S. 200, 210 (1979); **TERRY v. OHIO**, supra.

Assistant Vice Principal Choplick's thorough excavation of T.L.O.'s purse was undoubtedly a serious intrusion on her privacy. Unlike the searches in **TERRY v. OHIO, supra**, or **ADAMS v. WILLIAMS**, 407 U.S. 143 (1972), the search at issue here encompassed a detailed and minute examination of respondent's pocketbook, in which the contents of private papers and letters were thoroughly scrutinized. Wisely, neither petitioner nor the Court today attempts to justify the search of T.L.O.'s pocketbook as a minimally intrusive search in the TERRY line. To be faithful to the Court's settled doctrine, the inquiry therefore must focus on the warrant and probable-cause requirements.

A

I agree that schoolteachers or principals, when not acting as agents of law enforcement authorities, generally may conduct a search of their student's belongings without first obtaining a warrant. To agree with the Court on this point is to say that school searches may justifiably be held to that extent to constitute an exception to the Fourth Amendment's warrant requirement. Such an exception, however, is not to be justified, as the Court apparently holds, by assessing net social value through application of an unguided "balancing test" in which "the individual's legitimate expectations of privacy and personal security" are weighed against "the government's need for effective methods to deal with breaches of public order." Ante, at 337. The Warrant Clause is something more than an exhortation to this Court to maximize social welfare as

636

we see fit. It requires that the authorities must obtain
a warrant before conducting a full-scale search. The
undifferentiated governmental interest in law enforcement
is insufficient to justify an exception to the warrant
requirement. Rather, some special governmental interest
beyond the need merely to apprehend law breakers is
necessary to justify a categorical exception to the
warrant requirement. For the most part, special
governmental needs sufficient to override the warrant
requirement flow from "exigency" - that is, from the
press of time that makes obtaining a warrant either
impossible or hopelessly infeasible. See **UNITED STATES
v. PLACE,** supra, at 701-702; **MINCEY v. ARIZONA,** supra, at
393-394; **JOHNSON v. UNITED STATES,** supra, at 15. Only
after finding an extraordinary governmental interest of
this kind do we - or ought we - engage in a balancing
test to determine if a warrant should nonetheless be
required.

To require a showing of some extraordinary
governmental interest before dispensing with the warrant
requirement is not to undervalue society's need to
apprehend violators of the criminal law. To be sure,
forcing law enforcement personnel to obtain a warrant
before engaging in a search will predictably deter the
police from conducting some searches that they would
otherwise like to conduct. But this is not an unintended
result of the Fourth Amendment's protection of privacy;
rather, it is the very purpose for which the Amendment
was thought necessary. Only where the governmental
interests at stake exceed those implicated in any
ordinary law enforcement context - that is, only where
there is some extraordinary governmental interest
involved - is it legitimate to engage in a balancing test
to determine whether a warrant is indeed necessary.

In this case, such extraordinary governmental
interests do exist and are sufficient to justify an
exception to the warrant requirement. Students are
necessarily confined for most of the schooldays in close
proximity to each other and to the school staff. I agree
with the Court that we can take judicial notice of the
serious problems of drugs and violence that plague our
schools. As JUSTICE BLACKMUN notes, teachers must not
merely "maintain an environment conducive to learning"
among children who "are inclined to test the outer
boundaries of acceptable conduct," but must also "protect
the very safety of students and school personnel." Ante,

at 352-353. A teacher or principal could neither carry out essential teaching functions nor adequately protect students' safety if required to wait for a warrant before conducting a necessary search.

B

I emphatically disagree with the Court's decision to cast aside the constitutional probable-cause standard when assessing the constitutional validity of a schoolhouse search. The Court's decision jettisons the probable-cause standard - the only standard that finds support in the text of the Fourth Amendment - on the basis of its Rohrschach-like "balancing test." Use of such a "balancing test" to determine the standard for evaluating the validity of a full-scale represents a sizable innovation in Fourth Amendment analysis. This innovation finds support neither in precedent nor policy and portends a dangerous weakening of the purpose of the Fourth Amendment to protect the privacy and security of our citizens. Moreover, even if this Court's historic understanding of the Fourth Amendment were mistaken and a balancing test of some kind were appropriate any such test that gave adequate weight to the privacy and security interests protected by the Fourth Amendment would not reach the preordained result the Court's conclusory analysis reaches today. Therefore, because I believe that the balancing test used by the Court today is flawed both in its inception and in its execution, I respectfully dissent.

1

An unbroken line of cases in this Court have held that probable cause is a prerequisite for a full-scale search. In **CARROLL v. UNITED STATES**, 267 U.S. 132, 149 (1925), the Court held that "[o]n reason and authority the true rule is that if the search and seizure ... are made upon probable cause ... the search and seizure are valid." Under our past decisions probable cause - which exists where "the facts and circumstances within [the officials'] knowledge and of which they had reasonably trustworthy information [are] sufficient in themselves to warrant a man of reasonable caution in the belief" that a criminal offense had occurred and the evidence would be found in the suspected place, id., at 162 - is the constitutional minimum for justifying a full-scale search, regardless of whether it is conducted pursuant to a warrant or, as in Carroll, within one of the exceptions to the warrant requirement. **HENRY v. UNITED STATES**, 361 U.S. 98, 104 (1959) (Carroll "merely relaxed the requirements for a warrant on grounds of practicality," but "did not dispense with the need for probable cause"); accord, **CHAMBERS v. MARONEY**, 399 U.S. 42, 51 (1970) ("In enforcing the Fourth Amendment's prohibition against unreasonable searches and seizures, the Court has insisted upon probable cause as a minimum requirement for a reasonable search permitted by the Constitution").

Our holdings that probable cause is a prerequisite to a full-scale search are based on the relationship between the two Clauses of the Fourth Amendment. The first Clause ("The right of the people to be secure in their persons, houses, papers and effects, against unreasonable searches and seizures, shall not be violated ...") states the purpose of the Amendment and its coverage. The second Clause ("... and no Warrant shall issue but upon probable cause ...") gives content to the word "unreasonable" in the first Clause. "For all but ... narrowly defined intrusions, the requisite 'balancing' has been performed in centuries of precedent and is embodied in the principle that seizures are 'reasonable' only if supported by probable cause." **DUNAWAY v. NEW YORK**, 442 U.S., at 214.

I therefore fully agree with the Court that "the underlying command of the Fourth Amendment is always that searches and seizures be reasonable." Ante, at 337. But this "underlying command" is not directly interpreted in each category of cases by some amorphous "balancing test." Rather, the provisions of the Warrant Clause - a warrant and probable cause - provide the yardstick against which official searches and seizures are to be measured. The Fourth Amendment neither requires nor authorizes the conceptual free-for-all that ensues when an unguided balancing test is used to assess specific categories of searches. If the search in question is more than - a minimally intrusive TERRY stop, the constitutional probable-cause standard determines its validity.

To be sure, the Court recognizes that probable cause

"ordinarily" is required to justify a full-scale search
and that the existence of probable cause "bears on" the
validity of the search. Ante, at 340-341. Yet the Court
fails to cite any case in which a full-scale intrusion
upon privacy interests has been justified on less than
probable cause. The line of cases begun by **TERRY v.
OHIO**, 392 U.S. 1 (1968), provides no support, for they
applied a balancing test only in the context of minimally
intrusive searches that served crucial law enforcement
interests. The search in TERRY itself, for instance, was
a "limited search of the outer clothing." Id., at 30.
The type of border stop at issue in **UNITED STATES v.
BRIGNONI-PONCE**, 422 U.S. 873, 880 (1975), usually
"consume[d] no more than a minute"; the Court explicitly
noted that "any further detention . . . must be based on
consent or probable cause." Id., at 882. See also **UNITED
STATES v. HENSLEY**, ante, at 224 (momentary stop); **UNITED
STATES v. PLACE**, 462 U.S., at 706-707 (brief detention of
luggage for canine "sniff"); **PENNSYLVANIA v. MIMMS**, 434
U.S. 106 (1977) (per curiam)(brief frisk after stop for
traffic violation); **UNITED STATES v. MARTINEZ-FUERTE**, 428
U.S. 543, 560 (1976)(characterizing intrusion as
"minimal"); **ADAMS v. WILLIAMS**, 407 U.S. 143 (1972) (stop
and frisk). In short, all of these cases involved
"'seizures' so substantially less intrusive than arrests
that the general rule requiring probable cause to make
Fourth Amendment 'seizures' reasonable could be replaced
by a balancing test." DUNAWAY, supra, at 210.

Nor do the "administrative search" cases provide any
comfort for the Court. In **CAMARA v. MUNICIPAL COURT**, 387
U.S. 523 (1967), the Court held that the probable-cause
standard governed even administrative searches. Although
the CAMARA Court recognized that probable-cause standards
themselves may have to be somewhat modified to take into
account the special nature of administrative searches,
the Court did so only after noting that "because [housing
code] inspections are neither personal in nature nor
aimed at the discovery of evidence of crime, they involve
a relatively limited invasion of the urban citizen's
privacy." Id., at 537. Subsequent administrative search
cases have similarly recognized that such searches
intrude upon areas whose owners harbor significantly
decreased expectation of privacy, see, e.g., **DONOVAN v.**

DEWEY, 452 U.S. 594, 598-599 (1981), thus circumscribing the injury to Fourth Amendment interests caused by the search.

Considerations of the deepest significance for the freedom of our citizens counsel strict adherence to the principle that no search may be conducted where the official is not in possession of probable cause - that is, where the official does not know of "facts and circumstance [that] warrant a prudent man in believing that the offense has been committed." **HENRY v. UNITED STATES,** 361 U.S., at 102, see also id., at 100-101 (discussing history of probable-cause standard). The Fourth Amendment was designed not merely to protect against official intrusions whose social utility was less as measured by some "balancing test" than its intrusion on individual privacy; it was designed in addition to grant the individual a zone of privacy whose protections could be breached only where the "reasonable" requirements of the probable-cause standard were met. Moved by whatever momentary evil has aroused their fears, officials-perhaps even supported by a majority of citizens - may be tempted to conduct searches that sacrifice the liberty of each citizen to assuage the perceived evil. But the Fourth Amendment rests on the principle that a true balance between the individual and society depends on the recognition of "the right to be let alone - the most comprehensive of rights and the right most valued by civilized men." **OLMSTEAD v. UNITED STATES,** 277 U.S. 438, 478 (1928) (BRANDEIS, J., dissenting). That right protects the privacy and security of the individual unless the authorities can cross a specific threshold of need, designated by the term "probable cause." I cannot agree with the Court's assertions today that a "balancing test" can replace the constitutional threshold with one that is more convenient for those enforcing the laws but less protective of the citizens' liberty; the Fourth Amendment's protections should not be defaced by "a balancing process that overwhelms the individual's protection against unwarranted official intrusion by a governmental interest said to justify the search and seizure." **UNITED STATES v. MARTINEZ-FUERTE,** supra, at 570 (BRENNAN, J., dissenting).

2

I thus do not accept the majority's premise that "[t]o hold that the Fourth Amendment applies to searches conducted by school authorities is only to begin the inquiry into the standards governing such searches." Ante, at 337. For me, the finding that the Fourth Amendment applies, coupled with the observation that what is at issue is a full-scale search, is the end of the inquiry. But even if I believed that a "balancing test" appropriately replaces the judgment of the Framers of the Fourth Amendment, I would nonetheless object to the cursory and shortsighted "test" that the Court employs to justify its predictable weakening of Fourth Amendment protections. In particular, the test employed by the Court vastly overstates the social costs that a probable-cause standard entails and, though it plausibly articulates the serious privacy interests at stake, inexplicably fails to accord them adequate weight in striking the balance.

The Court begins to articulate its "balancing test" by observing that "the government's need for effective methods to deal with breaches of public order" is to be weighed on one side of the balance. Ibid. Of course, this is not correct. It is not the government's need for effective enforcement methods that should weigh in the balance, for ordinary Fourth Amendment standards - including probable cause - may well permit methods for maintaining the public order that are perfectly effective. If that were the case, the governmental interest in having effective standards would carry no weight at all as a justification for departing from the probable-cause standard. Rather, it is the costs of applying probable cause as opposed to applying some lesser standard that should be weighed on the government's side.

In order to tote up the costs of applying the probable-cause standard, it is thus necessary first to take into account the nature and content of that standard, and the likelihood that it would hamper achievement of the goal - vital not just to "teachers and administrators," see ante, at 339 - of maintaining an effective educational setting in the public schools. The seminal statement concerning the nature of the probable-cause standard is found in **CARROLL v. UNITED STATES**, 267

642

U.S. 132 (1925). CARROLL held that law enforcement authorities have probable cause to search where "the facts and circumstances within their knowledge and of which they had reasonably trustworthy information [are] sufficient in themselves to warrant a man of reasonable caution in the belief" that a criminal offense had occurred. Id., at 162. In **BRINEGAR v. UNITED STATES**, 338 U.S. 160 (1949), the Court amplified this requirement, holding that probable cause depends upon "the factual and practical considerations of everyday life on which reasonable and prudent men, not legal technicians, act." Id., at 175.

Two Terms ago, in **ILLINOIS v. GATES**, 462 U.S. 213 (983), this Court expounded at some length its view of the probable cause standard. Among the adjectives used to describe the standard were "practical," "fluid," "flexible," "easily applied," and "nontechnical." See id., at 232, 236, 239. The probable-cause standard was to be seen as a "common-sense" test whose application depended on an evaluation of the "totality of the circumstances." Id., at 238.

Ignoring what GATES took such great pains to emphasize, the Court today holds that a new "reasonableness" standard is appropriate because it "will spare teachers and school administrators the necessity of schooling themselves in the niceties of probable cause and permit them to regulate their conduct according to the dictates of reason and common sense." Ante, at 343. I had never thought that our pre-Gates understanding of probable cause defied either reason or common sense. But after GATES, I would have thought that there could be no doubt that this nontechnical," "practical," and "easily applied" concept was eminently serviceable in a context like a school, where teachers require the flexibility to respond quickly and decisively to emergencies.

A consideration of the likely operation of the probable-cause standard reinforces this conclusion. Discussing the issue of school searches, Professor LaFave has noted that the cases that have reached the appellate courts 'strongly suggest that in most instances the evidence of wrongdoing prompting teachers or principals to conduct searches is sufficiently detailed and specific to meet the traditional probable cause test." 3 W. LaFave, Search and Seizure section 10.11, pp. 459-460 (1978). The problems that have caused this Court difficulty in interpreting the probable-cause standard

643

have largely involved informants, see, e.g., **ILLINOIS v. GATES**, supra; **SPINELLI v. UNITED STATES** 393 U.S. 410 (1969); **AGUILAR v. TEXAS,** 378 U.S 108 (1964); **DRAPER v. UNITED STATES**, 358 U.S. 307 (1959). However, three factors make it likely that problems involving informants will not make it difficult for teachers and school administrators to make probable-cause decisions. This Court's decision in GATES applying a "totality of the circumstances" test to determine whether an informant's tip can constitute probable cause renders the test easy for teachers to apply. The fact that students and teachers interact daily in the school building makes it more likely that teachers will get to know students who supply information; the problem of informants who remain anonymous even to the teachers - and who are therefore unavailable for verification or further questioning - is unlikely to arise. Finally, teachers can observe the behavior of students under suspicion to corroborate any doubtful tips they do receive.

As compared with the relative ease with which teachers can apply the probable-cause standard, the amorphous "reasonableness under all the circumstances" standard freshly coined by the Court today will likely spawn increased litigation and greater uncertainty among teachers and administrators. Of course, as this Court should know, an essential purpose of developing and articulating legal norms is to enable individuals to conform their conduct to those norms. A school system conscientiously attempting to obey the Fourth Amendment's dictates under a probable-cause standard could, for example, consult decisions and other legal materials and prepare a booklet expounding the rough outlines of the concept. Such a booklet could be distributed to teachers to provide them with guidance as to when a search may be lawfully conducted. I cannot but believe that the same school system faced with interpreting what is permitted under the Court's new "reasonableness" standard would be hopelessly adrift as to when a search may be permissible. The sad result of this uncertainty may well be that some teachers will be reluctant to conduct searches that are fully permissible and even necessary under the constitutional probable-cause standard, while others may intrude arbitrarily and unjustifiably on the privacy of students.

One further point should be taken into account when considering the desirability of replacing the constitutional probable-cause standard. The question facing the Court is not whether the probable-cause standard should be replaced by a test of "reasonableness under all the circumstances." Rather, it is whether traditional Fourth Amendment standards should recede before the Court's new standard. Thus, although the Court today paints with a broad brush and holds its undefined "reasonableness" standard applicable to all school searches, I would approach the question with considerably more reserve. I would not think it necessary to develop a single standard to govern all school searches, any more than traditional Fourth Amendment law applies even the probable-cause standard to all searches and seizures. For instance, just as police officers may conduct a brief stop and frisk on something less than probable cause, so too should teachers be permitted the same flexibility. A teacher or administrator who had reasonable suspicion that a student was carrying a gun would no doubt have authority under ordinary Fourth Amendment doctrine to conduct a limited search of the student to determine whether the threat was genuine. The "costs" of applying the traditional probable-cause standard must therefore be discounted by the fact that, where additional flexibility is necessary and where the intrusion is minor, traditional Fourth Amendment jurisprudence itself displaces probable cause when it determines the validity of a search.

A legitimate balancing test whose function was something more substantial than reaching a predetermined conclusion acceptable to this Court's impressions of what authority teachers need would therefore reach rather a different result than that reached by the Court today. On one side of the balance would be the costs of applying traditional Fourth Amendment standards where a full-scale intrusion is sought, a lesser standard in situations where the intrusion is much less severe and the need for greater authority compelling. Whatever costs were toted up on this side would have to be discounted by the costs of applying an unprecedented and ill-defined "reasonableness under all the circumstances" test that will leave teachers and administrators uncertain as to their authority and will encourage excessive fact-based litigation.

645

On the other side of the balance would be the
serious privacy interests of the student, interests that
the Court admirably articulates in its opinion, ante, at
337-339, but which the Court's new ambiguous standard
places in serious jeopardy. I have no doubt that a fair
assessment of the two sides of the balance would
necessarily reach the same conclusion that, as I have
argued above, the Fourth Amendment's language compels -
that school searches like that conducted in this case are
valid only if supported by probable cause.

II

Applying the constitutional probable-cause standard
to the facts of this case, I would find that Mr.
Choplick's search violated T.L.O.'s Fourth Amendment
rights. After escorting T.L.O. into his private office,
Mr. Choplick demanded to see her purse. He then opened
the purse to find evidence of whether she had been
smoking in the bathroom. When he opened the purse, he
discovered the pack of cigarettes. At this point, his
search for evidence of the smoking violation was
complete.

Mr. Choplick then noticed, below the cigarettes, a
pack of cigarette rolling papers. Believing that such
papers were "associated," see ante, at 328, with the use
of marihuana, he proceeded to conduct a detailed
examination of the contents of her purse, in which he
found some marihuana, a pipe, some money, an index card.
and some private letters indicating that T.L.O. had sold
marihuana to other students. The State sought to
introduce this latter material in evidence at a criminal
proceeding, and the issue before the Court is whether it
should have been suppressed.

On my view of the case, we need not decide whether
the initial search conducted by Mr. Choplick - the search
for evidence of the smoking violation that was completed
when Mr. Choplick found the pack of cigarettes - was
valid. For Mr. Choplick at that point did not have
probable cause to continue to rummage through T.L.O's
purse. Mr. Choplick's suspicion of marihuana possession
at this time was based solely on the presence of the
package of cigarette papers. The mere presence without

646

more of such a staple item of commerce is insufficient to warrant a person of reasonable causation in interfering both that T.L.O. had violated the law by possessing marihuana and that evidence of that violation would be found in her purse. Just as a police officer could not obtain a warrant to search a home based solely on his claim that he had seen a package of cigarette papers in that home, Mr. Choplick was not entitled to search possibly the most private possessions of T.L.O based on the mere presence of a package of cigarette papers. Therefore, the fruits of this illegal search must be excluded and the judgment of the New Jersey Supreme Court affirmed.

III

In the past several Terms, this Court has produced a succession of Fourth Amendment opinions in which "balancing tests" have been applied to resolve various questions concerning the proper scope of official searches. The Court has begun to apply a "balancing test" to determine whether a particular category of searches intrudes upon expectations of privacy that merit Fourth Amendment protection. See **HUDSON v. PALMER**, 468 U.S. 517, 527 (1984) ("Determining whether an expectation of privacy is 'legitimate' or 'reasonable' necessarily entails a balancing of interests"). It applies a "balancing test" to determine whether a warrant is necessary to conduct a search. See ante, at 340; **UNITED STATES v. MARTINEZ-FUERTE**, 428 U.S., at 564-566. In today's opinion, it employs a "balancing test" to determine what standard should govern the constitutionality of a given category of searches. See ante, at 340-341. Should a search turn out to be unreasonable after application of all of these "balancing tests," the Court then applies an additional "balancing test" to decide whether the evidence resulting from the search must be excluded. See **UNITED STATES v. LEON**, 468 U.S. 897 (1984).

All of these "balancing tests" amount to brief nods by the Court in the direction of a neutral utilitarian calculus while the Court in fact engages in an unanalyzed exercise of judicial will. Perhaps this doctrinally destructive nihilism is merely a convenient umbrella under which a majority that cannot agree on a genuine rationale can conceal its differences. Compare ante, p.

327 (WHITE, J., delivering the opinion of the Court) with ante, p. 348 (POWELL, J., joined by O'CONNOR, J., concurring), and ante, 0. 351 (BLACKMUN, J., concurring in judgment). And it may be that the real force underlying today's decision is the belief that the Court purports to reject - the belief that the unique role served by the schools justifies an exception to the Fourth Amendment on their behalf. If so, the methodology of today's decision may turn out to have as little influence in future cases as will its result, and the Court's departure from traditional Fourth Amendment doctrine will be confined to the schools.

On my view, the presence of the word "unreasonable" in the text of the Fourth Amendment does not grant a shifting majority of this Court the authority to answer all Fourth Amendment questions by consulting its momentary vision of the social good. Full-scale searches unaccompanied by probable cause violate the Fourth Amendment. I do not pretend that our traditional Fourth Amendment doctrine automatically answers all of the difficult legal questions that occasionally arise. I do contend, however, that this Court has an obligation to provide some coherent framework to resolve such questions on the basis of more than a conclusory recitation of the results of a "balancing test." The Fourth Amendment itself supplies that framework and, because the Court today fails to heed its message, I must respectfully dissent.

JUSTICE STEVENS, with whom JUSTICE MARSHALL joins, and with whom JUSTICE BRENNAN joins as to Part I, concurring in part and dissenting in part.

Assistant Vice Principal Choplick searched T.L.O.'s purse for evidence that she was smoking in the girls' restroom. Because T.L.O.'s suspected misconduct was not illegal and did not pose a serious threat to school discipline, the New Jersey Supreme Court held that Choplick's search of her purse was an unreasonable invasion of her privacy and that the evidence which he seized could not be used against her in criminal proceedings. The New Jersey court's holding was a careful response to the case it was required to decide. The State of New Jersey sought review in this Court, first arguing that the exclusionary rule is wholly inapplicable to searches conducted by school officials, and then contending that the Fourth Amendment itself provides no protection at all to the student's privacy. The Court has accepted neither of these frontal assaults on the Fourth Amendment. It has, however, seized upon this "no smoking" case to announce "the proper standard" that should govern searches by school officials who are confronted with disciplinary problems far more severe than smoking in the restroom. Although I join Part II of the Court's opinion, I continue to believe that the Court has unnecessarily and inappropriately reached out to decide a constitutional question. See 468 U.S. 1214 (1984) (STEVENS, J., dissenting from reargument order). More importantly, I fear that the concerns that motivated the Court's activism have produced a holding that will permit school administrators to search students suspected of violating only the most trivial school regulations and guidelines for behavior.

I

The question the Court decides today - whether Mr. Choplick's search of T.L.O.'s purse violated the Fourth Amendment - was not raised by the State's petition for writ of certiorari. That petition only raised one question" "Whether the Fourth Amendment's exclusionary rule applies to searches made by public school officials and teachers in school. The State quite properly declined to submit the former question because "[it] did not wish to present what might appear to be solely a factual dispute to this Court." Since this Court has twice had the threshold question argued, I believe that it should expressly consider the merits of the New Jersey Supreme Court's ruling that the exclusionary rule applies.

The New Jersey Supreme Court's holding on this question is plainly correct. As the state court noted, this case does not involve the use of evidence in a school disciplinary proceeding; the juvenile proceedings brought against T.L.O. involved a charge that would have been a criminal offense if committed by an adult. Accordingly, the exclusionary rule issue decided by that court and later presented to this Court concerned only the use in a criminal proceeding of evidence obtained in a search conducted by a public school administrator.

Having confined the issue to the law enforcement context, the New Jersey court then reasoned that this Court's cases have made it quite clear that the exclusionary rule is equally applicable "whether the public official who illegally obtained the evidence was a municipal inspector, **SEE v. SEATTLE**, 387 U.S. 541 [1967]; **CAMARA [v. MUNICIPAL COURT,]** 387 U.S. 523 [1967]; a firefighter, **MICHIGAN v. TYLER**, 436 U.S. 499, 506 [1978]; or a school administrator or law enforcement official. It correctly concluded "that if an official search violates constitutional rights, the evidence is not admissible in criminal proceedings.

When a defendant in a criminal proceeding alleges that she was the victim of an illegal search by a school administrator, the application of the exclusionary rule is a simple corollary of the principle that "all evidence obtained by searches and seizures in violation of the Constitution is, by that same authority, inadmissible in a state court." **MAPP v. OHIO**, 367 U.S. 643, 655 (1961). The practical basis for this principle is, in part, its deterrent effect, see id., at 656, and as a general matter is tolerably clear to me, as it has been to the Court, that the existence of an exclusionary remedy does deter the authorities from violating the Fourth Amendment by sharply reducing their incentive to do so. In the case of evidence obtained in school searches, the "overall educative effect" of the exclusionary rule adds important symbolic force to this utilitarian judgment.

Justice Brandeis was both a great student and a great teacher. It was he who wrote:

"Our Government is the potent,the omnipresent teacher. For good or for ill, it teaches the whole people by its example. Crime is contagious. If the Government becomes a lawbreaker, it breeds contempt for law; it invites every man to become a law unto himself; it invites anarchy." **OLMSTEAD v. UNITED STATES**, 277 U.S. 438, 485 91928) (dissenting opinion).

Those of us who revere the flag and the ideals for which it stands believe in the power of symbols. We cannot ignore that rules of law also have a symbolic power that may vastly exceed their utility.

Schools are places where we inoculate the values essential to the meaning full exercise of rights and responsibilities by a self-governing citizenry. If the Nation's students can be convicted through the use of arbitrary methods destructive of personal liberty, they cannot help but feel that they have been dealt with unfairly. The application of the exclusionary rule in criminal proceedings arising from illegal school searches makes an important statement to young people that "our society attaches serious consequences to a violation of constitutional rights," and that this is a principal of "liberty and justice for all."

Thus, the simple and correct answer to the question presented by the State's petition for certiorari would have required affirmance of a state court's judgment suppressing evidence. That result would have been dramatically out of character for a Court that not only grants prosecutors relief from suppression orders with distressing regularity, but also is prone to rely on grounds not advanced by the parties in order to protect evidence from exclusion. In characteristic disregard of the doctrine of judicial restraint, the Court avoided that result in this case by ordering reargument and directing the parties to address a constitutional question that the parties, with good reason, had not asked the Court to decide. Because judicial activism undermines the Court's power to perform its central mission in a legitimate way, I dissented from the reargument order. See 468 U.S. 1214 (1984). I have not modified the views expressed in that dissent, but since the majority has brought the question before us, I shall explain why I believe the Court has misapplied the standard of reasonableness embodied in the Fourth Amendment.

II

The search of a young woman's purse by a school administrator is a serious invasion of her legitimate expectations of privacy. A purse "is a common repository for one's personal effects and therefore is inevitably associated with the expectation of privacy." **ARKANSAS v. SANDERS**, 442 U.S. 753, 762 (1979). Although such expectations must sometimes yield to the legitimate requirements of government, in assessing the

651

constitutionality of a warrantless search, our decision must be guided by the language of the Fourth Amendment: "The right of the people to be secure in their persons, houses, papers and effects, against unreasonable searches and seizures, shall not be violated. . ." In order to evaluate the reasonableness of such searches, "it is necessary 'first to focus upon the governmental interest which allegedly justifies official intrusion upon the constitutionally protected interests of the private citizen,' for there is 'no ready test for determining reasonableness other than by balancing the need to search [or seize] against the invasion which the search [or seizure] entails.'" **TERRY v. OHIO**, 392 U.S. 1, 20-21 (1968) (quoting **CAMARA v. MUNICIPAL COURT**, 387 U.S. 523, 528, 534-537, (1967)).

The "limited search for weapons" in TERRY was justified by the "immediate interest of the police officer in taking steps to assure himself that the person with whom he is dealing is not armed with a weapon that could unexpectedly and fatally be used against him." 392 U.S., at 23, 25. When viewed from the institutional perspective, "the substantial need of teachers and administrators for freedom to maintain order in the schools," ante, at 341 (majority opinion), is no less acute. Violent, unlawful, or seriously disruptive conduct is fundamentally inconsistent with the principal function of teaching institutions which is to educate young people and prepare them for citizenship. When such conduct occurs amidst a sizable group of impressionable young people, it creates an explosive atmosphere that requires a prompt and effective response.

Thus, warrantless searches of students by school administrators are reasonable when undertaken for those purposes. But the majority's statement of the standard for evaluating the reasonableness of such searches is not suitably adapted to that end. The majority holds that "a search of a student by a teacher or other school official will be 'justified at its inception' when there are reasonable grounds for suspecting that the search will turn up evidence that the student has violated or is violating either the law or the rules of the school." Ante, at 341, 342. This standard will permit teachers and school administrators to search students when they

652

suspect that the search will reveal evidence of even the most trivial school regulation or precatory guideline for student behavior. The Court's standard for deciding whether a search is justified "at its inception" treats all violations of the rules of the school as though they were fungible. For the Court, a search for curlers and sunglasses in order to enforce the school dress code is apparently just as important as a search for evidence of heroin addiction or violent gang activity.

The majority, however, does not contend that school administrators have a compelling need to search students in order to achieve optimum enforcement of minor school regulations. To the contrary, when minor violations are involved, there is every indication that the informal school disciplinary process, with only minimum requirements of due process, can function effectively without the power to search for enough evidence to prove a criminal case. In arguing that teachers and school administrators need the power to search students based on a lessened standard, the United States as amicus curiae relies heavily on empirical evidence of a contemporary crisis of violence and unlawful behavior that is seriously undermining the process of education in American schools. A standard better attuned to this concern would permit teachers and school administrators to search a student when they have reason to believe that the search will uncover evidence that the student is violating the law or engaging in conduct that is seriously disruptive of school order, or the educational process.

This standard is properly directed at "[t]he sole justification for the [warrantless] search." In addition, a standard that varies the extent of the permissible intrusion with the gravity of the suspected offense is also more consistent with common-law experience and this Court's precedent. Criminal law has traditionally recognized a distinction between essentially regulatory offenses and serious violations of the peace, and graduated the response of the criminal justice system depending on the character of the violation. The application of a similar distinction in evaluating the reasonableness of warrantless searches and seizures "is not a novel idea." **WELSH v. WISCONSIN**, 466 U.S. 740, 750 (1984).

In WELSH, the police officers arrived at the scene

653

of a traffic accident and obtained information indicating that the driver of the automobile involved was guilty of a first offense of driving while intoxicated - a civil violation with a maximum fine of $200. The driver had left the scene of the accident, and the officers followed the suspect to his home where they arrested him without a warrant. Absent exigent circumstances, the warrantless invasion of the home was a clear violation of **PAYTON v. NEW YORK**, 445 U.S. 573 (1980). In holding that the warrantless arrest for the "noncriminal, traffic offense" in Welsh was unconstitutional, the Court noted that "application of the exigent-circumstances exception in the context of a home entry should rarely be sanctioned when there is probable cause to believe that only a minor offense . . . has been committed." 466 U.S., at 753.

The logic of distinguishing between minor and serious offenses in evaluating the reasonableness of school searches is almost too clear for argument. In order to justify the serious intrusion on the persons and privacy of young people that New Jersey asks this Court to approve, the State must identify "some real immediate and serious consequences." **MCDONALD v. UNITED STATES**, 335 U.S. 451, 460 (1948) (Jackson, J., concurring, joined by Frankfurter, J.). While school administrators have entirely legitimate reasons for adopting school regulations and guidelines for student behavior, the authorization of searches to enforce them "displays a shocking lack of all sense of proportion." Id, 459.

The majority offers weak deference to these principles of balance and decency by announcing that school searches will only be reasonable in scope "when the measures adopted reasonably related to the objectives of the search and not excessively intrusive in light of the age and sex of the student and the nature of infraction." Ante, at 342 (emphasis added). The majority offers no explanation why a two-part standard is necessary to evaluate the reasonableness of the ordinary school search. Significantly, in the balance of its opinion the Court pretermits any discussion of the nature of T.L.O.'s infraction of the "no smoking" rule.

The "rider" to the Court's standard for evaluating the reasonableness of the initial intrusion apparently is the Court's perception that its standard is overly generous and does not, by itself, achieve a fair balance between the administrator's right to search and the student's reasonable expectations of privacy. The Court's standard for evaluating the "scope" of reasonable school searches is obviously designed to prohibit physically intrusive searches of students by persons of the opposite sex for relatively minor offenses. The Court's effort to establish a standard that is, at once, clear enough to allow searches to be upheld in nearly every case, and flexible enough to prohibit obviously unreasonable intrusions of young adults' privacy only creates uncertainty in the extent of its resolve to prohibit the latter. Moreover, the majority's application of its standard in this case - to permit a male administrator to rummage through the purse of a female high school student in order to obtain evidence that she was smoking in a bathroom - raises grave doubts in my mind whether its effort will be effective. Unlike the Court, I believe the nature of the suspected infraction is a matter of first importance in deciding whether any invasion of privacy is permissible.

III

The Court embraces the standard applied by the New Jersey Supreme Court as equivalent to its own, and then deprecates the state court's application of the standard as reflecting "a somewhat crabbed notion of reasonableness." Ante, at 343. There is no mystery, however, in state court's finding that the search in this case was unconstitutional; the decision below was not based on a manipulation of reasonable suspicion, but on the trivial character of the activity that promoted the official search. The New Jersey Supreme Court wrote:

"We are satisfied that when a school official has reasonable grounds to believe that a student possesses evidence of illegal activity or activity that would interfere with school discipline and order, the school official has the right to conduct a reasonable search for such evidence.
"In determining whether the school official has reasonable grounds, courts should consider 'the child's age, history, and school record, the prevalence and seriousness of the problem in the school to which the search was directed, the

655

exigency to make the search without delay, and the probative value and reliability of the information used as a justification for the search.'"

The emphasized language in the state court's opinion focuses on the character of the rule infraction that is to be the object of the search.

In the view of the state court, there is a quite obvious and material difference between a search for evidence relating to violent or disruptive activity, and a search for evidence of a smoking rule violation. This distinction does not imply that a no-smoking rule is a matter of minor importance. Rather, like a rule that prohibits a student from being tardy, its occasional violation in a context that poses no threat of disrupting school order and discipline offers no reason to believe that an immediate search is necessary to avoid unlawful conduct, violence, or a serious impairment of the educational process.

A correct understanding of the New Jersey court's standard explains why that court concluded in T.L.O.'s case that "the assistant principal did not have reasonable grounds to believe that the student was concealing in her purse evidence of criminal activity or evidence of activity that would seriously interfere with school discipline or order. The importance of the nature of the rule infraction to the New Jersey Supreme Court's holding is evident from its brief explanation of the principal basis for its decision:

> "A student has an expectation of privacy in the contents of her purse. Mere possession of cigarettes did not violate school rule or policy, since the school allowed smoking in designated areas. The contents of the handbag had no direct bearing on the infraction.
>
> "The assistant principal's desire, legal in itself, to gather evidence to impeach the student's credibility at a hearing on the disciplinary infraction does not validate the search."

Like the New Jersey Supreme Court, I would view this case differently if the Assistant Vice Principal had reason to believe T.L.O.'s purse contained evidence of criminal activity, or of an activity that would seriously disrupt school discipline. There was, however, absolutely no basis for any such assumption - not even a "hunch."

In this case, Mr. Choplick overreacted to what appeared to be noting more than a minor infraction - a rule prohibiting smoking in the bathroom of the freshmen's and sophomores' building. It is, of course, true that he actually found evidence of serious wrongdoing by T.L.O., but no one claims that the prior search may be justified by his unexpected discovery. As far as the smoking infraction is concerned, the search for cigarettes merely tended to corroborate a teacher's eyewitness account of T.L.O.'s violation of a minor regulation designed to channel student smoking behavior into designated locations. Because this conduct was neither unlawful nor significantly disruptive of school order or the educational process, the invasion of privacy associated with the forcible opening of T.L.O.'s purse was entirely unjustified at its inception.

A review of the sampling of school search cases relied on by the Court demonstrates how different this case is from those in which there was indeed a valid justification for intruding on a student's privacy. In most of them the student was suspected of a criminal violation; in the remainder either violence or substantial disruption of school order or the integrity of the academic process was at stake. Few involved matters as trivial as the no-smoking rule violated by T.L.O. The rule the Court adopts today is open-ended that it may make the Fourth Amendment virtually meaningless in the school context. Although I agree that school administrators must have broad latitude to maintain order and discipline in our classrooms, that authority is not unlimited.

IV

The schoolroom is the first opportunity most citizens have to experience the power of government. Through it passes every citizen and public official, from schoolteachers to policemen and prison guards. The values they learn there, they take with them in life. One of our most cherished ideals is the one contained in the Fourth Amendment: that the government may not intrude on the personal privacy of its citizens without a warrant

657

or compelling circumstance. The Court's decision today is a curious moral for the Nations youth. Although the search of T.L.O.'s purse does not trouble today's majority, I submit that we are not dealing with "matters relatively trivial to the welfare of the Nation. There are village tyrants as well as village Hampdens, but none who acts under color of law is beyond reach of the Constitution." **WEST VIRGINIA STATE BOARD OF EDUCATION v. BARNETTE**, 319 U.S. 624 (1943).

I respectfully dissent.

U.S. v. Andrew SOKOLOW
490 U.S. 794, 109 S.Ct. 1581, 104 L.Ed.2d. 1 (1989)
ON WRIT OF CERTIORARI TO THE UNITED STATES COURT
OF APPEALS FOR THE NINTH CIRCUIT
. . .

MR. Chief Justice Renhquist delivered the opinion of the Court.

Respondent Andrew Sokolow was stopped by Drug Enforcement Administration (DEA) agents upon his arrival at Honolulu International Airport. The agents found 1,063 grams of cocaine in his carry-on luggage. When respondent was stopped, the agents knew, *inter alia*, that (1) he paid $2,100 for two airplane tickets from a roll of $20 bills; (2) he traveled under a name that did not match the name under which his telephone number was listed; (3) his original destination was Miami, a source city for illicit drugs; (4) he stayed in Miami for only 48 hours, even though a round-trip flight from Honolulu to Miami takes 20 hours; (5) he appeared nervous during his trip; and (6) he checked none of his luggage. A divided panel of the United States Court of Appeals for the Ninth Circuit held that the DEA agents did not have a reasonable suspicion to stop respondent, as required by the Fourth Amendment. 831 F. 2d. 1413 (1987). We take the contrary view.

This case involves a typical attempt to smuggle drugs through one of the Nation's airports.[1] On a Sunday in July 1984, respondent went to the United Airlines ticket counter at Honolulu Airport, where he purchased two round-trip tickets for a flight to Miami leaving later that day. The tickets were purchased in the names of "Andrew Kray" and "Janet Norian," and had open return dates. Respondent paid $2,100 for the tickets from a large roll of $20 bills, which appeared to contain a total of $4,000. He also gave the ticket agent his home telephone number. The ticket agent noticed that respondent seemed nervous; he was about 25 years old; he was dressed in a black jumpsuit and wore gold jewelry; and he was accompanied by a woman, who turned out to be Janet Norian. Neither respondent nor his companion checked any of their four pieces of luggage.

---

[1] The facts in this case were developed at suppression hearings held in the District Court over three separate days. The parties also stipulated to certain facts.

After the couple left for their flight, the ticket agent informed Officer John McCarthy of the Honolulu Police Department of respondent's cash purchase of tickets to Miami. Officer McCarthy determined that the telephone number respondent gave to the ticket agent was subscribed to a "Karl Herman," who resided at 348-A Royal Hawaiian Avenue in Honolulu. Unbeknownst to McCarthy (and later to the DEA agents), respondent was Herman's roomate. The ticket agent identified respondent's voice on the answering machine at Herman's number. Officer McCarthy was unable to find any listing under the name "Andrew Kray" in Hawaii. McCarthy subsequently learned that return reservations from Miami to Honolulu had been made in the names of Kray and Norian, with their arrival scheduled for July 25, three days after respondent and his companion had left. He also learned that Kray and Norian were scheduled to make stop-overs in Denver and Los Angeles.

On July 25, during the stop-over in Los Angeles, DEA agents identified respondent. He "appeared to be very nervous and was looking all around the waiting area." App. 43-44. Later that day, at 6:30 pm, respondent and Norian arrived in Honolulu. As before, they had not checked their luggage. Respondent was still wearing a black jumpsuit and gold jewelry. The couple proceeded directly to the street and tried to hail a cab, where Agent Richard Kempshall and three other DEA agents approached them. Kempshall displayed his credentials, grabbed respondent by the arm and moved him back onto the sidewalk. Kempshall asked respondent for his airline ticket and identification; respondent said that he had neither. He told the agents that his name was "Sokolow," but that he was traveling under his mother's maiden name, "Kray."

Respondent and Norian were escorted to the DEA office at the airport. There, the couple's luggage was examined by "Donker," a narcotics detector dog, which alerted to respondent's brown shoulder bag. The agents arrested respondent. He was advised of his constitutional rights and declined to make any statements. The agents obtained a warrant to search the shoulder bag. They found no illicit drugs, but the bag did contain several suspicious documents indicating respondent's involvement in drug trafficking. The agents had Donker reexamine the remaining luggage, and this time the dog alerted to a medium sized Louis Vuitton bag. By now, it was 9:30 pm, too late for the agents to obtain a second warrant. They allowed respondent to leave for the night, but kept his luggage. The next morning, after a second dog confirmed Donker's alert, the agents obtained a warrant and found 1,063 grams of cocaine inside the bag.

Respondent was indicted for possession with the intent to distribute cocaine in violation of 21 U.S.C. § 841 (a)(1). The United States District Court for Hawaii denied his motion to suppress the cocaine and other evidence seized from his luggage, finding that the DEA agents had a reasonable suspicion that he was involved in drug trafficking when they stopped him at the airport. Respondent entered a conditional plea of guilty to the offense charged.

The United States Court of Appeals for the Ninth Circuit reversed respondent's conviction by a divided vote, holding that the DEA agents did not have a reasonable suspicion to justify the stop. 831 F.2d., at 1423.[2] The majority divided the facts bearing on reasonable suspicion into two categories. In the first category, the majority placed facts describing "ongoing criminal activity," such as the use of an alias or evasive movement through an airport; the majority believed that at least one such factor was always needed to sup
port a finding of reasonable suspicion. Id., at 1419. In the second category, it placed facts describing "personal characteristics" of drug couriers, such as the cash payment for tickets, a short trip to a major source city for drugs, nervousness, type of attire, and unchecked luggage. Id., at 1420. The majority believed that such facts, "shared by drug couriers and the public at large," were only relevant if there was evidence of ongoing criminal behavior and the Government offered "[e]mpirical documentation" that the combination of facts

---

[2] In an earlier decision, the Court of Appeals also reversed the District Court, but on the basis of different reasoning. UNITED STATES v. SOKOLOW, 808 F.2d. 1366 (CA9), vacated, 831 F.2d. 1413 (1987). The Court of Appeals' second decision was issued after the Government petitioned for rehearing on the ground that the court had erred in considering each of the facts known to the agents separately rather than in terms of the totality of the circumstances.

at issue did not describe the behavior of "significant numbers of innocent persons." Ibid. Applying this two-part test to the facts of this case, the majority found that there was no evidence of ongoing criminal behavior, and thus that the agents' stop was impermissible. The dissenting judge took the view that the majority's approach was "overly mechanistic" and "contrary to the case-by-case determination of reasonable articulable suspicion based on *all* the facts." Id., at 1426.

We granted certiorari to review the decision of the Court of Appeals, 486 U.S. — (1988), because of its serious implications for the enforcement of the federal narcotics laws. We now reverse.

The Court of Appeals held that the DEA agents seized respondent when they grabbed him by the arm and moved him back onto the sidewalk. 831 F.2d. at 1416. The Government does not challenge that conclusion and we assume—without deciding—that a stop occurred here. Our decision, then, turns on whether the agents had a reasonable suspicion that respondent was engaged in wrongdoing when they encountered him on the sidewalk. In **TERRY v. OHIO**, 392 U.S. 1, 30 (1968), we held that the police can stop and briefly detain a person for investigative purposes if the officer has a reasonable suspicion supported by articulable facts that criminal activity "may be afoot," even if the officer lacks probable cause.

The officer, of course, must be able to articulate something more than an "inchoate and unparticularized suspicion or 'hunch'." Id., at 27. The Fourth Amendment requires "some minimal level of objective justification" for making the stop. **INS v. DELGADO**, 466 U.S. 210, 217 (1984). That level of suspicion is considerably less than proof of wrongdoing by a preponderance of the evidence. We have held that probable cause means "a fair probability that contraband or evidence of a crime will be found." **UNITED STATES v. GATES**, 462 U.S. 213, 238 (1983), and the level of suspicion required for a *Terry* stop is obviously less demanding than that for probable cause. See **UNITED STATES v. MONTOYA DE HERNANDEZ**, 473 U.S. 531, 541, 544 (1985).

The concept of reasonable suspicion, like probable cause, is not "readily, or even usefully, reduced to a

662

neat set of legal rules." **GATES**, supra, at 232. We think the Court of Appeals' effort to refine and elaborate the requirements of "reasonable suspicion" in this case create unnecessary difficulty in dealing with one of the relatively simple concepts embodied in the Fourth Amendment. In evaluating the validity of a stop such as this, we must consider "the totality of the circumstances—the whole picture." **UNITED STATES v. CORTEZ,** 449 U.S. 411, 417 (1981). As we said in **CORTEZ:**

> "The process does not deal with hard certainties, but with probabilities. Long before the law of probabilities was articulated as such, practical people formulated certain common-sense conclusions about human behavior; jurors as fact-finders are permitted to do the same—and so are law enforcement officers." Id., at 418.

The rule enunciated by the Court of Appeals, in which evidence available to an officer is divided into evidence of "ongoing criminal behavior," on the one hand, and "probabilistic" evidence, on the other, is not in keeping with the quoted statements from our decisions. It also seems to us to draw a sharp line between types of evidence, the probative value of which varies only in degree. The Court of Appeals classified evidence of traveling under an alias, or evidence that the suspect took an evasive or erratic path through an airport, as meeting the test for showing "ongoing criminal activity." But certainly instances are conceivable in which traveling under an alias would not reflect ongoing criminal activity: for example, a person who wished to travel to a hospital or clinic for an operation and wished to conceal that fact. One taking an evasive path through an airport might be seeking to avoid a confrontation with an angry acquaintance or with a creditor. This is not to say that each of these types of evidence is not highly probative, but they do not have the sort of ironclad significance attributed to them by the Court of Appeals.

On the other hand, the factors in this case that the Court of Appeals treated as merely "probabilistic" also have probative significance. Paying $2,100 in cash for two airplane tickets is out of the ordinary, and it is even more out of the ordinary to pay that sum from a roll of $20 bills containing nearly twice that amount of cash.

Most business travelers, we feel confident, purchase airline tickets by credit card or check so as to have a record for tax or business purposes, and few vacationers carry with them thousands of dollars in $20 bills. We also think the agents had a reasonable ground to believe that respondent was traveling under an alias; the evidence was by no means conclusive, but it was sufficient to warrant consideration.[3] While a trip from Honolulu to Miami, standing alone, is not a cause for any sort of suspicion, here there was more: surely few residents of Honolulu travel from that city for 20 hours to spend 48 hours in Miami during the month of July.

Any one of these factors is not by itself proof of any illegal conduct and is quite consistent with innocent travel. But we think taken together they amount to reasonable suspicion. See **FLORIDA v. ROYER**, 460 U.S. 491, 502 (1983) (opinion of WHITE, J.); id., at 515-516 (BLACKMUN, J., dissenting); id., at 523-524 (REHNQUIST, J., dissenting).[4] We said in **REID v. GEORGIA**, 488 U.S. 438 (1980) (*per curiam*), "there could, of course, be circumstances in which wholly lawful conduct might justify the suspicion that criminal activity was afoot." Id., at 441.[5] Indeed, *Terry* itself involved "a series

---

[3]Respondent also claims that the agents should have conducted a further inquiry to resolve the inconsistency between the name he gave the airline and the name, "Karl Herman," under which his telephone number was listed. Brief for Respondent 26. This argument avails respondent nothing; had the agents done further checking, they would have discovered not only that respondent was Herman's roommate, but also that his name was "Sokolow" and not "Kray," the name listed on his ticket.

[4]In **ROYER**, the police were aware, <u>inter alia</u>, that (1) Royer was travelling under an assumed name; (2) he paid for his ticket in cash with a number of small bills; (3) he was traveling from Miami to New York; (4) he put only his name and not an address on his checked luggage; and (5) he seemed nervous while walking through Miami airport. 460 U.S., at 493, n. 2, 502 (opinion of WHITE, J.).

[5]In **REID**, the Court held that a DEA agent stopped the defendant without reasonable suspicion. At the time of the stop, the agent knew that (1) the defendant flew into Atlanta from Fort Lauderdale, a source city for cocaine; (2) he arrived early in the morning, when police activity was believed to be at a low ebb; (3) he did not check his luggage; and (4) the defendant and his companion appeared to be attempting to hide the fact that they were together. The Court held that the first three of these facts were not sufficient to supply reasonable suspicion because they "describe a very large category of presumably innocent travelers," while the last fact was insufficient on the facts of that case to establish reasonable suspicion. 488

of acts, each of them perhaps innocent" if viewed separately, "but which taken together warranted further investigation." 392 U.S., at 22; see also **CORTEZ**, 449 U.S., at 417-419. We noted in **GATES**, 462 U.S., at 243-244, n.13 (1983), that "innocent behavior will frequently provide the basis for a showing of probable cause," and that "[i]n making a determination of probable cause the relevant inquiry is not whether particular conduct is 'innocent' or 'guilty,' but the degree of suspicion that attaches to particular types of noncriminal acts." That principle applies equally well to the reasonable suspicion inquiry.

We do not agree with respondent that our analysis is somehow changed by the agents' belief that his behavior was consistent with one of the DEA's "drug courier profiles."[6] Brief for Respondent 14-21. A court sitting to determine the existence of reasonable suspicion must require the agent to articulate the factors leading to that conclusion, but the fact that these factors may be set forth in a "profile" does not somehow detract from their evidentiary significance as seen by a trained agent.

Respondent also contends that the agents were obligated to use the least intrusive means available to verify or dispel their suspicions that he was smuggling narcotics. Id., at 12-13, 21-23. In respondent's view, the agents should have simply approached and spoken with him, rather than forcibly detaining him. He points to the statement in **FLORIDA v. ROYER**, 460 U.S., at 500 (opinion of WHITE, J.), that "the investigative methods employed should be the least intrusive means reasonably available to verify or dispel the officer's suspicion in a short period of time." That statement, however, was directed at the length of the investigative stop, not at whether the police had a less intrusive means to verify their suspicions before stopping Royer. The reasonableness of the officer's decision to stop a suspect does not turn on the availability of less

---

U.S. 438, 441 (1980).

[6]Agent Kempshall testified that respondent's behavior "had all the classic aspects of a drug courier." App. 59. Since 1974, the DEA has trained narcotics officers to identify drug smugglers on the basis of the sort of circumstantial evidence at issue here.

665

intrusive investigatory techniques. Such a rule would unduly hamper the police's ability to make swift on-the-spot decisions—here, respondent was about to get into a taxicab—and it would require courts to "indulge in 'unrealistic second-guessing.'" **UNITED STATES v. ELVIRA MONTOYA de HERNANDEZ,** 473 U.S. at 542, quoting **UNITED STATES v. SHARPE,** 470 U.S. 675, 686, 687 (1985).

We hold that the agents had a reasonable basis to suspect that respondent was transporting illegal drugs on these facts. The judgment of the Court of Appeals is therefore reversed and the case remanded for further proceedings consistent with our decision.

It is so ordered.

UNITED STATES, Petitioner v.
ROSA ELVIRA MONTOYA DE HERNANDEZ.
437 U.S. 531, 105 S.Ct. 3304, 87 L.Ed.2d. 381 (1985)

Justice REHNQUIST delivered the opinion of the Court.

Respondent Rosa Elvira Montoya de Hernandez was detained by customs officials upon her arrival at the Los Angeles airport on a flight from Bogota, Columbia. She was found to be smuggling 88 cocaine-filled balloons in her alimentary canal, and was convicted after a bench trial of various federal narcotics offenses. A divided panel of the United States Court of Appeals for the Ninth Circuit reversed her convictions, holding that her detention violated the Fourth Amendment to the United States Constitution because the customs inspectors did not have a "clear indication" of alimentary canal smuggling at the time she was detained. 731 F2d 1369 (1984). Because of a conflict in the decisions of the Courts of Appeals on this question and the importance of its resolution to the enforcement of customs laws, we granted certiorari. 469 U.S.—, 105 S.Ct. 954, 83 L.Ed.2d 961. We now reverse.

Respondent arrived at Los Angeles International Airport shortly after midnight, March 5, 1983, on Avianca Flight 080, a direct 10-hour flight from Bogota, Columbia. Her visa was in order so she was passed through Immigration and proceeded to the customs desk. At the customs desk she encountered Customs Inspector Talamantes, who reviewed her documents and noticed from her passport that she had made at least eight recent trips to either Miami or Los Angeles. Talamantes referred respondent to a secondary customs' desk for further questioning. At this desk Talamantes and another inspector asked respondent general questions concerning herself and the purpose of her trip. Respondent revealed that she spoke no English and had no family or friends in the United States. She explained in Spanish that she had come to the United States to purchase goods for her husband's store in Bogota. The customs inspectors recognized Bogota as a "source city" for narcotics. Respondent possessed $5,000 in cash, mostly $50 bills, but had no billfold. She indicated to the inspectors that she had no appointments with merchandise vendors, but planned to ride around Los Angeles in taxicabs visiting retail stores such as J. C. Penney and K-Mart in order to buy goods for her husband's store with the $5,000.

Respondent admitted that she had no hotel reservations, but stated that she planned to stay at a Holiday Inn. Respondent could not recall how her airline ticket was purchased. When the inspectors opened respondent's one small valise they found about four changes of "cold weather" clothing. Respondent had no shoes other than the high-heeled pair she was wearing. Although respondent possessed no checks, waybills, credit cards, or letters of credit, she did produce a Columbian business card and a number of old receipts, waybills, and fabric swatches displayed in a photo album.

At this point Talamantes and the other inspector suspected that respondent was a "balloon swallower," one who attempts to smuggle narcotics into this country hidden in her alimentary canal. Over the years Inspector Talamantes had apprehended dozens of alimentary canal smugglers arriving on Avianca Flight 080. See App. 42; **UNITED STATES v. MENDEZ-JIMENEZ**, 709 F2d 1300, 1301 (1983).

The inspectors requested a female customs inspector to take respondent to a private area and conduct a patdown and strip search. During the search the female inspector felt respondent's abdomen area and noticed a firm fullness, as if respondent were wearing a girdle. The search revealed no contraband but the inspector noticed that respondent was wearing two pair of elastic underpants with a paper towel lining the crotch area.

When respondent returned to the customs area and the female inspector reported her discoveries, the inspector in charge told respondent that he suspected she was smuggling drugs in her alimentary canal. Respondent agreed to the inspector's request that she be X-rayed at a hospital but in answer to the inspector's query stated that she was pregnant. She agreed to a pregnancy test before X- ray. Respondent withdrew the consent for an X-ray when she learned that she would have to be handcuffed en route to the hospital. The inspector then gave respondent the option of returning to Columbia on the next available flight, agreeing to an X-ray, or remaining in detention until she produced a monitored bowl movement that would confirm or rebut the inspectors' suspicions. Respondent chose the first option and was placed in a customs' office under observation. She was told that if she went to the toilet she would have to use a wastebasket in the women's restroom, in order that female customs inspectors could inspect her stool for balloons or capsules carrying narcotics. The inspectors refused respondent's request to place a telephone call.

Respondent sat in the customs office, under observation, for the remainder of the night. During the night customs officials attempted to place respondent on a Mexican airline that was flying to Bogota via Mexico City in the morning. The airline refused to transport respondent because she lacked a Mexican visa necessary to land in Mexico City. Respondent was not permitted to leave, and was informed that she would be detained until she agreed to an X-ray or her bowels moved. She remained detained in the customs office under observation, for most of the time curled up in a chair leaning to one side. She refused all offers of food and drink, and refused to use the toilet facilities. The Court of Appeals noted that she exhibited symptoms of discomfort consistent with "heroic efforts to resist the usual calls of nature." 731 F2d, at 1371.

At the shift change at 4:00 p.m. the next afternoon, almost 16 hours after her flight had landed, respondent still had not defecated or urinated or partaken of food or drink. At that time customs officials sought a court order authorizing a pregnancy test, an X-ray, and a rectal examination. The federal Magistrate issued an order just before midnight that evening, which authorized a rectal examination and involuntary X-ray, provided that the physician in charge considered respondent's claim of pregnancy. Respondent was taken to a hospital and given a pregnancy test, which later turned out to be negative. Before the results of the pregnancy test were known, a physician conducted a rectal examination and removed from respondent's rectum a balloon containing a foreign substance. Respondent was then placed formally under arrest. By 4:10 a.m. respondent had passed 6 similar balloons; over the next 4 days she passed 88 balloons containing a total of 528 grams of 80% pure cocaine hydrochloride.

After suppression hearing the District Court admitted the cocaine in evidence against respondent. She was convicted of possession of cocaine with intent to

669

distribute. 21 U.S.C. § 841(a)(1) and unlawful importation of cocaine, 21 U.S.C. §§ 952(a), 960(a).

A divided panel of the United States Court of Appeals for the Ninth Circuit reversed respondent's convictions. The court noted that customs inspectors had a "justifiably high level of official skepticism" about respondent's good motives, but the inspectors decided to let nature take its course rather than seek an immediate magistrate's warrant for an X-ray. 731 F.2d, at 1371. Such a magistrate's warrant required a "clear indication" or "plain suggestion" that the traveler was an alimentary canal smuggler under previous decisions of the Court of Appeals. See **UNITED STATES v. QUINTERO-CASTRO**, 705 F.2d 1099 (CA9 1983); **UNITED STATES v. MENDEZ-JIMENEZ**, 709 F.2d 1300, 1302 (CA9 1983);but cf. **SOUTH DAKOTA v. OPPERMAN**, 428 U.S. 367, 370, n. 5, 96 S.Ct. 3092, 3096, 3097, n. 5, 49 L.Ed.2d 1000 (1976). The court applied this required level of suspicion to respondent's case. The court questioned the "humanity" of the inspectors' decision to hold respondent until her bowels moved, knowing that she would suffer "many hours of humiliating discomfort" if she chose not to submit to the x-ray examination. The court concluded that under a "clear indication" standard "the evidence available to the customs officers when they decided to hold [respondent] for continued observation was insufficient to support the 16-hour detention." 731 F.2d, at 1372.

The government contends that the customs inspectors reasonably suspected that respondent was an alimentary canal smuggler, and this suspicion was sufficient to justify the detention. In support of the judgment below respondent argues, *inter alia*, that reasonable suspicion would not support respondent's detention, and in any event the inspectors did not reasonably suspect that respondent was carrying narcotics internally.

[1, 2] The Fourth Amendment commands that searches and seizures be reasonable. What is reasonable depends upon all of the circumstances surrounding the search or seizure and the nature of the search or seizure itself. **NEW JERSEY v. T.L.O.**, 469 U.S. 325, 105 S.Ct. 733, 741-744, 83 L.Ed.2d 720 (1985). The permissibility of a particular law enforcement practice is judged by "balancing its intrusion on the individual's Fourth

670

Amendment interests against its promotion of legitimate governmental interests." **UNITED STATES v. VILLAMONTE-MARQUEZ**, 462 U.S. 579, 103 S. Ct. 2573, 2579, 77 L.Ed.2d 22 (1983); **DELAWARE v. PROUSE**, 440 U.S. 648, 654, 99 S.Ct. 1391, 1396, 59 L.Ed.2d 660 (1979); **CAMARA v. MUNICIPAL COURT**, 387 U.S. 523, 87 S.Ct. 1727, 18 L.Ed.2d 930 (1967).

Here the seizure of respondent took place at the international border. Since the founding of our Republic, Congress has granted the Executive plenary authority to conduct routine searches and seizures at the border, without probable cause of a warrant, in order to regulate the collection of duties and to prevent the introduction of contraband into this country. See **UNITED STATES v. RAMSEY**, 431 U.S. 606, 616-617, 97 S.Ct. 1972, 1978-1979, 52 L.Ed.2d 617 (1977), citing Act of July 31, 1789, ch. 5, 1 Stat. 29. This court has long recognized Congress' power to police entrants at the border. See **BOYD v. UNITED STATES** 116 U.S. 616, 623, 6 S.Ct. 524, 528, 29 L.Ed. 746 (1886). As we stated recently:

"'Import restrictions and searches of persons or packages at the national border rest on different considerations and different rules of constitutional law from domestic regulations. The Constitution gives Congress broad comprehensive powers "[t]o regulate commerce with foreign Nations," Art. I, § 8, cl. 3. Historically such broad powers have been necessary to prevent smuggling and to prevent prohibited articles from entry.'" *Ramsey, supra*, 431 U.S. at 618-619, 97 S.Ct., at 1979-1978, quoting **UNITED STATES v. 12 - 100 FT. REELS OF FILM**, 413 U.S. 123, 125, 93 S.Ct. 2665, 2667, 37 L.Ed.2d 500 (1973).

[3-4] Consistently, therefore, with Congress' power to protect the Nation by stopping and examining persons entering this country, the Fourth Amendment's balance of reasonableness is qualitatively different at the international border than in the interior. Routine searches of the persons and effects of entrants are not subject to any requirement of reasonable suspicion, probable cause, or warrant, and first-class mail may be opened without a warrant on less than probable cause, *Ramsey, supra*. Automotive travelers may be stopped at fixed check points near the border without individualized

suspicion even if the stop is based largely on ethnicity, **UNITED STATES v. MARTINEZ-FUERTE**, 428 U.S. 543, 562-563, 96 S.Ct. 3074, 3085, 49 L.Ed.2d 1116 (1976), and boats on inland waters with ready access to the sea may be hailed and boarded with no suspicion whatever. **UNITED STATES v. VILLAMONTE-MARQUEZ**, supra, 462 U.S. at ——, 103 S.Ct., at 2582.

These cases reflect longstanding concern for the protection of the integrity of the border. This concern is, if anything, heightened by the veritable national crisis in law enforcement caused by smuggling of illicit narcotics, see **UNITED STATES v. MENDENHALL**, 446 U.S. 544, 561, 100 S.Ct. 1870, 1880, 64 L.Ed.2d 497 (1980) (POWELL, J., concurring), and in particular by the increasing utilization of alimentary canal smuggling. This desperate practice appears to be a relatively recent addition to the smugglers' repertoire of deceptive practices, and it also appears to be exceedingly difficult to detect. Congress had recognized these difficulties. Title 19 U.S.C. § 1582 provides that "all persons coming into the United States from foreign countries shall be liable to detention and search authorized .... [by customs regulations]." Customs agents may "stop, search, and examine" any "vehicle, beast or person" upon which an officer suspects there is contraband or "merchandise which is subject to duty." § 482; see also §§ 1467, 1481; 19 CFR §§ 162.6, 162.7 (1984).

[5, 6] Balanced against the sovereign's interests at the border are the Fourth Amendment rights of respondent. Having presented herself at the border for admission, and having subjected herself to the criminal enforcement powers of the Federal Government. 19 U.S.C. § 482, respondent was entitled to be free from unreasonable search and seizure. But not only is the expectation of privacy less at the border than in the interior, see, e.g., **CARROLL v. UNITED STATES**, 267 U.S. 132, 154, 45 S.Ct. 280, 285, 69 L.Ed. 543 (1925); cf. **FLORIDA v. ROYER**, 460 U.S. 491, 515, 103 S.Ct. 1319, 1333, 75 L.Ed.2d 229 (1983) (BLACKMUN, J. dissenting), but the Fourth Amendment balance between the interests of the Government and the privacy right of the individual is struck much more favorably to the Government at the

border. *Ante*, at 3308-3309.

We have not previously decided what level of suspicion would justify a seizure of an incoming traveler for purposes other than a routine border search. Cf. *Ramsey, supra*, 431 U.S., at 618, n. 13, 97 S.Ct., at 1979, n. 13. The court of Appeals held that the initial detention of respondent was permissible only if the inspectors possessed a "clear indication" of alimentary canal smuggling. 731 F.2d, at 1372, citing *Quintero-Castro*, 705 F.2d 1099 (1983); cf. *Mendez-Jimenez*, 709 F.2d 1300 (1983). This "clear indication" language comes from our opinion in **SCHMERBER v. CALIFORNIA**, 384 U.S. 757, 86 S.Ct. 1826, 16 L.Ed.2d 908 (1966), but we think that the Court of Appeals misapprehended the significance of that phrase in the context in which it was used in *Schmerber*. The Court of Appeals for the Ninth Circuit viewed "clear indication" as an intermediate standard between "reasonable suspicion" and "probable cause." See *Mendez-Jimenez, supra*, at 1302. But we think that the words in *Schmerber* were used to indicate the necessity for particularized suspicion that the evidence sought might be found within the body of the individual, rather than as enunciating still a third Fourth Amendment threshold between "reasonable suspicion" and "probable cause."

No other court, including this one, has ever adopted *Schmerber's* "clear indication" language as a fourth Amendment standard. See, e.g., **WINSTON v. LEE**, 470 U.S. 753, 105 S.Ct. 1611, 1616-1617, 84 L.Ed.2d 662 (1985) (surgical removal of bullet for evidence). Indeed, another Circuit Court of Appeals, faced with facts almost identical to this case, has adopted a less strict standard based upon reasonable suspicion. See **UNITED STATES v. MOSQUERA-RAMIREZ**, 729 F.2d 1352, 1355 (CALL 1984). We do not think that the Fourth Amendment's emphasis upon reasonableness is consistent with the creation of a third verbal standard in addition to "reasonable suspicion" and "probable cause"; we are dealing with a constitutional requirement of reasonableness, not *mens rea*, see **UNITED STATES v. BAILEY**, 444 U.S. 394, 403-406, 100 S.Ct. 624, 631-633, 62 L.Ed.2d 575 (1980), and subtle verbal gradations may obscure rather than elucidate the meaning of the provision in question.

[7] We hold that the detention of a traveler at the border, beyond the scope of a routine customs search and

673

inspection, is justified at its inception if customs agents, considering all the facts surrounding the traveler and her trip, reasonably suspect that the traveler is smuggling contraband in her alimentary canal.

[8] The "reasonable suspicion" standard has been applied in a number of contexts and effects a needed balance between private and public interests when law enforcement officials must make a limited intrusion on less than probable cause. It thus fits well into the situations involving alimentary canal smuggling at the border: this type of smuggling gives no external signs and inspectors will rarely possess probable cause to arrest or search, yet governmental interests in stopping smuggling at the border are high indeed. Under this standard officials at the border must have a "particularized and objective basis for suspecting the particular person" of alimentary canal smuggling. **UNITED STATES v. CORTEZ**, 449 U.S. 411, 417, 101 S.Ct. 690, 695, 66 L.Ed.2d 621 (1981), *id.*, at 418, 101 S.Ct., at 695, citing **TERRY v. OHIO**, 392 U.S. 1, 21, N.18, 88 S.Ct. 1868, 1879, n. 18, 20 L.Ed.2d 889 (1968).

[9] The facts, and their rational inferences, known to customs inspectors in this case clearly supported a reasonable suspicion that respondent was an alimentary canal smuggler. We need not belabor the facts, including respondent's implausible story, that supported this suspicion, see *supra*, at 1-4, 88 S.Ct., at 1868-1871. The trained customs inspectors had encountered many alimentary canal smugglers and certainly had more than an "inchoate and unparticularized suspicion or 'hunch,'" *Terry, supra*, at 27, 88 S.Ct., at 1883, that respondent was smuggling narcotics in her alimentary canal. The inspector's suspicion was a "'common-sense conclusio[n] about human behavior' upon which 'practical people,'—including government officials, are entitled to rely." T.L.O., 469 U.S., at 325, 105 S.Ct., at 746, citing **UNITED STATES v. CORTEZ**, supra.

The final issue in this case is whether the detention of respondent was reasonably related in scope to the circumstances which justified it initially. In this regard we have cautioned that courts should not indulge in "unrealistic second-guessing," **UNITED STATES v. SHARPE**, 470 U.S. 675, 105 S.Ct. 1568, 1576, 84 L.Ed.2d

605 (1985), and we have noted that "creative judge[s], engaged in *post hoc* evaluations of police conduct can almost always imagine some alternative means by which the objectives of the police might have been accomplished," *Ibid*. But "[t]he fact that the protection of the public might, in the abstract, have been accomplished by 'less intrusive' means does not, in itself, render the search unreasonable." *Ibid*., citing **CADY v. DOMBROWSKI**, 413, U.S. 433, 447, 93 S.Ct. 2523, 2531, 37 L.Ed.2d 706 (1983). Authorities must be allowed "to graduate their response to the demands of any particular situation." **UNITED STATES v. PLACE**, 462 U.S. 696, 709, n. 10, 103 S.Ct. 2637, 2646, n. 10, 77 L.Ed.2d 110 (1983). Here, respondent was detained *incommunicado* for almost 16 hours before inspectors sought a warrant; the warrant then took a number of hours to procure, through no apparent fault of the inspectors. This length of time undoubtedly exceeds any other detention we have approved under reasonable suspicion. But we have also consistently rejected hard-and-fast time limits, *Sharpe, supra; Place, supra*, 709, n. 10, 103 S.Ct., at 2646, n. 10. Instead, "common sense and ordinary human experience must govern over rigid criteria." *Sharpe, supra*, 470 U.S., at 675, 105 S.Ct., at 1575.

The rudimentary knowledge of the human body which judges possess in common with the rest of humankind tells us that alimentary canal smuggling cannot be detected in the amount of time in which other illegal activity may be investigated through brief *Terry*-type stops. It presents few, if any external signs; a quick frisk will not do, nor will even a strip search. In the case of respondent the inspectors had available, as an alternative to simply awaiting her bowel movement, an X-ray. They offered her the alternative of submitting herself to that procedure. But when she refused that alternative, the customs inspector were left with only two practical alternatives: detain her for such time as necessary to confirm their suspicions, a detention which would last much longer than the typical *"Terry"* stop, or turn her loose into the interior carrying the reasonably suspected contraband drugs.

The inspectors in this case followed this former procedure. They no doubt expected that respondent, having recently disembarked from a 10-hour direct flight with a full and stiff abdomen, would produce a bowel movement without extended delay. But her visible efforts

675

to resist the call of nature, which the court below labeled "heroic," disappointed this expectation and in turn caused her humiliation and discomfort. Our prior cases have refused to charge police with delays in investigatory detention attributable to the suspect's evasive actions, see *Sharpe*, 470 U.S., at 675, 105 S.Ct., at 1576; *id.*, at 675, 105 S.Ct., at 1584 (MARSHALL, J., concurring in judgment), and that principle applies here as well. Respondent alone was responsible for much of the duration and discomfort of the seizure.

[10] Under these circumstances, we conclude that the detention in this case was not unreasonably long. It occurred at the international border, where the Fourth Amendment balance of interests leans heavily to the Government. At the border, customs officials have more than merely an investigative law enforcement role. They are also charged, along with immigration officials, with protecting this Nation from entrants who may bring anything harmful into this country, whether that be communicable diseases, narcotics, or explosives: See 8 U.S.C. §§ 1182(a)(23), 1182(a)(6), 1222; 19 CFR §§ 162.4-162.7 (1984). See also 19 U.S.C. § 482; 8 U.S.C. § 1103(a). In this regard the detention of a suspected alimentary canal smuggler at the border is analogous to the detention of a suspected tuberculosis carrier at the border: both are detained until their bodily processes dispel the suspicion that they will introduce a harmful agent into this country. Cf. 8 U.S.C. § 1222; 42 CFR pt. 34 (1984); 19 U.S.C. §§ 482, 1582.

Respondent's detention was long, uncomfortable, indeed, humiliating; but both its length and its discomfort resulted solely from the method by which she chose to smuggle illicit drugs into this country. In **ADAMS v. WILLIAMS**, 407 U.S. 143, 92 S.Ct. 1921, 1922, 32 L.Ed.2d 612 (1972), another *Terry*-stop case, we said that "[t]he Fourth Amendment does not require a policeman who lacks the precise level of information necessary for probable cause to arrest to simply shrug his shoulders and allow a crime to occur or a criminal to escape." *Id.*, at 145, 92 S.Ct., at 1923. Here, by analogy, in the presence of articulable suspicion of smuggling in her alimentary canal, the customs officers were not required by the Fourth Amendment to pass respondent and her 88 cocaine-filled balloons into the interior. Her detention for the period of time necessary to either verify or dispel the suspicion was not unreasonable. The judgment of the Court of Appeals is therefore

Reversed.

Justice STEVENS, concurring in the judgment.

If a seizure and a search of the person of the kind disclosed by this record may be made on the basis of reasonable suspicion, we must assume that a significant number of innocent persons will be required to undergo similar procedures. The rule announced in this case cannot, therefore, be supported on the ground that respondent's prolonged and humiliating detention "resulted solely from the method by which she chose to smuggle illicit drugs into this country." *Ante,* at 3312.

The prolonged detention of respondent was, however, justified by a different choice that respondent made; she withdrew her consent to an X-ray examination that would have easily determined whether the reasonable suspicion that she was concealing contraband was justified. I believe that Customs agents may require that a non-pregnant person reasonably suspected to this kind of smuggling submit to an X-ray examination as an incident to a border search. I therefore concur in the judgment....

FLORIDA v. MICHAEL A. RILEY
488 U.S. 445, 109 S.Ct. 693, 102 L.Ed.2d. 835 (1989)
ON WRIT OF CERTIORARI TO THE SUPREME COURT OF FLORIDA
. . .
MR. Chief Justice White announced the judgment of the Court and delivered an opinion, in which The Chief Justice, Justice Scalia and Justice Kennedy join.

On certification to it by a lower state court, the Florida Supreme Court addressed the following question: "Whether surveillance of the interior of a partially covered greenhouse in a residential backyard from the vantage point of a helicopter located 400 feet above the greenhouse constitutes a 'search' for which a warrant is required under the Fourth Amendment and Article I, Section 12 of the Florida Constitution." 511 So. 2d 282 (1987). The Court answered the question in the affirmative, and we granted the State's petition for certiorari challenging that conclusion. 484 U.S. —(1988).[1]

Respondent Riley lived in a mobile home located on five acres of rural property. A greenhouse was located 10 feet behind the mobile home. Two sides of the greenhouse were enclosed. The other two sides were not enclosed but the contents of the greenhouse were obscured from view from surrounding property by trees, shrubs and the mobile home. The greenhouse was covered by corrugated roofing panels, some translucent and some opaque. At the time relevant to this case, two of the panels, amounting to approximately 10% of the roof area, were missing. A wire fence surrounded the mobile home and the greenhouse, and the property was posted with a "DO NOT ENTER" sign.

This case originated with an anonymous tip to the Pasco County Sheriff's office that marijuana was being

---

[1] The Florida Supreme Court mentioned the State Constitution in posing the question, once_in the course of its opinion, and again in finally concluding that the search violated the Fourth Amendment and the State Constitution. The bulk of the discussion, however, focused exclusively on federal cases dealing with the Fourth Amendment.. and there being no indication that the decision "clearly and expressly...is alternatively based on bona fide separate, adequate, and independent grounds," we have jurisdiction. MICHIGAN v. LONG, 463 U.S. 1032, 1041 (1983).

grown on respondent's property. When an investigating officer discovered that he could not see the contents of the greenhouse from the road, he circled twice over respondent's property in a helicopter at the height of 400 feet. With his naked eye, he was able to see through the openings in the roof and one or more of the open sides of the greenhouse and to identify what he thought was marijuana growing in the structure. A warrant was obtained based on these observations, and the ensuing search revealed marijuana growing in the greenhouse. Respondent was charged with possession of marijuana under Florida law. The trial court granted his motion to suppress; the Florida Court of Appeals reversed but certified the case to the Florida Supreme Court, which quashed the decision of the Court of Appeals and reinstated the trial court's suppression order.

We agree with the State's submission that our decision in **CALIFORNIA v. CIRAOLO**, 476 U.S. 207 (1986), controls this case. There, acting on a tip, the police inspected the back yard of a particular house while flying in a fixed-wing aircraft at 1,000 feet. With the naked eye the officers saw what they concluded was marijuana growing in the yard. A search warrant was obtained on the strength of this airborne inspection and marijuana plants were found. The trial court refused to suppress this evidence, but a state appellate court held that the inspection violated the Fourth and Fourteenth Amendments of the United States Constitution and that the warrant was therefore invalid. We in turn reversed, holding that the inspection was not a search subject to the Fourth Amendment. We recognized that the yard was within the curtilage of the house, that a fence shielded the yard from observation from the street and that the occupant had a subjective expectation of privacy. We held, however, that such an expectation was not reasonable and not one "that society is prepared to honor." Id., at 214. Our reasoning was that the home and its curtilage are not necessarily protected from inspection that involves no physical invasion. "'What a person knowingly exposes to the public, even in his own home or office, is not subject of Fourth Amendment protection.'" Id., at 213, quoting **KATZ v. UNITED STATES**, 389 U.S. 347, 351 (1967). As a general proposition, the police may see what may be seen "from a public vantage point where [they have] a right to be" 476 U.S., at 213. Thus the police, like the public, would have been free to inspect the backyard garden from the street if their view had been unobstructed. They were likewise, free to inspect the yard from the vantage point of an aircraft flying in the navigable airspace as this plane was. "In an age where private and commercial flight in the public airways is routine, it is unreasonable for respondent to expect that his marijuana plants were constitutionally protected from being observed with the naked eye from an altitude of 1,000 feet. The Fourth Amendment simply does not require the police traveling in the public airways at this altitude to obtain a warrant in order to observe what is visible to the naked eye." Id., at 215.

We arrive at the same conclusion in the present case. In this case, as in **CIRAOLO**, the property surveyed was within the curtilage of respondent's home. Riley no doubt intended and expected that his greenhouse would not be open to public inspection and the precautions he took protected against ground-level observation. Because the sides and roof of his greenhouse were left partially open, however, what was growing in the greenhouse was subject to viewing from the air. Under the holding in **CIRAOLO**, Riley could not reasonably have expected the contents of his greenhouse to be immune from examination by an officer seated in a fixed-wing aircraft flying in navigable airspace at an altitude of 1,000 feet or, as the Florida Supreme Court seemed to recognize, at an altitude of 500 feet, the lower limit of the navigable airspace for such an aircraft. 511 So. 2d. at 288. Here, the inspection was made from a helicopter, but as is the case with fixed-wing planes, "private and commercial flight [by helicopter] in the public airways is routine" in this country, **CIRAOLO**, supra, at 215, and there is no indication that such flights are unheard of in Pasco County, Florida.[2] Riley could not reasonably

---

[2]The first use of the helicopter by police was in New York in 1947, and today every State in the country uses helicopters in police work. As of 1980, there were 1,500 of such aircraft used in police work. E. Brown, The Helicopter in Civil Operations 79 (1981). More than 10,000 helicopters, both public and private, are registered in the United States. Federal Aviation Administration. Census of U.S. Civil Aircraft, Calendar Year 1987, p. 12, and there are an estimated 31,697 helicopter pilots. Federal Aviation Administration, Statistical Handbook of Aviation,

have expected that his greenhouse was protected from public or official observation from a helicopter had it been flying within the navigable airspace for fixed-wing aircraft.

Nor on the facts before us, does it make a difference for Fourth Amendment purposes that the helicopter was flying at 400 feet when the officer saw what was growing in the greenhouse through the partially open roof and sides of the structure. We would have a different case if flying at that altitude had been contrary to law or regulation. But helicopters are not bound by the lower limits of the navigable airspace allowed to other aircraft. Any member of the public could legally have been flying over Riley's property in a helicopter at the altitude of 400 feet and could have observed Riley's greenhouse. The police officer did no more. This is not to say that an inspection of the curtilage of a house from an aircraft will always pass muster under the Fourth Amendment simply because the plane is within the navigable airspace specified by law. But it is of obvious importance that the helicopter in this case was *not* violating the law, and there is nothing in the record or before us to suggest that helicopters flying at 400 feet are sufficiently rare in this country to lend substance to respondent's claim that he reasonably anticipated that his greenhouse would not be subject to observation from that altitude. Neither is there any intimation here that the helicopter interfered with respondent's normal use of the greenhouse or of other parts of the curtilage. As far as this record reveals, no intimate details connected with the use of the home or curtilage were observed, and there was no undue noise, no wind, dust, or threat to injury. In these circumstances, there was no violation of the Fourth Amendment.

The judgment of the Florida Supreme Court is accordingly reversed.

So ordered.

Calendar Year 1986, p. 147. 1988 Helicopter Annual 9.

While FAA regulations permit fixed-wing aircraft to be operated at an altitude of 1,000 feet while flying over congested areas and at an altitude of 500 feet above the surface in other than congested areas, helicopters may be operated at less than the minimums for fixed-winged aircraft "if the operation is conducted without hazard to persons or property on the surface. In addition, each person operating a helicopter shall comply with routes or altitudes specifically prescribed for helicopters by the [FAA] Administrator." 14 CFR § 91.79 (1988).

UNITED STATES, PETITIONER, v. NEW YORK TELEPHONE COMPANY
434 U.S. 159, 98 S.Ct. 364, 54 L.Ed.2d 376,
22 Cr.L. 3001 (1977)
ON WRIT OF CERTIORARI TO THE UNITED STATES COURT OF
APPEALS FOR THE SECOND CIRCUIT.[December 7, 1977]
. . .
MR. Justice White delivered the opinion of the Court.

This case presents the question of whether a United States District Court may properly direct a telephone company to provide federal law enforcement officials the facilities and technical assistance necessary for the implementation of its order authorizing the use of pen registers to investigate offenses which there was probable cause to believe were being committed by means of the telephone.

I
On March 19, 1976, the United States District Court for the Southern District of New York issued an order authorizing agents of the Federal Bureau of Investigation (**FBI**) to install and use pen registers with respect to two telephones and directing the New York Telephone Company (the company) to furnish the **FBI** "all information, facilities and technical assistance" necessary to employ the pen registers unobtrusively. The **FBI** was ordered to compensate the Company at prevailing rates for any assistance which it furnished. App. 6-7. The order was issued on the basis of an affidavit submitted by an **FBI** agent which stated that certain individuals were conducting an illegal gambling enterprise at 220 East 14th Street in New York City and that, on the basis of facts set forth therein, there was probable cause to believe that two telephones bearing different numbers were being used at that address in furtherance of the illegal activity. App. 1-5. The District Court found that there was probable cause to conclude that an illegal gambling enterprise using the facilities of interstate commerce was being conducted at the East 14th Street address in violation of Title 18, United States Code, §§ 371 and 1952, and that the two telephones had been, were currently being, and would

682

continue to be used in connection with those offenses. Its order authorized the **FBI** to operate the pen registers with respect to the two telephones until knowledge of the numbers dialed led to the identity of the associates and confederates of those believed to be conducting the illegal operation or for 20 days, "whichever is earlier."

The Company declined to comply fully with the court order. It did inform the **FBI** of the location of the relevant "appearances," that is, the places where specific telephone lines emerge from the sealed cable. In addition, the Company agreed to identify the relevant "pairs," or the specific pairs of wires that constituted the circuits of the two telephone lines. This information is required to install a pen register. The Company, however, refused to lease lines to the **FBI** which were needed to install the pen registers in an unobtrusive fashion. Such lines were required by the **FBI** in order to install the pen registers in inconspicuous locations away from the building containing the telephones. A "lease line" is an unused telephone line which makes an "appearance" in the same terminal box as the telephone line in connection with which it is desired to install a pen register. If the leased line is connected to the subject telephone line, the pen register can then be installed on the leased line at a remote location and be monitored from that point. The Company, instead of providing the leased lines, which it conceded that the court's order required it to do, advised the **FBI** to string cables from the "subject apartment" to another location where pen registers could be installed. The **FBI** determined after canvassing the neighborhood of the apartment for four days that there was no location where it could string its own wires and attach the pen registers without alerting the suspects, in which event, of course, the gambling operation would cease to function. App. 15-22.

On March 30, 1976, the Company moved in the District Court to vacate that portion of the pen register order directing it to furnish facilities and technical assistance to the **FBI** in connection with the use of the pen registers on the ground that such a directive could be issued only in connection with a wiretap order conforming to the requirements of Title III of the Omnibus Crime Control and Safe Streets Act of 1968, 18 U.S.C. §§ 2510-2520 (Title III). It contended that neither Fed. Rule Crim. Proc. 41 nor the All Writs Act,

28 U.S.C. § 1651(a), provided any basis for such an order. App. 10-14. The District Court ruled that pen registers are not governed by the prescriptions of Title III because they are not devices used to intercept oral communications. It concluded that it had jurisdiction to authorize the installation of the pen registers upon a showing of probable cause and that both the All Writs Act and its inherent powers provided authority for the order directing the Company to assist in the installation of the pen registers.

On April 9, 1976, after the District Court and the Court of Appeals denied the Company's motion to stay the pen register order pending appeal, the Company provided the leased lines.

The Court of Appeals affirmed in part and reversed in part, with one judge dissenting on the ground that the order below should have been affirmed in its entirety. Application of the United States of America in the Matter of an Order Authorizing the Use of a Pen Register or Similar Mechanical Device (Application) 538 F.2d 956 (CA2 1976). It agreed with the District Court that pen registers do not fall within the scope of Title III and are not otherwise prohibited or regulated by statute. The Court of Appeals also concluded that district courts have the power, either inherently or as a logical derivative of Fed. Rule Crim. Proc. 41, to authorize pen register surveillance upon an adequate showing of probable cause. The majority held, however, that the District Court abused its discretion in ordering the Company to assist in the installation and operation of the pen registers. It assumed, *arguendo*, "that a district court has inherent discretionary authority or discretionary power under the All Writs Act to compel technical assistance by the Telephone Company," but concluded that "in the absence of specific and properly limited Congressional action, it was an abuse of discretion for the District Court to order the Telephone Company to furnish technical assistance." Id., at 961. The majority expressed concern that "such an order could establish a most undesirable, if not dangerous and unwise, precedent for the authority of federal courts to impress unwilling aid on private third parties" and that "there is no assurance that the court will always be able to protect [third parties] from excessive or overzealous Government activity or compulsion." Id., at 962-963. We granted the United States' petition for certiorari challenging the Court of Appeals' invalidation of the District Court's order against respondent.

II
We first reject respondent's contention, which is renewed here, that the District Court lacked authority to order the Company to provide assistance because the use of pen registers may only be authorized in conformity with the procedures set forth in Title III for securing judicial authority to intercept wire communications. Both the language of the statute and its legislative history establish beyond any doubt that pen registers are not governed by Title III.

Title III is concerned only with orders "authorizing or approving the *interception* of a wire or oral communication. . . ." 18 U.S.C. § 2518 (1) (emphasis added). Congress defined "intercept" to mean "the *aural* acquisition of the *contents* of any wire or oral *communication* through the use of any electronic, mechanical, or other device." 18 U.S.C. § 2510 (4) (emphasis added). Pen registers do not "intercept" because they do not acquire the "contents" of communications, as that term is defined by 18 U.S.C. § 2511 (8). Indeed, a law enforcement official could not even determine from the use of a pen register whether a communication existed. These devices do not hear sound. They disclose only the telephone numbers that have been dialed—a means of establishing communication. Neither the purport of any communication between the caller and the recipient of the call, their identities, nor whether the call was even completed are disclosed by pen registers. Furthermore, pen registers do not accomplish the "aural acquisition" of anything. They decode outgoing telephone numbers by responding to changes in electrical voltage caused by the turning of the telephone dial (or the pressing of buttons on push button telephones) and present the information in a form to be interpreted by sight rather than by hearing.

The legislative history confirms that there was no congressional intent to subject pen registers to the requirements of Title III. The Senate Report explained that the definition of "intercept" was designed to exclude pen registers:

"Paragraph 4 [of § 2510] defines 'intercept' to include the aural acquisition of the contents of any wire or oral communication by any electronic, mechanical, or other device. Other forms of surveillance are not within the proposed legislation. . . . The proposed legislation is not designed to prevent the tracing of phone calls. The use of a 'pen register,' for example, would be permissible. But see **UNITED STATES v. DOTE**, 371 F.2d 176 (7th 1966). The proposed legislation is intended to protect the privacy of the communication itself and not the means of communication." S.Rep. No. 1097, 90th Cong., 2d Sess., p. 90 (1968).

It is clear that Congress did not view pen registers as posing a threat to privacy of the same dimension as the interception of oral communications and did not intend to impose title III restrictions upon their use.

III
    We also agree with the Court of Appeals that the District Court had power to authorize the installation of the pen registers. It is undisputed that the order in this case was predicated upon a proper finding of probable cause, and no claim is made that it was in any way inconsistent with the Fourth Amendment. Fed. Rule Crim. Proc. 41 (b) authorizes the issuance of a warrant to

"Search for and seize any (1) property that constitutes evidence of the commission of a criminal offense; or (2) contraband, the fruits of crime, or things otherwise criminally possessed; or (3) property designed or intended for use or which is or has been used as the means of committing a criminal offense."

This definition is broad enough to encompass a "search" designed to ascertain the use which is being made of a telephone suspected of being employed as a means of facilitating a criminal venture and the "seizure" of evidence which the "search" of the telephone

686

produces. Although Rule 41 (h) defines property "to include documents, books, papers and any other tangible objects,: it does not restrict or purport to exhaustively enumerate all the items which may be seized pursuant to Rule 41. Indeed, we recognized in **KATZ v. UNITED STATES**, 389 U.S. 347 (1967), which held that telephone conversations were protected by the Fourth Amendment, that Rule 41 is not limited to tangible items but is sufficiently flexible to include within its scope electronic intrusions authorized upon a finding of probable cause. 389 U.S., at 354-356, and n. 16. See also **OSBORN v. UNITED STATES**, 385 U.S. 323, 329-331 (1966).

Our conclusion that Rule 41 authorizes the use of pen registers under appropriate circumstances is supported by Fed. Rule Crim. Proc. 57 (b), which provides: "If no procedure is specifically prescribed by rule, the court may proceed in any lawful manner not inconsistent with these rules or with any applicable statute." Although we need not and do not decide whether Rule 57(b) by itself would authorize the issuance of pen register orders, it reinforces our conclusion that Rule 41 is sufficiently broad to include seizures of intangible items such as dial impulses recorded by pen registers as well as tangible items.

Finally, we could not hold that the District Court lacked any power to authorize the use of pen registers without defying the congressional judgment that the use of pen registers "be permissible." S. Rep. No. 1097, supra, at 90. Indeed, it would be anomalous to permit the recording of conversations by means of electronic surveillance while prohibiting the far lesser intrusion accomplished by pen registers. Congress intended no such result. We are unwilling to impose it in the absence of some showing that the issuance of such orders would be inconsistent with Rule 41. Cf. Rule 57(b), supra.

IV

The Court of Appeals held that even though the District Court had ample authority to issue the pen register warrant and even assuming the applicability of the All Writs Act, the order compelling the Company to provide technical assistance constituted an abuse of discretion. Since the Court of Appeals conceded that a compelling case existed for requiring the assistance of the company and did not point to any fact particular to this case which would warrant a finding of abuse of discretion, we interpret its holding as generally barring district courts from ordering any party to assist in the installation or operation of a pen register. It was apparently concerned that sustaining the District Court's order would authorize courts to compel third parties to render assistance without limitation regardless of the burden involved and pose a severe threat to the autonomy of third parties who for whatever reason prefer not to render such assistance. Consequently the Court of Appeals concluded that courts should not embark upon such a course without specific legislative authorization. We agree that the power of federal courts to impose duties upon third parties is not without limits; unreasonable burdens may not be imposed. We conclude, however, that the order issued here against respondent was clearly authorized by the All Writs Act and was consistent with the intent of Congress.

The All Writs Acts provides:

"The Supreme Court and all courts established by Act of Congress may issue all writs necessary or appropriate in aid of their respective jurisdictions and agreeable to the usages and principles of law." 28 U.S.C. § 1651 (a).

The assistance of the Company was required here to implement a pen register order which we have held the District Court was empowered to issue by Rule 41. This Court has repeatedly recognized the power of a federal court to issue such commands under the All Writs Act as may be necessary to appropriate to effectuate and prevent the frustration of orders it has previously issued in its exercise of jurisdiction otherwise obtained: "This statute has served since its inclusion, in substance, in the original Judiciary Act as a 'legislatively approved source of procedural instruments designed to achieve the rational ends of law.'" **HARRIS v. NELSON**, 394 U.S. 286, 299 (1969), quoting **PRICE v. JOHNSTON**, 334 U.S. 266, 282 (1948). Indeed, "[u]nless appropriately confined by Congress, a federal court may avail itself of all auxiliary writs as aids in the performance of its duties, when the use of such historic aids is calculated in its sound judgment to achieve the ends of justice entrusted to it." **ADAMS v. UNITED STATES** ex rel. McCann, 317 U.S. 269, 273 (1942).

The Court has consistently applied the Act flexibly in conformity with these principles. Although § 262 of the Judicial Code, the predecessor to § 1651, did not expressly authorize courts, as does § 1651, to issue writs "appropriate" to the proper exercise of their jurisdiction but only "necessary" writs, Adams held that these supplemental powers are not limited to those situations where it is "necessary" to issue the writ or order "in the sense that the court could not otherwise physically discharge its duties." Ibid. In **PRICE v. JOHNSTON**, supra, § 262 supplied the authority for a United States Court of Appeals to issue an order commanding that a prisoner be brought before the court for the purpose of arguing his own appeal. Similarly, in order to avoid frustrating the "very purpose" of 28 U.S.C. § 2255, § 1651 furnished the District Court with authority to order that a federal prisoner be produced in court for purposes of hearing. **UNITED STATES v. HAYMAN**, 342 U.S. 205, 220-222 (1952). The question in **HARRIS v. NELSON**, supra, was whether, despite the absence of specific statutory authority, the District Court could issue a discovery order in connection with a habeas corpus proceeding pending before it. Eight Justices agreed that the district courts have power to require discovery when essential to render a habeas corpus proceeding effective. The Court has also held that despite the absence of express statutory authority to do so, the Federal Trade Commission may petition for, and a Court of Appeals may issue, pursuant to § 1651, an order preventing a merger pending hearings before the Commission to avoid impairing or frustrating the Court of Appeals appellate jurisdiction. **FEDERAL TRADE COMM'N v. DEAN FOODS CO.**, 384 U.S. 597 (1966).

The power conferred by the Act extends, under appropriate circumstances, to persons who though not parties to the original action or engaged in wrong doing are in a position to frustrate the implementation of a court order or the proper administration of justice. **MISSISSIPPI VALLEY BARGE LINE CO. v. UNITED STATES**, 273 F. Supp. 1, 6 (FD Mo. 1967), aff'd 389 U.S. 579 (1968); **BOARD OF EDUCATION v. YORK**, 429 F.2d 66 (CA10 1970), cert. denied, 401 U.S. 954 (1971), and encompasses even those who have not taken any affirmative action to hinder justice. **UNITED STATES v. MCHIE**, 196 Fed. 586 (ND Ill. 1912); **FIELD v. UNITED STATES**, 193 F.2d 92, 95-96 (CA2), cert. denied, 342 U.S. 894 (1951).

Turning to the facts of this case, we do not think that the Company was a third party so far removed from the underlying controversy that its assistance could not be permissibly compelled. A United States District Court found that there was probable cause to believe that the Company's facilities were being employed to facilitate a criminal enterprise on a continuing basis. For the Company, with this knowledge, to refuse to supply the meager assistance required by the **FBI** in its efforts to put an end to this venture threatened obstruction of an investigation which would determine whether the Company's facilities were being lawfully used. Moreover, it can hardly be contended that the Company, a highly regulated public utility with a duty to serve the public, had a substantial interest in not providing assistance. Certainly the use of pen registers is by no means offensive to it. The Company concedes that it regularly employs such devices without court order for the purpose of checking billing operations, detecting fraud, and preventing violations of law. It also agreed to supply the **FBI** with all the information required to install its own pen registers. Nor was the District Court's order in any way burdensome. The order provided that the Company be fully reimbursed at prevailing rates, and compliance with it required minimal effort on the part of the Company and no disruption to its operations.

Finally, we note, as the court of Appeals recognized, that without the Company's assistance there is no conceivable way in which the surveillance authorized by the District Court could have been successfully accomplished. The **FBI**, after an exhaustive search, was unable to find a location where it could install its own pen registers without tipping off the targets of the investigation. The provision of a leased line by the Company was essential to the fulfillment of the purpose—to learn the identities of those connected with the gambling operation—for which the pen register order had been used.

The order compelling the Company to provide assistance was not only consistent with the Act but also with more recent congressional actions. As established in Part II, supra, Congress clearly intended to permit the use of pen registers by federal law enforcement officials. Without the assistance of the Company in circumstances such as those presented here, however, these devices simply cannot be effectively employed. Moreover, Congress provided in a 1970 amendment to Title III that "[a]n order authorizing the interception of a wire or oral communication shall, upon request of the applicant, direct that a communication common carrier .... shall furnish the applicant forthwith all information, facilities, and technical assistance necessary to accomplish the interception unobtrusively...." 18 U.S.C. § 2518 (4). In light of this direct command to federal courts to compel, upon request, any assistance necessary to accomplish an electronic interception, it would be remarkable if Congress thought it beyond the power of the federal courts to exercise, where required, a discretionary authority to order telephone companies to assist in the installation and operation of pen registers, which accomplish a far lesser invasion of privacy. We are convinced that to prohibit the order challenged here would frustrate the clear indication by Congress that the pen register is a permissible law enforcement tool by enabling a public utility to thwart a judicial determination that its use is required to apprehend and prosecute successfully those employing the utility's facilities to conduct a criminal venture. The contrary judgment of the Court of Appeals is accordingly reversed.

So ordered.

KATZ v. UNITED STATES
389 U.S. 347, 88 S.Ct. 507, 19 L.Ed.2d 576 (1967)
CERTIORARI TO THE UNITED STATES COURT OF APPEALS
FOR THE NINTH CIRCUIT
Argued October 17, 1967.—Decided December 18, 1967
. . .

MR. Justice Stewart delivered the opinion of the Court.

The petitioner was convicted in the District Court for the Southern District of California under an eight-count indictment charging him with transmitting wagering information by telephone from Los Angeles to Miami and Boston, in violation of a federal statute. At trial the Government was permitted, over the petitioner's objection, to introduce evidence of the petitioner's end of telephone conversations, overheard by FBI agents who had attached an electronic listening and recording device to the outside of the public telephone booth from which he had placed his calls. In affirming his conviction, the Court of Appeals rejected the contention that the recordings had been obtained in violation of the Fourth Amendment, because "[t]here was no physical entrance into the area occupied by [the petitioner]." We granted certiorari in order to consider the constitutional questions thus presented.

The petitioner has phrased those questions as follows:

"A. Whether a public telephone booth is a constitutionally protected area so that evidence obtained by attaching an electronic listening recording device to the top of such a booth is obtained in violation of the right to privacy to the user of the booth.

"B. Whether physical penetration of a constitutionally protected area is necessary before a search and seizure can be said to be violative of the Fourth Amendment to the United States Constitution."

We decline to adopt this formulation of the issues. In the first place, the correct solution of Fourth

Amendment problems is not necessarily promoted by incantation of the phrase "constitutionally protected area." Secondly, the Fourth Amendment cannot be translated into general constitutional "right to privacy." That Amendment protects individual privacy against certain kinds of governmental intrusion, but its protections go further, and often have nothing to do with privacy at all. Other provisions of the Constitution protect personal privacy from other forms of governmental invasion. But the protection of a person's *general* right to privacy—his right to be let alone by other people—is, like the protection of his property and of his very life, left largely to the law of the individual States.

Because of the misleading way the issues have been formulated, the parties have attached great significance to the characterization of the telephone booth from which the petitioner placed his calls. The petitioner has strenuously argued that the booth was a "constitutionally protected area." The Government has maintained with equal vigor that it was not. But this effort to decide whether or not a given "area," viewed in the abstract, is "constitutionally protected" deflects attention from the problem presented by this case. For the Fourth Amendment protects people, not places. What a person knowingly exposes to the public, even in his own home or office, is not a subject of Fourth Amendment protection. See **LEWIS v. UNITED STATES**, 385 U.S. 206, 210; **UNITED STATES v. LEE**, 274 U.S. 559, 563. But what he seeks to preserve as private, even in an area accessible to the public, may be constitutionally protected. See **RIOS v. UNITED STATES**, 364 U.S. 253; Ex parte Jackson, 96 U.S. 727, 733.

The Government stresses the fact that the telephone booth from which the petitioner made his calls was constructed partly of glass, so that he was as visible after he entered it as he would have been if he had remained outside. But what he sought to exclude when he entered the booth was not the intruding eye—it was the uninvited ear. He did not shed his right to do so simply because he made his calls from a place where he might be seen. No less than an individual in a business office, in a friend's apartment, or in a taxicab, a person in a telephone booth may rely upon the protection of the Fourth Amendment. One who occupies it, shuts the door behind him, and pays the toll that permits him to place a call is surely entitled to assume that the words he utters into the mouthpiece will not be broadcast to the world. To read the Constitution more narrowly is to ignore the vital role that the public telephone has come to play in private communication.

The Government contends, however, that the activities of its agents in this case should not be tested by Fourth Amendment requirements, for the surveillance technique they employed involved no physical penetration of the telephone booth from which the petitioner placed his calls. It is true that the absence of such penetration was at one time thought to foreclose further Fourth Amendment inquiry, **OLMSTEAD v. UNITED STATES**, 277 U.S. 438, 457, 464, 466; **GOLDMAN v. UNITED STATES**, 316 U.S. 129, 134-136, for that Amendment was thought to limit only searches and seizures of tangible property. But "[t]he premise that property interests control the right of the Government to search and seize has been discredited." **WARDEN v. HAYDEN**, 387 U.S. 294, 304. Thus, although a closely divided Court supposed in Olmstead that surveillance without any trespass and without the seizure of any material object fell outside the ambit of the Constitution, we have since departed from the narrow view on which that decision rested. Indeed, we have expressly held that the Fourth Amendment governs not only the seizure of tangible items, but extends as well to the recording of oral statements, overheard without any "technical trespass under .... local property law." **SILVERMAN v. UNITED STATES**, 365 U.S. 505, 511. Once this much is acknowledged, and once it is recognized that the Fourth Amendment protects people—and not simply "areas"—against unreasonable searches and seizures, it becomes clear that the reach of that Amendment cannot turn upon the presence or absence of a physical intrusion into any given enclosure.

We conclude that the underpinnings of Olmstead and Goldman have been so eroded by our subsequent decisions that the "trespass" doctrine there enunciated can no longer be regarded as controlling. The Government's activities in electronically listening to and recording the petitioner's words violated the privacy upon which he justifiably relied while using the telephone booth and thus constituted a "search and seizure" within the meaning of the Fourth Amendment. The fact that the electronic device employed to achieve that end did not happen to penetrate the wall of the booth can have no constitutional significance.

The question remaining for decision, then, is whether the search and seizure conducted in this case complied with constitutional standards. In that regard, the Government's position is that its agents acted in an entirely defensible manner: They did not begin their electronic surveillance until investigation of the petitioner's activities had established a strong probability that he was using the telephone in question to transmit gambling information to persons in other States, in violation of federal law. Moreover, the surveillance was limited, both in scope and in duration, to the specific purpose of establishing the contents of the petitioner's unlawful telephonic communications. The agents confined their surveillance to the brief periods during which he used the telephone booth, and they took great care to overhear only the conversations of the petitioner himself.

Accepting this account of the Government's actions as accurate, it is clear that this surveillance was so narrowly circumscribed that a duly authorized magistrate, properly notified of the need for such investigation, specifically informed of the basis on which it was to proceed, and clearly apprised of the precise intrusion it would entail, could constitutionally have authorized, with appropriate safeguards, the very limited search and seizure that the Government asserts in fact took place. Only last Term we sustained the validity of such an authorization, holding that, under sufficiently "precise and discriminate circumstances," a federal court may empower government agents to employ a concealed electronic device "for the narrow and particularized purpose of ascertaining the truth of the .... allegations" of a "detailed factual affidavit alleging the commission of a specific criminal offense." **OSBORN v. UNITED STATES**, 385 U.S. 323, 329-330. Discussing that holding, the Court in **BERGER v. NEW YORK**, 388 U.S. 41, said that "the order authorizing the use of the electronic device" in Osborn "afforded similar protections to those .... of conventional warrants authorizing the seizure of tangible evidence." Through those protections, "no greater invasion of privacy was permitted than was necessary under the circumstances." Id., at 57. Here, too, a similar judicial order could have accommodated "the legitimate needs of law enforcement" by authorizing the carefully limited use of electronic surveillance.

The Government urges that, because its agents relied upon the decisions in Olmstead and Goldman, and because they did no more here than they might properly have done with prior judicial sanction, we should retroactively validate their conduct. That we cannot do. It is apparent that the agents in this case acted with restraint. Yet the inescapable fact is that this restraint was imposed by the agents themselves, not by a judicial officer. They were not required, before commencing the search, to present their estimate of probable cause for detached scrutiny by a neutral magistrate. They were not compelled, during the conduct of the search itself, to observe precise limits established in advance by a specific court order. Nor were they directed, after the search had been completed, to notify the authorizing magistrate in detail of all that had been seized. In the absence of such safeguards, this Court has never sustained a search upon the sole ground that officers reasonably expected to find evidence of a particular crime and voluntarily confined their activities to the least intrusive means consistent with that end. Searches conducted without warrants have been held unlawful "notwithstanding facts unquestionably showing probable cause," **AGNELLO v. UNITED STATES**, 269 U.S. 20 33, for the Constitution requires "that the deliberate, impartial judgment of a judicial officer .... be interposed between the citizens and the police...." **WONG SUN v. UNITED STATES**, 371 U.S. 471, 481-482. "Over and again this Court has emphasized that the mandate of the [Fourth] Amendment requires adherence to judicial processes," **UNITED STATES v. JEFFERS**, 342 U.S. 48, 51, and that searches conducted outside the judicial process, without prior approval by judge or magistrate, are per se unreasonable under the Fourth Amendment—subject only to a few specifically established and well-delineated exceptions.

It is difficult to imagine how any of those exceptions could ever apply to the sort of search and seizure involved in this case. Even electronic surveillance substantially contemporaneous with an

696

individual's arrest could hardly be deemed an "incident" of that arrest. Nor could the use of electronic surveillance without prior authorization be justified on grounds of "hot pursuit." And, of course, the very nature of electronic surveillance precludes its use pursuant to the suspect's consent.

The Government does not question these basic principles. Rather, it urges the creation of a new exception to cover this case. It argues that surveillance of a telephone booth should be exempted from the usual requirement of advance authorization by a magistrate upon a showing of probable cause. We cannot agree. Omission of such authorization

> "bypasses the safeguards provided by an objective redetermination of probable cause, and substitutes instead the far less reliable procedure of an after-the-event justification for the .... search, too likely to be subtly influenced by the familiar shortcomings of hindsight judgment." **BECK v. OHIO,** 379 U.S. 89, 96.

And bypassing a neutral predetermination of the *scope* of a search leaves individuals secure from Fourth Amendment violations "only in the discretion of the police," Id., at 97.

These considerations do not vanish when the search in question is transferred from the setting of a home, an office, or a hotel room to that of a telephone booth. Wherever a man may be, he is entitled to know that he will remain free from unreasonable searches and seizures. The government agents here ignored "the procedure of antecedent justification .... that is central to the Fourth Amendment," a procedure that we hold to be a constitutional precondition of the kind of electronic surveillance involved in this case. Because the surveillance here failed to meet that condition, and because it led to the petitioner's conviction, the judgment must be reversed.

It is so ordered

ILLINOIS v. PERKINS
496 U.S. 292, 100 S.Ct. 2394, 110 L.Ed.2d 243 (1990)
CERTIORARI TO THE APPELLATE COURT OF ILLINOIS,
FIFTH JUDICIAL DISTRICT

JUSTICE KENNEDY delivered the opinion of the Court.
An undercover government agent was placed in the cell of respondent Perkins, who was incarcerated on charges unrelated to the subject of the agent's investigation. Respondent made statements that implicated him in the crime that the agent sought to solve. Respondent claims that the statements should be inadmissible because he had not been given MIRANDA warnings by the agent. We hold that the statements are admissible. MIRANDA warnings are not required when the suspect is unaware that he is speaking to a law enforcement officer and gives a voluntary statement.

I

In November 1984, Richard Stephenson was murdered in a suburb of East St. Louis, Illinois. The murder remained unsolved until March 1986, when one Donald Charlton told police that he had learned about a homicide from a fellow inmate at the Graham Correctional Facility, where Charlton had been serving a sentence for burglary. The fellow inmate was Lloyd Perkins, who is the respondent here. Charlton told police that, while at Graham, he had befriended respondent, who told him in detail about a murder that respondent had committed in East St. Louis. On hearing Charlton's account, the police recognized details of the Stephenson murder that were not well known, and so they treated Charlton's story as a credible one.

By the time the police heard Charlton's account, respondent had been released from Graham, but police traced him to a jail in Montgomery County, Illinois, where he was being held pending trial on a charge of aggravated battery, unrelated to the Stephenson murder. The police wanted to investigate further respondent's connection to the Stephenson murder, but feared that the use of an eavesdropping device would prove impractible and unsafe. They decided instead to place an undercover agent in the cellblock with respondent and Charlton. The plan was for Charlton and undercover agent John Parisi to pose as escapees from a work release program who had been arrested in the course of a burglary. Parisi and Charlton were instructed to engage respondent in casual conversation and report anything he said about the Stephenson murder.

Parisi, using the alias "Vito Bianco," and Charlton, both clothed in jail garb, were placed in the cellblock with respondent at the Montgomery County jail. The cellblock consisted of 12 separate cells that opened onto a common room. Respondent greeted Charlton who, after a brief conversation with respondent, introduced Parisi by his alias. Parisi told respondent that he "wasn't going to do any more time" and suggested that the three of them escape. Respondent replied that the Montgomery County jail was "rinky-dink" and that they could "break out." The trio met in respondent's cell later that evening, after the other inmates were asleep, to refine their plan. Respondent said that his girlfriend could smuggle in a pistol. Charlton said: "Hey, I'm not a murderer, I'm a burglar. That's your guys' profession." After telling Charlton that he would be responsible for any murder that occurred, Parisi asked respondent if he had ever "done" anybody. Respondent said that he had and proceeded to describe at length the events of the Stephenson murder. Parisi and respondent then engaged in some casual conversation before respondent went to sleep. Parisi did not give respondent MIRANDA warnings before the conversations.

Respondent was charged with the Stephenson murder. Before trial, he moved to suppress the statements made to Parisi in the jail. The trial court granted the motion to suppress, and the State appealed. The Appellate Court of Illinois affirmed, 176 Ill. App. 3d 443, 531 N.E. 2d 141 (1988), holding that **MIRANDA v. ARIZONA**, 384 U.S. 436 (1966), prohibits all undercover contacts with incarcerated suspects that are reasonably likely to elicit an incriminating response.

We granted certiorari, 493 U.S. 808 (1989), to decide whether an undercover law enforcement officer must give MIRANDA warnings to an incarcerated suspect before asking him questions that may elicit an incriminating response. We now reverse.

II

In **MIRANDA v. ARIZONA,** supra, the Court held that
the Fifth Amendment privilege against self-incriminating
prohibits admitting statements given by a suspect during
"custodial interrogation" without a prior warning.
Custodial interrogations means "questioning initiated by
law enforcement officers after a person has been taken
into custody . . . ." Id., at 444. The warning mandated
by MIRANDA was meant to preserve the privilege during
"incommunicado interrogation of individuals in a police-
dominated atmosphere." Id., at 445. That atmosphere is
said to generate "inherently compelling pressures which
work to undermine the individual's will to resist and to
compel him to speak where he would not otherwise do so
freely." Id., at 47. "Fidelity to the doctrine announced
in MIRANDA requires that it be enforced strictly, but
only in those types of situations in which the concerns
that powered the decision are implicated." **BERKEMER v.
McCARTY,** 468 U.S. 420, 437 (1984).

Conversations between suspects and undercover agents
do not implicate the concerns underlying MIRANDA. The
essential ingredients of a "police-dominated atmosphere"
and compulsion are not present when an incarcerated
person speaks freely to someone whom he believes to be a
fellow inmate. Coercion is determined from the
perspective of the suspect. **BEKEMER v. McCARTY,** supra, at
442. When a suspect considers himself in the company of
cellmates not officers, the coercive atmosphere is
lacking. MIRANDA, 384 U.S., at 449 ("[T]he 'principal
psychological factor contributing to a successful
interrogation is privacy - being alone with the person
under interrogation'"); id., at 445. There is no
empirical basis for the assumption that a suspect
speaking to those whom he assumes are not officers will
feel compelled to speak by the fear of reprisal for
remaining silent or in the hope of more lenient treatment
should he confess.

It is the premise of MIRANDA that the danger of
coercion results from the interaction of custody and
official interrogation. We reject the argument that
MIRANDA warnings are required whenever a suspect is in
custody in a technical sense and converses with someone

who happens to be a government agent. Questioning by captor, who appear to control the suspect's fate, may create mutually reinforcing pressures that the Court has assumed will weaken the suspect's will, but where a suspect does not know that he is conversing with a government agent, the pressures do not exist. The state court here mistakenly assumed that because the suspect was in custody, no undercover questioning could take place. When the suspect has no reason to think that the listeners have official power over him, it should not be assumed that his words are motivated by the reaction he expects from his listeners."[W]hen the agent carries neither a badge nor gun and wears not 'police blue' but the same prison gray" as the suspect, there is no "interplay between police interrogation and police custody." **KAMISAR, BREWER v. WILLIAMS, MASSIAH** and **MIRANDA**: What is "Interrogation"? When Does it Matter?, 67 Geo. L. J. 1, 67 63 (1978).

MIRANDA forbids coercion, not mere strategic deception by taking advantage of a suspect's misplaced trust in one he supposes to be a fellow prisoner. As we recognized in MIRANDA, "[c]onfessions remain a proper element in law enforcement. Any statement given freely and voluntarily without any compelling influences is, of course, admissible in evidence." 384 U.S., at 478. Ploys to mislead a suspect or lull him into a false sense of security that do not rise to the level of compulsion or coercion to speak are not within MIRANDA'S concerns. Cf. **OREGON v. MATHIASON**, 429 US. 492, 495-496 (1977)(per curiam); **MORAN v. BURBINE**, 475 U.S. 412 (1986) (where police fail to inform suspect of attorney's efforts to reach him, neither MIRANDA nor the Fifth Amendment requires suppression of prearraignment confession after voluntary waiver).

MIRANDA was not meant to protect suspects from boasting about their criminal activities in front of persons whom they believe to be their cellmates. This case is illustrative. Respondent had no reason to feel tht undercover agent Parisi had any legal authority to force him to answer questions or that Parisi could affect respondent's future treatment. Respondent viewed the cellmate-agent as an equal and showed no hint of being intimidated by the atmosphere of the jail. In recounting the details of the Stephenson murder, respondent was motivated solely by the desire to impress his fellow inmates. He spoke at his own peril.

The tactic employed here to elicit a voluntary confession from a suspect does not violate the Self-Incrimination Clause. We held in **HOFFA v. UNITED STATES**, 385 U.S. 293 (1966), that placing an undercover agent near a suspect in order to gather incriminating information was permissible under the Fifth Amendment. In Hoffa, while petitioner Hoffa was on trial, he met often with one Partin, who unbeknownst to Hoffa, was cooperating with law enforcement officials. Partin reported to officials that Hoffa had divulged his attempts to bribe jury members. We approved using Hoffa's statements at his subsequent trial for jury tampering, on the rationale that "no claim ha[d] been or could [have been] made that [Hoffa's] incriminating statements were the product of any sort of coercion, legal or factual." Id., at 304. In addition, we found that the fact that Partin had fooled Hoffa into thinking that Partin was a sympathetic colleague did not affect the voluntariness of the statements. Ibid. Cf. **OREGON v. MATHIASON**, supra, at 495-496 (officer's falsely telling suspect that suspect's fingerprints had been found at crime scene did not render interview "custodial" under MIRANDA); **FRAZIER v. CUPP**, 394 U.S. 731, 739 (1969); **PROCUNIER v. ATCHLEY**, 400 U.S. 446, 453-454 (1971). The only difference between this case and Hoffa is that the suspect here was incarcerated, but detention, whether or not for the crime in question, does not warrant a presumption that the use of an undercover agent to speak with an incarcerated suspect makes any confession thus obtained involuntary.

Our decision in **MATHIS v. UNITED STATES**, 391 U.S. 1 (1968), is distinguishable. In MATHIS, an inmate in a state prison was interviewed by an Internal Revenue Service agent about possible tax violations. No MIRANDA warning was given before questioning. The Court held that the suspect's incriminating statements were not admissible at his subsequent trial on tax fraud charges. The suspect in MATHIS was aware that the agent was a Government official, investigating the possibility of non-compliance with the tax laws. The case before us now is different. Where the suspect does not know that he is speaking to a government agent there is no reason to assume the possibility that the suspect might feel coerced. (The bare fact of custody may not in every instance require a warning even when the suspect is aware that he is speaking to an official, but we do not have occasion to explore that issue here.)

This Court's Sixth Amendment decisions in **MASSIAH v. UNITED STATES**, 377 U.S. 201 (1964), **UNITED STATES v. HENRY**, 447 .S. 264 (1980), and **MAINE v. MOULTON**, 474 U.S. 159 (1985), also do not avail respondent. We held in those cases that the government may not use an undercover agent to circumvent the Sixth Amendment right to counsel once a suspect has been charged with the crime. After charges have been filed, the Sixth Amendment prevents the government from interfering with the accused's right to counsel. MOULTON, supra, at 176. In the instant case no charges had been filed on the subject of the interrogation, and our Sixth Amendment precedents are not applicable.

Respondent can seek no help from his argument that a bright-line rule for the application of MIRANDA is desirable. Law enforcement officers will have little difficulty putting into practice our holding that undercover agents need not give MIRANDA warnings to incarcerated suspects. The use of undercover agents is a recognized law enforcement technique, often employed in the prison context to detect violence against correctional officials or inmates, as well as for the purposes served here. The interests protected by MIRANDA are not implicated in these cases, and the warnings are not required to safeguard the constitutional rights of inmates who make voluntary statements to undercover agents.

We hold that an undercover law enforcement officer posing as a fellow inmate need not give MIRANDA warnings to an incarcerated suspect before asking questions that may elicit an incriminating response. The statements at issue in this case were voluntary, and there is no federal obstacle to their admissibility at trial. We now reverse and remand for proceedings not inconsistent with our opinion.

It is so ordered.

JUSTICE BRENNAN, concurring in the judgment.
The Court holds that **MIRANDA v. ARIZONA**, 384 U.S. 436 (1966), does not require suppression of a statement made by an incarcerated suspect to an undercover agent.

Although I do not subscribe to the majority's characterization of MIRANDA in its entirety, I do agree that when a suspect does not know that his questioner is a police agent, such questioning does not amount to "interrogation" in an "inherently coercive" environment so as to require application of MIRANDA. Since the only issue raised at this stage of the litigation is the applicability of MIRANDA, I concur in the judgment of the Court.

This is not to say that I believe the Constitution condones the method by which the police extracted the confession in this case. To the contrary, the deception and manipulation practiced on respondent raise a substantial claim that the confession was obtained in violation of the Due Process Clause. As we recently stated in **MILLER v. FENTON**, 474 U.S. 104, 109-110 (1985):

> "This Court has long held that certain interrogation techniques, either in isolation or as applied to the unique characteristics of a particular suspect, are so offensive to a civilized system of justice that they must be condemned under the Due Process Clause of the Fourteenth Amendment . . . Although these decisions framed the legal inquiry in a variety of different ways, usually through the 'convenient shorthand' of asking whether the confession was 'involuntary,' **BLACKBURN v. ALABAMA**, 361 U.S. 199, 207 (1960), the Court's analysis has consistently been animated by the view that 'ours is an accusatorial and not an inquisitorial system,' **ROGERS v. RICHMOND**, 365 U.S. 534, 541 (1961), and that, accordingly, tactics for eliciting inculpatory statements must fall within the broad constitutional boundaries imposed by the Fourth Amendment's guarantee of fundamental fairness."

That the right is derived from the Due Process Clause "is significant because it reflects the Court's consistently held view that the admissibility of a confession turns as much on whether the techniques for extracting the statements, as applied to this suspect, are compatible with a system that presumes innocence and assures that a

704

conviction will not be secured by inquisitorial means as on whether the defendant's will was in fact overborne." Id., at 116. See **SPANO v. NEW YORK**, 360 U.S. 315, 320-321 (1959)("The abhorrence of society to the use of involuntary confessions does not turn alone on their inherent untrustworthiness. It also turns on the deep-rooted feeling that the police must obey the law while enforcing the law; that in the end life and liberty can be as much endangered from illegal methods used to convict those thought to be criminals as from the actual criminals themselves"); see also **DEGRAFFENREID v. McKELLAR**, 494 U.S. 1071, 1072-1074 (1990) (MARSHALL, J., joined by BRENNAN, J., dissenting from denial of certiorari).

The method used to elicit the confession in this case deserves close scrutiny. The police devised a ruse to lure respondent into incriminating himself when he was in jail on an unrelated charge. A police agent, posing as a fellow inmate and proposing a sham escape plot, tricked respondent into confessing that he had once committed a murder, as a way of proving that he would be willing to do so again should the need arise during the escape. The testimony of the undercover officer and a police informant at the suppression hearing reveal the deliberate manner in which the two elicited incriminating statements from respondent. See App. 43-53 and 66-73. We have recognized that "the mere fact of custody imposes pressures on the accused; confinement may bring into play subtle influences that will make him particularly susceptible to the ploys of undercover Government agents." **UNITED STATES v. HENRY**, 447 U.S. 264 (1980). As JUSTICE MARSHALL points out, the pressures of custody make a suspect more likely to confide in others and to engage in "jailhouse bravado." See post, at 307-308. The State is in a unique position to exploit this vulnerability because it has virtually complete control over the suspect's environment. Thus, the State can ensure that a suspect is barraged with questions from an undercover agent until the suspect confesses. Cf. **MINCY v. ARIZONA**, 437 U.S. 385, 399 (1978); **ASHCRAFT v. TENNESSEE**, 322 U.S. 143, 153-155 (1944). The testimony in this case suggests the State did just that.

The deliberate use of deception and manipulation by the police appears to be incompatible "with a system that presumes innocence and assures that a conviction will not be secured by inquisitorial means," MILLER, supra, at

116, and raises serious concerns that respondent's will was overborne. It is open to the lower court on remand to determine whether, under the totality of the circumstances, respondent's confession was elicited in a manner that violated the Due Process Clause. That the confession was not elicited through means of physical torture, see **BROWN v. MISSISSIPPI**, 297 U.S. 278 (1936) or overt psychological pressure, see **PAYNE v. ARKANSAS**, 356 U.S. 560, 566 (1958), does not end the inquiry. "[A]s law enforcement officers become more responsible, and the methods used to extract confessions more sophisticated, [a court's] duty to enforce federal constitutional protections does not cease. It only becomes more difficult because of the more delicate judgments to be made." SPANO, supra at 321.

EDWARD SOLDAL et ux., Petitioner
v.
COOK COUNTY, ILLINOIS et al.
506 U.S. ___, 121 L.Ed.2d 450, 113 S.Ct. (1992)

JUSTICE WHITE delivered the opinion of the Court.

I

[1a] Edward Soldal and his family resided in their trailer home, which was located on a rented lot in the Willoway Terrace mobil home park in Elk Grove, Illinois. In May, 1987, Terrace Properties, the owner of the park, and Margaret Hale, its manager, filed an eviction proceeding against the Soldals in an Illinois state court. Under the Illinois Forcible Entry and Detainer Act, Ill Rev Stat, ch 110, ¶ 9-101 et seq. (1991), a tenant cannot be dispossessed absent a judgment of eviction. The suit was dismissed on June 2, 1987. A few months later, in August, 1987, the owner brought a second proceeding of eviction, claiming nonpayment of rent. The case was set for trial on September 22, 1987.

Rather than await judgment in their favor, Terrace Properties and Hale, contrary to Illinois law, chose to evict the Soldals forcibly two weeks prior to the scheduled hearing. On September 4, Hale notified the Cook County's Sheriff's Department that he was going to remove the trailer home from the park, and requested the presence of sheriff deputies to forestall any possible resistance. Later that day, two Terrace Properties employees arrived at the Soldals' home accompanied by Cook County Deputy Sheriff O'Neill. The employees proceeded to wrench the sewer and water connections off the side of the trailer home, disconnect the phone, tear off the trailer's canopy and skirting, and hook the home to a tractor. Meanwhile, O'Neill explained to Edward Soldal that "'he was there to see that [Soldal] didn't interfere with [Willoway's] work.'" Brief for Petitioner 6.

By this time, two more deputy sheriffs had arrived at the scene and Soldal told them that he wished to file a complaint for criminal trespass. They referred him to deputy Lieutenant Jones, who was in Hale's office. Jones asked Soldal to wait outside while he remained closeted with Hale and other Terrace Properties employees for over

707

twenty minutes. After talking to a district attorney and making Soldal wait another half hour, Jones told Soldal that he would not accept a complaint because "'it was between the landlord and the tenant . . .[and] they were going to go ahead and continue to move out the trailer.'" Id., at 8. Throughout this period, the deputy sheriffs knew that Terrace Properties did not have an eviction order and that its actions were unlawful. Eventually, and in the presence of an additional two deputy sheriffs, the Willoway workers pulled the trailer free of its moorings and towed it onto the street. Later, it was hauled to a neighboring property.

On September 9, the state judge assigned to the pending eviction proceedings ruled that the eviction had been unauthorized and ordered Terrace Properties to return the Soldal's home to the lot. The home however, was badly damaged. The Soldals brought this action under 42 USC § 1983 [42 USCS § 1983], alleging a violation of their rights under the Fourth and Fourteenth Amendments. They claimed that Terrace Properties and Hale had conspired with Cook County deputy sheriffs to unreasonably seize and remove the Soldals' trailer home. The District Judge granted defendant's motion for summary judgment on the grounds that the Soldals had failed to adduce any evidence to support their conspiracy theory and, therefore, the existence of state action necessary under § 1983.

The Court of Appeals for the Seventh Circuit, construing the facts in petitioner's favor, accepted their contention that there was state action. However, it went on to hold that the removal of the Soldals' trailer did not constitute a seizure for purposes of the Fourth Amendment or a deprivation of due process for purposes of the Fourteenth.

On rehearing, a majority of the Seventh Circuit, sitting en banc, reaffirmed the panel decision. Acknowledging that what had occurred was a "seizure" in the literal sense of the word, the court reasoned that, because it was not made in the course of public law enforcement- and because it did not invade the Soldals' privacy, it was not a seizure as contemplated by the Fourth Amendment. 942 F.2d 1073, 076 (1991). Interpreting prior cases of this Court, the Seventh

Circuit concluded that, absent interference with privacy or liberty, a "pure deprivation of property" is not cognizable under the Fourth Amendment. Id., at 1078-1079. Rather, petitioners' property interests were protected only by the due process clauses of the Fifth and Fourteenth Amendments.

We granted certiorari to consider whether the seizure and removal of the Soldals' trailer home implicated their Fourth Amendment rights, 503 U.S. ___, 117 L.Ed.2d. 514, 112 S.Ct. 1290 (1992), and now reverse.

II

[2] The Fourth Amendment, made applicable to the States by the Fourteenth, **KER v. CALIFORNIA**, 374 U.S. 23, 30, 10 L.Ed.2d, 83 S.Ct. 1623 (1963), provides in pertinent part that the "right of the people to be secure in their persons, houses, papers, and effects, against unreasonable searches and seizures, shall not be violated. . ."

A "seizure of property we have explained, occurs when "there is some meaningful interference with an individual's possessory interests in that property." **UNITED STATES v. JACOBSEN**, 466 U.S. 109, 113, 80 L.Ed.2d 85, 104 S.Ct. 1652 (1984). In addition, we have emphasized that "at the very core" of the Fourth Amendment "stands the right of a man to retreat into his own home." **SILVERMAN v. UNITED STATES**, 365 U.S. 505, 511, 5 L.Ed.2d. 734, 81 S.Ct. 679, 97 ALR2d 1277 (1961). See also **OLIVER v. UNITED STATES**, 466 U.S. 170, 178-179, 80 L.Ed.2d 214, 104 S.Ct. 1735 (1984); **WYMAN v. JAMES**, 400 U.S. 309, 316, 27 L.Ed.2d. 408, 91 S.Ct. 381 (1971); **PAYTON v. NEW YORK**, 445 U.S. 573, 601, 63 L.Ed.2d 639, 100 S.Ct. 1371 (1980).

[1b, 3] As a result of the state action in this case, the Soldals' domicile was not only seized, it literally was carried away, giving new meaning to the term "mobile home." We fail to see how being unceremonious dispossessed of one's home in the manner alleged to have occurred here can be viewed as anything but a seizure invoking the protection of the Fourth Amendment. Whether the Amendment was in fact violated is, of course, a different question that requires determining if the seizure was reasonable. That inquiry entails the weighing of various factors and is not before us.

The Court of Appeals recognized that there had been a seizure, but concluded that it was a seizure only in a "technical" sense, not within the meaning of the Fourth Amendment. This conclusion followed from a narrow reading of the Amendment, which the court construed to safeguard only privacy and liberty interests while leaving unprotected possessory interests where neither privacy nor liberty was at stake. Otherwise, the court said,

> "a constitutional provision enacted two centuries ago [would] make every repossession and eviction with police assistance actionable under - of all things - the Fourth Amendment[, which] would both trivialize the amendment and gratuitously shift a large body of routine commercial litigation from the state courts to the federal courts. That trivializing, this shift, can be prevented by recognizing the difference between possessory and privacy interests." 942 F2d, at 1077.

Because the officers had not entered Soldal's house, rummaged through his possessions, or, in the Court of Appeals' view, interfered with his liberty in the course of the eviction, the Fourth Amendment offered no protection against the "grave deprivation" of property that had occurred. Ibid.

[4a] We do not agree with this interpretation of the Fourth Amendment. The Amendment protects the people from unreasonable searches and seizures of "their persons, houses, papers, and effects." This language surely cuts against the novel holding below, and our cases unmistakably hold that the Amendment protects property as well as privacy. This much was made clear in Jacobsen, supra, where we explained that the first clause of the Fourth Amendment:

> "protects two types of expectations, one involving 'searches,' the other 'seizures.' A 'search' occurs when an expectation of privacy that society is prepared to consider reasonable is infringed. A 'seizure' of property occurs where there is some meaningful interference with an individual's possessory interests in that property." 466 U.S.,

710

at 113, 80 L.Ed.2d. 85, 104 S.Ct. 1652.

See also id., at 120, 80 L.Ed.2d 85, 104 S.Ct, 1652; **HORTON v. CALIFORNIA**, 496 U.S. 128, 133, 110 L.Ed.2d 112, 110 S.Ct. 2301 (1990); **ARIZONA v. HICKS**, 480 U.S. 321, 328, 94 L.Ed.2d 347, 107 S.Ct. 1149 (1987); **MARYLAND v. MACON**, 472 U.S. 463, 469, 86 L.Ed.2d 370, 105 S.Ct. 2778 (1985); **TEXAS v. BROWN**, 460 U.S. 730, 747-748, 75 L.Ed.2d 502, 103 S.Ct. 1535 (1983) (STEVENS, J., concurring in judgment); **UNITED STATES v. SALVUCCI**, 448 U.S. 83, 91, n 6, 65 L.Ed.2d 619, 100 S.Ct. 2547 (1980). Thus, having concluded that chemical testing of powder found in a package did not compromise its owner's privacy, the Court in Jacobsen did not put an end to its inquiry, as would be required under the view adopted by the Court of Appeals and advocated by respondents. Instead, adhering to the teachings of **UNITED STATES v. PLACE**, 462 U.S. 696, 77 L.Ed.2d 110 , 103 S.Ct. 2637 (1983), it went on to determine whether the invasion of the owners' "possessory interests" occasioned by the destruction of the powder was reasonable under the Fourth Amendment. Jacobsen, 466 U.S., at 124-125, 80 L.Ed.2d 85, 104 S.Ct. 1652. In Place, although we found that subjecting luggage to a "dog sniff" did not constitute a search for Fourth Amendment purposes because it did not compromise any privacy interest, taking custody of Places's suitcase was deemed an unlawful seizure for it unreasonably infringed "the suspect's possessory interest in his luggage." 462 U.S., at 708, 77 L.Ed.2d 110, 103 S.Ct. 2637. Although lacking a privacy component, the property rights in both instances nonetheless were not disregarded, but rather were afforded Fourth Amendment protection.

Respondents rely principally on precedents such as **KATZ v. UNITED STATE**, 389 U.S. 347, 19 L.Ed.2d 576, 88 S.Ct. 507 (1967), **WARDEN, MARYLAND PENITENTIARY v. HAYDEN**, 387 U.S. 294, 18 L.Ed.2d 782, 87 S.Ct. 1642 91967), and **CARDWELL v. LEWIS**, 417 U.S. 583, 41 L.Ed.2d 325, 94 S.Ct. 2464 (1974), to demonstrate that the Fourth Amendment is only marginally concerned with property rights. But the message of those cases is that property rights are not the sole measure of the Fourth Amendment violations. The Warden opinion thus observed, citing **JONES v. UNITED STATES**, 362 U.S. 257, 4 L.Ed.2d 697, 80 S.Ct. 725, 78 ALR2d 233 (1960) and Silverman , that the "principal" object of the Amendment is the protection of

711

privacy rather than property and that "this shift in emphasis from property to privacy has come about through a subtle interplay of substantive and procedural reform." 387 U.S., at 304 18 L.Ed.2d 782, 87 S.Ct. 1642. There was no suggestion that this shift in emphasis had snuffed out the previously recognized protection for property under the Fourth Amendment. Katz, in declaring violative of the Fourth Amendment the unwarranted overhearing of a telephone booth conversation, effectively ended any lingering notions that the protection of privacy depended on trespass into a protected area. In the course of its decision, the Katz Court stated that the Fourth Amendment can neither be translated into a provision dealing with constitutionally protected areas nor into a general constitutional right to privacy. The Amendment, the Court said, protects individual privacy against certain kinds of governmental intrusion, " but its protections go further, and often have nothing to do with privacy at all." 389 U.S., at 350 19 L.Ed.2d 576, 88 S.Ct. 507.

As for Cardwell, a plurality of this Court held in that case that the Fourth Amendment did not bar the use in evidence of paint scrapings taken from and tire treads observed on the defendant's automobile, which had been seized in a parking lot and towed to a police lockup. Gathering this evidence was not deemed to be a search, for nothing from the interior of the car and "no personal effects, which the Fourth Amendment traditionally has been deemed to protect" were searched or seized. Cardwell, 417 U.S., at 591, 41 L.Ed.2d 325, 94 S.CT. 2464 (opinion of Blackmun, J.). No meaningful privacy rights were invaded. But this left the argument, pressed by the dissent, that the evidence gathered was the product of a warrantless and hence illegal seizure of the car from the parking lot where the defendant had left it. However, the plurality was of the view that, because under the circumstances of the case there was provable cause to seize the car as an instrumentality of the crime, Fourth Amendment precedent permitted the seizure without a warrant. Id., at 593, 41 L.Ed.2d 325, 94 S.Ct. 2464. Thus, both the plurality and dissenting Justices considered defendant's auto deserving of Fourth Amendment protection even though privacy interests were not at stake. They differed only in the degree of protection that the Amendment demanded.

The Court of Appeals appeared to find more specific support for confining the protection of the Fourth Amendment to privacy interests in our decision in **HUDSON v. PALMER** 468 U.S. 517, 82 L.Ed.2d 393, 104 S.Ct. 3194 (1984). There, a state prison inmate sued, claiming that prison guards had entered his cell without consent and had seized and destroyed some of his personal effects. We ruled that an inmate, because of his status, enjoyed neither a right to privacy in his cell nor protection against unreasonable seizures of his personal effects. Id., at 526-528, and n 8, 82 L.Ed.2d 393, 104 S.Ct. 3194 (O'Connor, J., concurring). Whatever else the case held, it is of limited usefulness outside the prison context with respect to the coverage of the Fourth Amendment.

[1c, 5a, 6a] We thus are unconvinced that any of the Court's prior cases supports the view that the Fourth Amendment protects against unreasonable seizures of property only where privacy or liberty is also implicated. What is more, our "plain view" decisions make untenable such a construction of the Amendment. Suppose for example that police officers lawfully enter a house, by either complying with the warrant requirement or satisfying one of its recognized exceptions - e.g., through a valid consent or a showing of exigent circumstances. If they come across some item in plain view and seize it, no invasion of personal privacy has occurred. Horton, 496 U.S., at 133-134, 110 L.Ed.2d 112, 110 S.Ct. 2301; Brown, 460 U.S., at 739, 75 L.Ed.2d 502, 103 S.Ct. 1535 (opinion of Rehnquist, J.). If the boundaries of the Fourth Amendment were defined exclusively by rights of privacy, "plain view" seizures would not implicate that constitutional provision at all. Yet, far from being automatically upheld, "plain view" seizures have been scrupulously subjected to Fourth Amendment inquiry. Thus, in the absence of consent or a warrant permitting the seizure of the items in question, such seizures can be justified only if they meet the probable cause standard, **ARIZONA v. HICKS**, 480 U.S. 321, 326-327, 94 L.Ed.2d 347, 107 S.Ct. 1149 (1987), and if they are unaccompanied by unlawful trespass. Horton, 496 U.S., at 136-137, 110 L.Ed.2d 112, 110 S.Ct. 2301. That is because, the absence of a privacy interest notwithstanding, "[a] seizure of the article . . .would obviously invade the owner's possessory interest." Id., at 134, 110 L.Ed.2d 112, 110 S.Ct. 2301; see also Brown, supra, at 739, 75 L.Ed.2d 502, 103 S.Ct. 1535 (opinion of Rehnquist, J). The plain view doctrine "merely reflects an application of the Fourth Amendment's central requirement of reasonableness to the law governing seizures of property," ibid.; **COOLIDGE v. NEW HAMPSHIRE**, 403 U.S. 443, 468, 29 L.Ed.2d 564, 91 S.Ct 2022 (1971); id., at 516, 29 L.Ed.2d 564, 91 S.Ct. 2022 (WHITE, J. concurring and dissenting).

[7a] The Court of Appeals understandably found it necessary to reconcile its holding with our recognition in the plain view cases that the Fourth Amendment protects property as such. In so doing, the court did not distinguish this case on the ground that the seizure of the Soldal's home took place in a noncriminal context. Indeed, it acknowledged what is evident from our precedents - that the Amendment's protection applied in the civil context as well. See **O'CONNOR v. ORTEGA**, 480 U.S. 709, 94 L.Ed.2d 714, 107 S.Ct. 1492 (1987), **NEW JERSEY v. T.L.O.**, 469 U.S. 325, 334-335, 83 L.Ed.2d 720, 105 S.Ct. 733 91985); **MICHIGAN v. TYLER**, 436 U.S. 499, 504-506, 56 L.Ed.2d 486, 98 S.Ct. 1942 (1978); **MARSHALL v. BARLOW'S, INC.**, 436 U.S. 307, 312-313, 56 L.Ed.2d 305, 98 S.Ct. 1816 (1978); **CAMARA v. MUNICIPAL COURT OF SAN FARANSICO**, 387 U.S. 523, 528, 18 L.Ed.2d. 930, 87 S.Ct. 1727 (1967).

Nor did the Court of Appeals suggest that the Fourth Amendment applied exclusively to law enforcement activities. It observed, for example, that the Amendment's protection would be triggered "by a search or other entry into the home incident to an eviction or repossession," 942 F2d, at 1077. Instead, the court sought to explain why the Fourth Amendment protects against seizures of property in the plain view context, but in this case, as follows:

"[S]eizures made in the course of investigations by police or other law enforcement officers are almost always, as in the plain view cases, the culmination of searches. The police search in order to seize, and it is the search and ensuing seizure that the Fourth Amendment by its reference to 'searches and seizure' seeks to regulate. Seizure means one thing when it is the outcome of a search' it may mean something else when it stands apart form a search or any other investigative activity. The Fourth Amendment may still nominally apply, but, precisely because there is no invasion of privacy , the usual rules do not apply." Id., 942 F2d, at 1079 (emphasis in original).

[1d,8] We have difficulty with this passage. The court seemingly construes the Amendment to protect only against seizures that are the outcome of a search. But our cases are to the contrary and hold that seizures of property are subject to Fourth Amendment scrutiny even though no search within the meaning of the Amendment has taken place. See, e.g., Jacobsen, 466 U.S., at 120-125, 80 L.Ed.2d 85, 104 S.Ct. 1652; Place, 462 U.S., at 706-707, 77 L.Ed.2d 110, 103 S.Ct. 2637; Cardwell, 417 U.S., at 588-589, 41 L.Ed.2d 325, 94 S.Ct. 2464. More generally, an officer who happens to come across an individual's property in a public area could seize it only if Fourth Amendment standards are satisfied - for example, if the items are evidence of a crime or contraband. Cf. **PAYTON v. NEW YORK**, 445 U.S. 573, 587, 63 L.Ed.2d 639, 100 S.Ct. 1371 (1980). We are also puzzled by the last sentence of the excerpt, where the court announces that the "usual rules" of the Fourth Amendment are inapplicable if the seizure is not the result of a search or any other investigative activity "precisely because there is no invasion of privacy." For the plain view cases clearly state that, notwithstanding the absence of any interference with privacy, seizures of effects that are not authorized by a warrant are reasonable only because there is probable cause to associate the property with criminal activity. The seizure of the weapons in Horton, for example, occurred in the midst of a search, yet we emphasized that it did not "involve any invasion of privacy." 496 U.S., at 133, 110 L.Ed.2d 112, 110 S.Ct 2301. In short, our statement that such seizures must satisfy the Fourth Amendment and will be deemed reasonable only if the item's incriminating character is "immediately apparent," id., at 136-137, 110 L.Ed.2d 112, 110 S.Ct. 2301, is at odds with the Court of Appeals' approach.
[9,10] The Court of Appeals' effort is both interesting and creative, but at bottom it simply reasserts the earlier thesis that the Fourth Amendment protects privacy but not property. We remain unconvinced

715

and see no justification for departing from our prior cases. In our view, the reason why an officer might enter a house or effectuate a seizure is wholly irrelevant to the threshold question of whether the Amendment applies. What matters is the intrusion on the people's security from governmental interference. Therefore, the right against unreasonable seizures would be no less transgressed if the seizure of the house was undertaken to collect evidence, verify compliance with a housing regulation, effect an eviction by the police, or on a whim, for no reason at all. As we have observed on more than one occasion, it would be "anomalous to say that the individual and his private property are fully protected by the Fourth Amendment only when the individual is suspected of criminal behavior." Camara, 387 U.S., at 530, 18 L.Ed.2d 930, 87 S.Ct. 1727; see also O'Connor, 480 U.S., at 715, 94 L.Ed.2d 714, 107 S.Ct. 1492; T.L.O., 469 U.S., at 335, 83 L.Ed.2d 720, 105 S.Ct. 733.

[11] The Court of Appeals also stated that even if, contrary to its previous rulings, "there is one element or tincture of a Fourth Amendment seizure, it cannot carry the day for the Soldals." 942 F2d, at 1080. Relying on our decision in **GRAHAM v. CONNOR**, 490 U.S. 386, 104 L.Ed.2d 443, 109 S.Ct. 1865 (1989), the court reasoned that it should look at the "dominant character of the conduct challenged in a section 1983 case [to] determine the constitutional standard under which it is evaluated." 942 f2d, at 1080. Believing that the Soldals' claim was more akin to a challenge against the deprivation of property without due process of law than against an unreasonable seizure, the court concluded that they should not be allowed to bring their suit under the guise of the Fourth Amendment.

But we see no basis for doling out constitutional protections in such fashion. Certain wrongs affect more than a single right and, accordingly, can implicate more than one of the Constitution's commands. Where such multiple violations are alleged, we are not in the habit of identifying as a preliminary matter the claim's "dominant" character. Rather, we examine each constitutional provision in turn. See, e.g., Hudson (Fourth Amendment and Fourteenth Amendment Due Process

Clause); **INGRAHAM v. WRIGHT**, 430 U.S. 651, 51 L.Ed.2d 711, 97 S.Ct. 1401 (1977)(Eighth Amendment and Fourteenth Amendment Due Process Clause). Graham is not to the contrary. Its holding was that claims of excessive use of force should be analyzed under the Fourth Amendment's reasonableness standard, rather than the Fourteenth Amendment's substantive due process test. We were guided by the fact that, in that case, both provisions targeted the same sort of governmental conduct and, as a result, we chose the more "explicit textual source of constitutional protection" over the "more generalized notion of 'substantive due process.'" 490 U.S, at 394-395, 104 L.Ed.2d 443, 109 S.Ct. 1865. Surely, Graham does not bar resort in this case to the Fourth Amendment's specific protection for "houses, property, and effects" rather than the general protection of property in the Due Process Clause.

III

Respondents are fearful, as was the Court of Appeals, that applying the Fourth Amendment in this context inevitably will carry it into territory unknown and unforeseen: routine repossessions, negligent actions of public employees that interfere with individuals' right to enjoy their homes, and the like, thereby federalizing areas of law traditionally the concern of the States. For several reasons, we think the risk is exaggerated. To begin, our decision will have no impact on activities such as repossessions or attachments if they involve entry into the home, intrusion on individuals' privacy, or interference with their liberty, because they would implicate the Fourth Amendment even on the Court of Appeals own terms. This was true of the Tenth Circuit's decision in Specht with which, as we previously noted, the Court of Appeals expressed agreement.

[12] More significantly, "reasonableness is still the ultimate standard" under the Fourth Amendment, Camara, supra, at 539, which means that numerous seizures of this type will survive constitutional scrutiny. As is true in other circumstances, the reasonableness determination will reflect a "careful balancing of governmental and private interests." T.L.O., supra at 341, 83 L.Ed.2d 720, 105 S.Ct. 733. Assuming for example that the officers were acting pursuant to a court order,

717

as in **SPECHT v. JENSON**, 832 F2d 1516 (CA10 1987), or
FUENTES v. SHEVIN, 407 U.S. 67, 32 L.Ed.2d 556, 92 S.Ct
1983 (1972), and as often would be the case, a showing of
unreasonableness on these facts would be a laborious task
indeed. Cf. Simms and **WISE v. SLACUM**, 3 Cranch 300, 301,
2 L.Ed. 446 (1806). Hence, while there is no guarantee
against the filing of frivolous suits, had the ejection
in this case properly awaited the state court's judgment
it is quite unlikely that the federal court would have
been bothered with a § 1983 action alleging a Fourth
Amendment violation.

Moreover, we doubt that the police will often choose
to further an enterprise knowing that it is contrary to
the law, or proceed to seize property in the absence of
objectively reasonable grounds for doing so. In short,
our reaffirmance of Fourth Amendment principles today
should not foment a wave of new litigation in the federal
courts.

IV

[1f] The complaint here alleges that respondents,
acting under color of state law, dispossessed the Soldals
of their trailer home by physically tearing it form its
foundation and towing it to another lot. Taking these
allegations as true, this was no "garden-variety"
landlord-tenant or commercial dispute. The facts alleged
suffice to constitute a "seizure" within the meaning of
the Fourth Amendment, for they plainly implicate the
interest protected by that provision. The judgment of the
Court of Appeals is, accordingly, reversed, and the case
is remanded for further proceedings consistent with this
opinion.

So ordered.